The unique qualities of James Smith's *Daily Remembrancer* can be summarised as pastoral, doctrinal, experiential, and practical. Readers will find there concise and memorable readings, warming the heart, searching the conscience, comforting the soul, endearing the Lord Jesus, and directing the life in the God's ways. Preachers will find Smith's terse and orderly style enormously suggestive for sermon outlines, and will be amazed at the fresh shafts of light that fall upon familiar themes. Having gone through Smith for many years, I can heartily recommend this new and attractive edition.

JOHN THACKWAY
Minister, Emmanuel Church, Salisbury.
Editor, *Bible League Quarterly*.

I love this daily devotional from the pen of James Smith, the predecessor of Charles Spurgeon at the New Park Street Chapel in London. Smith is beautifully clear and simple (much like Ryle and Spurgeon), but he is often more experiential than Ryle and more succinct than Spurgeon. Through your daily 'visits' with Pastor Smith, may you grow in your walk with the Lord as you taste more of His grace, goodness, and gospel in these savory and spiritually warm meditations.

JOEL R. BEEKE
Chancellor and Professor of Systematic Theology and Homiletics,
Puritan Reformed Theological Seminary, Grand Rapids, Michigan.

THE DAILY REMEMBRANCER

A MORNING AND EVENING DEVOTIONAL

JAMES SMITH

CHRISTIAN HERITAGE

Scripture quotations are taken from the Authorised Version (AV).

Copyright © Christian Focus Publications 2025
Print ISBN: 978-1-5271-1256-8
E-book ISBN: 978-1-5271-1331-2

Published in 2025
in the
Christian Heritage Imprint
by
Christian Focus Publications,
Geanies House, Fearn, Tain, Ross-shire,
IV20 1TW, Scotland, UK
www.christianfocus.com

Cover design by Rubner Durais

Printed and bound by Gutenberg, Malta

FOREWORD

James Smith (1802–1862) served as pastor of the New Park Street church from 1841 until he left London under health concerns around 1850. That church had prospered under the Christ-centered biblical exposition of gifted ministers from its inception. The man who gathered this church in London during a period of oppression of dissenters was William Rider. Under his influence, Henry Jessey, minister at St. George the Martyr, adopted Baptist views and became one of the early and influential leaders of the Particular Baptist movement.

Rider was succeeded as pastor by Benjamin Keach, who had been persecuted, arrested, put on trial, placed in the stocks, fined, and put in jail for his Baptist views. Among his forty-something publications was a giant volume of exposition entitled *Exposition of the Parables* and another entitled *Preaching from the Types and Metaphors of the Bible*. Also, he evoked controversy and an excision from the church by his defence of corporate singing as a regulated part of corporate worship. "'Tis a hard case that any Christian should object against that Duty which Christ and his Apostles, and the Saints in all Ages in their publick Assemblies were found in the practice of: but 'tis no easy thing to break People off of a mistaken Notion, and an old Prejudice taken up against a precious truth of Christ.' [Benjamin Keach, *The Banquetting-House or A Feast of Fat Things* (London: Printed by J. A. for H. Barnard, 1692), 11.] The book contains 209 hymns beginning with 'God as Father' containing 16 hymns on the doctrine of God followed by 49 hymns on the Person and Work of Christ and 13 hymns on the Holy Spirit. After that 16 hymns on Scripture are followed by hymns on other subjects arranged systematically culminating with three on hell: 'Hell, a Furnace of Fire,' 'Hell, a Lake of Fire,' and, number 146, 'Hell, a Bottomless Pit.' Hymns 147-209 treat a variety of other subjects beginning with 'Sin Laid on Christ' and closing with 'Wrath Against Persecutors.'

Keach died in 1704 and was succeeded by his son-in-law, Benjamin Stinton (1676–1719), when he was close to thirty years old. Stinton was a convinced Baptist who defended those views while at the same time 'endeavored to cultivate harmony among Christians of different sentiments.' [Ivimey, 3:413] He was active in providing education for the children of

Dissenters and The Baptist Fund. He collected historical data on the Baptist churches of England, hoping that Daniel Neal would use it in his *History of the Puritans*, but later used by Thomas Crosby in his *History of the English Baptists*. Among several sermons that he had published by request was a theological celebration of the changes prompted in the life of the Dissenters by the death of Queen Anne: 'Of Divine Providence; occasioned by the demise of her late Majesty Queen Anne, and the happy accession of our present Sovereign King George to the Throne of Great Britain.' Ivimey observed that Stinton was 'a consistent Calvinist; stearing [sic] clear of Arminianism on the one hand, and Antinomianism on the other.' [3:413]. Stinton died unexpectedly on February 11, 1718.

After some controversy in the church which led to the establishing of another congregation, John Gill (1697–1771) was installed as pastor. Although self-taught, his scholarship was profound and his writings were abundant in length and type. He published sermons, controversial and polemical literature, commentaries, and systematic theology. *The Cause of God and Truth* displayed the skill with which he negotiated and intertwined polemical, exegetical, historical, and theological disciplines. His commentary of nine volumes dealt with every verse of the Bible and was completed before he wrote his two-volume *Complete Body of Doctrinal and Practical Divinity* (1769). He served the church from March, 1720, until his death on October 14, 1771. During his time as pastor, the Baptist cause was defended in public through his pen. The church, however, declined in membership, did not spawn the founding of other Baptist churches, and saw few men called to ministry. For his scholarship, his orthodoxy, his purity of life, and his unwavering faithfulness to his call as a preacher, teacher, and defender of the word of God and its gospel, Gill was admired and celebrated by many of his contemporaries. Even Ivimey, who had his reservations about some of the doctrinal propensities of Gill, wrote that he was 'an ornament to the denomination to which he considered it his honour to belong.' [3:444].

Upon the death of Gill, the church selected a young man from Bristol College, the twenty-year-old John Rippon (1750–1836). Another secession occurred at his coming. Showing early, however, his proverbial prudence, he managed the occasion with compassionate wisdom, suggesting that the leaving party be granted £300 with which to construct a chapel. The church prospered under his ministry of sixty-three years. His preaching has been described as 'lively, affectionate and impressive.' Rippon loved hymns, wrote several, and produced a hymnal in 1787, *A Selection of Hymns*, containing 588 hymns. This set a standard for hymnals and was widely popular in England and America. His alteration of Perronet's 'All Hail the Power of Jesus' Name' is probably his best known contribution. He remained as pastor until his death, although in his last years he was 'supposed to have outlived his usefulness.' [G. H. Pike, *The Life and Work of C. H. Spurgeon*, 6 vols., 1:121] Having begun at Horsley Down, moved to Goat Street, then Carter Lane, the construction of London Bridge made another move necessary. Factors

INTRODUCTION

dictated that a chapel be constructed at the south end of London Bridge at New Park Street. It was a damp, low-lying, unhealthy location.

Joseph Angus (1816–1902) succeeded Rippon—he was twenty-one—but remained for only four years. He served for a decade (1840–1850) as secretary of the Baptist Missionary Society and then served as Principal at Stepney College. During his 44 year span as principal, he moved the college to Regent's Park.

Coming to New Park Street after Joseph Angus was James Smith (1802–1862), the author of this book of devotions. Reared in the Church of England, upon conversion he concluded from his own reading of Scripture that he should be baptised in the manner practiced in the book of Acts. He applied, therefore, to the Baptist church in Brentford and was baptised and received as a member. Having natural gifts of speech and manifesting a deep commitment to evangelical truth, he was encouraged to pursue ministry. Smith was hesitant but, by 1829, became pastor of a church in Cheltenham. When he grew to a persuasion that he should address the unconverted, objections arose to his preaching, and he formed a new congregation in 1835. This church had remarkable success under his preaching and leadership. In 1841, he moved to London to serve as pastor of New Park Street after the removal of Joseph Angus. For almost a decade, he laboured faithfully and with true evangelical zeal for the growth of the members and the salvation of the lost. Smith recalled that 'the Lord enabled him in simplicity, not in the words of man's wisdom, but in the words of Scripture, in the language of the heart rather than the language of the head, – to preach the same doctrines [the Calvinistic doctrines of grace] in connection with their influence upon the heart and their effects in the life.' He found himself unable to sustain his health in the environment in London, particularly in the location of New Park Street. He left for health reasons resisting the protest of friends who 'told him how very wrong it was for him to leave Park Street.' Eventually he made his way back to Cheltenham where his ministry was blessed with spiritual fruit and a steady stream of conversions. Under his leadership, the congregation built a new building, Cambray Chapel, in 1855.

In 1861, Smith was invited to the celebration of the opening of the Metropolitan Tabernacle. He reminisced concerning the pessimism that some had about the prospects for the church when he left. He had assured his melancholy friends that God knew where to find a man and how to prepare him for just such a situation. Smith told the gathered crowd that 'He now felt confirmed in that opinion, for if he had not left Park Street, humanly speaking, they would never have had that Tabernacle, they would not have had the Church they now possessed, nor would have seen the wonder wrought in the land which they had witnessed.' On a visit to New Park Street after Spurgeon had come, Smith recalled this pleasing conversation: In the words of one recording Smith's speech, we read:

He remembered coming to London on one occasion, after New Park Street Chapel was thronged, and a member of the Church, not very comfortably seated on account of the crowd that surrounded him, speaking to him of the wonderful success that was given, and the glorious work that was being wrought, said, 'Ah! Sir, your prayers are answered. Did you not use to pray Sunday after Sunday that God would crowd the place? Have I not heard you say, "Lord, cram the place?" And he has done it, and I think now you ought to be satisfied; however uncomfortable it may be for us, you ought to be very comfortable to think that God had answered your prayers.' [MTP, 1961, 259.]

Smith preached on Thursday evening, April 11, 1861, on Effectual Calling. It was the fourth of a five part series on the doctrines of grace. Smith reviewed the doctrines covered leading to his topic showing his mental grasp and heart commitment to those doctrines. He affirmed the Father's infinite wisdom and mercy in electing a portion—'the vast majority of the fallen inhabitants of this world'—to be redeemed by the Son. The Son received this commission and in receiving it knew that the people of the Father's election had been given to him. The fall had brought them into a state of being 'so depraved, so polluted, so rotten, that nothing could effect a change but the omnipotent energy of the omnipotent God.' In order to perform an effectual redemption, the Son came and 'assumed humanity, and united it with Deity. The two natures constitute the one person of the glorious Mediator.' In this way he stood as the representative of his people, a Surety of the purchase, the 'Substitute of the multitude of his fallen ones.' He was the necessary sacrifice to whom sin was transferred by imputation so that by such an expiation sin no longer stood as a barrier to the free flow of divine mercy. Even as omnipotent and infinite wisdom devised the way, the infinite glory of the Son accomplished the redeeming and atoning work, so must a commensurate divine omnipotence operate through the Spirit to 'renew, to transform, to remodel, to fit human nature to gaze upon the unveiled glories of the Deity, and to render to God the homage due unto his name.' In consonance with his conviction about evangelistic urgency, Smith described the necessity of a general call of the gospel as prelude to the effectual call of the Spirit. 'While we speak and give the call as we are commanded and commissioned, the Holy Spirit works – the infinite power of the Eternal Spirit comes into contact – direct, immediate contact with the mind of man.' This covenantally-directed, infinitely-gracious, omnipotent third Person of the Triune God gives a life impossible for an iniquity-bound, transgressionally-dead sinner to obtain apart from the invincible, grace-determined power of a new creation. This life as granted sovereignly of irresistible power and imperishable seed can never be lost. Smith gives a moving narrative of the process of conviction wrought by the Spirit in the conscience and mental consciousness of the person being drawn with effectual grace. After this scripture-impregnated and experientially rigorous description, he preached, 'He has now experienced the effectual call. It has been a call from darkness into marvellous light, from bondage into glorious liberty; out of prison the man comes to reign; from the dunghill he is lifted up to sit among the princes, even among the princes of God's people.' This call is heavenly, distinguishing, and irreversible. 'Thus,'

INTRODUCTION

he summarized, 'you perceive, my friends, all originated in God's thought, which though sprung into a perfect plan, to carry out which plan provision was made, and this plan will be perfectly carried out to the praise of the glory of his grace.' [MTP, 1862, 318-322.]

This theological system of thought informs the day-by-day devotions that constitute this present work. One example may serve to illustrate the intense theological foundation to Smith's 'Remembrancer.' On the evening of December 25, these sentences constitute a portion of the intended encouragement to believing sinners:

> He was one with, and equal to the Father. But He became man. He was conceived in Mary's womb. He was born in Bethlehem. He was a weak and helpless infant, and yet at the same time the Mighty God, the Everlasting Father, the Prince of peace. Deity and humanity united in His person. He took our nature to take away our sins. He became a man in order to be a Saviour. He came on purpose to save sinners. This was His object. This was His work. For this He lived, and laboured, and suffered, and died. He came to be our substitute. He was born once, that we might be born again. He died once, that we might not experience the second death, but live forever. His love passeth knowledge. His birth was the greatest display of condescension, which heaven or earth ever witnessed. It was introductory to His obedient life, meritorious death, victorious resurrection, triumphant ascension, and glorious second advent. He was born in Bethlehem, in weakness and poverty; He will soon come to earth again, with power and great glory.

Cathcart's Baptist Encyclopedia (1881) recorded accurately and succinctly the spirituality and literary talent of Smith. The article noted that he was 'widely known and the author of "The Daily Remembrancer" and other evangelical works of large circulation.' [Cathcart, 2:1066, s.v. Smith, Rev. James.] The article recognized that Smith had 'the pen of a ready writer' from which 'no fewer than forty productions were given to the press.' He also contributed articles regularly to religious periodicals. 'His writings are characterized,' so the writer described, 'by great plainness of diction, remarkable felicity of Scripture quotation and illustration, and an exuberant richness of Christian experience.' [Cathcart] These lovely literary traits run throughout this book of more than 700 concise, spiritually-energetic, biblically-rich, heart engaging devotions.

Smith is not afraid to use the time of devotion to challenge and chasten the reader. Reflecting on Genesis 42:36, 'All these things are against me,' Smith looked the complaint straight in the face and wrote: 'They are not against you but for you; you forget that they come according to the arrangements of a gracious providence, and that your heavenly Father sends them for your good. Leave off complaining, for it springs from ignorance of God's Word, or forgetfulness of your many mercies and sins; or from unbelief and a bad temper; and it reflects upon the love, care, and kindness of your God. These things are painful, trying, and perplexing; but they are intended to do you good, and while you are complaining, they are working together under divine direction for your present and everlasting welfare. Beloved, how apt we are to mistake the design of our trials, and to lose sight of God's promises.'

Smith often deals in provocations to deeper devotion and a sense of the goodness and privilege of single-hearted discipleship. From 'Let Him Deny Himself' the reader is challenged to know that 'We are not our own, nor is any thing we have our own; it is the Lord's. Our appetites, pleasures, and pursuits, must all be brought into subjection to the obedience of Christ. His glory is to be sought at all times, in all things, under all circumstances; and when this is done, we are safe and happy.'

Each devotion ends with a verse or two of a hymn sung regularly by the Evangelicals of the mid-nineteenth century. They demonstrate Smith's alacrity in selecting fitting hymns to seal in poetic form the biblical principle devotionally composed. Hymns are from Joseph Addison, Isaac Watts, Philip Doddridge, Joseph Bromehead, Thomas Kelly, Thomas Haweis, Charles Wesley, Jane Hore, Walter Shirley, John Newton, and others. The hymn selections not only show depth of knowledge of present hymnody but carry an independent source of worship as well as a thematic cap to the devotion.

The devotions for a day often reflect juxtaposition of ideas that complemented and expand each other. We find such kinships in 'Be ye thankful,' based on Colossians 3:15 and 'Now will I praise the LORD' based on Genesis 29:35. Another is 'A mediator' based on Galatians 3:20 and 'One mediator between God and men' based on 1 Timothy 2:5. 'I will help thee' from Isaiah 41:13 teamed with 'Hitherto hath the LORD helped us.' Based on 1 Samuel 7:12, After a morning devotion on January 9 called 'Gethsemane' from Matthew 26, Smith closed the evening with 'The place which is called Calvary' based on Luke 23:33. These sentences introduced the evening devotion: 'We visited Gethsemane this morning; let us visit Calvary tonight. There Jesus suffered immediately from the hand of a holy God; here He suffered by the hands of wicked men.' 'Why are ye so fearful?' from Mark 4:40 is paired with 'Fear not, thou worm Jacob' from Isaiah 41:14. 'If ye love me, keep my commandments,' Christ's stern but loving call from John 14:15, is a morning text that comes before an evening text from 1 Corinthians 7:22, 'Christ's servant.' The narrative for the evening shows it is in pure earnestness in demonstrating the morning call: 'Every Christian is a servant. Jesus is his Master. The precepts of the gospel are his rule. He is bound to obey. He has pledged himself to do the will of God from the heart. He that is not willing to serve Christ, has no evidence whatever that he is interested in Him.' 'We joy in God' from Romans 5:11 is supplemented by 'The joy of the LORD is your strength' from Nehemiah 8:10. That day ends with this observation, 'It is as much our duty to be happy, as to be holy; both are recommended, and provision is as much made for the one as the other.'

Sometimes Smith uses a day to pair concepts that emphasize temporality under the governance of eternity, or the human viewed in light of the divine, or tottering weakness bolstered by unvanquished strength. He begins on January 1 with 'Look Unto Me,' from Isaiah 45:22 for the morning reading.

INTRODUCTION

The evening then is based on Isaiah 66:2: 'To this Man Will I look.' This pattern is repeated frequently with such striking combinations as 'The Fear of Death' and 'To Die is Gain;' 'Blessed be ye poor' from Luke 6:20 and 'All things are yours' from 1 Corinthians 3:21; 'Let him deny himself' expressing Matthew 16:24 and 'I will honour him' based on Psalm 91:15; 'Let him ask in faith' from James 1:6 paired with 'Help thou mine unbelief' from Mark 9:24; 'But thou art the same,' taken from Psalm 102:27 contrasted with 'We all do fade as a leaf' from Isaiah 64:6. That evening devotion begins with the humbling words, 'What a contrast between an unchangeable God, and a sinner fading like a leaf! Yet, this is a true picture of us, and of all temporal things. We began to look green and gay not long since, and in a little time we shall wither, fade, and die.'

Many days do not contain an intended pairing of ideas with complementary emphases or ironical distinctions. They all, however, generate knowledge of divinely revealed truth. Whether the devotions have some intended pairing or stand alone, each is resonant with biblical concepts designed to edify, challenge, and encourage the Christian, and remind him ever that all the glory belongs to the Lord. The subjects are so richly varied and the admonitions so well-distributed between challenge, encouragement, evangelistic appeal, theological instruction, and exhortation to wonder that an accurate summary statement defies complete accuracy. One of the closing applications from Smith himself, however, expresses his desire in a pleasing summary:

> To know God is to be truly wise, and to possess everlasting life; for 'This', said Jesus, 'is life eternal, to know thee the only true God, and Jesus Christ, whom thou hast sent.' The knowledge of God comes from reading His Word, watching His providence, studying His works, and the teaching of His Holy Spirit. Can we say tonight, 'My God, I know Thee? My God, I love Thee?'

Tom J. Nettles

JANUARY 1

🍀 MORNING 🍀

'Look unto me'
Isaiah 45:22

A New Year's morning opens upon us, and we are still exposed to sorrow, Satan, and disappointment; sin lives in us; and a thousand things are ready to distress us; but our God says, 'Look unto me.' 'Look unto me' as the source of happiness, the giver of grace, and your Friend. 'Look unto me' in every trial, for all you want, and in every place. 'Look unto me' *today*. I have blessings to bestow. I am waiting to be gracious. I am your Father in Jesus. Believe that I am deeply interested in your present and eternal welfare; that all I have promised, I will perform; that I am with you, purposely to bless you. I cannot be unconcerned about anything that affects you; and I pledge Myself to make all things work together for your good. You have looked to self, to others, in times past; but you have only met with trouble and disappointment; now look unto Me *alone*, to Me *for all*. Lift up the eye and the heart to Me today, and every day throughout the year; and walk before Me in peace and holiness. Prove Me hereby, if I will not thus make you holy, useful, and happy; try Me, and find My word of promise true; true to the very letter.

> *Look to Him, till His mighty love*
> *Thy ev'ry thought control,*
> *Its vast, constraining influence prove*
> *O'er body, spirit, soul.*

🍀 EVENING 🍀

'To this man will I look'
Isaiah 66:2

To what man? the poor in spirit; the humble; the man who trembles at His Word; who lies low in self-abasement at His throne; who mourns over his follies and his faults; who fears to offend a God so good, so holy, so great; the man who looks to Jesus for life, peace, and everlasting salvation. To such, the Lord will look. He will observe them. He will admire them. He will manifest His approbation of them. He will look and love; look and listen to their prayers; look and accept their persons and services; look and honour them, visiting them as His friends, dwelling with them as His children, owning them as His jewels, and using them as instruments for His glory. He will look upon them and strengthen them as He did Gideon; look, and restore them as He did Peter; look, and so lift up the light of His countenance upon them, and give them peace. My soul, hast thou been looking to the Lord today? Hast thou looked unto Him as thy Father? If so, doubtless He has been looking upon thee with a Father's love. He is now looking down upon thee with approbation. Sweet thought! The look of God is more than wealth, more than honour. Retire to rest this night with the thought: Jehovah is looking upon me with love.

> *He proves His love, displays His grace,*
> *Through the redemption of His Son;*
> *He turns my feet from sinful ways,*
> *And pardons what my hands have done.*

JANUARY 2

🌿 MORNING 🌿

'Be ye thankful.'
COLOSSIANS 3:15

What cause to be thankful; what reason to be grateful have we! Surrounded by mercies, both temporal and spiritual. If we look back, we ought to rejoice that God hath chosen us in Christ Jesus, before the foundation of the world; that He sent His only-begotten Son into the world, to be a propitiation for our sins; that He sent His Holy Spirit into our hearts, to convince us of sin, lead us to Jesus, and make us meet for heaven. We have His Word in our hands, His grace in our hearts, His mercies in our houses, and His heaven before our eyes. O for a thankful heart! But let us take our poor, hard, ungrateful hearts to Jesus; He can soften them and fill them with gratitude. Let us confess our ingratitude before Him, and mourn over our unthankfulness at His feet. He is ready to forgive. He can sanctify us wholly. He will hear our cry, and pity our complaints. O Jesus, grant us a deep sense of our utter unworthiness, and of Thine unmerited goodness, that our souls may daily praise Thee with joyful lips! May we live as thoughtful dependents; as grateful, loving children, before our Father and our God; and daily be thankful.

Through all eternity, to Thee
A joyful song I'll raise;
But O! eternity's too short
To utter all Thy praise!

🌿 EVENING 🌿

'Now will I praise the LORD'
GENESIS 29:35

Ingratitude is a great sin, and yet it is very common. Mercies come unnoticed; they are enjoyed without gratitude, and depart without praise. How many favours have we enjoyed which we have never acknowledged. Yet the Lord has said, 'He that offereth praise glorifieth me.' Let us reflect upon our mercies, repent of our ingratitude, and say with Leah, *'Now will I praise the LORD.'* Who can have more reason? When shall we have a more favourable opportunity? Let us begin at once, and praise Him for temporal favours, but especially for spiritual blessings. Let us bless Him for what He has done, and for what He has promised; for what was given us in Adam, but more for what was given us in Christ; that He has generously provided all we can need, and has presented all He has provided to be received by us without money and without price. All He sends us is in love, all He does to us is in mercy, whether it be pleasant or painful. Therefore let us attend to the apostle's exhortation, and 'in everything give thanks; for this is the will of God in Christ Jesus concerning us.' 'Giving thanks always for all things unto God even the Father, in the name of our Lord Jesus Christ.' 'Praise is comely for the upright.'

Bless, O my soul, the living God;
Call home my thoughts, that rove abroad;
Why should the wonders He hath wrought,
Be lost in silence, and forgot.

JANUARY 3

❦ MORNING ❦
'A mediator'
GALATIANS 3:20

God is, and must be, the eternal enemy of sin. He cannot be reconciled to it; it is the abominable thing which He hates. He cannot look upon it but with abhorrence. How then can God receive, bless, or commune with us? Only through a Mediator. Jesus fills this office: He stands between God and us; He honours all the Father's perfections, and renders us and our services acceptable through His glorious righteousness and precious blood. God can only love us, receive us, commune with us, or bless us, in Jesus. He represents us to God, and we are accepted in the *Beloved*. He represents God to us, and we prove Him to be gracious. When going to the throne of grace, never forget that Jesus is the Mediator, the Middle-man: present your persons, your petitions, and your praises to God through Him. You have nothing to fear, for Jesus wears your nature; He has a heart that beats in unison with yours; He calls you *brother*; He uses all His influence with the Father on your behalf; all He did and suffered is employed for you, and at this moment He pleads your cause.

> *Oft as guilt, my soul, torments thee,*
> *Turn thine eyes to Jesu's blood;*
> *This will comfort, cheer, and cleanse thee,*
> *Seal thy peace, and do thee good:*
> *Peace and pardon*
> *Flow to thee through Jesu's blood.*

❦ EVENING ❦
'One mediator between God and men'
1 TIMOTHY 2:5

There is but one Mediator; man has invented more, but God has appointed, revealed, and accepted but one. One is sufficient: Jesus alone is the Mediator of reconciliation. His atonement is infinite in its value and efficacy; it honoured the law, satisfied justice, and glorified all the perfections of God. It perfected for ever them that are sanctified. It is a sacrifice of a sweet-smelling savour unto God. On the ground of the one sacrifice of Jesus, sinners are received, pardoned, and accepted of God. Let nothing else engage your attention when seeking acceptance with God. Go through Jesus, through Jesus only, however vile, however sinful you may be; there is reconciliation to God through the death of His Son. There is but one Mediator of intercession. One is sufficient. Jesus ever lives to make intercession. The Father always hears Him. We need no one to dispose His mind to pity, listen to, or plead for us; His nature is love. It is His office and work to save, and He delights in His work. Therefore He is able to save them to the uttermost, who come unto God by Him, seeing He ever liveth to make intercession for them. Go to God, then, by Jesus; and acceptance is certain, a blessing is sure.

> *He ever lives to intercede*
> *Before His Father's face:*
> *Give Him, my soul, thy cause to plead,*
> *Nor doubt the Father's grace.*

JANUARY 4

🌿 MORNING 🌿

'Blessed be ye poor'
LUKE 6:20

The Lord's people are all poor; they see and feel that sin has stripped them of every excellence; and has left them wretched, and miserable, and poor, and blind, and naked. They can do nothing of themselves; they can procure nothing, but free grace has made ample provision for them, and the gospel informs them that Jesus has everything they want, and that all He has is for them. When they look at, or into themselves, they are discouraged; but when they look to Jesus, they rejoice. He has riches of grace, and riches of glory; and He says, 'Every one that asketh, receiveth.' He giveth liberally, and upbraideth not. Here then is the present blessedness of the Lord's poor; Jesus has all they need. He is their Friend; and they that seek Him shall not want any good thing. Am I poor? If so, Jesus bids me come to Him, and buy gold, clothing, wine, and milk; all that is necessary to comfort and support in time, and render me happy throughout eternity. Poor in self, rich in Jesus; poor at present, rich by and by; for theirs is the kingdom of heaven. 'All things are yours, ye are Christ's, and Christ is God's.' 'All things are for your sakes.'

> *What want shall not our God supply*
> *From His redundant stores?*
> *What streams of mercy from on high*
> *An arm almighty pours!*

🌿 EVENING 🌿

'All things are yours'
1 CORINTHIANS 3:21

'Hearken, my beloved brethren, hath not God chosen the poor of this world rich in faith, and heirs of the kingdom which He hath promised to them that love Him?' What a paradox is this, poor yet rich, as having nothing, yet possessing all things! All things are ours: For our use and benefit; to enjoy even when we do not actually possess; made over to us in covenant, presented to us in the promises, to be realized and enjoyed by faith, to claim and possess by and by. We shall have all that is really needful in time, and the whole when Jesus shall appear the second time without sin unto salvation. We are heirs of God, and joint heirs with our Lord Jesus Christ; and whether we reflect on things temporal or spiritual, things present or future, things painful or pleasant, things on earth or in heaven, we may justly say, 'All things are ours.' God is ours, our portion; Jesus is ours, our Bridegroom; the Holy Spirit is ours, our Comforter; earth is ours, our school-room; heaven is ours, our eternal home. But do we believe this? Do we live realizing this glorious truth? Can we lay down tonight on our pillows and say with confidence, 'All things are mine?' If so, it may be well said to us, 'I know your poverty, but *you are rich*.'

> *God is our joy and portion still,*
> *When earthly good retires;*
> *He will our hearts sustain and fill,*
> *When earth itself expires.*

JANUARY 5

❦ MORNING ❦
'Fear of death'
HEBREWS 2:15

All must die, but all do not die alike; some are cut off suddenly, others by a lingering illness; some die only safe, others happy. Some fear death all their lives, others do not. But death must be viewed through Jesus, or fear it we shall, if we think seriously. Death is a separation from the body; the second death is a separation from God. The former we must pass through, not so the latter. What shall separate us from the love of God? Death? No, we are more than conquerors through Him that hath loved us. Death only opens the prison-door, and sets the captive free. It is an answer to our many prayers for deliverance, for freedom from sin, and for perfect happiness. If we are united to Jesus by a living faith, death cannot disunite us; but will only introduce us into His presence, that we may forever enjoy His love. If we walk with God; if we believe the Saviour's Word; if we look beyond the valley, we shall not fear death. Jesus will not leave us then. He will be present according to His Word, and we shall prove His faithfulness, veracity, and love. 'Thanks be unto God who giveth us the victory, through our Lord Jesus Christ.'

> Why should I shrink at pain and woe,
> Or feel at death dismay?
> I've Canaan's goodly land in view,
> And realms of endless day.

❦ EVENING ❦
'To die is gain'
PHILIPPIANS 1:21

If we look at death as creatures, we shall fear it; but if we look at it as Christians, we shall not. It was once a curse; it is now a blessing. It was a loss; it is now a gain. Dying we gain our freedom from every foe, trial, and trouble; and obtain possession of innumerable blessings. We are freed from sin, and made perfect in holiness. We are delivered from sickness and pain, and enjoy perfect health and happiness. We shall gain knowledge, for then shall we know even as we are known. We shall gain holiness, for then we shall be with Christ and be like Him. We shall gain honour, for then white robes shall be given us, and we shall be acknowledged as victorious over Satan, the world, and sin. We shall sit down with Jesus on His throne. Death to every believer is gain. It is immediate gain. It is great gain. It is everlasting gain. It may be painful to pass through, but its results will be glorious. And shall we fear death? Why should we? Jesus says, 'He that keepeth my sayings, shall never taste of death.' He may sleep, he may depart to be with his Lord, he may go home to rest after the toils and conflicts of life, but he shall never die. Death hath no dominion over him. Look through Jesus at death, and look through death to Jesus.

> Soon will the Lord, my life, appear;
> Soon shall I end my trials here,
> Leave sin and sorrow, death and pain;
> To live is Christ – to die is gain.

JANUARY 6

🌿 MORNING 🌿

'Be careful for nothing'
PHILIPPIANS 4:6

The Lord careth for us. He knows our wants, and has promised to supply them; our foes, and will deliver us from them; our fears, and will make us ashamed of them. All creatures and things are in His hand, and at His disposal; all circumstances are absolutely under His control. He directs the angel, feeds the sparrow, curbs the devil, and manages the tempest. He is thy *Father*. His love to thee is infinite. Thou art His *delight*, His dear son, His pleasant child. Will He neglect thee? Impossible. Cast then thy cares upon Him. Tell out all thy desires, fears, and troubles to Him; let Him know everything *from thee*, keep nothing back; and then in the confidence of faith expect Him to fulfil His Word, and act a parent's part. Bless Him for all He has given, for all He has promised; plead with Him for all you may need; but never for one moment, or under any circumstances, distrust Him. He cannot love thee more. He is a present help. He will make all His goodness pass before thee. He will rejoice over thee to do thee good, with His whole heart, and with His whole soul.

> Then let me banish anxious care,
> Confiding in my Father's love;
> To Him make known my wants in prayer,
> Prepared His answer to approve.

🌿 EVENING 🌿

'Martha, Martha, thou art careful'
LUKE 10:41

Jesus loved Martha, and Martha loved Jesus; but Martha was too anxious about temporal things, and therefore Jesus lovingly reproved her. She was entangled and hurried, and His aim was to set her free. Her care was intense, and while it irritated her temper, it hindered her enjoying His society, or receiving with meekness His Word. This is a common fault among our Lord's disciples. How many Marthas have we in the church; how very few Marys? Let us take our seat at the feet of Jesus by Mary's side, let us listen to His Word, let us realize His care for us, and let us try and cast all our care on Him. All our concerns are in His hands, all circumstances are under His control, all events are managed by His wisdom. He exhorts us to seek first His kingdom, to aim always at His glory, to be satisfied with His arrangements, and to live in peace. Let the peace of God rule in your hearts. Whatever happens will be overruled for your good. You will soon leave the present scene, and leave behind you all the objects about which you have been careful. Be prayerful, but not careful. Attend to Martha's duties in Mary's spirit. Receive thy Lord's reproof this evening as spoken to thee, and try to bury thy cares where He has buried thy sins.

> How often we like Martha vex'd,
> Encumber'd, hurried, and perplexed?
> While trifles so engross our thought,
> The one thing needful is forgot.

JANUARY 7

🌿 MORNING 🌿
'Let him deny himself'
MATTHEW 16:24

It is required by Jesus that every disciple should practice self-denial. We must deny and crucify the workings of self-righteousness, and venture alone upon His work and worth for salvation; and we must mortify the pride of reason and intellect, and believe as His Word reveals, and walk as His Word directs. Our nearest relatives, dearest friends, and choicest comforts, must be resigned, if they are opposed to His glory and the furtherance of His cause. A Christian must lay everything at the feet of Jesus, and say, 'Lord, do with it as Thou wilt.' We are not our own, nor is any thing we have our own; it is the Lord's. Our appetites, pleasures, and pursuits, must all be brought into subjection to the obedience of Christ. His glory is to be sought at all times, in all things, under all circumstances; and when this is done, we are safe and happy. The servant must obey his master, and the child submit in all things to his wise, judicious and loving father. But for whom am I called to deny myself? For Jesus, who lived and died to save me, who is now in heaven interceding for me; and who is the great pattern of self-denial, having humbled Himself even unto death.

> *Beloved self must be denied,*
> *The mind and will renew'd;*
> *Passion suppress'd, and patience tried,*
> *And vain desires subdued.*

🌿 EVENING 🌿
'I will honour him'
PSALM 91:15

'Them that honour me I will honour.' Self-exaltation dishonours the Lord, and will bring us into discredit and disgrace; but self-denial is the road to advancement and honour. If the Christian deny himself, and keep his eye and his heart steadily fixed on the Lord's glory, the Lord will honour him. He shall be brought through all difficulties with credit, be cleared of all slanders and scandals that may be thrown upon him, and enjoy his Father's smile in the darkest day. The Lord will visit him, hold sweet communion with him, and raise his mind above all the circumstances that surround him. In sickness He will soothe and comfort him, in health guide and direct him; in poverty He will bless him with contentment, and in plenty with a liberal spirit; through life He will sustain and supply him, and in death animate and receive him. While he lives he shall be a blessing, and after death have a station near the throne. Beloved, deny self, mortify the flesh, rise above the world, live by faith, walk with God, honour the Lord, and He will honour you. Leave your concerns in His hands, while you seek to promote His kingdom and glory; and you will find that He will bless your provision, and satisfy you with the bread of heaven.

> *He that denies himself for Me,*
> *My kingdom to extend;*
> *Shall taste My love, My glory see,*
> *And I will be His friend.*

JANUARY 8

🌿 MORNING 🌿
'I will help thee'
Isaiah 41:13

Wherever the Lord leads us, He will support us; nor shall the difficulties of the way, or the weakness we feel, be too much for us. His hand is stretched out to us, and it is for faith to lay hold of it and proceed, confident of assistance. The arm of His power is the protection of His people in danger, and the strength of His people in weakness. He is a very present help in trouble, a God at hand. Are you weak, or in difficulty? Plead His Word; it is plain, positive, and sure. He cannot lie. He will not deceive. His strength is made perfect, and is glorified in your weakness. Fear not; underneath are everlasting arms. He will strengthen you with strength in your soul. He *can* help, for He is omnipotent. He *will* help, for He has given you His Word. Trust in the Lord at all times; yea, trust in the Lord forever, for in the Lord Jehovah is everlasting strength. That strength is promised to you, and will be employed for you in answer to prayer. Why then are you so fearful? Why cast down? He says, *'I will help thee.'* 'He hath said, and shall He not do it? He hath spoken, and shall He not make it good?'

> Fear not; I am with thee; O be not dismay'd!
> I, I am thy God, and will still give thee aid!
> I'll strengthen thee, help thee, and cause thee to stand,
> Upheld by My righteous, omnipotent hand.

🌿 EVENING 🌿
'Hitherto hath the LORD helped us.'
1 Samuel 7:12

God is faithful: and He hath written out His faithfulness in our experience in very legible characters. He promised to help us, and though we have passed through fire and through water, though our journey has been long, our road rough, our foes many, our sins great, and our faith feeble, He has ever been to us a very present help in trouble. He has helped us in darkness and light, in summer and winter, in soul and body. Let us tonight record His mercies; let us lift up the Ebenezer; let us bear witness to His faithfulness; and from the past let us draw encouragement for the future. He who hath helped us in time past, will help us now, will help us in all time to come. He says, 'I will not fail thee, nor forsake thee, until I have done that which I have spoken to thee of.' Let us rejoice and be glad, singing with the psalmist, 'Our help is in the name of the LORD, who made heaven and earth.' And as He hath said, 'I will never leave thee nor forsake thee,' let us boldly say, 'The Lord is my helper, and I will not fear what man can do unto me.' Remember, whatever may change, whoever may change, thy God is in one mind, and none can turn Him; therefore trust in Him, and He will help you out of every trial.

> Thus far His arm hath led us on;
> Thus far we make His mercy known;
> And, while we tread this desert land,
> New mercies shall new songs demand.

JANUARY 9

❦ MORNING ❧

'Gethsemane'
Matthew 26:36

This was a garden at the foot of Mount Olivet; here Jesus, as the *substitute* of His people, received the cup of wrath from the hand of His offended Father. It was the wrath of God, all we had deserved; the punishment we should have endured. The Son of God in our nature, in our stead, for our salvation, was punished by divine justice. No human hand touched Him, no human voice spoke to Him, when He sweat great drops of blood falling down to the ground. It was the baptism He expected, and O how great was His love! The baptism He longed to undergo. See the wonderful Sufferer; hear His dreadful groans; listen to His heart-breaking sighs; heaven and hell are astonished; only man remains unaffected. Beloved, it is our *surety*. He is paying our debt, redeeming our souls, purchasing our happiness, and making our peace. He went to *Gethsemane* that we might not go to hell. He was punished that we might be glorified. Often, very often, visit this sacred spot; here have fellowship with Christ in His sufferings by faith. O my soul, I charge thee to visit Gethsemane, and visit it very often for fellowship with Jesus!

> Go to the garden, sinner; see
> Those precious drops that flow;
> The heavy load He bore for thee:
> For thee He lies so low.

❦ EVENING ❧

'The place which is called Calvary'
Luke 23:33

We visited Gethsemane this morning; let us visit Calvary tonight. There Jesus suffered immediately from the hand of a holy God; here He suffered by the hands of wicked men. He is led as a lamb to the slaughter. See Him passing through the gates of Jerusalem, weary, weak, and faint, His cross laid on His shoulders. He ascends the eminence, the common place of execution. The cross is laid on the ground, He is stretched upon it, His arms and legs are strained, and the nails are driven through His hands and feet. It is raised up and thrust into its socket with a violent jerk, all His bones are out of joint, and He hangs a spectacle of misery and woe. See His attenuated frame, His pale cheeks, His sunken eye, His thorn-crowned brow, His death-stricken countenance, and hear Him cry, 'My God, my God, why hast thou forsaken me?' Was ever sorrow like unto His sorrow! He is accursed, He is made sin for us; He suffers, the innocent for the guilty; He dies, the just for the unjust. It is the Shepherd, dying for His sheep; the Bridegroom redeeming His bride; and the Head ransoming His body. He died for us, in our stead, that we might never die. Often let us visit Calvary, and muse upon its tragic scene, the scene of suffering love.

> When the dread scene of death, the last
> Important hours draws nigh,
> Then with my dying eyes, I'll cast
> A look on Calvary.

JANUARY 10

🌿 MORNING 🌿

'I am a worm'
PSALM 22:6

Man is naturally poor and proud, but grace strips him and humbles him in the dust. Here the highly favoured David, the man after God's own heart, cries out, 'I am a worm.' How little, how despicable he appeared in his own eyes. Every one that humbleth himself shall be exalted. You have looked at Bible saints, and have sighed out, 'Ah! they were not like me!' My brother, are you not a poor, weak, worthless worm? Do you not feel so? Well, so did David. The less you are in your own eyes, the more fit you are for the Lord Jesus, and the more welcome will you be at the throne of grace. But this was the language also of David's Lord; this was the view the Jews had of Him, and they treated Him accordingly. The brightness of glory is compared to a vile reptile; the express image of the Father's person is treated with the greatest contempt. But it was for us men, and for our salvation. O mystery of mercy! Jesus is reduced to a level with the worm, that we may be raised higher than the angels.

From Bethlehem's inn, to Calvary's cross,
Affliction mark'd His road;
And many a weary step He took,
To bring us back to God.

By men despised, rejected, scorn'd,
No beauty they can see;
With grace and glory all adorn'd,
The loveliest form to me.

🌿 EVENING 🌿

'God hath highly exalted him'
PHILIPPIANS 2:9

No one ever sunk so low as Jesus; no one is, or ever will be raised so high. He was considered as unfit to live, He was treated as a despicable worm, He was put to death in the flesh; but God hath highly exalted Him. He is gone into heaven, He is seated at the right hand of God, He wears a name which is above every name, He possesses all authority in heaven and on earth, thrones, and dominions, and principalities, and powers are made subject unto Him. His crown glitters with sparkling gems brighter than the morning sun, His sceptre extends over all creation, His kingdom is an everlasting kingdom, and His dominion endureth throughout all generations. He is the object of angelic admiration and adoration, the subject of every song. His exaltation is the reward of His humiliation, sufferings, and death; but it is a sweet thought that He is exalted for His people's good, for His people's glory. Exalted to give them repentance and remission of sins, to sanctify their sorrows, supply their wants, secure their safe arrival around His throne, and glorify them with Himself for ever. Immortal Saviour! May I know the power of Thy resurrection, glorify Thy grace, be raised up, and be made to sit together with Thee in Thy glory!

To Him whom men despise and slight,
To Him be glory given;
The crown is His, and His by right,
The highest place in heaven.

JANUARY 11

❦ MORNING ❧

'Come unto me'
Matthew 11:28

Jesus calls you to His throne; He is there waiting to hear, relieve, and bless you. You are to go to Him just as you are, and receive from Him all you need. He will give you wisdom, to direct your steps; peace, to keep your hearts; strength, to do His will; righteousness, to justify your souls; and rest, unspeakably sweet. He is glorified in bestowing these blessings upon you. He calls you this *morning*, this *moment*, to receive without money and without price. What a precious Saviour is Jesus! What a kind and tender Friend! Let us go boldly to the throne of grace, that we may obtain mercy, and find grace to help in time of need. 'Come,' He says, 'come to Me; go not to self, to the world, to the empty cisterns which creatures idolize; but come unto Me, and I will do for you exceeding abundantly, above all you can ask or think. Your sins I will pardon; your graces I will revive; your comforts I will restore; your holiness I will increase; your efforts to glorify Me I will crown with success; I will bless you, and you shall be a blessing.' O how great is Thy goodness, which Thou hast laid up for them that seek Thee; which Thou hast wrought for them that trust in Thee, before the sons of men!

> *Jesus, with Thy Word complying,*
> *Firm our faith and hope shall be;*
> *On Thy faithfulness relying,*
> *We will cast our souls on Thee.*

❦ EVENING ❧

'Draw me'
Song of Solomon 1:4

Sweet and precious is the invitation of Jesus, but we feel that something more than the invitation is necessary. There is often a want of inclination, the soul is sluggish, the heart is heavy, a host of things interpose to keep us from His fulness. His invitation is a full and sufficient warrant: we *may* go to Him, we may go with confidence, we may go when we will, and for all we need; His heart is kind, His resources are thrown open, His Word is true; but we need the drawings of the Holy Spirit. Our weakness, our reluctance, the difficulties we meet with, make us cry, 'Draw me;' He has drawn us, else we had never approached Him; for He has said, 'No man can come unto me, except the Father which hath sent me draw him.' This drawing is the effect and proof of eternal love; hence we read, 'I have loved thee with an everlasting love, *therefore with lovingkindness have I drawn thee.*' The Lord's drawings are so sweet that we yield before we are aware: 'I draw them with cords of love.' They are so natural, that they always prevail: 'I draw them as with the bands of a man.' May Jesus draw us from the world, from sin, and from self tonight; may He draw us to His footstool, and to His throne.

> *O lead me to Thy mercy-seat,*
> *Attract me nearer still;*
> *Draw me like Mary to Thy feet,*
> *To sit and learn Thy will.*

JANUARY 12

🌿 MORNING 🌿

'I go mourning'
Psalm 38:6

But what is the cause of thy mourning? There is nothing apart from Jesus worth mourning for, or beside sin worth mourning over. Is it because of the unevenness of thy walk with God? On account of the deep depravity of thy nature? Because men keep not God's law? Or because Jesus hides His face, and your evidences fade and wither? You may well mourn after Jesus, but you must not despond; for He will turn again, He will have compassion upon you. The depravity of the heart is enough to make an angel weep; but forget not the precious blood that cleanseth, or the promised grace that sanctifies. Look not too much at the defects which appear in your walk, nor at the corruption which works in your heart; but deal with the blood and grace of Jesus, as the means of thy cure. Read and believe His promises; confess and plead at His throne; wait and watch in His ways; be careful, lest by inordinate mourning you grieve His Spirit. He cannot be unkind; He never will forsake you; He was anointed 'to comfort all that mourn.'

> Cease, O believer, cease to mourn;
> Return unto thy rest, return;
> Why should thy sorrows swell?
> Though deep distress thy steps attend,
> Thy warfare shall in triumph end;
> With thee it shall go well.

🌿 EVENING 🌿

'Good tidings of great joy'
Luke 2:10

There is everything in our hearts to cast us down, and fill us with dejection; and we daily meet with things in the world, or the family, or the church, to make us sorrowful; but the gospel brings us glad tidings of great joy. It sets before us a Saviour, and such a Saviour! One who is God and can deliver us, One who is man and will sympathise with us; One who knows by experience what our trials mean, and who brings all the resources of God to meet our case; so that we may well ask, 'Why art thou cast down, O my soul?' In His blood, there is a full, a certain pardon for all sin; in His obedience, a righteousness, to justify us freely and for ever before God; in His fulness, an endless variety of blessings, to supply our needs; and in His promises, comfort to cheer us in our most gloomy hours. He is a Saviour for sinners; all He did, He did for sinners; just such sinners as we daily feel ourselves to be. For such He obeyed the law, for such He made atonement, for such He now pleads before His Father; it is just such sinners that He invites to His bosom, and for such He is preparing mansions in heaven. Whatever is necessary to constitute any tidings good, is in the gospel; and all that is requisite to fill us with great joy, is there too.

> This love exceeds our highest thought;
> Its length and breadth in vain are sought:
> No tongue can tell its depth and height,
> The love of God is infinite.

JANUARY 13

❦ MORNING ❦

'Let him ask in faith'
JAMES 1:6

The believer's prayers should be regulated by God's promises; he often fancies he wants what would only do him harm; and, therefore, if he ask, he is denied, not in anger but in love. God has promised all good, and only good, to His beloved people. Ask for what God has promised to bestow, and ask believing that God will honour and fulfil His own precious Word. He cannot deny Himself; all He hath promised He will perform. You can therefore have no reason to doubt whether the Lord will give you, if you really need it, and He has plainly promised it; therefore ask desiring and expecting, and then look to receive. What are thy wants this morning? Where hath God promised such things in His holy Word? Search out the promise, take it to His throne, plead in the name of Jesus for its fulfilment, and never doubt for one moment, but that the Lord will make it good. Stay yourself therefore on the Word of the Lord; but if you will not believe, surely you shall not be established. Faith honours God by trusting Him; and God always honours faith by answering it. 'Come boldly to the throne of grace, that you may obtain mercy, and find grace to help in time of need.'

> *Beyond thy utmost wants*
> *His love and power can bless;*
> *To praying souls He always grants*
> *More than they can express.*

❦ EVENING ❦

'Help thou mine unbelief'
MARK 9:24

Our faith is often weak, and our unbelief very strong. It is so natural for a sinner to disbelieve God, and it is often difficult for a Christian to give full credit to God's promises. Sometimes His Word appears to be too good to be true; at other times we have such a vivid sense of our sinfulness, that we cannot admit that such great and glorious blessings are for us. Indeed, it is very difficult to believe that God is as good as His Word declares; that His promises belong to *such sinners*; and that we may, *should*, believe, appropriate, and plead them as made to us. We fear presumption, and so yield to unbelief. We listen to Satan, and so doubt and fear. But Jesus asks, 'If I say the truth, why do ye not believe me?' Is then the promise true? Is the promise plain? Is it made to sinners? Does it flow from grace? Is it given us that God may be glorified in His mercy, love, and kindness? Then let us endeavour to believe, to rest on the Word, to expect that God will do as He has said. Let us take our unbelief where we take our other sins – to Jesus; let us confess it, deplore it, and cry with His disciples of old, 'Lord, increase our faith.' Or with the poor man in the text, 'Help thou mine unbelief.' Help me to conquer it, and to triumph over it.

> *Lord, Thou hast said, Thou wilt forgive,*
> *Now help me to believe and live:*
> *A living, vigorous faith impart,*
> *And seal my pardon on my heart.*

JANUARY 14

🌿 MORNING 🌿

'Walk circumspectly'
EPHESIANS 5:15

You are in an enemy's land; surrounded by temptations; and have a heart that is deceitful above all things, and desperately wicked. To honour Jesus in your spirit, communications, and every action, should be your constant aim. You are to live *unto* the Lord, for Him who died for you and rose again. To this end, provision was laid up in the everlasting covenant, for this purpose the precious promises were made, and with this design the Holy Spirit is given; that you may serve Him in righteousness and holiness all the days of your life. This world is not your home; Satan's family are not to be your associates; riches, honours, or pleasure, are not to be your objects; you are to walk as in the midst of snares; watchful, prayerful, depending upon Jesus, and cultivating fellowship with Him. O keep your eye on Jesus as your example; walk by His Word as your rule; be not venturesome or presumptuous, but avoid the very appearance of evil. Never leave the Lord's ways or ordinances, to join the world's parties or to please a carnal fancy. Keep close to Jesus, and follow on to know the Lord. Act as a loving child going home to his father's house.

> *So let our lips and lives express*
> *The holy gospel we profess;*
> *So let our works and virtues shine,*
> *To prove the doctrine all divine.*

🌿 EVENING 🌿

'Hold up my goings in thy paths'
PSALM 17:5

Failures, follies, and mistakes should lead us to our forgiving God, and teach us the necessity of close walking with God. We need to be constantly upheld by divine power, and to be guided by divine wisdom. We are prone to start aside as a broken bow. Many have fallen into sin; many do fall; we are as much exposed to temptations as they were, and are as liable to be overcome. Satan is watchful, temptations are powerful, and our hearts are weak. Let us therefore cry to the Strong One for strength, and let it be our daily prayer, 'Hold up my goings in thy paths.' In every duty, as well as in every trial; in the calm, as well as in the storm; we need to be upheld, for unless the Lord uphold us, we shall fall into presumption, or despair; into self-righteousness, or licentiousness; into open sin, or secret backsliding. We are never safe, but as the Lord keeps us; and He keeps by teaching us our weakness, our proneness to wander, and by leading us to walk softly before Him, in faith, and humility of mind. We are never so liable to wander, as when we fancy there is no fear of it; nor so likely to fall as when we think it impossible. Beloved, if you are not daily seeking divine protection, you are in danger of being overcome. Examine. Watch. Pray.

> *Now, Holy Spirit, to my heart,*
> *Wisdom and holiness impart;*
> *Uphold me by Thy mighty power,*
> *In every dark or dangerous hour.*

JANUARY 15

❧ MORNING ❧

'But thou art the same.'
PSALM 102:27

Everything below is liable to change; health may give place to sickness, pleasure to pain, plenty to poverty, love to enmity, honour to disgrace, strength to weakness, and life to death. Remember the days of darkness, for they shall be many. But though all our circumstances and friends should change, there is One who never changes. He is in one mind, and none can turn Him. With Him is no variableness. He is the same yesterday, today, and forever; and He is our best Friend, our nearest relation, our gracious Saviour. Yesterday, His name was Jesus; His nature was love; His purpose was to do us good with His whole heart and soul. Today, He is the same; we cannot expect too much from Him, or be too confident in Him, if we are walking humbly with Him. He will be our God, and we shall be His people. Let us cultivate intimacy with Him, dependence upon Him, concern to please Him, fear to offend Him, zeal to glorify Him; and it must be well with us in health and sickness, plenty and poverty, life and death; for He is the same, and will never turn away from doing us good, but remain the fountain of love and holiness for ever. Praise ye the Lord.

> *This God is the God we adore,*
> *Our faithful, unchangeable Friend;*
> *Whose love is as great as His power,*
> *And neither knows measure nor end.*

❧ EVENING ❧

'We all do fade as a leaf'
ISAIAH 64:6

What a contrast between an unchangeable God, and a sinner fading like a leaf! Yet, this is a true picture of us, and of all temporal things. We began to look green and gay not long since, and in a little time we shall wither, fade, and die. 'Man that is born of a woman is of few days and full of trouble. He cometh forth like a flower, and is cut down.' Humbling consideration this. But it may be rendered very useful. Let us endeavour to turn it to account. Shall we soon fade and die? Then let us not be much affected by anything that occurs below. Let us set our affections on things above, and lay up for ourselves treasures in heaven. Let us live by faith on Jesus, walk with God, and aim principally to please Him in all we do. Let us also watch against a worldly spirit, and pass the time of our sojourning here in fear. We shall soon find health give place to sickness; strength, to weakness; youth, to age. The dying bed, the coffin, the grave, are just before us; let us therefore make our calling and our election sure; let us cultivate close and filial fellowship with God; let us dig deep and lay our foundation upon the rock. Brethren, the time is short, eternity with all its glories is just before us; we all do fade as a leaf.

> *On the tree of life eternal,*
> *O let all our hopes be staid!*
> *This alone, for ever vernal,*
> *Bears a leaf that shall not fade.*

JANUARY 16

❦ MORNING ❧

'Is it well with thee?'

2 KINGS 4:26

Is Jesus precious to thy soul? Are you mourning over sin, or after the presence of your beloved Saviour? Are you strong in faith, giving glory to God? Are you panting for communion with your heavenly Father? Is the world beneath your feet? Are you glowing with love to all saints? Are you seeking first the kingdom of God and His righteousness? Are you lying at the feet of Jesus, in trouble, crying, 'Lord, help me?' If so, it is well with thee: there is spiritual life in thy soul, and the blessed Spirit is thy Teacher. But if the world is preferred to Jesus, the pleasures of time to fellowship with God, if self-examination is neglected, and the Bible is become dry and unsavoury, it is not well. Health of soul is manifested by habitual prayer, zeal in the Lord's cause, an appetite for the bread of life, and activity in the Lord's ways. Is thy soul sick? If so, apply at once to Jesus, as the great physician; and plead with Him to restore unto thee the joys of His salvation, and to uphold thee with His free Spirit. He will heal thy backslidings, and love thee freely.

> *'Tis well; my soul is fill'd with joy,*
> *Though in myself a feeble worm:*
> *For Jesus will His power employ,*
> *And save my soul in every storm;*
> *He will His gracious Word fulfil,*
> *And guard my soul from every ill.*

❦ EVENING ❧

'It is well'

2 KINGS 4:26

What a mercy to be able to say so! Still, if we are in Christ, if clothed with His righteousness, if living upon Him as the bread of life, 'it is well.' For all our sins are blotted out, the Holy Spirit dwells in our hearts, and God looks down upon us and loves us with an infinite love. It is well, for our names are in the book of life, our cause is in the Saviour's hands, and our peace with God is made. It may be a day of darkness with us, but the Lord is our everlasting light and the days of our mourning will soon be ended. Providence may frown upon us, but temporal trials are only intended to endear spiritual blessings. We may feel weak, very weak, but the strength of Jesus shall be made perfect in our weakness. Satan may sorely harass and hunt us like the partridge upon the mountains, but God will bruise Satan under our feet shortly. Our hearts may appear barren, and all within may wear a wintry aspect; but this is only permitted to drive us out of self, to prevent spiritual pride, and to render Jesus and His finished work more precious. It is well with them that fear the Lord, let outward things be as they may; for He watches over them to do them good, rejoices to bless and make them holy, and turns every thing to their account.

> *Though you may trials sharp endure,*
> *From sin, or death, or hell;*
> *Your heavenly Father's love is sure,*
> *And therefore, 'It is well.'*

JANUARY 17

🌿 MORNING 🌿
'I would do good'
Romans 7:21

Every believer has experienced the renewing of the Holy Ghost; sin has not dominion over him. He perceives the beauty of holiness, and loathes himself on account of sin. He would be internally holy, and externally conformed to the precepts of the Bible. He would pray with fervour; praise with gratitude; believe with confidence; war against sin, Satan, and the flesh with courage; and glorify God by every feeling, thought, word, and action. Thus he feels, and for this he prays in his best moments; but he finds that he needs the frequent renewing of the Holy Spirit, for he is prone to sink into coldness, deadness, darkness, and stupidity, and he is obliged to cry out, 'My soul cleaveth unto the dust; quicken thou me according unto thy word.' The Lord must work in us to *will* as well as to *do*; for by nature we are unwilling, and the desire after holiness, proved by effort to obtain it, is from God. Beloved, you must be coming to Jesus daily for fresh supplies of the Spirit, or you will find yourself not only weak, but careless; not only will the power of godliness decline, but you will become indifferent. Watch against temptation. Watch unto prayer. Watch over your own heart.

> O Lord, assist me through the fight,
> My drooping spirit raise;
> Make me triumphant in Thy might,
> And Thine shall be the praise.

🌿 EVENING 🌿
'Thy people shall be willing'
Psalm 110:3

No man by nature is willing to come to Christ for salvation, or to be saved by free and sovereign grace alone. Human nature is too blind, obstinate, and proud; if we are willing God has made us so. Nor is anyone desirous, or even willing, to be made truly holy, except he is taught of God. If therefore we would do good, if we are heartily desiring and earnestly seeking to be made holy in heart and life, it is because we are under the teaching of the Holy Spirit. What a mercy to know this! How often do we give human nature credit for being better than it is, and fancy that what we feel, desire, and do, is merely from an enlightened mind, and not from a sanctified heart. The Lord's people are made willing by the Lord's power; but that power works so secretly, so silently, in such strict accordance with our nature and faculties, that we do not perceive it. Are you in doubt, whether God hath really called you by grace or no? Enquire, am I willing to be saved by Jesus as a poor, lost sinner? Am I concerned to be made holy, as well as to be made happy? Do I pray to be made useful, as well as to be safe? If so, you are one of the Lord's people, and He has made you willing in the day of His power.

> Willing to be saved by grace,
> Let me see Thy glorious face;
> Willing to be holy too,
> Work in me to will and do.

JANUARY 18

❦ MORNING ❧

'Evil is present with me'

ROMANS 7:21

But what a mercy that it does not reign in you, and over you; it did once, and would now but for free and sovereign grace. If sin makes you groan, leads you to the throne to plead with God, and to the fountain of the Saviour's blood to be cleansed from it, it does not, it cannot reign. It may disturb your peace, distress your mind, hinder you in duty, mix with all your efforts to do good; and even make you cry out, 'O wretched man that I am, who shall deliver me?' But even then you should not doubt. Jesus still loves you, grace will reign in your experience, and you shall be more than a conqueror. Paul had known the Lord many years; he had been in the third heaven, and daily triumphed in Christ; yet he felt just as you feel; when he would do good evil was present with him, and he could not do the things that he would. If sin annoys you, if it is your burden, and causes you grief, holiness lives in you, and the present painful conflict will end in everlasting peace. You may even now sing, 'Thanks be unto God, who giveth us the victory, through our Lord Jesus Christ.' Live upon Christ, and you will live down all evil.

Crosses and changes are our lot,
Long as we sojourn here;
But since our Saviour changes not,
What have the saints to fear?

❦ EVENING ❧

'Ye that love the LORD, hate evil'

PSALM 97:10

Exhortations to the plainest duties are necessary, for sometimes we forget, but more often sink into a lukewarm, indifferent frame of soul. Do we love the Lord? If so, we love His people, His ordinances, His gospel, and His law. We love His prohibitions as well as His promises, knowing that He only prohibits what would do us an injury. Can we tonight join with David, and say, 'O how I love thy law, it is my meditation all the day!' The law prohibits all evil. Let us hate evil thoughts, and strive against them. Let us hate evil words, and keep the mouth as with a bridle. Let us hate evil works, and abstain from all appearance of evil. The evils of the heart are the worst, as all other evils flow from them; especially let us beware of an evil heart of unbelief in departing from the living God. Would you hate evil? Then walk close with God, be much in fellowship with Him, and so will holiness become your element, and every species of evil your abhorrence. Lovers of God, set your hearts, set your fears against evil; 'follow peace with all men, and holiness, without which no man shall see the Lord.'

Lord, whom I love, to Thee I give
My soul, my life, my all:
To Thee would I devoted live,
And ne'er the gift recall.

JANUARY 19

❦ MORNING ❧
'My brother'
Matthew 12:50

And who is the brother of Jesus? Every one who does the will of His Father; every believer who proves the truth of his faith by the goodness of his works; who shows the excellence of his nature, by the piety, benevolence, and charity of his life. Believer, Jesus calls thee *brother*. He has for thee a brother's love. O how tender! O how tried! Stronger than death; passing knowledge. He bears with thy infirmities, reproves thy follies, encourages thy faith, forbids thy fears, and will certainly provide for thy wants. Joseph in Egypt supplied his brethren during the famine, and shall not Jesus supply His? If He seem to speak roughly, He will act kindly, and perform a brother's part. He has all power in heaven and in earth. He doeth according to His will, and He is not ashamed to call us brethren. He will correspond with us, and bid us daily, yea hourly, correspond with Him. O remember, when you go to the throne of grace, that your *brother* fills it. He calls you to it, and will withhold no good thing from you. Precious Lord Jesus, manifest to me a brother's love; help me to rely on Thy fraternal kindness.

> Our nearest friend, our brother now,
> Is He to whom the angels bow;
> They join with us to praise His name,
> But we the nearest interest claim.

❦ EVENING ❧
'Joint-heirs with Christ'
Romans 8:17

Related to Jesus now, we shall inherit with Him by and by; not only as brethren of the same family, but as the bride inherits with her bridegroom. Jesus is constituted heir of all things, we are one with Him, and as such, are 'heirs of God and joint-heirs with Jesus Christ.' What dignity! What an unspeakable privilege is this! We are heirs of salvation, the heirs of promise. Connection with Adam involved us in guilt, ruin, and misery; connection with Jesus brings us righteousness, peace, and everlasting salvation. Now we suffer with Him, but we shall soon be glorified together. Now we taste the cup of His sorrow, but we shall soon drink of the cup of His joys. But are we indeed joint-heirs? Are we children of God by faith in Jesus Christ? Do we love our heavenly Father? Are we jealous for His honour and glory? Is sin the object of our hatred, and holiness our desire and delight? If so, Jesus calls us brethren, Jehovah calls us children, and in Jesus, 'we have obtained an inheritance, being predestinated according to the purpose of him who worketh all things after the counsel of his own will.'

> Children of God, through Jesus' love
> We rise undoubted heirs;
> His rich inheritance above,
> He with His brethren shares.

JANUARY 20

❦ MORNING ❧
'The wisdom of the just'
Luke 1:17

The Lord's people are justified freely, by His grace, through the redemption that is in Christ Jesus. The work of Jesus is their justification before God; in this they trust; in this they plead; and in this they rejoice. Taught by the Holy Spirit, they manifest wisdom in readily believing God's faithful Word, and trusting Him to make good the same to them. They resign themselves and all they value into His hands for preservation, and to be entirely at His disposal, persuaded that His wisdom and love will do better for them, than they possibly could for themselves. They refer all things to God for His decision, and cheerfully abide by His sentence. They live in simple, child-like dependence upon His providence and grace, for body and soul, for time and eternity, seeking to make His will theirs. They walk in charity with their fellow-Christians, who differ in some things from them, and would do good to all, especially to them that are of the household of faith. Beloved, do you manifest this wisdom? Do you walk by this rule? Do you mind the same things? Have you the wisdom that is from above, which is pure, gentle, easy to be entreated, full of mercy and good fruits?

> *Boundless wisdom, power divine,*
> *Love unspeakable, are Thine;*
> *Wisdom, Lord, to me be giv'n,*
> *Wisdom pure, which comes from heav'n.*

❦ EVENING ❧
'The LORD giveth wisdom'
Proverbs 2:6

In order to this He gives us to feel that we need it, ardently to long for it, and earnestly to seek it at His throne. We need wisdom to walk circumspectly, to overcome temptations, to work consistently in the Lord's vineyard, and to glorify God in our bodies, souls, and spirits which are His. The wisdom we need we may have, not by labour, but by prayer; we cannot produce it, but God has promised to bestow it. Hear His own word, 'If any of you lack wisdom, let him ask of God, that giveth to all liberally, and upbraideth not; and it shall be given him. But let him ask in faith, not wavering.' God is willing to bestow it, He promises to impart it; we ought therefore to believe His Word, ask Him for it, as though He really meant what He had said in His promise. 'The wisdom that is from above is first pure, then peaceable, gentle, easy to be entreated, full of mercy and good fruits, without partiality and without hypocrisy.' Would you be wise unto salvation? Wise to win souls? Wise to avoid evil, and secure all possible good? Then seek wisdom of God, seek it instantly, seek it earnestly, seek it in faith, and *'it shall be given you.'*

> *That wisdom, Lord, on me bestow,*
> *Gentle, and peaceable, and pure;*
> *That I may walk with Thee below,*
> *And make my own salvation sure.*

JANUARY 21

🌿 MORNING 🌿
'Ye cannot serve God and mammon'
Matthew 6:24

Our God is a jealous God. He requires the devotion of the heart, the consecration of all the powers, and we cannot enjoy religion without these. Persons who try to unite God and the world, the service of sin and the service of God, cannot be happy. We must be decided. Well, who is to be God *today*? Who is to have the heart, the talents, the affections, *today*? Is gain, carnal pleasure, or worldly company, to be the idol today? Or, is Jesus to have the thoughts, the desires, and the talents? Shall we seek His glory, and aim at His honour? Or, shall we say to some worthless bramble, 'Come thou, and reign over us?' Choose you. Whom will you serve? Attempt not to reconcile opposing claims, but let God or mammon have the whole. Surely, you are ready to cry out, 'Thine am I, Jesus, and Thee only will I serve!' But you can only serve Him acceptably, as you serve Him with the grace He imparts; He has provided, He has promised, and He invites you to receive it. Let us therefore have grace whereby we may serve God acceptably, with reverence and godly fear. Serving God in the spirit of adoption is true happiness.

> O let Thy love my soul inflame!
> And to Thy service sweetly bind;
> Transfuse it through my inmost frame,
> And mould me wholly to Thy mind.

🌿 EVENING 🌿
'O LORD, truly I am thy servant'
Psalm 116:16

Yes, we are the Lord's servants, created for His glory, redeemed to show forth His praise, regenerated to exhibit His virtues; we are His by the strongest ties. Jesus is our Master, His will is our law, and His pleasure should be our delight. Our Master is also our example; as the servant of the Father He appeared in our world, consulted the Father's will in all that He did, and suffered without complaining, all the Father saw fit to inflict. He humbled Himself and became obedient, and now He is exalted, and extolled, and is very high; and to us He says, 'If any man serve me, let him follow me: and where I am there shall also my servant be: if any man serve me him will my Father honour.' Obedience to Christ may sink us in the eyes of men, but it exalts us in the sight of God; it may expose us to suffering and contempt before the world, but God will honour us with His presence and smiles, and will afterwards receive us to glory. Well, whose servants have we been today? Whom have we been seeking to please? Whose cause have we been endeavouring to promote? Can we retire to rest as the servants of Christ, willing to go to Him whenever He calls us, or to stay and labour below so long as He sees proper to continue with us?

> Jesus, how great Thy servants are!
> What dignity on man bestow'd!
> We, who rejoice Thy yoke to bear,
> Are honour'd with the esteem of God.

JANUARY 22

❧ MORNING ☙

'I am thy shield'
GENESIS 15:1

They that believe are blessed with believing Abraham. The promises God made to him, He will fulfil to us. We are surrounded by foes; fiery darts fly in every direction; but Jehovah, in Jesus, interposes Himself as our Shield. Our safety and protection is from our relation to Him. We should soon be overcome if He did not preserve and defend. How safe and how happy we feel, when we realize that our God is our Defence, and the Most High God our Protector! If foes alarm, or dangers affright, yet remember, 'The name of the LORD is a strong tower,' you may run into that, and be safe. Faith is the arm. Jehovah is the Shield; with Satan, sin, and the world, we are in conflict; but we are preserved, as in a garrison, by the power of God, through believing, unto salvation. My brother, look to Jesus, through this day, as thy Shield, and expect safety and protection alone from Him; He will be present to protect thee, and answer thy prayers. He will thus preserve thy going out and coming in, from this time forth, and even for evermore. He will give thee the shield of His salvation, and His gentleness will make thee great.

His righteousness to faith reveal'd,
Wrought out for guilty worms,
Affords a hiding-place and shield,
From enemies and storms.

❧ EVENING ☙

'Keep me as the apple of the eye'
PSALM 17:8

Through another day the Lord has shielded us, and we should tonight record His faithful love. But while we record His past kindness, we should pray for protection for the future. What a beautiful, expressive, striking prayer is this! Keep me, for Thou art omnipotent, omniscient, and all-wise. Keep me, for I am exposed to enemies and storms; I am in danger from various quarters; I am weak and inexperienced as the newly fledged bird; I fear I shall fall! I have no one on whom I can repose but Thee. Keep me as the apple of the eye, carefully, constantly, tenderly and graciously. Keep me so, that I may be useful and ornamental as the apple of the eye. Keep me in Christ my head, watching, expecting, and enjoying Thy presence and Thy blessing. Keep me, for I see many fall into sin, and I feel I am as liable as they. Keep me, for such numbers decline, grow lukewarm, and leave the world under a cloud. Keep me by night and by day; and may I realise Thy preserving goodness, that I may with confidence say, 'The Lord is my keeper; the Lord is my shade upon my right hand. The Lord will preserve my coming in from this time forth, and even for evermore.'

Jehovah, by His ceaseless care,
Whose eye can never sleep,
From earthly foes, from Satan's snare,
My soul shall safely keep.

JANUARY 23

❧ MORNING ❧

'Why are ye so fearful?'
MARK 4:40

The disciples appeared to be in danger, and fear filled their hearts. They did not realize that they were the care and charge of Jesus, or else, knowing Him, their fears could have had no place. Beloved, you are in the hands of your loving Saviour. He has charge of you and all your concerns. He has numbered the very hairs of your head, and watches over you every moment, by night, as well as by day. He is ever present, His eye cannot be diverted from you, His omnipotence is engaged to defend you, His fulness to supply you, His wisdom to guide you, and all His perfections will be glorified in your everlasting holiness and happiness. He says, 'I am glorified in them.' Why are you so fearful? Jesus is a very present help; He is a Friend that loveth at all times; He is your shield, and will be your exceeding great reward. But perhaps you have wandered from Him; your conscience accuses you, and Satan tempts you to despond; go, go, and return unto Him, delay not a moment, cast yourself, guilty as you are, at His feet, confess all, and give yourself to Him afresh. He will receive you graciously, love you freely, and restore to you the joys of His salvation.

> *The saints should never be dismay'd,*
> *Nor sink in hopeless fear;*
> *For when they least expect His aid,*
> *The Saviour will appear.*

❧ EVENING ❧

'Fear not, thou worm Jacob'
ISAIAH 41:14

However mean and despicable we may appear in the eyes of others, however weak and feeble we may feel in ourselves, still our God says, 'Fear not.' Though but a worm, yet if a praying Jacob, we need not fear, we should not fear; our God forbids it because it injures our souls, encourages our enemies, dispirits our friends, and dishonours His glorious name. How precious, unspeakably precious these 'Fear nots' are! How thickly they are strewed through the divine Word! But why should we fear? The Lord expressly tells us that 'the race is not to the swift, nor the battle to the strong, neither bread to the wise, nor yet riches to men of understanding, nor yet favour to men of skill; but time and chance happeneth to them all.' Are we believers in Jesus? Then we should not fear, for our God is our friend, and His care extends over all time; embraces every event; supplies every want; anticipates every emergency; comprehends every believer from the beginning to the end of time; and shall everlastingly secure the safety and happiness of every worm that trusts in Him. His strength is almighty, His wisdom is omniscient, His love is unequalled, and His resources are unbounded. Therefore, 'Fear not, thou worm Jacob.'

> *On God thy constant Helper trust*
> *Thou abject worm despised by all;*
> *No one shall crush thee in the dust,*
> *Since He has raised thee from the fall.*

JANUARY 24

❦ MORNING ❧

'Ye are not your own'
1 Corinthians 6:19

No: Jesus has purchased you with His own blood, quickened you by His Spirit, espoused you to Himself, and intends to glorify you with Himself for ever. He claims you, and says, 'I have called thee by thy name; thou art mine.' He will provide for you as His own, and spare you, as a man spareth his own son that serveth him. You are His beloved bride; His portion; a member of His body, of His flesh, and of His bones. In loving you, He loveth Himself. He requires you to live under the daily conviction that you are His; that all you have is His. You have nothing of your own; all you have He freely gave, and all you have you profess to have surrendered to Him. Think more of Jesus than of His gifts, cleave to Him, and not to what you may be called to surrender. He will never take anything from you, but He will give you something better. If He strip you, it is to teach you, to lead you to live upon Himself, and to find your heaven in His company, grace, and offices. Do you live, walk, and act, so as to leave the impression upon the minds of observers that you are the Lord's? Do you expect Him to preserve, guide, and supply you? Let conscience answer.

> *Lord! am I Thine, entirely Thine?*
> *Purchased and saved by blood divine?*
> *With full consent, Thine I would be,*
> *And own Thy sovereign right in me.*

❦ EVENING ❧

'Christ died for us'
Romans 5:8

What an unspeakable blessing is this! Let us very seriously consider it tonight. Christ died, Jehovah's only begotten Son, the fountain of being and blessedness, the centre and source of all excellence and glory. Jesus, who united the divine and human natures in Himself, He died; died as our great friend, who stood up for us in covenant, who stooped for us from heaven to earth, whose love was stronger than death. He died for us the objects of His love and His Father's choice; died for us though we were base, the ungodly; weak, without strength; rebellious, His enemies. He died for us, as the Head for His body, as the Surety for the debtors He had undertaken to set free, as the Redeemer for captives He was pledged to deliver, as the Husband for His beloved, but fallen, bride, as the Shepherd to the flock entrusted for His care, as the Servant of the Father, who came to do His will and maintain His honour. He died for us to redeem us from death, to raise us to eternal life, to restore us to friendship with God, to fit us for His holy service, and that we might be crowned with glory at last. Let us therefore live looking to Jesus.

> *Christ bore our sins upon the tree,*
> *To seek and save the lost He came,*
> *There was He doomed to set us free*
> *From death and everlasting shame;*
> *The captive flock from hell was freed*
> *And ransom'd when their Shepherd bled.*

JANUARY 25

❦ MORNING ❧
'Ye are my friends'
John 15:14

What infinite condescension in Jesus, to call us worms, His friends! But He not only calls us so, but treats us as such, and expects us as friends to do whatsoever He commands us. Is Jesus thy friend? Then visit Him often, let Him hear thy voice in prayer and praise; then trust Him confidently, let Him see a proof of thy faith in thy dependence; then walk with Him in love, let Him enjoy much of thy company; then expect Him to be thy Friend in sickness and health, in poverty and plenty, in life and in death. If Jesus is our Friend, we can never be destitute; if father and mother forsake, He will take us up and take us in; we can never be miserable, He will receive us and be a Father unto us; we can never be neglected, for He will never fail us nor forsake us, but will do for us all He has promised in His Word. He will defend us from foes, visit us in sickness, and cheer and support us in death. Precious Lord Jesus, be Thou my Friend; call me Thy friend, and treat me as such, in life, in death, at the judgment, and before Thy Father's face for ever.

> O let us make His name our trust!
> He is a Saviour wise and just:
> On His almighty arm depend;
> He is a tried and faithful Friend;
> And all His friends shall shortly prove,
> The power and glory of His love.

❦ EVENING ❧
'Is this thy kindness to thy friend?'
2 Samuel 16:17

The conduct of Jesus towards us is the perfection of kindness; but our conduct toward Him is often just the reverse. How often we treat Him with neglect, and instead of prayer being a delightful privilege, it is an irksome task. How often we violate His positive precepts, or omit to perform known and acknowledged duties. How often we doubt His love, distrust His Word and complain of His dealings. How often we encourage the flesh, which He has directed us to mortify; prefer the world, which He has commanded us to forsake; and yield to Satan, whom He has exhorted us to resist. And have we not sometimes been afraid or ashamed to confess Him before the world; or at least to bear a plain, honest, decided testimony for Him? Well may our cheeks burn with shame, and our bosoms fill with confusion, if the question be put to us, in reference to much of our conduct toward our kind and gracious Redeemer. Let us seek afresh the tokens of His forgiving love, and in future when about to yield to temptation, or give way to any sin, put the question to our consciences, 'Is this thy kindness to thy friend?'

> Sure, were I not most vile and base,
> I could not thus my friend requite!
> And were not He the God of grace,
> He'd frown and spurn me from His sight.

JANUARY 26

❧ MORNING ❧

'I will instruct thee'
PSALM 32:8

At best we know but little, and we are slow to learn; but as the Lord has promised to instruct us, we may yet expect to be made wise unto salvation. The Lord's teaching always produces humility, self-loathing, confidence in God, zeal for His glory, and devotes the heart to His praise. It brings us to the feet of Jesus, and delivers us from the present evil world. Under divine instruction we learn the true nature of sin, the vanity of the world, the emptiness of creatures, and the fulness and preciousness of Christ. Is God willing to instruct us? Then let us be early and often at His throne, praying, as the psalmist did, 'Lead me in thy truth, and teach me: for thou art the God of my salvation; on thee do I wait all the day.' Then shall we exclaim, as Elihu did, 'Behold, God exalteth by his power: who teacheth like him?' The Lord will teach us to profit, and sanctify us through the truth He imparts. Christ is our great lesson, and to know Him rightly, is life, peace, and joy. Is Jesus thy Teacher? Then sit at His feet, treasure up His words, and show forth His praise. He says, 'Learn of me.' Learn to know Him, love Him, obey Him, and live upon Him.

Eternal life Thy words impart;
On these my fainting spirit lives:
Here sweeter comforts cheer my heart,
Than the whole world around me gives.

❧ EVENING ❧

'I have learned by experience'
GENESIS 30:27

So said Laban in reference to the benefit he derived from Jacob's services, and so may the Christian say in reference to the effects of divine teaching. Experience is knowledge derived from trial, and thus we learn the truth and value of real religion; the importance and dignity of the holy Scripture; the true state and condition of human nature; the character and suitableness of the Saviour; the need and nature of the operations of the Holy Spirit; the malice and cunning of Satan; and the power and efficacy of believing prayer; the beneficial tendency of afflictive dispensations; the emptiness and vanity of the present world; and the love and faithfulness of a covenant God. No knowledge is like that which is gained by experience; it is far preferable to what we gain from report, or reading, or mere opinion; it is above every other kind of knowledge in point of certainty, in its tendency to usefulness, and in its power to establish the mind. Young people should be modest, they can know but little from experience yet. Established Christians should communicate the results of their experience to others; nothing is more likely to be useful. We should all be careful, that our statements of experience and our practices agree.

Teacher divine! instruct me still
To know, to love, to do Thy will;
And let me by experience prove
Thy sanctifying power and love.

JANUARY 27

❦ MORNING ❦

'Lacked ye anything?'

LUKE 22:35

The Lord will always provide for His own people, who keep His company, do His will, and aim at His glory. If He sends us, though He chooses to carry the purse, our bread shall be given, and our water shall be sure. The disciples went out unfurnished, but then Jesus commanded them; they return, and confessed that they lacked nothing; the God of providence supplied them. If we are in the Lord's way, we may rest assured that we shall meet the Lord's messengers bringing our supply. They that seek the Lord shall not want any good thing. He notices our wants, remembers His promises, times His mercies, and proves Himself a faithful God. Have you lacked anything? for body? for soul? He who has supplied the past, will provide for the future. Jesus is full of grace. Go, and receive, that your joy may be full. Jesus is the God of providence. Look to Him, trust in Him, plead with Him, and you shall never be destitute. Believe His Word, He cannot deny Himself; trust in His faithfulness, and He will put honour upon thy faith, fulfilling His own Word. 'Thy bread shall be given thee, and thy water shall be sure.'

> *His love in times past, forbids me to think*
> *He'll leave me at last, in trouble to sink;*
> *Each sweet Ebenezer I have in review*
> *Confirms His good pleasure to help me quite through.*

❦ EVENING ❦

'He will not fail thee'

DEUTERONOMY 31:6

The expectations raised by His Word shall never be disappointed, the promises He has made shall never be broken, the trust reposed on His faithfulness shall never be dishonoured. He will not forget His Word, or neglect our interests. He never did fail His people, He never will. Your faith may be weak, your fears may be strong, your doubts may be painful, your weakness may be great, your temptations may be very distressing, and your wants may be numerous and alarming, but thy God will not fail thee. Why should He? He foresaw all thy wants, thy woes, and thy unworthiness before He called thee by His grace; thy present circumstances are not new to Him. He had them in His eye when He made His promises, and He will get honour to Himself by bringing thee through them. Fail not to trust Him. Fail not to apply to Him by prayer. Fail not to believe His faithful Word. He will not fail to support thee under thy burdens, to listen to thy requests, to provide for thy necessities, or to honour thy faith. However singular your experience, or strange the path may appear to you, His Word is true. *'He will not suffer you to be tempted above that ye are able.'*

> *Why should'st thou fear when God is thine,*
> *When all He is, He is for thee?*
> *If thou art weak, His strength divine*
> *To perfect in infirmity.*

JANUARY 28

🌿 MORNING 🌿

'We have an advocate'

1 JOHN 2:1

Yes: Jesus pleads for us in heaven. By His own blood He entered once into the holiest, there to appear in the presence of God *for us*. He pleads for us against Satan, answering all his accusations; and for us with the Father, that we may be kept, supplied, and glorified. O what a comfort when the heart is straitened in prayer, when the mouth is closed by guilt, when the spirit is harassed by temptation, to know that Jesus as our Advocate appears and pleads for us above! Beloved, Jesus is before God for *you* this morning, and every morning; and the benefit of His intercession you daily enjoy. When doubting and fearful, put your cause afresh into His hands, and leave Him to carry it; He can plead well; His arguments are powerful, and His manner is divine. Keep Jesus before thee this day as thy Advocate; rejoice in His office and name, and remember He is saying, 'Father, I will that those whom Thou hast given Me, be with Me where I am, to behold My glory.' Him the Father heareth always; and all for whom He pleads are safe and shall be happy.

> Look up, my soul, with cheerful eye;
> See where the great Redeemer stands,
> The glorious Advocate on high,
> With precious incense in His hands;
> And on His pleading still depend,
> Who is thy Advocate and Friend.

🌿 EVENING 🌿

'He ever liveth to make intercession'

HEBREWS 7:25

He died for our sins once; but He lives to plead for us daily, hourly, moment by moment. He possesses an endless life, an unchangeable priesthood; He appears in heaven as the great High Priest of our profession, our names are on His breastplate, He is intimately acquainted with our affairs, and He lives above on purpose to intercede for us. He presents His precious blood, His perfect righteousness; and He pleads them for our pardon, preservation, and glorification. He has the Father's ear, the Father's heart; and He improves all He has for our welfare. How wonderful His love: He first left heaven for us, and on earth He laboured, suffered, died, in our stead; He then returned to heaven for us, and there He lives, pleads, and secures our best interests. He witnesses all our changes, but He changes not; He is often grieved by our inconsistencies, but still pleads on our behalf; He undertook our cause, when there was nothing in us to move or induce Him to do so, and He still feels the deepest interest in us, pleads for us, and rejoices to do us good. What a source of comfort, what a ground of confidence is this. 'If when we were enemies, we were reconciled to God by the death of His Son, much more being reconciled, we shall be saved by His life'.

> There, as our great High Priest, He stands,
> And pleads before the mercy-seat;
> Our cause is in His faithful hands,
> Our enemies beneath His feet.

JANUARY 29

🌿 MORNING 🌿
'Search the scriptures'
John 5:39

The Bible is God's book, a favour bestowed on man; intended to lead him to a knowledge of the nature, perfections, purposes, will, providence, and salvation of God. It contains all that is really necessary to be known. It should be read carefully, prayerfully, frequently, and in course; every part of the Bible should be read, meditated upon, and prayed over. It makes us wise unto salvation, through faith which is in Christ Jesus. We cannot understand the Scriptures, or gather spiritual profit there from, but by the Holy Ghost; nor should we expect to be taught the mind of God but by the Scriptures. Praying, reading, and thinking, should go together; and no one, but he who has proved it, can possibly tell the profit which may be thus gained. Let the Bible be the every-day-book. In it God speaks to your soul; by it He will sanctify your nature, direct your steps, and give you joy and peace. Let not the works of man occupy the place of the book of God; but search the Scriptures daily, and exercise faith therein. 'Open thou mine eyes, that I may see wondrous things out of thy law.' Unfold to me the riches of Thy grace, revealed in Thy Word.

> O may Thy counsels, mighty God,
> My roving feet command!
> Nor I forsake the happy road
> That leads to Thy right hand.

🌿 EVENING 🌿
'Thy word have I hid in mine heart'
Psalm 119:11

The tables of the old covenant were laid up in the ark, and hidden in the holy place; the contents of the new covenant should be laid up in the believer's heart. By close, daily, prayerful meditation, we should seek to understand, enjoy, and lay up God's holy Word. It is the manna we are to gather for our daily food, the light in which we are to walk, and the rule by which we are to work. Let us lay up the gracious doctrines, which are the ground of our confidence; the exceeding great and precious promises, which are inexhaustible sources of comfort; and the kind and holy precepts, which are unerring guides. If hidden in the heart, no one can deprive us of this precious treasure; nor shall we have it to seek, when we want it to enjoy. But in order to this, we must know its value, prize its contents, search its pages, ponder it in our minds, and feed upon it as our daily food. Except we hide it in our hearts, we shall not be sanctified by it, nor will it be written out in our lives; from the heart it flows into the life. May it be our daily prayer, that God would put His laws into our minds, and write them upon our hearts, that we may be the epistles of Christ, known and read of all men.

> Its promises rejoice the heart,
> Its doctrines are divinely true;
> Knowledge and pleasure it imparts,
> It comforts and instructs us too.

JANUARY 30

🌿 MORNING 🌿

'And shalt thou be delivered?'

ISAIAH 37:11

This is plainly the language of an insulting foe; he had triumphed, and now he boasted, but his power was bounded, and his pride procured his fall. Often when in trouble, when distressed, when tried by a sense of sin and unworthiness, unbelief and Satan join, and pointing to others who have fallen and to our acknowledged unworthiness, insultingly ask the question, 'And shalt thou be delivered?' Yes, Satan, we shall be delivered; the God of Hezekiah is our God, and He hath said, 'I will deliver thee in six troubles, and in seven I will not forsake thee.' We believe His Word, we rely on His faithfulness, we plead at His throne; and so sure as He can deliver, He *will*. He hath often done so in times past, He doth deliver all His praying people now, and in Him we trust that He will deliver us. Not on account of anything in us, or of anything done by us, but because He hath said! 'I will be with him in trouble, I will deliver him and honour him; I will set him on high, because he hath known My name.' He is faithful, His Word cannot fail, nor should our faith be shaken. Deliverance is certain, for God hath spoken, and God is true.

> The same His pow'r, His love the same,
> Unmoved the promise shines;
> Eternal truth surrounds His name,
> And guards the precious lines.

🌿 EVENING 🌿

'We know that we are of God'

1 JOHN 5:19

What an honour! What a comfort is this! Yes, we are of God, created anew in Christ Jesus, by the power and agency of the Holy Spirit; consecrated to His service and glory, by the death of our great High Priest, and the sprinkling of His blood upon us; set apart in His eternal purpose for His praise, and now brought into holy and profitable relation to Him. We were rebels against Him; we are now His willing servants. We were His avowed enemies; we are now His attached friends. We were the children of wrath, but we are now the children of His love. We know that we are of God, by faith in His Word, by love to His saints, by sympathy with Himself, by the grief we feel when we sin, by our pleasure in obeying His will, by the contrast there is between us and the world, in our principles, pleasures, and pursuits. What we are, as distinguished from others, is of God; being thus distinguished, we are peculiarly the Lord's: His property, His treasure, His portion, His delight. What an astounding fact! We are the Lord's. The grace that made us so must be free and infinite. To know that we are His, is an invaluable blessing; but no one should rest satisfied without it.

> O Lord, be daily near my heart,
> And let my spirit feel Thee near;
> Then willingly with all I'd part,
> Nor count it worthy of a tear.

JANUARY 31

❧ MORNING ❧
'We joy in God'
ROMANS 5:11

This is every believer's privilege; God is reconciled to him in the person and through the work of Jesus; all charges against him are blotted out; all his sins are freely and fully forgiven; he is justified from all things; and stands before God in Christ, accepted, beloved, and blessed. To him God is love; with him God is at peace; and he is now a son of God. If this is believed on the testimony of God, and realized in the soul as the effect of faith, then God becomes our exceeding joy, and we rejoice with joy unspeakable and full of glory. If we joy in frames, they change; if we joy in friends, they die; if we joy in possessions, they are vanity; but if we joy in God, though the exercise of joy may be interrupted, yet the object remains eternally the same, and we shall joy for evermore. Beloved, look at Jehovah in Jesus; there you see Him as the Father of mercies and God of all comfort; joy and rejoice in Him as your God, your Portion, your everlasting All. Throughout this day, joy in God as your Father, your Friend, and your Saviour. In this rejoice and be exceeding glad.

> O that I could now adore Him,
> Like the heavenly host above,
> Who for ever bow before Him,
> And unceasing sing His love!
> Happy songsters!
> When shall I your chorus join?

❧ EVENING ❧
'The joy of the LORD is your strength'
NEHEMIAH 8:10

Fear and sorrow naturally weakens us, but faith and joy give us strength. Joy is the cordial of the soul: it quickens, enlivens, emboldens, and makes us strong. Our heavenly Father is called, 'The blessed, or *the happy* God.' He is also the happy-making God. He loves to see His people happy; therefore, as the God of all comfort, He has made great provision for our happiness. There are wells of salvation, and we should draw from them with joy. There is an inexhaustible fulness in Jesus, and from that fulness we should receive, for every want, for every duty, for every trial. We cannot apply to it too often; we cannot go to it for too much. Hear our beloved Lord, 'Ask and receive, that your joy may be full.' It is only as we live out of self, upon Jesus, above the world in the region of God's free grace, that we can be happy. The happy Christian is the strong Christian, and it is the strong Christian that brings much glory to God, much credit to His cause, and does much good in the world. It is as much our duty to be happy, as to be holy; both are recommended, and provision is as much made for the one as the other.

> Rejoice evermore
> In the truth and the power,
> And the grace of your heavenly Friend,
> Till to us who believe He His glory doth give,
> And a kingdom that never shall end.

FEBRUARY 1

🌿 MORNING 🌿

'Immanuel'
ISAIAH 7:14

Consider Jesus through this day as God with thee; God in thy nature; God become man for thy salvation and consolation. None but God was able to save; thy Jesus is God: it was necessary that the Saviour should be man, and Jesus is man. He has the nature of His Father – here is His ability; He has thy nature also – here is His suitability. Jesus is God with thee, to hear thy prayers, check thy fears, redress thy grievances, sympathize with thee in thy sorrows, and be thy everyday Friend. God is with us, observing our conduct, directing our ways, reproving our follies, providing our supplies, and making all things work together for our good. Always remember, Jesus is with you; every sin is committed under His eye, against His love, and goes to His heart; think, when tempted to sin, that you hear Immanuel, the suffering, bleeding, dying, reigning Saviour, say, 'O do not that abominable thing which I hate!' Walk before Him in love, peace, holiness, and zeal for His glory and praise. He is God for thee, as well as with thee. Look to His wisdom, power, and love, for safety and supply; and with filial confidence trust His Word, so shall you be safe and happy.

Sweeter sounds than music knows
Charm me in Immanuel's name;
All her hopes my spirit owes
To His birth, His cross, His shame.

🌿 EVENING 🌿

'A people near unto him'
PSALM 148:14

Jesus took our nature, and became one with us. Thus He is near unto us; He gives us His Holy Spirit, brings us into union with Himself, and we are near to Him. This is our highest honour, an unfailing source of happiness and peace. We are near to Him in point of relation, being His children; near to Him in point of affection, being loved with an everlasting love; we are near to Him in point of union, being members of His body, of His flesh, and of His bones; we are near to Him in point of fellowship, walking with Him as a man walketh with His friend; we are near to Him in point of attention, being the objects of His daily, hourly, tender care; we shall soon be near to Him in point of locality, when our mansion is prepared, for we shall depart to be with Christ, which is far better. We are near to Him though poor, when deeply tried, if ever nearer one time than another, we shall be nearest to Him in death. If we are near unto Him, He will sympathise with us in all our sorrows; assist us in all our trials; protect us in all our dangers; hold intercourse with us in all our lonely hours; provide for us in all seasons of necessity; and honourably introduce us to glory. Let us realise this fact daily: we are near and dear to our God.

And am I near to God,
His friend, His child, His care!
O may I walk with Him in love,
By faith and fervent prayer!

FEBRUARY 2

❦ MORNING ❦

'The spirit of grace and of supplications'
ZECHARIAH 12:10

All spiritual prayer is produced by the Holy Spirit. He convinces us of need, discovers to us the fulness of Jesus, leads us to the throne of grace, and helps our infirmities there. The very desire to pray is from Him, and the liberty we enjoy in prayer is His gift. But how dreadful a thing is sin, and how condescending is the Holy Spirit. He sympathizes with us, and maketh intercession for us, with unutterable expressions of distress; with groanings which cannot be uttered. Sin has rendered us so vile, that no sacrifice but that of the Son of God Himself could atone for sin; and so weak, that none but the Holy Spirit can enable us to pray with fervour, faith, and success. See, beloved, how deep your obligations are, and how great your dependence upon this blessed Spirit of grace and supplications. Be careful, lest you grieve Him by your lightness, worldliness, or lukewarmness; but sow unto the Spirit, and you shall reap life everlasting. He will testify to you of Jesus, and bless you with liberty and peace.

I want a heart to pray,
To pray and never cease,
Never to murmur at Thy stay
Or wish my sufferings less.

I want a godly fear,
A quick-discerning eye,
That looks to Thee when sin is near,
And sees the tempter fly.

❦ EVENING ❦

'The Spirit of adoption'
ROMANS 8:15

The same Spirit that leads us to seek for mercy as poor sinners, afterwards leads us to claim relationship with God as His beloved children. He unfolds Jehovah's gracious character, draws out and fixes the desires of the soul upon Him, sheds abroad His love in the heart, and then we cry, 'My Father, my Father.' To the privilege of adoption, we were predestinated before the world began; but we can only know our interest in it, or claim and enjoy that interest, as we are taught by the Holy Spirit. As the Spirit of adoption, He enlarges the heart, elevates the desires, sanctifies the spirit, ennobles the aims, guides into the truth, and leads out the soul in free and familiar fellowship with God. He imparts holy peace, deepens penitence, and fills with glowing gratitude. Under His influences, prayer becomes delightful, meditation profitable, and the ordinances of the gospel yield us pleasure. Have you the Spirit of adoption? Do you feel led to approach God as a child does its father? Do you look upon the Word as a volume sent from a father to his child, to instruct, reprove, and comfort him; and do you read it as such? Do you long, pray, and desire above all things to enjoy this sweet relationship?

Send forth the Spirit of Thy Son,
O God, into my panting heart,
That govern'd by Thy love alone,
From Thee I never may depart.

FEBRUARY 3

🌿 MORNING 🌿

'Cleave unto the Lord'
ACTS 11:23

Every believer is united to Christ, and is one with Him. Jesus is the vine, he is a branch; Jesus is the husband, he is the bride. Satan's design is to lead him from the Lord; he knows well he can do little or nothing, while the Christian cleaves to Jesus. O, then, cleave to Him by faith, in love, with perseverance! Cleave to His truth, to His people, to His ordinances, to His Word, and to His throne. Think of Jesus as the affectionate child thinks of his beloved father, as the tender bride thinks of her devoted bridegroom, as the way-worn traveller thinks of his cheerful home. Let Jesus be uppermost in thy thoughts, let His love rule thy heart, and let nothing steal away thy affections from Him. Live upon His fulness, live according to His Word, live in the element of His love; no living safely, no living happily, but as you cleave unto the Lord. Never let Satan find thee at a distance from Jesus, or he will assuredly be too much for thee. He is ever on the watch to find thee wandering, that he may worry, deceive, and distress thee. Therefore cleave unto the Lord, with full purpose of heart. Cleave to Him as the ivy to the oak, or the child to the mother's breast.

Saviour, let me cleave to Thee;
Love the bond of union be;
And, lest I should e'er depart,
Keep thy dwelling in my heart.

🌿 EVENING 🌿

'I press toward the mark'
PHILIPPIANS 3:14

The believer is a racer. He has a prize set before him, even the perfection of knowledge, holiness, and happiness. His course is marked out by God's holy Word. It lies through difficulties, foes, and trials. He has a mark on which to fix his eye, at which to aim, to arrive at which he should daily strive. His mark is Jesus in His holy exemplary life. We aim to be like Him: to oppose sin, overcome Satan, conquer the world, bear troubles, endure trials, and do good, as He did. He ran His race, keeping 'the joy set before Him' in view; He arrived at His mark, won His crown, and is now seated as conqueror at God's right hand. He is our pattern and example. On Him the eye and the heart should be set; after conformity to Him we should press; laying aside every weight, and the easily besetting sin, we should run the race set before us, looking unto Jesus. We should, like the apostle, pursue one object, keep to the point, press toward the mark. This will ensure the prize, for Jesus says, 'To him that overcometh will I grant to sit with Me in My throne, even as I also overcame, and am set down with My Father in His throne.'

The moment we begin our race,
We must the Saviour's cause embrace,
Press toward the mark, the prize obtain,
And then with Christ in glory reign.

FEBRUARY 4

❦ MORNING ❧
'Precious faith'
2 Peter 1:1

Faith is the gift of God. It is the fruit of everlasting love, the effect of grace; we believe through grace. The faith which is the evidence of salvation, includes giving credit to the gospel report, of a free and full salvation for poor, unworthy sinners; an application to Jesus on the throne of grace, founded on that report; and a trusting in the Word, work, and death of Jesus, for life and salvation. This always produces love to Jesus, and leads the soul to obey Him out of gratitude. It is precious; being scarce, few thus believe; being valuable, without it we cannot please God, cannot be justified, cannot rejoice in hope, or enjoy gospel blessings; but he that believeth is entitled to every precious promise, to all the fulness of Christ, to enjoy God in every new-covenant relation, and shall never see death. He is passed from death to life, and shall never come into condemnation. Gracious God! Give unto Thy people, and unto me especially, much precious faith, that believing in Jesus, I may rejoice with joy unspeakable and full of glory. O to believe this day without wavering! O to be strong in faith, giving glory to God!

> *O for a strong, a lasting faith,*
> *To credit what th' Almighty saith!*
> *To embrace the message of His Son,*
> *And call the joys of heav'n our own.*

❦ EVENING ❧
'See that ye be not troubled'
Matthew 24:6

That is agitated, anxious, dejected, confused, or alarmed. See that you meet troubles with courage, endure them with patience and fortitude, and yield entire submission to God. The world may be troubled, but you should not. 'You are one of the sheep of My fold, one of the children of My love. You should not be troubled, for all things that concern you are appointed by infinite wisdom and love; you are safe in My hand; I shall always be with you, to keep you from evil; your trials will be moderate, so that you will be able to bear them; every event will be directed to work your good; and if you are troubled you will dishonour Me. Therefore watch, pray, and guard against anxiety and dejection.' But, how can we prevent being troubled? 'Believe My word of promise, walk close by My side, whisper all your fears into My ear; cast all your cares and burdens at My feet; look often to the end of your trials; expect the support necessary to bear them from a faithful, a present God; and remember, *you are one with Me.*' Beloved, we are always safe if we are with Jesus. You should endeavour to be composed, for He bids you, and bids you in love.

> *O let my trembling soul be still,*
> *And wait Thy wise, Thy holy will,*
> *I cannot, Lord! Thy purpose see,*
> *Yet all is well – since ruled by Thee.*

FEBRUARY 5

❦ MORNING ❧
'Precious blood'
1 Peter 1:19

The blood of Jesus is the price of our redemption, the object of our faith, the ground of our peace, the subject of our meditation, and our constant plea at the throne of grace. It satisfied divine justice, and speaks peace to the humble sinner's heart. It overcomes Satan, and cleanseth from all sin. It purges the conscience from dead works, and leads us to joy in God. We build on it as our foundation, flee to it as our refuge, look to it as the cure for sin, and sing of it as the joy of our heart. It has made a perfect, a satisfactory, an infinite atonement; and no sinner can perish who relies upon it, washes in it, and pleads it before God. It is indeed precious blood! It is invaluable! Whenever you feel guilt on your conscience, fears rising in your mind, or a gloom come over your spirit; look to, meditate upon, make use of, the precious blood of Jesus. It made peace, it gives peace, and it secures peace. It cleanses, heals, and sanctifies; and we could not live happy one day without it. The blood of Jesus Christ cleanseth us from all sin. To this alone we must look as the foundation of our hope, and the ground of our peace.

> Dear dying Lamb! Thy precious blood
> Shall never lose its power,
> Till all the ransom'd church of God
> Be saved to sin no more.

❦ EVENING ❧
'The God of peace'
Hebrews 13:20

Through the precious blood of Jesus, God is fully pacified towards us, and perfectly reconciled to us. He is the peaceful God. We have nothing to fear from Him, but may expect every blessing which we plead for in the name of Jesus. He was angry with us, but His anger is turned away, and He comforts us. He is at peace with us, and we are at peace with Him. He seeks our welfare, and we seek to promote His glory. What a sweet view of Jehovah is this! 'The God of peace.' As such, let us approach Him, pour out our hearts before Him, exercise confidence in Him, and anew commit ourselves unreservedly into His hands. He has accepted the finished work of Jesus for us, He brought Him again from the dead, He placed Him at His own right hand in heavenly places, and He delights to bless our souls for His sake. He will never be more at peace with us than He is at this moment, though we may more confidently believe it, and more sweetly enjoy it. The resurrection of Jesus our substitute proves that He is fully satisfied; and the gift of the Holy Spirit shows that He delights to do us good. Beware therefore of mistaken views, or hard thoughts of God. He is 'the God of peace.'

> O God of peace! to me impart
> The quiet, peaceful frame:
> Sprinkle the blood upon my heart,
> And there engrave Thy name.

FEBRUARY 6

🌿 MORNING 🌿

'He is precious'
1 Peter 2:7

Yes, Jesus is precious to every believer. However Christians may differ upon some points, they all agree in this: *Jesus is precious.* They cannot always feel towards Him as they wish, but they have always one and the same opinion of Him. He is precious in His person, Word, work, blood, righteousness, and intercession; as Prophet, Priest, and King; in every name He wears, every character He bears, every relation He fills, and every office He sustains; so precious that none can be compared with Him. His people love Him, but none of them think they love Him enough; they adore Him, but mourn over their want of fervour when addressing Him; they prefer Him above all things, and consider Him altogether lovely. Do you find Christ precious this morning? If He was to be sold, what would you give for Him? If you could be gratified, how would you feel towards Him? He is precious to poor, sensible sinners; to strong believers; to holy angels; and to God our heavenly Father. Is He so to you? Live near to Him, be intimate with Him, and you will feel Him precious. The more you know of Him, the more you will prize Him.

Our Jesus is more precious far
Than life, and all its comforts are;
More precious than our daily food;
More precious than our vital blood.

🌿 EVENING 🌿

'The precious sons of Zion'
Lamentations 4:2

As the Lord Jesus is precious to His people, so are they precious to Him. He calls them His jewels, His peculiar treasure, His portion. His love to them is wonderful. He values them at an infinite price: therefore He redeemed them with His own precious blood; and having purchased them at so great a cost, He will never part with them. That Jesus should be precious to His people, is not surprising; He has done so much for them, He bestows so many blessings upon them, He stands in such a sweet relation to them, and He is so perfectly lovely in Himself: but that we should be precious to Him, is astonishing; we are so poor, so vile, so degraded, so deformed, and daily treat Him with such neglect. But His ways are not our ways, nor are His thoughts our thoughts. We are His precious children, His beloved bride; He loves us tonight with all the strength and tenderness of His nature. Glorious truth! May we receive it into our hearts, meditate upon it, and retire to rest this night, rejoicing that whatever men may think of us, or however they may feel toward us, we are precious in the sight of the Lord. Precious in the sight of the Lord are the persons and the death of His saints.

Hear, O my soul, what Jesus saith,
Nor tremble to depart;
For all His saints in life and death
Are precious to His heart.

FEBRUARY 7

🌿 MORNING 🌿

'My times are in thy hand'
PSALM 31:15

Every event is under divine control. Nothing is left to chance. The hand of God is in all that occurs, directing, overruling, and sanctifying to our good. He appointed all that concerns us, and appointed all in infinite wisdom and love; therefore we should not judge rashly, or conclude hastily. We know not what may occur today, but we know that the purpose of God cannot be frustrated, nor can His promise fail. He worketh all things after the counsel of His own will. He says, 'My purpose shall stand, and I will do all My pleasure.' But this is our comfort, that He taketh pleasure in His people, and in the prosperity of His servants. Let us consider, then, everything passes under our Father's eye; is overruled by our Saviour's power; is directed by the Holy Spirit to do us good. It shall not be as our enemies wish, or as our hearts fear; but as our God and Father pleases and has ordained. Be not therefore anxious, troubled, or cast down; the Lord God omnipotent reigneth, and He is God. He shall preserve thee from evil; He shall preserve thy soul.

> *I know not what may soon betide,*
> *But Jesus knows, and He'll provide;*
> *My life is by His counsel plann'd,*
> *And all my times are in His hand:*
> *I'll therefore trust, nor yield to fear,*
> *But cast on Jesus all my care.*

🌿 EVENING 🌿

'Therefore trust thou in him'
JOB 35:14

Forget not that thy times are in His hands, that thy name is in His book of life, that He has promised to be thy God, and that He is faithful to His Word. Every blessing we can need is promised; every promise is firm and sure; therefore trust thou in Him. Thy heart may 'misgive' thee, thy way may perplex thee, thy fears may overcome thee, thy foes may insult over thee; but thy way is not hid from the Lord; therefore trust thou in Him. His Word is true from the beginning, His people in every age have proved it so, its verity is its crown; therefore you may trust it firmly, fearlessly, and constantly; and His faithful Word should calm thy fears, strengthen thy hopes, sweeten thy comforts, and lead thee to cheerful, filial obedience. His hand may seem to go out against thee, but His heart beats with unutterable love to thee; He may appear to thy mistaken fancy, to be armed with a sword to destroy thee; but even then you should say with Job, 'Though He slay me, yet will I trust in Him;' and you will find, that instead of destroying, He will honour your confidence, and bring you out into a wealthy place.

> *Thy ways O Lord, with wise design,*
> *Are framed upon Thy throne above,*
> *And every dark and bending line*
> *Meets in the centre of Thy love:*
> *Therefore I trust in Thee alone,*
> *And humbly pray, 'THY WILL BE DONE.'*

FEBRUARY 8

🌿 MORNING 🌿

'That I may win Christ'
PHILIPPIANS 3:8

The aim of men in general is to make a fortune, enjoy the world, and live respectably; the aim of the believer is to win Christ. Jesus possesses all he desires, and to possess Christ would satisfy every wish. We have now a title to Him, we receive much from Him, and we often enjoy His love; but we want to be present with Him, and to have full possession of Him as our everlasting All. He is set before us as our mark, He is held out as the prize, and is promised as the everlasting portion of every overcomer. Where is the heart this morning? Which way do the desires tend? What is to be the object of pursuit today? If Jesus is the principal object, failing in our pursuit after other things, losses, or crosses, will not much affect us; but our conduct will say, 'I aim to win Christ; if He is mine, all is well, other things are but trifles compared with Him.' Keeping Jesus in view thus, will prevent murmuring, cure our impatience, and keep our hearts in comparative peace. O may our every action cry in the ears of every observer, 'That I may win Christ.' He who has Christ has an infinite portion, unsearchable wealth, and boundless resources.

> Not softest strains can charm mine ears,
> Like His beloved name;
> Nor aught beneath the skies inspire
> My heart with equal flame.

🌿 EVENING 🌿

'Thou knowest that I love thee'
JOHN 21:15

Notwithstanding all my imperfections, though I often grieve Thee, wrong Thy love, and fear to trust Thy Word; though I am too much influenced by the things of time, though dark and direful corruption work within me, though Satan sometimes overcomes me; Thou searchest the heart, Thou readest the inmost workings of the soul, and Thou knowest that I love Thee. Thou knowest that there is imbedded in the depths of my nature, a principle that cannot, will not be satisfied without Thee. Therefore I sigh for Thy presence, long for Thy love to be shed abroad in my heart, pray for Thy glory to be revealed to my soul, and desire above all things to claim and enjoy Thee as mine. I love Thee: therefore I am jealous of my heart. I love Thee: therefore I am dissatisfied with the world. I love Thee: therefore I desire to please Thee. I love Thee: therefore nothing wounds me so deeply as the thought of being separated from Thee. O that I loved Thee more! I want to feel my heart glow whenever I think of Thy name. I want to do always those things that please Thee, and to stand ready and willing at any moment, in any way, to depart and be forever with Thee. Lord, increase my love to Thee!

> Lord, it is my chief complaint,
> That my love is weak and faint!
> Yet I love Thee, and adore,
> O for grace to love Thee more!

FEBRUARY 9

🌿 MORNING 🌿

'Be watchful'
Revelation 3:2

Satan is watching to ensnare us, the world is watching to exult over us, and God is watching to protect us. Jesus, our best friend, says to us, 'Be watchful.' Watch against the spirit of the world, against thy easily besetting sins, against seasons of temptation, and against Satan, the sworn enemy of thy soul. Watch for opportunities to do good, for answers to prayer, for the appearance of God as a God of providence. Unite prayer to God, dependence on His holy Word, and watchfulness, together; pray to be kept *from* sin, *in* temptation, unspotted *from* the world; trust in God to answer, but do not leave the throne; and then watch as though all depended upon thy diligence and efforts. Blessed is he that watcheth and keepeth his garments. 'Watch ye therefore, and pray always.' But trust not to thy watchfulness, but while watching trust in God. He who keepeth thee will not slumber. He is with thee when on guard, as well as when thou art feasting on His Word and rejoicing at His table. He withdraweth not His eyes from the righteous. 'The eyes of the LORD are upon the righteous, and his ears are open to their cry.' Watch ye, therefore, and pray always.

> O gracious God, in whom I live,
> My feeble efforts aid;
> Help me to watch, and pray, and strive,
> Though trembling and afraid.

🌿 EVENING 🌿

'I give myself unto prayer'
Psalm 109:4

Watchfulness and prayer should be always united. The praying Christian should watch, and the watching Christian should pray. The one exercise helps us in the other. We should be given to prayer as to our business, our daily occupation. It will preserve us from innumerable evils, and bring invaluable blessings into our possession. God loves to hear us pray. The prayer of the upright is His delight. May we be impressed with this idea whenever we go upon our knees: God loves to see me approach Him. He delights to hear me plead with Him. He listens to me with a Father's ear. He rejoices over me with a Father's heart. He is grieved when I neglect His throne, and cannot approve of my hurrying over my devotions, as I sometimes do. He says, 'Come.' 'Come boldly.' If we disregard His Word or slight His invitation He will send some trial, raise some storm, or let loose some enemy to drive us to His throne. If we could hear the voice of our troubles distinctly, or understand its language, we should hear it shout, 'To your knees. To your knees. To your closets. Arise and call upon thy God.'

> Father, into my heart convey
> The power incessantly to pray,
> And plead a Saviour's blood:
> In love Thy Holy Spirit give,
> In me to work, and breathe, and live,
> That I may walk with God.

FEBRUARY 10

🌿 MORNING 🌿
'God is for me'
Psalm 56:9

Beloved, the greatest mercy a sinner can enjoy is to have God on his side, engaged in his quarrel, and employed in his most important concerns; this mercy is yours. God is for you. He chose you in Christ before the world began. He formed you to show forth His praise. He preserved you in Christ until He called you by grace. He quickened you by His Spirit, and led you to Jesus. He has given you His Son, and promised every additional good. He has said to you, 'Thou art mine.' You have said, 'I am thine.' He is now your refuge and strength; He is tenderly concerned for your welfare, devotedly attached to your cause, and observes every step you take. He may try your faith, but will certainly supply your wants. He may exercise your patience, but will never turn a deaf ear to your cries, except you indulge iniquity in your heart. No parent ever felt so deeply interested in the welfare of a beloved child, as thy God does in thine. He says, 'Fear thou not; for I am with thee; be not dismayed, for I am thy God: I will strengthen thee; yea, I will help thee: yea, I will uphold thee with the right hand of my righteousness.' Trusting such a promise, who can fail!

> *If God is mine, I need not fear*
> *The rage of earth and hell;*
> *He will support my feeble frame,*
> *Their utmost force repel.*

🌿 EVENING 🌿
'My soul thirsteth for God'
Psalm 42:2

It is not enough for the true Christian to know that God is for him; he wants to realize His presence, to hold sweet fellowship with Him, and to enjoy His love. Being created anew in Christ Jesus, he has an appetite to feed upon, and enjoy divine communications; nor can he be satisfied without them. He longs and prays for the gracious presence of his God, and finds it his joy, his strength, and his delight; but if denied this favour he is depressed, dissatisfied, and cast down. Ordinances, without God, are to him dry breasts; the Scriptures, without God, are a light without heat; the choicest privileges, without God are like provisions presented to one parched up with fever. God is his life, the presence of God is his element, the joy of the Lord is his strength, and without God he is lifeless, sickly, and sorrowful. My friend, is this your experience? Are you in any degree acquainted with it? Can you be satisfied with cold knowledge, empty forms, or what is called religion without the enjoyment of God? If you can, your state is very suspicious. Beware of a religion without God, without personal dealings with God, without daily intercourse with God.

> *Lord of heaven and earth, my trust*
> *Seeks in Thee its only rest:*
> *For Thy love I thirst, I sigh,*
> *To my longing soul draw nigh:*
> *Now Thy glorious face unveil,*
> *Let my faith and prayer prevail.*

FEBRUARY 11

🌿 MORNING 🌿
'I will spare them'
Malachi 3:17

Precious assurance! But whom will the Lord spare? All His children: especially those who speak of His goodness, witness to His faithfulness, think upon His name, and honour Him before an evil generation. He says, 'They shall be Mine, in that day when I make up My jewels, and I will spare them as a father spareth his obedient son.' If we are aiming at the Lord's glory, and walking by the Lord's Word, we have nothing to fear from any of His dispensations. He will shield us from danger, sanctify our troubles, and secure our best interests. If we are living to His praise, we may safely leave our wants and our comforts in His hands; He will supply the one and preserve the other. He says, 'Fear thou not, for I am with thee.' 'Bring every trouble to My throne, every want to My fulness; I am El-Shaddai, God all-sufficient; enough in the absence of every one and everything. I am your God; I may punish the nations, but I will spare you. Believe this, and be happy. Rejoice in this, and you glorify Me. You are no more a servant, but a son; and if a son, then an *heir* of God through Christ. Though I punish the world, I will spare you.'

> Jesus, my Saviour and my Lord,
> 'Tis good to trust Thy name;
> Thy power, Thy faithfulness, and love,
> Will ever be the same.

🌿 EVENING 🌿
'He spared not his own Son'
Romans 8:32

He would not spare His Son, that He might spare His people. He punished Him that He might comfort them. He spared not the angels that sinned. He spared not the old world. But He promises to spare us. How wonderful is this! He hath spared us, He doth spare us, and He will spare us. But Jesus was not spared. Let us reflect on this. For us He engaged in covenant, for us He came into the world, for us He fulfilled all righteousness, for us He offered an atoning sacrifice, for us He lay in the grave, for us He rose from the dead, for us He ascended into heaven, and for us He ever liveth to make intercession; He was our substitute, the Surety of the better covenant, therefore He was not spared. But if God did not spare Him, He may justly spare us, and He will; and not only so, but with His beloved Son, and for His sake, He will freely give us all things which pertain to life and godliness. Precious Saviour, Thy Father did not spare Thee; Satan did not spare Thee; guilty man did not spare Thee. May it therefore be my concern to spare Thee; may I avoid and abstain from everything which would grieve Thy heart, or dishonour Thy dear name! May I never wound Thee, my best, my changeless Friend!

> Thy cruel thorns, Thy shameful cross,
> Procure us heavenly crowns;
> Our brightest gain springs from Thy loss;
> Our healing from Thy wounds.

FEBRUARY 12

🌿 MORNING 🌿
'Hope thou in God'
Psalm 42:11

However gloomy the day, however strange the trials, however distressing the visitation, hope thou in God. He is with you, He is your God, He hath promised to befriend you, He is the faithful God. He will turn darkness into light, make crooked things straight, and make all grace abound towards you, so that you, having all sufficiency, may abound to every good work. The changes that affect you, cannot affect Him. You cannot rely too simply upon Him, or expect too much from Him. If all, within and without, seem to conspire to distress you, still say, 'I will hope in God.' Expect Him to be to you all a gracious and powerful God can be; expect Him to do all a loving Father and infinite God can do. Hope for light in darkness, for relief in distress, for strength in weakness, for joy in sorrow, for deliverance when sinking beneath the wave, and for life in death. Hope for all you need, and for all God has promised. Hope thou in God, and in God alone. Hope because God has spoken, because He is true and faithful, and you cannot hope in vain. The foundation of your hope is laid in the blood of Jesus, and the oath of God.

> *Hope in the Lord, whose mighty hand*
> *Can all thy woes remove;*
> *For thou shalt yet before Him stand,*
> *And sing restoring love.*

🌿 EVENING 🌿
'I will hope continually'
Psalm 71:14

I am warranted to do so, for the foundation of my hope remains immutably the same. The character of my gracious God, the faithful promises of His Word, the recorded history of His saints, and my own past experience, all conspire to say, 'Hope continually.' I will hope, that God will be merciful to my unrighteousness; that He will support me under all my trials, that He will send me seasonable relief, and timely deliverance; that good will flow from all my troubles; that grace will be brought unto me at the appearing of Jesus; and that eternal life will be my final portion. 'I will hope,' for I shall be injured if I do not, anxiety will torment my bosom, despondency will brood over my soul, and I shall be filled with fearful forebodings. 'I will hope continually,' for hope honours God; it brightens the prospects, it stimulates to prayer and exertion, and is the sweetener of human life. But I will also remember, that my hope will be sorely tried; Satan will try it, the God of hope will try it, a thousand things will try it, but a good hope will live, strengthen, and work until it gives place to possession. I will not despond. Why should I? I will not fear. What will it profit me?

> *Let the winds blow, and billows roll,*
> *Hope is the anchor of my soul:*
> *It fastens on a land unknown,*
> *And moors me to my Father's throne!*

FEBRUARY 13

🌿 MORNING 🌿

'Search me, O God'
Psalm 139:23

None can search the heart but God; none are desirous or willing for the heart to be searched but real Christians. A believer desires to know the worst. He dreads deception. Grace has made him honest, and he prays, 'Lord, search me.' If a man was to search, he would expose, irritate, and injure us; but if God search, He will humble, strengthen, and heal us. The man who sees himself in the light of truth, and knows himself as the effect of divine searching, cannot trust himself for one moment. He flees from self to Jesus, from law to grace; he loathes himself; and while he confidently trusts in Jesus, and rejoices in hope, he walks humbly with his God. He cannot boast, he dares not presume; but walks in holiness, and ascribes all to free grace. Beloved, take the heart to Jesus to be searched. He says, 'I am He that searcheth the hearts and trieth the reins.' If He search you, He will save you from deception, self-righteousness, and every false way. Be this your daily prayer, 'Search me, O God, and lead me in the way everlasting. Examine me, O Lord, and prove me: try my reins and my heart.' Let a man examine himself. You need searching.

> Lord, search my heart, and try my ways,
> And make my soul sincere;
> Then shall I stand before Thy face,
> And find acceptance there.

🌿 EVENING 🌿

'Thou hast tried me'
Psalm 17:3

Then prayer has been answered, graces have been exercised, and discipline has been used. The Lord trieth the righteous, and his trials discover, prove, and brighten his character. His fire is in Zion, and His furnace in Jerusalem; and there He tries His people. Every trial is necessary for our good; is ordained by eternal love; and is continued just as long as requisite, but not one moment longer. Every saint needs trials, and every saint is tried. If the Lord intends to make us holy, He will put us into the fire. Every time we pray for holiness, we pray for trials; but trials enhance the value of the promises, endear the throne of grace, render the ordinances profitable, and make the Saviour exceedingly precious. In trials we learn to read our own hearts, see the insufficiency of the world, look more closely to our evidences, humble ourselves before our God, and look with a longing eye to the end of our course. The tried Christian is likely to be a stable Christian; very few who walk in a smooth path are either remarkably spiritual, extensively useful, or very happy. Trials, like the frosts of winter, prepare our hearts to receive the good seed of the Word, and then we bring forth fruit with patience.

> Brought into the fire, Thy wonderful pow'r,
> Unburnt we admire, unhurt we adore;
> Brought thro' our temptation, we shortly shall prove
> Thine utmost salvation, Thy perfecting love.

FEBRUARY 14

❦ MORNING ❧

'The LORD delighteth in thee'
Isaiah 62:4

And is it possible, that such poor, depraved, unworthy creatures, can be the objects of Jehovah's delight? Yes: the infinite love of God has been fixed upon us from eternity; because He loved us, He sent His only-begotten Son to die for us; He sent His Holy Spirit into our hearts, and gave us a good hope through grace. Hear the apostle: 'But God, who is rich in mercy, for his *great love* wherewith He loved us, even when we were *dead in sins*, hath quickened us together with Christ: by whose grace ye are saved.' Jehovah views us in Jesus, and loves us with an infinite love. Yea, He has loved us, as He has loved Him. Every believer, though his faith may be weak, his fears many, his corruptions strong, his troubles great, and his temptations sore, is the object of Jehovah's delight. Let us therefore endeavour to pass through this day, yea, and every day, believing and realizing, 'I am Jehovah's delight; the object of His highest love; the subject of His sweetest thoughts; and His portion for evermore.' O incomparable privilege! Source of comfort, holiness, and love! Thou hast more cause for gratitude than an angel.

> The greatness of eternal love
> What angel tongue can tell?
> O may I to the utmost prove
> The gift unspeakable!

❦ EVENING ❧

'Delight thyself also in the LORD'
Psalm 37:4

As the Lord delights in us, we ought to delight ourselves in Him. In order to do this, we must receive correct views of His loveliness into our minds; we must meditate on His glorious perfections, as they are revealed to us in Jesus; we must realize our interest in His love, and perfect salvation; and turn from every other object to contemplate His beauty, His benevolence, and constant love to us. We should look to Him, as the fountain of all good; hope in Him as the promise-performing God; wait on Him, as our bountiful benefactor; trust in Him, as our Father and Friend; and delight in Him, as our portion and everlasting all. Let us endeavour to take off our affections more and more from things below, and fix them upon the Lord. How few delight in God! How seldom do we! If we read of Him, think of Him, call on Him, believe in Him, hope in Him, and feel a little love to Him, we think it enough. But it is not. We should delight ourselves in the Lord. We may delight ourselves in the Lord. We may delight in His love, which is set upon us; in His vast resources, which are open to supply us; in His truth, which secures us; in His holiness, which is His beauty; and in His grace, which rejoices to do us good.

> O Lord, I would delight in Thee,
> And on Thy care depend;
> To Thee in every trouble flee,
> My best, my only friend.

FEBRUARY 15

❦ MORNING ❧

'Grieve not the holy Spirit'
EPHESIANS 4:30

We are absolutely dependent upon the Holy Spirit for life, light, teaching and sanctification. Without His presence, power, and operations, we are dead, dark, ignorant, and carnal. We should therefore be very careful not to grieve or dishonour Him. We do so when we neglect, slight, or make any improper use of God's holy Word; when we indulge in hard thoughts of God, or low thoughts of the Lord Jesus; when we mind the things of the flesh, in preference to spiritual things; when we trifle with, or indulge in any sin of omission or commission; when we slight His intimations, abuse His gifts, and listen to Satan, the world, or the flesh, in preference to Him. When He is grieved, He suspends His influence, and we find no assistance in duty; we get cold, carnal, and indifferent; we taste no sweetness in spiritual things, and the ministry of the Word becomes dry and lifeless; the Bible is a sealed book; there is no power in prayer; no gratitude for mercies received; and religion becomes a task. O grieve not the Holy Spirit of God, by whom ye are sealed unto the day of redemption; but sow unto the Spirit, and ye shall reap life everlasting!

> Return, O holy Dove, return,
> Sweet messenger of rest!
> I hate the sins that made Thee mourn,
> And drove Thee from my breast.

❦ EVENING ❧

'The holy Spirit of promise'
EPHESIANS 1:13

The great blessing promised in the Old Testament, is the Son of God; but the great promise of the New Testament, is the Holy Spirit. He was promised to Jesus as the reward of His work; and He has promised Him to us, to all who ask Him. Jesus gives this living water, and all who receive it, find it to be a spring of water, welling up into everlasting life. The Spirit is promised to us, to teach us, lead us, comfort us, and assist us in every duty; and we are dependent upon Him for light, life, joy, peace, and power, as we are upon Jesus for atonement, righteousness, and acceptance with God. He is the Spirit of promise also, as it is part of His work to unfold, apply, and prompt us to plead the promises before God. Without Him, we read the promises but do not perceive their fulness, realize their glory, or appropriate them to ourselves; but under His teaching, the promises appear new, exactly suited to us, exceeding great, and very precious. Every Christian is learning out in the school of painful experience, his dependence upon, and daily need of the Holy Spirit of promise. Beloved, let us guard against grieving Him; with double diligence let us cherish His influence, consult His will, obey His intimations, and seek His operations.

> Father, the sealing Spirit give,
> In me to live and reign!
> Let me the promise now receive,
> And never thirst again.

FEBRUARY 16

❦ MORNING ❦
'I will be to them a God'
HEBREWS 8: 10

That is, to all His people: the object of their adoration and trust, the subject of their meditation, and the source of all their happiness. To be our God, is more than being our friend, helper, or benefactor – (creatures may be so); He engages to do us good according to His all-sufficiency, to bestow upon us blessings which none else can. He will pardon us, and pardon like a God; He will sanctify us, and sanctify us like a God; He will comfort us, and comfort us like a God; He will glorify us, and glorify us like a God. If He is our God, He is our All; and all He has is ours. He is our inheritance, and a glorious inheritance He is. Consider, when in danger, in darkness, in distress, in temptation, in duty, or in pain: God will be to you a God, delivering, enlightening, comforting, strengthening, and sanctifying you. Make a God of Him; look to Him for all He has promised, which is all you want; adore His divine perfections, and rejoice that they are all engaged to make you blessed. Live to His glory, walk by His Word, and He will glorify Himself in your present and everlasting welfare. He rejoiceth to do good unto His people; He delights to bless them.

> Here would I dwell, and ne'er remove;
> Here I am safe from all alarms;
> My rest is 'Everlasting love,'
> My refuge, 'Everlasting arms.'

❦ EVENING ❦
'By grace ye are saved'
EPHESIANS 2:5

What a mercy to be saved! To be saved by mere favour! But our salvation from first to last is of grace. It originated in the mind of God, before time began; and it will be completed before the throne of God, when time shall be no more. We are chosen to salvation, chosen in Christ; and this choice of our persons was eternal, sovereign, and immutable. Election gave us a name in God's book, an interest in the Saviour's undertaking, and a part in the saints' inheritance. We are redeemed from among men, and this is a favour. In redemption, a price is paid for us, power is exerted to rescue us, and a plea is put into our mouths. We are called to God's kingdom and glory, and this is a favour: it is personal, powerful, effectual. Calling gives us a new life, a spiritual taste, and an evidence of interest in all covenant blessings. We are kept by the power of God, and this is a favour; prevented from being overcome by foes, crushed by dangers, and from apostatising from the faith; and this proves that we are appointed to salvation. We shall soon be glorified, and heaven will be conferred on us as a favour. If salvation is a favour, then the vilest may receive it; and all the glory of it from first to last must be the Lord's.

> Salvation is a favour God bestows,
> Through Jesu's blood on aliens and on foes;
> By sovereign grace, to make His glory known
> He raises sinners to surround His throne.

FEBRUARY 17

🌿 MORNING 🌿

'Now is the day of salvation'
2 CORINTHIANS 6:2

What an unspeakable mercy to live at such a period! We are poor, lost, ruined sinners; but this is the day when salvation is freely bestowed, without money and without price. The Lord saves from the love, power, and consequences of sin, gives His Holy Spirit, writes His law in the heart, and directs our feet into the way of peace. He gives us Jesus, who is the Saviour; gives us grace, which conquers sin; and gives us heaven, to enjoy when the journey of life is ended. This is the day in which He works deliverance for His people; He employs His power, His wisdom, His Word, His providence, and His angels, for our deliverance. What then shall we fear? Of whom shall we be afraid? Let us go to His throne, remembering that it is the day of salvation; let us plead for deliverance from all that mars our peace, prevents our enjoyment, or hinders us in our Christian course. Let there be no despondency, for this is a day of glad tidings; it is, 'Believe, and be saved; pray, and be delivered; wait on the Lord, and He will strengthen your heart.' 'By grace are ye saved, through faith; and that not of yourselves, it is the gift of God.'

> Salvation! O the joyful sound!
> 'Tis pleasure to our ears!
> A sovereign balm for every wound,
> A cordial for our fears.

🌿 EVENING 🌿

'My soul cleaveth unto the dust'
PSALM 119:25

How common is the complaint, and how discreditable! What is the world? *Dust*! Its pleasures, profits, employments, honours, all dust. That is comparatively worthless, beneath an immortal mind, unsuitable to a child of God; yet our thoughts are filled with them, our affections are entangled by them, and our graces are weakened through them. Worldlings are at home in the dust, they appear to be satisfied with it; but the Christian when he cleaves to it most, is not at home, cannot be satisfied with it. This is a mercy. O to look on high! To rise and plume the wing! To treat the things of time as they deserve! My soul, rouse and shake thyself from the dust, and put on thy beautiful garments. It is the day of salvation, thy God calls thee, He waits to hold fellowship with thee, He hath blessings of immense value to bestow upon thee. It is beneath thy dignity to lie here. It is contrary to thy profession. It is opposed to thy best interests. Heaven is thy home. Holiness is thy element. The King of kings is thy husband. Glory is thy eternal portion. Earth is but a wilderness through which thou hast to pass, a lodging-place for a few days. It is not thy rest; it is polluted.

> Strange that my soul should cleave to dust,
> With death and heaven so nigh;
> Begone, vain world; my spirit must
> Ascend to dwell on high.

FEBRUARY 18

❧ MORNING ❧

'Be ye also patient'
JAMES 5:8

Our God is a God of patience. The Lord Jesus is the great Example of patience. The Holy Spirit is the Agent producing patience. Trials, troubles, and disappointments, are the means which exercise and strengthen it. The patience required is a disposition to bear all that God has appointed for us, without complaining; yea, with resignation and hope: to wait God's time for the mercies we need, or for answers to the prayers we put up. Patience is the daughter of faith; and it is only as we believe that God has appointed, overrules, or commands, for our good and His glory, that we can be patient. Patience produces self-possession, shuts the mouth from complaining, keeps back the heart from seeking revenge, and is a principal point in self government. Are you impatient? Then confess it, and mourn over it, before God; it will make you miserable, and lead you to dishonour God. Watch against it; the coming of the Lord draweth nigh. Look at the prophets, apostles, martyrs, at Jesus; and be ye also patient. 'In your patience possess ye your souls.' 'Be patient, for the coming of the Lord draweth nigh.'

> *O for Thy grace to aid us on,*
> *And arm with fortitude the breast,*
> *Till, life's tumultuous voyage o'er,*
> *We reach the shores of heavenly rest!*
> *O may we still with patience strive,*
> *Till we at Zion's gates arrive!*

❧ EVENING ❧

'To wait for his Son from heaven'
1 THESSALONIANS 1:10

Jesus came in the flesh to redeem us, He sent His Holy Spirit to sanctify us, He will soon come again and receive us to Himself, that where He is we may be also. This is a most glorious event. It is constantly kept before the minds of the Lord's people in the New Testament. It is our blessed hope. We are deeply interested in it, should frequently meditate upon it, daily prepare for it, and be found in a waiting posture. We are servants, and our Master is coming to call us to account. We are sons, and our Father is coming to fetch us home. We are the espoused bride of the Son of God, and He is coming to marry us, and introduce us to His glorious kingdom. He will come very suddenly. He will come when very few expect Him. The virgins will all slumber and sleep, but 'Let us not sleep as do others, but let us watch and be sober.' Jesus may come before morning; He will certainly come soon. Are we ready for His coming? Should we be glad to hear the trumpet sound, see the heavens pass away, and behold Him come in like manner as His disciples saw Him go into heaven? If He should not come to us very soon, we shall go to be with Him. Let us therefore prepare at once.

> *The Saviour comes! He comes to reign,*
> *To banish sorrow, sin, and pain;*
> *Prepare my soul and patient wait,*
> *So shall thy peace and joy be great.*

FEBRUARY 19

❦ MORNING ❦

'He careth for you'
1 Peter 5:7

The Lord knows all His people, their persons, wants, and trials; He thinketh upon them to benefit, deliver, and supply them. He keeps His eye upon them in all places, at all times, and under all circumstances. He has them in His hand, and will not loose His hold. He looks upon them always as His own; the objects of His love, the purchase of His Son's blood, the temples of the Holy Spirit. They are precious in His sight. He knows they are weak, fearful, and have many enemies. He teaches them to cast themselves and all their cares into His hands; and He has given them His Word, that He will care for them. It is a Father's care which He exercises. It is wise, holy, tender, and constant. Therefore all will be well, only trust. Believe that He cares for you this day; carry all your concerns to Him in the faith of this; leave all with Him, persuaded that He will manage all by His infinite wisdom, and bring all to a good issue by His omnipotent power. Cast all your cares upon Him as fast as they come in; be anxious for nothing. 'Cast thy burden upon the LORD, and He shall sustain thee; He shall never suffer the righteous to be moved.'

> 'Cast,' He says, 'on Me thy care,
> 'Tis enough that I am nigh;
> I will all thy burdens bear,
> I will all thy wants supply.'

❦ EVENING ❦

'Take no thought for the morrow'
Matthew 6:34

That is, no anxious, perplexing, distressing thought. You know not that you shall live until tomorrow; the Lord may take you home tonight; but if you do, the Lord will be as thoughtful of you, as kind to you, and as watchful of you, as He has been today. There is daily grace as well as daily bread. You cannot be fatherless; you will not be neglected. Whatever your circumstances may be, your Father knows them, He has provided for them, He will bring you through them, and get glory to Himself by them. Let the peace of God rule in your heart. Stay yourself upon the Word of the Lord. Your loving Saviour wishes you to be free from anxiety, to wait upon Him without distraction, to honour His Father's love, by living in the exercise of calm, patient, waiting faith. Go to rest this night, obeying your Redeemer's word, 'Seek ye first the kingdom of God and His righteousness; and all temporal things shall be added unto you. Take therefore no thought for the morrow; for the morrow shall take thought for the things of itself. Sufficient for the day is the evil thereof.' When you awake in the morning your God will be with you, and having delivered you in six troubles, in seven He will not forsake you.

> By day, by night, at home, abroad,
> Still I am guarded by my God:
> By His incessant bounty fed,
> By His unerring counsel led.

FEBRUARY 20

🌿 MORNING 🌿

'Is the LORD's hand waxed short?'
Numbers 11:23

No: what He hath done, He can do; and all He hath promised, or His people need, He will do. He has all power. He knows no difficulty. Why then are we cast down? Because we do not believe His Word, depend simply on His veracity, and expect all we need from His hand. He was displeased with Moses when he questioned His power, and He is displeased with us when we doubt His love, distrust His providence, or ask, 'How can this thing be?' Whatever may be your difficulty, trial, or want, plead with the Lord, and confidently expect deliverance; and if any temptation is presented to weaken your faith, rouse your fears, or disturb your tranquillity, meet it with this question, 'Is the LORD's hand waxed short?' Beloved, look not to the hand of man, but simply look to the hand of God; man may disappoint you, God will not. He is faithful that promised. He is a God at hand. He will be near you throughout this day; His hand is able and ready to help you; therefore trust, and be not afraid.

> In heaven, and earth, and air, and seas,
> He executes His firm decrees;
> And by His saints it stands confess'd,
> That what He does is ever best;
> Then on His powerful arm rely,
> And He will bring salvation nigh.

🌿 EVENING 🌿

'My counsel shall stand'
Isaiah 46:10

The counsel of man is often weak and unwise, his knowledge being imperfect, and his mind disordered. But the counsel of the Lord is the effect of infinite wisdom, and is sustained by omnipotent power. Men's purposes are often formed under evil influences, or when the mind is confused and perplexed; but the purposes of God were formed in the calm and quiet of the eternal mind, under the influence of justice, grace, holiness, truth, and love. Men's counsels are often frustrated, but God's purposes never can be. Men's purposes are frequently defeated, but our God worketh all things after the counsel of His own will. His counsel includes all that is essential to our eternal welfare; His purposes embrace all the events of this transitory life. Therefore we ought not to be much affected by anything which takes place around us. There may be confusion, conflict, injustice, oppression, cruelty, but our God who has His way in the whirlwind and in the storm, says, 'My counsel shall stand, and I will do all my pleasure.' Remember, beloved, our God is at work always and everywhere. He doeth according to His will in heaven, earth, and hell; and He says to us, 'Be still and know that I am God.'

> God will for all my wants provide,
> And save me for His mercy's sake;
> Me by His counsel He will guide,
> And afterwards to glory take.

FEBRUARY 21

❦ MORNING ❦

'The LORD trieth the righteous'
PSALM 11:5

Where the Lord gives grace, He always tries it; therefore His own people must expect to pass through the fire. He will try our faith, of what sort it is; our love, of what strength it is. He will also try our patience and our constancy. Let us not therefore be surprised at trials, nor let us be discouraged by them; for He tries out of pure love, with the best design, according to a wise rule, and at the fittest season. He considers our frame, our circumstances, and our foes; He does nothing rashly or unkindly. He would not put us to pain if we did not need it; trials are preservatives or restoratives; they keep us back from evil, or are intended to bring us out of the evil into which we have fallen. Thy trials then are from the Lord; His wisdom selected, His love appointed, and His providence brings them about. If you ask, 'Why, Lord, am I tried thus?' the answer is, 'To humble thee, and to prove thee, and to do thee good at thy latter end.' Receive every trial as from God, and go to Him for strength to bear it, grace to sanctify it, and deliverance from it; and so all will be well. It is not for His pleasure, but for your profit, that you are so tried.

> Often the clouds of deepest woe,
> A sweet love-message bear;
> Dark though they seem, we cannot find
> A frown of anger there.

❦ EVENING ❦

'Whom the Lord loveth he chasteneth'
HEBREWS 12:6

Every believer is beloved of his God, yet every believer is chastened, and chastisement is a proof of love. We are but children and need it; we are children and therefore receive it. Some are chastened by losses, some by sickness, some by the failure of their favourite schemes, some by domestic trials, some by the conduct of relatives or Christian friends. We are not all chastened with the same rod, but we are all chastened by the same hand. We are not all corrected in the same way, but we are all corrected by the same wise, holy, and loving Father. Some suffer most in mind, others in body; some are tried most in their own persons, others more in their relatives. But let us never forget, every correction flows from love; every stroke is in kindness. If it goes to our hearts, it touches our heavenly Father's heart. He does not afflict willingly, nor grieve us in sovereignty. Our follies call for strokes, and our sins for rebukes. Let us therefore humble ourselves under our Father's hand. Let us not question our relationship, or His love to us, because we are so tried; neither let us think the discipline unnecessary, and so despise His chastening.

> Afflicted by a gracious God,
> The stroke I patiently sustain;
> Grievous to feeble flesh and blood,
> Unable to rejoice in pain;
> Beneath a Father's hand I bow,
> And groan to feel the chastening now.

FEBRUARY 22

🌿 MORNING 🌿
'He delighteth in mercy'
Micah 7:18

The proper object of mercy is misery; sin has rendered us miserable, and God has revealed Himself as merciful. He delighteth in mercy; it is a pleasure to Him to have mercy upon us; He delights to pardon our sins, relieve our necessities, and save our souls. His own glory being secured, He delights to bless His people. He is styled, *'The Father of Mercies'*; and as a father takes pleasure in his children, so does our God in showing mercy. He always delights in mercy, therefore He does so this morning; go, then, and mourn over thy sins, which have grieved Him, and rendered you miserable; go, and plead for mercy at His throne, nor doubt for one moment His pity, His kindness, or His grace. Have you obtained mercy? Be zealous to glorify God in the day of visitation; be honest, and ascribe all to mercy which is her due; and be active to spread the good news abroad, assuring poor, miserable sinners, that *God delighteth in mercy*. With this, check thy fears, repel thy temptations, and comfort thy heart. Believe it as an undoubted truth, plead it as a powerful argument with God, and daily rejoice in it. It is sweet to be an infinite debtor to mercy.

> *'Tis mercy in Jesus exempts me from hell;*
> *Its glories I'll sing, and its wonders I'll tell;*
> *'Twas Jesus, my Friend, when He hung on the tree,*
> *Who open'd the channel of mercy for me.*

🌿 EVENING 🌿
'He will have compassion upon us'
Micah 7:19

His anger has been provoked by our sins, the effects of His displeasure have been felt, but He retaineth not His anger for ever; and though sin may have made us miserable, mercy shall make us happy. He will have compassion upon us, because of the benevolence of His nature, in accordance with His Word, to our comfort and salvation. He is full of compassion, plenteous in mercy, ready to forgive. These are His own words, and they contain enough, if we did but believe them, to banish our fears, conquer our doubts, and fill us with joy and peace. We have wandered, but He will have compassion, and the wandering sheep shall be restored; the prodigal shall be received with music and dancing. He will have compassion, let Satan suggest what he will; He will have compassion, let thy fears and sins be never so numerous. He will have compassion, for He has promised, His nature prompts Him to it, He has done so in innumerable instances, and His heart overflows with it. As soon as ever He sees you feel your sinfulness, hears you confess your follies, finds you broken down in contrition at His throne, He will have compassion, subdue your iniquities, and cast all your sins into the depths of the sea.

> *Moved with tenderest compassion,*
> *Jesus heals each wounded heart;*
> *And the richest consolation*
> *To His mourners doth impart.*

FEBRUARY 23

❦ MORNING ❦
'Who loved me'
GALATIANS 2:20

And what was Paul? A blasphemer, a persecutor, one who injured the church of God. And did Jesus love Paul? Yes: 'He loved me.' Then the love of Jesus is free, and not on account of anything man is. The cause of love is in God, not in the objects loved. You may have looked for some reason to conclude that God has loved you, but you have been disappointed; the Lord says, 'I will love them freely.' When we were dead in sins, He quickened us because He loved us; He revealed Jesus to us because He loved us; He has given us His Holy Spirit because He loved us. Whom once He loves He never leaves. Jesus loves us this morning with a free, infinite, and eternal love. He loves our persons, apart from our graces and acts; these are the effects of His love, and not strictly the objects of His love. O Holy Spirit! Whisper to our hearts this morning, 'Jesus loved *thee*, even thee.' O to love Him in return! To love Him above health, wealth, comfort, yea, life itself! O to show forth the praises of His love by humility, faith, constancy, and zeal!

> Great God, to Thy almighty love
> What honours shall I raise?
> Not all the raptured songs above,
> Can render equal praise:
> Thy love to me surpasses thought!
> O could I praise Thee as I ought!

❦ EVENING ❦
'She loved much'
LUKE 7:47

She hath been a great sinner; convinced of her sin, she sought the Saviour; applied for pardon, and she found mercy. Deeply affected with the love of Christ, and the manner in which He displayed it, her soul glowed with love to Him in return. She not only loved Him, but she loved Him *much*: and therefore she could endure scorn, contempt, and persecution, in order to enjoy His presence and listen to His Word. Her love would not be confined in her bosom, it sought to show itself; she therefore brought the alabaster box of precious ointment, washed His feet with her tears, wiped them with the hair of her head, and anointed them with the ointment. Here is an example for us: we also are great sinners; Jesus has kindly received us and pardoned our sins; *His* love to us is as great as it was to this woman, but is *our* love to Him equal to hers? I fear not. But why? Because our conviction of sin is not as clear, our views of our unworthiness are not as vivid, our apprehensions of danger are not as painful, or our sense of pardoning mercy is not as deep. We cannot force ourselves to love. But we can direct our thoughts to Jesus, and seek for the Holy Spirit to shed abroad His love in our hearts.

> For love like Thine, O God of heaven,
> What grateful honours shall we show?
> Where much transgression is forgiven,
> Let love in equal ardour glow.

FEBRUARY 24

🌿 MORNING 🌿
'Who gave himself for me'
GALATIANS 2:20

Jesus was our Substitute. He lived, suffered, and died, in our stead. Our sins were imputed to Him, punished in Him, and removed by Him. God had cursed us, but Jesus gave Himself to bear the curse in our stead; every threatening of the law was executed on Him; every one of the claims of justice was answered by Him; and now God is just and yet the justifier of everyone that believeth in Jesus. The debt-book is crossed, the handwriting that was against us is destroyed, and every foe is overcome. Do we think of the law we have broken, of the justice we have provoked, of the hell we have deserved? Let us also think, Jesus gave Himself for me. He satisfied justice, fulfilled the law, and brought glory to God, in my nature, name, and stead; and God is infinitely more honoured by the life and death of my Substitute, than He could have been either by my obedience had I never sinned, or by punishing me for sin. This is our rejoicing, that God can be just, in justifying us who believe in Jesus. Thanks be unto God for His unspeakable gift.

> *Jesus is the chiefest good;*
> *He hath saved us by His blood:*
> *Let us value nought but Him;*
> *Nothing else deserves esteem.*

> *Jesus, when stern justice said,*
> *'Man his life has forfeited;*
> *Vengeance follows My decree,'*
> *Cried, 'Inflict it all on Me.'*

🌿 EVENING 🌿
'Therefore glorify God'
1 CORINTHIANS 6:20

Whatever God does is for the glorification of Himself. This is the great end of all things. We are created for His glory, but we sinned and came short of it. We came short of the glory of His law, in not obeying it; we came short of the glory of His image, not resembling it; we came short of the glory of His favour, not desiring it; and we came short of the glory of His presence, not seeking it. But Jesus died for us, paying the price of our ransom, wrought out a perfect righteousness, and saves us with an everlasting salvation. Therefore we are not our own, but are bought with a price, and should now glorify God in our bodies, and in our spirits, which are God's. To glorify God, therefore, is the only legitimate business of life. We can do this by believing His doctrine, trusting His promises, and obeying His precepts. By endeavouring to benefit His creatures *for His sake*; especially by visiting, relieving, and comforting His poor saints; also by spreading His gospel, by governing our tempers, training up our families in His fear, and seeking the honour of His name in all we do. To glorify God is our duty, our reasonable service. O may it be our pleasure and delight!

> *O Thou who didst my person buy,*
> *And paid the price in blood,*
> *Assist me now to glorify,*
> *And only live to God!*

FEBRUARY 25

❦ MORNING ❧
'Christ is all'
COLOSSIANS 3:11

Yes: this is God's purpose, which cannot be frustrated, that Christ shall be all. He is all in our justification and sanctification, for we are justified and sanctified *in His name*. He is all in our preservation and glorification, for we are kept by His power, and enter heaven through His merits. He should be all in our pursuits, pleasures, hopes, motives, and aims. Many put their comforts in the place of Christ, and then God puts comfort out of their reach; others put their graces in the place of Christ, and then faith, hope, and love, are concealed by a cloud. There must be nothing between God and us, but Jesus; we must look away from sin, from graces, and from works, and expect to be accepted, blessed, and honoured only in the name and for the honour of Jesus. Christ is our conquering weapon, by which we overcome our foes; our plea, by which we prevail with God; our righteousness, by which we are justified; and our peace, which supports and comforts us in life and in death. Christ is all we want, or God can give. He is our sun and shield, our present joy and endless portion. He is our all on earth; He will be our all in heaven.

> *Saviour! the knowledge of Thy love*
> *Into my soul convey;*
> *Thyself bestow! for Thee alone,*
> *My all in all, I pray.*
> *I would be only, always Thine,*
> *And prove the power of love divine.*

❦ EVENING ❧
'My meditation of him shall be sweet'
PSALM 104:34

To meditate is to think closely, seriously, and for some time upon one subject: if the subject is spiritual, the exercise is peculiarly profitable; if the mind is spiritual, meditation of Jesus will be sweet. Let us think of Him frequently, intently, and seriously. Let us meditate on the glory of His person, the riches of His grace, the strength of His love, the tenderness of His sympathy, the power of His arm, the merit of His blood, the magnificence of His righteousness, the completeness of His conquest, the splendour of His ascension; the prevalence of His intercession, the exalted station He fills in heaven, His constant care of His people on earth, what He gives to them, what He requires of them, and the glory to which He will raise them, when He comes again the second time, without sin unto salvation. Let us meditate, and let Jesus be our subject. Let us go over in meditation all that regards His person, His office, His work, His kingdom, His humiliation, His exaltation, and His character. Such meditations will be sweet. Let us see Him in nature, in providence, and in grace. Such views of Him will cheer, strengthen, and spiritualise us. Let us meditate on Him *tonight*, and let our last thoughts be of Jesus.

> *Sweet are the thoughts which fill my breast,*
> *When on His various works they rest;*
> *God my CREATOR lifts my voice!*
> *In God my SAVIOUR I rejoice!*

FEBRUARY 26

🌿 MORNING 🌿
'Ye do dishonour me'
JOHN 8:49

This is a complaint brought against us by our Lord Jesus Christ. Let us listen to it. He has assured us of His love, that He seeks our good, that He will not be wroth with us. We dishonour Him therefore by our fretfulness under trials and troubles; by our murmuring when all is not as we wish; by our impatience to be delivered from pain; by our unbelief in reference to His promises and providence; by our unthankfulness for the many mercies we receive; by employing His favours in Satan's service; by limiting His power or His goodness; by omitting duties, from want of love or zeal; by relying on our services instead of free grace; and by looking to others, instead of looking only and always to Him for all. Dishonouring Jesus must be a great sin: it produces deadness, darkness, and misery. Let us realize its criminality, lament it before God, seek repentance for it, and forgiveness of it. O let us aim to honour Jesus by gratitude, patience, faith, love, forbearance, penitence, zeal, and by constantly aiming at His glory! To honour Him in life, death, and for ever!

> *Lord, draw my heart from earth away,*
> *And make it only know Thy call;*
> *Speak to my inmost soul, and say,*
> *'I am thy Saviour, God, thine ALL!'*
> *Nor let me more dishonour Thee,*
> *But Thy devoted servant be.*

🌿 EVENING 🌿
'Repent and do the first works'
REVELATION 2:5

Repentance implies thought, serious thought in reference to the conduct and state of the heart; it proceeds from conviction, deep and solemn conviction of our sin and sinfulness in the sight of God; it proves concern, a concern to escape danger, obtain pardon, and enjoy peace; it includes sorrow, enlightened, hearty, and abiding sorrow, that we have grieved the Lord, dishonoured His cause, and slighted His mercy; it always leads to reformation. There may be some degree of reformation without repentance, but there can be no repentance without reformation. Let us think upon our ways, reflect on the dishonour we have done the Saviour, be concerned to enjoy anew the tokens of His forgiving love, mourn over our follies and faults, and begin again to do our first works. Look to Jesus, wait upon God, search His holy Word, diligently attend His ordinances, speak of Jesus and for Jesus, and abstain from the very appearance of evil, as we did at first. What love, what zeal, what caution, what carefulness, what entire consecration to God, we manifested then! Let us search and try our ways, and turn again to the Lord. Jesus charges us with dishonouring Him, but He also says, 'Repent and do thy first works.'

> *Recall to mind the happy days,*
> *When thou wast fill'd with joy and praise;*
> *Repent, thy former works renew,*
> *Then I'll restore thy comforts too.*

FEBRUARY 27

🌿 MORNING 🌿
'All things come of thee'
1 Chronicles 29:14

Every good gift and every perfect gift is from above; creatures apart from God are empty cisterns, dry wells, deceitful brooks. All good dwells in thy God, and flows from Him to thee. Every crumb is from Christ. What He gives freely, cost Him groans, sweat, and blood, to procure for thee. View Him as the source of all good, and His atonement as the medium through which all flows to thee. He gives thee thy temporal mercies, and thy spiritual blessings; He gives thee also the ability to enjoy them, and employ them for His glory. He directs all events, whether pleasing or painful. 'Be not angry with yourselves,' said Joseph to his brethren; 'it was not you, but God.' To Him therefore your mind should be directed in prayer, dependence, and praise. Look above creatures, and see the Lord's hand, as did Job, Eli, David, and Paul. Rest with unshaken confidence and filial resignation on His Word, power, providence, and love, ever remembering that all things come of Him. The Lord will give us that which is good, and a blessing with it, if we are looking to, and walking with Him. Every good gift and every perfect gift is from above, from Jesus.

> He sank beneath our heavy woes,
> To raise us to His throne;
> There's ne'er a gift His hand bestows,
> But cost His heart a groan.

🌿 EVENING 🌿
'Rest in the LORD'
Psalm 37:7

The sinner is naturally restless, he is removed from his natural basis, and the wandering of the desire keeps him in constant agitation. To him Jesus says, 'Come unto me, and I will give you rest.' The believer has accepted this invitation, and has found rest; but he is often led away by temptations, worldly cares, and unbelief; and then he becomes restless again. Beloved, you are directed to rest, not in your circumstances, attainments, or enjoyments, but *rest in the Lord*. Rest in the *will* of God, for whatever He wills is for your good, your highest good: 'This is the will of God, even your sanctification.' Rest in the *love* of God, and often meditate on the words of Jesus on this point, 'Thou hast loved them, *as thou hast loved me*.' Rest in the *mercy* of God, from which flows endless streams of blessings for your supply. Rest in the *Word* of God, for it is true, immutable, and pledges Him to do you good. Rest in the *relation* thy God fills to thee; He is thy Father; kind, careful, wise, and ever-present. Rest in the Lord as He is manifested in Jesus, thy God in covenant, working all things after the counsel of His own will, directing all things for thy good and His glory. Rest in the Lord and be happy.

> Safe in the Lord His saints may rest,
> And calmly wait His will;
> Though poor and tried they yet are blest,
> Their God is gracious still.

FEBRUARY 28

❦ MORNING ❧
'I am he that liveth'
REVELATION 1:18

Jesus once died in our stead. He now liveth at the right hand of God. He is the fountain of life. Because He lives, His people shall live also. He lives in heaven to see of the travail of His soul, in the regeneration, sanctification, preservation, and glorification of His beloved family. He lives to intercede for them, to sympathize with them, and to pour down blessings upon them. He lives to watch over them, to counsel and direct them, and to save them for evermore. He lives to execute the purposes of the Father, to manage all the concerns of His church, and to glorify us with Himself for evermore. Gracious Saviour! Earthly friends may die, but Thou livest; temporal comforts may be lost, but we still have a place in Thy heart; Thou art our Friend before Thy Father's throne! May we ever remember, Jesus liveth who was dead; and He is alive for evermore, and has the keys of hell and of death. O to live for Him on earth, who lives for us in heaven! O to live like Him, that as He is, so we may be in this world, representatives of God and holiness! O to live by faith on Him, in sweet and holy fellowship with Him.

> *His saints He loves, and never leaves;*
> *The chief of sinners He receives;*
> *Cheer up, my heart! with this revive,*
> *The sinner's Friend is yet alive.*

❦ EVENING ❧
'Because I live, ye shall live also'
JOHN 14:19

Christ and His people are one. He is the head, and they are the members of His body. From Him they receive life, wisdom, power, holiness, and every grace. He has a fulness on purpose to supply them, and out of that fulness He daily gives them grace, as their circumstances may require. We have hitherto been supplied with grace by Jesus, and He who hath supplied us until now, will continue to do so. He lives, necessarily, as God; officially, as God-man. He lives in high authority, possessing unbounded influence. He lives to use what He possesses, to fulfil His Word, complete His work, and lead His people on to the enjoyment of eternal life. They shall live – that is exist – as Christians, persevere in their journey, and be happy in His love for ever. They shall live because Jesus who ever lives is their Life, their Representative, and their Surety. He lives *for* them, ruling, over-ruling, securing and loving. He lives *in* them and their life is hid with Him in God. Beloved, see the ground of your safety, the source of your joy, the wisdom of your God. Your life and happiness are identified with the life and happiness of Jesus. Christ who is your life will soon appear, and then you will live like Him, and be with Him for ever.

> *If my immortal Saviour lives,*
> *Then my immortal life is sure;*
> *His Word a firm foundation gives,*
> *Here let me build, and rest secure.*

FEBRUARY 29

❦ MORNING ❧

'Love not the world'
1 John 2:15

What is the world? A shadow; a deception; the enemy of God. What can it do for us? It may enchant, but it will deceive. It may please for a time, but will sting in the end. It is an enemy's country; we must pass through it, but we should not be too intimate with the inhabitants of it. It crucified our Saviour; it is in open rebellion against our God; it has allured, deceived, and injured many of our brethren; it is reserved unto fire at the judgment of the great day. We *shall* soon be called to leave it, we *may* be called today; 'For what is our life? It is even as a vapour, which appeareth for a little while, and then vanisheth away.' Let us fix and spend our love upon a worthier object; let us turn our thoughts to heaven, to Jesus; and let us seek grace that we may daily and heartily say, 'Whom have I in heaven but thee, and there is none upon earth I desire beside thee.' Precious Saviour! Engross our attention, fix our affections, and be always our *all in all!* None but Jesus, none but Jesus, should be our motto every day. He alone is worthy of our love; and He is worthy of it, for He died and lives to win it.

> Lord, from this world call off my love,
> Set my affections right;
> Bid me aspire to joys above,
> And walk no more by sight.

❦ EVENING ❧

'The Lord is at hand'
Philippians 4:5

Jesus is coming. When He will come is uncertain, therefore we should always be ready. If we realized the certainty and nearness of the Lord's coming, we should not be ensnared by the world as we too often are. Our love would be withdrawn from present things, and we should be daily laying up for ourselves treasures in heaven. Jesus will come to close the present dispensation, to judge the people, to be glorified in His saints, and reward every one according to his works. The Lord is at hand: we should think of this, we should realise it, it would preserve us from temptation, it would prevent our backsliding, and it would deepen our seriousness and spirituality. He will come: therefore we should expect Him, prepare for Him, invite Him, and be found waiting, looking, and longing for His appearing. When He comes, He will bring us grace, destroy all our foes, conform us to His own lovely image, and then introduce us to glory. When Jesus comes, His people will be made completely happy; sighs, groans, and cries will be exchanged for pleasures, songs, and triumphant hallelujahs. 'Even so, come Lord Jesus, come quickly.'

> Saviour, hasten Thine appearing,
> Bring, O bring the glorious day,
> When the awful summons hearing,
> Heaven and earth shall pass away:
> Then with golden harps we'll sing
> Glory, glory to our King.

MARCH 1

❧ MORNING ❧
'Thy Maker is thine husband'
Isaiah 54:5

Sweet assurance! Surprising condescension. Does Jesus, by whom all things were made, fill this sweet relation? Is He my nearest and dearest relative? Yes: He loves thee more than any other. He is more closely united to thee, and more deeply interested in thee. He is the Bridegroom, thou art the bride; He has espoused thee to Himself, has made full provision for all thy present wants, and is gone to prepare thy everlasting habitation, where thou art to dwell with Him and enjoy His love. The relation really subsists. He regards thee as His beloved bride, and He would have thee live daily in the recollection that He is thy Lord. O love Him above all! Call upon Him with confidence. Look for Him with ardent longing. He will come to be glorified in His saints, and admired in all them that believe. Think not that He will ever forget the person, neglect the concerns, or turn a deaf ear to the requests of His beloved, blood-bought bride. His love is infinite, and the whole is set on thee; and will remain fixed on thee forever. He is in one mind, and none can turn Him. Having loved thee, He will love thee unto the end.

> Jesus, my Shepherd, Husband, Friend,
> My Prophet, Priest, and King,
> My Lord, my Life, my Way, my End,
> Accept the praise I bring.

❧ EVENING ❧
'Show thy marvellous lovingkindness'
Psalm 17:7

He has already shown it, by taking us into the nearest, sweetest, and most profitable relation to Himself. What love to call a worm His child; a sinful and polluted worm His bride; to pledge Himself to us, in order to banish our fears, encourage our confidence, and raise our expectations. Lovingkindness is love in the most attractive form; love acting in the kindest manner; or, love robed in tenderness, benevolence, and condescension. To show marvellous lovingkindness is to bestow distinguished favours, such as reason or custom, could not warrant us to expect; favours which only faith would look for, or a God of love bestow. Yet such favours we may ask, and having asked in faith, expect. Beloved, never forget, our God rejoices to do us good, He takes pleasure in the prosperity of His servants, and He delights to give us good things. If we were but humble, simple-minded, living in the daily exercise of faith, He would deny us nothing. We have not, but it is because we ask not, or because we ask in an improper spirit, or with an unbecoming design, that we may consume it upon our lusts.

> O Thou, all gracious Lord, most high.
> On Thee alone I now rely;
> To me Thy gracious ear incline,
> And aid me with a power divine.
> To me while sojourning below,
> Thy wondrous lovingkindness show.

MARCH 2

🌿 MORNING 🌿

'Resist the devil'
JAMES 4:7

Every believer must expect to be visited by Satan; he is our adversary; he is always watching for an opportunity to injure us. He first tempts us to sin, and then accuses us of sinning. He misrepresents every subject. He endeavours to make the world appear lovely, sin trifling, death terrible; he generates hard thoughts of God, perverts His holy Word, and leads believers into bondage. His fiery darts are very terrible. Thoughts the most blasphemous, horrible, and unnatural, are often thrown into the mind by him; and then he lays them to our charge, and distresses our souls on account of them. But we are called upon to resist him steadfast in the faith, believing what God is to us; what Christ has done for us; what He has promised to give us; and that God will bruise him under our feet shortly. The triumph of this *wicked one* is but short, for we shall overcome him by the blood of the Lamb, and the word of His testimony. Look to Jesus, call upon thy God, and oppose the blood and righteousness of Jesus to all his charges. He is mighty, but thy Jesus is *almighty*. Take this shield of faith, and thou shalt quench all the fiery darts of the wicked one.

Temptations everywhere annoy;
And sins and snares my peace destroy;
Lord, let Thy presence be my stay,
And guard me in this dangerous way.

🌿 EVENING 🌿

'They overcame him'
REVELATION 12:11

What a formidable representation of Satan the context gives us. He is called 'the great dragon, that old serpent, called the Devil, and Satan, which deceiveth the world.' His power is great; his cruelty is greater. His cunning is deep, and his designs are dreadful. He hates the Saviour, and he hates all who love Him. He attempts to destroy, but he will distress those whom he cannot devour. He has tried all means to injure the Church of God, and he still tries to injure every believer. He is dreadful as a roaring lion; but he is more likely to harm us, when he comes slyly, and quietly, as a serpent. He is always most dangerous when he assumes the garb of an angel of light, for then we are apt to mistake him. But the saints overcame him, yet they were as weak, and as liable to be overcome, as we are. They overcame him, but not by reason, or argument, or eloquence; they conquered by the blood of the Lamb, and the word of their testimony. To that blood they looked, when he tempted them to despair; by that Word they walked, when he tried to draw them aside. The blood was their plea, the ground of their hope, and the subject of their rejoicing; the Word was their shield, their solace, and their rule.

By the blood of the Lamb the saints overcame,
And its virtue continues for ever the same,
The world and its good shall again be subdued
By the virtue divine of our Advocate's blood.

MARCH 3

❧ MORNING ❧
'Let us have grace'
Hebrews 12:28

We daily need grace to sustain us in troubles; to subdue our corruptions; to sanctify our tempers; to preserve us in temptation; to quicken our languid affections; to enlarge our experience; to render us useful to others; to enable us to endure to the end; and to meet death with confidence and joy. Our God is the God of all grace. Jesus is full of grace, and He giveth more grace. He has promised it. 'He will give grace.' He has invited us to come and receive it. 'Come boldly to the throne of grace, that ye may obtain mercy, and find grace to help in time of need.' His grace is sufficient for us; but without grace we are dull, lifeless, and sure to fall. O let us look to Jesus for grace to strengthen us, sanctify us, and make us useful! Let us never attempt anything in our own strength; but let us receive from the Lord, that we may live to the Lord; and ascribe all that we do that is good, to the grace of God which is with us. Grace is always free. It is free for us, for us this morning, and our God bids us come and receive. Come then boldly to the throne of grace, and you *shall* obtain mercy, and find grace to help you this day.

> On me, my King, exert Thy power,
> Make old things pass away;
> Transform and draw my soul to Thee,
> Still nearer every day.

❧ EVENING ❧
'As obedient children'
1 Peter 1:14

The believer should daily realize the pleasing fact that God is his Father, and this being the case he is treated as a child. His heavenly Father has made ample provision for all his wants. In Jesus, he will find all he needs as a sinner, and all he requires as a saint. Whatever is in Jesus is for him, and it is his duty as well as his privilege, to receive out of the fulness of Jesus grace for grace. As a child, he should listen to his Father's voice, learn his Father's will and do his Father's commands. He has only to obey, his Father will provide. He has to do with duty, not with consequences. Only let him ascertain his Father's will upon any point, and it becomes at once his duty, his honour, and his happiness to do it. Believer, you have a Father; a Father that loves you more than tongue can tell; a Father who has blessed you in Jesus with all spiritual blessings; a Father who is now waiting for you to approach Him in prayer and praise; a Father who wishes you to cast every care upon Him, to leave every burden at His feet, to trust Him to do you good. As an obedient child, resign all your will to His; leave all your concerns in His hands; and your safety, comfort, and supplies are certain.

> Lord, my heart is bare before Thee,
> Let me now Thy mercy prove;
> Help me, for my wants implore Thee,
> Love me with a Father's love.

MARCH 4

🌿 MORNING 🌿
'Only believe'
Mark 5:36

That is, take God at His Word. Give Him credit for meaning what He says, for being faithful to His own Word; and then what will become of your fears? God speaks to you in a language which you can understand; He promises all you can possibly need; He bids you put Him in remembrance, and plead with Him; and He pledges His character for the comfort of your heart. If you believe not, you make God a liar; you bring darkness on your own soul; you give Satan an occasion against you; and a thousand fears, doubts, and suspicions distress you. Is it any wonder? Can you offer a greater insult to God than deliberately to disbelieve His Word? But you ask, 'Are the promises made to me?' Yes, to every one that believeth, and to you if you believe. And the Spirit is promised to work faith in your heart; complain not then of the difficulty of believing, or of the power of unbelief; but go to thy God, and plead with Him, crying, 'Lord, increase my faith;' and go to His Word, as to the word of a gracious father, and endeavour to believe it.

> O that closer I could cleave
> To Thy bleeding, dying breast!
> Give me firmly to believe,
> And to enter into rest:
> Lord, increase, increase my faith;
> Make me faithful unto death.

🌿 EVENING 🌿
'The Strength of Israel will not lie'
1 Samuel 15:29

Then He ought to be believed. It is impossible for God to lie; then He ought to be trusted. His promises are the fruits of His love, they are changeless as His nature, and *must* be made good. He is the *Omnipotent*, and can fulfil His Word; He is the *Unchangeable*, and certainly will. His strength is pledged to His people, to sustain them; His resources, to supply them; and His faithfulness, to comfort them. He speaks to us in His Word, He speaks to us as sinners; He speaks to us as fearful, as tried, as suffering, just as we are tonight. He speaks to quell our fears, to cheer us under our trials, and to soothe our minds while suffering. Do we believe His Word? Do we treat Him as a truth-speaking God? Has He our confidence? Do we stay ourselves upon His Word? Are we looking at His promise, and while we look at it do we say, 'This is the faithful Word of my heavenly Father; this is certainly true; this must be fulfilled; this is more durable than heaven or earth, for Jesus has said, "Heaven or earth may pass away, but My Word shall not pass away".' Fix your eye on His Word, and while you do, say:

> Yes, since God Himself has said it,
> On the promise I rely;
> His good Word demands my credit,
> What can unbelief reply!
> He is strong, and can fulfil,
> He is truth, and therefore will.

MARCH 5

❦ MORNING ❦
'Fear thou not'
Isaiah 41:10

The Lord's people are prone to fear, because they do not realize their relation to God, their interest in the promises of God, and that they are always in the presence of God. How graciously our God forbids our slavish fears, and encourages confidence in Himself! Our slavish fears dishonour Him; our filial confidence glorifies Him. He loves to be trusted; He is grieved by our doubts and fears. We should fear nothing but sin; and if we fear sin, follow holiness, and preserve a conscience void of offence toward God and man; if we live upon His Word, daily use the open fountain, and cultivate communion with our God, we can have no cause to fear. Beloved, leave anxiety, distrust, and slavish fear, to the poor godless worldling; but trust thou in the living God always, and everywhere. Hope in God; wait upon God; expect from God; follow hard after God; and all you want will be given, and all that would injure you will be frustrated. Be not afraid, only believe; Jesus is with thee, and will preserve, bless, and keep thee; therefore, *'Fear thou not.'*

> *And art Thou with me, gracious Lord,*
> *To dissipate my fear?*
> *Dost Thou proclaim Thyself my God,*
> *My God for ever near?*
> *Then farewell, anxious, gloomy care,*
> *Since God forbids my soul to fear.*

❦ EVENING ❦
'Wait on thy God continually'
Hosea 12:6

A waiting frame is a holy frame. It is a calm quiet mind, living before the Lord's throne, exercising faith in His Word, hoping in His mercy, endeavouring to do His will, and patiently submitting to His pleasure. The waiting soul sees God in all things, realizes God as present everywhere, and acknowledges His hand in every event. Wait on thy God continually, so will you be safe in every season of danger, happy under all your numerous trials, and find the Lord putting honour upon you in His ordinances. Wait on the Lord as the industrious servant, on his kind and careful master; as the consistent maiden, on her thoughtful and benevolent mistress; as the affectionate child, on his loving and beloved parent. Wait on Him, for He approves of the exercise. Wait on Him, for He requires it at your hand. Wait on Him, for He rewards it with a blessing. 'Wait on the LORD, be of good courage, and He shall strengthen thine heart; wait, I say, on the LORD.' Have you been waiting on your God today? Are you in a quiet waiting frame tonight? Can you say, 'I wait for the Lord, … and in His word do I hope?' Beware of impatience.

> *Wait, believing on the Lord,*
> *Still let courage cheer thy heart;*
> *Wait, for faithful is His Word,*
> *He will grace and strength impart.*

MARCH 6

🌿 MORNING 🌿

'Walk worthy of God'

1 Thessalonians 2:12

God hath called us with a holy calling, to enjoy a holy Saviour, believe a holy Gospel, possess a holy nature, and walk in a holy way. All the provisions of free grace, all the promises of infinite love, and all the precepts of reigning holiness, unite to require us to be a holy people unto the Lord our God. We are to imitate the conduct of our God. He feeds His foes, loves His people, and always acts becoming His glorious character. Enemies will lie in wait to deceive you, errors will be broached to mislead you; but beware, lest being led away by the error of the wicked, ye fall from your own steadfastness. Consider your character: children of God; your high privileges: united to Jesus, temples of the Holy Ghost, companions of saints and angels, the friends of God; your destination: to fill a throne of glory, wear a blood-bought crown, and reflect the praises of Jehovah for ever. Walk worthy of God, suitable to your character, profession and destination. Walk with God; walk as Jesus walked; walk circumspectly; walk in love; walk honestly, as in the day; so will you adorn your profession, and secure to yourself comfort and peace.

> *When thus we walk with God and men,*
> *The life and conscience clean,*
> *Our faith assumes a body then,*
> *And may be felt and seen.*

🌿 EVENING 🌿

'There is therefore now no condemnation'

Romans 8:1

Every believer is in Christ: united to His person, interested in His offices, clothed with His righteousness, and sanctified by His Spirit. 'There is therefore now no condemnation.' Doubts there may be. Fears may harass. Sin there is in us, but no sin is imputed to us. The believer is under no charge. By virtue of oneness with Christ, he has been acquitted from every charge, he stands justified from all things, he is accepted of God as a beloved child, and is entitled to all the provisions of grace and glory. If he sins, he is chastened; being chastened, he confesses his sins with contrition; confessing his sins, God in faithfulness and justice forgives; he is led afresh to claim and plead the finished work of Jesus, and finds that he is not condemned, but acquitted. No one can lay any thing to his charge, for God justifies him; he does so, because Christ died for him; yea, rather, because as his Surety He is risen again, and is now at His own right hand as his Advocate, ever living to make intercession for him. Blessed state! Unspeakable privilege! I would lay down on my pillow tonight, impressed with the great fact: 'I am not a condemned sinner, but a justified and beloved child of God.' Astonishing grace!

> *No condemnation, O my soul,*
> *'Tis God that speaks the Word;*
> *Perfect in comeliness art thou*
> *In Christ, thy glorious Lord.*

MARCH 7

❦ MORNING ❧

'Ephraim my dear son'
JEREMIAH 31:20

Poor, fickle, backsliding Ephraim, is thus called by our infinitely gracious God. Adopted by grace into the heavenly family, taught by the Spirit, and united to Jesus, God views us through Him; and having predestinated us to be conformed to the image of His Son, He views things which are but purposed as accomplished, and we are comely through the comeliness He has put upon us. His love to us is wonderful; He says, 'He that toucheth you, toucheth the apple of His eye.' He rejoices to do us good, and gives His angels charge over us. He will not suffer anyone really to hurt us; but, lest this should be the case, He will keep us night and day. Let us then abide in Jesus; let us cultivate communion with this gracious God; let us follow on to know the Lord; trust in Him at all times; wait upon Him continually; and rejoice in this delightful fact, that God calls us *'His dear sons, His pleasant children.'* He not only calls us so, but treats us as such; and addresses us as such in His holy Word. Let us call Him our Father, and look to Him for all we need; so shall we honour Him, conquer Satan, and enjoy peace. Our Father is God; our God is our Father.

> *If I've the honour, Lord, to be*
> *One of Thy numerous family,*
> *On me the gracious gift bestow,*
> *To call Thee, ABBA, FATHER! too.*

❦ EVENING ❧

'Thy Father which seeth in secret'
MATTHEW 6:6

Can anyone hide himself in secret places from the Lord? Can a Christian under any circumstances escape His notice? Impossible! The eye of God has been fixed upon me every moment of this day; it is now at this moment fixed full upon me. But it is a Father's eye. My Father seeth us in secret. He sees every secret workings of my foes, and will save me from them. He sees every secret influence which is likely to injure me, and will prevent it. He sees the secret workings of my heart, my hidden thoughts, my unuttered desires, my soul conflicts, my private temptations. He sees me withdraw for prayer, or sees me cast up my imploring eye to Him when I cannot. He sees my wants and woes. But He sees also my secret sins, every evil thought, every improper action, every unbecoming word, passes under His eye. Solemn consideration this! May it make me cautious. May it preserve me from yielding to temptation, from encouraging improper suggestions, and from acting inconsistent with my profession. My heavenly Father seeth me, seeth me at this moment, seeth me every moment, seeth my most secret motives, thoughts, and purposes; and He who thus seeth me, hateth with an infinite hatred every sin.

> *O may these thoughts possess my breast,*
> *Where'er I rove, where'er I rest!*
> *Nor let my weaker passions dare*
> *Consent to sin, for God is there.*

MARCH 8

❦ MORNING ❦
'They need not depart'
MATTHEW 14:16

How many things concur to lead or drive us away from Jesus! But we need not depart from Him; He has everything we can possibly want, for body or soul, for time or eternity. He gives grace and glory, and no good thing will He withhold from them that walk uprightly. Having called us, and drawn us to Himself, He wishes us to abide with Him; and if tempted to leave Him, to whom can we go? He will supply every want, sanctify every trial, enable us to overcome every difficulty, and make us happy in His own love. The world will allure you, Satan will try to drive you, and inward depravity will prompt you to wander; but keep near to Jesus this day: think of Him, look to Him, call upon Him, converse with Him; make Him your Companion, Friend, and God. There is no real happiness, or solid peace, but in the presence and blessing of Jesus; and when He giveth quietness, none can make trouble. If you wander, if you look to others, if you set your affections on anything below, you cannot justify your conduct, for you need not depart. He is all. He has all. He will give all. You have only to believe His Word, and your wants shall be all supplied.

> O let us ever walk in Him,
> And nothing know beside;
> Nothing desire, nor aught esteem,
> But Jesus crucified.

❦ EVENING ❦
'Will ye also go away?'
JOHN 6:67

Many left the Saviour in the days of His flesh, and many decline from His ways now. How many like Lot's wife, look back; like the man of God who came from Bethel, yield to temptation; or like Demas, forsake the Saviour, having loved the present world? 'Let us therefore fear, lest a promise being left us of entering into His rest, any of you should seem to come short of it.' Go away, what from Jesus! This would be going from light to darkness, from plenty to poverty, from happiness to misery, from life to death. Go from Jesus! To whom can we go? We profess to have discovered the emptiness of the world, the insufficiency of temporal things to satisfy an immortal soul, and the pre-eminent excellency of the things of God. Still many go back and walk no more with Him. This should lead us to serious consideration. It should make us walk softly and cautiously. It cries to us with a loud voice and in clear accents, 'Let him that thinketh he standeth, take heed lest he fall.' There can be no cause to leave Jesus for one moment. It is folly to stir from His side; it is dangerous to neglect His ordinances; it is madness to turn the back on His ways. My soul, He asks thee tonight, 'Will you also go away?'

> Dear Lord, one bliss impart,
> ('Tis not from heaven I pray,)
> But let me not from Thee depart,
> No, never go away.

MARCH 9

🌿 MORNING 🌿

'Hear ye him'
MATTHEW 17:5

Jesus speaks to us in His Word; He tells us all His mind; and the Father commands us to hear Him. He speaks to us on a variety of subjects: He instructs, exhorts, warns, directs, and comforts. He always speaks in love. Every word is intended to do us good. Let us then take up His Word and say, 'I will hear what God the LORD will speak.' How much better this than to listen to Satan, unbelief, carnal reason, or men. Let us believe what He says, for He speaks truth; expect what He promises, for He intends to bestow; practise what He commands, for His ways are peace; and abstain from what He prohibits, for it is sure to be injurious. Hear Him, and plead His Word in prayer. Hear Him, and oppose what He says, to fear, Satan, and appearances. Hear Him, and compare all doctrines with His Word. Hear Jesus every day, give Him your attention at least for a few minutes; you can hear nothing better than what He speaks; no one that has a greater claim upon your attention. Hearing Jesus with attention, prayer, and faith, will prevent a great number of real evils.

Jesus, my Prophet, heavenly Guide!
Thy sweet instructions I will hear;
The words that from Thy lips proceed,
O how divinely sweet they are!
Thee, my great Prophet, I would love,
And imitate the blest above.

🌿 EVENING 🌿

'Ye shall know the truth'
JOHN 8:32

If Jesus is our Teacher, if we are of a childlike disposition, if we are willing to do as well as learn, we shall know the truth. All Zion's children shall be taught of the Lord. Every one who is divinely taught comes to Jesus. He that comes to Jesus is made wise unto salvation. He that is wise unto salvation knows the truth. The truth is in Christ. He is its centre. To know Him, so as to trust His Word, rely on His sacrifice, and do His will, is to know the truth. The knowledge of the truth makes us free. It frees us from ignorance, prejudice, and folly. It frees us from the slavery of Satan, the bondage of the law, and the terrors of God. It frees us from the guilt of sin, the accusations of conscience, and the cruel fetters of carnal custom. It makes us free, by imparting a true knowledge of God, by discovering the way of salvation, and by proclaiming pardon, peace, and reconciliation. If we know the truth as it is in Jesus, we shall conquer the world, enter the Redeemer's kingdom, enjoy peace with God, and render hearty and cheerful obedience to the will of God. Godliness will be our calling, our profession, and our delight.

Saviour! to me the truth reveal,
Thy teaching, Lord, I need;
Its power and unction may I feel,
To make me free indeed:
Each fetter break that binds my heart,
And sanctifying grace impart.

MARCH 10

🌿 MORNING 🌿

'Trouble is near'
PSALM 22:11

Trouble and the Christian are seldom far apart, or long apart. This may sound discouraging, but Jesus and the Christian are never apart. He will never leave us, and trouble is intended to prevent our leaving Him, or to bring us back if we have already wandered. His loving heart guides the hand which smites; and nothing is done by Him, or permitted, but that it may be over-ruled for our good. Trouble may be near, but the throne of grace also is near; His Word of promise is near; and He is near who justifieth us. In trouble God can glorify His grace, deepen His work in your heart, brighten your evidences, and fill you with joy and peace in believing; plead with Him to do so, let not trouble fill you with confusion, weaken your faith, or drive you from Him; but listen to, and act upon His Word. He says, 'Call upon me in the day of trouble: I will deliver thee, and thou shalt glorify me.' 'I will be with him in trouble, I will deliver him and honour him.' 'Hath He said, and shall He not do it? Or hath He spoken, and shall He not make it good?' Every trouble is intended to endear Jesus to your heart.

> This land, through which His pilgrims go,
> Is desolate and dry;
> But streams of grace from Him o'erflow,
> Their thirst to satisfy:
> Jesus has all His saints can want,
> And when they need He'll freely grant.

🌿 EVENING 🌿

'Neither be ye of doubtful mind'
LUKE 12:29

We are all prone to doubt, and to doubt that most, which there is no reason at all to doubt. But some seem to nurse their doubts, as though doubting was a part of religion. This is wrong. It is sinful. Our Lord often bids us believe, but He never encourages doubts. Doubting dishonours Him, distresses us, and gives Satan an advantage over us. Let us not doubt His providence, for it is kind; nor His Word, for it is true. Let us not judge by appearances, which often mislead; but let us rest on divine promises, which can never change or deceive. Let us not look too much at ourselves, our abilities, or our circumstances; but let us look to the Lord, to His wisdom, power, and love. Let us not tremble at poverty, because God can make us happier in poverty, than we ever have been in plenty. Let us not be affected by the changeableness of men, for our God is in one mind and none can turn Him. If we yield to a doubtful mind, it will spoil our present comforts, hinder us in holy duties, dim the eye of our hope, and feed and nourish our fears. But what is worse than all, it will reflect upon the kindness, care, and providence of our gracious God.

> Cast thy burdens on the Lord,
> Leave them with thy Saviour;
> He (whose hands for thee were bored)
> Can and will deliver;
> He is true and faithful still,
> Yield thyself unto His will.

MARCH 11

🌿 MORNING 🌿

'Beloved now are we the sons of God'

1 JOHN 3:2

What surprising grace is this! For what are we? Poor, vile, depraved, unworthy sinners; so base by nature that we had not one redeeming quality, and even now, apart from the work of the Spirit, there is in us no good thing. But we were predestinated to the adoption of children; we were born again of the Spirit; and grace has put us among the children, for its own glorification. Beloved, now, while we feel so much corruption, while despised by the world, harassed by Satan, tormented with fears, *now* are we the sons of God. And will God neglect or disregard His beloved sons? No. Let us then cherish the thought, believe the fact, and rejoice in the relationship. Let us walk and act as the sons of God, coming out from among the formal, the self-righteous, and the profane; and devoting ourselves entirely to the Lord's service and glory. Let us remember in trouble, in sickness, and in death itself, God is our Father, Jesus is our Brother, and heaven is our home. Let us approach God as children, and plead with Him as sons. He says to us, 'Come near unto Me, My son, that I may bless thee.' His blessing maketh rich.

> The God who reigns above, we call
> Our Father and our Friend:
> And, blessed thought! His children all
> Shall see Him in the end.

🌿 EVENING 🌿

'We love him because he first loved us'

1 JOHN 4:19

Our love to God is but a feeble reflection of His love to us. He loved us in eternity, that we might love Him in time. He loved us without any cause in us; but being infinitely lovely, He should be loved for His own sake. But it is the display of His love, which awakens love in our bosoms towards Him and His love being shed abroad in our hearts we love Him in return. No man in his natural state can love God, for 'the carnal mind is enmity against God, it is not subject to the law of God, neither indeed can be.' If therefore we love Him, or even heartily desire to love Him, it is a proof that our hearts have undergone a change; and that change is the effect and proof of His love to us. Every spiritual blessing flows naturally from His love, and whatever comes to us from Him is a covenant blessing, and leads us back to Him in return. Our faith in His Word, our hope in His mercy, our love to His people, our zeal for His cause, our sorrow for sin, and our desires after holiness are all so many proofs of His love to us. But our sonship crowns the whole. This is unparalleled love, that such sinners as we are, should be called *'the sons of God.'*

> How can I doubt Thy love to me,
> Thy love which doth my soul constrain,
> To seek an influence from Thee,
> To love my gracious Lord again?

MARCH 12

🌿 MORNING 🌿
'We shall be like him'
1 John 3:2

Like whom? Like Jesus in His glorified humanity: as free from sin, as perfect in holiness, as completely happy. His likeness will appear in every believer. What a contrast with the present! Now we appear to ourselves, at times, as like Satan as possible. O the depth of depravity we discover, the powerful corruptions we feel, the fearful opposition to God we sometimes experience! But we shall be like Him. God has purposed it, the Gospel plainly reveals it, and the Holy Spirit is engaged to effect it. Every evil shall be purged out, every virtue shall be produced and perfected, and we shall be pure as He is pure. Let us then look forward to, and anticipate that glorious period; let us consider the end of our election, redemption, and calling; and let us pray, pant, and strive to be holy. If holiness is our element, heaven will be our home, and unspeakable happiness our eternal portion. But we know not what we shall be, only that we shall be like Him, for we shall see Him as He is. If we suffer, we shall also reign with Him.

> O, when shall I, like Jesus, be,
> In soul and body clean?
> The true, eternal Sabbath see,
> A perfect rest from sin?
>
> Thy great salvation I shall know,
> And perfect liberty;
> And, free from all my chains below,
> My soul ascend to Thee.

🌿 EVENING 🌿
'So shall we ever be with the Lord'
1 Thessalonians 4:17

Now the Lord visits His people, and manifests Himself unto them, as He does not unto the world; and such visits are very sweet, such manifestations cheer and confirm our faith. But in a little time He will come to fetch us home. He may send death first, to introduce our souls into His presence; we may be called upon to depart and be with Christ, which is far better than our present circumstances. But He will come Himself soon; He will raise our bodies from the grave, conform both soul and body to His own likeness; we shall be caught up to meet Him in the air, and, 'so shall we ever be with the Lord.' This will be our heaven. This will be our portion. We shall be forever like Him, and forever with Him. How different to our present lot. What a glorious object for faith to fix upon. What a cheering subject for the mind to be engaged with. For ever with the Lord: what will it not include, that is glorious! For ever with the Lord: what will it not exclude, that is unpleasant or disagreeable! Let me close this day, reflecting upon this glorious prospect, anticipating this delightful change. And under all my future trails and exercises, let me look forward and say, 'Well, I shall soon be for ever with the Lord!'

> For ever with the Lord!
> Amen, so let it be;
> Life from the dead is in that word,
> 'Tis immortality.

MARCH 13

🌿 MORNING 🌿
'Seek those things which are above'
COLOSSIANS 3:1

And what are the things which are above? Holiness, or conformity to Jesus, and entire devotedness to His service. Happiness, flowing from the manifestation of Jehovah's glory, the presence of Jesus, and the soul's delight in His will. Unity: saints above realize close, intimate, and indestructible union to Father, Son, and Spirit; they enjoy sweet and constant union with each other, and the holy angels; they have unity of design, work, and enjoyment. Seek those things which descend from above: as faith, which believes, trusts, and prefers God's Word; love, which has God for its author, Christ for its principal object, and spiritual things for its chosen subjects; fellowship, with Father, Son, and Spirit, and all spiritual persons and subjects. In a word, all spiritual gifts, graces and operations. Seek them earnestly, principally, and constantly. Think much and often upon them. Highly value and esteem them. Constantly prefer them to earthly things. Labour to possess and enjoy them. God giveth liberally, and upbraideth not. You have not, because you ask not. Ask, and receive. Receive and be happy. Your God bids you, 'Rejoice.'

> Rise, my soul, and stretch thy wings,
> Thy better portion trace;
> Rise from transitory things,
> Towards heaven, thy native place.

🌿 EVENING 🌿
'Draw nigh to God'
JAMES 4:8

Sin thrusts us to an infinite distance from God, and unbelief keeps us there. Grace brings us back, and brings us nigh by the blood of the cross. When we sin, we still wander from God, but real prayer is drawing nigh to God. He is on the throne of grace, Jesus our intercessor is before the throne, and we are invited to draw nigh. We are to come up to the throne, to realize God as present, to exercise confidence in Him, through Jesus, and to pour out our hearts before Him; to tell Him all – all we fear, all we desire, all we want; to praise Him for all we possess, or have received in time past, or expect in time to come. We are to be frank; there is to be no reserve. We are to be serious; there must be no lightness. We are to be fully assured that our God is love; there is to be no dread or alarm. Draw nigh to God, to ascertain His will, to enjoy His love, to unburden your mind, to engage Him afresh on your side, and that you may rise above the present cheerless world. 'He will draw nigh to you.' What an inducement is this! Draw nigh and unveil His glories. Draw nigh and dissipate your fears. Draw nigh and confirm your faith.

> Let us now approach the throne
> Through the living way made known.
> Way of faith which Jesus made,
> Through the veil of flesh displayed;
> Through His rent humanity,
> God our Friend in heaven, we see.

MARCH 14

🌿 MORNING 🌿

'LORD, what is man!'
PSALM 144:3

By nature he is an enemy to God, in open rebellion against Him, and justly condemned by Him. He is in love with sin, a slave to lust, a servant of Satan. He is blind to his best interests, deaf to the call of God, and dead in trespasses and sins. He is an open sepulchre, a mass of wretchedness and disease, abominable and filthy beyond description. And can such a creature be the object of Jehovah's love, the purchase of a Saviour's blood, and the habitation of the Holy Spirit? Yes: as such, they were chosen to salvation; as such, Jesus was sent into the world to redeem them; as such, the Holy Spirit came to quicken, cleanse, justify, and save them! O amazing grace! Astonishing mercy! And will God in very deed dwell with such creatures upon earth? Yes: 'To this man will I look…' and with him will I dwell, '… even that is poor, and of a contrite spirit, and that trembleth at my word.' Well may the patriarch exclaim, 'What is man, that thou shouldest magnify him? and that thou shouldest set thine heart upon him?'

> O, what is feeble, dying man,
> Or any of his race,
> That God should make it His concern
> To visit him with grace!
>
> That God, who darts His lightnings down,
> Who shakes the worlds above,
> And mountains tremble at His frown,
> How wondrous is His love!

🌿 EVENING 🌿

'He laid down His life for us'
1 JOHN 3:16

This is a most stupendous fact, and amazing mystery, that God should take our nature, in order to labour, suffer, and die in our stead. Jesus was God. He became man. He was God and man in one person. As such He laid down His life for us. He laid it down willingly; no one took it from Him; He laid it down of Himself. He laid it down with a perfect knowledge of what we should be, and do, and deserve. He was not moved to do so by anything in us; it was His own pure, infinite, and sovereign love alone, which led Him to do so. 'Herein is love.' And there is no such love anywhere else. Nor has His love been so gloriously displayed in anything else. Beloved, let us dwell on the love of Jesus. We can never think of Him enough. We can never praise Him for it enough. Let us think of our state before God, our sins against God, and our desert at the hands of God; and then let us dwell upon this great fact, that instead of dealing with us according to our sins, or rewarding us according to our iniquities, 'He laid down His life for us.' Laid it down as the price of our ransom. Stupendous, astonishing love!

> How hath He loved us? How?
> Can man or angel tell?
> Before His cross we bow,
> The power of love to feel;
> To see Him love, and bleed and die,
> That we may live and reign on high.

MARCH 15

❦ MORNING ❧
'A Christian'
1 Peter 4:16

A Christian wears the name, possesses the nature, breathes the spirit, lives the life, and devotes himself entirely to the glory of Jesus. All Christ has is his, all Christ has done was for him, and all Christ has promised he may expect. Are you a Christian? Is the matter doubtful? Does Jesus live in you? Are you living by faith upon Him? Is He your daily bread? Do you find that you could as well live without food, as without Jesus? This is a sure evidence. This is the certain effect of the Spirit's work. If you are a Christian, you pant, pray, and strive to be Christ-like; to bear about in your body the dying of the Lord Jesus, that the life also of Jesus may be made manifest in your mortal body. You put off the old man which is corrupt, and put on the new man which is created in righteousness and true holiness. You would live in newness of life, as one raised from the dead; exhibiting the effects of His death in deadness to the world, love to immortal souls, bearing testimony to the truth, and looking for, and hastening to, the coming of the day of God. O to be a Christian indeed!

Father, in me reveal Thy Son,
And in my inmost soul make known
How merciful Thou art:

The secret of Thy love reveal,
And by Thine hallowing Spirit dwell
For ever in my heart!

❦ EVENING ❧
'In hope of eternal life'
Titus 1:2

Thus the consistent Christian lives. His heart is not set upon anything below, but he is looking for the mercy of our Lord Jesus Christ unto eternal life. This is the object of his hope. He hopes for life in perfection, in the highest state of existence, in another and better world; perpetual existence in health, in peace, in plenty, and in pleasure. This life is certain. It is promised, promised by God who cannot lie, promised before the world began; to Jesus as the Head of His church, to all believers. This is the gospel testimony, that God hath given to us eternal life, and this life is in His Son. He that hath received Christ by faith hath life. We have the first-fruits, we shall have the glorious harvest. We live in the daily exercise of hope, and this hope cheers us in trouble, strengthens us under persecution, animates us in our daily warfare, and defends us in the hour of danger. It is the helmet of salvation. Believer, you should not be looking *at* death, but *for* life, eternal life. Faith is a firm persuasion of the existence of this blessing, and a confident expectation of enjoying it.

Billows of disappointment roll
Along the restless tide of time;
But gospel-hope bears up my soul,
Till an eternal calm shall shine;
In hope of life eternal given
I live, anticipating heaven.

MARCH 16

❦ MORNING ❦
'Thy God reigneth!'
ISAIAH 52:7

Jesus has power over all flesh. He is upon the throne of the universe. He superintends all things. His will cannot be frustrated. His designs must be accomplished. Nothing is left to chance. His hand is in every event. He rules over the world by His power. He rules in the church by His Word. He rules in the heart by His Spirit. He reigns to crush or convert thy foes; to secure thy well-being and His glory. Let this truth calm and compose thy mind at all times: 'My God reigneth.' He sitteth above the water-floods, He remaineth a King for ever. He is entitled to all honour. He is the proper object of thy fear, faith, and love. See Him on His throne and rejoice, for it involves thy safety, happiness, and honour. Do men oppress? Does Satan annoy? Are things going cross? This is thy comfort: God reigneth. He directs and controls every being and every event. Gracious God! May I ever live believing that the reins of government are in Thy hands; that Thy counsel shall stand, and that Thou wilt do all Thy pleasure! My God, reign in me!

His kingdom cannot fail;
He rules o'er earth and heaven;
The keys of death and hell
Are to our Jesus given:
Lift up your heart, lift up your voice,
Rejoice aloud, ye saints, rejoice.

❦ EVENING ❦
'Oh that thou wouldest bless me indeed'
1 CHRONICLES 4:10

Thus prayed Jabez, and so prays every Christian. He knows that the blessing of the LORD it maketh rich, and He addeth no sorrow with it. There is a reality in the Lord's blessing. Well, He hath blessed us with all spiritual blessings in heavenly places in Christ. All is treasured up in Jesus for us, and by faith and prayer we receive out of His fulness and grace for grace. The Lord still blesses us. He says, 'I will bless thy bread and thy water,' and our temporal mercies are peculiarly sweet, when seasoned with His love. He blesses us with renewing grace, reviving grace, restoring grace, sanctifying grace, and preventing grace. He blesses with blessings costly beyond calculation, vast as our miseries, numerous as our sins, and lasting as our existence. He delights to bless. He gave His Son to die for us, that He might bless us honourably, suitably, and eternally. He has promised to bless us, and to make us blessings. It is a blessing to feel our need of His blessings, and everyone who does so, ardently desires and earnestly seeks it, is taught of God and blessed by God. Let us then read His Word, believe His love, plead for His blessing, and receive the answer as Jabez did.

All is finished: do not doubt it,
But believe your dying Lord;
Never reason more about it,
Only take Him at His word.

MARCH 17

🌿 MORNING 🌿

'God was manifest in the flesh'

1 Timothy 3:16

The manifestation of God is in the person and work of Christ, and we are here from to learn what our God is, and what we may expect Him to do for us. What Jesus was to those about Him, such Jehovah is; what Jesus did and was willing to do, that our God is willing to do for us. In Jesus we see tender love, melting compassion, and gracious forbearance; mercy and power, rectitude and pity, holiness and long-suffering, justice and harmlessness, united. Such is our God. Fury is not in Him. Love is His name and His nature. And can you slavishly fear such a God? Can you wilfully sin against and grieve such a Being? Cannot you believe His Word, depend upon His veracity, rejoice in His name, and expect from Him every promised good? For this purpose His Word was written, His name is published, and Jesus died. Always look at God in Christ; attempt not to learn God from nature. 'No man hath seen God at any time; the only-begotten Son, which is in the bosom of the Father, He hath declared Him.' *'I have manifested thy name.'*

Till God in human flesh I see,
My thoughts no comfort find;
The holy, just, and sacred THREE,
Are terrors to my mind:
But if IMMANUEL's face appear,
My soul surmounts each slavish fear.

🌿 EVENING 🌿

'Give unto the LORD the glory due unto His name'

1 Chronicles 16:29

The Lord has written out His name, in its greatness and graciousness, on the works of His power, and on all the gifts of His love. He that would learn God's name must study creation and providence; but must more earnestly study the gospel. Here he will see God writing out His name or displaying His glorious character and perfections, in the conversion, justification, sanctification, preservation, and glorification of multitudes of sinners. God has revealed His name in His Word, and it is to be read in its proclamations, doctrines, promises, precepts, and prospects. If we read and study Jehovah's name aright, we shall be filled with admiring views and adoring gratitude; and as the effect we shall glorify Him in our prayers, praises, and general conversation. To give Him the glory due unto His name will require all our talents, all our time, and even eternity itself. But to attempt to do so is a plain duty, and if the heart be right, it will be a real pleasure. Still, it is a duty much neglected, and while we neglect it, we rob God of His right, and our own souls of much comfort. Let us therefore learn to read God's name, to exalt His grace, and to give Him the glory due unto His name.

Nature and time and earth and skies,
Thy heavenly skill proclaim;
What shall we do to make us wise,
But learn to read Thy name?

MARCH 18

❦ MORNING ❧

'But He answered her not a word'
MATTHEW 15:23

Delays are not denials. Jesus delayed to answer, but He did not deny her request. He hath said, 'Ask, and it shall be given you. Whatsoever ye shall ask the Father in My name, He will give it you.' Heaven and earth may pass away, but His Word must stand for ever. He delays the answer to try our faith, patience and perseverance; but when He sends the blessing He proves His faithfulness, pity and love. Be not discouraged though your prayers remain unanswered for a time; it will not always be so. This poor woman had to wait, though her case was very trying, and her request very urgent; but at last Jesus commended her faith publicly, and dismissed her with, 'Be it unto thee even as thou wilt.' Prayer will prevail, if it is the prayer of faith. Pray on, then, and do not faint. Say, as Jacob on the plains of Peniel, 'I will not let thee go, except thou bless me.' Plead with Him; be importunate; wait His time; be willing to receive in His own way; be concerned that He should be glorified in giving to you, or doing for you; and you cannot fail. His mercy is from everlasting to everlasting, upon them that fear Him.

> Wait for His seasonable aid,
> And though it tarry, wait;
> The promise may be long delay'd,
> But cannot come too late.

❦ EVENING ❧

'Fear not, neither be discouraged'
DEUTERONOMY 1:21

Though the Lord tries us, He also encourages us. More than fifty times, He says to us in His Word, 'Fear not.' Yet we are often fearing. He knew this would be the case, therefore He provided so much to cheer and encourage us. Let us not be discouraged, the Lord hath set the good land before us, He hath promised it to us, He bids us go up and take possession of it. Our enemies may be mighty, but our God who goes with us and fights for us is Almighty. Our foes may be crafty, but on our side is 'the only wise God.' If providence should frown, if the Lord does delay to answer our prayers, if our case should appear to be almost desperate, it is only to exercise our graces, try our sincerity, to stir us up to importunate prayer. Let us therefore press on in hope; let us persevere in faith. The Lord will appear for us. His faithful Word shall be made good in our experience; and though now He may not answer us a word, He will soon give us the desire of our hearts. Yield not then to discouragement: it dishonours God, it weakens faith, it cheers on your foes. Fear not, for God is with you. God is for you.

> Arm'd with the presence of my Lord
> I would be of good cheer,
> Confiding in His faithful Word

> Why should I faint or fear?
> Though fierce the foe, though rough the road,
> I can do all things through my God.

MARCH 19

🌿 MORNING 🌿

'In his favour is life'

PSALM 30:5

That is, in the favour of God in Christ. If He have a favour towards us, all will be well; but He has, and as a proof of His favour He gave Jesus for us, and to us; He sent the Holy Spirit to quicken, teach, and sanctify us. By believing we enter into the enjoyment of His favour; and enjoying His favour we learn to despise all that is opposed to it. Our spiritual life flowed from His favour; our happiness stands in the enjoyment of His favour; and heaven will be the full display and realization of His favour. To His favour we ascribe all our present comforts and future hopes. By the favour of God we are what we are. By His favour we are saved. This is the source of every good, the joy of every true believer's heart. Let us endeavour to ascertain beyond a doubt, that we are the favourites of God; let us prize His favour above thousands of gold and silver; and let our daily prayer be, 'Remember me, O LORD, with the favour that thou bearest unto thy people: O visit me with thy salvation, that I may see the good of thy chosen, that I may rejoice in the gladness of thy nation, and glory with thine inheritance.' Amen, even so, Lord Jesus.

> Fain would I my Lord pursue,
> Be all my Saviour taught;
> Do as Jesus bids me do,
> And think as Jesus thought.

🌿 EVENING 🌿

'He restoreth my soul'

PSALM 23:3

'I have gone astray like a lost sheep.' We are prone to wander, and having wandered we never return till the good Shepherd seeks us. But His eye is upon the wanderer. His heart yearns unto it. He follows it with reproofs, rebukes, and expostulations; and at length He restores it. He convinces of the folly of wandering from the fold, the soul becomes unhappy in its wandering state, a spirit of prayer is awakened, concern to return deepens, the sheep creeps to the Shepherd's feet, acknowledges its sin and folly, implores mercy, and cries, 'Restore unto me the joy of thy salvation.' It is taken up by the Shepherd's power, and carried back with gentle reproofs to the fold. Every restoration is of grace. In every instance it is the Shepherd's care that restores the wandering soul. The restored wanderer always feels deeply humbled, flies to the precious blood of atonement, admires restoring mercy, becomes more cautious, careful, and circumspect; his conscience is more tender, his hatred of sin is deeper, and his jealousy of his own heart is more lively. He abhors himself and repents in dust and ashes. He pants for the presence of God, prizes the ordinances of religion, and watches unto prayer.

> Prone to wander, Lord, I feel it;
> Prone to leave the God I love;
> Here's my heart, Lord, take and seal it,
> Seal it from Thy courts above.

MARCH 20

❦ MORNING ❦

'The Lord is risen'
LUKE 24:34

Jesus once died for our sins, and He rose for our justification. He lay in the grave as our Substitute; He rose as our Representative. He died that we may live. He lives, and we shall live through Him, and with Him forever. He is risen, having conquered death, reconciled us to God, perfumed the grave, and finished the work which the Father gave Him to do. As He arose, so shall we. As He is gone into heaven, thither should our thoughts, our hopes, and our affections ascend. Jesus is risen, to plead our cause; manage our affairs; fulfil His precious promises; and to prepare for us mansions in our Father's house. Sin was atoned for by His death, heaven is secured by His life. He is our risen, ascended, and reigning *Brother*. He is our conquering and crowned *Captain*. O let us think of, speak for, and devote ourselves to Jesus! He is above the world; let us live above its vanities, amusements, and trammels; let us look beyond death to that glorious resurrection, when we shall be raised from the dead, and possess bodies which shall be incorruptible, glorious, powerful, and spiritual.

> Jesus triumphs! sing His praises!
> 'Twas by death He overcame:
> Thus the Lord His glory raises;
> Thus He fills His foes with shame.
> Sing His praises!
> Praises to the Victor's name.

❦ EVENING ❦

'Risen with Christ'
COLOSSIANS 3:1

Christ as our Substitute died in our stead. He died as a public person, representing His people; and as such He rose from the dead. All His people are said to have died in Him, when He died, and rose with Him, when He arose. By virtue of this, we are quickened by the Spirit of life from Christ, and we arise and ascend to Him in our hopes, desires, and affections. His life is put forth in us, and we are to make manifest the resurrection life of Christ in our bodies. We are to reckon ourselves to be dead indeed unto sin, but alive unto God through Jesus Christ our Lord. It is also stated of all believers that He hath raised us up together, and made us sit together with Christ in the heavenlies. Christ and His people are one. They were represented by Him when He fulfilled the law, when He made the atonement, when He arose from the dead, and when He entered into the holiest of all with His own blood. They live through His death. They live in union to His person. They live for His honour and glory. Being risen with Christ, they should not grovel on earth, or be very much affected by anything that occurs below; but as their head, their portion, and their life is in heaven, there their thoughts, desires, affections should be.

> Believing souls, whom Jesus know,
> If risen indeed with Him ye are,
> Superior to the joys below,
> His resurrection power declare.

MARCH 21

❧ MORNING ❧

'I will give you rest'
MATTHEW 11:28

There is no rest for the Christian in the world. There will be always something to disturb, perplex or distress him; it is an enemy's land. But Jesus says, 'I will give you rest.' He does so by enabling us to rely on His Word, recognise His hand, submit to His will, and trust in His perfect work. He assures us that our sins are forgiven us; that our persons are safe in His keeping; that His presence shall always be with us; and that all things shall work together for the best. We can rest on His faithfulness; He has been tried, and found faithful. We can rest on His love, for it knows not the shadow of a turn. We can rest on His power; it is ever engaged on our behalf. We can rest on His covenant; it is ordered in all things and sure. We can rest on His blood; it speaks peace, pardon, and acceptance with God. We can rest at His feet; there we are safe, and can never be injured. We cannot rest on our graces, on our comforts, on our friends, or on our possessions; but we may rest on Jesus. We should rest on Him with unshaken confidence and ardent love, for His promises are plain, His power is infinite, and His love passeth knowledge.

In the ark, the weary dove
Found a welcome resting place;
Thus my spirit longs to prove,
Rest in Christ, the Ark of grace.

❧ EVENING ❧

'They desire a better country'
HEBREWS 11:16

Not only a better state or a better frame, but a better country. This was the experience of the patriarchs; the apostles felt the same; so have all true Christians. Do we desire a better country? Do we desire a heavenly country? There is a better: it is set before us in the gospel, it is promised to all who believe in Jesus, and continue faithful unto death. Heaven is a country where all enjoy rest; there is no pain, no vexation, no toil, no trials there. All are active, yet all enjoy perfect repose. Heaven is the home of love; there are no foes, no envious professors, no jealous brethren. All is love – pure, perfect, perpetual love. All love God, and God loves all. Each loves his fellow, and loves his fellow as he loves himself. It is the residence of holiness. There are no sinners, for all are righteous; there is no sin, for each exactly resembles Jesus. Holiness is the element, the joy, the characteristic of the place. It is the abode of perfect satisfaction, unbroken joy, and undisturbed tranquillity. There Jesus is seen face to face; there God unfolds His glories; there every desire is gratified, every heart is full, every countenance beams with benevolence and joy. Truly it is a better country, it is the *rest* which remaineth for the people of God.

Then let the hope of joys to come
Dispel our cares, and chase our fears;
If God be ours, we're travelling home,
Though passing through a vale of tears.

MARCH 22

❦ MORNING ❦
'Precious promises'
2 Peter 1:4

The promises of Scripture are the promises of the great God; they are all of free grace; they are confirmed by the blood of Jesus; and are exceeding great and very precious. They are so plain that a child can understand them, and so great that no angel could fulfil them. There is such a variety that they meet every case, and such a fulness that they include every want. They are breasts of consolation for the poor, tried, and distressed believer; and are the strength and support of every child of God. They are our plea at the throne of grace, our confidence in the hour of trial, and our rejoicing in prospect of death. Beloved, God's promises are to be your daily comfort: it is for you to search them out, store them up, believe them, trust in them, plead them, and be assured of their fulfilment, because 'He is faithful who promised.' The promises are more precious than gold or silver; sweeter than honey or the honeycomb; more lasting than the earth; and more stable than the pillars of heaven. Let us think of them, plead them, and expect their fulfilment today; our God is a faithful God, keeping covenant and mercy unto a thousand generations.

Praise to the goodness of the Lord,
Who rules His people by His Word;
And there, as strong as His decrees,
He sets His kindest promises.

❦ EVENING ❦
'The heirs of promise'
Hebrews 6:17

We were by nature children of wrath, even as others. In character we were unrighteous; in circumstances, destitute; in state, lost. We had no claim upon God for one good thing, for we were traitors against His throne and government. But by an ancient and gracious appointment, He constituted us as believers in Jesus, *'heirs of promise.'* We were promised to Jesus as a seed, to reward the travail of His soul; and are entitled to all the promises, which in Him are yea, and in Him amen, to the glory of God by us. By virtue of our relation to Christ, by our interest in the testament of Christ, as well as to the appointment of God, we are entitled to all promised blessings. To us is promised life, eternal life; righteousness, everlasting righteousness; supplies, both temporal and spiritual; a kingdom, the kingdom of grace and glory; salvation, eternal salvation. We are heirs, and all these things are included in our estate. Heirship flows from grace. It stands in Christ. It leads us to heaven. It calls for gratitude. Ought we not to ask, 'Am I an heir? Can I prove my title? Do I view the promises as my title deeds? Do I live as a person entitled to such possessions?' Let a man examine himself.

As heirs of promise, let us live
By faith in Jesus' word;
Expect His fulness to receive,
And glorify the Lord.

MARCH 23

❦ MORNING ❦

'Where is your faith?'
Luke 8:25

The disciples were in a storm, surrounded by danger, and filled with fear; they apply to Jesus. This was right. They doubt His care, question His love, and cry, 'We perish.' This was wrong. Jesus demands, *'Where is your faith?'* May He not put the same question to us? We have His Word, but do we heartily believe it? We speak of His love, but do we confidently trust it? We read of His care, but do we see our safety in it? We often seem to believe anyone sooner than Jesus; to trust any word more than His Word; and therefore we are cast down, fearful and distressed. Let us this day endeavour to fix our faith steadily upon His precious Word. Let us believe in His particular providence. Let us commune with Him as our firm and faithful Friend. He says, 'Let not your heart be troubled: ye believe in God, believe also in me.' He is worthy of credit. He cannot deceive. He deserves our confidence. He will not neglect. He encourages our hope, and promises, 'If ye ask anything of the Father in my name, I will do it.' Do you believe this? Do you believe it when you pray? If not, 'Where is your faith?'

> O how wavering is my mind,
> Toss'd about with every wind;
> O how quickly doth my heart
> From the living God depart;
> O my God, Thy grace impart,
> To fix and bind my wandering heart.

❦ EVENING ❦

'Ready to forgive'
Psalm 86:5

Jehovah is revealed as a God who delights in showing mercy, who is slow to anger; as 'a God ready to pardon.' This is always a fact, and it should always be believed by us. It should also be daily kept before our minds, that we may seek, expect, and enjoy a daily pardon. The Lord is never indisposed, or backward to pardon a believing, penitent, confessing sinner. But He is faithful to His Word, and just to the merit of His Son, in pardoning every one who applies in the Saviour's name. *'Ready to forgive!'* Then our fears have been groundless, our distress without cause, and our suspicions have been sinful. The goodness of His nature is such that He devised a way in which He could honourably pardon the vilest transgressor; and though this cost Him the life of His only begotten and well-beloved Son, He freely gave Him up, to show that He was 'a God ready to pardon.' Without an atonement, pardon would have been impossible; but through the atonement of Jesus, God can easily, completely, and daily pardon the greatest sinners. What He *can* do, He *will* do and He *does* do. And tonight, He is 'ready to forgive' the sins of this day, and of every previous day; to forgive us, and to do it at this moment. Blessed truth!

> Believing let us raise our eye
> To Him who liveth and hath died;
> That look will lift our souls on high,
> And God pronounce us justified.

MARCH 24

❦ MORNING ❧

'Thy sins are forgiven'
LUKE 7:48

Whose sins? Thine, if thou believest in Jesus. For to Him give all the prophets witness, that through His name *whosoever* believeth in Him shall receive remission of sins. If we confess our sins, God is faithful and just to forgive us our sins, and to cleanse us from all unrighteousness. God pardons, for Christ's sake, every one who believeth, confesseth and forsaketh sin. He thus proves Himself ready to forgive, plenteous in mercy, and full of compassion, to all who call upon Him. He never refuses to pardon, nor manifests the least reluctance. Nor ought we to doubt for one moment upon the subject, seeing His Word is so plain; His grace is so great; His mercy is so free; and His faithfulness so clearly proved. What then do we want? Only faith to believe God's Word, that we, being believers in Jesus, having confessed sin at His throne, and prayed for pardon in Christ's name, are forgiven all our trespasses. And this is needful, for we can never mortify sin, live above the world, rejoice in God, and honour the Gospel, but as we believe these sweet words of Jesus, 'Thy sins are forgiven thee.'

> How high a privilege 'tis to know
> Our sins are all forgiven!
> To bear about this pledge below,
>
> This special grant of heaven!
> O Lord, this privilege bestow
> To cheer ME while I dwell below.

❦ EVENING ❧

'Go in peace'
LUKE 7:50

True peace flows from the pardon of sin. If we believe that God for Christ's sake hath forgiven us all trespasses, our souls will enjoy peace, for being justified by faith, we have peace with God. We have nothing to fear from God, for having pardoned us, He has no charge against us; but we may expect every good thing from God, for having given us His Son, will He not with Him also *freely* give us all things? If therefore we have no evil to fear, but every good to expect, may we not, ought we not, to be at peace? When Jesus pardoned the woman, He said to her, 'Go in peace.' So He says to us. Mind not what Satan says. Fear not what man can do. Go in the path of duty. Go, and face trials and persecutions. Go, and enjoy your temporal mercies. Go, and enjoy your religious privileges. Go, though dangers surround you. Go, though you feel weak and feeble. Go in peace, for God accepts you. Go, for your reconciliation to God is honourable and perfect. Go, and spread a Saviour's fame. Go, and tell of Jehovah's pardoning love. Go, and bear your personal testimony to the truth of His Word. Go, and conquer all your foes. Go, this night, to rest in peace, and comfort your soul with this: 'God is at peace with me.'

> O Lamb of God, in tender love,
> Now bid my sorrow cease;
> Kindly my doubts and fears remove,
> And bid ME, 'Go in peace.'

MARCH 25

🍂 MORNING 🍂
'Bring them hither to me'
Matthew 14:18

Our compassionate Lord was surrounded by a starving, fainting multitude; His disciples had only five small coarse loaves, and two little fishes, and yet He had bidden them to feed the company. The commands of Jesus are often intended to try our faith, and bring us as children to His feet. He says, 'Bring them to Me.' Things are not what they appear, but what Jesus makes them. His blessing produces a wonderful change. He bids you bring everything to Him. Have you a family? He says, 'Suffer the little children to come unto me, and forbid them not.' Have you trials? Take them to Him; His blessing sweetens and lessens trials. Are you in poverty? Carry your poverty to Him; He can increase your little and bless it with a peculiar flavour. Whatever troubles you this day, or any day, think that you hear Jesus saying, 'Bring it hither to me.' Carry all things to Him, small things as well as great ones; it is only by so doing, that you can surmount trials, conquer foes, glory in tribulation, and joy in God.

The privilege I greatly prize,
Of casting all my cares on Him,
The mighty God, the only wise,
Who reigns in heaven and earth supreme.

How sweet to be allow'd to call
The God whom heaven adores my Friend;
To tell my thoughts, to tell Him all;
And then to know my prayers ascend.

🍂 EVENING 🍂
'That I may know Him'
Philippians 3:10

Paul appears to have had seven principal wishes, and they are all expressed in this brief epistle. They all have reference to Christ. Indeed Christ was Paul's centre, to which he constantly tended, and the circle within which all the desires of his soul were included. He especially desired to know Christ; to win Christ; to magnify Christ both in his body and soul; to be found in Christ; to be conformed to Christ; to rejoice in the day of Christ; and to be with Christ. But the first lies at the root of all the rest. The knowledge of Christ is more excellent than *any* other, than *all* other knowledge. But how little do we know of Christ; therefore it is that we enjoy so little of Christ. But, is it the desire of our souls tonight, that we may know Him; that we may know Him clearly and correctly? Our knowledge of Christ should be powerful and influential, regulating our thoughts, desires, hopes, fears, confidence, and our conduct toward God and man, especially toward the saints; and we should *grow* in the knowledge of Christ. If we do really and sincerely desire to know Christ, we shall search His Word, frequent His ordinances, meditate on His truth, be often at His throne, and speak of Him to His people.

'Tis life to know the dying Lamb,
Eternal life is in His name;
O may I in this knowledge grow,
And daily more of Jesus know.

MARCH 26

❦ MORNING ❧

'He giveth power to the faint'
Isaiah 40:29

The Lord's people often feel faint, being burdened with a body of sin and death, pursued and assaulted by Satan, tried and hindered by the world; but though faint they continue to pursue. Waiting on the Lord they renew their strength. The Lord has said, 'I will strengthen thee.' Brother, remember the promise and faithfulness of thy God; yield not to fear, or you will surely faint. Believe because God is true. David says, 'I had fainted unless I had believed to see the goodness of the LORD in the land of the living.' Power is given in answer to prayer. Strength is proportioned to the day. The back is fitted for the burden. Our God will not lay upon us more than He will enable us to bear. He strengthens by His Word, by His Spirit, and by His presence. Expect Him to be and to do according to His Word. This will honour Him, and He will strengthen you with might by His Spirit in the inner man. Go forth, however weak you may feel, assured that God will give you strength and courage: strength to do and suffer His will, and courage to face, fight and overcome every foe.

> Whence do our mournful thoughts arise?
> And where's our courage fled?
> Have restless sin, and raging hell
> Struck all our comforts dead?
> Chase, chase thy gloomy fears away,
> Strength shall be equal to the day.

❦ EVENING ❧

'The Father of mercies'
2 Corinthians 1:3

Jehovah is a Father, a merciful Father, a tenderly merciful Father, a Father of mercies, with whom all mercies originate, from whom all mercies proceed. Our chief mercy is a Saviour; that Saviour His only begotten Son; that Son freely delivered up for us all. He was the author of the mercy which quickened us, comforted us, and still keeps us. All our merciful afflictions, deliverances, shuttings up, and relief, flow from His sovereign will. He is the fountain and source of mercy, and from Him all our mercies flow. This should correct the views we sometimes take of Him, as if He were difficult to please, or soon angry with us. It should also encourage our faith, hope, prayers, and love. What a comfort to a seeking soul, to know that the God he is seeking is the Father of mercies. What a shield this is to ward off the fiery darts of Satan. What an inducement to love our God more than all the gifts we receive from Him. Beloved, what do you need this evening? If it is a mercy, your God has it, and if it will really do you good, He is willing to bestow it. Look up to heaven tonight, and call upon the Father of mercies in confidence; He will produce and present the very mercy you need, be it what it may.

> My soul, Thou hast (let what will ail)
> A never-changing Friend;
> When brethren, friends and helpers fail,
> On Him alone depend.

MARCH 27

❧ MORNING ❧

'Ask, and ye shall receive'

JOHN 16:24

These are the words of Jesus. He addresses them to us this morning. They suppose want, and inability to supply ourselves. They intimate that provision is made, and may be obtained. They invite us to ask with confidence, assuring us we shall receive. Jesus has a boundless fulness of blessings, and a loving, tender heart to bestow them. He will supply all our needs. Let not want, then, lead you to despond, but look to Jesus; He has, He gives. He tells you to ask and receive. Can any terms be more easy, more suitable, more encouraging than these? But ask in faith, believing because Jesus has promised; ask with earnestness, as though you valued the blessings; ask with importunity; go again and again, until you obtain them. Go to Jesus for all you want; make everything a matter of prayer. In everything, by prayer and supplications, with thanksgiving, let your requests be made known to God. Doubt not, for His Word is plain; He is full of compassion; He waits to be gracious; and He has thousands of witnesses to attest His faithfulness, veracity, and love. Look to the generations of old. Did any ever seek the Lord in vain? No: every one that asketh receiveth.

> My soul, ask what thou wilt;
> Thou canst not be too bold;
> Since His own blood for thee He spilt,
> What else can He withhold?

❧ EVENING ❧

'Ye ask, and receive not'

JAMES 4:3

Is God then unwilling to bestow? Will He forfeit His Word? No; but He never promised to sanction sin, or encourage folly; and this He must do if He answered all our prayers. In prayer, God looks at our motives. He reads our hearts while He listens to our words. If we pray for temporal things to pamper our appetites, or gratify our lust, we have no reason to expect that God will give them. If we ask for spiritual things with a carnal end, God is just in withholding them. We may ask for good things that we may become eminent in the estimation of men, be respected by our fellows, or applauded by the multitude. Even grace and holiness may be prayed for in order to get a name. Our object should be simply to honour God, to exalt Jesus, and to promote His cause; or, we may ask in an unbecoming manner. We may be too anxious for temporals. We may be indifferent about spirituals. Lust may set us praying, and keep us praying, as pride, covetousness, or envy. See, then, the cause why our prayers are not always answered; the motive, or the end in view or the spirit displayed, is not good. The prayer is as the design is. Let us ask then – *Why* do we pray? *How* do we pray? For *what* do we pray?

> I fear I often ask amiss,
> Lord, search my heart and see;
> My motives purify, nor cease
> To draw my soul to Thee.

MARCH 28

❧ MORNING ❧

'I am the LORD's'
Isaiah 44:5

Not only because He has chosen me from others, in Jesus His beloved Son; nor merely because I am redeemed from among men, by the precious blood of Immanuel; but also because I have surrendered myself up into the Lord's hand, with all I have and am, to be taught by His Spirit, ruled by His Word, supplied by His providence, and devoted to His praise. The Lord claimed me, and I was enabled to acknowledge the claim; He has a right to me, and that right should never be forgotten by me. Am I tempted to sin? to murmur? to despond? Let this be my preservative, *'I am the LORD's.'* How base, ungrateful, and wicked for *me* to yield to sin; for me to complain of any of His dispensations; or for me to doubt His goodness or His grace. I am the Lord's for life; I shall be the Lord's in death; and then (O delightful thought!) I shall be the Lord's for evermore. He will guide me by His counsel, and afterwards receive me to glory. I have only to aim at His glory, walk by His Word, and live at His throne, until He takes me to Himself. My only business on earth is to please God, and my heaven will be to enjoy Him forever. Blessed truth, *'I am the LORD's!'*

> *Jesus, Thy boundless love to me,*
> *No thought can reach, no tongue declare;*
> *O knit my thankful heart to Thee,*
> *And reign without a rival there!*

❧ EVENING ❧

'I will fear no evil'
Psalm 23:4

Why should I, if I am the Lord's? Let this matter be settled, and then farewell to the fear of evil, for the Lord shall preserve thee from all evil. Not from all trials, for they are not all evils, but only benefits. Only two things can be said to be evils: the one sin, but to the believer, sin is pardoned; in the believer, sin is crucified; and over the believer, it shall not have dominion. The other evil is separation from God, but nothing can separate us from the love of God which is in Christ Jesus our Lord. The Lord is our keeper; He will preserve our souls. We may be tried by losses and crosses, by Satan and by men, by poverty and pain, but all these will work together for our good. And even death is not an evil; therefore we should not fear it. Let us live upon Christ; let us live for Christ; let us live like Christ; and then to die, will only be to depart and be with Christ, which is far better than remaining here. To die will be gain, or best of all. Let us then grasp the promise with a firm faith, walk close to the bleeding side of Jesus, aim to glorify God in our day and generation, and go through life saying, *'I will fear no evil.'*

> *Fear not, believe His Word,*
> *You are to Jesus given;*
> *'Tis the good pleasure of the Lord*
> *To bring you safe to heaven.*

MARCH 29

❧ MORNING ❧

'Cease ye from man'
Isaiah 2:22

Never trust him, for his heart is deceitful; never expect from him, for he is an empty cistern; never follow him, for he is a false guide. Cursed be the man who trusteth in man, and maketh flesh his arm, and whose heart departeth from the Lord. Trust ye not in a friend. One object of trust is enough. He has all you want, and has offered to give whenever you ask. He never did deceive, He never can. It is impossible for God to lie. Looking to man dishonours His fulness; trusting in man, is pouring contempt on His Word; expecting from man, is overlooking His agency. If you neglect this loving direction, expect to suffer; if you walk by it, your peace will be like a river, and your soul like a well-watered garden. He knows what is in man; you do not. He cautions you, because He loves you. He would save you from disappointment, sorrow, and woe. Come then to the conclusion of the prophet, 'Therefore will I look unto the Lord; I will wait for the God of my salvation: my God will hear me.' Never expect from man, but always from God.

Happy they who trust in Jesus!
Sweet their portion is, and sure:
When destruction others seizes,
God will keep His own secure:
Happy people!
Happy, though despised and poor.

❧ EVENING ❧

'I am with you alway'
Matthew 28:20

Then Jesus is with us tonight. He is, and He will be with us as He has promised in all future time. He is with us to afford protection, to impart consolation, to subdue our fears, to inspire with hope. He identifies us with Himself. He makes our cause His own. His presence is pledged to us, and it is the shield of our protection, the strength of our hearts, and the source of our joy. He will not leave us to go a step alone. He will not take His eye off us, or close His ear to us for one moment. He tells us that we are more endeared to Him than the loveliest infant is to the fondest mother. The ties of nature are not so strong, or so tender, or so lasting as the ties of grace. Let us endeavour to keep this fact in view: Jesus is with us, ever *will* be with us. He will be the last to comfort us in time, and the first to welcome us in eternity. He will go through the whole journey with us, and then place us before His face forever. We are therefore sure of one thing, and that is, the presence of Jesus; and His presence is the joy of angels, the bliss of heaven, and the glory of immortality. Turn, then, from every creature to Him. Lay down this night, resting upon the word of Jesus, 'Lo, I am with you always!'

Lord, I commend to Thee
The remnant of my days;
O that my chief concern may be
To spend them to Thy praise.

MARCH 30

🌿 MORNING 🌿
'Yea, He loved the people'
Deuteronomy 33:3

And what were the people whom He loved? Poor, oppressed, rebellious, stiff-necked, hard-hearted, unworthy creatures. Just such are His people by nature now. Such are we. Yet He loves us, pities us, and distinguishes us from others around us. He spared not His own Son, but delivered Him up for us all; and with Him He will freely give us all things. Though He has not yet all His people with Him, yet He has Jesus sitting at His right hand, who is their Representative, the express image and exact likeness of His elect. All the rays of His love centre in Him, who is the Head of His body the Church. All the streams of delight empty themselves into Him, and through Him flow down to every believer on earth. As He loveth Jesus, so He loveth us; while He loveth Jesus, He will love us, for Christ and we are one. What is done to us is done to Him; and what is done to, or bestowed upon Him, as man and Mediator, is done to and bestowed upon us. O glorious mystery of infinite and eternal love! O direct my heart into this love of God!

> O love of unexampled kind!
> That leaves all thought so far behind;
> Where length, and breadth, and depth, and height,
> Are lost to my astonish'd sight:
> Lord, shed abroad that love of Thine
> In this poor sinful heart of mine.

🌿 EVENING 🌿
'I fear God'
Genesis 42:18

So said Joseph to his brethren, when he sent them home with provisions to their needy father. So may we say whenever tempted to act unbecoming our Christian character. The true fear of God springs from love, and is deepened and strengthened by filial fellowship with God. It is not a dread of His majesty, but a fear to offend or grieve His heart. It is produced by the Holy Spirit, and is a great preventive to sin. If I fear to offend God, I shall certainly strive to please Him. If I love Him, I shall fear to offend Him. This fear makes us cautious, careful, and watchful. It will often lead us to prayer. It will prompt us to self-examination. It will lead us to compare our conduct with God's Word. It will preserve us from presumption, levity, and dishonesty. He that fears God will not go in the way of sinners, stand in the counsel of the ungodly, or sit in the seat of the scornful; but his delight will be in the Word of God, and in His book will he meditate day and night. Has the fear of God influenced us this day? Have we said by our conduct, in our dealings with our fellow men, *'I fear God?'* Reflecting upon the inconsistency of others, can we say, *'So did not I, because of the fear of the Lord.'*

> It gives religion life,
> To warm as well as light;
> Makes mercy sweet, salvation great,
> And all God's judgments right.

MARCH 31

🌿 MORNING 🌿
'I will be with him in trouble'
Psalm 91: 15

Sin is the parent of trouble; all sorrow originated in departing from God. It is generally occasioned by transgression, or sent as a preventive to a greater evil; it may be occasioned by good, for saints are sometimes persecuted for righteousness' sake. It is intended to correct, improve, and to bring us near to God. Whatever may be our trouble, if we are the Lord's, He is with us; and with us for the most gracious purposes. He fixes the period of our troubles; nor can they continue longer than He sees needful. He regulates the heat of the furnace; nor will He suffer us to be tried more than we are able to bear. He sanctifies our troubles, and causes them to work our good. He delivers out of trouble, when the purposes of His love are accomplished. In every trouble, remember, God is now especially present. He is with you to hear your prayer, increase your strength, direct your way, and make you a conqueror. His grace is sufficient; His presence is sure; your deliverance, in His time and way, is certain. Therefore, 'Wait on the LORD: be of good courage, and He shall strengthen thine heart: wait, I say, on the LORD.'

> He that hath made his refuge God,
> Shall find a most secure abode;
> Shall walk all day beneath His shade,
> And there at night shall rest his head.

🌿 EVENING 🌿
'The LORD shall give that which is good'
Psalm 85:12

Whatever is good for His people the Lord will certainly bestow: grace to sanctify, provision to sustain, and glory to crown them at last. But He will only give that which is good; therefore He will refuse them many things which they may desire. But all that is good for them they shall have, and He will give every good thing in its proper season. He will so give them good now, as to secure the greatest good at last; and every good thing shall come to them through the hands of Jesus. That He will give that which is good, is certain from the relation in which He stands to them: He is their Father; from His infinite wisdom which is engaged for them, and His tender love, which is set upon them; from the plan of His grace, and the word of His promise; from the testimony of His people, and His conduct towards His very enemies, for He will not feed His foes, and starve His friends. Let His assurance then check your impatience: wait for the Lord. Let it rouse you to prayer: ask good things of the Lord. Let it feed your faith: believe the Word of the Lord. Let it produce contentment: be satisfied with the provision of the Lord. Let it encourage hope: expect every good thing from the Lord.

> The Lord will grace and glory grant,
> And every good supply;
> No blessing which His people want,
> His bounty can deny.

APRIL 1

❦ MORNING ❦
'The LORD is my Shepherd'
PSALM 23:1

Then David was one of the Lord's sheep. All His sheep know Him, love Him, and follow Him. They possess His disposition; He was meek, and lowly in heart. Are you a sheep of Christ? Are you looking to, following of, and rejoicing in, your Shepherd? If so, it is His province to lead you, feed you, protect you, and heal you. Your person, life, health, comforts, and safety, are committed to His care. He is the good Shepherd, He laid down His life for His sheep; He searches and seeks out His sheep wherever they have been scattered; He feeds His flock; He gathereth the lambs with His arm, and carrieth them in His bosom. He loved His sheep more than His own life; He cares for His sheep more than for all the world beside. He feeds them in the most suitable pasture, and leads them in the paths of righteousness for His name's sake. O view Jesus as your Shepherd! Expect Him to lead you, feed you, fold you, and present you to His Father with exceeding joy. Cleave to Him; let nothing tempt you to leave His feet, His flock, or His fold. He will never leave you, nor forsake you.

> Jehovah is my Shepherd's name,
> Then what have I, though weak, to fear?
> My sin and folly I proclaim,
>
> If I despond while He is near:
> In every danger He is nigh,
> And will my every want supply.

❦ EVENING ❦
'The God of all grace'
1 PETER 5:10

How sweet and refreshing are the views which Jehovah gives us of Himself! Too often we allow our minds to be led away from the spiritual representation of our God, and view Him through some improper and injurious medium. He is the God of all grace, but still He is the just God. He is gracious naturally, sovereignly, infinitely, and eternally. He has riches of grace: grace to quicken the dead, to pardon the guilty, to comfort the disconsolate, to strengthen the weak, to restore the wandering, and to save the lost. In His dealings with His people, His grace is displayed: how *free*, in the conversion of Saul of Tarsus; how *seasonable*, in the salvation of the dying robber on the cross; how *unexpected* by Zaccheus, when called down from the sycamore. But these are but samples, or patterns, intended to show us what the God of all grace can and will do. Let us look to our God as infinitely gracious. The extent, the greatness, the riches, the freedom of His grace, is displayed in the undeserving, in the ill-deserving. Let this check our fears. Let it spur us on to diligence. It calls for confidence, gratitude, and consecration from us. Let us lay the head on the pillow tonight, cheered with the thought: our God is 'the God of all grace.'

> Great God, to us Thy grace afford,
> That far from Thee we ne'er may rove,
> Our guard – the presence of the Lord,
> Our joy – the sense of pardoning love.

APRIL 2

🌿 MORNING 🌿

'I shall not want'
PSALM 23:1

This was David's conclusion, from the belief that the Lord was his Shepherd. If we are the sheep of Christ, He will supply us. He has all things in His possession: the silver and the gold are His, and the cattle upon a thousand hills. His private mark is upon all. All spiritual blessings are in His possession also; and He has a kind, tender, and liberal heart. He will give. He has engaged to supply, conduct, protect, and present His flock upon Mount Zion. He has promised to be to us, do for us, and bestow upon us, all that our circumstances require. His conduct towards His flock in old times is a sufficient guarantee. Whenever were the righteous forsaken, or His sheep left neglected and unheeded? Did David ever want? Few passed through greater changes, or severer trials; yet upon his dying bed he tells us, he had all his desire. If you belong to Christ, you may safely conclude, 'I shall not want.' Your fears are follies; your anxieties are groundless; your forebodings are sinful; you have a God to provide for you, and you ought to rejoice. 'My God,' says the apostle, 'shall supply all your needs, according to His riches in glory by Christ Jesus.'

> *What want shall not our God supply*
> *From His redundant stores?*
> *What streams of mercy from on high*
> *An arm almighty pours!*

🌿 EVENING 🌿

'Occupy till I come'
LUKE 19:13

Our Lord has provided for all our wants. He forbids our fears. He has given us talents, or entrusted us with His money. He is gone home to His Father for a time; He will soon return again, and He bids us 'occupy until He comes.' We are to be busy for God, to be active for the Lord Jesus Christ. He will soon come to take an account of *what* we have done, *how* we have done it, and *why* we have done it. When He comes He will praise or blame as the case may require. He will reward every one according to his works. Do we believe this? Are we living under the impression of this fact? Do we often say to ourselves, 'I must stand before the judgement seat of Christ.' 'I must give an account.' Beloved, our time, our talents, as well as our persons are the Lord's. To Him they should be consecrated. For Him they should be all employed. Have we been living for Christ today? Have we been transacting our business, or doing our work, in the prospect of appearing before the Lord Jesus to give an account of it? Let us not sleep as do others. Let us not stand idle in the market place. Let us not live to ourselves. Let us live upon Christ, and live for Him alone.

> *O may I live on Jesus still,*
> *And use the talents given;*
> *Daily consult and do His will,*
> *And thus prepare for heaven.*

APRIL 3

🌿 MORNING 🌿

'I flee unto thee to hide me'
PSALM 143:9

This implies *danger*. The Christian may be in danger from sin, self, foes. *Fear* – his fears may be groundless, but they are often very painful; *inability* – to defend himself or overcome his opposers; *foresight* – he sees the storm in the distance, and looks out for the covert; *prudence* – he hides before the storm, ere the enemy comes upon him. A laudable *concern* for safety and comfort. The believer, if wise, will at all times flee to Jehovah. Jacob flies to Laban; the manslayer to the refuge; the bird to his mountain; and the Christian to his God. Asa may seek to physicians; Ephraim to king Jareb; and Saul to the witch: but the believer looks to his God. The Lord receives, befriends, and secures him. Let us flee to Him by prayer, in faith, with hope, for salvation; and He will receive us, shelter us, and be our refuge and strength. Flee from sin, from self, from the world; but flee to Jesus. His heart is ever toward us, His ear is open to us, and His hand is ready to help, protect, and deliver us. His throne is our asylum, His promise is our comfort, and His omnipotence is our guard.

> *Happy soul that, free from harms,*
> *Rests within his Shepherd's arms!*
> *Who his quiet shall molest?*
> *Who shall violate his rest?*
> *He who found the wandering sheep,*
> *Loves, and still delights to keep.*

🌿 EVENING 🌿

'The obedience of faith'
ROMANS 16:26

The obedience required of faith is the entire submission of the intellect, the heart and the life to God. The law of faith is the gospel; this requires us to believe that 'God is love.' That Christ died for sin instead of sinners: to embrace mercy as freely presented, and receive forgiveness as the gift of God; to accept of the righteousness of Jesus, to trust in it alone for acceptance before God, and to plead it at the throne of grace for all we need; to come daily to Jesus for all we want, and to expect to receive at His hands all He has promised; to live for God; to live to God; to live like God. It requires us, in one word, so to live that God may be *all* and man nothing. God requires the obedience of a believing heart. We must believe what He says, expect what He has promised, and do what He bids. This is the life of faith. Satan will oppose it. The carnal mind will throw a thousand obstacles in the way. Every thing that is of a worldly character will hinder us. But we must wrestle, strive, break through, and say, 'I will believe my God. I will obey my Lord. I will imitate my Saviour. I will be a follower of them, who through faith and patience now inherit the promises.'

> *Spirit of faith, unfold Thy law,*
> *Thy quick'ning power impart:*
> *My soul to sweet obedience draw,*
> *Fill and control my heart.*

APRIL 4

🌿 MORNING 🌿
'It is I; be not afraid'
JOHN 6:20

The fears of the Christian are a dishonour to his Lord, a denial of his creed, and a fruitful source of distress to his own soul. All things are of God. He worketh all things after the counsel of His own will, and in every event He says to us, 'It is I; be not afraid.' If friends turn to foes and distress us, if death enters our dwellings and bereaves us, if sickness lays us aside and fills us with pain, He says, 'It is I; be not afraid.' If losses, crosses, and sore trials come upon us, and discourage, distress, and perplex us, He says, 'It is I; be not afraid.' If death approaches, and calls upon us to leave the body and close our eyes upon our beloved relations, friends, and connections, He says, 'It is I; be not afraid.' Should we hear the pillars of heaven crack, and feel the strong foundation of the earth give way; should the heavens be rolled up like a scroll, and the great white throne appear; still, amidst the wreck of matter and the crash of worlds, He cries, 'Be not afraid; it is I.' Happy Christian! Thy fears are groundless and thy brightest hopes well founded. Rejoice in Jesus.

> O, that I might so believe,
> Steadfastly to Jesus cleave;
> Only on His love rely,
> Smile at the destroyer nigh:
> Free from care and servile fear,
> Feel the Saviour always near.

🌿 EVENING 🌿
'I know whom I have believed'
2 TIMOTHY 1:12

It is unspeakable mercy to know Christ. It lays at the root of our happiness. It is essential to our confidence. But unto us it is given to know Him. We know Him from His Word. We know Him from the testimony of His saints. But what is still better, we know Him by the teaching of the Holy Spirit. But we only know in part. We know His person, so as to love Him; His character, so as to trust in Him; His perfect work, so as to rely upon it alone for our acceptance with God; His infinite fulness, so as to repair to it for all we need; His tender compassion, so as to go to Him for sympathy in suffering and sorrow; His willingness to receive sinners, so as to recommend poor sinners to go to Him for life and peace. We know He is able to save. We know He is trustworthy. We know He will never leave or forsake one poor soul who trusts in Him. We know Him, and therefore trust our all in His hands. We know Him and therefore are not ashamed to avow that He is our Lord and our God. We know who He is: the Son of God; what He is: the Saviour; where He is: at the right hand of God; what He has done: He died for our sins, and rose again for our justification; what He will do: come again and receive us unto Himself.

> I know in whom I have believ'd,
> His Spirit doth my heart assure,
> That what He hath from me receiv'd,
> His constant love will keep secure.

APRIL 5

🌿 MORNING 🌿

'Without me ye can do nothing'
JOHN 15:5

Never forget that in the Lord is our righteousness and strength. We are not sufficient to think rightly of ourselves, but through Him we can do all things. Never attempt anything without looking to Jesus for power. Let a knowledge and constant sense of weakness keep you near to Him, sensibly depending on Him, and ascribing all good unto Him. You cannot; He can. You have destroyed yourself; in Him is your help found. It is only by union to Him, and receiving from Him, that you can glorify God, adorn your profession, enjoy your privileges, and obey the holy precepts of the Gospel. Never presume, but come up out of the wilderness leaning on Him, your Beloved. Live as one deeply sensible of your dependence upon, and obligation to, the Lord Jesus. He is the strength of the poor, the strength of the needy in his distress, and your strength too. Beloved, Jesus is your life-giving Head, the Fountain from which you are to draw all your supplies, and the Friend to whom you are to carry all your cares. He will work in you to will and to do of His own good pleasure.

Jesus, immutably the same!
Thou true and living vine!
Around Thy all-supporting stem

My feeble arms I twine;
Thou art my strength, my life, my hope,
Nor can I sink with such a prop.

🌿 EVENING 🌿

'Peace, peace'
ISAIAH 57:19

Such are the soft, soothing sounds which the gospel whispers in the believer's ear. In all times of tribulation, in all times of temptation, in all times of bodily disease and suffering, it softly cries 'Peace, *peace*.' Peace, for Jesus died to put away your sins. Peace, for Jesus lives to intercede for you in heaven. Peace, for Jesus reigns, and your concerns are in His hands. Peace, for Jesus loves, and His love is immutably fixed on you. Peace, for God is love. Peace, for you are reconciled to Him by the death of His Son. Let not your heart be troubled. Every thought of God respecting you is peaceful. Every purpose of God toward you which providence has to work out is peaceful. Heaven is at peace with you. You also are at peace with heaven. Your peace was made, when Jesus died in your stead, when He put away your sin by the sacrifice of Himself. Look to Him as your *Peacemaker*. Live in the atmosphere of Gethsemane and Golgotha. View God as your peaceful Father, and heaven as your peaceful home. Often meditate upon that precious verse, 'Thou wilt keep him in *perfect peace*, whose mind is stayed on thee; because he trusteth in thee.' Let your mind *rest* in the Lord.

Jesus, my feeble faith increase,
And sweetly multiply my peace,
And when I always trust Thy power,
My sin shall trouble me no more.

APRIL 6

🌿 MORNING 🌿

'Worthy is the Lamb that was slain'
REVELATION 5:12

This is an ascription of praise to Jesus, thy Jesus, as the sacrifice for sin, the atonement of the church, the Saviour of His body. Jesus, who died for thy sins, is worthy to receive power, and riches, and wisdom, and strength, and honour, and glory, and blessing. We never can ascribe too much to Jesus. But He is worthy also to be *believed*, in preference to Satan, unbelief, the world, or appearances; to be *trusted* with all, for all, before all; to be *loved*, more than any other, in opposition to any other that would rival Him; to be *obeyed*, though He commands us to cut off a right hand, or pluck out a right eye; to be *followed*, wherever He may lead us, through evil report and good report; to be *preferred*, to ease, pleasure, wealth, health, to anything and everything. Jesus is worthy to be our Example, our Confidant, our King, and our All. He is worthy of all He requires, all we can give, all His people have done for Him, or suffered in His cause. Believe His Word, trust His grace, love His name, obey His commands, and prefer Him before all others. Make it your daily business to endeavour to bring sinners to His feet. He is worthy of every effort you can make.

> Jesus is worthy to receive
> Honour and power divine;
> And blessings more than we can give,
> Be, Lord, for ever Thine.

🌿 EVENING 🌿

'The resurrection of the just'
LUKE 14:14

The dead in Christ shall rise first. They shall rise incorruptible, powerful, spiritual, and glorious, in exact conformity to the glorious body of Christ. His voice will rouse them, His power will raise them, and His glory will surround and adorn them. They shall be like Him, for they shall see Him as He is. What a glorious morning will the resurrection morning be! How deeply we are interested in it, and yet, how little it exercises our thoughts, or draws out our anticipations. It may be the very next morning we shall see, for we may die in our sleep; or for aught we can tell, Jesus may come tomorrow. Are we ready? Are we justified before God through faith in Jesus? Are we just with men, rendering to all their due? The resurrection of the just will be most glorious; they will come forth perfect in holiness and beauty; they will rise to be openly united to Jesus, to share His glory, and be with Him where He is. We ought often to think of that day; to prepare for it daily; to live and act as if it was just at hand; to do as Paul did, who laboured, suffered and prayed, 'if by any means he might attain unto the resurrection of the dead.' 'Blessed and holy is he that hath part in the first resurrection.'

> Sing with glad anticipation,
> Mortals and immortals sing,
> Jesus comes with full salvation,
> Jesus doth His glory bring.

APRIL 7

🌿 MORNING 🌿
'One thing is needful'
Luke 10:42

The things of time are transient; the things of eternity are permanent. The world passeth away. The body must die; earthly connections must be dissolved; but the soul must live forever. The welfare of the soul is the one thing needful. If the soul is in a sanctified and healthy state, it will be found at the feet of Jesus; it will relish His words; and enjoy His communications more than the richest feast. We shall be seeking to know Him, love Him, believe Him, obey Him, and enjoy Him. Fellowship with Jesus is needful as an evidence of interest in Him, and as a source of satisfaction and comfort. He that finds a home at the feet of Jesus will enjoy an eternal heaven in the presence of Jesus. Let not then the many trifles of time affect, distract, and bewilder you; but let the one thing needful be the constant object of pursuit and desire. Live at the feet of Jesus, and you are safe. Seek, above all things, to enjoy Jesus, and you will be happy. Aim in all things to glorify Jesus, and you will be holy. Look daily for the coming of Jesus, and you will be consistent. O Jesus! Manifest Thyself to me; draw me to Thy feet, and keep me there!

> *Engage this roving, treacherous heart*
> *To fix on Mary's better part;*
> *To scorn the trifles of a day,*
> *For joys that none can take away.*

🌿 EVENING 🌿
'One thing I do'
Philippians 3:13

The concentration and fixation of the thoughts, desires, and aims upon the great object and end of life, is an invaluable blessing. David desired 'one thing,' even to dwell in the house of the LORD. Mary chose the good part. Paul kept his eye and his heart upon 'one thing,' even the prize of his high calling. He forgot the past, and was constantly pressing on after higher attainments, sweeter enjoyments, and more extensive usefulness. Nothing past or present could satisfy his soul. His desires were large. His hopes were exalted. His heart was set upon doing all he could for God, obtaining all he could from God, and becoming as much as possible like God. Beloved, how does this reprove us! Are not our minds often distracted, our hearts divided, and our attention diverted from the object, which we should keep in view? Jesus kept His eye upon the joy that was set before Him. Moses had respect unto the recompense of the reward. Paul did not aim at any of the things which are seen and temporal, but at the things which are not seen, which are eternal. O to have the heart set, and the eye fixed, upon 'one thing;' and that one thing, the prize which Jesus holds out to stimulate His people, and which He will give them at that day!

> *Lord, help me this one thing to do;*
> *To keep the glorious prize in view;*
> *Fain would I leave the things behind,*
> *And heaven on earth in Jesus find.*

APRIL 8

❦ MORNING ❦

'He will save'

ZEPHANIAH 3:17

Whom? The lost, the wretched, the unworthy. Every applicant, for 'Whosoever shall call upon the name of the Lord shall be saved.' 'Him that cometh to me I will in *no wise* cast out.' *How?* Freely, without money and without price; fully, by His blood, power, and providence; eternally, all who flee to Him for refuge; all who build on Him for pardon, peace, and life, shall be saved with an everlasting salvation; they shall not be ashamed nor confounded, world without end. *Why?* Because it is His Father's will; because He delighteth in mercy; because it will eternally glorify His name. *From what?* From sin, in its guilt, filth, and power; from the present evil world; from Satan; from the wrath of God; from every evil work; and from all the evil designs of men. He has saved us, by receiving grace for us and dying in our stead. He does save us, by His presence, Word, providence, and the renewing of the Holy Ghost. He will save in every trouble, from every foe, even unto the end. Look to Him then, and to Him alone, to deliver, direct, relieve, and preserve. He says, 'Look unto me, and be ye saved, all ye ends of the earth; for I am God, and there is no other.'

> *Why should I doubt His love at last,*
> *With anxious thoughts perplex'd!*
> *Who saved me in the troubles past,*
> *Will save me in the next.*

❦ EVENING ❦

'Who hath saved us'

2 TIMOTHY 1:9

Salvation is a present blessing. If we are in Christ we are saved. Our God hath pardoned our sins, He hath justified our persons, He hath changed our natures and He hath given to us eternal life. We now receive the end of our faith, even the salvation of our souls. We are not perfectly delivered from all evils, foes, and fears yet; but then deliverance is certain. We are not in the exact likeness of our Lord now, but we shall be, for we shall see Him as He is. Every believer is in a justified state, and as such we should *walk* with God, *work* for God, and *suffer* all the will of God. Christ is ours, and all He has is ours. The promises are ours, and all they contain is ours; God is ours, and all He can do for us consistently with His perfections and government, He will do. In the assurance of this we should live; the apostle did so. It is this that will strengthen us to labour, give us courage in the conflict, cast out all slavish fear, and consecrate us entirely to the Lord. Let this then be the subject of meditation tonight, until we fall into the arms of sleep. God hath saved me. He may not have given me health, or wealth, or kind relatives, or a happy home; but He hath saved me, and saved me with an everlasting salvation.

> *Sav'd in Christ from hell and death,*
> *O may I seek the things above,*
> *And evermore the spirit breathe*
> *Of praise, sobriety, and love.*

APRIL 9

🌿 MORNING 🌿

'Lord, increase our faith'
Luke 17:5

The believer is as his faith is. If faith is weak, he is fearful, fretful, and troubled; if faith is strong and rightly placed, he is courageous, active, and happy. Faith comes from Jesus. He is its Author. It leads to Jesus; He is its object. Faith is like a grain of mustard-seed: it grows and increases; but Jesus alone can increase our faith. Let us apply to Him this morning, and let this be our prayer, *'Lord, increase my faith.'* Strong faith will believe without feeling, yea, against feelings or appearances. It will trust God where it cannot trace Him; it assures the soul that what He has promised He is able to perform, and will assuredly do so. Great faith will have great trials, for God never gives faith without trying it; and the heat of the furnace is in proportion to the strength of our faith. Little faith lays hold on Christ, and brings salvation; strong faith receives much and often from Christ and brings great consolation. Go to Jesus with the faith thou hast, and plead with Him for the faith He requires. He gives freely to every importunate pleader; and He will assuredly give to thee.

> *O Jesus, now Thyself impart*
> *And fix Thy presence in my heart,*
> *Give strong and living faith!*
>
> *Then will I throw off every load,*
> *And walk delightfully with God,*
> *Observing all He saith.*

🌿 EVENING 🌿

'Your faith groweth exceedingly'
2 Thessalonians 1:3

Such was the happiness of the believing Thessalonians. Their faith grew. It grew exceedingly. The seed became the plant; the plant soon became the tree. The blade grew into ear; the ear ripened into the full corn. The babe became a young man; the young man became a father in Christ. Faith roots itself in the truth. It firmly grasps the rock. It stands against, and defies the storm. It reposes on the covenant, and immutable faithfulness of God. It grows by exercise. It grows in the way of upright walking. It grows by the proper use of gospel ordinances. If our faith grows, Christ will become more precious. We shall earnestly long for more conformity to Him. We shall learn better to distinguish between faith and feeling. We shall be able to trust a naked promise. Our love to the saints will strengthen and become strong. Our zeal for God and His glory will increase. Our attention to the precepts will become close and influential. Our confidence in God's Word will be steady and vigorous. Our liberality and benevolence will grow in proportion to our faith. See then how important it is that our faith should grow. Look to it, that your faith be a growing faith.

> *How blest it is to live by faith,*
> *And cast our burden on the Lord:*
> *To credit what the Saviour saith,*
> *And rest, confiding in His Word.*

APRIL 10

❦ MORNING ❧
'He shall glorify me'
John 16:14

If Jesus is to be glorified, our pride must be mortified, and our spirits humbled. It is the Spirit's office and work to glorify Jesus; this He does, by discovering to us our wretched and ruined state, and leading us to Him to crave salvation as a favour at His hands; by daily emptying us and leading us to Him for all we need; by giving us to see, that all God has created cannot satisfy an immortal spirit for one moment of time, but that there is enough in Jesus to satisfy it throughout eternity. Jesus is glorified when we mourn over sin, and wash in the fountain of His blood; when we renounce our own doings and feelings, and desire to be found in His righteousness alone; when we refuse to look to any other quarter for help, relief, or comfort, but to Him; when His dear name fills all our songs; and when we long to have a crown to cast at His feet, and a harp that will worthily sound forth His praise. 'He shall glorify me.' This decrees the death of pride, self, and creature excellence. Beloved, whatsoever you do in word or deed, do all to the glory of Jesus. He is the Lord of all.

> Lord, draw my heart from earth away
> And make it only know Thy call;
> Speak to my inmost soul, and say,
> 'I am thy Saviour, God, thine all!'
> O dwell in me, and fill my soul,
> And all my powers by Thine control.

❦ EVENING ❧
'Thou shalt glorify me'
Psalm 50:15

When trouble drives us to the Lord in prayer, He kindly listens to us, and graciously answers us. But when prayer is answered and deliverance is enjoyed, then He expects to be acknowledged and adored. We glorify God when our hearts are grateful for His mercies; when we praise Him for His undeserved favours; and when we commend Him to others, as faithful to His Word, merciful to His enemies, and gracious to all who apply at His throne. But we glorify Him also when we exercise filial confidence in His promises; when we expect all He has promised, because He is true; when we call upon Him first, in every trial and trouble; and when we carry all our cares to His feet, and leave them at His throne. By silent submission under bereavements, by calm resignation in trials, by the daily offering up of the heart as a sacrifice, by tender concern for His honour, by steady attachment to His cause, by fraternal affection to His people, by preferring His will to our own, we glorify Him. Let us make *this* the one business of our lives. Let us charge ourselves every morning, saying, 'My soul, see to it that thou glorify God today.' And let us examine ourselves every evening, whether the Lord's glory has been kept in view through the day.

> He who offers grateful praises,
> Best exalts Jehovah's name:
> He whose mind His law embraces,
> Will aright his conduct frame.

APRIL 11

🌿 MORNING 🌿

'And she went to inquire of the LORD'
GENESIS 25:22

Excellent example! Let us imitate Rebekah, for God commands us to do so. In all thy ways acknowledge Him, and He shall direct thy steps. Commit thy way unto the LORD, trust also in Him, and He shall bring it to pass. Are you in trouble? Go, and inquire of the Lord: What is the cause? Unite with holy Job in praying, 'Show me wherefore thou contendest with me.' Are you in perplexity? Go, and inquire: What is the design? He will instruct thee and teach thee in the way thou shouldest go; He will guide thee with His eye. Go in an inquiring spirit. Go, persuaded whatever thy circumstances or trials may be, that, as a believer in Jesus, wrath and curse can have nothing to do with thee. They were exhausted when Jesus died in thy stead. Be assured that whatever comes from God is a blessing, a benefit, a favour, a proof of love, however painful, perplexing, or distressing it may be. Do not reason, but believe in the promise of thy God; do not despond, grieve, or complain; but go, and *inquire of the Lord*, at His throne, of His Word. He says, 'I will be inquired of.'

> Prayer was appointed to convey
> The blessings God designs to give;
> Long as they live should Christians pray,
> For only while they pray they live.

🌿 EVENING 🌿

'I will not be inquired of by you'
EZEKIEL 20:3

These persons were living in sin under a profession of religion. Such characters are peculiarly loathsome in the sight of God; He will not allow them to have any fellowship with Himself. 'If I regard iniquity in my heart, the Lord will not hear my prayer.' 'He that turneth away his ear from the law, even his prayer shall be an abomination.' Are our hearts sincere? Are our lives consistent? If we love sin, if we live in sin, if we can make excuses for sin, God will hold no communion with us. He says, 'Wash you; make you clean.' Sin is the pollution of the soul. Holiness is cleanliness of soul. Sinners are filthy. They are offensive to God. But none are so offensive as they, who while professing to be holy, live in sin. Sin spoils our services. One sin fostered and encouraged, will cause our services to be rejected, our prayers to be refused, and our persons to be loathed by a holy and righteous God. Christ will not be the minister of sin, or allow His work to be used as an excuse or cloak for transgression. If we are justified by grace, we are sanctified by the truth. If God accepts our prayers, our hearts are set against sin. Beloved, if tempted to indulge in sin, remember God says, '*I will not be inquired of by you*.'

> Lord, wash my soul from sin,
> Cleanse every secret part;
> And put Thy Spirit's grace within,
> To purify my heart.

APRIL 12

🌿 MORNING 🌿

'He cannot deny Himself'
2 Timothy 2:13

God has opened His heart to us in His Word. He has told us all His mind; He intends every word He has spoken, and will fulfil every promise He has made. He cannot deny Himself or falsify His Word; He can have no temptation to do so. Man may be fickle, he is but a bruised reed; Jehovah is always the same, He is the Rock of Ages. He will have compassion on the miserable, who seek His face; and show mercy to all who plead with Him in Jesus' name. He cannot cast out a coming sinner, or refuse to receive a confessing backslider. He cannot turn a deaf ear to our cries, or refuse to deliver us when we call on His name. He will take His own time, but will never dishonour His faithful Word. He will be rigidly faithful, both to His threatenings and promises. Let us take courage and trust in Him; we have His Word – it is true, from the beginning; we have this assurance, that *He cannot deny Himself*. Let us then stay ourselves on the Word of our God; let us trust Him, though the night be dark and the burden be heavy. He exhorts, 'Trust ye in JEHOVAH for ever, for in JAH, JEHOVAH there is everlasting strength.'

> *Engraved as in eternal brass*
> *The mighty promise shines;*
> *Nor can the powers of darkness rase*
> *Those everlasting lines.*

🌿 EVENING 🌿

'The will of the Lord be done'
Acts 21:14

If God is love, if His promises are true, if He is faithful to His Word, if His will is influenced by justice and mercy, holiness and love, if He only wills what is for our good and for His own glory, ought we not daily to use this language? Should not wishing give way to acquiescence? His wisdom is infinite, and He wills wisely. His heart is set upon our welfare, and He works with this object in view. Still we want our own way. We fancy that something else would be better than that which is. We cast dishonour upon the skill, the kindness, and the truth of our God. What folly is this! But it arises in part from want of reflection; more from want of faith; and most of all from the sinful selfishness of our natures. Most of our anguish springs from our wilfulness. Our distresses are generated by our opposition to God. We daily pray, 'Thy will be done.' We often talk of the excellency and perfection of the will of God, and yet if our wills are crossed, if our fortitude is tried, if our professions are put to the test, we either fret and complain, or sink in fears and gloom. Believer, God wills thy holiness, thy true happiness, thy everlasting welfare. Give up then at once, and strive to say at all seasons, 'The will of the Lord be done.'

> *Thy favour all my journey through,*
> *Thou art engaged to grant;*
> *What else I want, or think I do,*
> *'Tis better still to want.*

APRIL 13

🌿 MORNING 🌿
'Why are ye troubled?'
Luke 24:38

Consider what Jesus has done for you, promised to you, and is gone to prepare for you. Consider what He is to you: your loving Bridegroom, faithful Friend, and gracious Saviour. What troubles you? Is it sin? He will pardon, subdue, and destroy it. The world? He has overcome it, redeemed you from it, and is leading you through it. Satan? He is conquered, condemned, and will soon be imprisoned. The cares and troubles of life? Jesus says, 'Bring them to Me by prayer, cast them on Me in faith, leave them with Me; I know what you want, I have provided of My goodness, I will supply all your needs; your bread shall be given you, and your water shall be sure. I will make a way in the wilderness of trouble, and a path in the desert of perplexity. Let not your hearts be troubled, ye believe in God, believe also in Me. Try Me. Trust Me. In all your ways acknowledge Me, and I will direct your paths. I have wisdom, power, and love; and all that I have is yours, to be employed for your good.' Commit thy way unto the LORD, trust also in Him, and He will bring it to pass.

> Yield to the Lord, with simple heart,
> All that thou hast, and all thou art;
> Renounce all strength, but strength divine,
> And peace shall be for ever thine:
> Behold the path the saints have trod,
> The path which led them home to God.

🌿 EVENING 🌿
'Your names are written in heaven'
Luke 10:20

What an unspeakable blessing is this: to be registered among the family of God; to have a name in the Lamb's book of life; to be written among the living in Jerusalem. Election is the earliest effect of grace. We were chosen in Christ, chosen to holiness, chosen to eternal life. Our persons were given to Jesus; our salvation was entrusted to His hands; our interests were made His care; our names were recorded in the register of His members; and we are called upon by Him to rejoice in the fact. God has thought of us. He has thought of us in love. He has ordained us to eternal life. He has made a full provision for all our wants in the covenant. He has given us exceeding great and precious promises. He has proved His exceeding kindness towards us in a thousand ways. Let us daily write His name upon our memories. Let us so record His mercies as they shall never be forgotten. Let us make holiness the business of our life, for no one can know his election but by its results, of which holiness is the principal. If we are not holy, we have no proof whatever that our names are in the book of life. If our hearts, our hopes, and our desires are not in heaven, it is a great question if our names are written there.

> Thus did eternal love begin
> To raise us up from death and sin;
> Our characters were then decreed,
> Blameless in love, a holy seed.

APRIL 14

🌿 MORNING 🌿

'Ye are complete in him'
COLOSSIANS 2:10

Look not too much at thyself; there is nothing but vanity, weakness, sin, and misery there; but thy God hath united thee to His beloved Son. Jesus is one with thee, and all that He has is thine. Thou art unholy, but He is made unto thee sanctification; and He will sanctify thee wholly, body, soul, and spirit. Thou art foolish, but He is made unto thee wisdom; and He will make thee wise unto salvation. Thou art weak, but He is thy strength; and thou canst do all things through His strengthening thee. Thou art unrighteous, but He is made unto thee righteousness; and thou art not only righteous, but the righteousness of God in Him. Thou art lost, but He is made unto thee redemption; He has redeemed thee from the curse of God, and from the present evil world, and He will redeem thee from death. In thyself thou art not only incomplete, but wretched, miserable, poor, blind, and naked; but in Jesus thou art holy, wise, strong, righteous, rich, happy; in a word, *complete*. View thyself, then, at least occasionally, as *complete in Christ*, who is the head of all principality and power.

> *Still onward urge your heavenly way,*
> *Dependent on Him day by day,*
> *His presence still entreat;*
>
> *His precious name for ever bless,*
> *Your glory, strength, and righteousness,*
> *In Him you are complete.*

🌿 EVENING 🌿

'That ye be not slothful'
HEBREWS 6:12

That were to pervert truth, abuse mercy, dishonour God, and gratify the prince of darkness. Slothfulness is a disgrace, both in reference to temporals and spirituals. Not slothful in business, but active, diligent, and industrious, carrying on business from a pure motive, in a proper spirit, with becoming zeal. So should every Christian do. But in reference to spiritual things the apostle speaks: that ye be not slothful in seeking blessings, in employing your talents, in exercising your graces, in copying your examples; even them who through faith and patience now inherit the promises. Let hope inspire you. Let the conduct of the ancient saints stimulate you. Let the love of Christ constrain you. Let the holy precepts of the gospel direct you. Let the glorious promises of grace animate and strengthen you. Be not slothful, for all around you are active. The world is active to ensnare you. Satan is active to deceive you. Angels are active in administering to you. Jesus is active in carrying on your cause before the throne. Time swiftly flies. Eternity is fast approaching. The day of account is at hand. The last opportunity will soon present itself.

> *Happy we live, when God doth fill*
> *Our hands with work, our hearts with zeal;*
> *For every toil, if He enjoin,*
>
> *Becomes a sacrifice divine,*
> *And like the holy ones above,*
> *The more we serve, the more we love.*

APRIL 15

🌿 MORNING 🌿
'Set your affection on things above'
COLOSSIANS 3:2

We are apt to be much affected by earthly things, but our affections should be permanently fixed on things above. Let us lift our eyes and hearts to heaven this morning; there are the proper objects of our love, desire, and esteem. There is Jehovah our heavenly Father, dwelling in unapproachable light. There is Jesus, our dear and adorable Saviour, exalted, dignified and glorified at the right-hand of the Father. There is the Holy Spirit, our divine, gracious and condescending Comforter. There the love, favour, and presence of God are fully enjoyed. There peace, rest, and happiness are eternally realized. There is the crown of righteousness, the throne of glory, and the rivers of pleasure which our God has promised, and set before us. There are our brethren who have gone home before us, and there our affections should be. What is earth? Whatever it is, we are leaving it. What is time? We shall soon have done of it. O, let us then *set our affections on things above, and not on things on the earth.*

> Why should my heart descend so low,
> To brood on earth – a world of woe,
> While heaven, where endless pleasures roll,
> Waits to entrance my new-born soul?

> Saviour! let Thine attractions be
> But felt in all Their force by me;
> Then shall I mount on wings of love,
> And fix and dwell on things above.

🌿 EVENING 🌿
'He humbled Himself'
PHILIPPIANS 2:8

Who did? He who was the brightness of glory, the express image of the Father's person; He who was with God, and was God; He who was the mighty God, the everlasting Father, and the Prince of peace. How did He humble Himself? By taking our nature; by becoming a servant; by stooping to obey, even unto death. Look at the manger; look at the carpenter's shop; look at the cottage of Nazareth; look at the Jordan; look at the homeless wanderer; look at Gethsemane; look at Golgotha; look at Joseph's tomb. Now you need not ask, 'How did He humble Himself?' The scene is before you. But *why* did He humble Himself? Because He *loved us*. It was the stoop of majesty, under the influence of infinite love. He humbled Himself that He might mingle with mankind; enter experimentally into our infirmities and wants; know our feelings; die in our stead; and having suffered, being tempted, know how to succour those that are tempted. He humbled Himself to exalt us. He stooped low, to raise us high. He sighed that we may sing; suffered, that we may rejoice; died, that we may live; was set at naught, that we might be raised to the throne of glory. Amazing humiliation! Wondrous love!

> Did pity ever stoop so low,
> Dress'd in divinity and blood?
> Was ever rebel courted so,
> In groans of an expiring God?

APRIL 16

🌿 MORNING 🌿

'He will subdue our iniquities'
Micah 7:19

Sin must not only be pardoned, but corruption must be subdued; the one is freely promised as well as the other. The grace of God pardons, the power of God subdues; but grace and power always go together in the salvation of a sinner. Pardon comes first, and sanctification follows. Light shining upon the understanding, discovers corruption working in the soul; holiness seated in the heart, produces hatred and opposition to it; prayer ascends to God for deliverance from it, and power descends and subdues it. But like fire apparently quenched, it will break out again and again; like rebels in a state, it will seize every opportunity of disturbing the peace and happiness of the soul. Hear, then, what the Lord says to you this morning, *'I will subdue your iniquities.'* Carry your complaint to His throne, plead His faithful Word, and expect His promised power to subdue your iniquities. Sin shall not have dominion over you, for you are not under the law, but under grace. Grace reigns, and will conquer every rival lust.

Jesus, Thy boundless love to me
No thought can reach, no tongue declare;
O knit my thankful heart to Thee,
And reign without a rival there.

O grant that nothing in my soul
May dwell, but Thy pure love alone:
O may Thy love possess me whole,
My joy, my treasure, and my crown.

🌿 EVENING 🌿

'I know that my Redeemer liveth'
Job 19:25

We live in a dying world. Friends and relatives are constantly being removed by death. But one relative ever lives. Jesus is our Kinsman. To Him the right of redemption belongs. He has paid the ransom demanded, and He lives to effect our complete deliverance. He lives in our nature at the right hand of God. He lives for us in the holiest of all. His existence is eternal. His office is untransferable. He will plead our cause. He will conquer our foes. He will perfect our graces. He will redeem us from death. He will be glorified in us, when He comes again the second time without sin unto salvation. *I know Him* from the revelation of His Word, and by the teaching of His Holy Spirit. I know Him as the object of my trust, confidence, and desire. I know Him as my Redeemer. He has already rescued me from Satan, old habits, and this present evil world. Into His hands I have committed my spirit, and I know that as He liveth in the character of my Kinsman Redeemer, I shall live also. Dear friends, it is sweet, peculiarly sweet, to have one ever-living, ever-loving Friend; one to whom our interests are dear, and in whose hands our interests are safe. O Jesus may I know and love Thee more!

I know that my Redeemer lives,
And ever pleads for me;
Salvation to my soul He gives,
And life and liberty.

APRIL 17

🌿 MORNING 🌿

'The forerunner is for us entered'
HEBREWS 6.20

Whatever Jesus did was for His people. He is gone into heaven as our Forerunner; as the *pioneer* goes before the army to remove obstacles, clear the road, and render the march more easy, so did Jesus go before us. As an interested and kind friend, He shows the practicability of the way; as a wise *guide*, He marks out the road for us; as our example, He is gone before, and says to us, *'Follow me.'* We have now an *Advocate* with the Father, a *Husband* preparing our mansions, a *Saviour* waiting to receive us. We have one in heaven to whom in our addresses to His throne we can say, 'Lord, Thou knowest from Thy own experience what I feel in my present situation, for Thou wast once tried in all points like as I am.' We have one in heaven who will welcome us home, and who when He sees us enter will be glad in His heart. We know Him below, and we shall know, and enjoy, and love Him for ever above. He is gone into heaven *for us*, nor shall we know until we arrive there, how much we are indebted to His intercession and pleading above. O my soul, look at Jesus as thy Forerunner, and follow in His steps!

> Before His heavenly Father's face,
> For every saint He intercedes:
> For mercy and abounding grace,
> There Jesus, our Forerunner, pleads.

🌿 EVENING 🌿

'The love of Christ constraineth us.'
2 CORINTHIANS 5: 14

Love is according to the nature and character of the lover. Jesus possesses a perfect character, and unites in Himself the most excellent natures. His love, therefore, is peculiar, peculiarly glorious. It includes pity for sinners, sympathy for, and delight in, His saints. He loves us *as* the Father loves Him; except therefore we could tell the strength of His Father's love to Him, we cannot tell the strength of His love to us. (John 15:9) Love dwells in His heart, looks through His eye, works with His hand, speaks with His tongue, and procures for us by His influence. He considered no condition too low to stoop to, no action too mean to perform, no failing too foul to pass by, no gift too great to bestow, no sufferings too painful to endure, nothing too mean in His people to prize, no distance too far to travel to do them good. The love of Christ is above expression or conception. It was this that influenced the apostles to labour, to suffer, and to die. And if we believe the love of Christ to us, it will constrain us to surrender ourselves to Him; to part with all for Him; to *do*, to *suffer*, or to *give* any thing in His cause; to proclaim His excellencies, and publish His fame. Does the love of Christ constrain you to be active, zealous, liberal?

> The love of Christ constrain, to what?
> With all our sins to part,
> To yield Him what His blood hath bought -
> Our dearly-purchased heart.

APRIL 18

🌿 MORNING 🌿
'Our sufficiency is of God'
2 Corinthians 3:5

Let us think of this, whenever we are cast down on account of our weakness, or the difficulties we meet with in our way. We are weak, but Jesus is strong; and His strength is made perfect in our weakness. He has given us His Word, that 'He will work in us to will and to do of His good pleasure.' He speaks, and it is done. The Word of the Lord knows no obstacles or difficulties; all things must obey Him. When He sent Moses to Pharaoh, He said, 'Certainly I will be with thee,' and the Lord's presence was his strength. He acts just so with us: His fulness is our sufficiency; it is opened to us in Jesus, and we receive from it according to our wants, weakness, and faith. 'Through God,' said David, 'we shall do valiantly.' 'I can do all things,' said Paul, 'through Christ which strengtheneth me.' Look not then at your own emptiness, or weakness; but look at what God is to His people, and what He has promised to give them, and sing, *'Our sufficiency is of God.'* 'God is our refuge and strength;' and as our days so shall our strength be. His grace is sufficient for us; His strength is made perfect in weakness.

When we cannot see our way,
We should trust, and still obey;
He who bids us forward go
Will instruct the way to know.

🌿 EVENING 🌿
'Where is mine honour?'
Malachi 1:6

The Lord expects to be honoured by His people; but how often do we lose sight of this important duty. We should honour Him by prompt obedience, as Matthew did; by active faith, as Abraham did; by patient suffering, as Job did; by an honest testimony, as Peter did; by glowing love, as John did; by fervent zeal, as Paul and the holy martyrs did. Beloved, would you honour God? Then trust His providence. Always act as under His eye. Prefer His children to all others. Assist to promote the extension of His cause. Diligently attend to His ordinances. Seek above all things to advance His declarative glory. If you do not, He may well ask, *'Where is mine honour?'* But if you would honour God as He requires, you must know His character. You must be reconciled to Him through Jesus. You must daily realize His presence. You must acknowledge His authority. You must believe His love to you. You must consult His revealed will. You must make it your aim and study to please Him. If you honour Him, He will honour you, by giving you solid peace, suitable and certain supplies, good success in His cause, help in every time of trouble, the frequent visits of His love, and final victory over every foe.

Is God my Father? Will He claim
So mean a sinner for His son?
Then let His honour be my aim,
IN me, BY me, His will be done.

APRIL 19

🌿 MORNING 🌿

'Quicken thou me in thy way'
PSALM 119:37

What poor, dull, lifeless creatures we often feel ourselves to be; and how needful is this prayer. It is our duty to *run* in the way of God's commandments; it is our misery that through sin, weakness, and temptation, we scarcely creep. We are dependent upon the Spirit for quickening. He only can strengthen, animate and enliven us. Let us sow unto the Spirit this morning. He is gracious, and a grace-giving Spirit. He delights to exalt and honour Jesus. Let us therefore beseech Him in Jesus' name, for His sake, that we may bring honour unto His cause, to quicken our souls. Let us pray to Him to bring us near to God, for the nearer to God the happier, and holier, and livelier, we shall be. Let us ask Him to shed abroad the love of Jesus in our hearts, for the love of Christ will make us live well, bear the cross well, perform duties well, and die well. The command furnishes us with a rule, and the promise finds us strength; but it is only the Spirit that can put us in possession of the latter, and without that we cannot attend to the former, in a gospel spirit. The presence of Jesus and the communications of His grace are daily necessary to keep us lively, devoted, and working for God. Lord, quicken me thus.

I need the influence of Thy grace
To speed me in Thy way,
Lest I should loiter in my race,
Or turn my feet away.

🌿 EVENING 🌿

'Lord, help me'
MATTHEW 15:25

This prayer came from the heart of a poor woman, and it went to the heart of Jesus. It is brief, but comprehensive. It is always suitable, but at times especially so. It is a mercy to know and feel our weakness, for it is only then that we heartily cry to the Lord for strength. In every duty we have to perform, in every trial we have to meet, in every trouble through which we pass, under all the pains and sorrows we have to endure, we may consistently cry, 'Lord, help me.' We need the help of God; He has freely promised it. Let us therefore seek and receive it. Let this be our daily prayer: 'Help me to cleave to Jesus with full purpose of heart; help me to do Thy will, cheerfully and constantly; help me to persevere through all difficulties, and press towards the mark for the prize of my high calling; help me gratefully to acknowledge Thy hand in prosperity, and meekly to submit to Thy will in adversity; help me to conquer my foes, master the corruptions of my own heart, and resist all the temptations presented to me; help me quietly to wait all the days of my appointed time until my change come.' If such petitions are presented in faith, if they are the language of the soul, we may daily say, 'The Lord is my helper, I will not fear what man can do unto me.'

Lord, assist me with Thy grace,
Helpless at Thy feet to lie,
Well to close my various race,
Well to suffer, and to die.

APRIL 20

✿ MORNING ✿

'Christ hath made us free'
GALATIANS 5:1

We were once the slaves of sin, Satan, and the world; we were under the law as a covenant of life; but Jesus has made us free. We are now delivered from the law, and are under grace. We are dead to sin, and are justified from it. We are delivered from Satan, and are at war with him. We overcome the world, and are hastening out of it. We are at liberty to serve God, and walk with Him in friendship and holy love. The price of our freedom was the life and death of Jesus; the efficient cause of our freedom was the power and operation of the Holy Spirit; the grand moving cause, was the infinite and everlasting love of God our Father; the instrument by which we are made acquainted with our freedom, is the holy gospel; the grace which puts us into possession of our freedom is faith; and the end of our freedom is, that we may serve our God in righteousness and holiness all the days of our life, and then be glorified with Him for ever. We are freed from sin, that we may be holy; and are introduced to and accepted of God, that we may be happy. Let us stand fast in the liberty wherewith Christ hath made us free.

Sweet is the freedom Christ bestows,
With which He makes His people free;
A liberty no mortal knows,

Till they His great salvation see:
Freedom from wants, and fears, and cares,
From worldly lusts, and dangerous snares.

✿ EVENING ✿

'The LORD searcheth all hearts'
1 CHRONICLES 28:9

Solemn thought! Does He search my heart? What does He find there? Evil thoughts, foul corruptions, fearful depravity. But is this all? I trust not. There is some good thing towards the Lord God of Israel. All my thoughts are not evil, and those which are I hate. It is not all corruption; there is a little correcting truth. It is not all depravity, for there are good desires, hopes, fears, and a little faith. But if God search my heart, how necessary it is that I do so myself. Especially when the LORD says, 'Take heed to yourselves that your heart be not deceived.' Satan will deceive us if he can. He will try to conceal our defects, that he may lead us to presumption; and he will obscure our evidences, that he may drive us to despair. If the Lord searches all hearts, hypocrisy must be the height of folly. It is impossible to deceive Him. We may provoke His wrath, but we cannot impose upon His mercy. Let us then lay open our hearts before God. Let us daily seek the renewings of the Holy Spirit. Let us fly to the open fountain of a Saviour's blood, and daily wash in the laver of God's holy Word. Often let us cry with the psalmist, 'Examine me, O LORD.' And let us be sincere in all we profess, in all we say, and in all we do.

In all my vast concerns with Thee,
In vain my soul would try
To shun Thy presence, Lord, or flee
The notice of Thine eye.

APRIL 21

🌿 MORNING 🌿
'Walk humbly with thy God'
Micah 6:8

Pride is one of our greatest evils: to indulge it is to nourish a serpent in the bosom. The grace of God always humbles us; and it is only as we are humble that we can be happy. God condescends to walk with the humble man, but He keeps the proud at a distance. Consider what you were by nature, what now lurks in your heart, what you would have been but for the grace of God, and be humble. All you have is the gift of free grace; all you do that is good, is the effect of God's working in you. What have you to be proud of? What reason to boast? O, lie low in the dust of self-abasement; cherish humbling thoughts of yourself; admire the mercy, condescension, and infinite compassion of God, in noticing so vile, so unworthy a worm! Study the character and conduct of the humble Jesus, learn of Him, and endeavour to walk as He also walked. Serve the Lord in all humility of mind. But beware of spurious humility; that is not humility which rests contented without seeking for the utmost God has promised, or aiming at the highest duties God has commanded.

> By faith in Christ I walk with God,
> With heaven, my journey's end, in view;
> Supported by His staff and rod,
> My road is safe and pleasant too:
> Though earth and hell my course withstand,
> JEHOVAH guards me by His hand.

🌿 EVENING 🌿
'That he might bring us to God'
1 Peter 3:18

Such was the design of Jesus in all His engagements, labours, and sufferings for our sakes. By nature we are afar from God, opposed to God, afraid of God; consequently far from happiness and peace. Jesus knew the blessedness of being with God, and being like God. His love to His people led Him to desire for them the same blessedness. His desire was so strong, that He was willing to do or to suffer anything in order to put them in possession of it. He therefore voluntarily suffered for our sins, and put them away by the sacrifice of Himself. His aim was to bring us to God honourably, and to keep us with God eternally. He brings us to God on *the throne of grace*. Here we receive pardon, obtain peace, and enjoy paternal love. At this throne we obtain a supply for all our wants, the fulfilment of great and precious promises, and sweet manifestations of acceptance and favour. He will bring us to God on *the throne of glory*. Then we shall be perfectly holy and eternally happy. Then *He* will be satisfied, and we shall be satisfied too. What satisfies Him, will satisfy us, and in our satisfaction and happiness, He will rejoice. Our coming to God *now*, is the effect of His death; our being with God *for ever*, will be the reward of His pains.

> Yes, Jesus left the realms of day,
> Suffer'd and shed His blood;
> The awful ransom price to pay,
> And bring our souls to God!

APRIL 22

🌿 MORNING 🌿

'I will surely do thee good'
GENESIS 32:12

Though this promise was given to Jacob, it was not confined to him, but is intended for all his spiritual seed. It is thus God speaks to us this morning. How gracious! We know not what a day may bring forth, but we know our God, who superintends every event, will do us good. We may mistake as to what will be for our good, but He is infinite in wisdom and goodness, and therefore cannot. We may look at afflictions, losses, and crosses, and cry out, 'All these things are against me!' But read the history of David. What a train of troubles attended him! Hear his acknowledgement: 'It is *good* for me that I have been afflicted.' Thy God will do thee good; therefore He will try thee, sift thee, humble thee, and prove thee. He will give thee medicine as well as food. He will consider nothing too expensive, or too painful, if necessary for thy soul's welfare. Look at your trials, and say, 'This also shall turn to my salvation.' Look on the past, and acknowledge, 'Goodness and mercy have followed me all the days of my life.' Look to the future, and rejoice, 'The Lord will give that which is *good*.' Look in every direction, and say, 'I will trust and not be afraid.'

I cannot doubt His bounteous love,
So full, so free, so kind;
To His unerring, gracious will
Be every wish resign'd.

🌿 EVENING 🌿

'What shall I render unto the LORD?'
PSALM 116:12

A very suitable inquiry after a day's mercies. But though we attempt to render praise tonight, we ought not to confine our views to the day. Rather let us ask, 'What has the Lord conferred upon us?' *Benefits*. Blessings without which we could neither be happy, useful, or holy. He has given grace, scattered fears, wrought deliverances, sent supplies, confirmed our faith, and promised glory. Everything we receive is a benefit. It springs from free grace, flows to the undeserving, suits our case, and lays us under deep obligations. The Father has given us His Son. The Son has given us His perfect work. The Holy Spirit has given us life, and taken up His residence in our hearts. Then what shall we render? What *can* we? What are we *willing* to render? Have we gifts? Let us devote them to His service. Have we time? Let us employ it to His praise. Let us work in His vineyard, war against His foes, suffer in His cause, and give of our substance to His poor. What will be acceptable to God? That you walk closely with Him, spread His gospel, visit His sick ones, relieve His poor people, show your gratitude to Him as opportunity offers. In a word, live the life of a consecrated disciple.

What shall I render? Render praise,
Walk close with God in love;
Observe His precepts, keep His ways,
And all His will approve.

APRIL 23

🌿 MORNING 🌿
'Have faith in God'
MARK 11:22

You have His Word: believe it; plead it; expect the fulfilment of it. He cannot deceive you. His ear is open to you. Try Him. What do you want? Why do you want it? If you really need, if your motives are good, plead with God for it; expect Him to bestow it; and receive it as coming from Him. In every trial, for all you need, have faith in God. He will be gracious unto you. He is ever with you. He is ready to help you. He rejoices over you to do you good. His Word is true from the beginning. He is the faithful God. He keepeth covenant and mercy. Believe in God for all your circumstances require. Patiently wait His time for your supplies. Never give over praying or expecting because He delays; never doubt Him, but trust in Him with all thy heart. He is a God; He is thy God; He is able to do exceeding abundantly above all that we can ask or think. This is thy direction, thy duty, thy privilege: *Have faith in God*. Walk with God. Talk with God. Expect from God. Use all for God. Be entirely devoted to God. 'Casting all your care upon Him; for He careth for you.' 'Therefore will I look unto the Lord.'

> *Begone, unbelief! my Saviour is near;*
> *And for my relief will surely appear:*
> *By prayer let me wrestle, that He will perform;*
> *With Christ in the vessel, I smile at the storm.*

🌿 EVENING 🌿
'Let us draw near with a true heart'
HEBREWS 10:22

Distance from God is the effect of unbelief. It is the cause of coldness and discomfort. God is in the holiest. He is enthroned on the mercy seat. He has accepted the atoning sacrifice. Sin is for ever put away. Jesus has rent the veil. The way is open and free. Our High Priest is there with the blood, and the incense is burning in the golden censer. The heart of God towards us is true; it was no make-believe love that gave His beloved Son. Jesus also is true-hearted towards us, or He had never died for our sins, or entered heaven to plead in our behalf. Let us therefore be true-hearted towards God, and with deep sincerity and childlike simplicity draw near to God. We have liberty to tell out all our minds. We should not stand silent in the distance as awe-stricken servants, but we should draw near as the child which runs into its father's arms, and lays its head on its father's bosom. Let us not then stand at a distance, trembling as before an angry God; but let us draw near, exercising unhesitating, unwavering trust in God. He is not glorified by the fear of slaves, but by the peaceful confidence of children.

> *Trusting in our Redeemer's blood,*
> *Now let our souls draw near to God,*
> *Upon the mercy-seat;*
>
> *Boldly into the holiest come,*
> *And feel ourselves with God at home,*
> *Where truth and mercy meet.*

APRIL 24

🌿 MORNING 🌿
'I am the bread of life'
John 6:35

Jesus proposeth Himself to be our daily sustenance; we need bread for the soul as well as the body. In Jesus is all we need to refresh, strengthen, and satisfy us; but He must be received by faith. He must be daily received. Feeding upon Jesus yesterday will not do for today. We must go to Him afresh this morning. He presents Himself; He says, 'Eat, O friends; yea, satisfy yourselves, O my beloved.' If the Holy Spirit has given us a spiritual appetite, if we are hungering after righteousness, Jesus, and Jesus only, will satisfy us; and we are heartily welcome to live upon Him. Let us set Him before us many times in the day; let us endeavour to feed upon Him; and if we feel weak, faint, or weary, let us make use of this life-giving bread; and let us ever retain the sweet assurance, that if we feed on Jesus we shall live by Him, and have eternal life. Beloved, if you can make a living of anything but Jesus; or if Jesus is not enough in your estimation, you are either in a carnal, or an unhealthy state of soul. Jesus only is *the bread of life, the bread which came down from heaven!*

> *Jesus, Thou art the living bread*
> *By which our needy souls are fed,*
> *In Thee alone Thy children find*
> *Enough to fill the empty mind;*
> *O let me evermore be fed*
> *With this divine, celestial bread!*

🌿 EVENING 🌿
'A God at hand'
Jeremiah 23:23

The Christian has never far to run for a friend. The Lord is always near to him. He is a God at hand; present to observe; ready to help. This fact we should endeavour to realize. It would cheer us in gloom; preserve us in temptation; support us in trouble; raise us above our fears; keep us back from sin; encourage us in duty; prove a stimulus to exertion when ready to decline. Friends may be removed to a distance; so may my nearest relatives; but my God is at hand. He is present with heaven and earth at command. He is present to pity, to reprove, to counsel, and to sustain. But while He is near us, He is equally in every place; He is with our friends in distant places, and He is with our enemies in their most secret hiding-places. Therefore He will frustrate their designs, and overrule their opposition for our good. Let us retire tonight impressed with the thought: *'God is at hand.'* He will watch over me while I sleep; He will guard me; nothing can happen but what He permits; He is never taken by surprise; He sees everything at the greatest distance; and He stands pledged to make all things work together for my good. My soul, I charge thee never to forget that thy God is nigh at hand!

> *Lord, to my spirit's gaze reveal*
> *Thy perfect majesty and grace,*
> *And let my heart Thine influence feel,*
> *Unworthy to behold Thy face.*

APRIL 25

❧ MORNING ❧

'Who maketh thee to differ from another?'
1 Corinthians 4: 7

There is a wide difference between a Christian and a worldling: the one is dead in trespasses and sins; the other is alive unto God, by Jesus Christ our Lord. He has been quickened by the Son of God, is born of the Spirit, and taught by the eternal Father. He is a new creature, being created anew in Christ Jesus unto good works, which God had before ordained that we should walk in them. Who made this difference? You are at once ready to answer, if really taught of God, 'By the grace of God I am what I am.' 'Of his *own will* begat he me by the word of truth.' Yes, it was the rich, free, and sovereign grace of God, and that alone, that made you to differ. Grace was given you in Christ before the world began; and the Spirit was given you in time, that you might know and enjoy the things which are freely given unto you of God. O, beloved, view yourself as an infinite debtor to grace; be humble before God who has thus made you to differ; and pity, pray for, and strive to benefit those who are still without. 'Look unto the rock whence ye are hewn, and to the hole of the pit whence ye are digged.'

> *What was there in you that could merit esteem,*
> *Or give the Creator delight?*
> *'Twas 'Even so, Father,' you ever must sing,*
> *'Because it seem'd good in Thy sight!'*

❧ EVENING ❧

'Looking for that blessed hope.'
Titus 2:13

The posture of the Christian should be that of expectation. His best things are before him. The promises refer to the glory which is to be revealed. The Old Testament saints lived expecting Jesus to come; He came, He wrought, He suffered, He made the atonement, He prepared to depart, He promised to come again in glory, He went into the holiest, He is now making intercession, He will soon come out to impart the blessing. Then, the dead in Christ will rise, the living saints will be changed, the adoption will be obtained, we shall be caught up to meet the Lord in the air, and so shall we ever be with the Lord. This is the object of our hope. In expectation of this glory we should live. Looking for this blessed hope we should labour. Death is nowhere represented as the object of our hope; we are not to live looking for death, but for the coming of Jesus. Thus Enoch lived, walked with God, and so pleased Him that he was translated. Thus the apostles and primitive Christians lived, and therefore they were not so much affected as we are with *present things*.

> *Fill'd with the blessedness of hope,*
> *And love which casts out fear;*
> *Divinely taught my soul looks up,*
> *To see my Lord appear;*
>
> *Jesus, the one great God supreme,*
> *My Saviour shall come down,*
> *And find me gazing after Him,*
> *And with His glory crown.*

APRIL 26

🌿 MORNING 🌿
'Behold the man!'
JOHN 19:5

Jesus is presented before thee crowned with thorns, scourged, with His face so marred more than any man's. His blood is flowing, His heart is breaking, and He is a Man of sorrows. Behold Him, then, for in this Man, under these circumstances, dwelt all the fulness of the Godhead bodily; all the treasures of wisdom and knowledge. In Him the love of God centred and shone forth. He is the only foundation of His church's hopes, the only source of eternal salvation. He is Jehovah's first-born, His only-begotten Son, the express image of His person. He is thy Substitute, Surety, and Redeemer. He is the holy, harmless, and undefiled Lamb of God, taking away the sin of the world. Behold Him, for He here discloses the depth of His love; and teaches thee patience, meekness, and resignation under insult, suffering, and disgrace. O, behold Jesus, and be ashamed of complaining, of repining, or indulging any revengeful feelings. Behold, and imitate! Behold, and love! Behold, and adore!

Wounded head! back plough'd with furrows!
Visage marr'd! behold the Man!
Eyes, how dim! how full of sorrows;
Sunk with grief, behold the Man!

Lamb of God, led to the slaughter!
Melted, poured out like water:
Should not love my heart inflame,
Viewing Thee, Thou slaughter'd Lamb!

🌿 EVENING 🌿
'His heart was lifted up'
2 CHRONICLES 32:25

It swelled with pride, and was lifted up with vanity. Yet he was a good man, and had just received a remarkable proof of God's distinguishing love. We are by nature *so proud*, that we are always in danger of being unduly elevated if God favours us; or of taking offence at God's dealings if He please to try us. The strongest temptations often succeed the sweetest manifestations; therefore we ought to be on our guard. There is nothing that God hates more than pride; He cannot tolerate it; and yet it is the very thing to which we are most prone. A proud heart is sure to be unfruitful; only the humble bring forth the fruits of righteousness. Pride generates fretfulness, discontent, envy, ill-will, hardness of heart, and a thousand other evils. Let us therefore beware lest our hearts be lifted up, for if they are, God will be sure to pull them down, and the means, as in Hezekiah's case, may be very severe. If Satan can make us proud, he will soon make us prayerless; if we become prayerless, we shall soon be careless; and if careless, we put ourselves into Satan's power. Let us therefore consider what we were before we received grace, what we might have been but for grace, and what we certainly should be for ever, if God did not save us by grace, and so be humble.

Jesus to us the grace impart,
Which shone so bright in Thee;
The humble, meek, and lowly heart
From pride and envy free.

APRIL 27

🌿 MORNING 🌿

'I am He that comforteth you'
Isaiah 51:12

The Lord's people are often low and desponding; they do not live up to their privileges; the things of time make too deep an impression, because they do not sufficiently realize eternal things. But Jehovah is their *Comforter*; as such He presents Himself unto us this morning. He is the God of all comfort. He comforteth those who are cast down. To Him alone we must look for comfort. Looking to creatures for what God promises, dishonours Him; and at such times the creature may well ask, *'Am I in God's stead?'* Our God comforts us by His Son, whom He hath given to us; by the Spirit, which He pours out upon us; by His Word, in which He speaks to us; by His ordinances, in which He meets with us; and by His providence, when He appears for us. Let us look unto God as the author and giver of all comfort; let us plead with Him to comfort us according to His Word; and let us be suspicious of all comfort which does not come from Him, and lead to Him. He must be the centre to which we always tend, and the circumference within which we move.

Jesus, all our consolations
Flow from Thee, the sovereign good;
Love, and faith, and hope, and patience,
All are purchased by Thy blood;
Now Thy richest grace impart,
Sanctify and fill my heart.

🌿 EVENING 🌿

'Accepted in the beloved'
Ephesians 1:6

Jesus is the *Beloved One*. His Father loved Him infinitely and eternally. All His people who know Him, love Him. All that is loveable is found in Him, and *'He is altogether lovely.'* His person, His character, and His conduct, are most lovely. All His people approach God through Him, placing their entire dependence upon Him. They are united to His person, and are viewed as one with Him. Viewed in Him they are pleasant, acceptable, and lovely in the sight of God. He calls them *'all fair,'* and pronounces them to be without *'spot.'* My dear friends, in ourselves we are deformed, loathsome, and most offensive to infinite purity; but in Jesus we are clean, righteous and comely. As clothed with His righteousness, God pronounces us just; as filled with His Spirit, God calls us lovely. Never let us expect acceptance with God, but through Jesus; nor let us doubt our acceptance if we come unto God by Him; for Jehovah glorifies and commends His grace to universal admiration, by accepting us in *'the beloved.'* As believers, we are *now* accepted, nor shall we ever be more accepted; we may perceive our acceptance more clearly, and enjoy it more sweetly, but we shall never be more accepted than we are.

Accepted in Jesus, and perfectly too,
I fain would in all things my gratitude show,
I'd live to His honour, and walk in His light,
Till perfectly holy I stand in His sight.

APRIL 28

❦ MORNING ❧
'Though I be nothing'
2 CORINTHIANS 12: 11

This was Paul's estimate of himself: less than the least of all saints, and the chief of sinners. The more we know of ourselves and of Jesus, the more shall we be humbled in the dust before God; and the lower we lie before God, the happier and holier we shall be. Man will, *must* be something; this is his pride and his misery; the Christian is willing to be nothing, that Christ may be all in all. If we daily felt that we are nothing, how many mortifications we should be spared; what admiring views of the grace of God would fill and sanctify our souls. Apart from Christ we are less than nothing, but in Christ we are something. We are empty, but He fills us; naked, but He clothes us; helpless, but He strengthens us; lost, but He finds us; ruined, but He saves us; poor, but He supplies us. All we are, is by Christ; all we have, is from Christ; all we shall be, is through Christ. Believer, thou art nothing: therefore beware of thinking too highly of thyself, or fancying that you deserve more than you receive, either from God or men. Humble souls are soon satisfied.

> O could I lose myself in Thee,
> Thy depth of mercy prove,
> Thou vast unfathomable sea
> Of unexhausted love!
> I loathe myself when God I see,
> Content if Christ exalted be.

❦ EVENING ❧
'Kept by the power of God'
1 PETER 1:5

All the Lord's people feel that they need keeping, and therefore they pray to be kept. But it is not enough that we pray for keeping; we must believe the promises, expect their fulfilment, and seek for divine keeping in faith. The power of God is exerted on our behalf through faith. Believing, we grasp the promise, keep near the throne, walk with God, and are kept in dangers and death. Unbelief departs from God, questions His promise, wanders from the throne, and we fall into folly and sin. 'Take heed, therefore, lest there be in any of you an evil heart of unbelief, in departing from the living God. But exhort one another daily, while it is called *today*; lest any of you be hardened through the deceitfulness of sin.' God will not keep you as brutes, but as rational beings; He will not hold you in with bit and bridle, as the driver does the horse or mule, but He will lead you as beloved children, and keep you as intelligent disciples. His power is necessary. His power is pledged to you. But it is only pledged to believers. It is only pledged to believers as exercising faith, hope, and prayer.

> See the power of God to save!
> Jesu's grace in me admire,
> Kept, like Peter, on the wave,
> Kept, like Shadrach, in the fire.
> Rescued from the lion's teeth,
> Safe within the jaws of death.

APRIL 29

❧ MORNING ❧
'But thou art rich'
REVELATION 2:9

Real saints always feel themselves to be poor sinners. Many of God's people are really poor in reference to the things of time, for God hath chosen the poor of this world, rich in faith, and heirs of the kingdom which He hath promised to them that love Him. They are often persecuted, tried, tempted and cast down; so was the church in Smyrna; but Jesus says to her, 'Thou art rich.' So are all the Lord's people: rich by *relation* – God is their Father, and Jesus their elder Brother; rich by *donation* – Jesus has bequeathed unsearchable riches to them; rich by *promises* – the Lord has promised all good things; rich by *faith* – for he that believeth shall inherit all things; rich in *expectation* – for they look for a city which hath foundations, whose builder and maker is God. Believer, thou art rich; Jesus has willed to thee His righteousness, to justify thee; His blood, to cleanse thee; His Spirit to sanctify thee; His name to procure for thee; His angels to minister unto thee; and His heaven to be thy everlasting habitation. Precious Saviour! I would admire and adore Thy love! O teach me to live out of self on Thy fulness!

> Call'd by grace, the sinner see,
> Rich, though sunk in poverty;
> Rich in faith that God has given,
> He's a legal heir of heaven.

❧ EVENING ❧
'Thou sayest, I am rich'
REVELATION 3:17

It is one thing for the Lord to assure His poor people that they are rich, on account of the provision He has made for them; and another for the conceited, lukewarm professor to say, 'I am rich.' Spiritual persons are always sensible of their poverty, and they are taught to live out of self upon the fulness of Christ for all they need. It is always a bad sign when we begin to admire our gifts, graces, actions, or usefulness; for it is evident that we have taken our eye off the Lord Jesus Christ, and Satan will soon gain advantage over us. We are never so safe, or so happy, as when we lie at the Saviour's feet, sensible of our poverty, and seek from His fulness grace to perform every action, and to enjoy every privilege. Those who fancy that they are rich, are declared by the Saviour to be poor, wretched, miserable, blind and naked; but He counsels them to buy of Him gold tried in the fire, white raiment, and eye-salve that they may see. Let *us* then beware of boasting of any attainments we fancy we have made. 'Blessed are ye poor, for yours is the kingdom of heaven.' Woe unto you that are rich, for ye have received your consolation.

> Saviour! my misery I confess, | Wretched, and blind, and stript of all,
> I deeply feel my want of grace, | O save me, at Thy feet I fall,
> A needy sinner I! | Or else I pine and die.

APRIL 30

🌿 MORNING 🌿

'That which I see not teach thou me'
Job 34:32

We were once blind, but now our eyes are open; but still we are absolutely dependent on divine teaching, or we shall never become truly wise. If God teach us, self will become vile; the world vanity; sin bitter; the blood of Christ most precious; His righteousness glorious; His name our only hope; His love our joy; His Spirit our strength; His glory our aim; and 'Teach thou me,' our daily prayer. We see but little of what Christ is in Himself; of what He hath done for His people; of what He possesses, and will give to all who call upon Him in truth; of what He has promised to work in us, and bestow upon us. Beloved, let us daily plead with God to teach us, that we may know Christ, and the power of His resurrection, and the fellowship of His sufferings, and be made conformable to His death. Let us beg the Spirit of wisdom and revelation in the knowledge of Christ, that we may know what is the hope of His calling, and what is the riches of the glory of His inheritance in the saints. Jehovah alone can teach us to profit.

O Jesus, teach my soul to know
Thyself, the Truth, the Life, the Way;
May I in grace and knowledge grow,
Till I arrive in perfect day:
From Satan, self, and sin set free,
And what I know not teach Thou me.

🌿 EVENING 🌿

'Blessed are the meek'
Matthew 5:5

Meekness is very different to weakness, and yet the one is sometimes mistaken for the other. The strongest minds are sometimes adorned with the grace of meekness. The meek quietly submit to the will of God, they reverence His Word, and tremble at His rod. Instead of the spirit rising against God, and murmuring at His dispensations, it bows like the yielding plant to the breeze, and says, 'The will of the Lord be done.' The meek silently receive God's commands, patiently copy the Saviour's example, and wisely cherish the influences of the Holy Spirit. They walk softly with God, and prudently with men; not seeking their own glory, but the honour of their God and Saviour. They are quiet lambs, not roaring lions; gentle doves, not destroying vultures. They benefit all around them, as the sheep; not bite and devour, as the wolf. Such are *like* Christ, and they are blessed *with* Christ. They can claim but little now, but they shall inherit the earth by and by. Their very state of mind is a blessing; they live above the storms that agitate others, or bow while others break. They are cool, while others are hot; resigned, while others resist; at rest, while others are anxious; and are a blessing, while others are a curse.

Jesus, to my poor sinful heart
The grace of meekness now impart!
Fain would I, Lord, though poor and weak,
Be like Thyself, in all things meek.

MAY 1

🌿 MORNING 🌿

'I ... will be a Father unto you'
2 Corinthians 6:18

No man can be a loser by adhering to God's holy Word, for he is promised a hundred-fold in the present life, and in the world to come life everlasting. Carnal connections must be broken off. Decision of character must be manifested. The world must be forsaken. Christ and the world will not unite. Carnality and spirituality cannot be reconciled. Our God says, 'Come out from among them, and be ye separate; ... touch not the unclean thing; and I will receive you, and will be a *Father* unto you.' What can we need more to encourage, embolden, and produce decision? Suppose men reject me, despise me, and persecute me; God will receive me. Suppose they injure me and try to starve me; God will be a Father to me. He will care for me, protect me, dwell with me, comfort me, supply me, and fill a Father's place. I cannot be friendless. I should not be fearful. Beloved, God says, '*Prove me.*' Are you called upon to forsake friends, to break off connections, lose trade, or endure persecutions? Fear not, act for God, look to God; He will receive you, and be a Father unto you.

> And wilt Thou, Lord, a Father be,
> To those who leave the world for Thee?
> Wilt Thou provide for every want,
> And tokens of Thy favour grant?
> Then, Lord, I bid the world farewell!
> And now Thy Word in me fulfil.

🌿 EVENING 🌿

'Ye ought to please God'
1 Thessalonians 4:1

Nothing can be more reasonable. Nothing can be more profitable. He is our Father. He continually consults our welfare. He has made provision for all our wants. He seeks to profit us, and we ought to seek to please Him. My friend, do you realize the importance of pleasing God? Do you desire to please Him, to please Him well in all things? Then rest alone for acceptance on the finished work of Christ. Believe the love that He hath to you. Receive His promises as worthy of the strongest confidence. Approach His throne often, but always expecting to be heard and answered for the sake of Jesus. Consult His Word to ascertain His will, and whenever you discover anything to be the will of God, *do it*; do it promptly; do it cheerfully; do it just because He requires it; do it without asking why it is required; do it with a view to please Him. Bow with submission to all the dispensations of His providence, and endeavour to centre all your desires, plans, and aims in this one object, *to glorify Him*. This *will* please Him. This *must* please Him. This always *has* pleased Him. You *ought* to please Him, you *owe* Him so much, you *expect* so much from Him, and you have *professed* so much.

> My soul, THIS point pursue,
> Make THIS thy business here,
> Thy God to please, His will to do,
> In faith, with love and fear.

MAY 2

🌱 MORNING 🌿
'But grow in grace'
2 Peter 3:18

Never rest satisfied with present attainments. God has much to bestow, and we are capable of receiving, enjoying, and using it to His glory. As the tree planted in a good soil grows both in the root and the branches, so should the Christian; he should be rooted in the love of God, and grow up in conformity to Jesus. If we grow in grace, we shall discover more of our own wretchedness, misery, and weakness; and more of the preciousness, fulness, and glory of Christ. We shall be humble before God, and active before men. We shall trust in Jesus more simply, having no confidence in the flesh. Grace always leads out of self to Jesus, and puts the crown of crowns upon His head. Grace is spiritual beauty; it is the very glory of God. To grow in grace is to grow like Jesus, meek and lowly in heart; active and devoted in life; blameless and harmless as the sons of God. Let us have grace, for God loves to bestow it; let us grow in grace, for God commands it; let us look forward for the grace that is to be brought unto us at the coming of Jesus, for God has promised it. Look for that blessed hope, even the glorious appearing of Jesus.

> Though holy deeds and fruits of grace
> Are in believers found,
> 'Tis Christ's command, that they increase
> And more and more abound;
> O Saviour, may I grow in grace,
> Till I behold Thee face to face!

🌱 EVENING 🌿
'Ye are no more strangers'
Ephesians 2:19

Grace has wrought a wonderful change in us, as well as wrought a wonderful work for us. We were once strangers to God, far off from peace, and unacquainted with the privileges of true religion. We were made nigh by the blood of Christ; reconciled to God by the death of His Son; led into the knowledge of His will by the Holy Spirit; created anew in Christ Jesus unto good works. Once everything in real religion was strange to us, and we were strangers to it. We did not understand its doctrines, we knew nothing of its experience, and we thoroughly disliked its practices. But now we *know* God. We are *one* with Jesus. We enjoy the *communion* of the Holy Spirit. We are *united* to the saints. We are become *citizens* of Zion. We feel at *home* in its ordinances. We *enjoy* its privileges. We are become *familiar* with the Word of God, the throne of grace, the open fountain, the way of peace, the wedding garment, and the peculiar conflict of the sons of God. We are a part of God's sanctified family, of the Saviour's folded flock. Divine things are become natural to us, and we love them, live upon them, and enjoy them. Brethren, ye were once in darkness, but are now light in the Lord; walk as children of the light.

> No more a stranger to the Lord,
> His family or throne;
> I trust His grace, believe His Word,
> And live to Him alone.

MAY 3

🌿 MORNING 🌿

'Is thy counsellor perished?'
Micah 4:9

The Lord's people need counsel, and Jesus is given to them as a *Counsellor*. He is exactly suited to their needs, being possessed of infinite wisdom, unbounded benevolence, great experience, and high honour. He never lost a cause. He counsels freely, cheerfully, and successfully. He turns the counsel of all our foes into foolishness. But though we have this wonderful Counsellor, we neglect to consult, employ or trust Him; and it may often be demanded of us, 'Is thy counsellor perished?' If not, why this perplexity? Why these mistakes? Why those fears and groans, and forebodings? Why this running to creatures for advice and succour? Beloved, let us stand reproved; we have walked in our own counsels; we have not *waited* for His counsel; we have neglected and forgotten Jesus in His office. Let us in future never act without His counsel, never employ men to His dishonour, never listen to Satan when he would persuade us not to apply to, trust in, and expect advice from Jesus as our *Counsellor*. He says, 'I will counsel thee; Mine eye shall be upon thee.'

> Lord, be my Counsellor,
> My Pattern, and my Guide;
> And through this desert land,
> Still keep me near Thy side;
> O let my feet ne'er run astray
> Nor rove, nor seek the crooked way.

🌿 EVENING 🌿

'The sin which doth so easily beset us'
Hebrews 12:1

Every Christian hath his easily besetting sins. Often do those prove so to which he has been the slave in his unconverted state. But there is one sin to which we are all peculiarly liable; it is called, 'The sin which doth so easily beset us.' This is *distrust of God*; the great hindrance in our heavenly race; the weight that obstructs our progress; the disease which weakens our powers; the cloud which fills us with gloom. God has revealed His character, He has pledged that character; He has raised up a great cloud of witnesses, all of whom attest His faithfulness; He has made promise upon promise, and all to encourage our confidence. Still we doubt Him. Continually do we mistrust Him. Yet nothing injures us more, nothing dishonours Him more. Therefore the apostle exhorts us 'to lay aside the sin which doth so easily beset us.' Leave off distrusting God. Exercise unhesitating confidence in God's Word and faithfulness. In this imitate Abraham among the patriarchs, Moses under the law, and Jesus the great example of faith under the gospel. You never will be strong, or patient, or vigorous in the Lord's ways, except you leave off distrusting God.

> O Lord, with sorrow I confess,
> I have distrusted Thee;
> Yet, now bestow the needful grace,
> That I may faithful be.

MAY 4

🌿 MORNING 🌿
'I will heal your backslidings'
Jeremiah 3:22

Sin brings sickness. The believer can only be healthful as he walks with God, lives above the world, and looks for the coming of our Lord Jesus Christ. At the feet of Jesus we are safe, and shall be healthy; but if we wander from Him, spiritual diseases will seize upon us. The backslider feels too weak to run in the way of God's commands; too confused to read his interest in God's promises; too guilty to call God Father; too wretched to rejoice in hope. He has no liberty in prayer; no enjoyment of his Bible; no peace in his conscience; no delight in God's ways. But the LORD says, 'Return, ye backsliding children; *I will heal your backslidings.*' This is a message from the great *Physician*, an invitation from our Father's throne, a promise of our Saviour's love. O, let us return unto Him with weeping and supplication, adopting David's prayer as our own, 'Heal my soul, for I have sinned against thee.' Let us take up the determination of the church, 'Behold, we come unto thee, for thou art the LORD our God.' He will receive us graciously, and love us freely.

> *Give me Thy pardoning love to feel,*
> *And freely my backslidings heal,*
> *Repair my faith's decay:*
> *Restore the sweetness of Thy grace,*
> *Reveal the glories of Thy face*
> *And take my sins away.*

🌿 EVENING 🌿
'A very present help in trouble'
Psalm 46:1

Religion is never so valuable as in seasons of trouble, sickness, or death. Then we want something which nature cannot supply; and this something true religion presents. Our God is our help in trouble. He helps us to bear it. He helps us to improve it. He helps us through it. His choicest communications and sweetest manifestations are afforded in times of trial and distress. Believer, thy God is thy refuge and strength, a very present help in trouble. He is never nearer than when you fancy that He stands afar off; He is never kinder than when you think He hath shut up His lovingkindness in displeasure. Do not doubt His love. Do not mistake His dealings. Do not listen to His foe. Do not forget His Word. But remember, if trouble comes, grace comes with it; and your God *is present* to help you to rise above it, and to derive solid advantage from it. Believe, when you cannot see. Trust, when you do not feel. Wait, when you do not receive a message from God. Your good is consulted in every trouble, and your God will be glorified by every trial. The Lord of hosts is with you; the God of Jacob is your refuge. Therefore fear not, neither be dismayed.

> *Jehovah, thy refuge and rock,*
> *In trouble, His help shall supply;*
> *Though earth be remov'd with a shock,*
> *Still God, thy Redeemer, is nigh.*

MAY 5

🌿 MORNING 🌿

'Being in an agony'
LUKE 22:44

Beloved, let us visit Gethsemane this morning, and see this strange sight. Here is our *Surety*, the only-begotten Son of God; the brightness of Jehovah's glory, and the express image of His person; groaning on the cold ground, and baptized in blood. He is sore amazed. His heart is filled with horror, and His mind with dread. His soul is troubled, tossed with tempests and not comforted. He is exceeding sorrowful, even unto death. The sorrows of death encompass Him, and the pains of hell have gotten hold upon Him. His heart like wax is melted in the midst of His bowels. His whole nature is convulsed. He sweats blood. He cries aloud, with an exceeding bitter cry, and His heart faileth Him. No human hand toucheth Him; but it is the hour and power of darkness. Our sins meet upon Him; His soul is made an offering for our sins; and it hath pleased Jehovah to bruise Him. Was ever sorrow like unto His sorrow? *He is 'in an agony.'* Here our sins are punished, our iniquities are expiated, and our justification is procured. O, to love Jesus, even to an agony!

> *Go to dark Gethsemane,*
> *Ye that feel the tempter's power;*
> *Your Redeemer's conflict see,*
> *Watch with Him one bitter hour;*
> *Turn not from His griefs away;*
> *Learn of Jesus Christ to pray.*

🌿 EVENING 🌿

'Reconciled to God by the death of his Son'
ROMANS 5:10

By nature our hearts were enmity against God, and in our lives we were enemies to Him by wicked works. Whatever He required, we avoided doing; and whatever He prohibited, we practised. Nothing could be more opposite to God than we were before called by His grace; and yet, while we were altogether sinners, Christ died for us. In dying for us, or in our stead, He did all that was requisite to reconcile us to God; so that when we see our state, feel our condition, and desire to be at peace with God, we have only to believe in Him, plead His death with the Father, and we are honourably reconciled. All our sins are forgiven us for His sake. We are accepted of God, solely on the ground of what He did and suffered. We are treated as if we had done what He did, because He did it for us, and it is imputed to us as soon as ever we build upon it, place confidence in it, and plead it before God for our acceptance. We *are* reconciled to God. We *are* His friends. He *is* our loving Father. He *has* accepted what Jesus did for us. He delights in us. He rejoices over us. He is preparing us to dwell with Him.

> *The glorious work is done,*
> *The firm foundation laid:*
> *Our God hath sent His Son,*
> *The Son His life hath paid;*
> *Justice and mercy fram'd the plan*
> *That reconcileth sinful man.*

MAY 6

❦ MORNING ❦

'Pray without ceasing'
1 Thessalonians 5:17

In prayer we must approach God as a Father, ask of Him what we really need, and expect to receive according to His wisdom and Word. Our wants are constantly returning; therefore our prayers should be constantly ascending. The ear of God is always open. He is ever ready to listen to us. He invites, exhorts, and commands us to pray always, in everything. Every object that meets the eye, every circumstance that occurs, every employment in which we engage, would afford matter for prayer if properly viewed. The believer should acquire the *habit* of prayer. He should look up to his God for all he needs, through all he sees, whenever he has a moment to spare. The prayers of a Christian are pleasant to his God; He says, 'Let me hear thy voice,' let me see thy countenance; '... for sweet is thy voice, and thy countenance is comely.' The believer should pray as naturally and as constantly as he breathes, for prayer is the breath of the soul. Beloved, if prayer dwindle into a mere duty, is but occasionally offered, or becomes burdensome, it is clear that you are in a most unhealthy state.

*Through the skies when the thunder
is hurl'd,
The child to its parent will flee;
Thus, amid the rebukes of the world,*

*I turn, O my Father, to Thee;
The spirit of prayer in Thy mercy impart,
And take up Thy constant abode
in my heart.*

❦ EVENING ❦

'The God of all comfort'
2 Corinthians 1:3

We are poor comfortless creatures in ourselves. We often seek comfort in the things of time, and meet with painful disappointment. Sin has banished all true comfort and solid happiness from our world. While God is excluded, comfort is excluded. Distance from God is distance from comfort. Our God is the Happy One. He is also the happy-making One. His comforts are pure, spiritual, and lasting. His comforts delight the soul. One ray of light from His countenance, one word of peace from His lips, will give more solid comfort than all earthly things. We must learn to live out of self upon our God for comfort, or we shall never know permanent happiness. He is willing to comfort us. He says of His Zion, 'I will comfort all her waste places.' He promises His disconsolate people, 'as one whom his mother comforteth, so will I comfort you, and ye shall be comforted in Jerusalem.' He commands His servants, 'Comfort ye, comfort ye my people ... Speak ye comfortably to Jerusalem.' He sent His beloved Son into our world 'to comfort all that mourn;' and it is of His favour that we enjoy 'the comforts of the Holy Ghost.' Let us ever bear in mind, that it is our God 'who comforteth those that are cast down,' and that He will comfort us.

*My God to me the grace impart,
Which all that mourn receive;
The only Comforter Thou art,
Who only can'st forgive.*

MAY 7

🌿 MORNING 🌿

'O Israel, thou shall not be forgotten of me'
ISAIAH 44:21

What tenderness, mercy, and love are here! Friends forget us, relatives are careless about us, and we sometimes fear our God has forgotten us; but here He assures us that we shall never be forgotten of Him. Our names are in His book, our Representative is always before His throne, and we are the objects of His constant care. He cannot forget us while Jesus pleads for us; and if He does not forget, He will never neglect. There is only one thing He is ever said to forget, and that is our sins; but He is always mindful of His covenant. He will not forget the circumstances in which we are placed, the wants by which we are pained, or the prayers we put up at His throne. But though we are assured our God will never forget us, yet we can find no satisfaction, but as the Holy Spirit humbles us, empties us, and exalts Christ before us, showing us our pardon, peace, and salvation in His life, death, and intercession. Beloved, let us mind the things of the Spirit, and daily seek humbling, quickening, and sanctifying grace.

O Lord, my God! Whose sovereign love
Is still the same, nor e'er can move;
Look to the covenant, and see,
Has not Thy love been shown to me?
Remember me, my glorious Friend,
And love me always to the end.

🌿 EVENING 🌿

'Beware lest thou forget the LORD'
DEUTERONOMY 6:12

We are prone to commit this sin, especially in temporal prosperity. We forget our infinite obligation to Him; our absolute dependence upon Him; our accountableness to Him. To make use of the knowledge we possess, we should daily remember to acknowledge Him in all things; to apply to Him for all we need, under all we suffer; to commit ourselves and our cause unto Him; to endeavour in all things and by all means to please Him; to expect His promised interposition in trials, and supplies in need. Let us henceforth beware lest we forget the Lord, for it dishonours Him. It deeply grieves Him. It is injurious to us, for it generates timidity or hardness; insincerity or worldliness; foreboding and prayerlessness; ingratitude and self-righteousness. To prevent this crying sin, let us open each day with solemn prayer and devout meditation on some portion of God's Word; let us cultivate the habit of ejaculatory prayer; let us always endeavour to have some suited subject ready at hand for meditation, some portion of Scripture, or some attribute of God, or some office of Christ, or some merciful providence, or some merciless foe, or some possible danger. 'Beware lest thou forget the Lord.'

Forget the Lord! and can it be
That I should so ungrateful prove;
Alas! I have forgotten Thee
Too long, too oft, Thou God of love.

MAY 8

🌿 MORNING 🌿

'Wait on the LORD, and He shall save thee'
PROVERBS 20:22

Beloved, it is your privilege in every perplexity and trial to go to the Lord, to spread your case before Him, to plead His precious promises, and to wait expecting Him to appear for you. Wait on Him for light to discover the nature and design of your trouble; for wisdom that you may act honourably, and endure scripturally; for power to sustain you under, and bring you through it; and for consolation to make you happy and resigned under it. Wait upon the Lord in earnest, simple, persevering prayer; in searching, reading, and meditating upon His holy Word; in self-examination as to your views, motives, and designs. Wait upon the Lord, believing that He will fulfil His Word, answer your prayers, and send you deliverance, patiently enduring until He shall see good to appear on your behalf. Waiting on the Lord you engage Him on your side; you put His mercy and faithfulness to the trial; you are assured your strength shall be renewed; and God has promised you shall never be ashamed. Beloved, let us look to, trust in, and wait upon our God continually.

> O teach me, Lord, to wait Thy will,
> To be content with all Thou dost;
> For me Thy grace sufficient still,
> With most supplied when needing most;
> O Saviour! give me grace to wait,
> And daily watch before Thy gate.

🌿 EVENING 🌿

'Having food and raiment let us therewith be content'
1 TIMOTHY 6:8

We cannot really *want* more, and if God see fit to withhold, we ought not even to *wish* for more. But our food may be coarse, and our raiment very common. What then! If we have God's blessing, if we enjoy His presence, we are better off than if we possessed a kingdom without them. If God gave us no more, we ought to believe that more would be injurious to us. God either loves us, or He does not. He cares for us. He provides for us, or He leaves things to chance. If we are believers in Jesus, God certainly does love us, He does care for us, He does provide for us; if He has numbered the very hairs of our head, fixed the bounds of our habitation, promised to supply all our needs, He cannot have left anything to chance. But such is the case. Let us then be content with such things as we have. Let us learn *in every state* therewith to be content. Let us bear in mind that godliness with contentment is great gain, or a good fortune. Remember that it is written, that *'all things* that pertain to life and godliness,' are given to us through the knowledge of our Lord Jesus Christ, so that knowing Jesus, we may expect all that is necessary to 'a godly life,' and ought therewith to be content.

> Great things are not what I desire,
> Nor rich repast, nor gay attire;
> Content with little would I be;
> That little, Lord, must come from Thee.

MAY 9

🌿 MORNING 🌿
'The glory of his grace'
EPHESIANS 1:6

The glory of grace is its *freeness*: it fixes upon objects that are most unworthy; bestows upon them the richest blessings; raises them to the highest honour; promises them the greatest happiness; and all for its own glory. Nothing can be freer than grace. The glory of grace is its *power*: it conquers the stubbornest sinner; subdues the hardest hearts; tames the wildest wills; enlightens the darkest understandings; breaks off the strongest fetters; and invariably conquers its objects. Grace is omnipotent. The glory of grace is its *benevolence*: it never injured one; it has delivered, supplied, conducted, supported, and glorified thousands; it brings the inexhaustible fulness of God to supply the creature's wants; it opens the treasury of heaven, to enrich poor, miserable, and wretched creatures on earth. Grace gives away all it has, reserving nothing for itself but the praise and glory of its acts. Jesus is grace personified; in Him it may be seen, in all its beauty, excellency, and loveliness; by Him it is displayed in all its native dignity. O Jesus! Glorify Thy free, powerful, and benevolent grace in me!

> O grace, thou bottomless abyss,
> My sins are swallow'd up in Thee;
> Cover'd is my unrighteousness;
>
> From condemnation I am free:
> For Jesus' blood, through earth and skies,
> Mercy, eternal mercy, cries.

🌿 EVENING 🌿
'God dealeth with you as with sons'
HEBREWS 12:7

In what He bestows, and in what He withholds; in what you suffer, and in what you enjoy, your God has made you His children by adopting you into His family, and new-creating you by His Holy Spirit. He ever looks upon you as children, loves you as children, treats you as children. He will not trust you with what will harm you, or where you will be in danger. He corrects you as a child, not in wrath, but in mercy. He never trusts the rod out of His own hand. Whatever is the means, your Father is the agent. He works *all things* after the counsel of His own will. You are at present under training: you are being educated for eternity. The lessons you have to learn *now*, are for your benefit and honour in the *future*. Every loss, every cross, every disappointment, every pain is necessary. Do you believe this? Do you recognize the hand of God in what befalls you? Can you say with Job, 'The LORD gave': health, wealth, children, friends, prospects; 'and the LORD hath taken away; blessed be the name of the LORD!' Or with Eli, 'It is the LORD, let Him do what seemeth Him good.' Your circumstances cannot be more trying, but your privileges are much greater.

> Whoe'er their heavenly Father fears,
> His loving chastisements sustain;
> Not one of all His children here
>
> Is privileg'd from grief and pain;
> Not one but feels in deep distress
> This token of paternal grace.

MAY 10

🌿 MORNING 🌿
'He doth not afflict willingly'
LAMENTATIONS 3:33

Our afflictions do not flow from sovereignty, but from our Father's wisdom, holiness and love. He finds no pleasure in our pains, groans, and sighs. He is never hasty in using the rod; mercy flies to help us, but He is slow to anger and of great kindness. He never afflicts us without a sufficient cause; either sin has been committed; duties neglected; mercies slighted; lukewarmness discovered; worldly-mindedness tolerated; privileges abused; warnings despised; temptations trifled with; or danger is near. He never afflicts without a good and gracious intention, to make us fear, loathe, and flee from sin; to show His disapprobation of our unholy course; to quicken us in His ways; to make us long for, seek, and partake of His holiness; to produce contrition and godly sorrow; or to prove that His authority is not surrendered because His love is great. He only afflicts partially, occasionally, and sparingly. He always strikes in love, and aims at our spiritual welfare; and we are often more benefited by afflictions, than we are by comforts and joys. O Saviour, sanctify to me every afflicting stroke.

In the floods of tribulation,
While the billows o'er me roll,
Jesus whispers consolation,
And supports my fainting soul:
Sweet affliction,
Thus to bring my Saviour near.

🌿 EVENING 🌿
'Your sorrow shall be turned into joy'
JOHN 16:20

The sorrow of the disciples was occasioned by the sufferings and death of their beloved Lord, and their sorrow was turned into joy when He arose from the dead, and manifested unto them His love. The sorrow of the Christian must be transient. It is like the passing cloud on the summer's day, or the chill of winter which must give place to the genial warmth of spring. Beloved, if you now have sorrow, your sorrow also shall soon be turned into joy; for joy is sown for the righteous, and gladness for the upright in heart. Heaviness may endure for the night, but joy cometh in the morning. Thy risen Saviour will appear to thee, and pronounce the words of peace. Thy God who may now hide Himself from thee, will appear to thy joy, and thou shalt not be ashamed. The sin that causes thy sorrow shall be pardoned and subdued. The foes that disturb thy peace shall be converted or destroyed. The clouds that obscure thy sun shall soon dissolve in showers of blessing on thy favoured head. The distance between thee and thy home will soon be passed; the days of thy mourning will be ended, and thou who now goest forth weeping, bearing precious seed, shall soon return with songs of everlasting joy.

On Jesus' plighted love,
In every state rely;
The very hidings of His face
Shall train thee up for joy.

MAY 11

❦ MORNING ❧

'Rejoice in the Lord alway'
Philippians 4:4

This is a very difficult precept; sometimes the Lord hides His face; we fear and doubt our interest in His love; we are almost bewildered through the powerful workings of corruption within us; we are bowed down by Satan's sore temptations; and the dispensations of providence are so perplexing, that we are ready to cry out, 'All things are against us.' But we are not bidden to rejoice in frames and feelings, or in the dispensations of providence, but in the Lord. He has loved us with an everlasting love, and His love is immutably the same; He is our God in Jesus, and has promised to be unto us, to do for us, and freely give us, all that our circumstances require, or that will be for our good and His glory. In weakness we may rejoice in His power; in darkness we may rejoice that He knoweth our path; in sickness and sorrow, that He careth for us; and under any circumstances, in His covenant relations; for He is always our Father, Friend, and God. We should rejoice in His free grace, rich mercy, omnipotent power, faithful promises, special providence, and unchangeable love.

> Rejoice in glorious hope!
> Jesus, the Judge, shall come,
> And take His servants up
> To their eternal home;
> We soon shall hear the archangel's voice,
> The trump of God shall sound, 'REJOICE.'

❦ EVENING ❧

'Him that loved us'
Romans 8:37

There is something peculiarly sweet and pleasant in being the object of another's love. No condition can possibly be more dreary than to feel that no one loves or cares for us. Even the love of a child is sweet. But to be loved by one who is wealthy, exalted in station, and honourable in character, must be peculiarly delightful. How, then, should *we* rejoice; how happy should *we* be who are the loved ones of the Lord Jesus! When we consider, on the one hand, how mean, how poor, how worthless, and how unlovely we are; and, on the other, how glorious, how wealthy, how worthy, how lovely He is. To be loved of Jesus, is to be preferred before the possession of a world. Think of the glory of His person, the vastness of His possessions, the number of His attendants, the unlimited sovereignty which He exercises, and the excellent character He bears. Bear in mind, that He knew what loving us would cost Him, how He would be treated by us and by others for our sakes. Yet He fixed His love upon us. He loved just because He would. There were others more dignified in nature, more exalted in station, but *He chose us.* He did not, could not need us, for He was infinitely happy and glorious without us. Yet He loved us. He still loves us.

> Resting on Christ, secure we stand,
> His love shall order all things well;
> We soon shall gain the promised land,
> Triumphant o'er the powers of hell.

MAY 12

❦ MORNING ❦

'Their righteousness is of me, saith the LORD'
Isaiah 54:17

The longer the Christian lives, the more he learns; and the more the Spirit teaches him, the more he loathes himself and renounces his own righteousness as filthy rags. He hoped sensibly to grow in holiness, to feel his corruptions subdued, and to enjoy without interruption the presence of his God; but instead of this he seems to grow more like Satan, corruption appears to get stronger and stronger, and the depravity of his nature appears so dreadful, that he enjoys scarcely anything. He thinks himself a monster of iniquity, and wonders how God can possibly love him, or show any favour unto him. This experience endears free grace, renders Christ unspeakably precious, and the gift of righteousness invaluable. How can such a man be just before God? Where is his righteousness to come from? Jehovah answers, 'His righteousness is of Me.' Jesus wrought it; the Father imputes it to us; the gospel reveals it; and faith receives it, puts it on, and pleads it before God. O Jesus! in Thee have I righteousness and strength.

> *My hope is built on nothing less*
> *Than Jesus' blood and righteousness;*
> *I dare not trust the sweetest frame;*
> *But wholly lean on Jesus' name;*
> *On Christ, the solid Rock, I stand;*
> *All other ground is sinking sand.*

❦ EVENING ❦

'Fear not, little flock'
Luke 12:32

The Saviour's flock is small. It is in the desert. Enemies surround it. His lambs, especially, are timid. But He says, 'Fear not.' You are your Shepherd's care, you are His property, you are His delight. He is always present; He is omnipotent to defend you. Every perfection of His nature is employed for you. He never lost one of His charge yet; He never will. It was said of Him by the prophet, 'He shall feed His flock like a shepherd: He shall gather the lambs with His arm, and carry them in His bosom, and shall gently lead those that are with young.' He gathers His sheep to His fold, He feeds them in good pasture, He restores them when they wander; He makes them pass under the rod, and marks them as His own. His care of them is incessant; His love to them passes knowledge. The provision He has made for them is suitable and abundant. Beloved, let us know our Shepherd, let us listen to His voice, let us keep close to His side, let us feed and rest among His sheep, let us exercise confidence in His kindness and care, let us banish our fears, for why should we be alarmed? Let us cast all our care upon Him.

> *Fear not; believe His Word;*
> *You are to Jesus given;*
> *'Tis the good pleasure of the Lord*
> *To bring you safe to heaven.*
> *Then listen to your Shepherd's voice,*
> *And in His constant care rejoice.*

MAY 13

🌿 MORNING 🌿

'The LORD hath blessed me hitherto'
Joshua 17: 14

Believer, cannot you join with the children of Joseph this morning, and bear a similar testimony? Thy God hath blessed thee in Jesus, and through Jesus; look back to the rock whence you were hewn, and to the hole of the pit whence you were digged; call to mind the time and place, when and where thy God first led thee to cry for mercy, and seek for salvation; remember the distress and bondage felt before mercy was manifested; and then remember how your soul was delivered, and the comforts of the Holy Ghost imparted. Think of thy difficulties and dangers, thy trials and fears, the deliverances the Lord has wrought, the favour He hath shown, and the comforts He has imparted, and surely you will gratefully acknowledge, 'He hath blessed me hitherto.' He promised to bless, and you have found Him faithful. He has manifested a father's love, and a mother's tenderness in dealing with you. But what have been your returns? O, be humble, for you have been ungrateful! But cleave to Jesus, for God gives no blessing but by and through Him.

> *Jesus found me, vile and guilty,*
> *I had broken all His laws;*
> *When He look'd, He saw me filthy;*
> *All corrupt my nature was:*
> *Mine appear'd a hopeless case,*
> *Such it had been, but for grace.*

🌿 EVENING 🌿

'Love the brotherhood'
1 Peter 2:17

All Christians are brethren. If we are born of God, He is our Father, Jesus is our elder Brother, and all believers are our brethren. They may differ from us in creed, in outward ceremonies and in many other things, but if they possess the same nature, they should be objects of our love. We cannot refuse to love them, to acknowledge them, to assist them, without sin, for our God says, 'Love them: love them with a brother's love.' Let us then look upon all Christians as in Christ, as the beloved children of God, as our brothers and sisters; and let us endeavour to feel for them, and exercise toward them a brother's love. Such love is natural, strong, tender, constant, complacent. Let us love them so as to pity them in distress, relieve them if in want, help them in difficulties, and prefer them to carnal persons, however excellent such may be in many respects. Let us love them for the sake of their elder Brother, for their Father's sake, and because they are so nearly related to us. Remember, every Christian is a brother. God loves every one of your brothers as He loves Jesus. Jesus commands *you* to love every Christian, *as He has loved you.*

> *Myself begotten from above,*
> *I must my Father's children love;*
> *Born of the Spirit and the Word,*
> *Are we not brethren in the Lord,*
> *Flesh of His flesh, bone of His bone,*
> *His body mystical, and one?*

MAY 14

🌿 MORNING 🌿

'They shall be mine, saith the LORD of hosts'
MALACHI 3:17

Who? They that fear the Lord and think upon His name; they who fear to offend Him because they love Him; who desire above all things to obey Him, be conformed unto Him, and glorify Him; they who think upon His name, call Him Father, and believe Him to be gracious, merciful, long-suffering, abundant in goodness and truth; who approach Him as children; who walk before Him, desiring to do every thing as under His eye; who are jealous of His honour, and concerned for His glory; who speak of His goodness, talk of His power, and adore the riches of His grace. *'They shall be mine, saith the LORD of hosts.'* He will treat them as His children, prize them as His jewels, and acknowledge them before assembled angels. He will put a difference between them and others, and will manifest Himself unto them as He does not unto the world. Beloved, are we entitled to claim this precious promise? Do we fear God? Are we grieved at sin, because it dishonours Him? Do we think upon His name with love and reverence? If so, He will spare us, preserve us, and place us among His jewels for ever.

> Hail, sacred day! that shall declare
> The jewels of the Son of God;
> Design'd to deck His crown they were,
> Chosen of old, and bought with blood.

🌿 EVENING 🌿

'Ye are the light of the world'
MATTHEW 5:14

We are situated in a dark world. We have received light, the light of truth and holiness, and we are to let our light shine. Jesus is the sun, from whom we receive our light; and like the moon we do not receive light only for ourselves, but to reflect it on others. Let us then inquire, *How* does the light shine? Is it bright and cheerful, attractive and steady, mild and free? *Where* does our light shine? In the school room, in the chamber of affliction, in the abodes of poverty and misery, in the lurking places of ignorance and vice? In *what form* does our light shine? In kind words, in occasional visits, in religious tracts, in well-timed donations? *What has our light done?* Has it dried the widow's tears, supplied the orphan's wants, conducted sinners to the house of prayer, induced some to repair to the cross, comforted others on the banks of the Jordan? If we are the lights of the world we should shine, or darkness will reign. As we are but lamps, we should be careful to get plenty of oil. Often go to be trimmed. Beware of the bed of sloth, the bushel of worldly conformity, and the dark lantern of sinful timidity.

> Not for ourselves the light of grace
> Didst Thou on us bestow,
> But for the world's benighted race,
>
> Thy darken'd house below:
> Thy candlesticks Thy churches are,
> Thy truth and goodness to declare.

MAY 15

🌿 MORNING 🌿

'We walk by faith'
2 Corinthians 5:7

The Christian's path is often very rough; thorns and briars grow on either side, dark clouds hang over it, and no cheering prospects appear to animate the heart. But if he acts consistently, he still believes it is the right path, that trials are mercies in disguise, and that the path of tribulation ends in the kingdom of God. He believes it is all needful; is the very best way his Father could select; that the design of God is gracious, and his present trials are to end in his eternal welfare. He believes his God is with him, though he does not enjoy His presence, and that all needful supplies will be sent, though he cannot tell from whence. He rests on the faithful Word, trusts in an immutable God, and says, when surrounded by trials, 'None of these things move me; I know that it is through much tribulation that I must enter the kingdom; my God will support me, His hand will defend me, and His grace shall be glorified in my present and eternal salvation. I know not the way, but my God knows, and He will lead me; He will never leave me, but will be my guide, even unto death.'

> O may I daily walk by faith,
> Believing what my God has spoke;
> Rely on His unchanging love,
> And cease to grasp at fleeting smoke;
> On His eternal truth depend,
> And know Him as my God and Friend.

🌿 EVENING 🌿

'We have peace with God'
Romans 5:1

The life of Jesus is our righteousness; His death is our atonement; believing in Him we are fully justified; being justified we are at peace. We know that our God does not impute our trespasses unto us, but viewing us in Jesus, loves us with an infinite, unvarying love. All our present blessings, and all our future prospects flow from His love; He never hated us, though He was angry with us. He loved us before the foundation of the world, therefore He drew the plan of our salvation; and it is such a plan as secures the honour of all His perfections, provides for our guilt and all our necessities, and lays a foundation for permanent and perfect peace. If we therefore believe His Word, exercise confidence in the perfect work of Jesus, and approach Him as a Father in the Saviour's name, we have peace. If we have not peace, it is because we do not see the perfection of the Saviour's work, or we do not exercise confidence in the faithful promise, or we do not believe the love which God hath to us, or we are looking into self, instead of looking simply to Jesus. Believing in Jesus, we are justified; being justified, we ought to enjoy peace.

> Justified by faith in Jesus,
> We have peace and joy in God;
> Faith from dread and terror frees us,

> While we trust His precious blood;
> Casting on Him all our care,
> He preserves from slavish fear.

MAY 16

🌾 MORNING 🌾

'Blessed are ye that hunger now'

Luke 6:21

Appetite supposes life, and is regulated by nature: the carnal appetite is satisfied with carnal things; but a Christian can only be satisfied with spiritual things. He hungers to enjoy an interest in Christ; for righteousness wrought in him by the Spirit, and given to him by Jesus; to be conformed to the image of Christ; to know Him extensively, experimentally, and practically; to enjoy God as his portion; and that Christ may be magnified in him by life or by death. His appetite is fixed on its object; no substitute can be found; it is only as he feeds upon Christ that he enjoys satisfaction. Beloved, how is it with you this morning? Are you hungering for Jesus? He filleth the hungry with good things; He pronounces them blessed. They are blessed with spiritual life; with an interest in the things for which they hunger; and with the operations of the Holy Spirit. None but God can produce this hunger, and only God can satisfy it; and He will, for He has said, *'They shall be filled.'* This is plain, positive, unconditional, and certain. Believe it and be happy.

> Bless'd are the souls that thirst for grace,
> Hunger and long for righteousness;
> They shall be well supplied, and fed
>
> With living streams and living bread:
> O, may my hungry soul receive
> The food on which Thy people live.

🌾 EVENING 🌾

'He shall choose our inheritance for us'

Psalm 47:4

Can you honestly and heartily say this? Are you so fully persuaded of the Lord's wisdom; have you such steady faith in the Lord's love; are you so resigned to the Lord's will; do you sufficiently desire that the Lord's glory should be advanced, as to say cheerfully, 'He shall choose my inheritance for me?' Do you approve of His general conduct in choosing for you? Are you jealous of your own judgment? If not, you cannot adopt this language tonight. It includes an entire surrender to the Lord; a desire to be wholly at His disposal; acquiescence in all His appointments, as to trials, comforts, gifts, place of residence, time and circumstances of death. You may be sure of this, that if the Lord choose for *you*, He will do for you as Joseph did for his father and brethren: He will choose *the best.* It is therefore your wisdom to commit all to the Lord, and leave Him to manage your affairs. It is a great privilege to have a God to choose for us, One who knows all persons, things, and events; and knows all perfectly. It is your duty to be content with the choice God has made for you; you *could* not have chosen better; you *would* not have chosen so well. May our hearts now say, 'He shall choose our inheritance.'

> Now as on rising ground I stand,
> Reviewing what is past,
> I see that love and wisdom plann'd
> My path from first to last.

MAY 17

🌿 MORNING 🌿

'He will rest in his love'

ZEPHANIAH 3:17

Man's love is changeable, being a passion; God's love is unchangeable, being a perfection. Having loved, He always will love. Nothing can occur in time, but what He knew from eternity; consequently there can be no reason today, why God should not love me, but what He knew would be before He set His heart upon me. He fixed His love upon us in the fore-view of all that would be done by us, or felt within us; and connected us with Jesus, that He might never withdraw His love from us. O, to be able to say with holy John, 'We have known and believed the love that God hath to us! God is love!' The love of God is from everlasting to everlasting, without variableness, or the shadow of a turn. Here God resteth, and here we should rest. Herein is love, that God should take such poor, vile, ungrateful, wretched creatures, and make them the bride of His Son, the delight of His soul, and His portion for evermore. O, the riches of divine love! Admire it, trust it, rejoice in it, and make it the subject of your daily meditation. *'He will rest in his love.'* On this Rock we may rest with confidence; on this Pillow we may repose in peace.

> The cov'nant of grace all blessings secures;
> Believer, rejoice, for all things are yours;
> And God from His purpose shall never remove,
> But love thee, and bless thee, and rest in His love.

🌿 EVENING 🌿

'He knoweth our frame'

PSALM 103:14

This is a sweet and encouraging thought. Others may fancy us strong when we are weak, healthy when we are diseased, out of temper when we are suffering; but He knoweth our frame. But it is not bare knowledge, but knowledge united with love; knowledge that awakens sympathy; knowledge that takes the will for the deed. He knows the weakness of our constitutions, the exact nature of our temperament, the shattered state of the nerves, the secret disease which causes irritability, or depression. He can distinguish between what proceeds from physical causes, and what flows from the depravity of our hearts. He knows every avenue by which temptation can enter, and the effects which external objects, or mental images have upon us. He knows and often pities when others blame. He knows and sympathises when others judge hardly of us. He knows and makes allowance, saying, 'The Spirit indeed is willing, but the flesh is weak.' Beloved, you may not know the cause of your depression, or irritability, or excitability, but your heavenly Father knows, and, 'like as a father pitieth his children, so the LORD pitieth them that fear Him.'

> He knows the frailty of our frame,
> Weakness and vanity our claim;
> But as the parent's bosom moves,
>
> In pity, o'er the child he loves,
> So will the Lord His servants view,
> He loves His pity to renew.

MAY 18

❦ MORNING ❧

'And went and told Jesus'
MATTHEW 14:12

When Herod beheaded John, his disciples took up his body and buried it, and went and told Jesus. Let us imitate their example, and carry all to Jesus. He loves to listen to the tale of human woe. He can and will sympathise with us in all our trials and troubles. He is our Father, and to whom should the child tell his troubles, but to his kind and tender parent? He will direct our steps, avenge our wrongs, and turn all things to our advantage. Does business go wrong? Are enemies active? Is corruption strong? Does faith flag? Are you tried in your family? Go and tell Jesus. It will ease your mind; prevent sin; ensure supplies; manifest relation; and frustrate the designs of Satan. Do not sit poring over your miseries; go not to creatures; neither murmur, complain, nor fret; but go to Jesus; go with speed; go in hope; go and tell Him all, without reserve. Go this morning, with all thy complaints, desires, and fears; lay them all before Him, and beseech Him to undertake for you. He loves to hear you, has promised to help you, and will certainly bless you. It is your duty, and your privilege, to pour out your heart before Him, and find Him a refuge for you.

Our sorrows and our tears we pour
Into the bosom of our God;
He hears us in the mournful hour,
And helps to bear the heavy load.

❦ EVENING ❧

'My beloved brethren, be ye stedfast'
1 CORINTHIANS 15:58

How affectionately the apostle writes, even to those who had grieved him, and dishonoured his Master's cause. He not only calls them brethren, but 'beloved brethren.' In this, he is our example. But it is to the exhortation he delivers, to which we wish to call your attention. Many of us are unstable, as were many in the apostle's day. Instability is a great evil. It is injurious to our own souls; it is a stumbling-block or a grief to others, and it gives Satan an advantage over us. He is never unstable, his purpose is fixed, his aim is steady, his efforts are persevering. 'Destroy if possible and distress if not,' is his motto. Brethren, let us be steadfast in our profession of Christ, and let us be steadfast in our efforts to promote the glory of Christ. But if we are to be steadfast, let us be sure that we are building on the right foundation, that we hold the truth of Christ, that we are vitally united to Him, and are entirely consecrated to His praise. Let us take nothing for granted here, but let us prove all things. To the law and to the testimony. Compare everything with God's Word. Seek earnestly the teaching of the Holy Spirit. Be much in prayer. That which thou hast already *hold fast*.

Then steadfast let us still remain,
Though dangers rise around,
And in the work prescrib'd by God
Yet more and more abound.

MAY 19

🌿 MORNING 🌿

'It shall be well'
2 Kings 4:23

This was the language of a believer in trouble; and it should be our language under similar circumstances. Our trials, troubles, and difficulties may be great; but it shall be well with them that fear God. Are you alarmed at the powerful working of corruption within you? It shall be well, for sin shall not have dominion over you, for you are not under the law, but under grace. Are you distressed by the evil suggestions and powerful temptations of Satan? It shall be well, for the God of peace will bruise Satan under your feet shortly. Is your soul cast down by the vexations, difficulties, and trials of the way? It shall be well, for all things shall work together for good, to them that love God, to them who are the called according to His purpose. Do you conclude your case is singular, and therefore fear? It shall be well, for no temptation hath taken you, but such as is common to man; and God is faithful, who will not suffer you to be tempted above that ye are able; but will also with the temptation make a way to escape, that ye may be able to bear it. O, precious promise of a gracious God! Lord, help me to believe, and rejoice. In life and death, 'It shall be well.'

> *What cheering words are these*
> *Their sweetness who can tell?*
> *In time, and to eternal days,*
> *'Tis with the righteous, well.*

🌿 EVENING 🌿

'The meek will he teach his way'
Psalm 25:9

The meek are conscious of their ignorance. They feel the need of teaching. They are desirous of being taught. They especially desire to be taught of God. They feel unworthy of the least mercy at God's hand; and yet, because He has promised, they seek and expect the greatest. Meekness is especially pleasing to God; and the meek may have any favour at His hands. 'Blessed are the meek: for they shall inherit the earth.' The Lord will teach them '*His way*': the way in which He pardons, justifies, and saves sinners; the way in which He would have them walk through this world; the way of escape which He opens in seasons of danger and temptation; the way in which He confounds the crafty, overturns the devices of His foes, and crushes the oppressors of His people. He will teach them the way of peace, and they shall enjoy it; the way of holiness, and they shall walk in it; the way of salvation, and they shall persevere in it. He will unfold to them His Word, confer on them His blessing, walk with them in fellowship, and make them to possess durable riches and righteousness. The meek are heaven's favourites, the churches' ornaments, and the world's truest friends. They are peaceful, and desire to spread peace in every direction.

> *Make me, Saviour, as Thou art,*
> *Poor in spirit, meek in heart;*
> *Then Thou wilt my Teacher be,*
> *And my soul shall cleave to Thee.*

MAY 20

🌿 MORNING 🌿
'He giveth more grace'
JAMES 4:6

It is impossible to be more welcome at the throne of grace than we are, or for God to be more willing to bestow. We are as welcome to the throne of grace, as angels are to the throne of glory. Our God has provided on purpose to give. He invites us to come that we may receive. He gives grace upon grace. He is never weary of bestowing, though we are of asking. We dishonour Him when we ask doubtfully, when we ask for small matters; He bids us ask in faith, nothing doubting; to open our mouths wide that He may fill them. Grace comprises all we need, to pardon our sins, sanctify our natures, conquer our foes, bear our trials, or perform our duties. If we have not, it is because we ask not, or because we ask amiss, to consume it on our lusts. There is grace for us this morning. Let us apply for it, expect to receive it, and determine to use it for God's glory and the good of souls. He will give grace and glory, and no good thing will He withhold from them that walk uprightly. They that seek the Lord shall not want any good thing. Ask, and *you* shall receive; seek, and *you* shall find. He giveth liberally, and upbraideth not.

> *Transporting truth; amazing Word!*
> *What! grace and glory from the Lord;*
> *O, may I feel the promise true,*
> *Fulfill'd in grace and glory too!*

🌿 EVENING 🌿
'She hath done what she could'
MARK 14:8

Mary was a believer. Her faith wrought by love. Love brought her where Jesus was, and she did what she could to honour Him and express her gratitude. An excellent example for us to copy. It cannot be said that we have done all we could. We dare not say this. Let us try and *feel* it. Have we loved Jesus as much as we could? Have we been as much in prayer and in praise as we could? Have we done as much as we could to spread the truth, to save souls, to commend the Saviour, to oppose Satan? Have we done all we could for the spiritual good of our families? Have we done all we could for the comfort and prosperity of the church? Have we done all we could for the Lord's poor? Have we done all we could for the neighbourhood where we reside? Have we done what we could for the world? Satan does all the mischief he can. Many wicked men do all they can to destroy souls. The times call upon us to do all we can. The Saviour loves to see us do all we can. Let us therefore feel reproof, encourage the conviction, seek more grace, daily remember this woman, and begin afresh. 'It is high time to awake out of sleep.' Let us not only work, but *abound* in the work of the Lord, for our labour is not in vain.

> *My God, inspire my soul with zeal,*
> *With glowing love to men;*
> *Make me my obligation feel,*
> *To do what good I can.*

MAY 21

🌿 MORNING 🌿

'Take heed to your spirit'
MALACHI 2:15

The spirit of the believer should be characterized by forbearance, humility, and love; he is exhorted to put away all anger, wrath, clamour, evil-speaking, and malice; and to put on bowels of mercy, kindness, humbleness of mind, meekness, longsuffering, and to be ready to forgive. A bitter, contentious, censorious spirit, is just the opposite of the Spirit of Christ; and an unforgiving person cannot be a Christian, for Jesus has said, 'If ye forgive men their trespasses, your heavenly Father will also forgive you.' Take heed then to your spirit, lest it be said, 'Ye know not what manner of spirit ye are of.' Learn of Jesus; He was meek and lowly, patient and forbearing, kind to His enemies, and ready to forgive. A proud, contentious, overbearing disciple cannot expect to have fellowship with a humble, lowly, and broken-hearted Master. Beloved, let us watch over our spirit; he that rules his own spirit, does more than he that conquers a city; and a spirit that is not under control, is like a city with the walls and gates broken down, open to the enemy on every side. Lord, sanctify my spirit!

Come, blessed Spirit, heavenly Dove,
Descend on balmy wings;
Come, tune my passions all to love,
And strike the peaceful strings;
Let every action, thought, and word,
Bring honour to my holy Lord.

🌿 EVENING 🌿

'When wilt thou comfort me?'
PSALM 119:82

The Lord's people often get into a very uncomfortable state, and sometimes they continue in that state for a long season. But there is always some cause for it, and we should seek to know what that cause is, that it may be removed. It is not easy to give an answer to the inquiry, for it must depend on the character of the inquirer. To one the Lord may say, 'When you humble yourself before Me, cordially approve of My method of salvation, and submit to My righteousness.' To another, 'When you frankly confess your sin, seek pardon through the blood of Christ, and engage to walk according to My Word.' To another, 'When you break off that unscriptural connection, come out from the world, and separate yourself unto Me.' To another, 'When you leave off seeking comfort from selfish motives, and aim at and endeavour to promote My glory.' To another, 'When you leave the bed of sloth, stir up yourself to take hold on Me, and seek to make others happy.' To another, 'When you enter upon that self-denying duty, mortify the flesh with its affections and lusts, or put off the old man with his deeds.' In a word, God will comfort you as soon as comfort will secure His glory and your good.

May holiness be my pursuit,
Thy promises my plea;
So shall I bring forth precious fruit,
And Thou wilt comfort me.

MAY 22

🌿 MORNING 🌿

'If ye shall ask any thing in my name, I will do it'
JOHN 14:14

This is the word of Jesus to us this morning; it is intended to encourage and embolden us at the throne of grace, and to comfort us under all our privations and wants. Jesus has all power in heaven and in earth; all things are delivered unto Him by the Father. He has a large store, and a kind and tender heart. Let us therefore go to Him with our wants, that He may supply them; with our fears, that He may quell them; with our sins, that He may pardon and subdue them; with every thing that troubles us, or is likely to harm us. Let us go to Him with confidence. He says, 'What wilt thou that I shall do for thee? If you ask any thing that will do you good, promote My cause, or glorify My name, *I will do it*. Be not afraid to ask, for I am omnipotent; do not doubt, for I give you My word, *I will do it*.' O, believer, what a friend is Jesus! How kind! How gracious! Never complain, never despond, never be cast down, while Jesus is thy *Friend*. He is, and will be thy Friend for ever. O, make a friend of Him! Visit Him daily; trust Him implicitly; and follow Him fully. Make Him your all in all. He is worthy. He will not deceive. It is impossible for Him to lie.

Jesus, my Lord, I look to Thee;
Where else can helpless sinners go?
Thy boundless love shall set me free
From all my wretchedness and woe.

🌿 EVENING 🌿

'My tongue shall speak of thy word'
PSALM 119:172

If all Christians had done so, how much less ignorance would there be now in the world. The tongue rightly used is our glory, but it is the disgrace of some, and of some professors too. If anything is worth speaking of, it is God's Word. We have it that we may learn it, believe it, love it, practice it, enjoy it, and publish it. It is the means of conversion: therefore speak of it to sinners. It tends to edification: therefore speak of it to saints. It is the instrument of restoration: therefore talk of it to backsliders. It brings comfort to our own souls: let us therefore meditate upon it and then publish it for our own sake. It honours God and exalts the Saviour: let us therefore out of love to God speak of His Word. Let us endeavour to speak of it at proper seasons, in a kind spirit, from a good motive, and with a right aim. It must do good, for it is incorruptible seed which never rots under the clods. It restrains the impetuous, soothes the sorrowful, directs the perplexed, restores the wanderer, and brings peace to the troubled. It is bread to the hungry, light to the benighted, a staff to the pilgrim, a sword to the warrior, and a downy pillow to the wayworn and weary. Then let us resolve in the Lord's strength that our tongues shall speak of His Word.

My lips in thankful strains shall flow,
When taught by THEE Thy truth to know;
My tongue shall spread that truth abroad,
The glorious gospel of my God.

MAY 23

🌿 MORNING 🌿
'We look for the Saviour'
Philippians 3:20

Our beloved Saviour is now at the right hand of God. He waits, expecting His enemies to be made His footstool. He will come again; the time is hastening on; and we should be living in expectation of His appearing. The Christian posture is that of waiting, looking, hasting to the coming of the day of God. He will come the second time, as certainly as He did the first. He will come as a thief in the night. He will come in His glory, and all the holy angels with Him. He will come to reign, to reward His people, and to punish His foes. Let us not be slothful, careless, or indifferent about the coming of our Lord. He comes for our salvation. Let us look for Him daily, with earnest desire, ardent hope, fervent love, importunate prayer, and diligent preparation. When He comes, the earth will be delivered from the bondage of corruption, into the glorious liberty of the children of God; the groans of creation will be silenced, the prayers of the Lord's people will be answered, and crowns of righteousness bestowed. Let us abide in Him, that we may have confidence, and not be ashamed before Him at His coming.

> Lo! He comes with clouds descending,
> Once for favour'd sinners slain;
> Thousand thousand saints attending,
> Swell the triumph of His train;
> Hallelujah!
> Jesus comes, and comes to reign.

🌿 EVENING 🌿
'The Lord knoweth them that are his'
2 Timothy 2:19

Doth a father know his child, or a husband his beloved bride; so the Lord knoweth them that are His. He knows them as the objects of His love, as the purchase of His Son's blood, as the temples of the Holy Ghost. He knows them as strangers and pilgrims upon the earth, as suffering for righteousness' sake. He knows them, though He may not seem to acknowledge them, though He causes men to ride over their heads, and lead them through fire and through water. He knows that they love Him, and grieve that they do not love Him more. He knows that they believe Him, and daily struggle with unbelief, mourning that their faith is so weak. He knows that they trust in Him, though doubts and fears will harass and perplex them. He knows that they obey Him, and often sigh, 'O that my ways were directed to keep Thy statutes always!' Beloved, the Lord knows you are His, and He loves you as His own child, cares for you as His chosen bride, leads you as the sheep of His pasture, keeps you as the apple of His eye, tries you as His gold and silver, keeps you safely as His jewels, and will soon lift you up as the stones in His crown. The Lord's knowledge of you is perfect.

> Dear by a thousand tender bonds,
> Thy saints to Thee are known;
> And, conscious what a name they bear,
> Iniquity they shun.

MAY 24

🌿 MORNING 🌿

'The enemy'
Luke 10:19

The Christian has many foes, but there is one who is emphatically called *'the enemy.'* He is the god of this world; all worship him, except those whom Jesus has delivered from him. He is the prince of the power of the air; he rules over, and works in, all unbelievers. He is a subtle serpent, endeavouring to deceive; a roaring lion, seeking to devour. He has the power of death. He gains access to our hearts, and is always attempting to lead us astray. He is well versed in Scripture, and will often quote it, in order to misapply it; he will use one part to fill us with terror, and another to lead us to make light of sin. He is always planning how he shall injure us, and is incessantly trying to draw us from God. Beloved, there is no safety for us but at the feet of Jesus; it is only as we abide in Him, and walk with Him, that we can overcome Satan. Our weapons are the blood of the Lamb, and the word of the divine testimony. Faith seizes the perfect work of Christ as its shield, and the Word of God as its sword, and thus overcomes the infernal foe. Let us put on the *whole armour* of God.

Jesus hath died for you;
What can His love withstand?
Believe, hold fast your shield, and who
Shall pluck you from His hand?
You shall o'ercome through Jesus' blood,
And stand complete before your God.

🌿 EVENING 🌿

'The just shall live by faith'
Galatians 3:11

It is by faith they become just. Being convinced of sin, sensible of their weakness, and understanding the gospel, they embrace the finished work of Christ; His righteousness becomes theirs, and they are justified from all things. Being justified they live – that is, they are freed from condemnation, they are entitled to all spiritual blessings, and they walk at liberty. They live by faith. By faith they overcome their foes. By faith they obtain supplies. By faith they perform the will of God. By faith they walk with God. The life which they live in the flesh, is by the faith of the Son of God. They believe His Word, rest alone on His work, have confidence in His faithfulness, and derive their supplies from His fulness. They work from principle, not for wages. They live as children in their Father's house, not as servants on a weekly allowance. They trust when they cannot trace, expect when they do not receive, wait when the promise delays, go forward though all appear dark, gloomy, and forbidding. At times they appear to have nothing but the bare promise. All within is cold, hard, and dead; all without seems to go against them. Then it is that they more particularly trust in the Lord, and stay themselves upon their God.

By faith accounted just,
By faith to God we live,
With patience wait His time, and trust
His fulness to receive.

MAY 25

❦ MORNING ❦
'Certainly I will be with thee'
Exodus 3:12

It is a great honour to be favoured with the presence of Jehovah; but in every enterprise for His glory, in every duty required by His Word, in every dangerous part of the pilgrim's path, in every trouble in this land of strangers, He has promised to be with us. His presence is to encourage, strengthen, protect, and prosper us. This promise should arm us against fear, nerve the mind against opposition, and embolden us in a good cause. Beloved, has God promised to be with us? Let us then seek to realize His presence; never let us be satisfied with any religion without the Lord's presence. If God be with us we shall be successful; all He requires He will provide; and display in our experience the exceeding riches of His grace. His presence is sure to His people; He is not always perceived by sense, but certainly He is present; for though heaven and earth may pass away, one jot or tittle of His Word shall in no wise pass away; all must be fulfilled. Let us then seek and expect the presence of Jehovah this day, and rejoice that He has said, 'I will never leave thee, nor forsake thee.' May we never forsake Him.

> Then rest, my soul, upon the Lord,
> Believe and plead His faithful Word;
> He will be with thee, He will guide,
> And for thy every want provide;
> O trust His faithful love and power,
> In every gloomy, trying hour.

❦ EVENING ❦
'Ye are all one in Christ Jesus'
Galatians 3:28

That is, all Christians are one in Christ. He is the centre of Christian union. We were all chosen in Him; we are all represented by Him; we are all vitally united to Him; we are all clothed with Him, for we have put on the Lord Jesus Christ. There is now no distinction or difference on account of nation, age, sex, or condition; but all are one in Christ, being entitled to the same privileges, pleasures, and prospects. The whole form one family, though of different ages; one flock, though in different fields or folds; one building, though composed of many stones of different sizes; one body, though there be different members and offices; one church, though its parts are scattered abroad; one beloved spouse of Jesus, which He purchased with His own blood. If it be indeed so, that we are all one in Christ, then we ought to love as brethren; occasionally at least to feed together; to cleave to each other in sincere affection; to act for each other, as the members in the natural body do; to refuse to divide in heart though separated by place, or other circumstances; and we should mutually rejoice in our dignity and destiny. Beloved, let us look at every Christian as in Christ, as a part of His mystical body, and treat Him accordingly.

> May the Lord our hearts impress,
> Make them like His own above,
> Fill'd with all the tenderness,
> And all the strength of love.

MAY 26

🌿 MORNING 🌿

'Let a man examine himself'

1 CORINTHIANS 11:28

This is necessary, that we may know upon what we are resting; and whether we are growing or declining. Let us examine this morning upon what foundation we are building for eternal life, and from what does our hope arise? What is the source of our satisfaction, pleasure, and peace? What do we possess to prove the reality of our religion? Have we been quickened by the Holy Spirit? Is Christ our life, and is He living in us? Are we enlightened to see sin, in its nature, character, and actings? Have we living faith which receives Christ, believes His Word, and lives to Him? Have we a good hope through grace? Is the love of God shed abroad in our hearts by the Holy Ghost? Do we love God because He first loved us, and walk with Him in peace and holiness? Have we the earnest and witness of the Spirit in our hearts? Are we conflicting with sin, and praying to be delivered from it, as from a tyrant, a plague, the most fearful evil? Let us examine carefully, deliberately, prayerfully, taking God's Word for our rule and guide. Let us prove our own work; so shall we have rejoicing in ourselves alone, and not in others.

> Searcher of hearts! O, search me still;
> The secrets of my soul reveal;
> My fears remove; let me appear
> To God and my own conscience clear:
> Each evidence of grace impart,
> And deeply sanctify my heart!

🌿 EVENING 🌿

'Love is strong as death'

SONG OF SOLOMON 8:6

Death has conquered all. The wisest, the strongest, the bravest, the kindest, the holiest, all have been conquered by death. It has triumphed over myriads, and turned our world into a vast graveyard. But love is equally strong; it conquers all. The love of Jesus is stronger, for it conquered death itself. And we are the objects of that love. He says, 'I have loved you.' He proves it: 'Greater love hath no man than this, that a man lay down his life for his friends.' He has proved the strength of His love by the gifts He has conferred upon us; by the visits He has paid us, by the tears He shed for us, by the labour He undertook to perform for us, by the sufferings He engaged to endure for us, by the death He died, by the desire He cherished, and by His constant intercession on our behalf. His love overcame all difficulties, triumphed over all opposition, conquered all foes, and now reigns in His bosom as a ruling passion of His manhood, and as a glorious perfection of His Godhead. His love passeth knowledge; it is beyond our conception. Let us retire tonight impressed with the thought, however wonderful the love of Jesus may be, however strong or glorious, it is unalterably fixed on us as believers in His name.

> My blessed Saviour, is Thy love
> So great, so full, so free?
> Behold I give my love, my heart,
> My life, my all, to Thee.

MAY 27

🌿 MORNING 🌿
'And He blessed him there'
GENESIS 32:29

Poor Jacob, full of fears and alarm, retired to plead with his God; he wept and made supplication, he had power with God, and prevailed. *'And he blessed him there.'* Our God delights to bless us; therefore He began so early, for He blessed us with all spiritual blessings in Jesus, before the foundation of the world; He gave us grace in His Son, before He gave us a being; but yet He will have us plead with Him, and weep before Him. He is *'The Blessing God.'* There never was a want, that ever pierced the heart of fallen humanity, or met the omniscient eye of Jehovah, but that want was anticipated, and provided for, in the person and fulness of Christ. And however great our conflicts and trials may be, we can have no reason to despond, for grace is given us; and grace always goes hand in hand with omnipotence. Our heavenly Father's love cannot fail, our divine Saviour's fulness cannot be exhausted, the faithful promise cannot be broken. Let us therefore plead in the valley of Achor, wrestle on the battle-plain, and it shall again be said, *'He blessed him there.'* O for the Spirit of prayer! O for living and lively faith!

> Lord, let me know the grace below,
> To all believers given:
> O, bid me feel Thy love, and go
> In perfect peace to heaven.

🌿 EVENING 🌿
'Trust in Him at all times'
PSALM 62:8

He always warrants us to trust in Him, and He is at all times worthy of our trust. We are constantly exhorted to it, but almost as constantly neglect it. It is the exercise of necessity, for a creature *must* trust in another; it is an evidence of dependence, therefore we should cultivate it. It is the exercise of a servant on his master; of a friend on his friend; of a child on his parent; of a believer on his God. Let us trust His Word, for it is true. Let us trust the Saviour's work, for it is perfect. Let us trust a special providence, for it is worthy. Nothing should be allowed to disturb our confidence in God, for His nature is always love, His solemn pledge is given, His resources are inexhaustible, and His mercy is everlasting. Let us trust Him then in joy and sorrow, in darkness and in the light, when increased or bereaved, when tempted or in repose. Let us trust Him and we shall conquer our fears; patiently endure our trials; successfully pursue our work; rise above our cares, and overcome our foes. That we may trust Him, He has revealed His character, pledged His Word, sworn that He will not be wrath with us, and assured us that He is unchangeable. Trust then in the Lord for ever.

> O may we with a steady faith
> Believe whate'er Jehovah saith!
> At all times trust our heavenly Friend,
> And on His faithful Word depend.

MAY 28

🌿 MORNING 🌿

'In all thy ways acknowledge Him'

Proverbs 3:6

Beloved, we are the Lord's, the creatures of His power, the purchase of His blood, the subjects of His grace. He has set His love upon us, employed His wisdom for us, and is deeply interested in all that concerns us. Every thing we do should be done with a view to His glory; and in every thing by prayer and supplication with thanksgiving, we should let our requests be made known unto Him. Every thing should be mentioned at His throne. His presence, direction, and blessing, should be sought in reference to every circumstance of our lives. Our misery can never exceed His mercy, or our application at His throne find His ear preoccupied. He is our Father, and as such ought to be honoured. We should ask of Him, and ask with the whole heart, for he that withdraws his heart in asking, will find God withdraw His hand in giving. Acknowledging God in all things will produce a steady peace of mind; preserve us from many temptations; and strengthen our faith in Him. He that always acknowledges God will find that God always acknowledges him.

> Stretch o'er my head Thy guardian wings,
> Secure my soul, O King of kings!
> My shield and refuge be;
>
> Thy grace and mercy, Lord, display
> Through Christ the Life, the Truth, the Way,
> That I may come to Thee!

🌿 EVENING 🌿

'Thou God seest me'

Genesis 16:13

The eye of the Lord is upon the righteous, and His ear is open unto their cry. He sees everything, but He observes His people with special attention. His eye has been upon us this day; He has seen every movement of the mind, and every action of the body. His eye is upon us now, and will be through the dark watches of the night. But it is a comfortable thought, that He who sees us always, loves us most, loves us notwithstanding all He sees amiss in us. Let us ever cherish the thought, my Father sees me. I am under His eye. He sees all I do, all I suffer, all my desires. Nothing can conceal the least circumstance from His eye. He sees me when I see not Him. He sees me in the furnace, and is with me. He sees me in the field of battle, and gives me the shield of His salvation. He sees me when my foot is slipping, and often has the hand of His mercy caught me and held me up. When tempted to sin, when giving way to fear, or when yielding to the world, let me call to mind this solemn fact: 'My God sees me.' If I sin, it must be immediately under His eye. If I yield to temptation, it must be in His presence. If I encourage His foe, it must be against the clearest light and tenderest love. Keep this daily before the mind.

> Lord, put within my heart Thy fear,
> Grant me from sin to fly,
> At all times to behold Thee near,
> And on Thy grace rely.

MAY 29

❦ MORNING ❧
'And be found in Him'
PHILIPPIANS 3:9

To be in Christ, is to be united to Him by faith and love; and it is of the utmost importance. Apart from Christ we are wretched, miserable, poor, blind, and naked. United to Christ, we are immensely rich; immutably safe; exalted to the highest honour; and shall appear without a fault before the throne of God. If we are in Christ, or one with Christ, we are justified by His obedience, as the debtor is cleared by the payment made by his surety; we are sanctified through Him, as the vessel is cleansed in the fountain; we are protected by Him, as Noah was in the ark; we are preserved from judicial proceeding, as the manslayer in the city of refuge; and are exalted to honour as the *bride* of the *King Eternal*, Immortal, the only wise God. Well may the apostle desire *to 'be found in him.'* No mind can conceive, no tongue can declare the blessedness that flows from being *one with Christ*. Let us therefore, beloved, ask, this morning, 'Am I in Christ at present? Am I living with Him as His faithful bride; for Him as His devoted servant; upon Him as His dependent child? Do I renounce all for Christ? Can I say, 'I am crucified with Christ? The world is crucified unto me, and I unto the world?"

> Yes, yes, I must and will esteem
> All things but loss for Jesus' sake;
> O, may my soul be found in Him,
> And of His righteousness partake.

❦ EVENING ❧
'The trying of your faith worketh patience'
JAMES 1:3

Whoever professes to believe in God, will have his faith put to the trial. Every believer is tried. By Satan, by the world, or by false professors, *we* shall be tried; but our God superintends the trial. He tries our faith in His Word, if it be sincere; our faith in His love, if we really credit it; our faith in His Son, if we trust in Him alone for complete salvation; our faith in His veracity, if we expect Him to make good His Word. He will try the nature of our faith, if it is divine; the strength of our faith, if it is rooted. He will try the constancy of our profession, if we hold fast the beginning of our confidence. This trial is for His own glory, for the good of others who observe us, and for our own advantage. It worketh patience. It gives us occasion to exercise what we have. It perfects the habit and strengthens the exercise of it. It is often a call to exchange ease for patience, wealth for contentment and our own opposing strength, for the power of Christ. Let us therefore remember that faith must be tried, that afflictions are to try our faith, that sanctified trials make us patient, and that when patience is complete, our trials will cease. Be ye therefore patient.

> Lord, whene'er my faith is tried,
> Keep me near Thy bleeding side;
> Make me patient, meek, and kind,
> To Thy sovereign will resigned.

MAY 30

🌿 MORNING 🌿

'All my springs are in thee'
PSALM 87:7

Jesus is the fountain of living water; the wells of salvation are found in His person, work and Word; He says, 'If any man thirst, let him come unto me, and drink.' The springs of comfort, peace, and salvation are all in Him, and in Him for us; they are therefore called our springs. These waters cleanse from all defilement; refresh the faint and weary; and satisfy the longing soul. The springs bespeak plenitude: whosoever will may come and take, for they are never dry. We are absolutely dependent on Jesus: this is our mercy; we are not absolutely dependent on any besides; this is our happiness. Our desires should concentrate in Him; our affections should be fixed upon Him; and our expectations should be only from Him. In Jesus is all possible variety: He can do, and bestow, all we can possibly want; for 'it pleased the Father that in him should *all* fulness dwell.' If all our springs are in Jesus, let us not then look to any other; but let us with joy draw water out of the fountains of the Saviour. Let us ask, and He will give us *living water*, that we may thirst no more. Only what comes from Jesus can satisfy the soul.

> To whom, dear Jesus, O, to whom
> Shall needy sinners flee?
> But to Thyself, who bid'st us come,
> Our springs are all in Thee:
> Now fill my soul with Thy pure love,
> And raise my thoughts and hopes above.

🌿 EVENING 🌿

'A sure foundation'
ISAIAH 28:16

The Lord Jesus in the glory of His person, and in the perfection of His work, is the only foundation of a sinner's hope. If we build on anything else, we must perish. If we mix anything with Christ as the basis of our hope, He will profit us nothing. It must be Christ, and Christ alone. His meritorious obedience, His atoning sacrifice, His prevalent intercession: on these we must build for eternity, they form the one foundation, and building on these we are safe, for it is a sure foundation. The dignity of His person, the perfection of His character, the merit of His work, and the veracity of His Word, make it so. It has stood firm in all times past, it is unshaken at present, and it will ever be the same. No sinner ever built on it and found it fail him. Storms cannot shake it, floods cannot loosen it, earthquakes do not affect it; it is firm as the perfections of God can make it, and lasting as eternity itself. Let us build upon it, upon it alone; and doing so, let us rejoice in our safety. Errors may spread, evil men and seducers may wax worse and worse, Satan may try all his arts, but 'the foundation of God standeth sure, having this seal: the Lord knoweth them that are His.' 'Other foundation can no man lay than that is laid, which is Jesus Christ.'

> When all foundations else will fail,
> Those built on Jesus shall prevail;
> And lift their heads with joyful praise,
> To Him who this foundation lays.

MAY 31

🌿 MORNING 🌿

'The just shall come out of trouble'
PROVERBS 12: 13

The Lord's people are justified by grace, through faith, in the righteousness of Jesus; and all who are thus justified and created anew, have immortal principles of holiness and justice implanted in their hearts, so that they hate sin, follow holiness, and walk uprightly. Sin has not dominion over them, nor will they be slaves to lust. They meet with many troubles, they have to pass through fire and water, but they shall come out into a wealthy place. They shall not perish in their affliction, for the Lord upholdeth them with His hand. Beloved, look beyond your present trials; remember if you suffer as a Christian, you suffer with Christ; and if you suffer, you shall also reign with Him. Your God is able to deliver; He has promised to do so; trust in Him without wavering; yield not to temptation; avoid the appearance of evil; and your God will bring you out of trouble. He will bring forth your righteousness as the light, and your judgment as the noonday. You shall also forget your misery, or remember it as waters that pass away. Present troubles will end in everlasting peace.

> Millions who now His throne surround,
> Here sought relief, here mercy found;
> The Lord dispell'd their gloomy fears,
> Heal'd all their wounds, and dried their tears;
> And thou shalt also mercy find,
> For God is faithful, just, and kind.

🌿 EVENING 🌿

'Restore unto me the joy of thy salvation'
PSALM 51:12

The psalmist had sustained a loss. Sin was the cause of it. He seeks a restoration. Salvation cannot be lost, the joy of salvation can. The joy of salvation flows from the gospel, which is good news and glad tidings; when it is received by faith, it fills us with joy and peace. It is intended to impart an immediate assurance of eternal life to every sinner that believes it, and when it is received as coming directly from God, under the influence of the Holy Spirit, it does so. When we realise our interest in Jesus, feel the burden of our guilt removed, and read our title to all the promises, we are filled with joy. This had been realised, but it was lost. There may be a sense of want, clear views of the gospel, but no appropriating faith, and then there is no joy. But what we cannot take, we may ask for; what we cannot apply ourselves, we may plead with God to impart. This prayer for a restoration of joy shows our weakness, we cannot produce it; it proves our folly, in that we sinned it away; it exhibits our dependence upon God, who alone can make us happy; and it warns us against backsliding from the Lord. Let us mourn over our sins. Let us watch against temptations. Let us not despair.

> Those joys, my God, which once I knew,
> Those saving joys restore;
> Thy Spirit's free! His grace renew,
> Nor let me wander more.

JUNE 1

❦ MORNING ❧
'THE LORD OUR RIGHTEOUSNESS'
Jeremiah 23:6

Jesus is Jehovah, the self-existent, eternal, and immutable God. He is our righteousness. To this end He assumed our nature; came into our place; laboured, suffered, bled, and died in our stead. We have no righteousness by nature, but we have the righteousness of God by grace. 'Their righteousness is of me,' saith the LORD. Jesus completed for us all that was necessary to justify us; He made an end of sin; He magnified the law and made it honourable; He brought in everlasting righteousness; and now He clothes us with the garments of salvation, and covers us with the robe of righteousness. In Him we possess all justice can demand or God require, for our full and eternal justification. This portion is not necessary merely for one day, but every day; it silences an accusing conscience, confounds Satan, strengthens the soul, and glorifies God. Let us look today, all the day, and every day to Jesus, as 'THE LORD OUR RIGHTEOUSNESS.' Let us go to duty, to conflict, to trials, in the strength of the Lord, making mention of His righteousness, even of His only. This is our plea at the throne of grace, our song in the house of our pilgrimage, and our confidence in the prospect of death.

> Saviour divine, we know Thy name,
> And in that name we trust;
> Thou art the Lord our Righteousness,
> Thou art our joy and boast.

❦ EVENING ❧
'Shew ye the proof of your love'
2 Corinthians 8:24

We profess to love God. We cannot be Christians without love. Christian love professes to prefer Christ and His cause to all besides; to submit to His authority and acquiesce in His will; to obey all His commands without partiality or insincerity; to delight in His saints as the excellent of the earth; to sympathise with sufferers, especially with those who suffer in His cause and for His sake; to be ready to every good work. Such is our profession if we are sincere and diligent Christians. The law of God requires this at our hands. Jehovah as a Sovereign promises to produce it. By the Holy Spirit it is brought forth within us. He convinces us that by nature we have it not. He leads us to admire it, desire it, and seek for it. By unfolding the gospel and shedding abroad the love of God in our hearts, He produces it. By daily and filial fellowship with God it is sustained. Beloved, do we profess to love God and His people? Then let us prove the sincerity of our love, by uniting with them, by assisting them in every good word and work, and by preferring them to all beside. Let us visit them in sickness, relieve them in poverty, defend them when oppressed, and show them all possible kindness for Jesus' sake.

> Mercy through Jesus we have found,
> Free mercy from above;
> May mercy move us to fulfil,
> The perfect law of love.

JUNE 2

🌿 MORNING 🌿

'I will deal well with thee'
GENESIS 32:9

So the Lord promised Jacob, and the promises made unto our fathers, He will fulfil unto us their children. But such a promise does not exclude great trials, sore temptations, deep personal afflictions, fiery persecutions, poverty, disappointments, and perplexity; all these things may happen unto us, and yet the Lord deal well with us. The promise secures the sanctification of our troubles, the communication of grace, deliverance from all real evils, the supply of all wants, and the satisfying of our best desires. Is not this enough, to know that Jehovah will deal well with us in sickness and health; in life and in death; in time and through eternity? This promise is Jehovah's bond, the believer's plea, the ground of the Christian's confidence, a reason for contentment and gratitude, and the cause of our enemies' confusion. Jacob, though tried, found the Lord faithful, and so shall we. Let us therefore rejoice that our God has said, 'I will deal well with thee: I will make all my goodness pass before thee. I will save thee with an everlasting salvation. I will be thy God and thy glory.' Gracious Lord, do as Thou hast said!

Jesus! in whom but Thee above,
Can I repose my trust, my love?
Thy counsels and upholding care,
My safety and my comfort are;
And Thou shalt guide me all my days,
Till glory crown the work of grace.

🌿 EVENING 🌿

'The household of God'
EPHESIANS 2:19

The Lord has a family which is peculiarly His own. It is a spiritual family, for every member of it is born of God, is taught by the Spirit, is inhabited by the Spirit, is led by the Spirit, and is baptised by the Spirit into the *one body*. It is wholly and entirely of God. It originated in His purpose. It expresses His sovereign pleasure. It is produced by His power. It is called His own. It is designated the household of God. His in opposition to Satan; His in distinction from the world; His as differing from man's. It is the family where He dwells, the home of God, the flock over which He presides. Here He manifests His paternal love in supplying every want, protecting every member, employing every child, loving and delighting in each and every one. All the members of this household are brethren, and all are blessed. It is designed to glorify His grace, to honour His Son, to maintain His cause, to execute His will. Here in His family He is known, trusted, praised, obeyed, loved, and enjoyed. Are you of this household? Do you attend the family feasts? Do you enjoy the family services? Do you sincerely love the Head and the members of this household? This honour have all His saints.

Lord, come and dwell with me,
Now make my heart Thy home;
Unite me to Thy family,
Unite me to Thy Son.

JUNE 3

❦ MORNING ❧

'The exceeding riches of His grace'
Ephesians 2:7

Jehovah glories in His grace. It is His riches, His wealth. All its riches are intended for us, to be expended upon us. They are all treasured up in Jesus to be received by us. They are promised and presented to us. They exceed our thoughts, our expectations, our faith; we do not believe that God has provided and promised so much for our good as He has; and therefore we do not ask for, and expect so much. Let us this day think of *'the exceeding riches of grace.'* Jesus was the gift of grace, so was the Holy Spirit, and so are all spiritual blessings. Grace includes, and is the source from which flows all the church has received, is receiving, and will receive throughout eternity. Grace freely gives, but never sells. It has a bountiful eye, a tender heart, and a liberal hand. We are not straitened in God, but in our own hearts. O, that we did but believe what God has revealed in reference to the riches of grace, and expect to receive according to His most liberal promises! There is an abundance of grace, and it is for us; for us this morning, for us whenever we apply. Let us therefore have grace, whereby we may serve God acceptably, with reverence and godly fear.

> *Amazing grace! how sweet the sound!*
> *That saved a wretch like me!*
> *I once was lost, but now am found;*
> *Was blind, but now I see.*

❦ EVENING ❧

'That God may be all in all'
1 Corinthians 15:28

The design of Jehovah, in all His ways and works, is the glorification of Himself. He will be all in all. He is all in the great scheme of salvation. The plan was drawn by infinite wisdom in eternity, and is carried out by divine power in time. Are we chosen to salvation? It is *of* God *in* Christ. Are we given to Jesus? It is by Jehovah. Are we ordained to eternal life? It is the act of the Most High. Are we blessed with all spiritual blessings? It is by the Father of mercies. Are we redeemed by the precious blood of Christ? He was foreordained to this work by the Father. He is all in the dispensation of grace. Are we quickened? It is by God. Are we taught? It is by God. Have we faith and repentance? They are the gift of God. Do we overcome Satan? It is because the God of peace bruises him under our feet. Are we laborious? It is the effect of His power which worketh in us mightily. Are we holy? By the grace of God we are what we are. Do we overcome all our foes? It is through Him that loved us. He will be all in the world of glory, in the arrival of every child at home; as the love of God, and the God of love will constitute our perfect bliss for ever. In our complete and everlasting salvation, God will be all.

> *Here the whole Deity is known,*
> *Nor dares a creature guess,*
> *Which of the glories brightest shone,*
> *The justice or the grace.*

JUNE 4

🌿 MORNING 🌿

'His kindness towards us'
EPHESIANS 2:7

What a subject is the kindness of God towards us! Let us think of it, as it appears in the place and circumstances of our birth; in happy Britain, not in a heathen land; in our education and preservation; especially in our regeneration, that we were born again, not of the will of the flesh, nor of blood, but of God. How many, born in the same place, about the same time, and educated in the same school, have been allowed to pass out of time into eternity, carnal, and under the curse of God; or are living in that state! Why were we distinguished? Called by grace! Justified from all things in the righteousness of Jesus! Kept by the power of God! Supplied according to the promises! Walking with God! Looking for the coming of Jesus with hope, holy longings, and steady faith! Having the promise of the life that now is, and of that which is to come! Warranted to say, 'All things are mine, for I am Christ's, and Christ is God's.' O, how great is the goodness of our God! How unsearchable His grace! His kindness to us is wonderful!

> *Who can have greater cause to sing,*
> *Who greater cause to bless,*
> *Than we, the children of a King,*
> *Than we who Christ possess?*
> *Our all we to His kindness owe,*
> *And grateful praise should ever flow.*

🌿 EVENING 🌿

'It is more blessed to give than to receive'
ACTS 20:35

These are very remarkable words. They are the words of the Lord Jesus. They were acted upon by Himself. They contain the very principle which influenced Him in eternity, which induced Him to leave heaven for earth, and which actuates Him still. He urged this saying upon His disciples, so that it is probable that it became a kind of proverbial saying among them. He has preserved it for our instruction and admonition. Receiving implies want and unfulfilled desires; giving supposes a possession, an honourable trust. Giving manifests a generous disposition, and a concern for the comfort of others. It is acting like God, who created that He might give, redeemed that He might give, glorifies that He may give. It is a source of pure pleasure. Let us remember these words of the Lord Jesus when we go to His throne, and draw encouragement from them to ask for great blessings, to ask often, to ask with confidence; and let us encourage others to go to Him, assuring them that He considers it more blessed to give than to receive. Let us walk by this rule, prudently, plainly, notwithstanding discouragement.

> *The man who marks from day to day,*
> *In generous acts His radiant way,*
> *Treads the same path the Saviour trod,*
> *The path to glory and to God.*

JUNE 5

🌿 MORNING 🌿

'Lord, what wilt thou have me to do?'
ACTS 9:6

A very proper inquiry to bring to the Lord's throne, for all the Lord's people should be employed in the Lord's vineyard, for the Lord's glory. There is something for each of us to do, and something for us to do today. *Jesus* is our *Master*, He has a right to reign over us, and employ us as He will. He should be obeyed. We especially, who are so deeply indebted, should obey Him willingly, cheerfully and habitually. Is our enmity subdued? How can we manifest it, but by seeking to be in His employment? Have we faith, hope, love, humility, peace, gratitude? Are we not then desirous of obeying Him, who gave us all these blessings? We ought to be employed, always employed, and so employed as if every day were our last. That is the best employment, which we can look at with satisfaction on a death-bed; and of which we shall not be ashamed at the Day of Judgment. Are you doing for Jesus? Are you doing in the spirit of Jesus? Beware lest you put your doings in the place of Jesus; do all you can, and then lay all you do at the feet of Jesus, it will need washing.

> Never did men by faith divine
> To selfishness or sloth incline;
> The Christian works with all his power
> And grieves that he can work no more;
> Commits his works to God alone,
> And seeks His will before his own.

🌿 EVENING 🌿

'The promises of God'
2 CORINTHIANS 1:20

The promises of God are the assurances He has given His people, that He will bless them and bestow favours upon them. They all originate in His divine sovereignty, and flow spontaneously from His will. They are but the effects and tokens of His love, the kind expressions and manifestations of His grace. They are acts of divine condescension which bring the promiser under a bond, and prove His fatherly care of us and concern for our welfare. They all rest on the same immutable basis, even His veracity and faithfulness, and are stored up in Jesus as the present property of His people. They are so comprehensive that they embrace time and eternity, and provide what is suitable for both. They open the heart of Jehovah, challenge the faith of the Christian, and animate the hopes of the penitent sinner. They are connected with the mediatorial office of Christ, for as Prophet He publishes them, as Priest He confirms them, and as King He fulfils them. They all belong to the same persons, believers; have the same design, our benefit; and aim at the same end, the praise of Jehovah's grace. They all lead us to the same fountain, the fulness of Christ, and produce the same effects, even admonition, gratitude, and praise.

> The promises surpass my thought,
> But faithful is my Lord;
> In unbelief I stagger not,
> For God hath spoke the Word.

JUNE 6

❦ MORNING ❦

'He hath done all things well'
MARK 7:37

This was the testimony of the multitude concerning Jesus. He did many things, but He did every thing well. Cannot we bear the same testimony this morning? He called us by His grace, and when we reflect upon the means, the manner, and the period, must we not say, 'He did it well?' He has tried us in many ways; but when we think of His design, the mercies He mingled with the afflictions, and the deliverance He granted us out of them, must we not say, 'He hath done all things well?' If we look back, and see Him standing forward as our *Surety* with the Father in eternity; or if we behold Him taking our nature, bearing our sins, procuring our righteousness, and sending His Holy Spirit to sanctify and save us; must we not say, 'He hath done all things well.' And when our mansions are prepared, our bodies raised from the grave, and our persons are perfectly conformed to His image; when we hear Him say, 'Come, inherit the kingdom', O, with what rapture, gratitude, and love shall we shout, '*He hath done all things well!*'

> How sovereign, wonderful, and free,
> Is all His love to sinful me;
> He pluck'd me as a brand from hell!
> My Jesus hath done all things well.
>
> And since my soul has known His love,
> What mercies has He made me prove;
> Mercies which all my praise excel:
> My Jesus hath done all things well.

❦ EVENING ❦

'The offence of the cross'
GALATIANS 5:11

The doctrine of salvation by a crucified Jew was in Paul's day peculiarly offensive; many stumbled at it and perished; and the doctrine of complete salvation by faith in Christ alone, is still offensive to many. Man naturally desires *to be* something, *to do* something, and *to be thought* something; but in the doctrine of salvation by grace, man is nothing, Christ is all. It presents the crucified One as the object of faith, the only ground of hope, and the medium through which every blessing flows. It places the cross in the centre, directs the eye to it, and makes it the constant object of attention and attraction. It places all upon a level, the harlot and the modest maiden, the thief and the honest man, the poor and the wealthy, the illiterate and the learned; and presents salvation to each on the same terms, requiring all alike to rest upon the finished work of Jesus, and allows no flesh to glory in God's presence. This is very offensive to the pride of man. In a word, the gospel knows no man after the flesh, but points all to Jesus, directs each to the strait gate and narrow way, inculcates self-denial and self-renunciation as necessary to salvation and shuts up every soul to this alternative: *it must believe in Christ, or perish.* This is the offence of the cross.

> Jesus is a perfect Saviour,
> Only source of all that's good;
> Every grace and every favour,
> Come to us through Jesu's blood.

JUNE 7

❧ MORNING ❧

'Ye are my witnesses, saith the LORD'
ISAIAH 43:12

We are to witness to the truth, power, and sweetness of religion, to the goodness, holiness, and faithfulness of God. We are to witness to the world, by our spirit, testimony, and conduct; we are to witness to poor, doubting, fearful souls. Our witness should be unequivocal, and should be borne with courage, constancy, and love. Our testimony should be from experience. Do we know the Lord? Do we daily experience the power of truth in our hearts? Does it free us from slavish fear, the love of the world, and the dominion of sin? Can we say we have known and believed the love which God hath to us? God is love. Are we saying to those around us, 'O, *taste* and see that the Lord is good ... there is no want to them that fear Him'? Suppose we should be called to bear witness before judges and kings; in the prison or at the stake. How would it be with us then? Could we witness that God is good and gracious; that He is enough to make us happy; if He were to strip us as He did Job, or try us as He did Paul? He says, *'Ye are my witnesses.'*

> Give me to bear Thy easy yoke,
> And every moment watch and pray;
> And still to things eternal look,
> And hasten to Thy glorious day!
> I would Thy daily witness be,
> And prove that I am one with Thee.

❧ EVENING ❧

'The breastplate of faith and love'
1 THESSALONIANS 5:8

We are surrounded by foes, and are in a state of perpetual conflict. Armour is provided for us by the great Captain of our salvation, and we are directed to take the whole of it and use it for our defence. The breastplate which is to guard the heart is composed of faith and love, the two principal graces of the Spirit. Faith is confidence in God. Love is affection for Him. They are distinct, yet united. They differ in nature, yet agree. Faith always begets love, and love strengthens faith; together they make the Christian a match for his foes. Faith always embraces the Lord Jesus as the Saviour, Friend, and Lord of poor sinners; and love delights in Him as the visible Jehovah, the fountain of grace, and the brightness of glory. Faith receives the promises and trusts them; love calls forth admiration and renders praise for the same. Faith appropriates the righteousness of Christ for justification; love delights in the person of Christ as supremely glorious. Faith daily leads to the open fountain for cleansing; love conducts to the throne for intercourse and communion. Faith looks to Christ for support; love goes forth to labour or suffer in His cause. Faith points to heaven as our home; love urges us to hasten there.

> Let faith and love, most holy God!
> Possess this soul of mine;
> So shall I conquer all my foes,
> And reach the joys divine.

JUNE 8

🌿 MORNING 🌿

'If God be for us, who can be against us?'
ROMANS 8:31

Beloved, if we are believers in Jesus, all the perfections of Jehovah's nature are arrayed for our defence and safety. He is engaged by covenant, by promise, and by oath, to support, supply, and befriend us. He is for us; engaged in our cause; opposed to our enemies; pledged to deliver us in six troubles, and not forsake us in the seventh. We may challenge our foes, for God is with us; what then is man? What devils? We may admire our safety, happiness, and honour; God, the Lord God omnipotent, is our ally. We should be grateful, for what is our desert? What do we possess? What were our expectations? What has God promised? We may triumph in Christ, but only in Christ. If God be for us, then supplies shall certainly be sent us. If God be for us, men or devils shall never prevail against us. If God be for us, we shall overcome the world, conquer death, and eternally inherit glory. But God is for us. Who then shall harm us? What then shall alarm or terrify us? God is ours; we are God's. This is our honour, our happiness, our boast and our glory.

Yes, God is above men, devils, and sin,
My Jesus' love the battle shall win:
On His mighty power I'll daily rely,
All evil before His presence shall fly:
I fear no denial, no danger I fear,
Nor start from a trial, when Jesus is near.

🌿 EVENING 🌿

'Brethren, we are debtors'
ROMANS 8:12

Favours bestowed on the undeserving always increase their obligations; we are debtors as creatures, but more so as new creatures. We are indebted to sovereign grace, for a name in God's book of purpose and promise; for an interest in the Saviour's person, office, and work; for the benefits resulting from His obedience, death, and intercession. We are debtors to atoning blood, for by it justice is satisfied; we are delivered from the wrath of God, and are rescued from the power of Satan. We are debtors to divine influence, for by it we were quickened when dead in trespasses and sins, are taught the will of God, and are introduced into liberty and safety. We are indebted to a special providence for daily, hourly, invaluable favours. Beloved, let us endeavour to feel our obligations; we owe a debt of love and gratitude. Let us therefore revere our heavenly Father's commands; observe and do our loving Saviour's precepts; attend to all the Holy Spirit's intimations; and bow with cheerful submission to all the dispensations of divine providence. As debtors, let us be humble, let us be honest, and acknowledge that we are not our own; our time is not our own; our talents are not our own, but all are the Lord's.

Thy love I owe for sin forgiven,
Through satisfaction made;
For present peace and promised heav'n,
Can never be repaid.

JUNE 9

🌿 MORNING 🌿

'Let Israel hope in the LORD'
PSALM 130:7

This title is applied to all the Lord's people. It sets forth their dignity: they are *princes*; it refers to their experience: they wrestle with God in prayer, and they prevail. Despondency does not become a prince, much less a Christian. Our God is *'the God of Hope'*, and we should hope in Him. Israel should hope in His mercy; in His patience; in His provision; in His plenteous redemption. They should hope for light in darkness; for strength in weakness; for direction in perplexity; for deliverance in danger; for victory in conflict; and for triumph in death. They should hope in God confidently, because He has promised; prayerfully, for He loves to hear from us; obediently, for His precepts are to be observed by us; and constantly, for He is always the same. Beloved, let not your hope rest on frames, or duties, or men or anything; but hope in the Lord, in the Lord only. Israel's God is at all times Israel's hope. The hope of Israel shall never be disappointed. Therefore hope in God, for it is good that a man should both hope, and quietly wait for the salvation of the Lord. This will keep you steady in storm and tempest.

> *The gospel bears my spirit up;*
> *A faithful and unchanging God*
> *Lays the foundation for my hope,*
> *In oaths, and promises, and blood;*
> *Then, O my soul, still hope in God,*
> *And plead thy Saviour's precious blood.*

🌿 EVENING 🌿

'Beloved of God'
ROMANS 1:7

What a privilege is this! It is the source of all real good. How are the Lord's beloved ones known? By their faith in Jesus, and obedience to His Word; by their love to God, and their zeal for His glory; by their hope in God, and patient endurance of His will. What are the honours they possess? They are the sons of God; they are the acknowledged brethren of Jesus; they are the companions of God, with whom he daily walks; they are the residence of the Holy Ghost; they are watched over, befriended, and supplied by providence; they are attended by angels; they are heirs of all things. What are their prospects? Victory and triumph over all their foes; freedom from all bondage and pain; the enjoyment of holiness, happiness, and God; likeness to Jesus in body and soul; the possession of the throne of glory, a diadem of beauty, and a harp of celestial sweetness. What are their duties? To be very decided for God and His cause; to be entirely consecrated to God and His service; to love His ordinances, practice His precepts, prefer His will, and walk with His people in all His ways. Reader, are you beloved of God? Do you love Him? Do you walk with Him?

> *Now let me rise in Jesus' name,*
> *His arm my stay, His praise my aim;*
> *Let unreserv'd obedience prove,*
> *The truth and ardour of my love.*

JUNE 10

❦ MORNING ❦
'I am Alpha and Omega'
REVELATION 22:13

Jesus is the first and the last. He began, He carries on, and He will complete the great work of our eternal salvation. He was the first object to which we were directed to look, and He will be the last we shall wish to see. He was the first subject we began to learn, and we shall be learning Him to all eternity. He is first with us in every trial and trouble, and will never leave us nor forsake us. He is the foundation on which we build, and He will be for a covering. We should look to Him first in every trouble, and go to Him first with every want. He includes all that is good, great, and glorious. He that hath Jesus hath all things. Let us begin with Jesus, and then go on with Jesus, so shall we end with Jesus, and a blessed ending it will be. He is our great lesson, and we have learned nothing to purpose until we know Him. O, to know Him, and the power of His resurrection, and the fellowship of His sufferings, and to be made conformable to His death! Let us endeavour to learn the happy art of looking to Jesus, expecting from Jesus, and glorifying Jesus as our *Alpha* and *Omega* from day to day.

> *Christ is my hope, my strength, my guide,*
> *For me He groan'd, and bled, and died;*
> *Christ is the source of all my bliss,*
> *My wisdom, and my righteousness;*
> *My Saviour, Brother, faithful Friend,*
> *On Him alone I now depend.*

❦ EVENING ❦
'He is not ashamed to call them brethren'
HEBREWS 2:11

This is truly wonderful, especially if we consider the amazing contrast between us. This is very great, as it respects His purity and our pollution; His wealth and our poverty; His strength and our weakness; His happiness and our misery; His knowledge and our ignorance; His dignity and our degradation; His society and our company. But though the contrast is so great He acknowledges us, and there is a degree of likeness: we have the same Father, even God; we possess His nature, spirit, and image in a degree; our work and His are the same, to glorify God; our cause and interest are identified with His; our aim and end are one with His; and His heaven is to be our eternal home. We are often ashamed of ourselves, and ashamed of one another; the world is ashamed of us, but Jesus never is. He owns us in heaven before His Father and His holy angels *now*, and He will call us brethren, blessed of His Father, on the throne of judgment *by and by*. If Jesus is not ashamed to call us brethren, never let us be ashamed to own each other, though in some things we differ. Jesus owns us all. Let us own all as our brethren, whom we have reason to believe are owned by Him.

> *Lord, what is man's distinguished race,*
> *Whom Thou dost for Thy brethren own,*
> *Crown'd with dignity and grace,*
> *To brightest seraphim unknown!*

JUNE 11

🌿 MORNING 🌿
'The LORD is my portion'
LAMENTATIONS 3:24

How poor is the worldling's possession, if compared with the Christian's portion: it is but for a few days; it cannot satisfy; it cannot bless. But, beloved, Jehovah hath given up Himself; He says, *'I am your inheritance.'* We are ever with Him, and all He has is ours. His power is ours to support us, His wisdom to guide us, His love to comfort us, His mercy to relieve us, His goodness to supply us, His justice to defend us, His covenant to secure us, and His heaven to receive us. He is a suitable, sufficient, and immutable portion. We are to live upon Him, draw from Him, rejoice in Him, and look to Him for all we need. For Him we renounce all other; to His glory all our efforts must be directed, and with Him we must daily walk. Men cannot deprive us of our portion, fire cannot consume it, nor rust corrupt it. Let us not therefore be much affected by any thing that occurs below. If the streams are dried, the fountain remains; if creatures fail or deceive us, our God is the portion of our inheritance and of our cup; He maintains our lot; He is our strength, and *our portion for ever.*

> *Begone, ye gilded vanities,*
> *I seek the only GOOD;*
> *To real bliss my wishes rise,*
> *The FAVOUR OF MY GOD;*
> *Thy love, my God, my portion be,*
> *And let me find my all in Thee.*

🌿 EVENING 🌿
'Thy comforts delight my soul'
PSALM 94:19

Our circumstances are often trying, and our thoughts very perplexing and depressing; but our God has provided comfort for us. A fulness of comfort; a supply of comfort for all times. What comfort is wrapped up in the precious promises, in the perfect work of Jesus, in the everlasting covenant, in the prospect of a complete and everlasting deliverance from all sin, suffering, and sorrow! We have everything in ourselves calculated to make us uncomfortable, but in our God we have everything that can make us happy. Our own thoughts are often a source of grief, but the thoughts of our God are full of love, peace, and holy joy. O what a comfort it is to us to have a friend that loveth at all times, a brother born for adversity, an advocate with the Father, ever making intercession for us; to know that we are in union with Jesus, that the union is so close that He knows every thought, sympathises with us in every pain, and will bring us where He is in exact likeness to Himself. He is our head; we are His body. Precious truth this, that Christ and His church are one! How full of holy comfort! What an antidote it is against despondency and despair! May I live on the Lord's comforts, when all within and around me is wintry, desolate, and depressing.

> *When mournful thoughts within me roll,*
> *And rush upon my labouring breast,*
> *Thy comforts shall my heart console,*
> *While on Thy promises I rest.*

JUNE 12

❦ MORNING ❦

'The LORD God is a sun and shield'
PSALM 84:11

To Him we must look for light, comfort, and fruitfulness. He is our light and our salvation. He will not leave us comfortless. From Him is our fruit found. The people who know Him, believe Him, and walk with Him, are blessed. He giveth light in darkness, joy in sorrow, and life in death. He is our defence; from Him we must expect protection. His salvation is our shield; faith lays hold of it, and employs it against all our foes. He will enlighten and protect us; He will never fail us, or leave us to want or perish. He communicates His favours as freely, as easily, and as plentifully as the sun shines. There is enough in Him, and He will cheerfully bestow. Let us therefore wait upon Him this day, and walk in the light of His countenance. Who is among you that feareth the Lord, and obeyeth the voice of His servant, that walketh in darkness and hath no light? Let him trust in the name of the Lord, and stay upon his God. His heart is ever more towards us, His promises shall be fulfilled to us, and He will glorify every perfection of His nature in us. O the riches of grace!

> Lord, be my safety and defence,
> My light, my joy, my bliss;
> My portion in the world to come,
>
> My confidence in this:
> Be Thou, O Lord, my Shield and Sun,
> As I the path of duty run.

❦ EVENING ❦

'God for Christ's sake hath forgiven you'
EPHESIANS 4:32

The pardon of all our sins is one of God's greatest blessings; and to know and enjoy it is one of our greatest privileges. Our God is a pardoning God. He pardons freely. He pardons frequently. He pardons willingly. He pardons heartily. He pardons justly. He pardons for ever, so that sin forgiven is sin forgotten. But He only pardons for Christ's sake. It is not for the sake of repentance, or faith, or good works, but for the sake of Christ alone. Jesus hath once suffered for our sins, the just for the unjust, that He might bring us to God. He hath made a full, complete, and everlasting atonement for our sins; He put them away by the sacrifice of Himself. So that when we believe in Jesus, receive the record God hath given of His Son, approach the throne of grace and plead for pardon in His name, the Father does honour to His Son by pardoning us. Every believer is pardoned. He is forgiven all transgressions. His sins are all blotted out. He is justified from every charge. Who is he that condemneth? God hath justified us. Jesus died for our sins according to His will. He obtained for us eternal redemption. For His sake, we stand before God this night, pardoned and accepted.

> O! may I practically show,
> My interest in this grace;
> Be all I am, and have, and do,
> Devoted to Thy praise.

JUNE 13

🌿 MORNING 🌿
'The angel of the LORD stood by'
ZECHARIAH 3:5

Who was it that thus stood by Joshua, when Satan accused and resisted him; when his filthy garments bore testimony against him, and he was cited to appear before God? Surely it was Jesus: Jesus, the messenger of the covenant; the minister of the true tabernacle, which God pitched, and not man; the angel of Jehovah's presence. This same Jesus stands by all His people; He stands by *us*. He stands on our side in prayer, in trouble, in temptation, in all our efforts to glorify His name. He stands by to instruct us in the will of God; to help us in the work of God; to enrich us with the wealth of God; and to watch over us for good. Beloved, whoever leaves us, Jesus still stands by us. Our eyes should always be fixed upon Him. We ought never to forget, there is one witness to every action; Jesus stands by observing. We should therefore be circumspect, grateful, and courageous. He stands at the right hand of the poor, to save him from those who condemn his soul. He stands ready to help, waiting to give, determined to bless. May we always realize that Jesus stands by, and expect counsel and help from Him!

> *Look up, my soul, with cheerful eye,*
> *See where the great Redeemer stands,*
> *The glorious Advocate on high,*
> *With precious incense in His hands!*
> *On Him alone thy hopes recline;*
> *His power and love are all divine.*

🌿 EVENING 🌿
'Thou standest by faith'
ROMANS 11:20

Faith in Jesus is of the greatest importance. We cannot overvalue it, unless we put it in the place of Christ. Are we justified? It is by faith. Are we sanctified? Our hearts are purified by faith. Do we fight? It is the fight of faith. Do we overcome? This is the victory which overcometh the world, even our faith. By faith we look to Jesus; by faith we receive Christ; by faith we walk with God; by faith we stand; for we are kept by the power of God, through faith, unto salvation. It is by believing what Christ is to us, what Christ has for us, what Christ will confer upon us, that we stand. It is by faith that we receive from Christ light to guide us in every difficult path; strength to act, to fight, and persevere in our Christian course. In a word, grace to help us in every time of need. Let us therefore take heed, lest there be in any of us an evil heart of unbelief, in departing from the living God. Let us strive against doubts, and encourage confidence in God. We cannot believe in God's Word too confidently; we cannot trust in the Saviour's finished work too steadily; we cannot confide in God's veracity too firmly. Let us endeavour to imitate Abraham, who was strong in faith, giving glory to God.

> *Christ is my Rock, and though my foes,*
> *Display their utmost wrath,*
> *Yet in the power which He bestows,*
> *I stand by precious faith.*

JUNE 14

🌿 MORNING 🌿

'As thy days, so shall thy strength be'
DEUTERONOMY 33:25

No man can possibly tell what is before him; but our God knoweth, and He has promised His people strength proportioned to their trials. We should not be anxious, for with the trial comes the strength. Our troubles are very generally to be numbered amongst our mercies. Temporal prosperity without a special blessing from God will prove to be a curse; and it always brings a solemn responsibility with it. We have always found our God faithful; He always has given strength according to the day; and why should we now doubt? We may look forward and suppose the worst, and then say, 'I will trust and not be afraid; for the LORD JEHOVAH is my *strength* and my song; he also is become my salvation.' We go from strength to strength, and every true believer shall appear in Zion before God. He will perfect that which concerneth us, but will never forsake the work of His own hands. Let us then expect the Lord to give *when* we want, *as* we want, and *all* we want; let us believe that our strength will be equal to our burden, to our day. The promise is plain: it is positive, it is sure, and our God is faithful.

> *God is love, and will not leave you,*
> *When you most His kindness need;*
> *God is true, nor can deceive you,*
> *Though your faith be weak indeed.*

🌿 EVENING 🌿

'They crucified Him'
MATTHEW 27:35

The Father delivered Him up, Judas betrayed Him, and then they crucified Him. Let us consider the design of God in His death. It was to satisfy the claims of justice, to clear His holiness in the salvation of the people, to display His wisdom, to manifest His mercy, to put away our sins, and to disclose the wonders of His love. Let us notice what Jesus displayed when He was crucified. Here we see His filial obedience to His Father, His implicit trust in God, His surprising patience under suffering, His meek forgiving spirit, His astonishing love to His people, and His entire submission to the divine will. Let us observe what man discovered in this transaction. What base ingratitude! What inexcusable cruelty! What insulting pride! What profound ignorance! What fickle instability! Judas shows the power and tendency of covetousness; the Pharisees, the envy and cruelty which lurks under self-righteousness; Pilate, the effect of the fear of man; His disciples, the weakness which may be found in honest hearts. Here, Jehovah is most clearly revealed. The nature of sin is set forth. The true condition of man is unfolded. The cross unveils heaven, earth, and hell. Go to the cross to repent, to believe, to pray, to set an example. It is –

> *The balm of life, the cure of woe,*
> *The measure and the pledge of love;*
> *The sinner's refuge here below,*
> *The angel's theme in heaven above.*

JUNE 15

🌿 MORNING 🌿

'Let not your heart be troubled'
JOHN 14:1

Jesus does not approve of your being in an agitated, perplexed, uncomfortable state. He wishes to see you steady, holy, and happy. He forbids your fear; He commands your faith. As He is with you, as He is engaged for you, you should leave your concerns very much with Him. But how can we attend to this exhortation? Get the mind assured of a covenant interest in God, as your God. Live under the impression: God is with me; He minutely observes every thing that takes place within and around me; He is watching for an opportunity to do me good; He will not allow any thing to hurt me; He will glorify Himself in me, and me in Himself; He bids me trust Him; I will trust and not be afraid. What will follow? He will keep them in perfect peace, whose minds are stayed on Him, because they trust in Him. Trust then in the Lord for ever, for in the Lord Jehovah is everlasting strength. Let nothing trouble you, for your souls are in the hands of Jesus; your life is hid with Christ in God; your times are at God's disposal; and all things are working together for your good.

> *Calmer of my troubled heart,*
> *Bid my unbelief depart;*
> *Speak, and all my sorrows cease;*
> *Speak, and all my soul is peace;*
> *And till I Thy glory see,*
> *Help me to believe in Thee.*

🌿 EVENING 🌿

'They are the sons of God'
ROMANS 8:14

Who are the sons of God? As many as are led by the Spirit of God. To what does the Spirit lead the sons of God? To know their need of a Saviour, to perceive the exact suitability of the Lord Jesus, to fly to Him for refuge, to rest alone on His perfect work, to receive from Him life, light, and holy peace. In brief, He leads them to loathe themselves, repent of sin, separate from the world, cleave to Jesus, walk with God, follow after holiness, and devote themselves to the Lord's service and praise. Those who are thus led by the Spirit of God, they are the sons of God. They were predestinated to the adoption of children before time. They are now declared to be the children of the Most High. They are born of God, they are taught of God, they are the beloved of God, they are treated as children, they are heirs of God, they are associated with the Lord Jesus, they are appointed to share in the highest honours, to enjoy the purest bliss. Beloved, are we led by the Spirit? Has He led us this day to Jesus? Has He humbled us? Is Christ precious to us? If we are the sons of God we are safe. We shall be supplied.

> *Send forth the Spirit of Thy Son,*
> *O God, into my panting heart,*
> *That govern'd by Thy love alone,*
> *From Thee I never may depart,*
> *But following my celestial guide,*
> *Be numbered with the glorified.*

JUNE 16

🌿 MORNING 🌿

'I go to prepare a place for you'

JOHN 14:2

See, beloved, what Jesus is doing. He is engaged for us; He did all He could for us on earth, and then ascended to heaven to carry on His work. The place He prepares will be worthy of Himself: 'His rest will be glorious.' It will just suit us; there the wicked cease from troubling, sin shall no more annoy, troubles shall no more beset, but the weary shall be at rest. He is preparing us for it, as well as it for us; therefore we are so tried and afflicted. Our light afflictions which are but for a moment, are working out for us a far more exceeding and eternal weight of glory. Let us daily think of Jesus as employed for us; let us consider death as going to take possession of the place He has prepared for us; and under all that tries us or casts us down, let us remember, Jesus will come again and receive us unto Himself, that where He is, we may be also. Our present cottage may be incommodious and uncomfortable; but our mansion will be spacious, magnificent, and worthy of a God. He that overcometh shall inherit all things, and Jehovah will be his God. Glorious privilege! Unspeakable blessing! Sweet prospect!

And art Thou, gracious Saviour, gone,
A mansion to prepare for me?
Shall I behold Thee on Thy throne,
And there for ever sit with Thee?
Then let the world approve or blame,
I'll triumph in Thy gracious name.

🌿 EVENING 🌿

'It knew him not'

1 JOHN 3:1

The world knew not Jesus when He sojourned below; the generality of men do not know Him now. They do not know the love which glows in His bosom, which brought Him to tabernacle in the flesh, and made Him a man of sorrows, and the familiar of grief. They knew not the sweetness of His disposition, or the kindness of His intention toward fallen, polluted man. They know not His willingness to receive, His determination to bless, and His engagement to save, all who flee for refuge to His arms. They know not the glory of His person, the extent of His authority, or the value of His atoning blood. They have no just idea of the condescension He displays, the extent of the sufferings He endured, or the invaluable blessings which He freely bestows on the lost and undone. No one knows the Saviour who does not love Him. Every one who believes in Him knows Him; and every one that knows Him will believe His Word, rests on His glorious atonement, and rejoices in His veracity. Jesus to be known must be revealed. The Holy Spirit must enlighten our minds, unfold His character, and apply the Word or we shall not know Him. May we daily behold His glory and be changed into the same image, from glory to glory, even by the Spirit of the Lord.

Come, Holy Spirit, now reveal,
The Son of God to me;
Thy powerful influence let me feel,
And all His glories see.

JUNE 17

🌿 MORNING 🌿
'Salvation is of the LORD'
Jonah 2:9

The love of the Father, the work of the Son, and the operations of the Holy Ghost, save the soul. The Father devised the scheme, the Son gave the ransom, and the Holy Spirit puts us in possession of the blessing. It is of God. It is by grace. It is through faith. Deliverance from dangers, trials, and wants, is of the Lord. He delivered Jonah when he cried, though he was a poor, proud, obstinate, peevish, fretful sinner; and He will deliver us. He says, 'Look unto Me and be delivered, for I am God. Look, for I bid you. Look, for I will attend you. Look, for I will deliver you.' He will deliver in six troubles, and in seven He will not forsake us. He will deliver our souls from death, our eyes from tears, and our feet from falling. He will deliver the needy when he crieth, the poor also, and him that hath no helper. Are you looking to others? Are you drooping, fearing, or desponding? Your God takes it unkindly; He asks, 'Is my hand shortened at all, that it cannot redeem? or have I no power to deliver?' 'Is there any thing too hard for me?' He says, 'I will work.' He asks, 'Who shall let it?' He swears, 'I will not be wroth with thee.'

> Of all the crowns JEHOVAH bears,
> Salvation is His dearest claim;
> That gracious sound well pleased He hears,
> And owns EMMANUEL for His name;
> He saves us by His precious blood,
> And proves Himself the MIGHTY GOD.

🌿 EVENING 🌿
'The kingdom of God is within you'
Luke 17:21

Jehovah erects His throne in the hearts of His people. He reigns over the world, but He reigns in them. The Christian is at once the habitation, the temple, and the kingdom of God. In us He dwells and reigns. He takes possession in regeneration, and is enthroned when we consecrate ourselves entirely to His service and praise. This kingdom includes reconciliation to God, friendship with God, and entire submission to the will of God, brought about by the application of the atonement, the manifestation of divine favour, and the comforts of the Holy Ghost. Where Jehovah reigns, the soul is justified through the righteousness of Christ, enjoys holy peace and fellowship with God, and is happy in a sense of the paternal love of God. The enmity of the heart is slain, the darkness of the mind is dispersed, the carnality of the affections is removed, and the person is brought into subjection to the obedience of Christ. The will of God becomes law, the person and work of Christ precious, and the glory of God the object sought. The enemy is a friend, the rebel a loyal subject, the alien a beloved child. If the kingdom of God is within us, we ought to be in the church of God by a scriptural profession, and should so walk as to please God.

> Reign in me, Jehovah, reign,
> Let my rebel lusts be slain;
> Righteousness and peace impart,
> Fill with holy joy my heart.

JUNE 18

🌿 MORNING 🌿

'I will not leave you comfortless'

JOHN 14:18

Believers when in darkness often fear that Jesus has forsaken them. This is natural, but it is unscriptural, for He has said, 'I will never leave thee, nor forsake thee.' His offices require His presence with us; His love secures His presence to us. He will not leave us orphans. We are absolutely dependent upon Him; our comfort is His gift, and the continuance of comfort depends on His presence and grace. He is the great source of comfort to His people. His presence and His comforts are generally connected. He may withhold them for a time to reprove, instruct, or correct us, but we may calculate upon His comforts returning, for His promise is plain. It stands unrepealed in His Word, and His nature and love are the same. His precious word of promise should be believed, pleaded and firmly trusted. We never shall be orphans, for our Father ever lives; our home waits to receive us, and our hope is imperishable. O, beloved, plead this precious word of Jesus; expect Him to make it good; aim at His glory, and your comforts are sure! He will not leave us comfortless.

Most Holy Spirit, give me faith,
To rest on what my Saviour saith;
May I the sweetest comforts prove,
Of His divine eternal love;
And daily trust His faithfulness,
Who will not leave me comfortless.

🌿 EVENING 🌿

'Thou restrainest prayer before God'

JOB 15:4

This charge, brought against Job, may often be justly brought against us, for though prayer is one of the most delightful privileges, and is enjoyed as such when under the influence of the Spirit of adoption, yet when a spirit of bondage prevails, or we get worldly-minded, it is rather a task than a pleasure. Often are we tempted to keep away from the Lord, because we are so lukewarm, or cold, or dead, whereas these are the very things which should drive us to Him. Never let us wait for a better frame, or more convenient season, but let us go as we are, and whenever an opportunity offers, to a throne of grace. For if we restrain prayer before God, we shall soon get cold, careless, and lifeless, if we are not so; sin will gather strength, all our graces will be weakened, and the gift of prayer will wither. Our tempers will become carnalised, our peace will be disturbed, and the enjoyment of religion will fade. The things of time will be preferred, gospel ordinances will become barren, and Satan will gain advantage over us. Restraining prayer is directly opposed to God's Word; it is yielding to Satan, grieving the Holy Spirit, and must end in mischief.

Father, to my heart appear,
Pleased and smiling in Thy Son;
Conscious of Thy presence near,
Bow'd and humble at Thy throne.
Then I in Thy sight shall stay,
Always fear, and always pray.

JUNE 19

🌿 MORNING 🌿

'All his saints are in thy hand'
DEUTERONOMY 33:3

Every believer is a saint, separated by the purpose of God, sanctified by the operations of the Holy Spirit, set apart for God, and devoted to His service. Every saint is in the hand of Jesus, in the hand of His mercy, in the hand of His power, and in the hand of His providence. The hand of Jesus is large enough to hold all, strong enough to defend all. They are in His hand as His property, purchased by His blood; as His charge, committed to Him by His Father; at His disposal, to do with them as seemeth good in His sight; under His protection, to be kept from Satan, death, and hell; to be guided through this desert world, to our Father's house above; to be moulded by His skill, and conformed to His own lovely image; to be covered from the storm, and preserved from the furious blast; to be used for His praise, and be lifted up to His eternal throne. They are His *saints*; He chose them for His *bride*; He rescued them from the hand of the enemy; He claims them as His right; He made them what they are; and He will glorify them for ever.

> Blessed are the saints of God!
> They are bought with Jesus' blood,
> They are ransom'd from the grave,
>
> Life eternal they shall have;
> With them number'd may I be,
> Now and through eternity!

🌿 EVENING 🌿

'I obtained mercy'
1 TIMOTHY 1:13

Paul was a blasphemer, a persecutor, and very injurious to the cause of Christ; but the Lord showed him mercy as a pattern to them which should hereafter believe. Here we see that mercy is free for the vilest; that the Lord has mercy upon sinners, just because He will have mercy. Paul obtained it without seeking; any one may by seeking it. The mercy which the Lord shows, and which Paul obtained, always brings a complete pardon for all past sins, however numerous or flagrant they may have been. It brings peace to the conscience, however troubled or distressed. It produces holiness in the heart which will appear in the life. It leads the soul to desire and seek the knowledge of Christ above all other things, and to count everything but dross and dung in comparison with it. It fortifies the mind to meet, endure, and pass through trials and tribulation for Christ's sake. It leads to friendship with God, concern for the salvation of souls, and binds us to the church of Jesus by strong and various ties. Reader, have you obtained mercy? Has mercy had the same effect on you as it had on Paul? Whenever mercy is obtained, the fruits and effects of its reception will appear. Precious must be that mercy which brings so many blessings in its train.

> Mercy I cannot claim,
> But since Thy mercy's free,
> And I so poor and helpless am,
> Have mercy, Lord, on me.

JUNE 20

❦ MORNING ❧
'It is God that justifieth'
ROMANS 8:33

To be justified is to be acquitted, and pronounced righteous. Every believer in Jesus, however ungodly he may have been, or however vile and unworthy he may feel, is justified by Jehovah. The perfect work of Jesus is imputed to him, free grace is glorified in him, and he is passed from death unto life. To him, there is no condemnation; no one can lay any thing to his charge; he is accepted in the Beloved; Christ lived and died for him, and now he liveth and shall be glorified through and with Jesus. All his trespasses are freely forgiven and eternally forgotten. God has cast all our sins behind His back, and now He pronounces us just. Let us approach God, believing that He has justified us; and let us look forward and rejoice that the Judge of all the earth will declare us righteous. Who shall lay anything to our charge? It is God that justifieth. Who is he that condemneth? It is Christ that died, yea, rather that is risen again, who is even at the right hand of God, who also maketh intercession for us. My soul, look to Jesus, to His perfect work and prevalent intercession, and there see thy salvation and find peace.

> *Turn then, my soul, unto thy rest;*
> *The merits of thy great High Priest,*
> *Speak peace and liberty;*
> *Trust in His efficacious blood,*
> *Nor fear thy banishment from God,*
> *Since Jesus died for thee.*

❦ EVENING ❧
'The LORD's portion is His people'
DEUTERONOMY 32:9

We are filled with gratitude and joy, when we say, 'The Lord is my portion,' but it is enough to fill us with wonder and astonishment to read, 'The LORD's portion is His people.' He is so great, and they are so insignificant; He is so holy, and they are so polluted; He is so glorious, and they are so mean. But He chose them in preference to others, when all lay before His eye. He redeemed them, when enslaved and alienated from Him. He claimed them, when held fast by their tyrannizing foe. He possesses and enjoys them as the objects of His love. He inhabits them as His temple, He protects them as His children, and He will dignify them in heaven for ever. They are the Lord's lot, His inheritance, His vineyard, His garden, His spouse. Think, believer, of the honour conferred upon you, in calling you the Lord's portion! Once a wandering sheep, but now returned unto the Shepherd and Bishop of your soul. Angels are never called His portion, His jewels, but you are. Walk as the Lord's chosen bride, who is going home to be openly united to her beloved bridegroom. Give to grace its righteous due, for it is by favour that you are distinguished. Let me lie down on my pillow tonight impressed with this thought: *'I am the Lord's portion.'*

> *His portion is His care,*
> *He keeps it day and night;*
> *No other can with this compare,*
> *'Tis Jesu's chief delight.*

JUNE 21

🌿 MORNING 🌿

'How is it that ye have no faith?'

MARK 4:40

Where there is little faith there are many fears. The disciples were filled with alarm, and Jesus inquires, 'How is it that ye have no faith?' May not our heavenly Father often address us in the same language? 'How is it that ye give no credit to My Word? How is it that ye place no dependence upon My relation, character, and veracity? How is it that ye have no confidence in My power, presence, and love? How is it that ye do not expect My interference, and look for My supplies? Have I not made promises which are plain, positive, and sure? Have I not fulfilled My promises again and again? Have I not summoned witnesses to attest the truth of My Word? Have I not promised you My Holy Spirit? Have I not pledged My holiness? Have I not given My Son for you and to you? Have I not appeared for you in every past difficulty? How is it, then, that ye have no faith?' Beloved, let us humble ourselves before God. Let us plead guilty of indulging in unbelief, and plead for faith. Let us look for God in every place and in every thing. Let us trust Him when we cannot trace Him.

> Why should my soul indulge complaints,
> And yield to dark despair?
> The meanest of my Father's saints,
> Are safe beneath His care.
> Dear Lord, increase my faith in Thee
> Till I Thy full salvation see.

🌿 EVENING 🌿

'For with the LORD there is mercy'

PSALM 130:7

Mercy has been shown to us, but it dwells in God. It is one of His perfections. The exercise of it is His delight. There is mercy with the Lord in all His fulness; He never was more merciful than now, nor He never will be. There is mercy with the Lord in all its tenderness; He is full of compassion, His bowels are troubled for us, His tender mercies are over us. There is mercy with Him in all its variety; it suits every case. Here is mercy that receives sinners, mercy that restores backsliders, mercy that keeps believers. Here is the mercy that pardons sin, that introduces to the enjoyment of all gospel privileges, and that blesses the praying soul far beyond its expectations. With the Lord there is mercy and He loves to display it, He is ready to impart it, He has determined to exalt and glorify it. There is mercy with the Lord. This should encourage the miserable to approach Him; this informs the fearful. They need bring nothing to induce Him to bless them. This calls upon backsliders to return to Him; and this is calculated to cheer the tried Christian, under all his troubles and distresses. Remember, mercy is like God: it is infinite and eternal; mercy is always on the throne; mercy may be obtained by any sinner.

> Believer, on the Lord recline;
> His mercy's boundless and divine!
> See from the cross how wide it flows,
> Beyond the extent of all thy woes!

JUNE 22

❦ MORNING ❦
'God is faithful'
1 Corinthians 10:13

This is the believer's sheet anchor; without this his comforts would droop, and hope would give up the ghost. We are at times shaken to pieces by unbelief, and filled with tormenting doubts. We feel nothing of the presence, power, or comforts of the Holy Ghost; faith, hope, and love seem to be quite extinguished. We have no power, and scarcely any inclination to pray; and we feel only hardness, fretfulness, and misery. We are tempted by Satan, and harassed with tormenting thoughts, so that we feel tired of this miserable life. But God is faithful; He never fails us, but appears again and again, restoring us to peace, joy, and satisfaction; and our most miserable times are often succeeded by peculiar joys. The Scriptures are opened up to our understandings, the promises are applied to our souls, and we are filled with the comforts of the Holy Ghost. Then our souls melt before God in contrition and holy penitence; we feel crumbled into dust before Him, and can only admire and adore the riches of free and sovereign grace. Beloved, in the darkest night, remember, 'God is faithful.'

> He will not His great self deny;
> A God all truth can never lie;
> True to His Word, God gave His Son
> To die for crimes which men had done;
> Blest pledge! He never will revoke
> A single promise He has spoke.

❦ EVENING ❦
'Holding forth the word of life'
Philippians 2:16

That is the gospel. It reveals life in the promise, and in the person and work of Christ. It presents life as God's free gift to the condemned and guilty. It is employed to produce life through the power of the Holy Ghost. The life which it reveals, presents, and produces, stands in the favour of God; in union to the person of Christ; in the possession of the Spirit; in fellowship with the fountain of life; in freedom from all condemnation; and in a title to eternal glory. This gospel is entrusted to us; it is entrusted to us for others, and we are to hold it forth as a light in a dark place, as food provided for hungry sinners, as a pardon for condemned criminals, and as a rule for quickened souls. It is to be held forth in the public ministry, by a holy conversation, and by every possible means. Beloved, let us view the gospel as 'the word of life.' Let us remember the obligation that is laid upon us to hold it forth. Let us ask ourselves, 'Are we holding it forth as we should?' Let us hold forth this word of life by speaking, by writing, by purchasing and distributing little works which have been printed for the purpose, and by assisting those who have consecrated their time and talents to the work.

> Come, let us with a grateful heart,
> In the bless'd labour share a part;
> Our prayers and offerings gladly bring,
> To aid the triumph of our King.

JUNE 23

❦ MORNING ❦

'What do these Hebrews here?'

1 Samuel 29:3

David's host wanted to mingle with the Philistines' army. This was decidedly wrong, and it is as wrong when God's people unite with the world, contrary to His holy Word. We may ask, 'What do these Christians here?' What do they joining with the world? Their Master has told them to 'come out and be separate.' What do they seeking a settlement below? He has said, 'Arise ye, and depart; this is not your rest.' What do they out of the path of duty, or by their presence sanctioning sin? He has said, 'Be ye holy, for I am holy.' What do they on Satan's ground, in the enemy's ranks? Do they intend to leave Jesus, and join the world? Are they tired of His company, set against His Word, and determined to throw off His yoke? Do they intend to share in what they have proclaimed as the sinner's doom, the frown of Jesus, the wrath of God, and the slavery of Satan? *What do they here?* Their conduct is unnatural, degrading and traitorous. Beloved, you should keep the company of Jesus, walk with spiritual persons, and keep yourselves unspotted from the world.

> Ye tempting sweets forbear,
> Ye dearest idols fall;
> My love ye must not share,
> Jesus shall have it all;
> Aid me, dear Saviour, set me free,
> And I will all resign for Thee.

❦ EVENING ❦

'The righteous shall flourish as a branch'

Proverbs 11:28

Such are justified by faith of Christ. To them, the Lord hath brought forth His righteousness; in them, the Lord hath put His Holy Spirit. They are just before God in Jesus, and they are consistent before men, bringing forth the fruits of righteousness to the praise of His glory. They are compared to a branch, which is united to, and forms part of the parent tree. So are they united to Jesus, and are one with Him. All their support is from Him, and they derive all their supplies from His fulness. He is the source of their life, beauty, strength, and fruitfulness. Apart from Him they are barren, withered, and dead. He supplies them secretly, as the tree does the branch with sap; but He sheds on them also the dew of His grace, and the showers of His blessing. In consequence of this they grow, flourish, and bear fruit. He prunes them by afflictions, but it is only that they may bring forth more fruit. Autumnal winds may strip them, and wintry frosts may lay them bare, but their life is in the root, hid with Christ in God. See, beloved, the effect of union to Christ: we flourish – the proof of a religious state.

> The trees of righteousness shall rise,
> Water'd each moment from above,
> And bear the fruit of paradise,
> The glorious fruits of faith and love.

JUNE 24

❦ MORNING ❦

'Ye are a chosen generation'
1 Peter 2:9

Religion does not originate in chance, but in the purpose of God; it flows not from the nature of man, but from the unalterable decree of the Most High. Every believer is a chosen vessel. The church had its origin in Jehovah's eternal election. Election flows from love; it is the exercise of sovereignty; it secures man's salvation and God's glory. It injures none, but it pours incalculable blessings upon thousands. It was the act of God before time. He chose us in Christ as our Head; it was of pure grace; it was to holiness. We were chosen to be redeemed from death; purified from sin; separated from the world; devoted to God; and raised to a state of oneness with Jehovah. Being chosen of God, we choose God in return. He chose us to be His people, we choose Him to be our God. He chose us to be the beloved Bride of Jesus, and we choose Jesus to be our beloved Bridegroom. His election is the cause; our choice is the effect. His choice prevented ours; or else we had chosen death, in the error of our ways. Beloved, if we are the elect of God, we are holy; we are in union with Jesus. Let us endeavour to prove and enjoy this.

All the elected train
Were chosen in their Head,
To all eternal good,

Before the worlds were made;
Chosen to know the Prince of peace,
And taste the riches of His grace.

❦ EVENING ❦

'Lead me to the rock'
Psalm 61:2

That rock was Christ. He was first promised, then prefigured, and then manifested. He is the smitten rock, which supplies His thirsty ones; the rock of ages, which sustains His feeble ones; the great rock, which revives His weary ones; the high rock, which protects His hunted ones; and the cleft rock, which hides His timid and fearful ones. In this rock we are safe. From this rock, we can see the land which is very far off. By this rock, we are sheltered from the storm, and screened from the scorching sun. We often wander from it. At a distance we learn its value, and sigh for the privilege it confers. But wherever we may be, it is accessible to us. Yet we need a guide to conduct us, and a friend to assist us. Then, let us determine with the psalmist, however far off we may be: 'From the end of the earth will I cry unto thee; when my heart is overwhelmed, lead me to the rock that is higher than I.' Jesus is all we need. He has all we can possibly want. Prayer is always allowed, approved, encouraged, rewarded. Led to Him, we shall be raised above our fears, above our foes, and above our expectations. He is able to do for us exceeding abundantly above all that we can ask or think.

When sorely afflicted, and ready to faint,
Before my Redeemer, I'll spread my complaint;
In every new trial, to Him will I cry,
'Lead me to the Rock that is higher than I.'

JUNE 25

❦ MORNING ❦

'What manner of persons ought ye to be?'

2 PETER 3:11

The people of God are expected to be different from the world; they profess to have another Spirit in them, and to be the sons of God. They believe the present frame of things is to be dissolved. They look for a new heaven and a new earth, wherein dwelleth righteousness. They are strangers and pilgrims here. What manner of persons then ought we to be? Surely we ought to set light by the things of time, and aim at the things which are eternal. We ought to be watchful, prayerful, diligent, holy, patient, thankful, and expectant. We ought to be contented with such things as we have; to give all diligence to prove our title, make sure of our election, and rejoice in our destination. We ought to walk as Jesus walked, to live as Paul lived, dying daily. Let us ask this morning, 'Do we habitually believe that present things will soon be dissolved?' If so, are we acting according to the same? Are we laying up for ourselves treasures in heaven? Are we doing good, that we may be rich in good works, and an honour to religion? Is the coming of Jesus the object of our desire and hope?

> Then let us wait the sound
> That shall our souls release,
> And labour to be found
> Of Him in spotless peace;
> In perfect holiness renew'd,
> Adorn'd with Christ, and meet for God.

❦ EVENING ❦

'Ye are Christ's'

1 CORINTHIANS 3:23

Who are Christ's? The saints whom He hath set apart for Himself; those who worship Him as their God and Saviour; or Christians who believe on His name, surrender at His call, and submit to His will. All Christians, though of low stature, though compassed about with infirmities, though often cast down through doubts and fears, they are Christ's and in consequence His Father is theirs; His Spirit is theirs; His righteousness is theirs; His atonement is theirs; His peace is theirs; His wealth is theirs; Himself and all He has is theirs. If they are Christ's, He will defend them as His property, support them as His children, and cherish them as His bride. If we are Christ's, then we should entirely listen to Him when He speaks; cheerfully obey Him when He commands; refuse to believe anything that may be suggested against Him by Satan or men. Always own Him as our Lord and Master. Frequently visit Him at the throne of grace, at His table, and in His house. Live upon Him now, in hope of living with Him for ever and ever. Reader, have you good evidence that you are Christ's? Are you daily looking to Him for wisdom, righteousness, sanctification, and redemption?

> All things I want, but One is nigh,
> My want of all things to supply;
> Pardon, and peace, and liberty,
> Jesus, I all things have in Thee.

JUNE 26

🌿 MORNING 🌿

'My grace is sufficient for thee'

2 CORINTHIANS 12:9

You need look to no other quarter for help, relief, or comfort. Jesus assures you that His grace is sufficient. You are welcome to it. You are exhorted to have it, to be strong in the grace which is in Christ Jesus. It is sufficient to support you under every privation, to help you over every difficulty, to strengthen you for every duty, to mortify every lust, and to fill you with all joy and peace in believing. His grace is almighty, it is free, it is durable, it brings salvation. Look not at difficulties, dangers, or thy own weakness; but look to the free, powerful, and promised grace of Jesus. Go to His throne of grace this morning, on purpose to receive grace for this day; go every day, and whenever you feel weak, timid, or cast down. His grace was found sufficient for Paul, for the martyrs and saints, in the deepest trials, and it will be found sufficient for thee. He says, 'I am the LORD thy God; ... open thy mouth wide, and I will fill it.' Come boldly to the throne of grace, that ye may obtain mercy and find grace to help you in time of need. 'Every one that asketh receiveth.' O Jesus, make good Thy Word in me!

> *Thy strength in weakness is display'd;*
> *My soul this truth can relish now:*
> *A worm upon Thy power is stay'd;*
>
> *The weaker he, the stronger Thou;*
> *My hope, my joy, is this alone:*
> *My strength is Christ, THE MIGHTY ONE.*

🌿 EVENING 🌿

'I am the way'

JOHN 14:6

This is a beautiful figure selected by Jesus to set forth His adaptation to us. We are at a distance from God; as sinners, there is by nature no way in which we can approach God with acceptance. But Jesus, by becoming the Mediator, became the way to the Father. He is the way from a state of sin to a state of holiness; from the dread of wealth, to the enjoyment of eternal love. He is the way to acquaintance with God, reconciliation to God, acceptance with God, relationship to God, enjoyment of God, conformity to God, and to the presence and glory of God. As a way He is suitable to all sinners, open to all who are willing to make use of Him, safe for all who venture upon Him, and the only way from the wrath to come. Observe, we are all out of the way by nature. We are convinced of this fact by the Holy Spirit. We discover our need of just such a way as Jesus is. We enter upon it by faith. We often moisten the way with our tears. We have to travel along the way with patience; and every one that really enters upon it, arrives at the end of it in safety. Beloved, the ground on which we stand is good, the way in which we walk is direct, and the end of the journey we have commenced – is everlasting life.

> *Thou art the WAY – to Thee alone,*
> *From sin and death we flee;*
> *And he who would the Father seek,*
> *Must seek Him, Lord, in Thee.*

JUNE 27

❦ MORNING ❦

'Remember Lot's wife'
LUKE 17:32

She received the angels, and hospitably entertained them; she believed their message, and prepared to act upon it; she obeyed their command, and left Sodom and her children behind her. She forsook the ungodly, and went in company with the saints; yet her heart was left in the city, and she looked back. She was deprived of life, for too highly prizing its comforts. She was cut off by a visible display of God's judgment. The situation in which she died was instructive: it was not in Sodom, but on the plain; she escaped one judgment, but was overtaken by another. She was left as a sad example of God's jealousy and displeasure against sin. Here is a warning to the covetous, whose hearts are set on things below; to the self-willed, who trifle with God's commands; and to the undecided, who stand between Sodom and Zoar. God will be honoured by our obedience, or by our sufferings. It is dangerous to trifle with the smallest of God's commands. We may overcome one temptation, and yet fall by another. Let us examine, 'Are our hearts detached from the world?' Be not high-minded, but fear. Remember Lot's wife.

> Waiting for our Lord's returning,
> Be it ours His Word to keep;
> Let our lamps be always burning;
>
> Let us watch, while others sleep.
> We're no longer of the night;
> We are children of the light.

❦ EVENING ❦

'My beloved is mine, and I am his'
SONG OF SOLOMON 2:16

This is the language of holy assurance. Christ is given by the Father to sinners; He is God's unspeakable gift. He is presented in the gospel to every one who hears or reads it, without money and without price. He is accepted and received by faith. The reception of Christ is ratified by solemn engagements; the party engages to be His, and His alone. It is confirmed by holy fellowship. He that claims Christ lives in communion with Him. My Beloved is to me: the Saviour in whom I believe and trust; the Husband whom I reverence and love; the Lord whom I adore and obey; the Portion on which I live; and the Beloved One upon whom my heart and affections are set. 'I am my beloved's.' He chose me, or I had never chosen Him. He redeemed me, or I had still been a slave. He called me, or I had still been wandering from God. He sanctified me, or I had still been vile and polluted. He manifested Himself to me, or I have never seen His glory. I am to my Beloved: His sister-spouse; His portion; His delight; His choice out of all worlds; His glorious crown, out of the spoils He has won. Beloved, seek assurance, nor ever be satisfied but as you say, 'He is mine, and I am His.'

> Jesus my love, my life, my peace,
> Jesus is mine, and I am His;
> His bride, His dear bought property,
> Who lov'd and gave Himself for me.

JUNE 28

❦ MORNING ❧

'The LORD will be the hope of His people'
JOEL 3:16

We know not what a day may bring forth; we are born to trouble; many unexpected trials may befall us; but our God will be our hope. He is the *refuge*, to which we may always repair, and find safety; the *fulness*, from which we shall receive a plentiful supply. His oath, His promises, His covenant character, and the blood of Jesus, lay a firm foundation for our hope; and His gospel warrants us to hope in Him at all times, for all things. Therefore, let what will come, we can have no reason to be disconsolate; we can have no reason to fear; our God is our hope. May the God of hope fill us with all joy and peace in believing, that we may abound in hope by the power of the Holy Ghost. Let us gird up the loins of our minds, be sober, and hope to the end for the grace that is to be brought unto us at the appearing of the Lord Jesus. Let us look for that blessed hope, even the glorious appearing of the great God, even our Saviour Jesus Christ, who gave Himself for us, that He might redeem us from all iniquity, and purify unto Himself a peculiar people, zealous of good works. As Jesus is our hope, let His glory be our aim, and His service our delight.

In Him I hope, in Him I trust,
His bleeding cross is all my boast;
Through troops of foes He'll lead me on
To victory and the Victor's crown.

❦ EVENING ❧

'Knowing the time'
ROMANS 13:11

We cannot know the future, but we may know the present time. Indeed, we ought to know it. What is its character? It is the time of Satan's power: he is active, energetic, and determined. It is the time of the world's danger: it is asleep, or deluded, or enraged against the cause of God. It is the time of God's forbearance: justice now waits, grace sits enthroned, mercy kindly warns, and it is called the accepted time, the day of salvation. It is the time of the church's duty: for it is working time, it is evening time, and therefore precious time. It is a singular time: we have such facilities for doing good, so many calls to action, so many encouragements to persevere, and our responsibility is so deep and solemn. Let us therefore know the time. We may learn its character, partly from God's Word, and partly from observation. Let us improve our knowledge and turn it to account by stirring up others who are drowsy, and embracing every opportunity of doing good ourselves. Let us employ every talent, and improve every opportunity to the utmost. Remember, the time to do good, and to get good, must be short. The end of the present time will be solemn, deeply solemn. We should be wakeful, watchful, laborious, liberal.

Divine Instructor; grace bestow,
Teach me the present time to know;
Help me each talent to improve,
And serve my God in faith and love.

JUNE 29

🌿 MORNING 🌿

'My son, give me thine heart'
Proverbs 23:26

Beloved, the Most High presents Himself as a Suitor this morning. He asks for thy heart. It is His workmanship; He wants it to be His habitation. He made it by His power; He wants to rule it by His grace. He will not be satisfied with anything else. If He have the heart, He has all; if He has not the heart, He has nothing. Let us surrender our hearts to Him this morning, and every morning. Let us ask Him to sanctify them by His grace, to fill them with His Spirit, to engrave on them His image, to keep them by His power, and to fill them with the fruits of holiness. If the heart is given to God, the life will be according to His Word. If He rule in us, we shall walk as Jesus walked. If our walk is not holy, our religion is but a form. 'He that saith, I know Him, and keepeth not His commandments, is a liar, and the truth is not in him.' O, how awful, to think and profess that we are the Lord's, and yet to have the heart under the influence of sin, Satan, and the world! Jesus says, '*My son, give me thine heart.*' Let our reply be, 'Lord, take my heart, reign and rule in it for ever.'

> O Jesus! wounded Lamb of God,
> Come, wash me in Thy cleansing blood;
> Take my poor heart and let it be
> For ever closed to all but Thee;
> Unloose my stammering tongue to tell,
> Thy love immense, unsearchable.

🌿 EVENING 🌿

'Christ in you, the hope of glory'
Colossians 1:27

The object of a Christian's hope is glory, but the exact nature of that glory is unknown. Its greatness is at present inconceivable. It is said to comprise an inheritance, a kingdom, a crown, gladness, exceeding joy. It is a crown of glory, a weight of glory, eternal glory, the glory of our Lord Jesus Christ. It is glory clothing us, glory in us. It will robe the body; it will fill the soul. It includes purity and power, wisdom and knowledge. It is waiting to be revealed. We expect this. This hope or expectation originates in grace; is produced by the Holy Spirit; springs from faith; rests on the promise and oath of God; waits God's time; and purifies its possessor. The evidence or proof of this hope is, *Christ in us*. He dwells in His people by His Word, by His grace, and by His Spirit. He dwells in us as a King in His kingdom, ruling; as a Master in His family, providing; as an Owner in His habitation, claiming; as the Sap in the tree, supplying; as God in His temple, to be adored. If Christ dwells in you, He dwells in your thoughts, desires, affections, enjoyments and aims. Is Christ in you? Are you hoping for glory? Is the glory you hope for the fruition of God?

> Jesus, in me for ever dwell;
> Thyself, the gift unspeakable;
> The hope of heavenly bliss impart,
> The glorious earnest in my heart.

JUNE 30

❦ MORNING ❦
'I am thine, save me'
PSALM 119:94

We profess to be the Lord's. We are not our own. We belong not to the world. We are no longer the servants of sin. We are solely and entirely the Lord's, having willingly given up ourselves into His hands, to be saved by His grace, devoted to His service, and employed for His glory. We are His children by grace and adoption; His servants by voluntary engagement; His soldiers by public profession; and His spouse by affection and union. Being the Lord's, we may expect His interference on our behalf; and we should call on Him and plead with Him in all straits and difficulties. He will save us. He will deliver us. Let us, therefore, lay our case before Him; and then ardently expect Him to glorify His grace in us. Let us walk worthy of God as beloved children, and live under the impression that He will make all grace to abound toward us, so that we having all sufficiency in all things, may abound in every good work. His mercy is great unto the heavens, and His faithfulness unto the clouds; and He never said to the seed of Jacob, *'Seek ye me'* in vain. But He saith, *'Seek ye me, and ye shall live.'*

Jesus, my Saviour, and my God,
Thou hast redeem'd me with Thy blood;
By ties both natural and divine,

I am, and will be ever Thine;
Save me from sin, and Satan's power,
Guide me and guard me every hour.

❦ EVENING ❦
'Partakers of the benefit'
1 TIMOTHY 6:2

The gospel is a benefit – one of God's greatest and best gifts. It benefits every person who receives it. It benefits his intellect, informing it. It benefits his heart, sanctifying it. It benefits his conscience, giving it repose. It benefits his temper, controlling and sweetening it. It benefits his life, preventing many evils, and directing to the attainment and possession of many blessings. It benefits the family where it rules. It makes the master kind, the mistress considerate, the servants attentive and industrious, the parents exemplary, and the children obedient. It benefits the commonwealth in which it works. It suggests good laws, requires good government, and makes good subjects. Have we partaken of this benefit? What is intended by this? It is to perceive its divinity, to approve its doctrines, to receive its blessings, to submit to its precepts, to observe its ordinances, to test its joys, and to employ it for every useful purpose. Some hear of it, others listen to it, others taste and disapprove of it, some partake and are benefited by it. In their state, they are justified; in their character, sanctified; and in their circumstances, happy; for all things work together for their good. Have you benefited by this gospel?

Lord, grant this benefit to me,
And let me feel, and taste, and see,
What glories in that gospel dwell,
Which saves believing souls from hell!

JULY 1

❦ MORNING ❧

'The LORD thy God is a merciful God.'

DEUTERONOMY 4:31

It is no uncommon thing to mistake the true character of our God, and conceive of Him so as to dishonour His name, and distress our own souls. It is plainly and plentifully asserted in the divine Word, that our God is merciful, and the same is satisfactorily proved in nature, providence, and redemption. It is to be firmly believed and constantly remembered, especially when burdened with guilt, or at the throne confessing sin; when enduring trials, or pleading with God for blessings; when performing duties, or suffering privations; when witnessing misery, or comforting mourners. *'Our God is a merciful God.'* But mercy and holiness are united in His nature, Word, and ways. He is not implacable or difficult to please, but He should be daily loved and constantly trusted. His mercy is the sun that enlightens, the ocean that supplies, and the army that guards us. But for His mercy we should soon sink into despair, or run into desperation; but now we may trust and not be afraid, walk with Him in peace, and rejoice in Him day by day.

Merciful God, Thyself proclaim,
In my polluted breast;
Mercy is Thy distinguished name,
Which suits a sinner best.
Thy mighty mercy now make known
In me, and claim me for Thy son.

❦ EVENING ❧

'Who forgiveth all thine iniquities.'

PSALM 103:3

We daily need to be pardoned, for we daily sin. Our sins are of an aggravated character. They are the sins of a ransomed captive against Him who redeemed him at the price of His blood. They are the sins of a peculiarly favoured servant, who lives in his master's house, sits at his master's table, and owes his all to his master's liberality, against the master who thus favours him. They are the sins of a beloved child, against the wisest, kindest, and best of fathers. Our faults are many, various, frequently repeated, and inexcusable. Yet the Lord forgiveth all our iniquities. He pardons like a God, fully, freely, consistently. Every pardon is the price of the blood of Jesus. When He pardons, He secures hatred to sin, sorrow for sin, and a departure from sin. He pardons like a father; He does so tenderly, frequently. David, who bore this testimony to God's pardoning mercy, was no common sinner. He had been guilty of adultery, deception, murder. He led others into sin, charged it upon providence, and slept under the guilt of it for months. He made the record with a smarting conscience, and with a grateful heart. Reader, are you pardoned? Are you guilty? God is ready to forgive; confess, pray, plead Jesus, and be forgiven.

Saviour, I long to testify,
The fulness of Thy gracious power!
Pardon my sins, Thy blood apply,
That I may sovereign grace adore!

JULY 2

❦ MORNING ❦

'He that toucheth you, toucheth the apple of His eye.'
ZECHARIAH 2:8

How infinitely tender is Jehovah of His people! They had lately been visited with sore judgments; reduced to great straits; appeared to be neglected of God; were generally despised; had only just escaped from the enemy's land; and returned with weeping and supplication, like brands plucked from the burning, to their own country. And now the LORD says, 'He that toucheth you, toucheth the apple of His eye.' How wonderful the ways of God! As the wise physician, He will touch to cure; but He will not allow others to touch to hurt. Like the tender mother, He can correct His children Himself; but will not allow others to do so. How close the union! How peculiar the affection! How tender the sympathy! How kind the care! How constant the attention! How merciful the provision! How safe and how happy they are! Beloved, take encouragement under all your persecutions and trials; be comforted in all your afflictions; you are as near and dear to Jehovah as the apple of His eye; and you are hid under the shadow of His wings. Holy Spirit, help me daily to realize this truth!

> No condemnation now I dread,
> Jesus, and all in Him, is mine,
> Alive in Him, my living Head,
> And clothed in righteousness divine.
> Bold I approach the eternal throne,
> And claim the crown, thro' Christ, my own.

❦ EVENING ❦

'The night cometh.'
JOHN 9:4

Night is the emblem of death. There is generally something dreary and gloomy in the night, and so there is in death. When death comes, all our opportunities of doing good in this world are over; let us therefore improve the present. When death comes, our work should be done; if it is not we must leave it unfinished; let us therefore work while it is called day. When death comes, we must bid our friends farewell; let us therefore treat them, and enjoy them, as those that must soon leave them. When death comes, we shall go home to rest; our bodies will find a home in the grave, and sleep quietly and soundly there; and our souls will find a home in the presence of Jesus, and enjoy the sweetest repose and satisfaction there. 'The night cometh,' it is not far off; it draws very nigh to some of us; it may overtake us suddenly; we are therefore warned that we may be ready. Let us endeavour as believers in Jesus, to realize the fact: let us redeem the time; let us work through the whole day; let us be ready for the night, having our work done, our limbs weary, our appetite for heavenly things sharp, and feeling glad to go home. The night of death is preparatory to the morning of the resurrection; then we shall arise refreshed, strong, glorious, immortal.

> O glorious hour! O bless'd abode!
> I shall be near and like my God,
> And flesh and sin no more control
> The sacred pleasures of my soul.

JULY 3

❧ MORNING ❧
'Their heart is divided.'
HOSEA 10:2

This is a very serious charge, for God demands the whole heart, and His people profess to surrender it. But have we not reason to fear that many are guilty on this point? They appear so undecided, that we must think that the heart is divided between God and the world; between sin and holiness; between truth and error; or between Christ and self. What are the symptoms of a divided heart? Habitual cleaving to earth; being satisfied with a form of godliness; backwardness to examine ourselves; a dislike to plain, close, soul-searching, rousing preaching; putting away eternal things to a distance. Beloved, how is it with you? God rejects half the heart; He will have all or none. Do you fear on this point? There is a remedy. Thoroughly examine your heart. Condemn whatever you detect amiss in it. Take it to Jesus, and beseech Him to heal it. Expose it to the keen edge of God's Word. Endeavour to keep up a constant sense of the presence of God. Converse much with eternal realities. As the heart is, so will the life be; so will the comfort and peace be. O Lord, unite my heart to fear Thy name!

Let me, according to Thy Word,
A tender, contrite heart receive,
Which grieves at having grieved its Lord,
And never can itself forgive;
A heart Thy joys and griefs to feel,
A heart where Christ alone may dell.

❧ EVENING ❧
'He retaineth not His anger for ever.'
MICAH 7:18

The wrath of God is dreadful, but this is only directed against His obstinate and determined enemies. The anger of the Lord is distressing; this is directed against His people for a time. Each one may say, 'Thou wast angry with me.' Let us look at this solemn fact: God had been angry. The cause of His anger is sin. The object with which He is angry is His child. The nature of His anger is paternal. The design of His anger is correction. The effects of His anger are various: sometimes it affects our temporal things; it always does our spiritual comfort and joy. The continuance of His anger is transient. His anger endureth but for a moment; in His favour is life. But when God is angry with us, every hour appears a day, and every month a year. But it is cheering to know that He retaineth not His anger for ever. He is not naturally angry. He is never sovereignly angry. He is not always, nor long angry. He looks to the atonement; He listens to the cry of the corrected one; love works in His heart; He remembers His covenant; and He proves that He delighteth in mercy. Wrath will burn for ever against impenitent sinners, being fed with the fuel of sin. Anger against a child soon burns out, or is quenched by the water of love.

He passes all our follies by,
And all our sins forgives,
His wrath doth in a moment die,
His love for ever lives.

JULY 4

❦ MORNING ❧

'He shall testify of me.'
JOHN 15:26

It is the office and work of the Holy Spirit to bear testimony of Jesus; He hath done so in the Word; there Christ is set forth in His glory and grace. He testifies of Jesus by the preaching of the gospel; for we preach Christ crucified, and are determined (when under divine teaching) to know nothing else among men. He testifies of Jesus to the heart; and then we see His loveliness, behold His glory, pant for an interest in His salvation, sigh for union to His person; or, trust in His promises, accept His invitations, rejoice in His name, and melt in love and gratitude before Him. We have then no doubt about His divinity, suitability, or love; all we want is to enjoy, possess, and glorify Him. Every idol falls before Him, every grace springs up and is in exercise upon Him; we love Him, believe Him, hope in Him, mourn for Him, are humbled before Him, and are zealous for Him; our language is, *'None but Jesus, none but Christ for me.'* O, for the Spirit, to testify of Jesus to our hearts and consciences, this day and every day, especially our last day; and to bear witness with our hearts that we are sons of God.

> *Saviour, I Thy Word believe,*
> *My unbelief remove;*
> *Thy testifying Spirit give,*
> *The unction from above;*
> *Show me, O Lord, how good Thou art,*
> *And fix Thy witness in my heart.*

❦ EVENING ❧

'Thy lovingkindness is better than life.'
PSALM 63:3

Life is existence. Here it means, existence under the most favourable circumstances: as life in ease, honour, plenty. The life of a social being in the enjoyment of gratification, as a merchant in his business, a student at his books, a monarch on his throne. Life surrounded by all that is desirable. But what then is God's loving-kindness? It is His love displaying itself in kind words; kind acts; kind discoveries of His divine excellencies; feasting the soul with spiritual delights. This is better than life, for it bestows greater blessings, it confers higher honours, it imparts sweeter pleasures, it raises higher expectations, and it throws around us greater security. It is better, for it is more lasting; it is more suited to the nature of the soul; it is truly glorious. It is unmixed good, unfading pleasure, inexhaustible wealth. Well, then, may the psalmist prefer it to life, and well may he say, *'My lips shall praise thee.'* I will commend thee in conversation. I will give Thee thanks in my devotions. I will praise Thee for its discovery, for my present enjoyment of it, and for the prospect of eternally enjoying it. Do you value life? Do you prefer God's lovingkindness to it?

> *Thy favour and love I prefer*
> *To life in its happiest hours;*
> *Possessed of a Paradise here,*
> *When mercy my spirit o'erpowers.*

JULY 5

❦ MORNING ❧
'I know their sorrows.'
Exodus 3:7

The Lord is acquainted with all the sorrows of His people; they do not suffer unnoticed; He sympathises with them, and will sanctify sorrow to them. Israel suffered, but Jesus sympathised. 'In all their affliction He was afflicted; and the angel of His presence saved them; in His love and in His pity He redeemed them; and He bare them, and carried them all the days of old.' Beloved, He knows our sorrows, and He will be our Comforter. Let us lay them before Him; let us plead with Him; He will be very gracious unto us at the voice of our cry; when He heareth, He will answer. He is touched with the feeling of our infirmities. He once suffered; He was *'the man of sorrows;'* and He is able to succour us who now suffer. His sorrows are ended, and so will ours be soon; weeping may endure for a night, but joy cometh in the morning. Light is sown for the righteous, and joy for the upright in heart. We shall obtain joy and gladness, and sorrow and sighing shall flee away. We shall enter into His joy, be filled with His love, and so be for ever with Him. O Jesus! suffer me not to dwell on my sorrows, but by Thy Spirit direct my heart into Thy love!

Away with our sorrow and fear,
We soon shall recover our home;
The city of saints shall appear,
The day of eternity come.

❦ EVENING ❧
'Faint, yet pursuing.'
Judges 8:4

Gideon's soldiers were in a painful situation; they were faint. Yet they were the Lord's selected host, and they were steadily following their Captain. But from their exertions, their conquests, and the want of food, they were faint. They were faint near the Jordan, where God had done such great things for their forefathers, and just as their victory was being completed. All this is true of the Lord's people now. Though the Lord's beloved ones, though the soldiers of the cross, from the burdens they have to bear, from the trials they have to endure, from the conflicts they are engaged in, and from the want of sufficiently feeding on spiritual provisions, they often feel very faint, dejected, and dispirited. Still these men were pursuing. They did not give up, nor give way to carnal reason, which may have suggested: 'If God were with us, He would supply us, or not allow us to feel thus faint.' They pursued their vanquished foes in obedience to God's commands, and as encouraged by the promise. They were pursuing in faith, in hope, with certainty. Brethren, let us imitate these worthy men. Do you feel faint? Does it appear in prayer? in labour? Still pursue. Pursue, though very weak. Pursue, because God is with you.

Wrestle on in prayer unceasing,
Till you see the foe destroy'd,
Bless'd with all the victor's blessing,
Crown'd with all the life of God.

JULY 6

MORNING
'God is with us.'
Isaiah 8:10

The Lord's people are never alone; therefore they should not feel lonely. God is with them as an *Observer*; He notices every thought, word, and action; every trial, every foe, and every danger. He is with them as a *Father*, loving and holding communion with them. He is with them as the *Lord of Hosts*, having all the armies of earth and heaven under His direction to befriend them. He is with them as a *Guide*, to lead them; as a *Counsellor*, to plead their cause; as a *Friend*, to supply and comfort them; as a *Saviour*, to deliver and exalt them; and as a holy, sin-hating God. He is present with them to try them, to reprove them, to humble them, to preserve them, to comfort them, and to save them with an everlasting salvation. Beloved, let us remember that God is with us, every where and always: this will check levity, prevent impatience, make us honest, encourage prayerfulness, inspire with fortitude, and produce diligence. If God is with us thus, He is for us; and if God be for us, who can be against us? But do we so walk, as by our conduct to say, 'God is with us?' O, to be always circumspect!

> Be it my only wisdom here,
> To serve the Lord with filial fear,
> With loving gratitude;
>
> Superior sense may I display,
> By shunning every evil way,
> And walking in the good.

EVENING
'Who healeth all thy diseases.'
Psalm 103:3

The Lord is the Physician; He heals both the body and the soul. He is especially the healer of the soul. The patient is a believer. The cause of all disease and suffering is sin. The seat of the malady is in the heart. The nature of it is most loathsome and afflictive. It affects the memory, the affections, the conscience, the will, yea the whole man. We are all the subjects of this disease. We all suffer from it. No one can heal us but the Lord Jesus. He is the great Physician; to Him we may repair and be restored to health. To encourage you to do so, look at His qualifications. He is infinitely wise, tender, and skilful. His experience is without a parallel; and so is His success. The remedies He employs are His precious blood, His holy Word, and His blessed Spirit. The mode of application is by afflictions, bereavements, convictions, and secret energy. He never failed in any case of affecting a cure. David's was a bad case, but he could say, 'He healeth all my diseases.' This testimony is personal, credible, undoubted. Sinner, thou art sick, mortally sick; go to Jesus. Backslider, thou art sick; go to Jesus. Believer, art thou not desiring perfect health? Then go to Jesus this night. Go and say, 'Lord, if Thou wilt Thou canst make me whole.'

> Forgive, and make my nature whole,
> My sinful maladies remove,
> To perfect health restore my soul;
> To perfect holiness and love.

JULY 7

🌿 MORNING 🌿

'I will not remember thy sins.'

Isaiah 43:25

We need fear nothing but sin; and we have no reason to fear whether God will pardon that, and save us from it, if we believe in Jesus, confess and forsake it. He has promised, 'I will be merciful to their unrighteousness, and their sins and their iniquities *will I remember no more.*' He will not impute sin unto us; but He will impute righteousness, even the righteousness of Jesus without works. He has made up His mind to glorify the riches of His grace, thus to display the wonders of His love. No one sin shall be charged upon us, He will blot them all completely out of His book, and banish them eternally from His mind. He will treat us as though we had not sinned, or rather as having received full satisfaction for all we have done amiss, and being infinitely delighted with our persons. If one sin were remembered, and laid to our charge, we were undone; but believing in Jesus, we are justified from *all sin*, we are saved from wrath, and are made *'the righteousness of God in Him.'* This is godlike, glorious, divine! When God forgives our sins, He always forgets them.

> Crimes of such horror to forgive,
> Such guilty daring worms to spare;
> This is Thy grand prerogative,
> And none shall in the honour share.
> Who is a pardoning God like Thee?
> Or who has grace so rich and free?

🌿 EVENING 🌿

'Let us not sleep as do others.'

1 Thessalonians 5:6

Sleep is here used in a figurative sense. The apostle does not refer to the repose of the body, but to the state of the mind. He refers to a suspension of the energies in faith, prayer, and holy affection; an improper withdrawment from the scenes of action; a state which is next door to death. Others are asleep. Many others are asleep. Professors are asleep. 'But let us not sleep as do others.' If we sleep, it is like sleeping, where? On the plains of Waterloo, after that dreadful battle, among the wounded, the dying, and the dead; in a city infected with the plague, while we possess the remedy, which if applied, would heal the infected; in an island of slaves, while we have the act of emancipation in our pockets; in a town of madmen, while we have the means of restoration; in a starving country, when we know where there is plenty of food. If we sleep, it is like sleeping, when? In the day, on a harvest day, the great day of opportunity. If we sleep, it is like, what? Like the labourer sleeping in the harvest field, when the storm is coming, and his master's crops are all exposed; like the soldier sleeping on duty, when the foe is in the field.

> See professors round thee sleeping,
> Rouse my soul, awake! arise!
> Carefully the precepts keeping,
> Labour for the glorious prize.

JULY 8

🌿 MORNING 🌿

'Follow after charity.'

1 Corinthians 14: 1

Charity is love; and what can be so worthy of the Christian's thought, care, and anxious desire, as *love?* Love to God, the centre and source of all excellence; to Jesus, the Mediator of the new covenant, the person-ification of everything that is lovely; to believers, for His sake, and because they are His children and represent-atives; and to sinners, because He commands us. The law requires it, and the gospel, when applied by the power of the Holy Ghost, produces it. It is not in our hearts by nature; we are *enmity*. It is not to be produced by human effort. It flows from grace. It is produced by the Holy Ghost. It is connected with evangelical sentiment. Its exercise is our happiness and our holiness. There is no real religion without love; and only so much true godliness as there is love. *Let us follow after charity*. Let us cultivate love to the Lord's people, for the Lord's sake; not merely those who see as we see, attend the place of worship we attend, and are our personal friends; this is love of party; but let us love all who love Jesus, though in some things they differ from us.

'Tis love that makes our cheerful feet
In swift obedience move;
'Tis love shall tune our joyful songs,
In the sweet realms above.
Jesus, to me this love be given;
Fill me with love, for love is heaven.

🌿 EVENING 🌿

'He will turn again.'

Micah 7.19

Here is a melancholy fact intimated. The Lord had turned away His face from His people. He was displeased. There were now no sweet visits; no love-tokens; no intimate communion. But He threatens. He frowns. He smites. He shows His displeasure. He is angry, but not wrathful. He has sworn that He will not be wroth with us. 'He will turn again.' Here confidence is expressed. He smites but to correct. He frowns but to bring us to repentance. He will turn again and look upon us, as He did on Peter when He broke his heart, and brought him back with weeping and supplication. He will speak to us as He did to Mary, when He said, 'Thy sins are forgiven thee, go in peace.' He will smile away our fears, take us to His bosom, and again assure us of His love. He will, for He has promised to do so. He will, for He has always done so. He will, for the love of His heart prompts Him to do so. He will, for He delighteth in mercy. Then let us mourn over our follies, but not despair of pardon. Let us weep, that we have grieved our kind and gracious God, but not yield to gloom. Let us confess our backslidings, and expect Him to return. Let us wait upon the Lord, who hideth Himself from the house of Israel, and let us look for Him.

Saviour, while after Thee we mourn,
Thou wilt compassion show,
In mercy to our souls return,
And all our sins subdue.

JULY 9

❦ MORNING ❦

'I will do all my pleasure.'
ISAIAH 46:10

The purpose of God cannot be frustrated. His holy mind can never be disappointed. His will is law. His counsel must stand. He is in one mind, and none can turn Him. He takes pleasure in them that fear Him, and in them that hope in His mercy. He chose them to salvation in Jesus, according to the good pleasure of His will. He works in us to will, and to do, of His good pleasure. He will fulfil in us all the good pleasure of His goodness, and the work of faith with power. He is pleased to save His people with an everlasting salvation. He is pleased with our obedience to His precepts. It is our Father's good pleasure that gives us the kingdom. He accomplishes the purposes of His will by angels – they are His ministers which do His pleasure; by men, good and bad; by devils; by Jesus Christ; the pleasure of the Lord prospers in His hand. For His pleasure all things are and were created; and He worketh all things after the counsel of His own will. Let us seek to be like-minded with our God, let us acquiesce in all that pleases Him, and let us take pleasure in glorifying Him. If God does His pleasure, our best interests are safe.

> God moves in a mysterious way,
> His wonders to perform;
> He plants His footsteps in the sea,
> And rides upon the storm.
> His power and wisdom will fulfil,
> The utmost counsel of His will.

❦ EVENING ❦

'I will be their God.'
JEREMIAH 32:38

This was spoken of the literal Israel, but it applies also to the spiritual Israel. It refers to all who are gathered to the Lord Jesus; to every penitent sinner, who is returning to God with weeping and with supplication; to every one to whom the Lord gives a heart to know Him, and who trusts in His gracious Word; to all true believers. What does this promise include? 'I will be their God': they shall own My authority; receive My Word; bow at My throne; engage in My service; do My will; prefer Me to all besides; make Me the object of their trust, worship, and love; 'their God'. 'I will be their God': they shall have My wisdom to guide them; My power to protect them; My love to assure them; My mercy to save them; My holiness to sanctify them; and My Spirit to comfort them. As their God I will be with them. I will be for them. I will be a God to them. I will never fail them, nor forsake them, but will do for them all I have promised in My Word; and confer upon them all I have provided in My covenant. Believer, see in this promise God's greatest mercy; He gives you Himself to be your God. Man's highest honour, to have God so nigh unto him, and engaged for him. Jehovah is his God for ever.

> On this support my soul would lean,
> And banish every care;
> The darkest path is cheer'd with smiles,
> If God is with me there.

JULY 10

🌿 MORNING 🌿
'He that waiteth on his master shall be honoured.'
PROVERBS 27:18

And who is our master but Jesus? One is your master, even Christ. We have chosen to serve Him, because He chose to save us. He has given us the knowledge of salvation by the remission of our sins, that we may serve Him without fear, in righteousness and holiness all the days of our life. Our happiness is found in obeying our Master's Word, and studying our Master's will. Let us wait on Him for the word of command, nor dare to proceed without it. Let us wait on Him for ability, to do and suffer all His righteous will. Let us wait His time for every promised blessing, and continue looking in faith until we receive it. Let us expect to live at His table, and wait on Him for a supply of all our needs, both spiritual and temporal. Let us wait on Him in private, and in public always form a part of His retinue. He will honour us, for He has said, 'If any man serve me, let him follow me; and where I am, there shall also my servant be; if any man serve me, him will my Father honour.' We shall know the truth, and the truth shall make us free; and all such are free indeed.

> That wisdom, Lord, on me bestow,
> From every evil to depart;
> To stop the mouth of every foe,
> While upright both in life and heart.
> The proofs of godly fear I give,
> And show them how true Christians live.

🌿 EVENING 🌿
'Examine me, O LORD.'
PSALM 26:2

The Lord says, 'Let a man examine himself.' The Christian does so, but not satisfied with his own searching, he turns to the Lord and says, 'Examine me, O LORD.' He is afraid of being deceived, and he knows that his heart is deceitful. He is really sincere. He desires to know the worst of his case, let it be ever so painful. He would have his heart right with God; therefore he comes to the light. This is a proof that there is grace in the soul; for only those who are taught of God cry, 'Examine me, O LORD.' Beloved, is this your prayer tonight? Are you willing to be examined? Are you desirous that God should examine you? Are you crying, 'Lord, examine my heart: am I a subject of Thy grace? Examine my motives: are they pure and scriptural? Examine my actions: are they according to Thy Word? Examine my objects: do I aim at Thy glory and the promotion of Thy cause?' You see the prayer is for *personal* examination. 'Examine *me*.' It is for *immediate* examination; *now* examine me. It is for *thorough* examination; therefore he prays God to do it. None but an honest man will court a thorough investigation into his affairs, and none but right-minded Christians will court the searching eye of God, or heartily pray:-

> Search me, O God, and cleanse my heart,
> Thy Spirit and Thy grace impart;
> Save from deceit, from guile set free,
> And let my soul Thy temple be.

JULY 11

❧ MORNING ❧

'The LORD will give strength unto His people.'
Psalm 29:11

However hot the war, or sore the trial, we may be sure of this, that 'as our days, so shall our strength be.' God has promised, and He will give. He gives because they are His people, as the father to his children, because He has covenanted to do so, and He is faithful; lest their foes should triumph over them, whereas He has said, 'They shall overcome at the last.' He has raised their expectations, and He will not disappoint them; He has commanded them to pray, and He will not refuse. He will give strength sufficient; enough, but perhaps none to spare; suitable to their circumstances and wants. Has the Lord pledged Himself to give strength to His people; yea, to be Himself their strength? Then let us fight courageously, look forward joyfully, bear every cross patiently, pray fervently, praise daily, and believe confidently. God hath spoken; saints in every age have found Him a truth-telling, promise-performing God. Satan is a liar, a deceiver, a false witness against God. Let us therefore resist him, and he will flee from us. The strong God is our support in every trial.

Give me Thy strength, O God of power;
Then let winds blow, or thunders roar;
Thy faithful witness will I be:

'Tis fix'd: I can do all through Thee:
Fulfil Thy sovereign counsel, Lord,
Thy will be done, Thy name adored!

❧ EVENING ❧

'Look thou upon me.'
Psalm 119:132

Here is a child seeking a father's notice. Whatever God does, He does with ease. A look is enough to relieve us in our deepest distresses, to rescue us from our greatest difficulties, and to fill us with peace and joy. The Lord's look will discover and detect us, if we are wrong; it will confirm and establish us, if we are right. His look humbled Job, strengthened Gideon, brought Peter to repentance, and filled dying Stephen with joy and peace. To look upon us, is to show us favour. 'To this man will I look, even to him that is poor and of a contrite spirit, and trembleth at my word.' If we would have God look down upon us, we must look up unto Him. If we would have Him look upon us, and be gracious unto us, we must look unto Him in prayer and with faith. Beloved, are you desiring that the eye of God should rest upon you? That you may realize this fact? If He look upon you in mercy, His look will dissipate your fears, disperse your darkness, and fill you with light and holy confidence. Is it too much to ask? It is not much for God to give, but it is much for us to receive. It betokens reconciliation. It evidences interest in us. It imparts blessings unto us. Let this then be our closing prayer tonight: 'Look thou upon me.'

O look upon Thy servant, Lord,
And pardon, peace, and joy afford;
May I with Thy sweet presence blest,
This night enjoy refreshing rest!

JULY 12

🌿 MORNING 🌿

'Happy is the man that feareth alway.'
PROVERBS 28:14

Godly fear flows from grace, and is always connected with spiritual knowledge. It is the fear of a tender child, who would not on any account grieve a kind and loving parent. It is a covenant blessing. Our God bestows it on all whom He loves; and they consequently fear to offend Him, their Father; dishonour their gracious Saviour; or grieve the Holy Comforter. They fear lest they should be led astray from God by their own hearts, by Satan, by professors, by the world, or any of the dispensations of providence. They fear to trust their own judgments, they reverence God's Word, and dread a lukewarm state. Happy is the man who *thus* feareth alway; he happily preserves a tender conscience, a humble mind, and a consistent walk. He proves his interest in all new-covenant blessings; has much to do with the blood of atonement; and enjoys a solid peace. He is in a happy state, standing high in the favour of God, walking in the comforts of the Holy Ghost, and keeping himself unspotted from the world. Oh, for godly fear to rule my heart, and preserve my goings! In the fear of the Lord is strong confidence, and solid peace.

This fear's the spirit of faith,
A confidence that's strong,
An unctious light to all that's right,
A bar to all that's wrong.

🌿 EVENING 🌿

'He shall be for a sanctuary.'
ISAIAH 8:14

That is, the Lord Jesus shall, for of Him the prophet speaks. He is the sanctuary in which we are safe from the wrath of God, the curse of a broken law, and the evil designs of Satan. This is our refuge to which we must repair from enemies, storms, and troubles. Here we can worship God, on a throne of grace, with confidence, faith, and acceptance. And by Him God will manifest Himself, and impart instruction on all matters of importance. In this sanctuary we may expect a supply of all our wants; deliverance from all our fears; defence from all our foes; help in all our troubles; the sanctification of all our sorrows; and safety while we continue below. Reader, you should fly to Jesus in every trouble. You should expect from Him whatever you really need. He shows you how gracious God is to you, and sets forth the blessedness of all true believers. Is He your sanctuary? Have you ever *met* God in Christ? Do you *worship* God in Christ? Do you look for all you *want* in Christ? If He is your sanctuary, seek to glorify Him. Expect to find every blessing in Him. In every difficulty and danger repair to Him, and praise the Lord for such a glorious dwelling. Here you are safe. Here you will enjoy peace. Here you will obtain grace.

In Christ I every glory view,
Of safety, strength, and beauty too;
Beloved Saviour! ever be
A sanctuary unto me.

JULY 13

🌿 MORNING 🌿

'Behold, I have given Him for ... a leader ... to the people.'
Isaiah 55:4

This was in consideration of our ignorance. We know not the way to our heavenly Father's house, but Jesus is sent to lead the blind by a way which they knew not. On account of the difficulties of the way, they are many and great, but Jesus comes as our Leader, saying, 'I have made, and I will bear; even I will carry, and will deliver you.' It manifests our heavenly Father's concern for our safety, comfort, and confidence. He sent His only Son, because He could trust us in His hands; He being infinitely wise, gracious, forbearing, and powerful. He came to lead us from the world to the church, from the law to the gospel, from sin to holiness, from wrath to love. He leads all His people to the throne of mercy, the house of prayer, the pastures of Jehovah's love, and the mansions of endless glory. He leads us against Satan, and we overcome; against lust, and we conquer. He leads us in the way He went Himself; in the footsteps of His flock, as we are able to bear; so as to cross and crucify the old man, and revive and strengthen the new. Lead me in truth and teach me, for Thou art my God.

> Lead me on, Almighty victor, Till on Canaan's shores I stand:
> Scatter every hostile band;   Shouts of victory
> Be my guide and my protector. Then shall fill the promised land.

🌿 EVENING 🌿

'God who is rich in mercy.'
Ephesians 2:4

In consequence of sin, our misery is great; but it cannot be so great as God's mercy. Our sufferings are many, but God's mercy is an antidote for all. Mercy is the wealth of God, which He lays out upon His people. It is the sympathy of God, which He displays toward His afflicted children. It is that by which He is affected, with a sense of all our sufferings; as it is written of His people of old, 'In all their affliction He was afflicted, and the angel of His presence saved them: in His love and in His pity He redeemed them: and He bore them, and carried them all the days of old.' The mercy of God is infinite. It flows through Jesus. It is glorified in soothing our sorrows, supplying our wants, pardoning our sins, relieving our distresses, and restoring us from all our wanderings. Beloved, God is rich in mercy tonight. He has mercy for thee; just that mercy which is necessary. He says, 'I will have mercy, and not sacrifice.' Believe His promise. Plead for mercy at His throne. Expect Him to glorify His mercy in thee. You need no recommendation, but your misery. No greater encouragement than this: 'He is rich in mercy, rich unto all that call upon Him.' Honour Him then tonight, by placing confidence in His Word.

> High as the heav'n o'er earth extends,
> His mercy all our sins transcends;
> Far as the east from western climes,
> He casts the guilt of all our crimes.

JULY 14

🌿 MORNING 🌿

'My people doth not consider.'
ISAIAH 1:3

This is a complaint preferred against us by our infinitely gracious God; let us attend to it a little this morning. What should we consider? Surely, how great things the Lord hath done for us, He hath delivered our souls from death, our eyes from tears, and our feet from falling, that we may walk before God in the land of the living. How God provides for all His creatures, even the meanest, and therefore will certainly provide for us; being engaged to do so as our Creator, Preserver, covenant God, and gracious Father. That He is the supreme and universal Governor, arranging, managing, and directing every event; so that accident can never happen, chance can have no place, but all is directed by infinite wisdom and omnipresent love. Why do we not consider? Because our hearts are fickle, false, and worldly; our minds are influenced by unscriptural notions; and we endeavour to walk by sight instead of faith. What are the consequences of our not considering? Our God is dishonoured and displeased; our souls are alarmed and misled; and Satan gains an advantage over us. Lord, fill our minds with serious and becoming thoughts!

> *Jesus, mighty to renew,*
> *Work in me to will and do;*
> *Stem my nature's rapid tide,*
> *Slay my vile self-righteous pride!*
> *All Thy power in me be shown,*
> *Take away the heart of stone!*

🌿 EVENING 🌿

'The LORD reigneth.'

PSALM 97:1

That Lord is thy Saviour. He wears thy nature. He knows thee well. He loves thee more than a mother does her first-born, her only son. He keeps thy welfare in view in all He does, and in all He permits. He reigns universally, over all worlds. He reigns supreme: thrones and dominions, and principalities, and powers, are made subject to Him. In His government He equally displays His wisdom and power; His justice and mercy; His sovereignty and grace. He reigns to advance the interests of holiness, the happiness, and endless welfare of His people. He reigns over His enemies, and secretly frustrates their designs, using their energies for the accomplishment of His purposes. He rules in as well as over His friends. Thus He preserves them from evils, manages their affairs, and fulfils His Word. 'The LORD reigneth.' Think of this when Satan besets and harasses you; when sin rises within you, perplexing and distressing you; when providence frowns on you, crossing your plans, blasting your gourds, and trying your faith; when you have fightings without, and fears within; when enemies oppose you, when sickness lays you low, and when death stares you in the face. Rejoice in this, that your Saviour reigns supreme, and therefore you are safe.

> *The Lord is king, rejoice and sing,*
> *My Lord and King Thou art,*
> *Thy Spirit reigns, Thy love maintains*
> *Its sway within my heart.*

JULY 15

❧ MORNING ❧

'What time I am afraid, I will trust in thee.'
PSALM 56:3

It is no unusual thing for the Lord's people to be cast down, and filled with tormenting fears. They fear their faith is presumption, their hope delusion, and that they shall one day disgrace that holy name by which they are called. They fear to rely on a naked promise, and want comfortable feelings to underprop their faith. But they should take up the psalmist's resolution, 'What time I am afraid, I will trust in thee.' Jehovah in Jesus is the only proper object of trust, and He should be trusted at all times. Beloved, it is well when we can say, 'I will depend upon the faithful promise of my gracious God; I will rely on the free grace of my adorable Saviour; I will hope in covenant mercy for evermore; I will fly to my Father's bosom and venture all in my Saviour's hands.' Let us trust in God, in opposition to frames and feelings. Let us trust in covenant love, though providence appears to frown. Our God has said, 'Trust ye in the LORD for ever.' Here is our warrant; let us seek grace to say with Job, 'Though He slay me, yet will I trust in Him.'

> O, let me then at length be taught
> What I am still so slow to learn,
> That God is love, and changes not,
> Nor knows the shadow of a turn:
> To cast on Him my anxious cares,
> And triumph o'er my doubts and fears.

❧ EVENING ❧

'Let us keep the feast.'
1 CORINTHIANS 5:8

Paul is referring to the Passover; when the lamb was slain, the doorposts sprinkled, the first-born of the Egyptians destroyed, and the deliverance of Israel secured. Christ is our passover lamb; His blood was shed for us, and is sprinkled upon us; our foes are destroyed, and our salvation secured. The Israelites were to feed on the lamb whose blood secured them; and we are to feed on Christ, by whose blood we are redeemed. 'Therefore let us keep the feast.' It is a feast upon a sacrifice, upon Christ as crucified for us. He is not only our ransom, but our food. Our souls are fed by taking in believing views of His glorious person; finished work; complete conquest; and eternal honours. The eye should be daily directed to Christ. The mind should be engaged with Christ. The heart should feed upon Christ. He is the life-giving bread. He says, 'He that eateth me, even he shall live by me.' We are invited to a feast; the substance of that feast is Christ. Let us then daily keep the feast. Let us keep it with much prayer, with hearty praise, in faith and hope, with humility and seriousness, with godly sorrow, and lively joy. Let us keep it for God has bidden us. Let us keep it, for we honour Jesus by doing so.

> On Jesus let us daily feed,
> And keep the gospel feast;
> In Him is all our souls can need,
> Life, health, and food, and rest.

JULY 16

🌿 MORNING 🌿

'Be clothed with humility.'

1 PETER 5:5

It is of great importance, to have and to cherish right views of our own littleness and insignificance; of our own vileness and unworthiness; and of our absolute and constant dependence on the mercy of our God. To possess a meek and quiet spirit, which is in the sight of God of great price; that so we may be humble under cross providences, considering our sin and ill-deservings, how we have requited the Lord; seeing the hand of God working all in all; acknowledging Divine providence, let who or what will be the instrument; to be contented with our lot, with such things as we have, uniting godliness with contentment; to be habitually looking at the Lord Jesus, what He was in His ancient glory; what He became for us; what He now is; and what we shall soon be with Him. Humility is the best garment for a justified sinner to wear, for God has said He will look to, and dwell with the humble. He giveth grace unto the humble. He that humbeth himself shall be exalted. He will hear the cry, grant the desire, and save the humble person. Humility attracts God's notice, and brings down God's blessing.

Jesus, from my proud heart remove
The bane of self-admiring love!
O, make me feel and own with shame,
I less and worse than nothing am!
The least of saints with pity see,
The chief of sinners save, in me!

🌿 EVENING 🌿

'Be no more children.'

EPHESIANS 4:14

This refers not to state, but to stature. We are always in the relation of children, but in understanding, we should be men. The Lord has made provision for the growth of His people, and He exhorts them to grow. We should advance in knowledge. Children are satisfied with trifles, we should not be. We should increase in strength, and become strong in the grace which is in Christ Jesus. We should also become more courageous against our foes, bold in the Lord's cause, and steadfast in our attachment to divine things. Our faith, our hope, our love, and our zeal should grow. We should not be stationary; but from babes, grow up to young men; and from young men, to fathers in Christ. In order to our growth we must make use of food, exercise, and devotion; we must feed upon Christ, exercise all our graces, and live in fellowship with God. That we may grow, the Lord has given us His book, His ordinances, and His Son. To perfect our character, He uses His ministers, His providence, and even His foes. He has promised that we shall 'grow as the vine,' and 'go forth and grow up as calves of the stall.' Let us set our heart upon growing, and attend to this salutary caution, 'That ye be no more children.'

Then, Lord, forbid, forbid that we
Should ALWAYS little children be;
But may our path shine more, we pray,
And more until the perfect day.

JULY 17

🌿 MORNING 🌿
'The faithful witness.'
Revelation 1:5

This is one of the titles of our adorable Saviour. His Father gave Him to be a witness, to testify unto us of His love, and His testimony is: 'God so loved the world, that He gave His only-begotten Son, that whosoever believeth in Him should not perish, but have everlasting life.' To testify of His will in reference to sinners, and this is His witness: 'This is the will of Him that sent me, that every one that seeth the Son…' (perceiveth His divinity, His authority, and office) '… and believeth on Him, may have everlasting life, and I will raise him up at the last day.' To testify of His delight in making His people happy; and this is the record: 'Fear not, little flock, for it is your Father's good pleasure to give you the kingdom.' He bare witness that our God and Father will do for us, and give unto us, all that our circumstances require; and we know that His witness is true. Let us therefore believe it, simply on the ground of His divinity, knowledge, integrity, veracity, and the interest He takes in our happiness and His Father's glory. Jesus is the faithful Witness, and our glorious Friend. Let us witness for Him, as He does for His Father.

> *Great Witness from above,*
> *My tongue would bless Thy name:*
> *By Thee the joyful news*
> *Of my salvation came;*
> *The joyful news of sins forgiven,*
> *Of hell subdued, and peace with heaven.*

🌿 EVENING 🌿
'Iniquities prevail against me.'
Psalm 65:3

The believer is in a state of warfare. Sin lives in him, works in him, and sometimes overcomes him. He is never free from sin, and has daily need to watch and strive against sin. Iniquities prevail against us at times, and then they break our peace; strengthen unbelief; lead away our affections from God; close the mouth in prayer; silence the voice of praise; weaken and pollute the soul; and raise a cloud between God and us, so that we cannot see His face, or enjoy His love. When we yield to sin and it prevails against us, we must expect to feel the rebukes and reproofs of the Holy Spirit within; the rod of affliction may also be laid on without; confusion and perplexity will be felt before the throne; and our state calls for humiliation, confession, and repentance toward God. If the Lord sanctify this experience to us, it will lead us to hate sin more, and loathe ourselves before God; we shall become more watchful and prayerful; we shall be more jealous of ourselves, and careful to avoid all appearance of evil; and when again set at liberty, we shall bless, praise, and adore the long-suffering mercy, and forgiving love of God. We shall be clothed with humility, and walk humbly with our God.

> *Lord, my iniquities prevail,*
> *My courage droops, my spirits fail;*
> *Do Thou my rebel lusts subdue,*
> *And all my inward powers renew.*

JULY 18

❦ MORNING ❦

'Blessed are the pure in heart: for they shall see God.'
MATTHEW 5:8

It is faith that purifies the heart; it brings home the atonement, and we enjoy pardon, peace, and reconciliation; it purges the conscience from dead works, and delivers us from all condemnation. It receives the truth of God, and Jesus through the truth; and we receive power to become the sons of God. We realize our relationship to God, read the gracious promises God has made, and anticipate the glorious kingdom He has prepared; hope rules in the heart, and every one that has this hope in Him purifies himself, even as Christ is pure. His conscience is made tender, his intentions are honest, and his heart is sound in God's statutes. He groans under a body of sin and death, proclaims eternal war with the flesh, and loathes himself on account of filthiness in the spirit. He would give a world to be free from sin, for holiness is the element of his soul. He is blessed. He shall see God, and enjoy Him as his Father, Portion, and everlasting all. He shall be with his God; and be like Him, in purity, happiness, and glory. The pure in heart daily groan under a painful sense of impurity.

Jesus, Thy crowning grace impart;
Bless me with purity of heart,
That now beholding Thee,

I soon may view Thy open face,
On all Thy glorious beauties gaze,
And God for ever see!

❦ EVENING ❦

'I am glorified in them.'
JOHN 17:10

The work of Jesus was to glorify the Father, and the Father is glorified in Him. Our work should be to glorify Jesus, and He is glorified in us. His blood is glorified, in our pardon, peace, and cleansing from all sin; His righteousness, in our complete, perpetual, and eternal justification; His power, in our separation from the world, and preservation unto eternal life; His mercy, in our quickening, and numerous comforts; His Word, in our liberty, and holy joy; His condescension, in our fellowship and communion; His faithfulness, in the answers we receive to our prayers and petitions; His love, in our boldness and access with confidence at His throne; His goodness, in our supplies and supports under trouble; His sympathy, in our afflictions and sorrows; His patience, in bearing with our perverseness and many infirmities; His grace, in our whole lives, in death, and in our eternal salvation. Jesus is glorified in us, for all we *are*, we owe to Him; all we *have*, we receive from Him; and all we *hope for*, we expect from Him. His church is His glory, and He will make her glorious. He will present her unto Himself a glorious church, not having spot, or wrinkle, or any such thing. Sweet thought, Jesus is glorified in me!

Now glorify Thyself in me,
Saviour, Redeemer, Friend!
Fain would I live and die for Thee,
On whom I now depend.

JULY 19

MORNING

'Whom having not seen ye love.'
1 Peter 1:8

We have never seen the glorified body of Jesus, but we have believed what His Word declares of Him, and believing we love Him. As the only-begotten Son of God, who was exalted, dignified, and glorified from everlasting; as the voluntary Saviour of poor lost sinners, who became incarnate, suffered, bled and died for them. We love His adorable person, His countenance is majesty, His heart is love, His hand is omnipotence, His eye is bountifulness, His bowels are compassion, and His presence and smile are heaven. We love His precious salvation, in its freeness, completeness, and glory. We love His delightful promises, which anticipate our wants, meet all our wishes, and fill our souls with peace. We love His throne, where He meets us, attends to our requests, and blesses us indeed. We love His holy precepts, which exhibit His authority, display His love, and call us to holiness. We love His heaven-born family, who wear His likeness, are the excellent of the earth, and resemble the children of a king. O to love Him more! To love Him with all our hearts, minds, souls, and strength! To manifest our love to Him by holy actions, and a useful life!

A bleeding Saviour, seen by faith;
A sense of pardoning love;
A hope that triumphs over death,
Give joys like those above.

EVENING

'I know that thou favourest me.'
Psalm 41:11

What believer does not know this! And yet who is sufficiently affected by the fact. If God had not favoured us, we had been still dead in sin; or we had been smarting under the lashes of a guilty conscience; or we had been shut up in despair; or our enemy had triumphed over us. He is superior to us in wisdom, power, experience, and perseverance. He has had great advantage given him by our weakness, timidity, and cowardice; by our powerful corruptions, and ignorance of his devices. He has endeavoured to lead us into sin, draw us into apostasy, or drive us to despair; but he has not prevailed. He certainly would if the Lord had not favoured us. But Jesus has interceded for us. The Holy Spirit has helped our infirmities. Our heavenly Father has faithfully fulfilled His Word, and has restrained, curbed, and kept him back. He has shielded us in the day of conflict, and protected us in the heat of the battle. He has given us strength equal to our day, and we have found His grace to be sufficient for us. Surely the Lord has favoured us, for we have stood, when many have fallen; we have persevered while many have gone back; we live tonight as the monuments of His mercy. Each of us may say, 'I am God's favoured child.'

Then will I trust His power and grace,
Deliverance to command,
Till with His saints, before His face
In endless bliss, I stand.

JULY 20

🌿 MORNING 🌿

'Pray that ye enter not into temptation.'
LUKE 22:40

Temptations are trials; but by temptations very generally we understand solicitations to evil. Satan is the arch-tempter; he uses every possible variety of instruments, to draw us into sin and folly; consequently we are always in danger from him. But we are liable to be led astray by his temptations often, because they are sudden, powerful, importunate, deceptive, so timed as to fall in with our peculiar circumstances; also because our hearts are weak, changeable, prone to evil, open to seduction. How many eminent saints have fallen! Let us beware! Falling into temptation dishonours God, disgraces religion, and distresses the soul. God is able to preserve and deliver us. He has promised. But prayer is implied in every promise. Beloved, daily remember you have a malicious and designing foe; he is present with you! he will use saints and sinners as instruments to lead you astray. Pray without ceasing. Pray in simplicity, in sincerity, with importunity. God is faithful, and will make a way for your escape. Take heed lest you tempt Satan to tempt you; some do.

> *Jesus, Redeemer, Saviour, Lord*
> *The weary sinner's Friend.*
> *Come to my help, pronounce the Word,*
> *And bid my troubles end:*
> *Wisdom and strength to me impart,*
> *To quench each flaming fiery dart.*

🌿 EVENING 🌿

'Him that overcometh.'
REVELATION 2:17

Every Christian is a soldier, and he is exhorted to conduct himself as a good soldier of Jesus Christ. Every Christian soldier must go to war. His enemies are numerous and powerful. They must be conquered, for they will never yield. He must never propose, or accept of any terms with them. He must fight until they are entirely subdued. He must overcome the world. He must conquer Satan. He must rule over his own spirit. Heaven is the home of conquerors. Honours unspeakably glorious are reserved for them. Jesus, the captain of their salvation, will give them to eat of the tree of life, and of the hidden manna; to possess the white stone, with the new name written; the morning star; the white raiment; to be a pillar in the temple of God; to wear a crown of life; and to sit with Him on His throne. All these are promised to him that overcometh. There is therefore something to animate, to stimulate, to encourage us. Every indulgence that can be granted, every honour that can be conferred, will be the portion of the conqueror. Let us therefore, wrestle, strive, and fight; using the whole armour of God, strong in the grace of Jesus, keeping the eye upon the prize, and stimulating each other in the conflict. By faith we conquer.

> *Then let me meet my threefold foe,*
> *And conquering on to conquer go,*
> *Arm'd with His sword, and mind, and name,*
> *Who hell, the world, and sin o'ercame.*

JULY 21

❦ MORNING ❦
'Abide in me.'
John 15:4

By nature, we are without Christ and are far from Him; by grace, we accept His invitation, and come to Him feeling our need of Him. We are brought to see that nothing but union to Jesus can make us safe and happy; and to give up ourselves to Him, praying to be one in Him; He receives us, sheds abroad His love in our hearts, and we become members of His body, of His flesh, and of His bones. He then bids us abide in Him, which we do by living in absolute dependence upon Him; by cleaving to Him in love as our beloved Saviour, God, and Friend; by openly professing our attachment to Him, and expectations from Him; by walking in daily fellowship and communion with Him; and by identifying our cause with His. Beloved, we must abide in Jesus if we would get sin mortified; our graces nourished; our lusts subdued; obtain victory over the world; prove a match for Satan; and obtain all necessary supplies. Abiding in Jesus will give us a single eye; a burning zeal; holy discretion; and enable us to seize all opportunities to glorify His adorable name. Keep the eye on Jesus at all times, and in all places.

> Hail, gracious Saviour, all divine!
> Mysterious, ever-living vine!
> To Thee united may I live,
> And nourished by Thine influence thrive;
> Still may my soul abide in Thee,
> From envy, pride, and malice free.

❦ EVENING ❦
'Ye are come … to the blood of sprinkling.'
Hebrews 12:22,24

The blood that was shed for sin, was sprinkled on the sinner: the former action made atonement; the latter declared the sinner clean. The blood of Jesus is the blood of sprinkling. It has made peace for sinners. It speaks peace to sinners. It cleanses from all sin, and it does this meritoriously, efficaciously, infallibly. It heals the wounded conscience, perfumes our services, and confirms the covenant. It secures us, as the blood of the Passover did the Israelites; and it satisfies the claims of infinite Justice. It procured pardon for the guilty; life for the dead; redemption for the captive; and all grace for graceless sinners. As believers, we come to this blood of sprinkling. We come to hear it, for it speaks better things than the blood of Abel. We come to trust in it, for it alone procures us acceptance with God. We come to prove it, and enjoy the blessedness that results from it. We come to plead it, that we may obtain mercy and find grace to help in time of need. We come to rejoice in it, for it is a source of comfort, consolation, and joy. We come by faith. We come whenever annoyed by guilt, disturbed by fears, beset by Satan, pinched by want, and when death is near.

> Upon the cross my Saviour hung,
> And shed His vital blood;
> And every wound is now a tongue
> To plead my cause with God.

JULY 22

❦ MORNING ❧

'A just God and a Saviour.'
ISAIAH 45:21

God cannot part with His justice even to gratify His love; and His justice shines equally with His grace in the present and eternal salvation of our souls. He gave His Son for a Substitute, He appointed Him to be our Surety, and punished Him in our stead. He justly condemned Him to die, though guiltless, because our sins were imputed to Him; and He justly raised Him from the dead, because our sins had been expiated by Him. His work was perfect; therefore His deliverance was just. He is a just God, and therefore never will exact the same debt of the sinner, which was paid by his Surety; nor condemn him for that for which his Substitute atoned. His justice will shine in our eternal acquittal, and be eternally honoured in our endless salvation. He drew the plan of salvation, sent His Son to execute it, gives His Spirit to put us in possession of the blessing, and at last receives us to Himself, of purest grace. 'He saved us, and called us with an holy calling, not according to our works, but according to His own purpose and grace, which was given us in Christ Jesus before the world began.'

> *Mystery of redemption this:*
> *All my sins on Christ were laid.*
> *Mine offence was reckon'd His.*
> *He the great atonement made!*
> *Here His justice He displays,*
> *While He saves my soul by grace.*

❦ EVENING ❧

'Blessed are they that keep my ways.'
PROVERBS 8:32

The Lord's ways are various, but they all lead to glory, honour, immortality, and eternal life. There is the way of salvation, or the way to be delivered from the guilt, power, and consequences of sin; the way of peace, or the way to obtain, enjoy, and maintain peace of conscience; the way of holiness, in which we acquire and increase it; the way of truth, or the way to learn, experience, and practice it; the more excellent way of charity, by which we recommend our religion, and benefit our fellow men. There is no entering upon, or walking in either of these ways but by faith. We are saved by grace through faith. By faith we have peace with God, purifying their hearts by faith. The truth of God must be believed, or it will never be practically known. Faith worketh by love. Here is the commendation: 'that keep my ways.' They keep the eye on them, the heart toward them, and the feet in them. They keep them with care, with fear, with constancy. Such are blessed. For they perceive correctly; they choose rightly; they walk safely; they live happily; they progress gradually; they proceed honourably; and they end gloriously. Reader, are you in the Lord's ways? Do you love and prefer His ways to all other?

> *Prone to stray and start aside,*
> *Saviour! keep me near Thy side.*
> *Make me walk in all Thy ways,*
> *Teach me to show forth Thy praise.*

JULY 23

🌺 MORNING 🌺
'Hold thou me up, and I shall be safe.'
PSALM 119:117

This should be the Christian's daily prayer; his way is rough, the dangers are many, his foes are powerful, and he is liable to fall. If we from the heart present this prayer, it proves that we have a sense of our own weakness; a knowledge of the Lord as our strength; genuine humility working within; and a desire to honour God ruling in the conscience. We are in the world, and unless the Lord hold us up, we shall bring guilt on the conscience, disgrace on the gospel, and dishonour to God. We are in the church, and unless the Lord hold us up, we shall prove roots of bitterness, stumbling-blocks, and grieve the godly. We shall be, if we are not, in affliction, and unless the Lord hold us up, we shall faint, be angry with God, as was Jonah, or be hardened through the deceitfulness of sin. O believer, lean not on earth; trust not in a friend; place no dependence on gifts; but let your daily, yea, hourly prayer be, 'Hold thou me up, and I shall be safe.' The ear of thy God is open, the heart of thy God is tender, the arm of thy God is strong. Live out of self upon God, if you would be safe.

> *Son of God! Thy blessing grant;*
> *Still supply my every want;*
> *Unsustain'd by Thee, I fall;*
> *Send the strength for which I call;*
> *Weaker than a bruised reed,*
> *Help I every moment need.*

🌺 EVENING 🌺
'All the promises of God in Him.'
2 CORINTHIANS 1:20

As all light is in the sun, so all grace is in Christ. The promises which are scattered over the Bible, all centre in Jesus. The promises of scripture are divine; they make known the nature and disposition of God. They all originated in grace; they are proofs of unbounded benevolence; they display infinite condescension; and they are intended to strengthen our faith and hope. They are in Christ. In His mouth as the true Witness; in His hand as the Surety of the better covenant; in His heart as the Bridegroom of His church; in His will as the gracious Testator; in His inheritance as the Heir of all things; and are all comprehended in Himself, as the mercy promised to our forefathers. He publishes them as a Prophet, confirms them as a Priest, and fulfils them as a King. Some of them relate to the world, and some of them exclusively to the church. Some of them regard the body, others the soul. They embrace all time, and run forward into eternity. In Christ, every promise is yea to the Greek, and amen to the Jew; that is, they are confirmed to all believers, whether Jews or Greeks. Beloved, let us believe them, plead them, and rest our souls upon them. They were made for us, and shall be fulfilled to us, for God is faithful.

> *Here I repose my trust,*
> *On these my hopes recline;*
> *Eternal truth and righteousness*
> *Appear in every line.*

JULY 24

🌿 MORNING 🌿
'The way of peace.'
ROMANS 3:17

Peace is an invaluable blessing, whether we consider it as reconciliation to God, or tranquillity and comfort of mind. It is not to be obtained by the works of the law, but if we would obtain peace, it must be by receiving the Saviour's word into our hearts; by believing on Him as able and willing to save; by trusting the testimony God hath given of His Son; by renouncing self, as loathsome in the sight of God; by relying simply and always on Jesus for all we need; and by daily making a hearty surrender of all to infinite love. If we would maintain peace, we must confide in the promises; walk by the precepts; be loyal to the King of Zion; commune daily with our heavenly Father; attend upon Him in the ordinances of His own appointment; rely on His special and particular providence; frequent the open fountain for purification; cleave to the saints in love, as the body of Christ; and disentangle our affections from the world, and set them on things above. This is the way, walk ye in it. Let nothing tempt you to leave it. Endeavour by all means to attract others to it. No peace but by Christ; therefore cleave to Christ.

> There is no path to heavenly bliss,
> Or solid joy, or lasting peace,
> But Christ, th' appointed road:
>
> O, may I tread the sacred WAY;
> By faith rejoice, and praise, and pray
> Till I sit down with God.

🌿 EVENING 🌿
'Fury is not in me.'
ISAIAH 27:4

It is easy to mistake the character of God. This is very often done. We think Him wrathful. We are afraid of Him. But in Jesus, God meets us, blesses us, and assures us, that there is no fury in Him. Here is a basis for hope. If there is no fury in God, there is love, and I may hope. He will not refuse my application, despise my prayer, or drive me from His throne. Here is a source of comfort. If there is no fury in God, the wrath of man is vain. The rage of hell is harmless. Here is an antidote for my doubts and fears. If there is no fury in God, my dread of death is unfounded, my fear of rejection is childish, my alarm at the approach of judgement is causeless. Here is a call for gratitude and praise. If there is no fury in God, I may draw near, I may confide in Him, I may expect good things from Him, I ought to praise Him. If there is no fury in God, whom shall I fear? Of what shall I be afraid? He is a refuge in trouble; a well of living water in the desert; a vineyard in the wilderness; a river, the streams whereof make glad the city of God. God is not wrath, but love. God is not darkness, but light. Christian, be careful what views you entertain of your God. Be sure that they are scriptural, that they are derived from the new covenant.

> Fury is not in Me – but love,
> Behold the proof, My Son I gave!
> And still My tender mercies move,
> From sin, and death, and hell to save.

JULY 25

❦ MORNING ❧

'Be still, and know that I am God.'
PSALM 46:10

The dispensations of divine providence are often very perplexing; our God has His way in the sea, and His path in the deep waters, and His footsteps are not known. Reason is confounded, and faith is staggered; but He hushes our fears, silences our cries, and bids us 'BE STILL.' We must lie before Him, as the lamb at the shepherd's feet; as the child in the parent's arms. He will not harm us Himself, nor will He let others do so. We must learn that He is God, infinitely wise, invariably good, always a Sovereign. He doeth according to His will in heaven, on earth, in the sea, and all deep places. None can stay His hand, or dispute His right to accomplish His will. Let us therefore keep silence before Him. He is our God, and we are His people; His mercy is everlasting, and His truth endureth throughout all generations. Let us not murmur, for He is gracious; let us not complain, for He is a Father unto us; let us not fear, for He is faithful: but let us wait upon Him, submitting in all things to His will, and surrendering ourselves into His hands with 'Here am I, do with me as seemeth Thee good.'

When I can trust my all with God,
In trial's fearful hour;
Bow, all resign'd beneath His rod,
And bless His sparing power;
A joy springs up amidst distress,
A fountain in the wilderness.

❦ EVENING ❧

'Jesus only.'
MATTHEW 17:8

Moses and Elias had been with them on the mount, but they were gone; Jesus only remained. How many things change, or pass away, as health; wealth; trade; comforts; ministers; relatives; youth; vigour; prosperity. But whatever changes, Jesus is the same. He is the same in His nature, which is love; in His purpose towards us, which is grace; in His promises, which are faithful; in His offices, as Priest-Intercessor-King; in His blood, which is always efficacious; in His relations, for He is the Father-Brother-Husband-Friend. The same yesterday, today, and forever. The passage forms a suitable motto for us. *Jesus only*, as my plea at the throne of grace; as the object of my faith, desire, and confidence; as my hope and ground of acceptance with God; as my pattern and example; as my joy and song; as my King and Lawgiver; as my all in all. Let us endeavour to keep the eye and the heart always on Jesus. Let us rejoice that when Moses and Elias depart, Jesus remains. Let us remember, that the dark cloud or the bright vision makes no change in Him. Let us expect Jesus to sweeten and sanctify all bereavements, and to preserve us from the snares which accompany prosperity.

He's all that's good and great,
All that I can admire;
All that Jehovah can bestow,
And all my soul's desire.

JULY 26

❦ MORNING ❦

'Receive not the grace of God in vain.'

2 CORINTHIANS 6.1

By 'the grace of God' in this passage, we are to understand the everlasting gospel; which is a glorious proclamation of favour manifested to the vile and unworthy. It proclaims that God has come down unto us in the person of Christ; that He has accepted the labours, sufferings, and death of Jesus, as the ground of our deliverance from death, and as our title to eternal life; and He now sends His ambassadors to assure us that He is our Friend; that He will not impute our trespasses unto us; that He views us in Jesus as a new creation; all former things are passed away and forgotten; and He will make all who receive His Word, and believe in His Son, the righteousness of God in Him. Let us not then receive this glorious message in vain; we do so if we indulge the thought that God is angry with us; if we doubt our acceptance of God in Christ; if we fear that He will be wrath with us. He informs us of His grace to encourage us to believe, to quicken us in His ways, to embolden us at His throne, to produce love to His name, and to furnish us with an answer to all objections.

> O, what amazing words of grace
> Are in the gospel found!
> Suited to every sinner's case,
> Who knows the joyful sound.
> May I this glorious grace receive,
> And to my Saviour's glory live.

❦ EVENING ❦

'Rejoice evermore.'

1 THESSALONIANS 5:16

The Christian is described as happy, 'rejoicing in Christ Jesus.' He is required to be happy: 'Rejoice evermore.' This joy is a fruit of the Spirit. It is the effect of faith. It is associated with hope. 'Rejoicing in hope.' It is the soldier, rejoicing in his courageous and conquering captain; the mariner, rejoicing in his wise and experienced pilot; the penitent, rejoicing in his pardoning and gracious God; the prodigal, rejoicing in his kind and loving father. The joy is sometimes unspeakable and full of glory. It is always holy joy, and is easily damped and weakened by sin. Christian, thy God bids thee rejoice. The Lord's people of old were exceeding joyful in all their tribulations. A solid foundation is laid for thy joy in God's holy Word; in His gracious covenant; in the fulness of Jesus; and in the glorious perfections of God. Our joy is very often injured, by our uncertainty about our calling and election – these should be made sure; by our unbelief, which insults God while it injures us; by low views of Christ; by a hasty spirit; by worldly entanglements; by an uneven walk with God; by selfishness in our religion. Believer, you ought to be happy.

> Rejoice evermore in the truth and the power,
> And the grace, of your heavenly Friend;
> Till to us who believe He His glory doth give,
> And a kingdom that never shall end.

JULY 27

❦ MORNING ❧
'I will wait upon the LORD.'
ISAIAH 8:17

The Lord hath concealed His face, His favour could not be discovered, but marks of displeasure appeared; yet the church determines not to despond or yield to fear, but to wait upon the Lord who was hiding Himself from the house of Israel, and to look for Him. It is a great trial to a real believer for his God to hide His face; but it is still his privilege to wait daily at His gates, and to watch at the posts of His doors, persuaded that He will turn again and display His forgiving love. We must not give up hope, nor abandon the Lord's ways, nor restrain prayer before Him; but we must wait in faith, believing His Word in expectation, trusting His faithfulness. Nothing should be allowed to weaken our faith in God's Word, or drive our souls from His throne. He waits for the fittest time to be gracious; and we should wait His time to be comforted, or delivered. Wait on the Lord and keep His way. Wait as a servant for his master's return; as a child for his father's blessing; as a bride for the tokens of her bridegroom's love. He says, 'Behold, I come quickly; blessed is he that watcheth.' A waiting posture is a blessed posture.

> *Still nigh me, O my Saviour, stand,*
> *And guard in fierce temptation's hour.*
> *Hide in the hollow of Thy hand,*
> *Show forth in me Thy saving power,*
> *Still be Thine arm my sure defence,*
> *Nor earth nor hell shall pluck me thence.*

❦ EVENING ❧
'This man receiveth sinners.'
LUKE 15:2

This was a charge brought against our Lord, but it is full of consolation to us. He did receive sinners, and He received them as sinners. He does receive sinners still, and receives them notwithstanding their sins; yea, because of them. He receives the very worst of sinners; however worthless, despised by others, or peculiar their circumstances may be; sinners of every clime, at any age, without making a distinction; every sinner that comes to Him, is received by Him. He receives them with all their sins upon them, however polluted, or however base. He receives them without any thing to recommend them; without any reluctance; most graciously. He receives them to pardon all their sins; to cleanse them from all their defilement; to justify them from all charges; to heal all their wounds; to make them new creatures; to use them to His glory; to make them a peculiar people, zealous of good works on earth; and to glorify them with Himself in heaven for ever. Beloved, if you feel that you cannot go to God as a saint, go to Jesus as a sinner. Are you doubting the character of your past experience? Go to Him as you did at first, or as though you never had gone. Go, for He will receive you. Go, for He is at this very moment waiting to bless you.

> *His blood can cleanse the blackest soul,*
> *And wash your guilt away;*
> *He will present you sound and whole*
> *In that tremendous day.*

JULY 28

❦ MORNING ❧

'He will yet deliver us.'

2 Corinthians 1:10

How many times has our God delivered us, from how many dangers, in how many ways; and He who hath delivered, doth deliver, and in Him we trust that He will yet deliver us. He delivered us from spiritual death, by the operations of His Holy Spirit, and from eternal death, by the sacrifice of His Son. We were dead, but we are now alive unto God, through Jesus Christ our Lord; and He who delivered from the greatest evil – spiritual death – will not refuse to deliver us from any lesser danger. Let us trust in Him, rely upon Him, and expect Him to deliver. It is written, 'Many are the afflictions of the righteous, but the Lord delivereth him out of them all.' He knoweth how to deliver the godly out of temptation. Let us triumph with Paul: 'The Lord stood with me, and strengthened me; and I was delivered out of the mouth of the lion; and the Lord shall deliver me from every evil work, and will preserve me unto His heavenly kingdom; to whom be glory for ever and ever. Amen.' If He had not intended to carry on the work, He would not have begun it, for He well knew what opposition it would meet with: but He that began will perfect it in the day of Jesus Christ. He is faithful who hath promised.

> *Yet I must fight, if I would reign:*
> *Increase my courage, Lord!*
> *I'll bear the toil, endure the pain,*
> *Supported by Thy Word.*

❦ EVENING ❧

'I know whom I have chosen.'

John 13:18

Some have been chosen to office who were not chosen to salvation. This was the case with Judas. But all believers are chosen to everlasting life. He chose them as an act of sovereignty, as presented to Him by the Father. He chose His people to be His bride, His servants, His witnesses, His glory. His choosing them was the cause of their choosing Him. He knows His chosen ones. His knowledge of them is perfect. He knows them by name and where they live; He knows their hearts, their faith, their hope, their love, their fears, their sorrows, their works, their wants. His knowledge of them is a source of comfort to them. He approves of them. He will put a difference between them and others. If Jesus knows all His people thus, He must be God; for who could distinctly know the number, names, residences, hearts, and entire circumstances of a number which no man can number, but God. Beloved, Jesus knows us so as to humble our pride, honour our faith, supply all our needs, guide our steps, and reward our good works. Ever remember, Jesus knows my ways in the family, in the business, in the church, in all places. He knows His chosen ones, as the father does His beloved child; as the husband does his tenderly attached bride. Thus He knows me.

> *No claim had we who now enjoy*
> *The smiles of our redeeming God;*
> *He only knows who chose us, why*
> *Our hearts are His divine abode.*

JULY 29

❦ MORNING ❧

'I am a stranger in the earth.'

PSALM 119:19

Beloved, we are strangers and pilgrims in the earth, as all our fathers were; our days are as a shadow, and there is no abiding. We are born from above, and are bound for glory. We are distant from home, where our kindred, our treasure, and our hearts are found. Here we have no fixed residence; nor should we have any fellowship with the unfruitful works of darkness, but rather reprove them. We are called to submit to many inconveniences. The Bible is our light, our food, our joy, and our directory. We want a guide, a guard, a companion, a comforter; but Jesus has engaged to fill each of these offices. We should pray for the peace of the country where we sojourn; we should not be meddlers with its concerns, but keep ourselves detached; we should be thankful for every advantage, but set and keep our affections on things above; we should neither be impatient nor reluctant in reference to going home, but submit to our Father's will; we should consider ill-treatment as permitted to do us good; and contrast the present with our own beloved country and home. As strangers and pilgrims, let us abstain from fleshly lusts.

There is my house and portion fair,
My treasure and my heart are there,
And my abiding home;

For me my elder brethren stay,
And angels beckon me away
And Jesus bids me come.

❦ EVENING ❧

'Let us draw near hither to God.'

1 SAMUEL 14:36

By nature we are far from God. By grace we are reconciled and brought nigh. But still we live at a great distance from Him. In prayer we meet with God on a throne of grace. We sometimes enjoy nearness, but we are near to Him whether we enjoy it or not. Let us keep this view of prayer before our minds; it is drawing near to God. Let us often pray and so draw nigh to Him. In order to this we must believe that He is; we must embrace the atonement; we must credit His Word, especially the promises; we must desire what we ask; we must expect what we ask, if we really need it, and He has promised it; we must plead as though argument and earnestness could prevail; we must place our entire confidence in the name of Jesus; we must importune until we succeed. How should we draw near? With confidence, as children; with reverence, as sinners; with frequency, as dependants; with a pure conscience; without wrath or doubting, being careful that we do not indulge iniquity in our hearts. Let us draw near in the closet, in the family, in the church, in the street. Let us draw near for we are invited; we are exhorted; we are commanded. Therefore we must or sin; we must or suffer.

O look with pity on me, Lord,
Thy precious influence afford!
From sin and Satan set me free,
And help me to draw near to Thee.

JULY 30

❦ MORNING ❦

'He that glorieth, let him glory in the Lord.'

1 Corinthians 1:31

It is unlawful to glory in ourselves, our descent, our possessions, our connections, or doings; if we glory it must be in the Lord. We must glory in Him as gracious and merciful, exercising lovingkindness and tender mercies in the earth; in what He is to His people, their God, their portion, and their Friend; in what He has for us, has already given to us, and will without doubt bestow upon us; in Christ, as crucified for our sins, raised for our justification, and ascended to heaven in order to plead our cause, and take possession of the kingdom in our names; in our relation to Him, interest in Him, and oneness with Him. This is our glory, that we are one with Christ, and one with the Father through Him; that we are heirs of God and joint-heirs with Jesus Christ; that all things are for our sakes, that the abundant grace might, through the thanksgiving of many, redound to the glory of God. Beloved, let us glory in the Lord, in His free grace, eternal love, well-ordered covenant, precious promises, splendid mansions, and glorious name. If we glory in the Lord now, we shall never regret it.

In Christ my full salvation stands,
In Him alone my glorying be;
Nothing shall pluck me from His hands,

From condemnation I am free:
Be holiness my costly dress,
And my best robe His righteousness.

❦ EVENING ❦

'To obey is better than sacrifice.'

1 Samuel 15:22

We are prone to attach too much importance to ceremonies. Israel did so. Thousands do so now to a very fearful extent. But obedience to moral precepts, out of love to God, while depending for life and peace on the finished work of Christ alone, is what pleases God. To obey is better than to sacrifice. The obedience intended requires the surrender of the judgment; the acquiescence of the conscience; the concurrence of the will; and the submission of the whole man to the authority of God. Such obedience pleases God better than any sacrifice which we can offer, because it is an acknowledgement of His wisdom and goodness in requiring, and it is a hearty compliance with His will. But in order to our obedience being thus acceptable, it must be scriptural, sincere, humble, uniform, and constant. Then it is better than any gifts which we can present, than any sufferings we can endure. We must obey God as a Sovereign, while we love Him as a Father. We must reverence His authority, while we trust in His promises. Our obedience must be that of children, of children living under the smile of a father's love. Our obedience is not to be considered a price paid for blessings, but as the proof of love, and the effect of union to Christ.

My God, with heavenly wisdom bless,
And teach me how Thyself to please:
Work in me both to will and do
That I Thy glory may pursue.

JULY 31

❦ MORNING ❦
'Things that accompany salvation.'
Hebrews 6:9

Let us inquire. What are they? Do we possess them? Spiritual life, evidenced by convictions of sin; hatred to sin; crying to God for deliverance from sin; groaning under the weight of the body of sin and death; a tender conscience, which trembles at sin, and feels deeply for God's glory; a filial fear of God, lest we should dishonour His name, disgrace His cause, and grieve His love; an anxiety and deep-rooted concern for holiness, both in the heart and the life; contrition or brokenness of heart for sin, accompanied with holy mourning before God; fervour in devotion, earnestly breathing out the desires of the heart before God, or grieving when it is not so; a jealousy of self, as to our sincerity and uprightness of intention, lest we should be led astray by the corruptions which are within; a chaste conversation coupled with fear; diligence in the means of grace; searching the scriptures, to ascertain our real state and condition. What is the Lord's will and our duty? An increasing discovery of our own weakness, imperfection, and misery. He that hath these things shall never finally fall.

> O, give me, Saviour, give me still
> My poverty to know;
> Increase my faith; each day in grace
> And knowledge may I grow:
> Unfold the glories of Thy cross,
> For which I count all else as loss.

❦ EVENING ❦
'The Father Himself loveth you.'
John 16:27

Loveth whom? All who love Jesus. And who are they? Such as believe His Word; rely on His merits; trust in His name; observe His ordinances; keep His precepts; and find Him to be precious to their souls. All such are beloved of the Father. This love includes His infinite good will toward them, and His delight in them. It is an infinite willingness to do them good, and to bestow blessings upon them. This appeared first in a purpose; then in a promise; and at length in the glorious work of His beloved Son. His love is eternal, immutable, and free. The proofs of it are the covenant; the gift of His Son; the bestowment of the Holy Spirit; the Bible; all gospel privileges and spiritual blessings; with the kingdom of glory at last. Does the Father Himself love us? Then let us believe the fact, especially when we go to prayer. Then let us love Him in return, and be willing to do and suffer all His will. Let us live above the world, and testify unto it, that the works thereof are evil. Let us seek the welfare of all He loves. Let us pity, plead for, and plead with sinners. Let us encourage all who are seeking the Lord, by assuring them of His love. Let us aim at the increase, union, and spirituality of the church, because God loves us.

> Let every tongue the Father own,
> Who when we all were lost,
> To seek and save us sent the Son,
> And gives the Holy Ghost.

AUGUST 1

❦ MORNING ❧

'We trust in the living God.'

1 Timothy 4:10

The living God is opposed to a dying world, to our dying frames, and to our dying friends; these must not be trusted, or we shall be wretched. Our God may, ought to be trusted, for He is the only suitable object of a Christian's trust; He is able to do exceeding abundantly above all we can ask or think. He is immutable. He never disappointed a sinner's hope, if founded on His Word; or refused a believer's petition, for deliverance or relief. If we trust in the living God, it will preserve us from perpetual disappointment; from bitter reflections on self and others; from many dangers; and from the threatened curse. If we trust in the living God we are blessed; we shall be fruitful; we shall be delivered from slavish fears; we shall enjoy perfect peace; we shall be provided for; we shall find a refuge in every storm; have an answer for all who reproach us; experience firmness and stability; and enjoy solid happiness. Let us ascertain: Are we trusting in the living God? Let us seek grace, daily to live in simple, child-like dependence upon Him. Blessed is the man that trusteth in the Lord; he shall be safe, fruitful, and happy.

> *In Thee, O Lord, I put my trust,*
> *Mighty and merciful and just*
> *Who hides my life above;*
>
> *Thou canst, Thou wilt my Helper be;*
> *My confidence is all in Thee,*
> *My faithful God of love.*

❦ EVENING ❧

'The LORD hath put away thy sin.'

2 Samuel 12:13

The sin of David was flagrant and fearful. He first committed adultery, then made Uriah drunk, then planned his murder, then ascribed it to divine providence, and lay comparatively careless under the whole for several months. At length he is aroused from his lethargy, and then he humbly confesses his transgressions unto the Lord. His confession was preceded by conviction; it was attended with compunction; it was confirmed by supplication; and it was crowned with forgiveness. 'The LORD hath put away thy sin.' Sin appears before God pleading against the sinner. The advocate appears also opposing it. He prevails, and God pardons the grievous offender. His sin is so forgiven, as to be forgotten. This is pardoning like a God. Observe, the man that frankly and honestly confesses his sins, will find that God fully and freely pardons. If God puts away our sin, our enemies shall search for it in vain. It shall not be found. If God casts your sins behind His back, you will often place them before your face, in order to humble you, to preserve you from turning again to folly, and to inspire you with gratitude and love. So did David. He says, 'My sin is ever before me.' Pardoned sinners are always sorry *for* sin, afraid *of* sin, and watchful *against* sin.

> *Jesus, Giver of contrition,*
> *Giver Thou of pardon art;*
> *Wound me, O my kind Physician,*
> *Break, and then bind up my heart.*

AUGUST 2

❦ MORNING ❦

'My son, despise not thou the chastening of the Lord.'

HEBREWS 12:5

The Lord speaketh to us as unto children; He speaks in reference to our afflictions: they are chastisements; they are sent in love; when we are chastened we are judged of the Lord, that we may not be condemned with the world. Let us not faint under them; let us not despise them. We do so when we think there is no occasion for them, and that we could do as well, or better without them; when we do not seek to ascertain the cause why they are sent, or to learn the lessons they are intended to teach; when we do not acknowledge the Lord's right to chasten, His love in doing it, and His wisdom in the time, nature, and duration of the trial; when we do not seek grace to submit cheerfully, or at least silently, and to glorify God in it, and after it; when we do not seek to be improved in our knowledge, sanctity, and spiritual vigour by it; when with a carnal, flesh-pleasing view, we seek to be delivered from it. Beloved, let us beware of despising divine chastisement in any of these ways; but let us glorify God in the day of visitation. God dealeth with us as with sons.

> *Father, if Thou must reprove*　*Chastise Thy wayward son:*
> *For all that I have done,*　*Correct with kind severity,*
> *Not in anger, but in love,*　*And bring me home to Thee.*

❦ EVENING ❦

'The last enemy.'

1 CORINTHIANS 15:26

The Christian has many enemies, but through grace he shall overcome them all. 'The last enemy that shall be destroyed is death.' Death is an enemy to kingdoms, cutting down the wise, the patriotic, and the philanthropic. It is an enemy to congregations, removing the active, the benevolent, and the unprofitable hearer. It is an enemy to churches, robbing them of their officers, their teachers, the youthful, the devoted, and the most zealous members. It is an enemy to families, taking away the parent, the husband, the wife, the offspring. It is an enemy to individuals, to saints, but especially to sinners. It was an enemy to our Lord Jesus Christ. It is the last enemy. The last in its introduction: Satan comes first, then sin, then death. It is the last in its attack: we have disease, often age, and then death. It is the last that will be destroyed: for God has decreed it, Christ has promised it, saints pray for it, the church anticipates it, and Jesus is coming to execute the judgement written. Yes, it shall be destroyed certainly, perfectly, for ever. But even now the saint may defy its power, be reconciled to its attack, long for its stroke, rejoice in its arms, and spring from its grasp to the enjoyment of unspeakable glory.

> *O Lord! that I may thus depart,*
> *Thy joys to share, Thy face to see,*
> *Impress Thine image on my heart,*
> *And teach me now to walk with Thee.*

AUGUST 3

🌿 MORNING 🌿
'The Lord thinketh upon me.'
PSALM 40:17

When we think of the greatness and glory of Jehovah, man appears so worthless and insignificant, that we are ready to ask, 'Will the Lord regard us, bless us, and dwell with us?' Yes, He has promised to do so in His Word, and He has informed us that His thoughts are perpetually taken up with us. He thinketh upon us, to supply our need, protect from foes, lead us in His ways, and make us meet for His kingdom and glory. His thoughts are thoughts of peace and not of evil, to give us an expected end. He thinketh upon us by day and by night, when at home or abroad; and He thinks of us with love as His children; with pleasure as His friends; with a purpose to bless us as His dependants. We think He may perhaps have mercy, He may do a little for us; but as high as the heavens are above the earth, so are His thoughts above our thoughts; and His ways above our ways. His thoughts are worthy of a God. What are the promises? Only His thoughts put into our language. And what do they prove? Truly that He thought of all our wants, wishes, and desires, and made full provision for them.

> Father, I want a thankful heart,
> I want to taste how good Thou art;
> To plunge me in Thy mercy's sea,
> And comprehend Thy love to me,
> The length, and breadth, and depth, and height,
> Of love divinely infinite.

🌿 EVENING 🌿
'O when wilt thou come unto me?'
PSALM 101:2

The presence of the Lord is the heaven of His people. They cannot be satisfied or happy without it. He is the object of their love, the source of their enjoyment, the centre of their desires, and the life of their souls. If He is present all is well, but if He is absent nothing can yield them satisfaction. They are restless; their souls can find no repose, their desires no rest. The reasons are many: in His favour is their life; in His fellowship is wealth and peace; in His presence is fulness of joy, safety, rest, refreshment and victory. His presence promotes their sanctification, enlarges their hearts, and ripens the fruits of grace. It proves the excellency of their religion. The Lord now visits His people. They sometimes lose the sense of His presence. Having once enjoyed it, they cannot but long for it again. The pleading, desiring, importunate soul shall be satisfied. Reader, have you enjoyed the presence of God? Do you enjoy it now? Can you find any substitute for it? Are you crying with David, 'My soul followeth hard after thee?' or, 'O when wilt thou come unto me?' or, 'Let thy tender mercies come unto me, that I may live; for thy law is my delight?' If you are careless about God's presence, you are a stranger to it.

> My thirsty soul with strong desires,
> To God, the living God, aspires.
> Come, gracious Lord, and let me know,
> The joys which from Thy presence flow.

AUGUST 4

❦ MORNING ❦
'Thou shall know hereafter.'
JOHN 13:7

We are often at a loss to account for many things in our feelings, in our circumstances, and in the Lord's dealings with us; but what we know not now, we shall know hereafter. This is our Saviour's promise; let us take the comfort of it, and expect its fulfilment to our perfect satisfaction by and by. We shall know some things before the coming of our Lord, and we shall know all things after. Every difficulty will then be cleared up, and all the trying dispensations of divine providence accounted for. Let us therefore be patient and wait the Lord's time; the coming of our Lord draweth nigh. Let us silently submit to our Father's will, for we shall see that it was wise and kind. Let us acknowledge the right of God to conceal the cause of His working, until He has fully accomplished His designs. Let us praise Him for all that is past, and trust Him for all that is to come. 'Now we see through a glass darkly', but we shall soon see Him face to face; 'now we know but in part, then shall we know even as also we are known.' May the Lord direct our hearts into His love, and into the patient waiting for Christ.

Jesus, we own Thy sovereign hand,
Thy faithful care we own,
Wisdom and love are all Thy ways,
When most to us unknown;
To Thee we cheerfully resign
For Thou art ours, and we are Thine.

❦ EVENING ❦
'Oh that God would speak!'
JOB 11:5

Job's friends mistook his case. They failed to convince him by their reasonings. They were desirous to do so; therefore one of them at length exclaims, 'Oh that God would speak!' Thus the believer often exclaims; it supposes a desire to accomplish a certain end; a persuasion of the insufficiency of all but God; a kind and benevolent feeling. To whom may we desire God to speak? To *ourselves*, to assure us of our interest in His love, to relieve us under our distresses, and to establish us in the truth; to *sinners*, to quicken them, to convert them, and to bring them forth on the Lord's side; to *mourners*, to comfort them, to strengthen them, and to set them at liberty; to *backsliders*, to reprove and restore them to holiness, to happiness, and to usefulness. What does the exclamation teach us? Confidence in God; to apply to God in all difficult cases. Tried believer, God will speak *for* thee. Devoted Christian, God will speak *with* thee. How does He speak? By His Word; by His providence; by His Spirit. Then let us listen to hear His voice. Let us look for the effects of His Word. Let us plead with Him often to speak to us, by His preachers, by His ordinances, by His Word, and by every dispensation.

Sweet is the voice of heavenly peace,
Which spreads His gospel o'er.
Then let His servants trust His grace
Nor turn to folly more.

AUGUST 5

❦ MORNING ❦

'He will ever be mindful of His covenant.'
PSALM 111:5

The Lord's people know their God as a covenant God, reconciled to them, at peace with them, and dwelling among them, through the work of Jesus. He has made a covenant in which they are interested, from which all their blessings flow, and on which their confidence is founded. Of this covenant, God is ever mindful. He is mindful of the engagements of Jesus as our Surety; of the relationship in which He was pleased to manifest Himself, as our Father; of the state in which He viewed us, as poor wretched sinners; of the provision He made for His own glory and our needs; of the promise made to Jesus, including all the promises made to us; of the oath He swore, that He would not be wroth with us; of the blood of His Son, as the Victim slain to confirm and ratify it; of the end He had in view in making it, even the display of all His glorious perfections in our eternal salvation. He will ever be mindful of this covenant; He cannot forget it; He will not act contrary to it, but will confirm it even to the end. Beloved, let us also be ever mindful of His covenant.

> Firmer than heaven His covenant stands,
> Tho' earth should shake, and skies depart;
> We're safe in our Redeemer's hands,
> Who bears our name upon His heart;
> For us He lived, and died, and rose,
> And triumph'd over all our foes.

❦ EVENING ❦

'Doing the will of God from the heart.'
EPHESIANS 6.6

Here is a point to be ascertained: What is the will of God? The will of God concerning a sinner is that he should believe Him, love Him, obey Him. His will concerning a believer is that he should reverence His authority, receive His Word, and observe His precepts. God's perceptive will revealed in the New Testament is plain, and that is to be the rule of our conduct. Here is a duty to be performed: to *do* the will of God. To do it, though it excite the opposition of our fellow men, though it cross our natural inclinations. We are to *do* a Father's will; to *perform* a Master's command; to *keep* a Sovereign's laws; to *obey* a Saviour's precepts. The manner in which that will is to be done is also pointed out: *from the heart*. As every evil proceeds from the heart as depraved by sin, so every good thing proceeds from the heart as renewed by grace. 'Doing the will of God from the heart' – that is, not by constraint, but willingly; from the heart – that is, from conviction, from love; doing it heartily, throwing the energies into it. Beloved, are you seeking to *know* the will of God? Are you willing to *do* it? Do you act up to the light you now have? Is your obedience hearty?

> Be Christ my pattern and my guide,
> His image may I bear;
> O may I tread His sacred steps,
> And His bright glories share!

AUGUST 6

🌿 MORNING 🌿

'Come ye near unto me.'

ISAIAH 48:16

The believer's happiness and Jehovah's pleasure are united: we are only happy as we are near to Him, and He is only pleased as we cleave unto Him. He has taken us into a near relationship as His children, people, and beloved bride; He has represented our union by the most striking figures: the branch in the vine, the member with the head, and the building with the foundation. He has made His name our strong tower, His Son our fountain of supply, and His secret place our home. In living near to Him, we enjoy the sweetest comforts, possess unutterable peace, realise the fullest liberty, and find safety and rest. Our assurances, light, holiness, and strength come from His presence; our misery, wretchedness, and woe, from living at a distance from Him. He invites us this morning, as Jacob did his beloved son, 'Come near unto me.' He intends to bless us, as that patriarch did his child; to discover Himself unto us; to show us His covenant and secret; to make us understand His will and Word; to preserve us from all evil, fill us with grace, and conform us to His image. O Saviour, be near to me this day, and keep me near to Thee!

> When trials vex my doubting mind,
> Jesus, to Thy dear wounds I'll flee;
> No shelter can I elsewhere find,
> No peace or comfort but in Thee:
> To Thee my cause I recommend,
> On Thee for future grace depend.

🌿 EVENING 🌿

'Wait thou only upon God.'

PSALM 62:5

What does waiting upon God suppose? *Dependence:* It is the posture of a subject, a servant, a child. *Promise:* Many things are promised us; indeed all good things. But we must believe, feel our need, seek for the blessings, wait God's time. *Hope:* It is expectation that brings us to God, keeps us waiting upon God, and is the spring of all spiritual action. *Desire:* Unless I desire to receive from God, I shall not look to God, nor shall I wait upon God. *Obedience:* We are commanded to wait upon the Lord, and the neglect of this duty is sin. What does waiting upon God include? It includes: faith in His Word; supplication at His throne; attendance upon His ordinances; habitual looking out for answers to prayer, and the interference of God on our behalf; eyeing God in all places, and in all things; acknowledging Him as the Source and Giver of all good things. Let us glance at the injunction: 'Wait thou only upon God.' Then and only then are you safe, holy, wealthy, content, thriving, and happy. Wait on the Lord for all you need, in all you do, and especially when perplexed and troubled. The waiting soul is sure of the blessing, for He has promised: 'They shall not be ashamed that wait for me.'

> With humble faith I wait,
> To see Thy face again;
> Of Israel it shall ne'er be said,
> He sought the Lord in vain.

AUGUST 7

🌿 MORNING 🌿

'Surely I come quickly.'

REVELATION 22:20

Who is this proposing to come quickly? Is it an enemy threatening us? Is it a stranger? No, it is Jesus whom we love, speaking to cheer us. It is Immanuel, to whom we are betrothed in righteousness, judgment, lovingkindness, mercies, and faithfulness. It is our Saviour, who saved us by His death, and preserves us by His life. He will come shortly; the period cannot be far distant. He will come gladly, with delight and pleasure to receive us to Himself. 'Surely,' He says, 'I come quickly;' and is it not a source of joy to us; does it not excite and draw forth holy expectation? He comes to end our persecutions, to silence our complaints, to conform us to His image, to fill us with His love, to clothe us with His glory, and to bring us grace. Do we say with the church, 'Amen, even so, come, Lord Jesus'? Or, are we indifferent about His coming? He says, 'Behold, I come quickly: blessed is he that watcheth and keepeth his garments, lest he walk naked and they see his shame.' Let us look for, and hasten to the coming of the day of God. He comes for our redemption. His coming completes our salvation.

Fly, ye seasons, fly still faster:
Let the glorious day come on,
When we shall behold our Master

Seated on His heavenly throne!
When the Saviour
Shall descend to claim His own.

🌿 EVENING 🌿

'Those that hope in His mercy.'

PSALM 147:11

Mercy sympathises with misery, and the miserable are the objects of mercy. God has revealed His mercy to us in Jesus, in whom it appears in its tenderness, plenitude, constancy, and power. We can expect nothing from justice, for we have sinned; but we may expect every thing from mercy, for God delighteth in it. The first thing the sinner seeks for is mercy; and the last thing the saint appeals to is mercy. There are many who have not the assurance of faith; they cannot say, 'He loved me and gave Himself for me.' They feel as if they dared not call God, 'Father.' It appears presumption in them to claim the promises, appropriate the doctrines, or to say, 'The LORD is my God.' But they do hope in God's mercy. Mercy cheers them, encourages them, and at times gives them joy. Because God shows mercy to sinners through Jesus, they hope He will show mercy to them. They do not feel that they are pardoned, but they hope that they shall be. They are not sure that they shall be saved, but they are looking for the mercy of our Lord Jesus Christ. How precious to them then is the fact, that 'the LORD taketh pleasure in them that fear Him, in those that hope in His mercy.' He is pleased to hear them call, and will answer.

Ye souls who fear His name, 'tis you
The glorious Lord delights to view;
And they, who on His mercy rest,
Shall with His richest love be blest.

AUGUST 8

❧ MORNING ❧

'Owe no man any thing.'
ROMANS 13:8

Rash speculations are inconsistent with Christianity; and getting in debt is as much a breach of the divine precept as robbery or murder. Every believer should live within his income, and not bring a disgrace on religion, by contracting debts which he is unable to pay. If he has done so, he should be very humble; he should confess his sin before God, and pray to be enabled to fulfil his engagements. It is not necessary that he should make an appearance, as it is called; but it is necessary that he should adorn the doctrine of God his Saviour. He that is in debt, and is not grieved by it, humbled under it, and striving to extricate himself from it, is a very suspicious character, whatever profession he may make. Our God says, and He speaks to all who profess His name, *'Owe no man any thing but love.'* A Christian's payments should be prompt and punctual; his word should be as firm as a bond, and his promise as sacred as an oath. O, may our God bring back His people to primitive simplicity! May they all be slow to promise, quick to perform, and so fulfil the law of Christ. May they dread getting into debt, and carefully avoid it.

> Let those who bear the Christian name
> Their holy vows fulfil;
> The saints – the followers of the Lamb,
> Are men of honour still.
> Their Saviour's precepts they obey,
> And hasten to the judgment day.

❧ EVENING ❧

'It pleased God.'
GALATIANS 1:15

Paul is speaking of being separated from his mother's womb, of being called by grace, of Christ being revealed in him, and of his being made a preacher, and an apostle of the Lord Jesus Christ, and he traces up the whole to the pleasure of God. It pleased God to convert, consecrate, and crown the apostle with such eminent success. There was nothing in him to deserve it, nothing to move God to do it. He did it, just because He would, because it pleased Him to do it. So in our case. Do we differ from others? From our former selves? Who made us to differ? Have we spiritual gifts and graces? Why were they conferred upon us, and not on others whom we know? We can trace it to no cause but the sovereign good pleasure of God. He hath mercy on whom He will have mercy, and hath compassion because He will have compassion. When all have more than they deserve, none have cause to complain. But where some are peculiarly favoured, it becomes them to trace their favours to their proper source, and be grateful. 'The LORD taketh pleasure in His people; He will beautify the meek with salvation.' 'The LORD will not forsake His people for His great name's sake, because it hath pleased the LORD to make you His people.'

> God's glorious arm the work hath wrought;
> My soul abhors a boasting thought;
> Before His feet I humbly own,
> Praise is due to grace alone.

AUGUST 9

❦ MORNING ❧

'That He might deliver us from this present evil world.'
GALATIANS 1:4

The whole world lieth in the wicked one, as the devoted child in the arms of Molech; or as the putrid corpse in the grave, over which is written, 'Here lieth….' We were once dead in sin, and buried in corruption, but Jesus Christ interfered for us. 'He gave Himself for our sins, that He might deliver us from this present evil world, according to the will of God and our Father.' The world is evil; therefore we are delivered from it. Jesus died to deliver us from its *spirit*, by which we are influenced in a state of nature; from the *love* of the world, which is enmity with God; from seeking *satisfaction* in the world, which is idolatry; from its fearful *doom*, which is eternal destruction. He intended to raise us above it, in our desires and pursuits; to lead us through it, and glorify us beyond it. Let us inquire this morning: Are we of the world, or are we delivered from it? Have we another spirit in us? Are we become dead to the world by fellowship with Christ in His death? Is Jesus loved, praised, and obeyed, out of gratitude for delivering us? The world is God's enemy; may it be your cross.

> *Jesus, I my cross have taken,*
> *All to leave and follow Thee:*
> *Naked, poor, despised, forsaken,*
> *Thou from hence my all shalt be:*
> *Thou hast my Deliverer been,*
> *I have Thy salvation seen.*

❦ EVENING ❧

'What do ye more than others?'
MATTHEW 5:47

What do you *possess* more than others? Look around at the asylum, at the union house, at the prison, at the hospital, at the sick room, at the hovel. Look at the blind, the deaf, the lame, the dumb, the insane, the idiot. Look back at what saints once were called to endure: see the wanderer covered only with a sheepskin, the confessor in his dungeon, the martyr at the stake, the praying slave under the lash of his cruel owner. Look at thy heart, at the Bible, at the sanctuary. Look up into heaven. Look down into hell. Can you count your mercies? Have you not received much? What do you *profess* more than others? That your principles are far better than those of the worldling, the pagan, the papist, and many professed protestants. You profess to give the Lord the heart, the head, the hand, the life, the property, the all. What *do* ye more than others? For the poor, the church, the world? for the young? for the spread of the gospel, and the honour of Christ? Do you do more than some heathens, or papists, or worldlings? You *know* more than others. You *talk* more than others. More is *expected* from you than others. See therefore that you *do* more than others, or your profession will be justly suspected.

> *Where is the holy walk that suits*
> *The name and character we bear?*
> *And where are seen those heavenly fruits*
> *That show we're not what once we were?*

AUGUST 10

❦ MORNING ❦

'O LORD, I beseech thee, deliver my soul.'
PSALM 116:4

The prayer of faith is generally short, and always to the point. It takes the soul and places it before God, in its real state and true character. It pleads with Him for what is really needed, what must be had. The believer often needs deliverance, and faith cries to God for it. His language is, 'O LORD, I beseech Thee, deliver my soul from doubts and fears, which continually beset me; from a spirit of bondage, which would daily entangle me; from Satan who worries, harasses, and hinders me; from *the sin* which so easily besets me; from men who would injure or mislead me; from my own feelings, which daily burden me.' Thus the Lord is acknowledged as the great Deliverer; our own inability is practically confessed; it is evident our trials and troubles are sanctified; the legitimate tendency of grace is discovered by the earnestness, simplicity, importunity, and success of our prayers. Be this our daily cry until deliverance be no longer needed; for our God says, 'Call upon me in the day of trouble; *I will deliver thee.*' He who delivered thee once, will deliver thee unto the end.

O, for that tenderness of heart
Which bows before the Lord,
Acknowledges how just Thou art,
And trembles at Thy Word!
Saviour, to me in pity give
The pledge Thou wilt at last receive.

❦ EVENING ❦

'Is not the LORD your God with you?'
1 CHRONICLES 22:18

Believer, it is your privilege to have the Lord always with you. He is pledged to you by promise. He has said, 'I am with you always.' 'I will never leave you nor forsake you.' He is with you as a Father to care for you; as the Omnipotent God to defend you. He is with you to counsel you in difficulty, to guide you in perplexity, to strengthen you in weakness, to deliver you in danger, and to comfort you in all your tribulations. Your God has always proved Himself to be true to His Word. Is not the Lord your God with you? Poor Christian! Tempted soul! Tried believer! Sick saint! Is not God with you? Who sustains you? Who supplies you? Who preserves you from desperation? He is with you. But if so, why fear? Why complain? Look up to Him. Call upon Him. Trust in Him. If the Lord be with you, you are a match for Satan, for the world, for every trouble, yea, for death itself. Endeavour to realize the fact: God is with me. Say, 'The LORD of hosts is with us, the God of Jacob is our refuge'; therefore will we not fear. 'I will trust and not be afraid, for the LORD JEHOVAH is my strength and my song; He also is become my salvation.'

With us is Jehovah of Hosts,
Our God, as in Jacob of old;
Our soul of His faithfulness boasts,
And in God we our refuge behold!

AUGUST 11

❦ MORNING ❧

'Heirs of the kingdom.'

JAMES 2:5

He raised the poor from the dust, and the beggar from the dunghill; such were we by nature, but through rich grace we shall inherit the throne of glory. He has prepared for us, promised to us, and will bestow upon us a *kingdom*: a kingdom in which His glory will be seen, felt, and enjoyed for ever; in which all His riches of grace, mercy, and glory will be displayed; in which peace, joy, and pleasure will eternally reign; a kingdom which cannot be moved, and will never know a change. But who are the acknowledged heirs? The poor of this world, who are poor in spirit; the rich in faith, who believe in God, in Jesus, who exercise faith on the precious promises, and whose faith is proved to be good by the works they produce; those who love God from a knowledge of His love to them, and as the effect of His love being shed abroad in their hearts, by the Holy Ghost. Am I an heir? Are you, my friend? If so, rejoice and be exceeding glad; imitate those who through faith and patience now inherit the promises, and the end will crown the whole. The heirs of the kingdom are in the way to the kingdom.

> There shall your eyes with rapture view
> The glorious Friend who died for you;
> That died to ransom, died to raise
>
> To crowns of joy and songs of praise
> Jesus, to Thee I breathe my prayer!
> Reveal, confirm my interest there.

❦ EVENING ❧

'I have loved you.'

JOHN 13:34

The love of Christ is an inexhaustible subject. It is full of sweetness. He loved us before we knew Him, and He manifested His love by preferring our nature to angels, by making a full and sufficient atonement for our sins, by conquering all our spiritual foes, by going to heaven as our Forerunner, by sending down the Holy Spirit, by acting as our Advocate and Intercessor, and by sympathising with us. He has displayed His love in His dealings with us. He found us enemies to God, and He reconciled us. He bore with us when under conviction of sin. He keeps us, for we cannot be trusted alone for one moment. He only chastens, when He might justly punish us. He restores us from all our wanderings. He carries on His work, and supplies all our needs. He rejoices to save us, though great sinners. He does every thing that is necessary for us, and does all cheerfully. His love is displayed in what He intends to do. He will come and fetch us as our Bridegroom. He will separate us from all sinners. He will clothe us with glory. He will publicly marry us. He will exalt us to His throne. He will bring us to reign where we served, to rejoice where we suffered, and to shine where we were put to shame. Glorious Saviour! Thy love indeed passeth knowledge.

> *Lord, in Thy love I yet behold*
> *An undiminished store,*
> *A depth unmeasured and untold,*
> *A sea without a shore.*

AUGUST 12

❧ MORNING ❧

'Thou shalt see greater things than these.'
JOHN 1:50

When the eyes of our understanding are opened by the eternal Spirit, we begin to see out of darkness and obscurity; but our sight is imperfect, we have seen but little yet, there is much more before us to be revealed by and by. We shall see greater depths of sin in our nature, and greater depths of grace in the person of Christ. We shall have clearer evidences of interest in Jesus, and see more of His love to us. We shall experience the cleansing efficacy of His precious blood to a greater extent; and see the power of His arm displayed more visibly for our deliverance. We shall see more of the emptiness, vanity, and deceitfulness of the world; and have greater reason to rejoice that we are delivered from it. We shall see greater things in our Bibles, and feel ourselves under greater obligation to the Holy Spirit for His teaching. We shall see Christ descending, present things abolished, and the glories of eternity unfolding. Let us seek greater things, for Jesus has promised them; and daily pray 'What I know not teach Thou me.' Let us expect to see greater things, for God is true.

> O Lord, how little do we know,
> How little of Thy presence feel;
> While we continue here below,
> And in these earthly houses dwell!
> When wilt Thou take us up above,
> To see Thy face without a cloud.

❧ EVENING ❧

'Give an account of thy stewardship.'
LUKE 16:2

We are in office. We were put into office by another. Our office is one of trust and responsibility. It requires the exercise of the head, the heart, the hand, the foot. A steward should be active, faithful, diligent, and keep the reckoning day in view. We must give an account. We may be called upon to do so soon, suddenly. Our Master is coming, and we must give an account of our *time*, how it has been occupied, for or against Him; of our *talents*, how engaged, as money, voice, influence; of our *souls*, and all their powers, as understanding, will, affections, and memory; of our *conduct* towards others, and the cause of God; of the *sentiments* we entertain and propagate; of our *opportunities* for usefulness. Beloved, you are a steward; do you realize this? Your Bible is the Master's rule, and your directory; do you search it as such? Your Master's eye is always upon you; do you constantly bear this in mind? Opportunities of usefulness are tests and trials, which prove your spirit and disposition; do you view them as such? The day of the Lord is at hand; then all our accounts will be settled, and then, however treated now, every faithful steward will 'have praise of God.' O to realize our responsibility, and act accordingly!

> All-righteous and eternal Judge,
> When summoned at Thy bar to stand,
> May I acquitted and approv'd,
> Be crown'd with bliss at Thy right hand.

AUGUST 13

❦ MORNING ❦
'Men shall be blessed in Him.'
PSALM 72: 17

Every thing out of Christ is under the curse; all blessings are treasured up in Him, and can only be received and enjoyed by union to and communion with Him. If in Him, He is made of God unto us wisdom, righteousness, strength, sanctification, and redemption; if separate from Him, His work will profit us nothing. How important then is union to Jesus! All who are in Him are blessed with the favour of God, which compasses them as a shield; with access to God, by the Spirit, as to a kind and indulgent Father; with the friendship of God – He calls them not servants but friends, and His friendship is a good fortune; with justification before God, as the great Lawgiver and Judge of all; with sanctification by God, to the praise, honour, and glory of His grace; and ultimately they will be glorified with God through eternal ages. All things are theirs, and for them is laid up a crown of righteousness, which fadeth not away; a treasure in Heaven which corrupteth not, and where thieves cannot steal. O, blessed state! O, happy persons! But this honour have all the saints.

> *Blessings abound where Jesus reigns:*
> *The prisoner leaps to lose his chains;*
> *The weary find eternal rest,*
> *And all the sons of want are blest.*
> *In Him the tribes of Adam boast,*
> *More blessings than their father lost.*

❦ EVENING ❦
'Ye are the children of the LORD your God.'
DEUTERONOMY 14:1

Important and interesting relation this: Children of God. Who are so? Those who are born again; in whom a new nature produces new desires, new tastes, new sorrows, new joys, new pursuits; those who are taught of God, who have received the Spirit of adoption, such are under obligation. Children should believe what their Father says, do what their Father bids, go where their Father sends, trust in a Father's care, expect what a Father promises, and look for a Father's supplies. What comfort such a relationship affords! You are not, you cannot be friendless. You are not orphans; you have a Father, and an incomparable Father. You should not despond, but remember, in all your trials, a Father's love; in poverty, your Father's wealth; under reproaches, your honourable relation; in sickness, your happy home; in death, your endless life. 'Behold what manner of love the Father hath bestowed upon us, that we should be called the sons of God ... Beloved, *now* are we the sons of God, and it doth not yet appear what we shall be: but we know that when He shall appear we shall be like Him; for we shall see Him as He is.'

> *O! let a sense of this Thy grace*
> *My best affections move,*
> *That, while my lips Thy praise proclaim,*
> *My heart may feel Thy love.*

AUGUST 14

🌿 MORNING 🌿
'In the day of adversity, consider.'
ECCLESIASTES 7:14

Circumstances sometimes regulate duties. The Lord's people have to pass through many changes; they are strangers and pilgrims here. Sometimes prosperity calls for rejoicing, and sometimes adversity calls for consideration. If our prayers appears to be shut out, our petitions seem to be denied, and we cannot enjoy the life and power of religion, it is the day of adversity; if providence frowns, and the heart contracts and becomes hard, it is a day of adversity. Now we should consider: Is there not a *cause*? What is it? Has sin been indulged? or mercy slighted? or duty neglected? or self deified? What is the *intention*? Is it to correct, reprove, and restore us? How should we now *act*? Let us take shame to ourselves, justify our God, confess sin, lament over our folly, crave pardon, and plead for restoration. It is our comfort to know that the Lord calls us to return, declares He is ready to forgive, promises a gracious reception, and assures us He will heal our backslidings and love us freely. Let us, believing, look for His blessing.

> *Of my extreme distresses*
> *The author is the Lord;*
> *Whate'er His wisdom pleases,*
> *His name be still adored.*
>
> *If still He prove my patience*
> *And to the utmost prove,*
> *Yet all His dispensations*
> *Are faithfulness and love.*

🌿 EVENING 🌿
'Give, and it shall be given unto you.'
LUKE 6:38

The teacher of this precept has set us the example: 'For ye know the grace of our Lord Jesus Christ, that, though He was rich, yet for your sakes He became poor, that ye through His poverty might be rich.' In Him also we see an illustration of the promise: 'He humbled Himself and became obedient unto death, even the death of the cross. Wherefore God also hath highly exalted Him, and given Him a name which is above every name.' The *precept* is *'Give.'* Be liberal. Give to every good cause if you have the means. Give from a good motive. Give with a good end in view: as to discharge a necessary duty, or to promote the welfare of mankind, or to honour God. Give by a good rule, according as God hath given to you. The *promise* is, *'It shall be given you.'* Who is it makes the promise? He who *can* fulfil it, for He is rich; He who *will* fulfil it, for He is good; He who *must* fulfil it, for He is faithful. The promise is made to every liberal soul. The promise extends to body and soul, to time and eternity. Its extent is 'good measure, pressed down, shaken together, and running over.' We sow a few grains, and reap a harvest. Are you liberal? Does your liberality flow from faith *in* Christ, and love to His name?

> *If profit by thy scope,*
> *Diffuse thine alms about:*
> *The worldling prospers laying up,*
> *The Christian, laying out.*

AUGUST 15

❦ MORNING ❧

'The expectation of the poor shall not perish for ever.'
PSALM 9:18

The promises of God raise the expectation of His people, and His providence tries it; what the promise has engaged to give, providence seems loath to bestow. But God is faithful. We may expect the Lord to appear for us in every trouble, if our faith is fixed on His Word, and prayer is daily sent up to His throne. We may expect to be supported under all our trials, and to be supplied with all necessary good, if we are making God our portion, and seeking to glorify Him. We may expect to be pardoned, justified, and saved, if we believe with the heart, confess with the mouth, and walk according to our profession. God notices our expectations, Jesus pleads that they may be realized; and nothing shall be able to turn away the bountiful hand of our God. He will regard the prayer of the destitute, and not despise their prayer. Our fears may be strong, and our doubts may be many; but our security is in the character, Word, and work of our God and Saviour. He will not fail us, nor forsake us, until He hath done all which He hath spoken to us of.

Soon the delightful day will come,
When my dear Lord will bring me home,
And I shall see His face;

Then, with my Saviour, Brother, Friend,
A blest eternity I'll spend,
Triumphant in His grace.

❦ EVENING ❧

'He will keep the feet of His saints.'
1 SAMUEL 2:9

The saints are the sanctified ones: those who were set apart by the Father for His praise; who were separated by the precious blood-shedding of our Lord Jesus Christ; who are regenerated, purified, and brought out of the world, by the agency and operation of the Holy Spirit. They are not of the world, even as Jesus was not of the world. But though thus privileged, they are entirely dependent. They need keeping, constant keeping. The keeping of a God; no one else is sufficient to preserve them. Their weakness is very great. Their road is rough, thorny, and dangerous. Their foes are many, and they are vigilant, experienced, and determined. Their fears are great, and their courage very small. Still they are safe, for the Lord is their keeper. He keeps them from pride, presumption, security, and final falling. He keeps them by His Word, by His Spirit, by trials, by disappointments, by bereavements, by His angels, and by His ordinances. They are safe whom God keeps, but only they. He keeps all His saints, without one exception. But He keeps none but saints; therefore many professors fall. Believers are kept through faith, by His power, unto salvation. 'Hold thou me up, and I shall be safe.'

Saviour! I trust Thy faithful grace,
To uphold my goings in Thy ways,
Till walking with my God I see
The glorious place prepared for me.

AUGUST 16

🌿 MORNING 🌿
'Remember the Lord.'
NEHEMIAH 4:14

He is the great author of your being, and the only proper object of your faith, fear, and worship. Remember the promises He has made, the deliverances He that wrought, the blessings He has conferred, the invitations He has given, and the relations He now fills. Remember Him in calamity, to trust Him; in prosperity, to praise Him; in danger, to call upon Him; in difficulty, to expect His interference. Remember to obey His commands; to attend to His exhortations; to keep His company; to seek His blessing; and to aim at His glory in all you do. Remember Him, for it is your duty; it is your privilege. Remember Him, in order to strengthen your faith; as an antidote to your fears; as a source of encouragement to your souls; and as a preventative to sin. Remember He is holy, just, and good, and He will be glorified in all them that draw nigh unto Him. Whatever or whoever you forget, always 'Remember the Lord.' He is your life, your strength, your food, your portion, your God, your all. Remember Him, for He never forgets you; cleave to Him, for He will never forsake you; live for Him, for He loves you.

O, may I still from sin depart!
A wise and understanding heart,
Jesus to me be given!

And let me through Thy Spirit know
To glorify my God below,
And find my way to heaven.

🌿 EVENING 🌿
'In thy righteousness shall they be exalted.'
PSALM 89:16

In whose righteousness? In the righteousness of God, for we have none of our own. He has provided a righteousness for us; He freely gives it to us; we receive it by faith. Our religion is peculiar, for we are wise in the wisdom of another, even our Head; we are rich in the wealth of another, even our elder Brother; and we are righteous in the righteousness of another, even the righteousness of our Saviour. This magnifies the law, fills the soul with joy, and endures for ever. In this righteousness we are exalted above the condemning power of the law, above the wicked designs of Satan, above the present evil world, and above the sting and power of death. It exalts us to peace and friendship with God, to the adoption of children, to boldness and access with confidence into the presence of God, to sit in the heavenlies with Christ, and to endless glory. It exalts our views of God's character and perfections, and of Jesus in His person, work, and love. Let us prize this righteousness, daily wear it, and plead it always for acceptance with God. It is our wedding dress, our impenetrable shield, and our title to the heavenly mansions. It secures, it comforts, it strengthens, it elevates us.

Let others in the gaudy dress
Of fancied merit shine;
The Lord shall be my righteousness,
The Lord for ever mine.

AUGUST 17

🌿 MORNING 🌿

'In quietness and in confidence shall be your strength.'

ISAIAH 30:15

Quietness is expressive of submission to the holy will of God, and supposes a waiting upon Him as directed by His Word. It is the believer's duty to be silent before God while He is working, being assured that his best interests are secured by the promises, and that all things will be made plain by and by. He should confide in the Lord's Word, and rely on the Lord's wisdom, love, and ability. Our confidence must arise from God's Word, a review of His dealings with His people, and the relation in which He stands to us. We may be confident, for God who has spoken is true, and hath confirmed His Word in every generation. Quietly confiding in God will give us strength; we then put His love and faithfulness to the trial; we honour Him by our confidence, and He will honour us by appearing for us. Let us endeavour to be *still*, to be *silent* before Him, when He is raised up out of His holy habitation. Let us wait for Him, for it is good that a man should both hope and quietly wait for the salvation of the Lord. Beware of complaining or replying against God.

> When, my Saviour, shall I be
> Totally resign'd to Thee?
> Poor and vile in my own eyes,
> Only in Thy wisdom wise,
> Only guided in Thy light,
> Only mighty in Thy might!

🌿 EVENING 🌿

'Continue in prayer.'

COLOSSIANS 4:2

Prayer is always necessary, and it is always profitable. But we often restrain prayer before God. This is sinful. It dishonours God, and it injures us. In prayer we do homage to the perfections of God. We exercise faith on His omnipresence. We express our dependence on Him for our supplies. We evince the sincerity of our profession. We acknowledge our poverty and weakness. We unburden the mind of our secret trials. We give vent to our feelings of joy and sorrow, of gratitude and grief. We confess our sins, acknowledge our backslidings, and obtain pardon and restoring grace. We give utterance to our desires, and spread our case before the Lord. Prayer is the medium of communication between God and our souls; we communicate our thoughts, feelings, fears, and desires; and He communicates light, strength, comfort, and grace to us. Prayer is a very important duty; it is a great privilege. Many things will conspire to lead us to neglect it. But in prayer we should be constant, fervent, believing, hopeful, incessant. God loves it, Satan hates it, and every true Christian values it. We should be always in a praying frame, though we cannot be always in a praying posture. It is always necessary, profitable and acceptable to God.

> We perish if we cease from prayer;
> Lord, grant us power to pray!
> And when to meet Thee we prepare,
> O! meet us by the way.

AUGUST 18

❦ MORNING ❦

'The LORD is nigh unto all them that call upon Him.'
PSALM 145:18

Real prayer is calling upon God. He is our Father; we are His children. We have nothing; He has all things to bestow; and is willing to give them. From a sense of need, we call on the Lord for a supply; from a sense of weakness, we call on Him for strength; from a sense of guilt, we call on Him for pardon; being diseased, we cry for health; being troubled, for comfort and peace; being in distress, for relief and deliverance. We go out of self to Jesus, accepting His invitation, to plead His promise, and find Him faithful. Our God is always near the praying soul, not merely as the omnipresent Jehovah, but as our faithful Friend. He is near us, lovingly to listen to what we have to lay before Him; mercifully to relieve our miseries, be they what they may; graciously to help us in every difficulty or danger. Beloved, our God is near us. He is attentive to us this morning; let us call upon Him in spirit and in truth; let us lay all our concerns before Him. He loves to listen to the often-told tale; He has patience with us, blessings for us, and will do us good. O, to walk closely with my gracious God today.

> O Lord, each day renew my strength,
> And let me see Thy face at length,
> With all Thy people yonder;
> With them in heaven Thy love declare,
> And sing Thy praise for ever there,
> With gratitude and wonder.

❦ EVENING ❦

'The upright love thee.'

SONG OF SOLOMON 1:4

None are upright by nature, for none seek to render to God the things which are God's, and to men the things which are men's. But this is uprightness. It flows from grace. It is the effect and proof of a new creation. The truly upright regard the eye of God, as fixed upon them; the Word of God, as binding upon them; the approbation of God, as the chief thing to be sought by them; and the judgment of God, as most important to them. The upright love Jesus. They all know Him, and highly esteem Him. They love Him uprightly, and as the proof of it, they rejoice in His presence; they are grieved at His absence; they desire the closest union with Him; they aim to please Him in all things; they will give up everything for Him; they love to speak of Him, and they always speak well of Him; they will do any thing for Him, perform any duty, avoid any sin; they will choose to suffer for Him rather than deny or dishonour Him. Reader, are you upright? Do you love Jesus? Sincerely? Supremely? Every upright soul loves Him. You are not upright if you do not. Terrible is the denunciation of the inspired apostle, 'If any man love not our Lord Jesus Christ, let him be accursed when the Lord cometh.'

> Jesus, my balm for every ill,
> My life in death Thou art;
> Thy lips as lilies pale, distil
> The myrrh that heals my heart.

AUGUST 19

❦ MORNING ❦

'My presence shall go with thee.'

EXODUS 33:14

So the Lord promised Moses, and so He has promised us. Let us never venture any where, if we have reason to think the Lord will not favour us with His presence there. The Lord's presence produces holiness, imparts power, fires with zeal, brings into union, and often fills with comfort, joy and peace. His presence is our glory, and it will yield us support under losses, crosses, and bereavements. Let us plead for the Lord's presence to go with us; let us expect it; let us not be satisfied with any thing else. He went with Moses, and he persevered; with Joshua, and he conquered; with David, and he reached the throne; with Paul, and he was more than a conqueror. Nothing can be a substitute for the Lord's presence; and as it is so graciously promised, let us not attempt to find a substitute, but daily cry, *'If thy presence go not with me, carry us not up hence.'* Jesus has said, 'If a man love me, he will keep my words; and my Father will love him, and we will come unto him, and make our abode with him.' Lord, dwell in me!

> O Lord, be ever near us,
> Fix in our hearts Thy home;
> By Thine appearing cheer us,
> And let Thy kingdom come:
> Fulfil our expectation,
> And give our souls to prove,
> Thine uttermost salvation,
> Thine everlasting love.

❦ EVENING ❦

'My soul refused to be comforted.'

PSALM 77:2

God has provided suitable and sufficient comfort for His people. He sends them comforters just as their circumstances require. But they at times refuse to hear the voice of the charmer. The Lord has perhaps taken away an idol; or He withholds His sensible presence, that they may learn to live by faith; or He has blighted their worldly prospects; or He has written vanity and emptiness upon all their gourds, cisterns, and delights. They give way to passion, as did Jonah; or they sink into sullen gloom; or allow unhumbled pride to rule the spirit; or yield to extreme sorrow, as Rachel did; or fall under the power of temptation; or imbibe the notion, that they have no right to comfort. This is wrong, all wrong, decidedly wrong. Look at what is left you: at what the gospel presents to you; at what heaven will be to you. But the psalmist was recovered from this state. He was convinced that he was wrong. He was sorry for his sin. He was reformed in his spirit and conduct. He wrote this psalm to instruct, caution, and warn us. Observe, they who are entitled to all comfort, often through their own folly, enjoy the least. The Lord's people are often their own tormentors: they put away the cup of comfort from them, and say they are unworthy of it.

> O Thou Source of every blessing,
> Chase my sorrows, cheer my heart,
> Till in heaven, Thy smiles possessing,
> Life, and joy, and peace impart.

AUGUST 20

MORNING

'The LORD preserveth all them that love Him.'
PSALM 145:20

All who know the Lord love Him, and none can love Him until taught by His Spirit. If we know God in Christ, as our covenant God, and enjoy our interest in Him, we shall love Him supremely, above our tranquillity, natural relations, earthly possessions, gifts, and reputation. We discover in Him greater glory, more real worth, pre-eminent beauty, and superior excellence. Those who love Him are preserved by Him. He preserves them in trouble, from its natural effects; in the world, from its spirit and doom; from enemies, evils, and wrath. His loving-kindness and truth will continually preserve them; yea, He will preserve them unto His kingdom and glory. But He preserves us in the use of means; let us therefore walk before Him, confide in Him, wait upon Him, and often demand of our hearts: Do we love the Lord? Are we desiring to love Him? Are we preserved from sin, the world, and all evil? If so, we must ascribe it to free and sovereign grace; if not, let us search and try our ways, and turn again to the Lord. He bids, He exhorts us to come.

Infinite grace! Almighty charms!
Stand in amaze, ye rolling skies!
Jesus, the God, extends His arms,
Hangs on the cross of love, and dies.
Sure I must love: my passions move:
This heart shall yield to death or love.

EVENING

'He is faithful that promised.'
HEBREWS 10:23

The promises of God were freely made; but being made, they must be fulfilled, for God is faithful. He has promised us as believers eternal life, the pardon of all sin, purity of heart, peace of conscience, growth in grace, perseverance in His ways, support under all our trials, supplies for all our wants, and that all things shall work together for our good. These promises we should believe, and expect the Lord to make them good. He is faithful to His promises: this is clear from the infinite perfection of His nature, the stability of His well-ordered covenant, His solemn oath, the testimony of all His saints, the gift of His beloved Son, the history of the church in all ages, and the design with which the promises were made. Let us therefore remember, that 'faithful is He that calleth you, who also will do it.' Believe that 'the Lord is faithful, who shall stablish you, and keep you from evil' or 'the evil one.' And let us commit the keeping of our souls to Him in well doing, as unto a faithful Creator. We cannot place too much confidence in His Word, nor too steadily expect its fulfilment. Heaven and earth may pass away, but His Word can undergo no change. It is changeless as His nature, and immutable as His throne. Nothing is so stable as God's Word.

True to His Word, God gave His Son
To die for crimes which men had done;
Blest pledge! He never will revoke
A single promise He has spoke.

AUGUST 21

❦ MORNING ❦

'Shall God avenge His own elect?'

LUKE 18:7

The Lord's people are often oppressed; they are tempted to be revengeful, but our God says, 'Vengeance is mine, I will repay.' Under man's wrath, remember you are the objects of the Lord's love; when men oppress you, rest assured that God will befriend you. Carry your case to Him, spread the whole of the matter before Him, plead with Him, and then rest assured that He will appear for you. The master will interfere for a servant he values; the parent for the child he loves; and the husband for the bride he has chosen: 'And shall not God avenge His own elect? ... I tell you that He will avenge them speedily.'Cry to Him day and night; look to no other quarter for relief or deliverance; never encourage any unholy feelings, but pray for grace to imitate your insulted, persecuted, and crucified Lord. Consider Him who endured such contradiction of sinners against Himself, lest ye be weary and faint in your minds. He will tread all your enemies under His feet shortly. He is able to avenge you, and His Word is passed. Only trust in Him, wait His time, and all shall be well.

> Shall we distrust our faithful God
> Or question His almighty power,
> Because He doth not our desires
>
> Accomplish in a little hour?
> He will avenge His own elect,
> And evermore His saints protect.

❦ EVENING ❦

'Perfect in Christ Jesus.'

COLOSSIANS 1:28

The believer painfully proves that he is imperfect in himself. Imperfection appears to be stamped upon all he *feels*: upon his desires, his joys and sorrows; and upon all he *does*: on his prayers, his praises, and all his performances. What says the sigh, which escapes from his full heart? Imperfect. What says the groan, which ascends from his troubled bosom? Imperfect. What says the tear, which glistens in his eye, or rolls down his cheek? Imperfect. But there is perfection in Christ. In Him there is a perfect atonement, to reconcile us; a perfect righteousness, to justify us; perfect holiness, to sanctify us; perfect wisdom, to direct and instruct us. We become perfect by union to Him, for as His bride we have fellowship with Him in all that He has; by receiving from Him, for of His fulness we receive, and grace for grace; by being with Him, for we are changed into the same image from glory to glory, even as by the Spirit of the Lord. Our full perfection is decreed, promised, provided for, and will be realized. Christ now represents us as perfect; He will make us perfect; and then present us in full perfection. Delightful thought! We shall be perfectly holy and perfectly happy.

> With Him His members on the tree,
> Fulfilled the law's demands.
> 'Tis 'I in them, and they in Me,'
> For thus the union stands.

AUGUST 22

❧ MORNING ❧
'They that seek the LORD shall not want any good thing.'
Psalm 34:10

What a comfortable promise is this to the poor, weak, and timid Christian; he has not attained to a state of assurance, but he is seeking the Lord, and here his God promises him that he shall not want any good thing. He feels that he has no good thing in him, finds he can do no good thing of himself, fears that good will never be enjoyed by him; but his God assures him, no good thing shall be withheld from him. His God will pardon his sin, justify his person, strengthen his soul, supply his needs, comfort his heart, conquer his foes, sanctify his trials, and give him victory over death. He shall not want long, if God is able to supply; he cannot be neglected, if our God is true; he shall receive all that is good, as it will do him most good. Let us therefore seek the Lord, and rest assured that He will withhold from us no good thing. The silver and the gold are His, and He says, 'If ye being evil know how to give good things unto your children, *how much more* shall your heavenly Father give good things to them that ask Him.'

> If earthly parents hear
> Their children when they cry,
> If they with love sincere
>
> Their children's wants supply,
> Much more will God His love display,
> And answer when His children pray.

❧ EVENING ❧
'Thou hast a little strength.'
Revelation 3:8

Sinners are strengthless. Saints are very weak, but they have a little strength. Strength is provided for us in Jesus; He is the strength of the poor. Strength is promised us in the Word. God says, 'I will strengthen thee.' Strength is presented to us by the gospel, which says, 'Be strong in the Lord, and in the power of His might.' Strength is to be received by faith, in answer to prayer, in the diligent employment of what we have, by virtue of our union to Jesus. We have a little strength; let us pray for more. Let us hold fast and hold on. We should be grateful for the provision made, the promise given, and the welcome we receive at the throne of grace. We should use what we have against Satan, sin, and the world; and for God, and the promotion of His cause. We ought to seek for more. God will not refuse us. He cannot deny His Word. We need more, and we may soon need more than we do at present. What a mercy that we have a little, for we were once without strength. We have a little now, we are promised enough, and we shall be strong by and by. It is sweetly testified of our God, that He giveth power to the faint; and to them that have no might, He increaseth strength. Believer, wait on Him, and He will strengthen thee with strength in thy soul.

> *Stand in the Saviour's might*
> *With all His strength endued;*
> *And take to arm you for the fight,*
> *The panoply of God.*

AUGUST 23

🌿 MORNING 🌿

'God, even our own God, shall bless us.'
PSALM 67:6

He has pledged Himself to do so in His Word, and He delights to make good His promise. He is our God by covenant, by a spiritual birth, through Christ Jesus, and at our own desire, request, and consent. He is the great God, who fills heaven and earth; the all-sufficient God, who has all resources in Himself; the unchanging God, who is eternally the same. He espouseth the quarrel of His people, He dignifies and ennobles them, and proves Himself gracious and merciful unto them. He blesseth them indeed; and if others curse, He turneth the curse into a blessing. We may rest fully assured of this pleasing fact: *'God, even our own God, will bless us.'* He has done so in Christ before time; He has promised to do so through time; and when time shall be no more. He will bless us in temporals and spirituals; He will bless us wherever we are. Let us believe the fact, and plead for its realization in our experience; this will embolden us in danger, fortify us against fear, and keep us in perfect peace. Let us trust in Him, and He will bless us; and so shall we rejoice in Him.

> Rise, my soul, with ardour rise!
> Breathe thy wishes to the skies;
> Freely pour out all thy mind,
> Seek, and thou art sure to find;
> Ready art thou to receive,
> Readier is thy God to give.

🌿 EVENING 🌿

'Acquainted with grief.'
ISAIAH 53:3

Strange acquaintance for the Son of God! – the brightness of glory, and the express image of the Father's person! But He came into our world on purpose, that He might know by experience all that His people had suffered; yea, all that His people deserved. He had heard of sorrow. He had seen it in others. But He had never felt it Himself. He took our nature. He came into our place. He began to suffer as soon as He was born, and He pursued a course of suffering until He died. In the sweat of His brow He ate His bread. The reproaches of them that reproached His Father fell on Him. He became intimate with grief. He knew it in all its varieties, in all its depth. No one ever suffered so much, or from so many causes, or so constantly as He. He visited joy occasionally, but He dwelt with grief. It was His companion. Christian, thy Lord suffered for thee; He suffered like thee; He suffered far, far more than thee; and now He can sympathise with thee. He knows by experience what human nature feels. He knows the effect of grief upon the nerves, and the spirits, and the temper. He suffered from all quarters: from heaven, earth, and hell, and therefore He is able; He is moved to succour thee in all thy sorrows, griefs, and woes.

> As man, He pities my complaints;
> His power and truth are all divine;
> He will not fail, He cannot faint;
> Lord, make Thy full salvation mine!

AUGUST 24

❦ MORNING ❦
'A living sacrifice.'
ROMANS 12:1

When a beast was set apart for sacrifice, it was considered sacred, and was carefully preserved from all injury. The Christian is devoted; he is intended for the altar, his body as well as his soul, and he is required to present it to God holy, acceptable, as a reasonable service. It is not to be defiled by fornication, by intoxication, by gluttony, by filth, or by pride; he is to look upon it as the Lord's: bought with the blood of Jesus; consecrated as the temple of the Holy Ghost; set apart to be the habitation of a Holy God. The believer's body should not be united by marriage to an unbeliever; this is *sacrilege*, for the vessel is holy; it is *rebellion*, for it is plainly and positively forbidden; it is *sinning wilfully*, and provoking the eyes of divine holiness; it is offering insult to the God of love, and calling upon Him to vindicate His injured mercy. Believer, present thy body daily to God, washed in pure water – that is, cleansed from defilement by observing His Word; never call that common which God has consecrated, or debase that which He has devoted to Himself. Let God have His own, and all that is His own, especially thyself.

> Lord, it is but just and right,
> That I should be wholly Thine;
> Only in Thy will delight,
> In Thy blessed service join.
> Now my sacrifice receive,
> Give me grace to Thee to live.

❦ EVENING ❦
'The whole family.'
EPHESIANS 3:15

The church of Christ is a family. Part of it is in heaven, part on earth, and part is not yet brought into existence. God is the Father of the whole. Every child is alike the object of His love, care, and compassion. Each one lives in His sight, and is dear to His heart. He will not part with one. Jesus, who is *Surety* for the whole, will never have to say with the troubled patriarch: 'One is not.' Those in heaven differ from us in place, in purity, in happiness, and employment; but they are not more loved than we are. The whole family is alike beloved, redeemed, adopted, and destined to perfect holiness and happiness. Every name is recorded in the book of life, and engraved on the Saviour's hands. Heaven is the family mansion, our Father's house. The kingdom is our Father's gift. For us He prepared it, before the foundation of the world; and with pleasure He bestows it upon us. We are all one in Christ. Let us therefore love the brotherhood. Let us endeavour to keep the unity of the Spirit in the bond of peace. Let us treat every Christian kindly, seeing the Saviour says of what is done to them: *'Ye did it unto me.'* You cannot hurt a saint, but you injure the Saviour. The Head suffers in the members, the Father in His family.

> Lord, may my spirit form a part
> Of that Thrice happy whole,
> Derive its pulse from Thee the HEART,
> Its life from Thee the SOUL!

AUGUST 25

❦ MORNING ❧

'The Spirit helpeth our infirmities.'
ROMANS 8:26

We are compassed with infirmities; we know but little of ourselves; we know not what would be best for us; we know not what is coming upon us; we know not Satan's position or design; we know but little of God's provision or intention. We are as weak as we are ignorant; weak to withstand evil; weak to perform good; weak to obtain benefits. Our infirmities: many of them are constitutional, arising from our tempers and dispositions; from bodily ailments; and from the smallness of our capacities. But though thus infirm, Jesus is touched with a sympathetic feeling for us, and the Holy Spirit is given to assist us. He teaches us what we want; leads us to the precious promises; furnishes us with the prevailing plea; excites us to pray, and assists us in prayer. He produces the ardent desire, bestows the wrestling power, and warms the affections while pleading; He gives us such a keen sense of what we need, and such an ardent desire after it, that unutterable groans are begotten, to which God attends. Let us daily seek the Spirit's power to help.

> Spirit of interceding grace,
> I know not how or what to pray.
> Relieve my utter helplessness,
> Thy power into my heart convey.
> That God, acknowledging my groan,
> May answer, in my prayers, His own.

❦ EVENING ❧

'On mine arm shall they trust.'
ISAIAH 51:5

And well they may, for it is nerved with omnipotence, it is directed by infinite wisdom, and it is employed by tenderest love. It is stretched out for us to lean upon, for support; to work for us, and to secure a supply; to fight for us, and defend us from our foes; and to carry us when we are unable to go, that we may make progress in weakness, and when sick. It is a Father's arm, yet the arm of God. It is a Saviour's arm, and yet the arm that sustains heaven and earth. It is our Brother's arm, and yet the arm that bars the gates of hell, and holds every fallen spirit in check. On *this* arm we must trust, not on our own. We must be weaned from trusting on all other. We must be brought to trust wholly and always on the Lord's. This is warranted by the Word. It is approved and commanded by our God. It is rewarded in our present experience. They shall trust in darkness and difficulty, for all my promises contain, because they feel the necessity of it, and when all besides fails and deceives them. God hath said, and He will surely bring to pass. He will have us trust in the arm of His power, follow the leadings of His providence, aim at the advancement of His cause, and live dependent on His bounty, or we shall not know happiness.

> Arm of the Lord, whose wond'rous power,
> The world and all things made,
> Thou art our strength, defence, and tower,
> Our ever present aid.

AUGUST 26

🌿 MORNING 🌿
'The unsearchable riches of Christ.'
EPHESIANS 3:8

Never forget that Jesus is our *Brother*, and that He has devoted all His riches to us, so that the riches of Jesus are the Christian's fortune. 'Ye know the grace of our Lord Jesus Christ, that, though He was rich, yet for our sakes He became poor, that we through His poverty might be rich.' He employed all He possessed for our redemption, sanctification, and salvation; and now, at the right hand of the Majesty on high, He giveth liberally, and upbraideth not. He has riches of grace, riches of mercy, and riches of glory. The residue of the Spirit is with Him. He has promised largely; He has proved His readiness to bestow, in the most wonderful way; let us therefore expect great things from Him, for He has *unsearchable riches*. O believer, look not at thy poverty, at thy wants, or thy circumstances; but look at Jesus; all things are under His feet, all blessings are at His disposal, and His heart is set upon thee to do thee good! He will supply all thy needs while on earth, and afterwards receive thee to glory. My soul, thy Jesus has all thou needest: therefore look to Him, and Him alone!

Possessing Christ, I all possess,
Strength, wisdom, sanctifying grace,
And righteousness complete:

Bold, in His name, I dare draw nigh,
Before the Ruler of the sky,
And all His justice meet.

🌿 EVENING 🌿
'We count them happy which endure.'
JAMES 5:11

Our afflictions are trials. Every professor shall be tried. Many faint in the day of adversity. Some go back and walk no more with the Saviour. The effect of the stroke is according to the nature of that on which it falls: the softened yields; the hardened flies. Some under this discipline fall at His feet, but others fly in His face. Happy is the man who meets his trials like a Christian, with humility, faith, fortitude, and patience; who endures them without repining, complaining, and rebelling against God. He looks not so much at the rod, as at the hand that uses it; nor only at the hand, but at the heart that guides the hand. He says, 'It is discipline. It is chastisement. It is my Father who strikes, and He never corrects for His own pleasure but my profit, to make me a partaker of His holiness. I have prayed for deeper sanctification; He is answering my prayer. I have desired brighter evidences for heaven, and He is granting them. Shall I then complain? The cup which my heavenly Father giveth me, shall I not drink it?' Such a man *endures* affliction; he meets it; he bears it; he proves it as a Christian. He is blessed. His trials must do him good. Nor will they continue long.

Wisdom and mercy guide my way!
Shall I resist them both?
A poor blind creature of a day,
And crush'd before the moth.

AUGUST 27

❦ MORNING ❦

'We should bring forth fruit unto God.'
Romans 7:4

Without union to Christ, there can be no good works; and until we are dead to the law we cannot be married to Christ. We must see that there is neither help nor hope for us in any law that God has given; that only grace can save us, before we shall be willing to take Christ as God hath set Him forth in the everlasting gospel. Being married to Christ, we renounce our own name and take His; we live upon His fulness, walk by His Word, and aim to please Him in all things. By His grace we perform good works; and through His merit, and His name, they are accepted as evidences of our love, proofs of our sanctification, and fruits of our oneness with Him. He that is joined to the Lord is one spirit with Him; and it becomes his meat and drink to do the will of God. Without union to Christ we can do nothing acceptable to God; being married to Him, our poor, imperfect, and (in themselves) worthless performances, are acceptable and well-pleasing to God. *No union no fruit, no fruit no union.* Beloved, are we bringing forth fruits unto God? Do we bring forth much fruit? Herein is our Father glorified, that we bear much fruit, and such are Christ's disciples.

> *Blest Jesus, animate my heart;*
> *Let Thy rich grace abound;*
> *So, to the honour of Thy name,*
> *Shall plenteous fruit be found.*

❦ EVENING ❦

'He preserveth the way of His saints.'
Proverbs 2:8

The believer's journey lies through an enemy's land. His course is lined with tribulation. His pilgrimage is exhausting and wearying. It is rendered more trying by his own weakness, and the inward conflict. But it is the only way to the city of habitation. It leads to the rest and inheritance promised; and the Lord always accompanies His saints, His holy ones. He suits His mercies to their condition, and adapts His communications to their wants. He preserves them from being overcome, so that at the worst, it may be said to them, 'There hath no temptation taken you, but such as is common to man: but God is faithful, who will not suffer you to be tempted above that ye are able; but will with the temptation also make a way of escape, that ye may be able to bear it.' He preserves them from being driven back when *buffeted* by Satan, making His strength perfect in their weakness, and proving that His grace sufficient for them. He preserves them with a watchful eye, a powerful arm, and a loving heart. Beloved, look back and see how He has preserved you. Look forward and trust Him to preserve you in all time to come; it is His practice to preserve His saints in their course.

> *The saints at all time are secure*
> *In Jesus' everlasting love;*
> *Through Him they shall all storms endure,*
> *And with Him reign enthron'd above.*

AUGUST 28

🌿 MORNING 🌿

'Being justified freely by His grace.'

ROMANS 3:24

It was a solemn question which was proposed in the days of old: 'How can man be just with God?' Man is without righteousness; he is chargeable with many crimes; he is brought in guilty, and condemned by God's holy law; and he has no excuse to make. His mouth is stopped. We feel this to be our situation by nature. But the Lord who is our Judge hath devised a way by which He can be just, and yet justify us. *It is by grace.* He justifies, or acquits us from all charges; pronounces us righteous; accepts us; and introduces us into His favour, friendship, and fellowship, *freely*; without anything being done or suffered by us. He *presents us* with the work of Jesus, by which all our debts are paid; our righteousness is wrought out; the law and government of God are honoured; and a good title to eternal life is made out. We *receive* this work by faith, which He also bestows, and we are '*justified from all things.*' Not one charge remains. There is no condemnation. But we are justified freely by grace without the works of the law, and being justified we have peace with God.

> Slain in the guilty sinner's stead,
> Jesus, Thy righteousness I plead,
> And Thine atoning blood:
>
> That righteousness my robe shall be,
> Thy merit shall avail for me,
> And bring me near to God.

🌿 EVENING 🌿

'A great high priest.'

HEBREWS 4:14

The Lord Jesus is in office for us. He is our Priest. He was appointed, anointed, and sent to do the priest's office on our behalf. He had to make an atonement for our sins, and He has made it: an atonement which is radiant with all the glories of Deity; infinite in its value, and eternal in its efficacy. It has expiated our guilt, and made a perfect satisfaction for our offences. Now He is employed in interceding for us. For this He lives. In this work He is always engaged. He also presents our prayers, our various services, and our poor gifts to the Father, having perfumed them with the incense of His own merits. He averts every evil from us, procures every good for us, and pours down innumerable favours upon us. He is now in the holiest, officiating before the throne; He has sprinkled the blood, He offers the incense, and He will soon come out to bless us. He is not only a Priest, but 'the High Priest'; not only the High Priest, but 'a great High Priest'; superior to all other, in the dignity of His person, in the completeness of His qualifications, and in the efficacy of His services. He is *our* great High Priest, and also the Son of God. He is gone to appear in the presence of God for us. He is there presenting the blood for us tonight.

> He ever lives to intercede
> Before His Father's face;
> Give Him, my soul, thy cause to plead,
> Nor doubt the Father's grace.

AUGUST 29

❦ MORNING ❦

'They all slumbered and slept.'
MATTHEW 25:5

When we think of the warning Jesus has given, the promises He has made, and the precepts He has delivered, we are ready to conclude that His people must be always active and always happy. But when we look around us, or when we look at our own course, we are obliged to lament that this is not the case. Jesus is gone to receive a kingdom and to return; He has given talents to His servants, and *to every man his work*, and commanded the porter to watch. But it is said of the wise, as well as the foolish virgins, *'They all slumbered and slept.'* Are we awake to our duties, to our privileges, to our expectations? Are we looking, longing, and preparing for the coming of Jesus? Are we sober and vigilant, because our adversary the devil, as a roaring lion, is going about seeking whom he may devour? Are we active for God? Are we hasting home? Do we pass the time of our sojourning here in fear? Is the talent in the *napkin*, or at the *bank*? Let us not sleep as do others, but let us watch and be sober. Behold the Judge standeth before the door. It is high time to awake out of sleep, for our redemption draweth nigh.

> He comes, He comes to call
> The nations to His bar;
> And take to glory all

> Who meet for glory are:
> Make ready for your full reward;
> Go forth with joy to meet your Lord.

❦ EVENING ❦

'The LORD hath comforted His people.'
ISAIAH 49:13

The Lord hath a people in the world which are peculiarly His own. This truth is constantly kept before us in His holy Word. He has always loved them. He chose them to salvation. He redeemed them by the precious blood of Christ. They are united to, and viewed as one with His beloved Son. They are dear to Him as the apple of His eye. Still they are deeply tried. They often sigh and groan. They are still sinners, and sin festers within them, when it does not break out into an open wound. It pains them when it does not openly disgrace them. They have more cause for gratitude than Gabriel has, yet they have much to distress and cast them down. But their God comforts them. He hath comforted His people by giving them His holy Word, by erecting for them the throne of grace, by freely and for ever pardoning all their sins, by bestowing His peace on them, by assuring them that He is their Father, by giving them Jesus as their portion, and with Him all things, and by unfolding before them the bright prospect of endless blessedness. What condescension is this, that the eternal God should stoop to comfort a worm! What grace, that He should comfort one who was but recently a rebel!

> This joy to strangers is unknown,
> Nor can it be expressed;
> It is revealed to those alone,
> Who on the Saviour rest.

AUGUST 30

❦ MORNING ❦
'He will not always chide.'
PSALM 103:9

If we sin, our heavenly Father will correct us, in order to reclaim us; His strokes often fall heavy, and the effects remain for a long time. But He will not always chide; when we repent and confess, He pardons and restores. His anger is but for a moment; but His mercy is everlasting. He loves when He frowns, and pities while He reproves. 'The Lord is merciful and gracious, slow to anger, and plenteous in mercy ... He hath not dealt with us after our sins, nor rewarded us according to our iniquities. For as the heaven is high above the earth, so *great* is His mercy toward them that fear Him.' Let us not therefore *despise* the chastening of the Lord, nor *faint* when we are rebuked of Him; for whom the Lord loveth He chasteneth, and scourgeth every son whom He receiveth. In a little wrath He may hide His face from us for a moment; but with everlasting kindness will He have mercy on us, and prove Himself our Redeemer. His frowns are transient, but His love is everlasting. His strokes are few and light, but He daily loadeth us with benefits, and crowns the year with His bounty. He will always love, but He will not always chide.

> God will not always chide,
> And when His strokes are felt,
> His strokes are fewer than our crimes,
> And lighter than our guilt:
> He chides us with a Father's heart,
> That we from Him may not depart.

❦ EVENING ❦
'Remember me, O LORD.'
PSALM 106:4

This is an important prayer. There is very much wrapped up in it. It is poverty appealing to wealth, misery to mercy, the necessitous to a friend. If the Lord remember us, He will preserve us from evils, deliver us from dangers, direct us in difficulty, supply us in want, comfort us in sorrow, and lay everything under tribute for our welfare. If the Lord remember us, then it is not of much consequence who forgets us. He is more than all creatures, and enough in the absence of all. But He does remember us: He remembers that we are dust, that we are weak, exposed, dependent, and often deeply tried. He remembers for us His covenant, His promises, the sufferings of His dear Son, and the relation in which we stand to Him. Still we may plead to be remembered, that we may share in the gifts of His providence, in the bestowment of His grace, and in the proofs of His love. We should pray that He will remember, to pardon our sins, to visit our souls, to revive our graces, to crown our labours, and to fill us with all joy and peace in believing, that we may abound in hope by the power of the Holy Ghost. Remember me, O Lord, and preserve me from all danger this night, and raise me on the morrow full of faith, fired with zeal, glowing with love, and clothed with humility.

> Thou wond'rous Advocate with God,
> I yield my soul to Thee;
> While Thou art pleading at His throne
> Dear Lord, remember me.

AUGUST 31

🌿 MORNING 🌿

'The LORD is good unto them that wait for Him.'

LAMENTATIONS 3:25

The Lord is good to all, and His tender mercies are over all His works; but He is especially benevolent, kind, and attentive to the praying, waiting soul. He has prepared of His goodness for the poor, and His goodness is ever great towards us. He bids us ask, promises to bestow, makes us wait, and then blesses us indeed. We have proved Him to be good; but if we had more faith in Him, and were more earnest with Him, we should see and enjoy His goodness in a much greater degree. He delivered David from the horrible pit; Jeremiah from the dungeon; Daniel from the lions; Peter from the waves; and Paul from the forty Jews. 'The LORD is good, a stronghold in the day of trouble; and He knoweth them that trust in Him.' He will renew our strength, illumine our path, take vengeance on our foes, and introduce us into the glorious liberty of the sons of God. Let us wait for Him in faith, look for Him in hope, and plead with Him to work in us all the good pleasure of His will, and the work of faith with power. Wait for the Lord, and prove Him good. Wait on the Lord, and glorify His name.

Jesus, preserve my soul from sin,
Nor let me faint for want of Thee;
I'll wait till Thou appear within,

And plant Thy heavenly love in me;
In every soul that waits for Thee,
Thou wilt Thy goodness, Lord, display.

🌿 EVENING 🌿

'I would seek unto God.'

JOB 5:8

This is sound advice. It is the counsel of a real friend. It is much better than seeking unto men, or poring over troubles, or indulging the fancy, or giving way to fears. Troubles generally look worst in the distance; they are seldom found to be so bad as they appeared to be. My friend, I know not what may be your case, but if I was in perplexity, I would seek unto God for wisdom; if I was in sorrow, I would seek unto God for comfort; if I was in weakness, I would seek unto God for strength; if I was under guilt, I would seek unto God for pardon; if I was in a severe conflict, I would seek unto God for victory; if I was in doubt and fear, I would seek unto God for confidence and a sense of His favour; if I was under the power of unbelief, I would seek unto God for faith; if I was harassed by Satan, I would seek unto God to lift up a standard against him; if I was afraid of falling, I would seek unto God to uphold me with the right hand of His righteousness; if I was alarmed at death, I would seek unto God to turn the shadow of death into the morning. Whatever you want, seek it of God; whatever you fear, carry it to God; whatever troubles you, lay it before God. You cannot seek Him in vain, or without profit.

Seek unto God, He loves to give,
Ask but in faith, it shall be given;
Go pray, expecting to receive
His grace, His image, and His heaven.

SEPTEMBER 1

MORNING

'The Deliverer.'
ROMANS 11:26

The Lord Jesus Christ is anointed and appointed to deliver His people whenever they need His aid; for this purpose all the treasures of wisdom and knowledge are stored in Him, authority over all flesh is given to Him, and every attribute of Deity can be exerted by Him. We are not left to the mercy of men; we are not expected to deliver ourselves, but we are to look to Jesus, who is glorified in delivering us from all evil, and preserving us to His eternal kingdom and glory. To Him we are to repair in every trial, from Him we are to expect deliverance in every danger; He is in office on purpose to hear us, appear for us, and bless us. He delivers in temporals as well as spirituals, from internal and external foes. Let us remember this title of our beloved Lord, and make use of Him as the *Deliverer*, in preference to every other; apply to Him first in every difficulty, rely on Him with confidence in every trial, and He will deliver you until deliverance is no longer required. 'He will deliver thee in six troubles, and in seven shall no evil touch thee.' No man can look to Jesus, or trust God in vain.

> *Why should His people now be sad,* *Jesus the mighty Saviour lives,*
> *None have such reason to be glad,* *To them eternal life He gives,*
> *As those redeemed to God;* *The purchase of His blood.*

EVENING

'Songs in the night.'
JOB 35:10

The presence of God, and the light of His countenance, make the Christian's day. His absence makes our night. But this figure is often employed to represent afflictions. Losses, crosses, sickness, poverty, old age, death: these constitute a very gloomy night. They are dark, cold, and tedious. But in the gloomiest night, the Lord can make us happy, His presence will make us sing. 'He giveth songs in the night.' He tunes the heart by the light of joy and grace. He furnishes matter for praise. He enables us to sing to the wonder and surprise of many. So did Paul and Silas at Philippi; the prophet Habakkuk, in prospect of famine; and so did many martyrs in their dungeons. Many have sung for joy in poverty, in sickness, and in death. Christian, thy God can make thee joyful in the gloomiest circumstances, and give a song in the dreariest night. Walk closely with Him. His presence will disperse gloom, and give joy, peace, and thankfulness; His love will make thee rejoice in His salvation. He loves to see His people happy, He is pleased to hear them sing; and those who walk with Him, will joy and rejoice in Him, both here and hereafter.

> *Thou giver of songs in the night,*
> *Of joy in the darkest distress,*
> *I sigh to be fill'd with Thy light,*
> *I long for a glimpse of Thy face.*

SEPTEMBER 2

🌿 MORNING 🌿

'Be not high-minded, but fear.'

ROMANS 11:20

Believers are sometimes tempted to think more highly of themselves than they ought to think; they forget that they are indebted to the free, sovereign, and distinguishing grace of God for all the difference there is between them and the vilest of the vile. They should consider they are still weak, and liable to be overcome; foolish, and prone to wander; sinful, and easily wrought upon; that Satan is strong and determined; subtle and insinuating; malicious and designing; active and persevering; that the world is alluring and ensnaring, treacherous and vain, attracting and deceitful; and this would preserve them from being too secure. A high-minded Christian is sure to be unfruitful, and is generally left to fall. Therefore let him that thinketh he standeth take heed. David fell, Peter fell, and thousands beside have fallen; and they exhort us with groans, sighs, and tears, *'Be not high-minded, but fear.'* 'Work out your own salvation with fear and trembling.' Let us cultivate humility of mind, and habitual dependence upon God; so shall we be safe, holy, and happy. God's fear is our preservative.

> *Jesus, if Thou withdraw Thy hand,*
> *That moment sees me fall;*
> *O, may I ne'er on self depend,*
> *But look to Thee for all;*
> *Lead me in all Thy righteous ways,*
> *Make plain Thy path before my face.*

🌿 EVENING 🌿

'Doest thou well to be angry?'

JONAH 4:4

Jonah quarrelled with his God. And who has not? We may not speak as plainly as he did, but we have been in the same temper, and manifested it. Very few are quite satisfied with the Lord's plans. Fewer still are always pleased with the Lord's works. How many quarrel with His sovereignty! What hard things have been spoken against it! How many complain of His providence, and think it partial, unkind, and almost unjust! Beloved, we are often angry with God. This temper, shows itself in fretfulness, complaining, and sullen gloom. Some are so angry that they will scarcely speak to Him, and they restrain prayer. Others will not acknowledge their obligations, therefore, they do not praise Him. But do we well to be angry? Angry with our Father, whose wisdom is infinite, whose love is as constant as the day, and who constantly showers His blessings upon us! Angry with God, who has pardoned our sins, justified our persons, provided for our wants, united us to His Son, and blessed us with all spiritual blessings! Surely it is a sin, a grievous sin, not to be pleased with all He does, with all He has provided, and with all He requires. Doest thou well to complain, to repine, or be angry?

> *Lord, I confess my sin to Thee;*
> *Pardon and peace impart;*
> *From evil passions set me free,*
> *And sanctify my heart.*

SEPTEMBER 3

🌿 MORNING 🌿

'My God shall supply all your need.'
PHILIPPIANS 4:19

So Paul assured believers at Philippi, and so he assures us. They had many wants, so have we; they were dependent on God, and so are we. The Lord engaged to supply them, and He is engaged to supply us. The Lord was faithful to them, and He will be faithful to us. His absolute promises are our invaluable treasure; His unchangeableness is our immutable security. While Jehovah lives we cannot be friendless, we shall never be left to want; and at last we shall be able to testify, 'Not one thing hath failed of all that the Lord our God hath promised.' We can this morning rejoice, and say, 'The Lord hath blessed me hitherto. Thou has dealt well with thy servant, O LORD, according to thy word.' Our wants should remind us of God's promises; the promises should be used to quell our fears, and comfort our hearts. We know not what a day will bring forth; but we know that 'our God will supply all our needs according to His riches in glory by Christ Jesus.' Let this banish care, and let us rejoice in the Lord as our *Provider*. He who supplies us will never fail us.

In Jesus is our store,
Grace issues from His throne;
Whoever says, 'I want no more',
Confesses he has none;
But they who come to be supplied
Will find Jehovah doth provide.

🌿 EVENING 🌿

'In all their affliction He was afflicted.'
ISAIAH 63:9

The union between the Lord and His people is real: it is close and it is vital. Whatever affects them, affects Him. He has a fellow-feeling with them. If they are punished, He is persecuted. They never suffer alone. He is always present, and as the parent suffers with the child, by sympathy; so the Lord is said to suffer with His people. Their afflictions are many, they are often deep, they are frequently very painful; but in *all* their afflictions He is afflicted, and the angel of His presence saves them. Believer, art thou suffering, in thy mind, in thy body? Jesus at the right hand of the Father knows it. He sympathises with thee. Sweet thought! Jesus, at this moment is sympathising with me! He knows my weakness, my fears, my many trials; He presents them all to the Father, and pleads for me that I may obtain mercy, and find grace to help me in time of need. Precious Lord Jesus! May I ever cherish the thought, that Thou takest part with me in all my trials and afflictions, and wilt honourably bring me through them all.

We have not an High Priest above
Unmov'd at what we suffer here;
In tenderest sympathy of love
He shares our pain, our grief, and fear;
Wounded with every wounded soul,
He bleeds the balm that makes us whole.

SEPTEMBER 4

🌿 MORNING 🌿

'The gospel of your salvation.'

EPHESIANS 1:13

Our salvation is our deliverance from sin, the curse, and the wrath of God; this was impossible to man, but God sent His own Son in our nature, to save us freely, fully and eternally. The gospel is the 'good news of our salvation.' It is sent to inform us that God is love; that grace reigns; that heaven is opened; that provision is made for our guilt, weakness, and fears; that God waits to receive us, bless us, and glorify us with Himself for ever. It sets before us all Christ has done, all He possesses, and invites us to come and receive, to use, and be happy. It requires nothing of us to entitle us, it presents all it has, and gives it freely to the poor, the halt, the maimed, and the blind. It has all our misery requires, all our wants demand; we cannot wish for more than it brings; it is full of grace, and full of glory. Precious gospel! Glorious news! May we receive it, act upon it daily, and so be happy. It is intended to fill us with joy and peace in believing, to lead us to abound in hope, and to make us more than conquerors over despondency, doubt, and fear. Strong faith in God's gospel will bring strong comfort to our souls.

> For you the purple current flowed,
> In pardons from His wounded side;
> Languished for you the eternal God;
> For you the Prince of glory died;
> Believe, and all your sins forgiven,
> Only believe, and yours is heaven.

🌿 EVENING 🌿

'Let me hear thy voice.'

SONG OF SOLOMON 2:14

This is the language of Jesus to His Church, to us. He loves to see us come to His throne; to hear us pour out our hearts before Him. The prayer of the upright is His delight. It may be as mournful as the cooing of the dove, and there may be as much sameness in it too, but He loves to hear it. We are wearied with telling the oft-repeated tale, we fancy that He will be so too, but no, He says, 'Let me hear thy voice.' Shall we refuse Him? Rather, let us go to Him more frequently. Let us confess our sins, mourn over our follies, lament our proneness to backslide, plead His precious promises, seek the enjoyment of His presence, beseech Him to pardon our sins, and crave every blessing which He has to bestow. We cannot go to Him too often. We cannot ask for too much at His hands. He asks us to pray. He exhorts us to come often to His throne. He sends troubles, trials, and afflictions to bring us near to Him. In every comfort, He says, 'Let me hear thy voice.' In every trial, He says, 'Call upon me, I will deliver thee.' Beloved, go this night to Jesus, tell Him thou art come in obedience to His call, and let Him hear thy voice, acknowledging His goodness, pleading His promises, and seeking His grace.

> 'Tis sweet to steal awhile away
> From ev'ry cumbering care;
> And spend the closing hours of day
> In humble, grateful prayer.

SEPTEMBER 5

🌿 MORNING 🌿

'I will in no wise cast out.'

John 6:37

The strongest believer is subject to fears, and may at times be strongly tempted to doubt, not only all that God has done for him, but his right and title to every promise in God's Book; at such times it is well to have recourse to those wells, from which we have drawn the choicest consolation in former times; and the words of Jesus which we have chosen for this day's portion stand foremost. Here He tells us, with peculiar tenderness and love, that He has made up His mind, that He will on no account refuse to receive the coming sinner, or allow him to be driven from His throne; neither the nature nor number of his transgressions, his age or circumstances, shall be found sufficient to procure him a rejection. His arms and His heart are open, He stands and calls us to Him, giving us this assurance, 'I will in no wise cast out.' Nearly two thousand years have rolled away since He spake the words; millions of sinners of every clime and character have made application, and all have found Him faithful. Let us not then grieve His love, and distress our own souls, by doubts and fears, but trust His Word. He will receive, pardon, and bless us.

When, gracious Lord, when shall it be,
That I shall find my all in Thee?
The fulness of Thy promise prove,
The seal of Thine eternal love?
Ah! wherefore did I ever doubt!
Thou wilt in no wise cast me out.

🌿 EVENING 🌿

'Yet I will rejoice in the Lord.'

Habakkuk 3:18

This was a wise determination. Everything around us, and everything within us may change, but the Lord changes not. He is the same. Light may give place to darkness, peace to war, health to sickness, plenty to poverty, ease to suffering, and society to loneliness. Still we may be happy. We may rise above circumstances. We may rejoice that though much is lost, we have more than we can ever lose. But if we would emulate the prophet, we must make sure of our interest in the Lord, of our title to all the promises of His Word; we must know that our sins are pardoned, that we are at peace with Him, that He is our best and faithful friend. Then we may rejoice in Him at all times, for His fulness is our fortune, His power is our defence, His love is our solace, His promises are our security, His throne is our place of safety, and His presence is our heaven. Everything *in* God has a tendency to make us happy; and everything that is done *by* God will promote our everlasting welfare. We may well say, 'Although the fig tree shall not blossom, neither shall fruit be in the vines, the flock shall be cut off from the fold, yet will I rejoice in the Lord, I will joy in the God of my salvation.'

God is the treasure of my soul,
The source of lasting joy,
A joy which want shall not impair,
Nor death itself destroy.

SEPTEMBER 6

🌿 MORNING 🌿
'I will love them freely.'
Hosea 14:4

The Lord loves His people naturally, as parents love their children; freely, without any cause whatever in them. He looks for nothing in them to move Him to love; nor will He allow any thing in them to prevent His love. He loves them as vessels of mercy, disciples of Jesus, as bearing His image, His name, and His nature. His love to them is infinite, fruitful, and unchangeable. He will love them, though they deserve hatred, merit wrath, and may be justly sentenced to perdition. Beloved, let us never look into ourselves to find out the cause of God's love; it is in Him, not in us; but let us believe Him when He says, 'I have loved thee with an everlasting love.' Let us plead with Him, encouraged by the words of Jesus, 'The Father Himself loveth you.' Let us rejoice before Him, and praise Him for distinguishing grace. If He will love, who shall forbid Him? If He will love us, who shall dispute with Him? If He love us, as His Word testifies He does, who shall estimate the honour, the advantage, or the happiness, which will eternally flow from His love? All glory to free grace, and unmerited love.

> O Jesus, full of truth and grace,   Open the ark and take me in:
> More full of grace than I of sin;   And freely my backsliding heal,
> Yet once again I seek Thy face;   And love the faithless sinner still.

🌿 EVENING 🌿
'Wherefore didst thou doubt?'
Matthew 14:31

This is the language of reproof, it was addressed to Peter, but to whom is it not applicable? Who of us have not doubted? Who does not often doubt? Who considers doubting as sinful? But it is so. Are not our doubts the offspring of unbelief? Do they not reflect on the love, care, constancy, and faithfulness of our Redeemer? Could He speak plainer than He has in His Word? Could He do more to lay a firm foundation for our confidence, peace, and joy? Has He not promised to receive, pardon, and bless every coming sinner? Has He not given us instances of the manner in which He proves His care, fulfils His Word, and answers the prayers of His people, in the historical portions of His Word? Has He spoken? Is He worthy of credit? Did He ever deceive? Can He trifle with an immortal soul? Is He not unchangeable? Then 'wherefore didst thou doubt?' Make no excuse for thy doubts, but at once acknowledge that they are sinful, and seek grace, that you may trust in the Lord with all your heart, and trust Him at all times. Doubts weaken the soul, exhaust the spirits, and hinder cheerful obedience; therefore strive against them.

> Within are fears, without a storm,
> And foes are round about;
> But Jesus will His Word perform,
> Then wherefore dost thou doubt?

SEPTEMBER 7

❦ MORNING ❧
'Rejoicing in hope.'
ROMANS 12:12

The believer cannot always rejoice in possession, for he appears stripped of every thing; but he may rejoice in hope even then. He is warranted to hope for eternal life; for righteousness by faith, that God may be magnified in his body, by life or by death; for the resurrection of the body, and its reunion with the soul; for the appearing of his beloved Saviour, and complete salvation through Him. The hope which is laid up for him in heaven, of which the gospel now informs him; a weight of glory, a crown of righteousness, and an eternal inheritance, are in reserve for him; and in hope of these he may rejoice. They are set before Him to excite desire, produce courage, prevent despondency, and fill with joy. They are freely given, plainly promised, and carefully preserved; therefore we shall never be ashamed of our hope. Let us not yield to our gloomy feelings, or to distressing forebodings; but let us lift up our heads, rejoicing that we shall so soon be made partakers of our hope. Let us hope in God, and daily praise Him more and more, making use of hope as the anchor of the soul, sure and steadfast. He that hopes in God will never be disappointed.

Come, Lord, and help me to rejoice,
In hope that I shall hear Thy voice,
Shall one day see my God;
Shall cease from all my painful strife,
Handle and taste the Word of life,
And feel the sprinkled blood.

❦ EVENING ❧
'They say unto God, Depart from us.'
JOB 21:14

That is the ungodly do so. His presence is offensive to them. They wish there was no God. But as there is one, they wish Him to keep at a distance from them. This is not your case. It was once. It would have been this evening but for grace. You desire the presence of God, this is the effect of His love. You have seen something of His glory, in the person of Jesus Christ. You have tasted that He is gracious. You are reconciled to Him, and are at peace with Him. You have nothing to fear from Him, therefore you desire that He would come unto you; and manifest Himself to your soul as He does not so unto the world. You say, 'My soul thirsteth for God, for the living God; when shall I come and appear before God.' Those who now say unto God, 'Depart from us,' will one day hear Him say 'Depart from me, ye cursed, into everlasting fire, prepared for the devil and his angels.' But you who now invite Him to your hearts and your homes, will hear Him invite you, saying, 'Come, ye blessed of my Father, inherit the kingdom prepared for you from the foundation of the world.'

My God, I cannot say 'Depart',
But, 'Come and dwell with me:
Take full possession of my heart,
And keep me close to Thee.'

SEPTEMBER 8

🌿 MORNING 🌿

'The word of our God shall stand for ever.'
ISAIAH 40:8

The Word of our God is like His nature, immutably the same; He saith, 'My covenant will I not break, nor alter the thing that is gone out of my mouth.' Believer, this is thy comfort; every promise is confirmed and shall be fulfilled. But what hath He said? He hath said, 'Though your sins be as scarlet they shall be white as snow. Many are the afflictions of the righteous, but the Lord delivereth him out of them all. No weapon formed against thee shall prosper. I will strengthen thee; I will help thee. I will never leave thee, nor forsake thee. No good thing will He withhold from them that walk uprightly.' All that He saith cometh surely to pass. Not one jot or tittle can fail. He never spake hastily, insincerely, or unwisely; He has drawn His plan, given His Word, and every thing shall answer the end He had in view. Man may be disappointed, God cannot. Man may change his mind, or break his Word, but God cannot. He abideth faithful, He cannot deny Himself. Trust, and be not afraid. God's Word is firmer than a rock, and changeless as His nature.

> *The Word of God shall still endure,*
> *Faithful, immutable, and sure;*
> *This solid rock shall never break,*
> *Though earth should to her centre shake;*
> *And while it stands we should not fear,*
> *For all we need is promised there.*

🌿 EVENING 🌿

'Testify against me.'
MICAH 6:3

By our conduct we often reflect upon the Lord. We treat Him with neglect and disrespect, preferring creatures or worldly things before Him. He speaks of this conduct as if it went to His heart. He says, 'O my people, what have I done unto thee? and wherein have I wearied thee? testify against me.' Have you neglected the closet? Have you slighted the means of grace? Have you laid your bible on one side and left it unopened? Have you withdrawn your thoughts and your affections from God, and given them to the world? Why is this? What reason have you for doing so? The Lord asks you why? He says, 'Have you any charges against me? Bring them forward. Have I treated you unkindly? Have I been false to my Word? Have I acted in any way unbecoming my character? Tell me, why do you treat me with neglect? Why do you prefer my enemy, the world, to me? Tell out your reasons, let me know all; anything but this shyness, this distance, this indifference.' O believer! are you not guilty? Have you not wounded your God? Have you not grieved His Holy Spirit? Return to thy injured Lord. Go, fall at His feet, confess your sins, crave His pardon, be reconciled, and embosomed in His love.

> *Behold again I turn to Thee,*
> *O, cast me not away, though vile;*
> *No peace I have, no joy I see,*
> *O Lord my God! but in Thy smile.*

SEPTEMBER 9

🌿 MORNING 🌿

'O, love the Lord, all ye His saints.'

PSALM 31:23

Our God has revealed Himself as the source, centre, and end of everything lovely. In Jesus He appears as the fairest among ten thousand, and the altogether lovely. The wealth of the universe is His. He is worthy of our highest love. He is all we could wish or desire. To possess Him is to be made for eternity. To have Him on our side is to be safe forever. But you may ask, What is His mind towards us? Emphatically, 'grace.' We have found favour in His eyes. He is the friend of penitent sinners. He loveth us with an infinite love. Do you doubt it? Read His Word. Look at Calvary. Ask His people. Prove for yourselves. See what He has already done for us. Have we a being? He gave it. Have we a good hope? He bestowed it. Have we liberty? He bought it. Have we holiness? He wrought it. Consider what we may have been but for His grace; what we certainly should have been but for His salvation; what we are now, and what we shall be, as the effect of His love; and, 'O, love the Lord, all ye His saints!' It is happiness! it is holiness! it is heaven! It is your first duty, and your sweetest privilege!

> *Love all defects supplies,*
> *Makes great obstructions small;*
> *'Tis prayer, 'tis praise, 'tis sacrifice,*
> *'Tis holiness, 'tis all!*

🌿 EVENING 🌿

'Thou hast known my soul in adversities.'

PSALM 31:7

Prosperity makes friends, but adversity tries them. How many will visit and smile upon us when the sun shines, but who will venture out to do us good in the wintry or stormy day? David had been in adversity; he had been forsaken and neglected by his friends, but not by his God. His God knew him, and visited him, and supplied him, and at length delivered him. This honour have all His saints. He knew Israel in the wilderness, in the land of great drought; and He will know us, that is, He will acknowledge us, and care for us, and approve of us. He hath done so. We have been in adversity. We have passed through a wilderness, but our God led us, and fed us, and preserved us, and brought us out into a wealthy place. We can witness for Him in reference to the past; and we ought calmly, quietly, and confidently to trust Him for the future. He hath passed His Word that He will deliver us in six troubles, and that in seven no evil shall touch us; and He is faithful who hath promised. He is emphatically the friend of His people in distress, and in our greatest trials He will glorify His richest grace.

> *Thy presence to my soul display,*
> *And shine my gloomy fears away;*
> *Let mercy to my thankful heart,*
> *Its saving health and joys impart.*

SEPTEMBER 10

🌿 MORNING 🌿

'To comfort all that mourn.'

ISAIAH 61:2

The Lord's people are all mourners; grace sets and keeps them mourning over sin committed, depravity discovered, evidences needed, comforts forfeited and lost, apparent uselessness, the sins of others, the state of the church, or for the salvation of relatives and friends. We mourn after Jesus when we do not enjoy His love, and over Him as suffering when we do. But He has declared, 'Blessed are they that mourn, for they shall be comforted.' Jesus Himself is anointed and appointed to be our Comforter; He has given Him the tongue of the learned, that He may speak a word in season to them that are weary. He comforts us by pardoning our sins, subduing our iniquities, restoring the joys of our salvation, employing us in His service, and making us successful. He comforts us by His Word, His servants, and His Spirit. Admire the wisdom of God in the person appointed; the love of God in the work to which He is appointed; and the faithfulness of God in the perpetuity of His office. He ever lives, and lives to comfort us. Sweet view of Jesus; let us dwell upon it, and especially do so in trouble and trial.

> Now in the Lord will I be glad,
> And glory in His love;
> In Him I'll joy, who will the God
> Of my salvation prove;
> My Saviour will my comfort be,
> And set my soul from trouble free.

🌿 EVENING 🌿

'Unite my heart to fear thy name.'

PSALM 86:11

To fear God includes faith in His Word, love to His character, zeal for His glory, concern to please Him, and the fear of offending Him. It sometimes signifies to worship Him. This embraces reverence, adoration, thanksgiving, and prayer. Worship without the heart is worthless. But how often in worship do we feel our hearts distracted and wandering, and at a distance from God! Well may we pray, 'Unite my heart to fear thy name.' That is, calm it, compose it, attract it, fix it, enflame it; that it may throw all its energies into Thy service. Such a prayer proves that we love the service, desire to honour God in it, feel our own weakness, and seek to obtain grace, whereby we may serve God acceptably with reverence and godly fear. But do all saints feel their hearts thus prone to wander, and find it difficult to engage them in the Lord's service? They do at times, though some suffer from this much more than others. Yet all occasionally feel some reluctance to duty, or distractions in it; they are the subjects of dulness, deadness, and conflict. Therefore they all pray as David did here, or sigh as he did elsewhere, 'O that my ways were directed to keep thy statutes' always'.

> How oft my heart's affections yield,
> Scattered o'er all the world's wide field?
> My vagrant passions, Lord, reclaim,
> Unite them all to fear Thy name.

SEPTEMBER 11

🌿 MORNING 🌿

'Wilt thou be made whole?'

John 5:6

The great Physician presents Himself to us this morning, and He asks, 'Wilt thou be made whole?' This is a searching question. Are you willing to be sanctified throughout? Willing that He should use what means He pleases, to conform you to Himself? Jesus is able to sanctify us wholly; the time of mercy is now; are we desirous of being healed? If so, let us put ourselves into His hands for the purpose; let us submit without hesitation to His terms; He performs the cure and receives all the glory. Let us not fancy that our case is hopeless, but let us look to Jesus, who will heal us, and heal us gratis. Open thy whole case to Him, consult Him daily, trust Him implicitly, and expect to shine before the Father's throne as a proof of His skill and kindness. No case can be desperate, while Jesus lives to heal; no sinner can be too poor, for He heals without money and without price. O Jesus! heal us this morning! Soften our hard hearts. Regulate our disorderly wills. Elevate our earthly affections. Fill us with holiness; fill us with love. We lie at Thy feet, and we trust in Thy Word. O to be made whole!

> *Jesus, to Thee for help I call,*
> *With pitying eye behold me fall,*
> *Diseased at Thy throne;*
>
> *O, heal my soul, remove my sin,*
> *Now make the filthy leper clean,*
> *Remove the heart of stone.*

🌿 EVENING 🌿

'He will be our guide even unto death.'

Psalm 48:14

What a precious assurance is this! Our God is our guide: He led us out of the world at first, directed us to the cross, and conducted us into the path of peace; He has led us through all our past difficulties and trials; He leads us by the hand at present, and He will never give up His charge, for He will be our guide even unto death. He will choose our way; lead us in the paths of righteousness; kindly converse with us on the road; point out the snares and dangers in our path; and keep us by His power through faith unto salvation. He undertook to guide us at first without our knowledge, He kindly appeared as our *Conductor* in answer to our prayers, and He will patiently bear with us unto the end. He may hide His face, refuse communion, withhold comforts, smite us for our follies, and teach us, by painful experience, our dependence on Himself; but He will never forsake us or give us up. He will guide us to the end of the journey, and will go with us through the last dark valley. He will not only lead us to the kingdom, but puts us in possession of it. This He has promised, and He will faithfully perform it. Beloved, it is our Father's good pleasure to give us the kingdom. He will guide us now, and by and by receive us to glory.

> *For God, whom Zion boasts her friend,*
> *Our God unchangeable is known;*
> *Our Guide – who will our steps attend,*
> *Till death advance us to His throne.*

SEPTEMBER 12

🌿 MORNING 🌿

'I lay down my life for the sheep.'

JOHN 10:15

Jesus has a flock peculiarly His own; His Father chose them and gave them to Him; He received them and became their Shepherd; they wandered and were doomed to die, but He interfered and died for them. O, what an infinite love was the love of Jesus! He left His Father's bosom, left the songs of angels, left the throne of glory, and became a man, that He might become a Substitute. He offered Himself for them: His blood for theirs, His life for theirs. The offer was accepted, and He redeemed them to God by His blood out of every nation, country, people, and tongue. They are doubly His, for He bought them when they had sold themselves, though before they were given Him by His Father in love. Herein is love; not that we loved Jesus, but that He loved us; and gave Himself to be the propitiation for our sins. Are we among His sheep? Are we like them? Do we love them, cleave to them, and walk with them? His sheep are gentle, harmless, peaceful, humble, dependent upon Him, and devoted to Him. They hear His voice, love His ways, and follow Him whithersoever He goeth.

> *When the Shepherd's life was needful*
> *To redeem the sheep from death,*
> *Of their safety ever heedful,*
> *Jesus yielded up His breath;*
> *Faithful Shepherd!*
> *Love like Thine no other hath.*

🌿 EVENING 🌿

'Noah walked with God.'

GENESIS 6:9

He was reconciled to God. He was intimate with God. He listened to the voice of God. He chose the way of God. He drank into the Spirit, and approved of the designs of God. His God was his *Friend*, with Him he could converse, to Him he could look for counsel, from Him he often received favours. His God was his *Companion*, he walked with Him, realizing that He was near, loving His presence, and improving by His society. He did not sit with the Lord on His throne, nor stand with Him in His sanctuary, but he walked with Him in his way. He made progress. He was diligent, as well as devout. The presence of God was his happiness, his security, and his honour. This privilege may be ours. It is, if we are really believers in the Lord Jesus. Our God is with us. He is with us as our Father, our Friend, our Companion. We walk with Him. We converse with Him. We receive from Him. We imbibe His spirit. Beloved, do you *walk with God*? Have you been walking with God *today*? Does the thought of God's presence with you give you joy? Does it soothe, and animate, and sanctify your spirit? Retire to rest rejoicing in the fact: God is with me, as my Father and my Guard.

> *I walk with God, though Lord of all,*
> *My nearest friend He is;*
> *On Him I lean, and cast my cares:*
> *O what a friendship this!*

SEPTEMBER 13

❧ MORNING ❧

'Let patience have her perfect work.'

JAMES 1:4

Patience supposes trials and troubles; it signifies to remain under a burden; it is opposed to fretfulness, murmuring, haste, and despondency; it produces submission, silence before God, and satisfaction with His dealings. The Holy Spirit produces this grace by means of afflictions; tribulation worketh patience. Every Christian is supposed to possess it, and is required to exercise it; yea, to let it have its perfect work. To this end let us study the examples of suffering and patience set before us in the Bible; let us take up and plead God's promises; let us remember that eternal love appointed every trial and trouble; that Jesus forewarned us of tribulation; that He has set us an example which we are required to imitate. Impatience dishonours our profession, and grieves the Spirit; patience benefits others, and is of great advantage to ourselves. Let us watch against temptations to impatience, and in patience possess our souls. So shall we fill up our character as Christians; complete the evidence of our sincerity; and prove our principles divine.

Dear Lord, though bitter is the cup
Thy gracious hand deals out to me,
I cheerfully would drink it up;
That cannot hurt which comes from Thee.
The gift of patience, Lord impart,
To calm and soothe my troubled heart.

❧ EVENING ❧

'Increasing in the knowledge of God.'

COLOSSIANS 1:10

Our knowledge at present is very imperfect. We know but in part. The means of knowledge are in our hands, but we have not always the heart to turn them to account. God must be known or He cannot be loved, or He will not be trusted: we shall neither adore His perfections, nor reverence His majesty, nor seek His favour, nor fear His frown, nor do His commandments, except we know Him. Paul knew this; therefore he prayed for the Colossians, that they might increase in the knowledge of God. If we would know Him, we must read His works, observe His providence, and study His Word. But it is in Jesus that He reveals Himself most clearly and most fully. Therefore He says, 'He that hath seen me hath seen the Father.' Do you know God at all? You did not once, therefore be thankful. But your knowledge is small and very imperfect, therefore seek an increase of it. Remember Jesus said, 'This is life eternal, that they might know thee the only true God, and Jesus Christ whom thou hast sent.' He that hath an extensive knowledge of God in Jesus, hath a never failing source of happiness. Beloved, make it your daily aim to increase in the knowledge of God.

Shine, mighty God, with vigour shine,
On this benighted heart of mine;
And let Thy glories stand reveal'd,
As in the Saviour's face beheld.

SEPTEMBER 14

🌿 MORNING 🌿

'And Jacob said, … I have enough' or, 'I have all things.'
Genesis 33:10,11

Poor Jacob left his father's house with only a staff, but he returned with two bands; so greatly had the Lord prospered him. But it was not his earthly possessions, but the kindness of his brother, and the grace of his God, which led him to exclaim, 'I have enough', or, 'I have all things.' Beloved, such language becomes us, as the objects of Jehovah's everlasting love; as interest in the well-ordered covenant; as entitled to all the promises; as invited to come to the Throne of grace to receive all we need; as directed to cast all our cares upon God; as having a warrant to expect every good thing on earth, and glory at the journey's end; ought we not to rejoice and shout, 'I have enough,' Enough to make me happy; enough to make me holy; enough to fill me with gratitude; enough to fill angels with wonder, and devils with envy and vexation. O Jesus! to what a height hast Thou raised us! With what great, lasting, and glorious blessings hast Thou blessed us! Everlasting praises to Thy name, and eternal glory to Thy sovereign grace! O to live in the world as one who has enough!

Jesus is all I wish or want!
For Him I pray, I thirst, I pant;
Let others after earth aspire,

Christ is the treasure I desire;
He is an all-sufficient store;
Possess'd of Him, I wish no more.

🌿 EVENING 🌿

'Peter followed Him afar off.'
Matthew 26:58

And have not we done so too? Once we thought that nothing could cool our love, damp our ardour, or turn our feet aside. But we have long since discovered our mistake. Still, it is better to follow at a distance, than turn our backs upon Him. For Peter there was some excuse, in the circumstances in which his Master was placed; for us there is none. Faith brings us near to Jesus, and love keeps us near; unbelief is the cause of our slow pace, and declining in His ways. Let us carefully guard against unbelief. It poisons our comforts, falsifies our profession, damps zeal, hinders our communion, thrusts us to a distance from Jesus, and alienates our souls from His ways. Let us encourage and feel our faith: it will strengthen our hearts, quicken our pace, endear our Saviour, fortify our minds, and keep us near to our beloved Lord. Reader, are you following the Lord closely? Or, are you, like Peter, afar off? If you are, beware. You know to what this conduct led in him; it is not possible to say, where it may lead you. Get close to Jesus, and keep close. Let your thoughts gather round Him, your affections fix upon Him, and your hope centre in Him. Cleave to the Saviour as the child to its parent, as the limpet to the rock.

The soul that would to Jesus cleave,
And hear His secret call,
Must his own strength and wisdom leave,
And let the Lord be all.

SEPTEMBER 15

🌿 MORNING 🌿
'The end of all things is at hand.'
1 Peter 4:7

The mountains shall depart, and the hills be removed; only Jehovah's Word, love, purposes, and perfections remain the same. The world passeth away, and the fashion of it; but he that doeth the will of God abideth for ever. The end of all things is at hand; our labours will soon cease; our commerce terminate; our earthly relationships dissolve; our pleasures and sorrows in this world be concluded; the last sermon will soon be preached; and the last opportunity for us to do good will make its appearance. The coming of the Son of God draweth nigh; let us be therefore preparing ourselves for so great, so solemn an event; and whenever tempted to trifle, to loiter, or to sin, let us remember *'the Lord is at hand.'* Let us be sober, temperate in reference to the body; and let us think soberly of ourselves, of others, of everything around us. Let us not be rash or hasty, careless, or indifferent; but let us speak and act soberly, as those that *must* give an account. He that shall come will come, and will not tarry; and He bids us be ready to receive Him with gladness, joy, and rejoicing.

> *When Thou, my righteous Judge, shalt come*
> *To fetch Thy ransom'd people home,*
> *Shall I among them stand?*
>
> *Shall such a worthless worm as I,*
> *Who sometimes am afraid to die,*
> *Be found at Thy right hand?*

🌿 EVENING 🌿
'None can stay His hand.'
Daniel 4:35

The hand of God is His providence, or His wisdom and power in operation for the accomplishment of His will. No one can possibly frustrate His designs. Nothing can throw confusion into His plans. He steadily pursues His object, easily accomplishes His purpose, performs all His pleasure. All His saints are in His hand; therefore they are safe. His hand is at work for them; therefore they shall not be injured. He always works in accordance with His Word. His predictions must come to pass. His promises must be fulfilled. His charge must be safe. Beloved, the hand of God is lifted up to defend you; therefore you are safe. His hand is opened to supply you; therefore you shall not want. His hand is beneath you; therefore you shall not fall. Trust in Jesus, in His wisdom and power. Exercise faith in His providence. His hand will crush or convert your foes, protect you and supply your wants, guide you through the desert, and lift you up for ever. Look from circumstances to the hand that guides and overrules them; it is your Father's hand, and His hand is moved by His heart, which heart glows with unutterable love to you. He is at work for you, and *'None can stay His hand.'*

> *Jehovah's arm shall be my strength,*
> *And His almighty power*
> *Will well fulfil His promises,*
> *And victory ensure.*

SEPTEMBER 16

🌿 MORNING 🌿

'Even to hoar hairs will I carry you.'
ISAIAH 46:4

What a sweet portion is this for the aged disciples of the Lord Jesus: heart and flesh may fail them, but God will not forsake them. Having begun a good work in them, He will carry it on. His gifts and callings are without repentance. He will be as kind, as tender, and as gracious at last as at the first. He will carry us. The eternal God is our refuge, underneath are the everlasting arms. He will carry us safely through every danger, over every difficulty, into His presence and glory. Aged pilgrim, lean upon thy God; look unto Him; and as the nurse carrieth the sucking child, so will thy God carry thee. He will prove Himself faithful to His Word, and ultimately call you forth as a witness to the same. Fear not then in reference to the evening of old age: thy God will supply thee; He will support thee; and at last land thee safe where the storms of trouble never blow, where weakness and fears are never felt. 'Take no anxious thought for the morrow; let the morrow take thought for the things of itself; sufficient unto the day is the evil thereof.' The promise of thy God cannot fail thee; He will guide thee and carry thee to His kingdom and glory. He says:

> *E'en down to old age, all My people shall prove*
> *My sov'reign, eternal, unchangeable love;*
> *And when hoary hairs shall their temples adorn,*
> *Like lambs they shall still in My bosom be borne.*

🌿 EVENING 🌿

'Will a man rob God?'
MALACHI 3:8

This is a very solemn question, for to attempt it must be very daring. But who can plead not guilty? If we will not take what He has, we have withheld what He claims. He charges us with the crime; He says, *'Ye have robbed me.'* We have robbed Him of His *time*. His own day, and other time which He claims, and which should be devoted to Him. We have robbed Him of *property*. What He lent us, we have claimed as our own. What was given us for others, we have squandered or hoarded for self. We have withheld from His cause what He entrusted to our care for its benefit. We have robbed Him of the *heart*. This we have given to others, to idols. They have been loved, trusted, adored, and feared before Him. We have robbed Him of our *talents*. Spending them in the service of others, and using them for the gratification and aggrandizement of ourselves. What can we say to such conduct? Is it not ungrateful? For He is our Father. Is it not daring? For He could crush us with a look. Let us reflect upon our characters, robbers of God. Let us confess our crimes, obtain a pardon, change our course, and render unto God the things that are God's. O for honesty of heart, and consistency of life, as Christians!

> *Guilty I plead before Thy throne:*
> *My God, my crimes forgive;*
> *I plead the Saviour's blood alone,*
> *Pardon, and bid me live.*

SEPTEMBER 17

❦ MORNING ❦
'Fight the good fight of faith.'
1 Timothy 6:12

Faith has to fight with the deep and direful depravity of the heart; with error and superstition; with despondency and early prejudices; with unbelief and carnal reason; with Satan and the world at large. Faith has to fight for victory, for a crown, for God's glory. True faith fights in God's strength; with certainty, arising from the faithful promise; in holy fear, produced by grace taking advantage of our weakness; with courage; principally on the knees; and looking to the Captain of our salvation, the end of the conflict, and the design of the combat. Believer, *'fight the good fight of faith.'* Thy God bids thee. His promises are intended to encourage thee. The example of Jesus should animate thee. The coward's doom should alarm and instruct thee. The connection between conflict and conquest should impel thee. Jesus says, 'To him that overcometh will I grant to sit with me in my throne, even as I also overcame, and am set down with my Father in His throne.' God is faithful, by whom ye were called unto the fellowship of His Son, Jesus Christ our Lord.

> Omnipotent Lord, my Saviour and King,
> Thy succour afford, Thy righteousness bring,
> On Thee, as my power, for
> strength I rely,
>
> All evil before Thy presence shall fly;
> Thy love everlasting will never depart,
> Thy truth and Thy mercy shall rule
> in my heart.

❦ EVENING ❦
'Their Redeemer is strong.'
Jeremiah 50:34

The Redeemer is the nearest of kin. No one is so nearly related to us or by so many and various ties, as the Lord Jesus; and He is our Redeemer. He gave His life a ransom for us. He sent His Holy Spirit to rescue us from the hands of our spiritual enemies. He will exert His almighty power to raise us from the dead, and so complete our redemption. What He undertook, He can accomplish, for He is strong. What He has promised He will perform, for He is faithful. We shall therefore be completely delivered from Satan, who held us captive; from sin, which tyrannised over us; from death, which is an enemy to us; and from hell, which we justly deserved. Our Redeemer is strong, therefore let us place confidence in Him; let us look to Him alone for deliverance from our foes and fears; let us never dishonour Him by supposing that He will allow our enemies to triumph over us. He cheerfully laboured for us. He willingly shed His blood for us. He graciously quickened us when dead in trespasses and sins, and He will perfect that which concerneth us, for He will not forsake the work of His own hands. Our Redeemer is strong, the Lord of Hosts is His name, and He will thoroughly plead our cause.

> Jesus our Lord, in Thee
> We a Redeemer have,
> Strong to set Thy people free,
> Omnipotent to save.

SEPTEMBER 18

❦ MORNING ❦

'He forgetteth not the cry of the humble.'
PSALM 9:12

The humble grateful soul, may have any thing from the Lord; so great is His love to them, and delight in them. He cries to the Lord to be kept from every false way, from falling into sin, and that he may be devoted entirely to the Lord's glory. He prays for his enemies, that they may be blessed, and for his friends, that they may be rewarded. His cry is constant, sincere, and hearty. But he is often tempted to think that because he is so unworthy, so insignificant, and so vile, God will not hear him, and especially when answers are delayed. But the cry of the humble cannot be forgotten. The Lord will not neglect or pass over such an one's prayer without notice; He will not despise, or contemn their petitions; but He will regard, attend to, and answer them. His wisdom will shine forth in the time when, and the means by which He answers their prayers; and He will get Himself a glorious name by their sanctification, salvation, and glorification. O believer, never harbour the thought that thy God will forget thy petitions; He will only forget thy sins!

Friend of sinners, King of saints,
Answer my minutest wants;
Let my cries Thy throne assail,
Entering now within the veil;
Free my soul from guilt and shame,
Lord, I ask in Jesus' name.

❦ EVENING ❦

'By love serve one another.'
GALATIANS 5:13

The root of all acceptable obedience is love. Love springs from faith, and produces all good. Nothing that we can do is good, except it flows from love. Love is the chief thing in religion. We may have gifts, honours, and benevolence; but without love, we are only as sounding brass or a tinkling cymbal. Nature desires to rule over others, but grace is willing to serve them. Look around you, are there not many whom you can serve, and serve effectually, without neglecting your other important duties? Are you willing to do so? If not, where is your love? If you have not loved, where is your religion? Love is the fulfilling of the law, and it is the chief production of the gospel. Love is Godlike. It is Christlike. Love is heaven. Love will visit the sick, cheer the sorrowful, clothe the naked, feed the hungry, and become all things to all men, if by any means it may save some. Love will make our wilderness world a garden; and our divided church a paradise. What we do from love we do easily, cheerfully, heartily, constantly, and acceptably. See then that ye love one another, with a pure heart fervently; serve Christ in His people, and imitate His conduct toward His foes. As you have therefore opportunity, do good to all men.

Heirs of the same immortal bliss,
Our hopes and fears the same,
With bonds of love our hearts unite,
With mutual love inflame.

SEPTEMBER 19

❧ MORNING ❧

'Sin shall not have dominion over you.'
ROMANS 6:14

What a precious promise. How many of the Lord's people have been cheered and encouraged by it. Sin lives in us, works in us, fights in us; but it shall not reign. It may annoy; it shall not destroy. Its authority is destroyed by the Lord; its power is weakened by grace; it is warned to quit its old residence, and it will soon be ejected. We are not under the condemning power of the law, it is not our rule of justification, but we are under favour; God dealeth with us as with children. He pardons, pities, and delivers us. He will not allow sin to hold us in perpetual bondage, or to condemn us at the last day; but He will set us at liberty, and justify us fully. The flesh will lust against the Spirit, corruption will rise and fight; but we shall be strengthened, assisted, and counselled until we finally overcome. Grace shall reign through righteousness unto eternal life, by Jesus Christ our Lord. The law will be honoured in our endless blessedness, and Jesus will be glorified in us throughout eternity. By grace we are saved, from sin now, and from wrath for ever.

> On such love, my soul, still ponder,
> Love so great, so rich, so free!
> Say, while lost in holy wonder,
>
> Why, O Lord, such love to me?
> Hallelujah,
> Grace shall reign eternally.

❧ EVENING ❧

'Therefore have they forgotten me.'
HOSEA 13:6

Why? He had brought them into the good land. They were placed in circumstances of prosperity. They gave way to self-indulgence. They were lifted up with pride. Therefore they forgot God their Saviour, who had done such great things for them. We often fancy that we could bear prosperity better than adversity, but those who have been tried have proved the reverse. The heart is secretly, and, at first, imperceptibly led away from God. The affections are set on things below. Indulging the flesh unfits for spiritual duties and exercises. Divine things lose their savour and power. The means of grace convey no grace to the soul. We relax in duty. Satan employs his influence to harden our hearts, to alienate our affections, to blind our minds, and to stupify our consciences. The warnings of God's Word are disregarded, the throne of grace is neglected, worldly company is preferred, and then God is forgotten. We forget His deliverances, His favours, His claims, His threatenings, until aroused by some painful visitation. Brethren, let us be cautious, circumspect, aware of our danger, and carefully examine into our present state. Are we just in the state in which we should wish death to find us? Why not?

> I left my guide to happiness,
> I lost the true internal peace;
> Nor can my soul retrieve its rest,
> Till lodg'd again in Jesus' breast.

SEPTEMBER 20

🌿 MORNING 🌿

'I have gone astray like a lost sheep.'

PSALM 119:176

This is the humble confession of a man of God, and may not we adopt it as our own this morning? Have not we also gone astray? Does not this display our *weakness*? How weak to wander from so kind a Shepherd, so rich a pasture, so good a fold! Is it not a mark of *inattention*? Jesus hath warned and cautioned us against it in His Word. Is it not a proof of our *ingratitude*? O, how ungrateful to forsake Him after so many favours, such rich blessings, such tokens of unmerited kindness! Does it not betray our *folly*? – to go from good to bad, from safety to danger, from plenty to want and wretchedness. O, the power of corruption! The deceitfulness of the human heart! Lord, seek Thy servants, for we do not forget Thy commandments. We smart for our folly; we grieve over our sin; we desire to return; restore us to Thy fold, to the enjoyment of Thy favour; and enable us to delight ourselves in Thy ways. Jesus, Shepherd of the sheep, bring us back from all our wanderings, and keep us near Thyself; for why should we turn aside from Thy flock and fold?

Thou know'st the way to bring me back,
My fallen spirit to restore;
O, for Thy truth and mercy's sake,
Forgive, and bid me sin no more;
The ruins of my soul repair,
And make my heart a house of prayer.

🌿 EVENING 🌿

'I will walk in thy truth.'

PSALM 86:11

God's truth is opposed to many of our customs, prejudices, and inclinations. It requires what our depraved nature thinks hard, and prohibits what we naturally love. The resolution therefore is noble. It reflects honour upon Him who formed it. Let us follow His example. To walk in the truth is to believe it; to receive it into the mind, as a communication from God; to place confidence in it. But faith without works is dead; therefore it includes the practice of it. The true Christian prays, 'Teach me to do thy will.' He purposes, 'I will run the way of thy commandments,' for there is the enjoyment of the truth. It brings us glad tidings. It furnishes us with a feast as well as a rule. It charms while it corrects. It consoles while it requires. It makes us happy as well as holy; or rather it makes us happy by making us holy. If we believe the truth, and do the truth, and enjoy the truth, let us profess the truth, and let our profession be open, sincere, and scriptural. If we have made a profession of the truth, let it be our daily study to adorn it; to walk worthy of the vocation wherewith we are called in all godliness and honesty. Let us hold fast the profession of our faith without wavering, for He is faithful that hath promised.

Thou great Instructor, lest I stray,
O teach my erring feet the way;
Thy truth with ever fresh delight,
Shall guide my doubtful footsteps aright.

SEPTEMBER 21

🌿 MORNING 🌿
'The Lord was ready to save me.'
ISAIAH 38:20

This is the testimony of a good man who had been in great danger. His heart was full of fears, and he gave up all for lost; but now he is recovered, and stands forth to acknowledge his mistake, and bear witness to this pleasing fact, that the Lord is ever ready to save His people in every time of trouble. The Lord hath saved us, and He will save us even to the end. He has power, and He will exert it; He has authority, and He will employ it; He has sympathy, and He will manifest it. He is a Saviour at hand and not afar off; He is ready and willing to deliver. Has He not proved Himself so in our past experience, and ought we not to trust Him for the future? Let us in every danger cry unto God to save us; wait upon Him in humble hope for the blessing; banish carnal and unscriptural fears far away; refuse to listen to Satan, sense, or unbelief; persevere in seeking until we obtain and enjoy the blessing. *The Lord is ready to save us.* Let us believe, hope, prove, and be happy. He will save, He will rest in His love, and joy over us with singing.

Salvation to God will I publish abroad,
Jehovah hath saved me through Jesus' blood;
The Lamb was once slain, but
He liveth again,
And I with my Jesus for ever shall reign;
Then fill'd with His love, in
the regions above,
I shall never, no never, from Jesus remove.

🌿 EVENING 🌿
'My God will hear me.'
MICAH 7:7

He has promised it, and He is faithful to His Word. He has done so in times past, and what He has done is the pledge of what He will do. Besides, He is my Father, as well as my God. He knows my nature. He appointed my lot. He has given me the Spirit of grace and supplication. He bids me call upon Him. He has assured me that He 'is nigh unto all them that call upon him, to all that call upon him in truth.' And that 'He will fulfil the desire of them that fear him; he also will hear their cry and will save them.' Beloved, let us then call upon God, let us pour out our complaints before Him, let us present our petitions to Him, let us seek His help, His presence, and His blessing, He will hear us. Men may become alienated from us; our God never will. Friends may turn a deaf ear to us; our God never can. Let us then come to the same determination as Micah did, and say, 'Therefore will I look unto the Lord; I will wait for the God of my salvation; my God will hear me. Rejoice not against me, O mine enemy; when I fall, I shall arise; when I sit in darkness, the Lord shall be a light unto me.' Though He delay, He will not deny, for 'no good thing will he withhold from them that walk uprightly.'

Praying on, and never ceasing,
Saviour! I Thy Word shall prove,
Bless'd with all the gospel blessing,
Fill'd with holy, heavenly love.

SEPTEMBER 22

🌿 MORNING 🌿

'Be ye imitators of God, as dear children.'

EPHESIANS 5:1

The Lord proposes Himself to us as our pattern, and He gives grace to every one who desires it to imitate Him. He exhorts us as His dear and tenderly beloved children, and in mildest strains proposeth Himself for our imitation. Let us imitate the Lord in the world, dealing justly, ever acting from holy principles, and by a righteous rule, adhering strictly to truth, for our God is *the God of truth*: choosing our company, being only familiar with them who are familiar with God; and doing good to all, especially unto them who are of the household of faith; for He causeth His sun to shine on the evil and on the good, and sendeth rain on the just and on the unjust. Let us imitate Him in the *church*, cultivating a spirit of love to all saints, notwithstanding their infirmities, exercising forbearance, and pity; being slow to anger and ready to forgive; accepting the will for the deed, and being always ready to help in trouble and distress. Let us imitate our God, for He commands us; our relation to Him requires it; and our peace is involved in it. Imitation of God is a sure evidence of saintship.

> This will solve th' important question,
> Whether thou art a real Christian,
> Better than each golden dream;

> Better far than lip expression,
> Towering notions, great profession;
> This will show your love to Him.

🌿 EVENING 🌿

'Thy blessing is upon thy people.'

PSALM 3:8

They were blessed in Christ, with all spiritual blessings, before the world was. They are blessed through Christ, with every good thing, while here below. And they will be blessed with Christ, with more than heart can conceive, in the world to come. The Lord's blessing is upon their persons, and they are set apart for His praise; upon their comforts, and they promote their holiness; upon their trials, and they work their real good; upon their labours, and they advance His kingdom and glory; upon their families, as the house of Obed-edom was blessed for the Ark's sake. Behold, thus is the man blessed that feareth the Lord. Beloved, this is your privilege: the blessing of God is upon you. Do you realize it? Do you manifest it? Remember, it flows from grace. It comes to you through Jesus. It is enjoyed in the exercise of faith, and in the way of obedience. It is insured by the oath and promise of God. It includes all you can need, or consistently desire. Retire to rest tonight impressed with the thought, 'The blessing of God is upon me.' Or, if afraid to claim it, with the prayer, 'Bless me, even me, O my Father.' 'Blessed are all they that put their trust in Him.'

> Lord, make it plain that I am Thine,
> In Jesus bless'd, with Jesus one;
> That all the promises are mine,
> As Thy belov'd, adopted son.

SEPTEMBER 23

🌿 MORNING 🌿

'Cast thy burden upon the Lord, and He shall sustain thee.'
PSALM 55:22

The Lord's people are often heavy laden, their burdens are heavy and their grief great; but the Lord kindly directs them to cast every burden upon Him, and promises to sustain them. Guilt in the conscience and a sense of sin in the soul, often prove an intolerable burden; but the Lord will remove it by the blood of His Son, and the whisper of His Spirit. The care of a family sinks the spirit, and fills with distress; but Jesus says, 'Cast them all on Me.' Losses, crosses, enemies, temptations, and the inward conflict, often burden the soul; but our God will sanctify them to us, sustain us through them, and deliver us out of them all. Our God has determined that we shall use Him, feel our dependence upon Him, and glory only in Him. Believer, He will sustain you by speaking peace to your troubled heart; by enabling you to leave your intricate affairs in His hands; by strengthening you with strength in your soul; and by enabling you to contrast the present with the future. Thanks be unto God who giveth us the victory. Let every burden lead us to the Lord, and let us leave it with Him. O Jesus, teach me to bring every burden to Thy feet, and to cast every care upon Thee!

Thou, O Lord, in tender love,
Wilt all my burdens bear!
Lift my heart to things above,
And fix it ever there!

🌿 EVENING 🌿

'Wherein hast thou loved us?'
MALACHI 1:2

This is a strange question, especially as proceeding from the Lord's people. But it is only speaking out, what many feel within. Do you ask, wherein has the Lord loved you? Look at the gifts He has conferred upon you: His Son to die for you; His Spirit to quicken, teach, and sanctify you; His ordinances to revive and refresh you; His angels to minister unto you; His covenant and oath to secure you; His glorious kingdom to be eternally possessed and enjoyed by you. Look at the account He makes of you: He calls you His love, the dearly beloved of His soul; His jewels, His crown, His dear son. If He compare you with the world: you are gold, that dross; you are wheat, that chaff; you are sheep, that swine; or goats, or serpents. Look at the relations He sustains to you: as a Father, a Husband, a Brother, a Friend. The offices He fills for you: an Advocate, a Captain, a Head, a King. Look at what He has already done for you: provided a righteousness, conferred a pardon, given His peace, appointed the Mediator, blessed you with all spiritual blessing. Surely you will exclaim, 'His love is wonderful, beyond comparison, beyond expression.'

Lord, give me with a grateful heart,
Thy mercy to improve;
And Ebenezers daily rear
To praise the God of love.

SEPTEMBER 24

🌿 MORNING 🌿

'In the mount of the Lord it shall be seen.'

GENESIS 22:14

Jehovah has provided supplies for His people. He arranges the bestowment of them, and hears and answers prayer for them. He may allow them to come into trials, dangers, and troubles; but in the mount the Lord will be seen, He will show Himself as rigidly faithful to His Word; as kind and merciful in all His dealings; as attentive to the wants and wishes of His people; as ready to supply them, and display His love and power in delivering them. In the mount of the Lord it shall be seen that Satan is a liar; that our fears were all groundless; that unbelief is a great sin; that prayer shall surely be answered; that faith and hope shall not be disappointed; that Jesus is touched with the feeling of our infirmities; and that none shall be ashamed who trust in, wait for, and obey the commands of the Most High God. Beloved, we have seen the Lord in the mount of trial; we have found it turned into the mount of mercy; and we shall see Him on the mount of glory.

'Tis in the mount the Lord is seen,
And all His saints shall surely find,
Though clouds and darkness intervene,
He still is gracious, still is kind.

Yes, in the mount, the Lord makes bare
His mighty, His delivering power;
Displays a Father's tender care,
In the most trying, darkest hour.

🌿 EVENING 🌿

'Rejoice the soul of thy servant.'

PSALM 86:4

It is a greater honour to be the Lord's servant, than to be the son of the greatest monarch upon earth. But all God's true servants are also His sons. He loves them as His children, while He employs them to accomplish His designs. They are all willing servants. They are convinced that they ought to be employed for Him, they have engaged themselves to serve Him, and they love their Master, their work, their fellow servants, and their wages. But though employed for God, they are not always happy in God. They lose sight of their true state, high relation, glorious prospects, and present privileges: or their evidences are clouded, or Satan harasses them, or providence appears to frown upon them, or the law in the members prevails against them, and they are cast down. Or, it may be that the Lord is rebuking them for some sin, or is displeased, because some idol is set up, some Agag is spared. They cannot claim comfort, or take joy, but they can pray for it. David did so, 'Restore unto me the joys of thy salvation.' 'Rejoice the soul of thy servant.' Do you do so? One ray of light, one word of grace, one whisper of His love, will fill you with joy and peace. He comforteth those that are cast down.

O bid my heart rejoice,
And every fear control,
Since at Thy throne, with suppliant voice,
To Thee I lift my soul.

SEPTEMBER 25

🌿 MORNING 🌿
'What think ye of Christ?'
Matthew 22:42

Beloved, let us inquire what do we think of Jesus this morning? What do we think of His divinity, as one with the Father; of His humanity, as one with us; of His complex person, as God and man in one Christ? What think we of His one sacrifice for sin? What think we of His grace as displayed in the whole work of our redemption? What think we of His Word, as the ground of our hope, the source of our comfort, and the rule of our lives? What think we of His kingdom? What think we of His coming? How do we think of Jesus? Do we think of Him frequently, as of a subject full of pleasure; naturally, as we do of refreshing food; pleasantly, as of choice and delightful music; or, only seldom, and then with gloom, and without love and ardent desire? What does our thinking of Christ produce? Does it produce desire, contrition, love, trust, resolution, prayer, action? What are we willing to suffer for Christ? What are we willing to part with for Christ? What can we cheerfully give to Christ, to feed His poor, or to help His cause?

If ask'd what of Jesus I think,
Though still my best thoughts are but poor,
I say, He's my meat and my drink,
My life, and my strength, and my store.

My Shepherd, my Husband, my Friend,
My Saviour from sin, and from hell;
My hope from beginning to end,
My portion, my Lord, and my all.

🌿 EVENING 🌿
'Submit yourselves to God.'
James 4:7

Human nature does not like submission, and yet there is no happiness without it. It is only as our wills accord with the will of God, as we cheerfully submit to all His dispensations, that we can be peaceful or joyful. Without submission there can be no holiness, for its opposite is rebellion. If I refuse to submit to God, I oppose His authority, question His wisdom, doubt His love, and despise His Word. In proportion as I am sanctified, I shall cheerfully bow to whatever I discover to be the will of God, receive with gratitude whatever comes from the hand of God, and endeavour to do whatever bears the stamp of the authority of God. Without submission, there is no salvation. We must acknowledge His justice; confess our sins; bow at His throne; seek for pardon on the ground of mercy; and acquiesce in His plan of salvation by grace, or we shall never be delivered from the wrath to come. Submit yourselves therefore to God, to be saved by His grace, to be ruled by His Word, to be disposed of by His providence, and to be employed for His glory as He will. Only submit, and you are happy; seek for deep and thorough sanctification, and you will submit; and submitting to God you are safe in life, in death, and for ever.

The Sov'reign Father, good and kind,
Wants but to have His child resign'd;
Wants but thy yielded heart, no more,
Thee with His richest grace to store.

SEPTEMBER 26

❦ MORNING ❦

'Partakers of the heavenly calling.'
HEBREWS 3:1

Beloved, God hath called us by His grace and gospel, into the knowledge of Christ; into the favour of Jesus; to partake of the Spirit of His Son; to enjoy fellowship with Christ; to wear the image of Christ; and to possess and enjoy His righteousness, strength, wisdom, unsearchable riches, and eternal glory. This calling is heavenly in its origin, nature, tendency, and consummation; it is from heaven and to heaven. All believers partake of the same calling; they are called by the same voice, to the same cross and throne, to possess and enjoy the same title, and to claim and use the same blessings. This calling is the greatest honour that can be conferred upon a sinner; it is altogether a favour, the fruit of free and everlasting love; its enjoyment calls for gratitude and praise. Are we called with an heavenly calling? Then we should come out from the world, walk with God, imitate the Saviour, set our affections upon things above, and prepare for, and hasten to, our blessed home, our glorious inheritance. Let us make our calling and our election *sure*, and then sing.

> As Thou wilt, dispose of me,
> Only make me one with Thee;
> Make me in my life express
> All the heights of holiness;
> Sweetly in my spirit prove
> All the depths of humble love.

❦ EVENING ❦

'Prove me now.'
MALACHI 3:10

That is, put my faithfulness and veracity to the test. God hath spoken; will He not make it good? He hath promised; will He not fulfil His Word? Who can doubt it? But if you do He says, *'Prove me.'* How is this to be done? Search His Word and see what He has said. Take His Word to His throne and plead it in prayer. Watch, wait, and work as He has directed; and see if He will not do as He has said. When should we prove Him? Under conviction, and see if He will not pardon sin; in affliction, and see if His grace is not sufficient for us; in perplexity, and see if He will not make darkness light before us, and crooked things straight; in difficulties and peculiar trials, and see if He will not appear for us, and make a way for our escape. When engaged in His service, and see if godliness is not profitable to all things, having a promise of the life which now is, and of that which is to come. Thousands proved Him, and all have found Him true and faithful. Let us prove Him for ourselves; so shall we become strong in faith, and be ready to bear witness whenever we are required, that His Word is true from the beginning. 'O taste and see that the Lord is good; blessed is the man that trusteth in Him.'

> He will not His great self deny,
> A God all truth can never lie;
> As well might He His being quit,
> As break His oath, or Word forget.

SEPTEMBER 27

🌿 MORNING 🌿

'Is the spirit of the Lord straitened?'

MICAH 2:7

Why then do you despond? Why are you satisfied to live so far below your privileges? The Holy Spirit is promised to teach us all things; to testify of Jesus to our hearts; to help our infirmities, to comfort us by taking of the things of Christ, and showing them to us; and to lead us in the way everlasting. Do we experience His love in these particulars? If not, what is the cause? 'Is the spirit of the Lord straitened?' No. But do we sow to the Spirit? Do we pray for the Spirit? Do we expect the Father to give Him, in answer to our prayers; that Jesus will send Him according to His promise? O, beloved, look at your doubts, your fears, your carnality, your coldness, your want of life, love, and power; and now ask, 'Are these his doings?' Is His arm shortened? Is His love changed? Is His Word false? Or, rather, have you not grieved Him, quenched His operations, and caused Him to withhold His hand? O, pray for the Spirit! You are absolutely dependent upon Him, for without Him you can do nothing.

> Come, Holy Ghost, all-quickening fire, │ Still to my soul Thyself reveal;
> My consecrated heart inspire, │ Thy mighty working may I feel,
> Sprinkle with the atoning blood: │ And know that I am one with God.

🌿 EVENING 🌿

'I am married unto you.'

JEREMIAH 3:14

This is the closest connection that can be formed between intelligent creatures. Two become one flesh. And this is the relation which the Lord selects, to represent His connection with His people. He is engaged to them, and they are engaged to Him. His love is fixed upon them, and their love is set upon Him. He has chosen them, and they have chosen Him. He finds pleasure in them, and they find all their happiness in Him. He communicates to them, and they have fellowship with Him. He treats them with confidence, and they make Him the sole object of their trust. He provides all they need, and they are to live in constant dependence upon Him. Christian, do you realize the fact, that the Lord is married unto you; that He is all that to you, that the kindest, wisest, and wealthiest husband can be? Are you walking with God, as His bride? Are you living with God, as one that is married to Him? Do you leave all for Him? Expect all from Him? Aim in all things to please Him? Rejoice, that though every earthly relative and friend may be torn from you, your Husband ever liveth, and will never leave you. Cleave to Him; let nothing draw you from Him, for He is 'married to you.'

> Lord, make me in this union shine,
> That heaven and earth may see,
> In heart, in life, I'm truly Thine,
> And married unto Thee!

SEPTEMBER 28

❦ MORNING ❦

'Be content with such things as ye have.'
Hebrews 13:5

We may not have what we wish, but we certainly have what our God thinks best for us. Every mercy is directed by infinite wisdom and eternal love, and never misses its road, or comes into the possession of any but the persons for whom it is intended. Let us therefore remember, that our God has chosen our inheritance for us, and it becomes us to be content; yea, to be very grateful. We have infinitely more than we deserve; we have more than many of our fellow-believers. We have liberty, while the apostles were shut up in prison; we have a home, while many of the primitive Christians wandered about in dens and caves of the earth; our lives are protected, while the martyrs were burned at the stake; we live in hope of heaven, while many are lifting up their eyes in hell, being in torments. Let us strive to be content with present things, and hope for better. Let us endeavour to learn Paul's lesson, 'I have learned, in whatsoever state I am, therewith to be content. I know both how to be abased, and I know how to abound.' O happy state! O blessed experience! Lord,

> Take my soul and body's powers,
> Take my memory, mind, and will,
> All my goods, and all my hours,
>
> All I know, and all I feel;
> Thine I live, thrice happy I!
> Happier still if Thine I die!

❦ EVENING ❦

'The Lord was with Joseph.'
Genesis 39:21

He has been torn from his father, deprived of his home, sold for a slave, falsely accused, and cast into prison. But the Lord was with him. Many have found the time of greatest trial, the season of peculiar manifestation. When persecuted for righteousness' sake, a special blessing rests upon us. The Lord's presence made up for all the losses he sustained, for that will turn a prison into a palace, a dungeon into a paradise. The Lord was with him to sustain him, to cheer him, to hold communion with him, to give him favour with the keeper, to teach him lessons of the greatest importance, to prepare him to rule over the land of Egypt, to make him an example to all who should suffer for His name, to bring him forth with honour, and crown him with peculiar dignity. Before exalted he must be humbled. The prison was the direct road to the palace. The way of the cross leads to the crown. If we reign with Christ in heaven, we must suffer with Christ on earth. Beloved, wherever duty leads you, or persecution drives you, the Lord will be with you. His presence is more frequently enjoyed when a cloud hangs over our outward circumstances, than when the sun of prosperity shines upon our tabernacle. Precious truth!

> Thy gracious presence, O my God,
> My every wish contains;
> With this beneath affliction's load,
> My heart no more complains.

SEPTEMBER 29

❦ MORNING ❦

'Trust ye in the Lord for ever.'

ISAIAH 26:4

We are often discouraged by the difficulties of the way, and cast down through the weakness of our faith: we look to creatures, instead of looking to the Lord; and reflect upon our weakness, instead of believing His promises, and trusting His faithfulness. But the Lord our God should be the only and the constant object of our trust; His Word warrants us to look to Him for all we need, both temporal and spiritual; and His character assures us that we cannot be disappointed. He will appear for us, and make all His goodness pass before us. If we connect prayer to God with trusting in God, and waiting for God, it is impossible that we should be left in trouble, or be neglected in distress. We may trust Him with the fullest confidence, and expect without doubting all He has promised to bestow. Are you at this time tried, tempted, and distressed? Cast your burden upon the Lord. Commit your way unto Him; He will bring to pass His largest promises and your best desires. Seek out His promises, confide in them, plead them with God, and expect their accomplishment. O trust in the Lord for ever!

> Trust Him, He's faithful to His Word,
> His promise cannot fail;
> He'll never leave you nor forsake,
> Or let your foes prevail;
> Then trust His Word, expect His grace,
> Until you see Him face to face.

❦ EVENING ❦

'And Aaron held his peace.'

LEVITICUS 10:3

He was in deep trouble. His trial was peculiarly great. It was death, the death of two sons at once. It was instantaneous death, in an act of presumptuous sin. It was in the presence of the people, as an example of Jehovah's jealousy and wrath. It was without time for repentance, or any knowledge of their eternal state. But God said, 'I will be glorified.' And Aaron held his peace. This was opposed to murmuring, to fretting, to questioning the right or justice of God, or refusing to be comforted. It was submission to the Lord's will, springing from a knowledge of His righteousness, from supreme love to God, from carnal reason being brought into subjection, from a sense of desert. My friend, this subject speaks to us. It says, 'In your most painful trials, imitate the saint of the Lord.' It reproves all our complainings, and questioning the Lord's love and mercy. It comforts us, by showing us that the greatest saints have sometimes had the greatest trials. It speaks caution, and says, 'Beware how you trifle, or presume, for Jehovah is a jealous God.' 'The Lord is righteous in all His ways, and holy in all His works.' Just and true are His ways.

> In all Thy dealings, Lord, with me,
> O stop the murmuring groan!
> Or let my only answer be,
> 'Father, Thy will be done!'

SEPTEMBER 30

❧ MORNING ☙

'Ye are under grace.'

ROMANS 6:14

Believers are delivered from the law, and are dead to it; they are married to Christ, and are alive unto God as a God of love. The curse is removed, sin is atoned for, and we stand as high in the favour of God as we possibly can. We should look upon ourselves as the favourites of God, His beloved children, whom He hath reconciled to Himself by the death of His Son. Grace reigns over us, rules in us, provides for us, and will glorify us. Why then should we fear? Of whom should we be afraid? Sin is pardoned. The law is magnified. Justice is satisfied. God is at peace with us; yea, He delights in us. The world is overcome for us, and even Satan shall be bruised under our feet shortly. What shall we say to these things? As God is for us, and with us, who shall injure, or prevail against us? All things must work together for good; nothing shall be able to separate us from the love of God; we shall be more than conquerors through Him who loved us; and why? Because we are not under the law, but under grace. Because Jesus lives, we shall live also. Our interests are identified with His.

> On Jesus only I depend,
> He is my Father, God, and Friend,
> My Prophet, King, and Priest;
>
> Had I an angel's holiness,
> I'd cast aside that glorious dress,
> And wrap me up in Christ.

❧ EVENING ☙

'The faithful God.'

DEUTERONOMY 7:9

'A *faithful* man who can find?' But suppose we cannot, we have found a faithful God. One who may be believed, without enquiry; who may be trusted, without fear; to whom we may open our hearts, without reserve. He is faithful, and therefore He corrects our follies, reproves us for our faults, teaches us His will, supports us in our trials, brings us through our troubles, holds our enemies in check, makes darkness light before us, and crooked things straight. Upon every mercy we receive, upon every danger we escape, upon every disappointment we meet, upon every history we read, and upon every cross we carry, we may see written, 'The faithful God.' He is faithful, to maintain the rights of His own Throne, to execute the threatenings of His Word, to fulfil the promises of His grace, to supply the wants of His dependents, to answer the prayers of His people, and to make all things work together for good, to those that love Him, and are called according to His purpose. His faithfulness is seen in expelling Adam from paradise; in destroying the world with the flood; in sending His Son to redeem us; and in giving His Holy Spirit unto us. He is *'the faithful God.'* This is our rock, our refuge, and our rest.

> Cast thy burden on the Lord;
> Plead His promise, trust His Word;
> So shalt thou have cause to bless
> His eternal faithfulness.

OCTOBER 1

🌿 MORNING 🌿

'Your heavenly Father.'
MATTHEW 6:32

When ye pray, say, 'Our Father.' When ye are cast down, remember you have a Father in heaven who loves you, cares for you, has given His Word to you, and is ever ready to do you good. It is truly blessed to begin this month, and every month, believing that we have a Father in heaven; and that 'like as a father pitieth his children, so the LORD pitieth them that fear Him. For He knoweth our frame; He remembereth that we are dust.' Let there be no reserve between us and our heavenly Father, but let us communicate everything to Him; let there be no hard thoughts of our Father encouraged; but let us take His own Word, which sets forth His own immutable mind, and rejoice. Our heavenly Father knoweth what we need, He hath provided all we need, and He will give all He has provided; but He will be acknowledged and sought unto. Nothing is too hard for Him to effect, nothing is too great for Him to produce, nothing is too good for Him to bestow upon His people. What a mercy to have a Father, and such a Father, in this inhospitable world! To Him let us carry, and with Him let us leave all our cares, griefs, and woes.

> Father, on me the grace bestow,
> To call Thee mine while here below,
> To love Thee as Thy law requires;
>
> To this my longing soul aspires:
> May every word and action prove
> My soul is fill'd with heavenly love.

🌿 EVENING 🌿

'We have now received the atonement.'
ROMANS 5:11

The Lord Jesus has made satisfaction to divine justice for our sins. He has done and suffered all that is necessary for our pardon and justification. His sacrifice is our expiation. What He did is presented to us in the gospel. By faith we receive it, rely on it, plead it before God for our acceptance, are accepted on account of it, and enjoy peace. The atonement was made on Calvary: it contains all that God requires, He is satisfied; but it must be received by the sinner, or he cannot enjoy peace. We must daily exercise confidence in it, or we cannot walk happily with God. We have *now* received the atonement; we had not once. We did not feel our need of it. We did not see its value. We did not understand its nature. What a mercy that we do now! The death of Jesus is our life: 'He bore our sins in His own body on the tree'; 'He … put away sin by the sacrifice of Himself'; 'He is our peace.' Let us never lose sight of His atoning sacrifice, or of His justifying righteousness; for if we do, Satan will prevail against us, guilt will soon fill us with gloom, duties will become irksome, and the prospect of death terrible. Nothing can make us bold and happy, but lively faith in the atonement.

> Saviour! may Thy atonement
> Be ever new to us,
> Grant we may every moment
> In spirit view the cross.

OCTOBER 2

🌿 MORNING 🌿

'Who is on the LORD's side?'
Exodus 32:26

Every believer is ready to answer, 'I am.' Well, the Lord has a cause upon the earth; it is weak, and wants your support; it is opposed, and needs your countenance. If you are on the Lord's side, you are on the side of truth, holiness, charity, of His worship and ordinances, of His people and His ways, and you are jealous of His honour. You unite with His people; go forth to Jesus without the camp, bearing His reproach. If you are on the Lord's side, He will spare you as obedient children; supply you as faithful servants; protect you as loyal subjects; and honour you as brave and courageous soldiers. You will never see any just occasion to change sides; or regret that you decided to serve so good a Master. You will find the Lord to be on your side, supporting you in affliction; comforting you in trouble; giving you victory in death; and pronouncing you just in the judgment. If you are on the Lord's side, avow it openly; prove it daily; and let your whole conduct say, *'I am the Lord's.'* Use all your influence for His glory, consecrate all your energies to His cause, and rejoice to suffer for His name.

> There shall your eyes with rapture view
> The glorious Friend who died for you;
> That died to ransom, died to raise
>
> To crowns of joy, and songs of praise:
> Jesus, to Thee I breathe my prayer!
> Reveal, confirm my interest there.

🌿 EVENING 🌿

'We are more than conquerors.'
Romans 8:37

This is marvellous. For the believer has to conflict with all that is depraved in his nature; with all that is opposed to God in the world; with all that is unholy in his family; with many painful and trying dispensations of providence; with Satan his grand adversary; and also with sickness and death. But he overcomes. He triumphs. But it is through Him that loves him – that is, through Jesus. The love of Jesus is his solace, his delight, and his encouragement. The loving Jesus supplies him with grace, strength, and wisdom: and by these he overcomes. He conquers by faith in Christ. He overcomes all by patience, fortitude, and confidence in his Saviour. He overcomes all and appears on the field uninjured. He overcomes and is benefited by the contest. He obtains a great, a signal, a complete victory; and will at length appear possessed of the spoils, and crowned as the conqueror. No one can overcome but by Jesus. But if united to Him, if living by faith upon Him, if copying His example, we shall not only overcome, but be more than conquerors. Believer, expect opposition. Christian, see your dependence: it is on the wisdom, power, care and interference of Jesus. Look to Him as your example, and conquer through His love.

> Conform'd to our Head in outward distress,
> In sorrow and need, in pain and disgrace,
> All happy and glorious we inwardly prove,
> And more than victorious through Jesus' love.

OCTOBER 3

❦ MORNING ❦
'Thou shalt be a blessing.'
GENESIS 12:2

We were by nature cursed of God, and a curse to others; but a God of love interferes for us, pours out His blessing upon us, and makes us a blessing. He gives grace to form the character; gifts to fit for usefulness; wisdom to choose the course; strength to do His will; supplies to complete the design; faith to trust His Word; patience to persevere and wait His time; and success to crown our efforts. The result of His thus blessing us is: we are a blessing to others, to sinners and to saints; we are a blessing by the spirit we breathe, if it is meek, gentle, and lovely; by the example we set, if it is an imitation of Jesus; by our prayers for the good of souls and the glory of God; and by our efforts to spread abroad the knowledge of the truth in every place. What a blessing to be the means of the conversion of but one soul! – to be used to instruct the ignorant, to strengthen the weak, or to comfort the desponding or distressed. O Jesus! make us a blessing. Thy grace is sufficient; fulfil to us Thy promise to Abraham. Beloved, let us look to Him, depend upon Him, act for Him, give praise daily unto Him, and *we shall be a blessing.*

Lord, make me faithful unto death,	Him whom I serve, and whose I am;
Thy witness with my latest breath,	On whom for strength I daily lean,
To tell the glories of the Lamb,	Whose strength is in my weakness seen.

❦ EVENING ❦
'Weak in the faith.'
ROMANS 14:1

This sometimes arises from a defect in our knowledge. Many of the Lord's people have a very imperfect acquaintance with the gospel. They know but little of God's real character, or of the nature and design of the Saviour's work, or of what really constitutes Christian experience. In consequence of this, they are full of fears, and are often harassed with doubts, when if well informed, they would be rejoicing in hope of the glory of God. They think they must *do* something, besides believing in Christ, in order to acceptance with God; or they must *feel* something more than they have done before they are entitled to joy in God. Such do not perceive that they are putting what they *do* or what they *feel* in the place of Christ, or are at least connecting these things with Christ, as if He alone were not sufficient. They are just doing what the Galatians did, who made circumcision necessary to salvation; and to whom Paul said, 'Christ is become of no effect unto you, whosoever of you are justified by the law, ye are fallen from grace.' Beloved, it must be grace alone, or works alone, which must form the ground of our acceptance with God. Let us therefore fix the eye, and place the dependence of our souls upon Christ, and upon Christ alone.

> Blest soul that can say, 'Christ only I seek!'
> Wait for Him alway, be constant though weak;
> The Lord whom thou seekest, will not tarry long,
> And to Him the weakest is dear as the strong.

OCTOBER 4

🌿 MORNING 🌿

'I will do you no hurt.'

JEREMIAH 25:6

How is it possible that a God of love, who is full of compassion, plenteous in mercy, ready to forgive, waiting to be gracious, should do His children hurt? It cannot be. His dealings may cause us pain, but nothing shall by any means harm us. We ought rather to argue with Paul, 'He that spared not His own Son, but delivered Him up for us all, how shall He not with Him also freely give us all things?' He sent His ancient people as captives to Babylon, but it was for their good; He allowed His children to be cast into the fiery furnace, into the lions' den, to be driven out to wander in sheep-skins and goat-skins, but He did not allow them to be hurt; all was sanctified to them, and the curse was turned into a blessing. If He scourge us with one hand, He will support us with the other, and at last we shall come up before His throne, out of great tribulation, having washed our robes and made them white in the blood of the Lamb. Not one who has arrived safe in heaven will say that his God allowed him to be hurt, notwithstanding the trials endured by the way. Nothing shall by any means hurt you.

Lord, I would my all resign,
Gladly lose my will in Thine,
Careless be of things below,
Thee alone content to know;
Simple, innocent, and free,
Seeking all my bliss in Thee.

🌿 EVENING 🌿

'Ye are the salt of the earth.'

MATTHEW 5:13

Sin has rendered it unsavoury, and exposed it to destruction. Only grace and truth can restore it to purity and order. These come by Jesus Christ, and they are retained and diffused by His people. He compares His saints to salt. They season and preserve others. Every Christian is a grain of salt. He should affect and impress all around him. His principles are to be diffused, and his character is to attract and instruct. The earth without the saints would be given up to putrefaction and destruction. Beloved, are you seasoning those around you? Is your conversation always with grace, seasoned with salt, that it may minister grace unto the hearers? Do you diffuse what you possess? Do you possess what you profess? Who is the better for you? Does your influence spread silently and penetrate deeply, like that of salt in nature? Or have you only the form of godliness without the power? If a Christian, you will benefit all with whom you may be brought into contact; you will not live unto yourself, but unto Him that died for you and rose again. If salt is present, it will discover itself; and so will grace. The world needs gracious persons; its present state calls for much salt; may the Lord season us with the salt of His grace.

Now to my Saviour I would live,
To Him who for my ransom died;
Nor would untainted Eden give
Such bliss as blossoms at His side.

OCTOBER 5

🌿 MORNING 🌿
'Only acknowledge thine iniquity.'
Jeremiah 3:13

Will the Lord receive us when we have backslidden from Him, and are desirous of returning to Him? O, yes, He invites, He exhorts, He beseeches us to return. Nor does He prescribe any hard conditions, but He says, *'Only acknowledge thine iniquity.'* He is so ready to forgive, so infinitely gracious in His nature, that if we confess our sins, He is faithful and just to forgive us our sins, and to cleanse us from all unrighteousness. Have we wandered? Have we left our first love? Let us go and return to our first husband, for then it was better with us than now. His bowels yearn over us, His arms are open to receive us, and He waits to fall upon our neck and kiss us. Let us go to His throne, and there confess our sins, crave His pardon, sigh for the enjoyment of His love, and He will restore unto us the joys of His salvation, and establish us with His free Spirit. Let us daily confess our iniquities unto the Lord, and He will pardon our numerous sins. In His favour is life. In His frown is distress and woe. He delighteth in mercy. He will receive us, pardon us, and bless us like a God, for His mercy endureth for ever.

His glorious news dispels my fears,
Makes glad my heart, wipes off my tears,
Displays the riches of His grace,
Inflames my love, and claims my praise.
A pardon'd sinner lives to prove
The height and depth of Jesus' love.

🌿 EVENING 🌿
'Approve things that are excellent.'
Philippians 1:10

Take nothing upon trust, but bring everything to the Word of God, and try it there. Learn to distinguish between the ornamental and the useful; the fundamental and the circumstantial; the beneficial and the hurtful. Try things that differ, and approve the things that are excellent. There are excellent institutions – assist them; excellent gifts – seek for them; excellent doctrines – embrace and hold them fast; excellent duties – perform them; excellent attainments – aspire to them; excellent ordinances – attend to them; excellent scriptures – search them; excellent enjoyments – pray for them. Prove that your eye is clear to discover, and that your heart is sanctified to approve. Endeavour to distinguish between the law and the gospel, between nature and grace, between conviction and conversion, between profession and possession, between graces and their counterfeits, between scriptural doctrines and the opposite errors, and approve the things that are excellent. Hold fast what you procure. Publish to others what you know and enjoy yourself. If you lack wisdom for this, ask it of God, who giveth to all liberally and upbraideth not, and it shall be given you. But ask in faith, nothing wavering.

My gracious Lord, I own Thy right
To every service I can pay,
And call it my supreme delight,
To hear Thy dictates and obey.

OCTOBER 6

🌿 MORNING 🌿

'The righteousness which is of God by faith.'
PHILIPPIANS 3:9

The righteousness here intended is that which God requires in His law; provided by the life and death of His Son; presents to sinners in the everlasting gospel; imputes to every believer, of richest grace; accepts when pleaded at the throne of His grace; and honours with a title to eternal life. This righteousness is by faith; it is the office of faith to receive it; plead it; trust it; rejoice in it; embolden the soul through it; and clothe the soul in it. It is not offered to anything but faith, nor can it be received and enjoyed in any other way. Every unbeliever and self-righteous person rejects it, but every man who is taught of God feels that he needs it; discovers the beauty, glory, and value of it; applies for it with ardent desire and earnest longing; embraces it as one of God's greatest favours; enjoys it as a rich and durable treasure; and dies confidently expecting to be accepted in it and admitted to glory through it. O, may we be found in Jesus, not having on our own righteousness, which is of the law, but the righteousness which is of God by faith! And while we pant for holiness with every breath, and aim at it in every action, may each of us devoutly say:

And even when I feel Thy grace,
And sin seems most subdued,
I'll wrap me in Thy righteousness,
And plunge me in Thy blood.

🌿 EVENING 🌿

'Abide with us.'
LUKE 24:29

The Saviour had accompanied His disciples to Emmaus, He had unfolded the Scriptures, He had endeared Himself to them, He made as if He would leave them, but they entreated Him to remain with them; they said, 'Abide with us, for it is toward evening.' Who ever enjoyed the presence of Christ and did not wish for its continuance? But who, among the Lord's people, has not had to mourn His absence? He is always present as our keeper, but we do not always enjoy His presence. Let us seek it, if we have it not at present; and let us beseech Him to abide with us, if we have. Let us ask Him to dwell with us, and open His Word to us, and kindle the flame of love in our souls, and fill us with admiring gratitude and joy. He desires us to abide with Him, more than we can desire Him to abide with us; and it is still true which was spoken of old, 'The LORD is with you, while ye be with Him; if ye seek Him He will be found of you.' Beloved, have you enjoyed the Saviour's presence today? Can you be happy without doing so? His presence is the sweetness and glory of heaven; and His presence is the balm for all our sorrows, and the antidote for all our miseries on earth. The presence of Jesus will make it a delightful evening.

Jesus, Thy presence I implore,
This blessing now bestow;
With me abide, nor leave me more,
While I remain below.

OCTOBER 7

🌿 MORNING 🌿

'He that loveth me shall be loved of my Father.'
John 14:21

Do we love Jesus? Are we cultivating an acquaintance with Him? If we love Him, we desire to know Him more fully; to serve Him more cheerfully; and to enjoy Him continually. If we love Jesus, we are willing to part with all things for Him, to renounce whatever He forbids, and pursue whatsoever He commands. If we love Him, we want to love Him more, and to be always with Him. If we love Him, He assures us His Father will love us; for He so delights in His beloved Son, that He visits, revives, and blesses every soul that loves Jesus. If God loves us, what good thing will He withhold from us? Will He suffer anyone to hurt us? O, no! He will manifest Himself to us. He will appear for us. He will glorify Himself in us. He will be to us all a God can be, and do for us far above our expectations and hopes. To be the object of the love of God is to enjoy the highest honour, and to possess a title to the greatest happiness which it is possible for rational creatures to enjoy. Let us therefore ascertain beyond a doubt, that we love Jesus, ardently and sincerely.

> *To His meritorious passion*
> *All our happiness we owe;*
> *Pardon, uttermost salvation,*
> *Heaven above and heaven below;*
> *Grace and glory*
> *From that open fountain flow.*

🌿 EVENING 🌿

'I shall come forth as gold.'
Job 23:10

Job was in the furnace. It was heated seven times hotter than it was wont to be. But he was conscious of his integrity. He knew that though he was imperfect, he was sincere. He knew that he had a living Redeemer; that his God knew his heart, his motives, his desires, and his course. Therefore he felt confident that he should not be consumed, but only refined. This is the design of all our trials. They are to make us meet for the Master's use; to make us reflect the Saviour's image; to fit us for eternal glory. However fierce the fire, we shall lose nothing but our dross. Our eternal interests are safe. Our God is immutably the same. This is our security. He says, 'I am the Lord, I change not, therefore ye sons of Jacob are not consumed.' He sits by the furnace as the Refiner, He superintends the whole process of purification, and He removes the fire the moment the design is accomplished. Tried Christian, thy God is refining thee; His design is most loving; He will take care of thee. Let not thy faith flag, or thy courage droop; but say with Job, 'He knoweth the way that I take; when He hath tried me, I shall come forth as gold.' Tried faith is more precious than gold; if God try your faith, it is to improve it and increase it.

> *In fiery trials and distress,*
> *I will Thy promise hold;*
> *Thou wilt my soul in trouble bless,*
> *I shall come forth as gold.*

OCTOBER 8

🌿 MORNING 🌿
'We will remember thy love.'
Song of Solomon 1:4

What subject is so sweet as the love of Jesus? The goodwill of His heart towards us, which He fixed on us sovereignly, immutably, and eternally. Let us remember this love of Jesus, for it is sufficient to fill us with joy, peace, and love. O, how it condescended to look upon us, come and die for us, and now to dwell with us! What benevolence it has and does display, giving everything that is necessary for life and godliness. How it dignifies its objects, raising them to glory, honour, immortality, and eternal life. Let us remember His love, to comfort our hearts amidst changing friendships; to encourage our souls in seasons of darkness; to produce confidence in times of trial; to inspire with fortitude in times of danger; to beget patience when burdened and oppressed; to reconcile the mind under bereaving dispensations; and to produce zeal and devotedness in the Lord's cause and service. O, love of Jesus! be Thou my daily subject and constant theme! Beloved, let us remember His love, if we forget everything beside; there is nothing so sweet, so valuable, so excellent as this! It will profit, please, and sanctify us.

> God only knows the love of God;
> O, that it now were shed abroad
> In this poor stony heart!

> Give me to know this love divine,
> This heavenly portion, Lord, be mine;
> Be mine this better part!

🌿 EVENING 🌿
'They have spoken lies against me.'
Hosea 7:13

'Who has?' The people whom He has redeemed. Awful as the sin is, it is so common, that we may rather ask, 'Who has not?' Spoken lies against God! Yes. When you said that He was unwilling to receive you, because you were such a wretched sinner. When you said that you should perish, though you were clinging to the cross, trusting in His grace, and seeking His mercy. When you exclaimed, 'The LORD hath forsaken me, and my Lord hath forgotten me.' When you said that He would allow you to want, leave you in distress, or turn a deaf ear to your prayer in the time of trouble. When you spoke of Him as the author and cause of your darkness, coldness, and deadness. But time would fail to enumerate the instances in which you have spoken lies against God. Sometimes plainly, and at other times more obscurely, you have said He does not mean what He says: He will not perform His promise; He will not make good His Word – at least, He will not to me. My friend, beware! Your unbelief gives God the lie; your doubts reflect on His veracity; He speaks the truth, and only the truth. 'Why then do you not believe Him?' 'He that believeth not God hath made Him a liar; because he believeth not the record which God gave of His Son.'

> I too have lied against my God,
> With shame and sorrow I confess;
> Pardon my sin through Jesus' blood,
> And give me sanctifying grace.

OCTOBER 9

❦ MORNING ❧

'The poor committeth himself unto thee.'

PSALMS 10:14

Those who appear the most friendless have the best and truest Friend. The Lord's people are poor, but they are not friendless nor forsaken. They have Jehovah for their God, Jesus for their Saviour, and the Holy Spirit for their Comforter and Guide. They know God and commit themselves and their all to Him. But how do they commit themselves to Him? As the debtor does to his surety; as a sick man does to his physician; as the client does to his lawyer or advocate; as the needy does to his rich and generous friend; as a sinner to the Saviour; as the loving bride does to her beloved bridegroom. But why do they commit themselves unto Him? They commit themselves to His grace, to be saved by it; to His power, to be kept by it; to His providence, to be fed by it; to His Word, to be ruled by it; to His care, to be preserved by it; and to His arms at death, to be safely landed in glory. This flows from grace, and produces peace, safety, satisfaction, and success. Let us, beloved, commit ourselves to the Lord daily, heartily, deliberately, and unreservedly.

My soul shall cry to Thee, O Lord,
To Thee, supreme, incarnate Word,
My rock and fortress, shield and Friend,
Creator, Saviour, source, and end;
And Thou wilt hear Thy servant's prayer,
Though death and darkness speak despair.

❦ EVENING ❧

'The hope of Israel.'

JEREMIAH 14:8

The *Author* of Israel's hope: It is begotten by the Spirit, through the promises of His Word. They hope because He has promised, because He is faithful, because His Word is true from the beginning. He is the *object* of Israel's hope: 'Let Israel hope in the LORD, for with the LORD there is mercy, and with Him is plenteous redemption.' They cannot hope in man, for he is poor, or weak, or fickle, or unwilling to help. But they do hope in God, for He is strong to deliver, wealthy to supply, present to help, pledged to befriend, ready to pardon, wise to direct, waiting to be gracious, and He delighteth in mercy. His compassion is a spring that never fails. His love is a sun that never sets. His Word is a paradise that cannot be forfeited. His grace is sufficient for us, and His strength is made perfect in our weakness. The hope of Israel is a rock: let us build upon it. The hope of Israel is a refuge: let us repair to it. The hope of Israel is a fountain: let us seek our supplies from it. The hope of Israel is a Saviour: let us put our trust in Him. The hope of Israel is God: let us therefore worship, adore and believe Him. 'Happy is he that hath the God of Jacob for his help, whose hope is in the Lord his God.'

Hope of Israel, hear my cry,
To Thee from self I flee;
Be Thou in every trial nigh
And I will hope in Thee.

OCTOBER 10

🌿 MORNING 🌿

'Who shall lay any thing to the charge of God's elect?'
ROMANS 8:33

God's elect are sinners; they know it, feel it, and deplore it. The world is against them, and Satan tries every means in his power to ruin them. But, blessed be God, he cannot prevail. The work of the Holy Spirit within them sets and keeps them panting for holiness; striving against sin; aiming at God's glory; and desiring to be a blessing to all around them. The work of Christ for them, brings forth a sentence of justification from the eternal Father; and believing His Word they realise their privilege, and may boldly ask: *'Who shall lay any thing to the charge of God's elect?'* Will God? No, for He is perfectly satisfied through the death of His Son. Will conscience? No, for it is cleansed by the blood of Jesus, silenced by the Word of God, and corroborates Jehovah's testimony. Can Satan? No, for he is cast out, his testimony cannot be received, having long since been proved a liar by the God of truth. Will Jesus as Judge of all? No, for He would rather die for us than condemn us. O beloved, see the perfection of the Saviour's work!

Complete atonement He has made,
And to the utmost farthing paid
Whate'er His people owed;
How then can wrath on me take place,
If shelter'd in His righteousness,
And sprinkled with His blood?

🌿 EVENING 🌿

'Call to remembrance the former days.'
HEBREWS 10:32

It is sometimes very profitable to look back. Reflection upon the past may do us good tonight. Our *land* was once immersed in pagan darkness, superstition, and barbarity; since then it has been under the dominion of papal ignorance, priestcraft, and cruelty. How different its state then to the present! Our *souls* were once the slaves of Satan, under the dominion of sin, and exposed to the curse of God. We were thoughtless, careless, and hardened. We loved our idols, and after them we would go. But God, who is rich in mercy, for His great love wherewith He loved us, even when we were dead in sins, quickened us together with Christ, and saved us by His grace. How delightful were the days of our first love! How precious the Saviour! How sweet the gospel! How delightful the Lord's day! How amiable the tabernacles of God! But our zeal declined, our joys faded, our prospects were overcast, because we wandered from God. We became like the heath in the desert, and we mourned in our complaint and made a noise. But the good Shepherd sought us out, reproved us for our follies, and restored us again. He hath led us and fed us; taught us and sanctified us; and now He bids us call to remembrance the former days.

I muse on the years that are past,
Wherein my defence Thou hast prov'd,
Nor wilt Thou relinquish at last,
A sinner so signally lov'd!

OCTOBER 11

🌿 MORNING 🌿

'Keep yourselves in the love of God.'
JUDE 21

The love of God to His people is free, unspeakably great, and eternal; our love to God is dependent on His love to us as its source, on faith and fellowship with Him as its fuel; therefore we are exhorted to keep ourselves in the love of God. This implies that we are beloved of God, and that we know it, and love Him in return; that we should endeavour to retain our standing, and keep ourselves sensibly in the love of God, by setting it always before our minds; exercising our faith on it; and seeking the enjoyment of it by prayer and in the Lord's ways. We should keep ourselves in the exercise of love to God, by avoiding temptations, walking by faith, and living as in His presence. We should keep ourselves in the exercise of love one to another, by exhortation, forbearance, and example. We should preserve ourselves by the love of God from the temptations of Satan, the snares of the world, and the lusts of the flesh. Beloved, consider how the love of God aggravates our sins; and how it should fire us with courage to oppose everything that is unholy or forbidden.

> *O love divine, how sweet Thou art!*
> *When shall I find my longing heart*
> *All taken up by Thee?*
>
> *Grant me, O gracious Lord, to prove*
> *The sweetness of redeeming love,*
> *The love of Christ to me.*

🌿 EVENING 🌿

'He feedeth among the lilies.'
SONG OF SOLOMON 6:3

Believers are compared to this lovely flower, not as it is in the field, but in the garden. They are all in the Saviour's garden, and He loves and prizes them greatly; He visits and walks among them. He is pleased with their persons: their graces, their prayers, their praises, their testimony, and their obedience. He manifests Himself to them, which they ardently desire, highly prize, and are much benefited by. See what a Christian should be: not a thorn, which wounds every one who comes in contact with it; not a nettle, which stings all who touch it; not a useless weed, which cumbers the ground, or poisons all who taste it. But a lily: one who has a sweet spirit; whose life and conversation is fragrant and inviting; of an ornamental character, who looks well in any situation; a good and useful neighbour, who benefits many, but injures none; of whom Jesus may not be ashamed, but in whom He can find satisfaction and pleasure. He feeds among lilies, or in His church; there you may find Him. True worship is exceedingly pleasant to Him. Invite Him to your heart, your house; expect Him to accept your invitation; aim to entertain Him suitably. He feedeth among lilies.

> *Saviour! mould me by Thy power,*
> *Fill me with Thy grace divine,*
> *Make me like the lily flower,*
> *To Thy praise and glory shine.*

OCTOBER 12

🌿 MORNING 🌿

'Be sure your sin will find you out.'
NUMBERS 32:23

Sin cannot be concealed; it meets the eye and affects the heart of God; and unless we find it out, confess it with sorrow, and forsake it with disgust, it will find us out, and expose us to the rod of God, and the contempt of godly men. It found Achan out, and proved his ruin; it found Noah out, and covered him with disgrace; and it found David out, so that the sword never departed from his house. God cannot be reconciled to sin; nor should we be. However secret the sin, God is a witness; and He will bring it to light. *'He that covereth his sin shall not prosper; but he that confesseth and forsaketh his sins shall find mercy.'* Let us be careful that we give sin no quarter, or vainly fancy that because God loves us He will not expose us; He assures us *our sin will find us out*. O, to hate sin as God hates it, to loathe it as Jesus loathed it, and to become dead to it, and be entirely delivered from it! It is the source of all our miseries, the cause of all our pains, and the occasion of all our troubles. It cannot be hid, it will find us out, and sorely wound us.

O God, our sins have found us out,
And melted us with grief!
Before Thy throne ourselves we cast,
And supplicate relief;
To Jesus' feet we now repair,
And seek, and find salvation there.

🌿 EVENING 🌿

'I am the light of the world.'
JOHN 8:12

The world without Christ is in a state of darkness: In the darkness of ignorance, crime, cruelty, and degradation. The Jews had a candlestick with its seven lamps, but it was confined to their tabernacle or temple. But Jesus is come a luminary into the world, a light to enlighten the Gentiles, and the glory of His people Israel. He is the source of knowledge, comfort, beauty or holiness, and safety. In Him there is a fulness of light. Like the light of the sun it is free, and it abideth for ever. He shines on the world by His Word; He shines into the heart by His Spirit. His light attracts sinners to His feet, and in His light they see light. They are by Him delivered from moral darkness, or guilt; from mental darkness, or ignorance; from legal darkness, or the yoke of the law; from spiritual darkness, or the hiding of the Lord's countenance; and from eternal darkness, or banishment from God for ever. Following Him they have the living light, by which they discover their path; escape the snares of the fowler; enjoy the scenery; discern the object; and rejoice in their privileges. Reader, are you enlightened by Jesus? Do you walk in His light? Are you directing others to do it? If you are dark, go to Him for light. Seek and obtain it.

Light of my soul! Thyself reveal;
Thy power and presence let me feel;
And know, and see the wondrous things
Concealed from prophets, priests, and kings.

OCTOBER 13

❦ MORNING ❧

'Return, ye backsliding children.'
JEREMIAH 3:22

We are prone to wander, and are daily going astray; our God may justly cast us off, but He lovingly invites us to return. He bids us take words and come to Him, and gives us every encouragement to hasten to His feet. We are *children*, though backsliding; and it is our *Father* who bids us return. Beloved, let us return to our God this morning, let us confess our sin, deplore our folly, crave His pardon, plead His Word, hope in His mercy, and expect the token of reconciliation and love. What an unspeakable mercy to have such a Father! So ready to forgive! So willing to receive! So desirous that we should be happy and blest! His love is wonderful, His forbearance beyond description. See His arms extended; hear His Word inviting; and hasten to be blest. Do not dwell on your miseries, or your wretchedness – they are the effects of your backsliding; but He says, 'I will heal your backslidings.' 'Come, and let us return unto the LORD; for he hath torn, and will heal us; he hath smitten, and he will bind us up.' His heart is grieved for us, His Word invites us, and His love will make us happy.

> Father of mercies, God of love!
> O! hear a humble suppliant's cry!
> Bend from Thy lofty seat above,
> Thy throne of glorious majesty;
> O, deign to listen to my voice,
> And bid this drooping heart rejoice.

❦ EVENING ❧

'O LORD, revive thy work.'
HABAKKUK 3:2

No one can revive the Lord's work but Himself. He began it. He must carry it on. He will complete it. But He does so by means; and one of the means He employs is prayer. He convinces us that we need a revival. He stirs us up to seek it. He makes us sensible of our insufficiency. He may perhaps keep us waiting at His throne for a time. The delay may cause us pain, and perplexity. If sanctified, it will make us more earnest for the blessing; and then we shall cry out with one of old, *'Wilt thou not revive us again, that thy people may rejoice in thee.'* When the Lord revives His work, He strengthens our faith, invigorates our hope, inflames our love, deepens our humility, animates our zeal, and stirs us up to seek the promotion of His cause. Then prayer becomes pleasant, praise sweet, ordinances profitable, the Sabbath a delight, and the sanctuary amiable. The church resembles a lovely garden, in which we walk with peculiar satisfaction; the gospel is a feast, most suitable and costly; and we look forward to heaven as to our country and our home. The Lord revives His work in us by His Spirit, by His providence, and by His holy ordinances. His power is unlimited. His grace is omnipotent. His mercy is free. Let nothing satisfy us but a revival.

> O! for His all-reviving grace,
> The quickening power divine,
> The deadness from my soul to chase,
> That I may rise and shine.

OCTOBER 14

🍂 MORNING 🍂
'I will restore health unto thee.'
JEREMIAH 30:17

Jesus is a skilful Physician. He heals all the falls, bruises, and dislocations of His people. He brings health to the heart. Believer, is thy heart hard, wandering, unbelieving, or wounded? Jesus can heal it, and to you He says, *'Come and be healed.'* He restores the fainting, the dying and the dead. He is the perfect master of every disease. His terms are *'No money: no price!'* But He will have an absolute surrender to Him: you must refuse all other medicines; and take all He prescribes, bitter or sweet. Touch; trust; and be happy. Jesus is *Jehovah Rophi*; therefore look for health to no other. Lodge in His neighbourhood. Consult Him daily. Lay open your whole case to Him. Never despond until His nature changes, His skill fails, or His advertisement is withdrawn from the book of God. Be grateful for healing, and show your gratitude by endeavouring to send others to Him. Recommend this gracious Physician. Trust Him and remember His question, 'Were there not ten cleansed, *but where are the nine?* They are not found that return to give glory to God, save this stranger.' Beloved, come to Jesus and be healed; and be sure you render again according to the mercy shown you.

> *Saviour, I wait Thy healing hand!*
> *Diseases fly at Thy command;*
> *Now let Thy sovereign touch impart,*
> *Life, health, and vigour to my heart.*

🍂 EVENING 🍂
'It is finished.'
JOHN 19:30

What was finished? The prophecies and predictions, which referred to His humiliations, sufferings, and death. The object and design of the ceremonial law. The sufferings of Christ were finished. His work below was finished. The debts of His people were paid. The price of their redemption was found. The righteousness by which they are to be justified was wrought out. All the demands of the law were met. The rights of justice were acknowledged and rendered. Satan was defeated and spoiled. Sin was for ever put away. The curse had been endured and was now removed. The flock was purchased by the Shepherd's blood. The foundation of peace, joy, and everlasting salvation was laid. The fountain to cleanse from all sin was opened. The grand plea of our interceding High Priest was provided. Death was abolished, and everlasting life was about to burst upon our world in all its glory. In a word, the Saviour had finished the work which the Father gave Him to do: He had redeemed His pledge, which He gave in the covenant of peace; He had ransomed His beloved bride; He had harmonized all the divine perfections in man's salvation; He had glorified the Father on earth; and manifested His name unto His chosen followers.

> *'Tis finished, the Messiah dies*
> *For sins, but not His own;*
> *The great redemption is complete,*
> *And Satan's power o'erthrown.*

OCTOBER 15

🌿 MORNING 🌿

'And he marvelled because of their unbelief.'
MARK 6:6

Unbelief is represented as filling Jesus with surprise; and is it any wonder, especially our unbelief? Consider what God hath done to remove doubt. He hath sent His character, 'God is love.' He hath made a proclamation, 'Behold, now is the accepted time; behold, now is the day of salvation.' He hath given an invitation, 'Look unto me, and be ye saved.' He hath employed entreaty, 'As though God did beseech you by us, we pray you in Christ's stead, be ye reconciled to God.' He hath issued a command, 'This is His commandment, that we should believe on the name of His Son Jesus Christ.' He hath sworn an oath, 'That by two immutable things in which it was impossible for God to lie, we might have strong consolation.' He hath given His Son as a pledge, to assure us that 'whosoever believeth in Him shall not perish, but have eternal life.' He hath added the testimony of all His saints. Well then may He marvel at our unbelief. Never let us attempt to excuse it, but let us plead and pray against it, until we conquer it.

O Lord, fulfil in me Thy Word,
Now let me feel Thy pardoning blood,
Let what I ask be given;

The bar of unbelief remove,
Open the door of faith and love,
And take me into heaven.

🌿 EVENING 🌿

'Let not your hearts faint.'
DEUTERONOMY 20:3

Remember the promise, 'As thy days, so shall thy strength be.' Prove the Saviour's testimony, 'My grace is sufficient for thee.' Accept the divine invitation, 'Call upon me in the day of trouble, I will deliver thee, and thou shalt glorify me.' Attend to the inspired direction, 'Cast thy burden upon the LORD, and he shall sustain thee; he shall never suffer the righteous to be moved.' Imitate the deeply tried psalmist, 'I had fainted, unless I had believed to see the goodness of the LORD in the land of the living.' Rest thy troubled spirit on the conduct of thy God, 'He giveth power to the faint, and to them that hath no might He increaseth strength.' Endeavour to carry out the apostolic exhortation, 'Be strong in the grace that is in Christ Jesus.' Let not your heart faint, for your sins are pardoned, your foes are all doomed, your mansion is being prepared, supplies will certainly be sent, your Saviour deeply sympathizes with you, your heavenly Father cares for you, and all things must work together for your good. Fear not, only believe. Wait on the Lord, and He shall save thee. Call upon God, and He will show thee great and mighty things that thou knowest not. 'Let not your heart faint.'

Every day the truth I prove,
Of Jesus my almighty Friend,
Kept by Him, whose constant love,
Shall keep me to the end.

OCTOBER 16

🌿 MORNING 🌿

'The LORD shall be thy confidence.'
PROVERBS 3:26

Our happiness consists in knowing God and believing Him; if we know His true character, we can believe His precious Word; and if we believe His holy Word, we enjoy peace and sacred satisfaction. He presents Himself to us in His Word, as able and willing to make us holy, happy, and honourable. To Him we may communicate all that troubles us; from Him we may receive all that our circumstances require; with Him we may walk and enjoy peace. We may be confident in God, for He has power, love, and faithfulness; He has spoken to us, will appear for us, and will never turn away from us; but will rejoice over us to do us good, with His whole heart and with His whole soul. Let us make Him our confidence, by believing His Word, frequenting His throne, and seeking His glory in all things. Are you troubled, fearful, and cast down? Acquaint now thyself with Him and be at peace; thereby shall good come unto thee. They that trust in the Lord shall be as mount Zion, which cannot be removed, but abideth for ever. Let us hold fast the confidence which we had at the beginning.

> *Thou, Lord, on whom I still depend,*
> *Wilt keep me faithful to the end:*
> *I trust Thy truth, and love, and power,*
> *Shall save me to the latest hour;*
> *And when I lay this body down,*
> *Bestow a bright immortal crown.*

🌿 EVENING 🌿

'Zealous of good works.'
TITUS 2:14

Being saved by free grace, we should lay ourselves out for God's glory. We are created anew in Christ Jesus unto good works. We should be active in God's cause for His creatures' good, not only doing good works, but being zealous for them; zealously doing them ourselves, and zealously encouraging them in others. We cannot do too much for Him, who has done so much for us. Our works should proceed from love to God, be regulated by the command of God, and be done for the glory of God. We cannot be too zealous in performing them, but we ought to be equally zealous in renouncing them as a ground of acceptance with God. Good works are the works of a child, who aims to please his Father: they are performed from a sense of what God has done for us, not in order to induce Him to confer blessings upon us. In working from a right motive we are happy, for working we shall be by and by rewarded: but though like Moses, we may have respect unto the recompense of the reward; yet like Paul, when we do more than others, we shall heartily exclaim, 'Not I, but the grace of God that was with me.' Free grace enjoyed in the soul will make all who enjoy it zealous of good works. Love is sure to be active.

> *What is my being but for Thee,*
> *Its sure support, its noblest end,*
> *Thy ever-smiling face to see,*
> *And serve the cause of such a friend.*

OCTOBER 17

🌿 MORNING 🌿

'My strength is made perfect in weakness.'
2 CORINTHIANS 12:9

The more the believer feels his weakness, the more should he expect his Saviour to appear for and strengthen him. The strength of Jesus is imparted, enjoyed, and displayed in our sorest trials and most distressing seasons. Never was Abraham so strong, as when offering up his beloved Isaac upon the mount; never were the martyrs so courageous, as when in prison they felt their entire weakness, cried to Jesus for strength, and depending on His faithfulness and love, left all and went to the stake. Then they could exclaim, 'None but Christ. None but Christ.' 'Farewell life, welcome the cross of Christ.' Beloved, let us walk by faith, not by feeling; when we feel weakest, the strength of Jesus is nearest, and He magnifies His mercy by giving power to the faint, and increasing the strength of the weak. Let us depend on Him, for we can do all things through Christ who strengtheneth us. He is our strength, a very present help in trouble. The Lord is our strength and song, He also is become our salvation. Strengthen, O Lord, that which Thou has wrought in us.

> Saviour, on earth, I covet not,
> That every woe should cease.
> Only, if trouble be my lot,
>
> In Thee let me have peace.
> Thy grace and strength display in me,
> Till I arrive at perfect day.

🌿 EVENING 🌿

'The chastening of the Almighty.'
JOB 5:17

Crosses are not curses. Frowns are sometimes favours. Every child is chastened – chastened by the Almighty. His chastisements are always wise. He never corrects but for faults, though His dispensations are sometimes intended to draw out our graces, and improve our principles. If the Lord chasten us, it is because He loves us. Let us not then mistake the character of our afflictions. They are really mercies. They are to do us good. They are indispensable, unless our wise and gracious Father would allow us to be injured. Let us therefore ask, 'Why am I corrected?' Let us prostrate ourselves before our Father's throne, and while we acknowledge His wisdom in the discipline, beseech Him to make His chastisement a blessing. The Lord's rod often blossoms and bears fruit. Better be a chastened child, than a pampered menial. Our present discipline is to prepare us for future duties, enjoyments, and glories. It is all right. It is really kind. It is for our good. The rod is not in a stranger's hand; we are not suffering from the stroke of a cruel one, but from the chastening of the Almighty. 'Now no chastening for the present seemeth to be joyous, but grievous: nevertheless afterward it yieldeth the peaceable fruits of righteousness unto them which are exercised thereby.'

> O Father of mercies on me,
> In deepest affliction bestow,
> A power of applying to Thee,
> A sanctified use of my woe.

OCTOBER 18

🌿 MORNING 🌿
'I will look unto the LORD.'
Micah 7:7

Looking to creatures always ends in disappointment; therefore it is forbidden by Him who loves us best, and consults our best interests at all times. The prophet had been weaned from this, by many and sore trials; and now he determines to look unto the Lord. Let us imitate his example. We cannot do better than look to the Lord, as our Captain, to command; as our Master, to direct; as our Father, to provide; and as our God, to defend. His name is a strong tower; the righteous run into it and are safe. Looking to Jesus will preserve us from a thousand snares; and prepare us to suffer as Christians and triumph as conquerors. The eyes of the Lord are always upon us; may our eyes be ever towards the Lord. Let us look to Him for all we need; from all we fear; through all that obstructs our progress; and so press on towards the mark for the prize of the high calling, which is of God in Christ Jesus. He says, 'Look unto me and be ye saved.' It is recorded, 'They looked unto Him and were lightened, and their faces were not ashamed.' Jesus is the same, yesterday, today, and for ever.

Lord, shine on my benighted heart,
With beams of mercy shine;
And let Thy Spirit's voice impart

A taste of joys divine:
To Thee I look, to Thee I cry,
O, bring Thy sweet salvation nigh.

🌿 EVENING 🌿
'LORD, be thou my helper.'
Psalm 30:10

Sweet and appropriate prayer this! We daily need help. The Lord *can* help us. He has said, 'Fear not, I *will* help thee.' But promises should be turned into prayers: and we never pray so spiritually as when we can say, 'LORD, ... do as thou hast said.' 'Be it unto me according to thy word.' Let us then earnestly cry unto our God this night, 'LORD, be thou my helper.' I see many fall, I shall fall too except Thou hold me up. I am weak. I am exposed to temptation. My heart is deceitful. My enemies are strong. I cannot trust in man. I dare not trust in myself. The grace I have received, will not keep me without Thee. 'LORD, be thou my helper' – in every duty; in every conflict; in every trial; in every effort to promote the Lord's cause; in every season of prosperity. Every hour we live, this short and inspired prayer is suitable. May it flow from our hearts, be often on our lips, and be answered in our experience. For if the Lord help us, there is no duty which we cannot perform; there is no foe which we cannot overcome; there is no difficulty which we cannot surmount. All things are possible; difficult things are easy; and painful things will be pleasant. 'The Lord is my helper, therefore I will not fear.'

Weak and inconsistent, Lord, I am,
On Thee alone can I depend;
0 let me not be put to shame,
But be my helper and my friend.

OCTOBER 19

🌿 MORNING 🌿

'I will call upon thee, for thou wilt answer me.'

Psalm 86:7

Such was David's purpose, and such his assurance; and we have the same warrant for confidence as he had. Our God will answer prayer. Let us inquire what is necessary, in order to the assurance that our God will answer us. We must *really mean* what we say when we pray. We must pray for a definite object. We must pray in accordance with the will of God, as revealed in His promises and precepts. We must pray in submission to the will of God, as to the time when, and the means by which He will answer us. We must heartily desire what we pray for. Our motives must be pure, as that God may be glorified, sin subdued, and Jesus exalted. We must pray with importunity and perseverance. We must offer all our prayers in the name of Jesus, and expect them to be accepted and honoured only for His sake. There must be no sin indulged; for if we indulge iniquity in our hearts, *God will not hear our prayer.* We must pray in faith, believing that God is, and that He is the rewarder of all them who diligently seek Him. Thus call, and God will answer you.

> Lord, on me Thy Spirit pour,
> Turn the stony heart to flesh;
> And begin from this good hour,
>
> To revive Thy work afresh.
> Lord, revive me!
> All my help must come from Thee.

🌿 EVENING 🌿

'His compassions fail not.'

Lamentations 3:22

This is an unspeakable mercy. The sympathy of friends may fail. The affection of relations may fail. The tender mother's love to her babe may fail. But the compassion of our God is unfailing. It is an ocean which we can never exhaust; a sun which will never set. It may be obscured. We may not enjoy its communications. But it is as full of light and glory as ever. Believer, thy God never was more compassionate than He is this night. His love was never more tender. His grace was never more free. His promise was never more true in reference even to His most favoured ones, than it is in reference to thee at this time. Turn from thy broken cisterns, from thy withered gourds, from thy dried brooks; turn from thy gloomy feelings, from thy painful circumstances; and turn to thy God, impressed with this fact, *'His compassions fail not.'* Did Jesus have compassion on the multitudes which followed Him, because they had nothing to eat; He will also have compassion on thee. He will bear with thy infirmities, He will pardon thy sins, He will sanctify thy sorrows, He will soothe thy griefs, He will restore thy soul, He will guide thee with His counsel, and afterwards receive thee to glory, for His compassions fail not.

> Though annoyed by doubts and fears,
> Though distressed by various cares,
> Though determined foes assail,
> Thy compassions never fail.

OCTOBER 20

🌿 MORNING 🌿

'Behold, thy salvation cometh.'
ISAIAH 62:11

The Lord's people may be now sorely tried and often cast down; but the present is the worst state they will ever be in; they are hastening to the day of God, which is to them the day of deliverance. Their salvation is on the road; they will soon be freed from all disease, from which they now suffer; from all sin, under which they now groan; from all foes, of whom they are now afraid; and from all cares and troubles, with which they are now burdened. Beloved, why are you so fearful, and why do desponding thoughts arise in your hearts? Behold, your salvation cometh; behold, His reward is with Him, and His work before Him. He will free you from all that pains you, and raise you above all you fear. The time of deliverance is at hand, the year of release is near; the trumpet of the Jubilee will soon be heard; our Saviour will arrive to lead us to our Father's house, to the mansions which He hath prepared for us, and so shall we be ever with the Lord. Comfort one another with these words, 'Behold, the bridegroom cometh; go ye out to meet him!' O to be ready for His coming, and to share in His glorious triumphs!

Jesus beckons from on high; | *Thine the righteousness of God!*
Fearless to His presence fly; | *Go, His triumphs to adorn,*
Thine the merit of His blood; | *Made for God, to God return!*

🌿 EVENING 🌿

'Is there anything too hard for me?'
JEREMIAH 32:27

Difficulties are for creatures; there can be nothing difficult to God. His wisdom is infinite. His power is omnipotent. His resources are boundless. His instruments are innumerable. His plan is formed, and He is working it out. 'He worketh all things after the counsel of His own will.' We are sometimes placed in very trying circumstances, creatures cannot help us, our faith falters, our minds are agitated, our spirits droop, we give way to fear, but the Lord reproves us and asks, 'Is anything too hard for me?' Bring the matter to Me, exercise faith in My Word, place yourself in My hand, wait upon Me in My way. 'I will work, and who shall let it?' Beloved, your inward evils, and outward trials, may be too hard for you; but they cannot be too hard for your God. He can subdue the one, and deliver you from the other, with the greatest ease; and His strength is made perfect in weakness. Let this demand then, silence our fears, strengthen our faith, revive our hope, increase our courage, animate our prayers; and let us go forward, saying, 'Nothing is too hard for the Lord.' Look from your own weakness to His strength, from your trials to His delivering mercy.

Nothing too hard can be
For my Almighty Lord;
Sufficient is Thy grace for me,
Who hang upon Thy Word.

OCTOBER 21

🌿 MORNING 🌿

'Thou shalt guide me with thy counsel.'
PSALM 73:24

This supposes a knowledge of the Lord as infinitely gracious, inflexibly just, inconceivably wise, and immutably faithful; except we know Him, we cannot trust Him. But here is an entire surrender to Him, to be led where He pleases, as He chooses, and by whom He will. This surrender is becoming, prudent, gainful; for godliness with such contentment is great gain. Such a surrender is the effect of faith in the Lord's promise, gracious presence, and covenant character; it exhibits expectation from the Lord. Whom the Lord guides He protects, He preserves, He supplies, and receives. He receives them now at the throne of grace, to be His charge and His care; and He will receive them at the throne of His glory, and introduce them to holiness, happiness, and honour. Beloved, have you thus surrendered? Are you daily surrendering? Can you say to your gracious God, 'Thou shalt guide me with thy counsel, and afterwards receive me to glory?' If so, happy are ye; the Spirit of glory and of God will rest upon you. The Lord is a wise, patient, infallible Guide.

Thy Word, O Lord, is light and food,
The law of truth, and source of good;
O, let it richly dwell within,
To keep me from the snares of sin;
And guide me still to choose my way
That I no more may go astray.

🌿 EVENING 🌿

'We are the Lord's.'
ROMANS 14:8

The Lord hath a people peculiarly His own. They are distinct from all others. They are preferred to all others, being the objects of His choice, the purchase of His blood, the temple of His Holy Spirit. He loves them with an everlasting love. He calls them His portion. He treats them as children. He prizes them as His peculiar treasure. He is united to them, loves them, and cares for them as His bride. He keeps them as the apple of His eye. This privilege Paul claimed for himself and his fellow-believers; and if we are Christians we can claim it too. 'We are the Lord's,' and we *know* it, for we have been quickened by the Holy Spirit, we have been received and acknowledged at the Lord's throne, and we are consecrated to His service and praise. 'We are the Lord's,' and we *prove* it, for we are united to His family, we are walking by His Word, we are living to His glory, and we can only be satisfied with His presence and His love. Beloved, let us rejoice in our privilege; it is great and glorious. Let us cleave to His saints; they are the excellent of the earth. Let us carefully observe His Word, believing its doctrines, trusting its promises, and keeping its commands. Let us realize in difficulty and danger the glorious fact, '*I am the Lord's.*'

Lord, I am Thine, entirely Thine;
Purchas'd and sav'd by blood divine;
My person claim, my soul possess,
And sanctify me by Thy grace.

OCTOBER 22

🌿 MORNING 🌿

'After He had patiently endured He obtained the promise.'
HEBREWS 6:15

Abraham was long tried, but he was richly rewarded. The Lord tried him by delaying to fulfil His promise; Satan tried him by temptations; men tried him by jealousy, distrust, and opposition; Hagar tried him by contemning her mistress; and Sarah tried him by her peevishness. But he patiently endured. He did not question God's veracity, nor limit His power, nor doubt His faithfulness, nor grieve His love; but he bowed to divine sovereignty, submitted to infinite wisdom, and was silent under delays, waiting the Lord's time. And so, having patiently endured, he obtained the promise. God's promises cannot fail of their accomplishment. Patient waiters cannot be disappointed. Believing expectations shall be realized. Beloved, Abraham's conduct condemns a hasty spirit, reproves a murmuring one, commends a patient one, and encourages quiet submission to God's will and way. Remember, Abraham was tried; he patiently waited; he received the promise and was satisfied; imitate his example, and you will share the same blessing.

All anxious cares I fain would leave,
And learn with sweet content to live
On what the Lord shall send;

Whate'er He sends, He sends in love,
And good or bad things blessings prove,
If blessed by this dear Friend.

🌿 EVENING 🌿

'I abhor myself.'
JOB 42:6

The more clearly the Lord manifests Himself to us, and the more He works in us by His Spirit, the deeper will be our humility and self-abhorrence. Self-admirers are strangers to close and holy fellowship with God. Nothing discovers to us the true state of human nature like nearness to God. Men may speculate, and reason, and boast of what man can do, so long as they are at a distance from God; but no sooner do they come into His presence, than their comeliness is turned into corruption. They not only see that they are vile, but they feel it. Job had boasted, and contended with God; but as soon as ever God came near to him, his views and feelings underwent an entire change, and he cried out, 'I have heard of thee by the hearing of the ear, but now mine eye seeth thee: wherefore *I abhor myself* and repent in dust and ashes.' We cannot think too meanly of ourselves as sinners, or feel too deeply on account of the baseness of our nature; except we allow our feelings to lead us to doubt either the ability or willingness of Jesus to save us, or to question our interest in our Father's love. Never does grace appear so glorious, or Christ so precious, as when we sink before God in self-loathing and self-abhorrence.

Appear, great God, appear to me,
That by myself abhorr'd,
Asham'd I may for ever be
Before my gracious Lord.

OCTOBER 23

🌿 MORNING 🌿

'We should walk in newness of life.'
ROMANS 6:4

All who profess Christ are supposed to possess a new nature; they are brought under new obligations; and are expected to keep new objects in view. Being baptized into the death of Christ, and participating in His resurrection, they should walk as influenced by new principles; the free grace, holy truth, and divine power of God, should lead them to newness of life. They should walk by new rules, no longer following custom, or imitating the world; they should walk according to God's Word, the Saviour's golden rule, and bright example. The love of God, gratitude to God, and zeal for His glory, should be the motives from which they act; while to honour God, to enjoy His presence, to exalt Jesus, to benefit others, to prove the power and purity of their principles, to justify their profession, and to evidence their faith and love, should be the ends they have constantly in view. A new life is expected from new creatures; and without it our religion is vain, and our profession a falsehood. Beloved, do we walk in newness of life? If not, we are yet in our sins; we are dead before God.

Jesus, my life! Thyself apply,
Thy Holy Spirit breathe;
My vile affections crucify,
Conform me to Thy death.
Teach me to keep the heavenly path,
And conquer sin and hell by faith.

🌿 EVENING 🌿

'The power of the Holy Ghost.'
ROMANS 15:13

The Holy Spirit is a divine person, equal with the Father and the Son, in power, majesty, and glory. Without His agency, salvation is impossible. He quickens us when dead in trespasses and sins. He teaches us when ignorant and bewildered. He sanctifies us when polluted and depraved. He comforts us when depressed and cast down. He helps us in prayer, against temptation, and out of many difficulties. His power produces our graces, quickens them when dull, and keeps them alive. He witnesses to our adoption, and seals us unto the day of redemption. We are His workmanship and His temple. He is our teacher, comforter, and inward intercessor. His power alone can make the gospel effectual, subdue the corruptions of our hearts, and conform us to the likeness of the Lord Jesus. Our obligation to Him is great, our dependence upon Him constant, and our love to Him should be fervent. He convinces us of sin, unfolds to us the glories of Jesus, works faith in our hearts, leads us to the fountain of His blood, clothes us in His perfect righteousness, unites us to His person, and teaches us to live upon Him. The great thing we want in the church, and in our hearts, is to experience *'the power of the Spirit of God.'*

Come, Holy Ghost, Thy power display,
Thy working let me prove;
Chase darkness, doubt, and fear away,
And fill my soul with love.

OCTOBER 24

🌿 MORNING 🌿

'I am Jesus.'

ACTS 9:5

Immanuel presents Himself this morning, and tells us He is exactly suited to us, whatever may be our circumstances or feelings; He says, 'I AM JESUS.' Are you seeking the Lord? He is Jesus, the gracious, powerful, tender-hearted, ready and willing *Saviour*. Are you tried, troubled, and cast down? He is Jesus, the constant, sympathizing, present, wise and unchangeable *Friend*. Are you a returning backslider, filled with your own ways? He is Jesus, and He says, 'I will receive you; I will heal you; I will restore you; I will rejoice over you, as the shepherd over the sheep he had lost.' Beloved, Jesus is the Lord our God, our all in all; our God is Jesus the Saviour, merciful, kind, and tender; this proclamation is cheering to the sinner, and delightful to the saint. Let us remember, whoever may change, whatever may change, He is Jesus still; still touched with the feeling of our infirmities; still able and willing to help us; still full of compassion and plenteous in mercy unto all that call upon Him; still ready to forgive, waiting to be gracious, full of pity, and pledged to receive us.

> When darkness veils His lovely face,
> I rest on His unchanging grace;
> In every high and stormy gale,
> My anchor holds within the veil;
> On Christ the solid Rock I stand,
> All other ground is sinking sand.

🌿 EVENING 🌿

'What is good for man in this life?'

ECCLESIASTES 6:12

This is a very difficult question, if we refer it to temporal things; and providence alone can furnish the answer. Sometimes prosperity is good, and sometimes adversity; sometimes sickness, and sometimes health; sometimes pain, and sometimes ease; sometimes success, and sometimes disappointment; sometimes plenty, and sometimes poverty. If we set our hearts strongly upon anything below, that is the thing that is not likely to be good for us. If God deny us, or take any thing from us, we may be sure at once that that is not good for us. What we have is good for us, if we rightly use it, and improve it for the Lord's glory. Beloved, have you been looking a few steps above you, and thinking what a good thing it would be for me, if I could obtain that situation? If so, you are wrong. Resignation to God's will, and acquiescence in God's plan, are far better than wishing for this, or longing for that. It is good for a man, daily to live by faith on Jesus, to walk with God, to lay up for himself treasure in heaven, and to endeavour to benefit all around him: but what is good for man in a temporal point of view is not for us to say. Prosperity is often dangerous, and adversity safe.

> 'Tis God appoints my earthly lot,
> And He does all things well;
> I soon shall leave this trying spot
> And rise with Him to dwell.

OCTOBER 25

🌿 MORNING 🌿

'In every thing give thanks.'

1 THESSALONIANS 5:18

Every thing we enjoy should be viewed as coming from the liberal hand of God: all was forfeited by sin; what we receive is of grace. The providence that supplies us is the wisdom, benevolence, and power of God in operation for us, as expressive of His infinite love and unmerited grace. Talents to provide supplies, opportunities to obtain, and ability to enjoy, are alike from the Lord. Every mercy increases our obligation and deepens our debt. Thanksgiving is the ordinance that God has appointed, that we may express our gratitude, and acknowledge our obligation; and our thanksgivings are acceptable and well-pleasing in His sight. Thanksgiving is never out of season, for we have always much to be thankful for. In everything, we should give thanks; to that end view that all things be as arranged by His wisdom, pendant on His will, sanctified by His blessing, according with His promises, and flowing from His love. All our blessings come through Jesus, and all our praises must ascend through Him, for our Father only accepts what is presented in the name of His beloved Son. Thank God, take courage, and press forward.

> Praise Him who by His Word
> Supplies our every need,
> And gives us Christ the Lord,
> Our hungry souls to feed:
> Thanks be to God for every good,
> Eternal thanks for Jesus' blood.

🌿 EVENING 🌿

'He is altogether lovely.'

SONG OF SOLOMON 5:16

This is the opinion formed of Jesus by all who really know Him. There is nothing lovely but it is in Jesus, and it is in Him in full perfection. He is the object of admiration and adoration to all who are taught by the Holy Spirit. His person as God-man is altogether lovely: for He possesses every grace that can adorn humanity, and all the glories of uncreated deity. His character is altogether lovely, for He is infinitely wise, dignified, condescending, and kind. Indeed there is nothing in Christ but what is lovely, and there is nothing lovely but it may be found in Him. The testimony borne by the spouse will apply to His offices, as Prophet, Priest, and King; to His government, universal and particular; to His work for us on earth and in heaven; to His design in all His dealings with us, even to purify, elevate, and honour us. Reader, do you *know* Him? Do you *admire* Him? Do you *love* Him? Do you *recommend* Him? Will you *try* Him? If so, be reconciled to Him; cordially embrace Him; and meekly learn of Him. The more you know Him, the more you will love Him; and the more you love Him, the more happy you will be. Let us ask, 'What are our views of Christ tonight?' If our minds are spiritual, *'He is altogether lovely'*.

> All-over glorious is my Lord;
> Must be beloved, and yet adored;
> His worth if all the nations knew,
> Sure the whole earth would love Him too.

OCTOBER 26

🌿 MORNING 🌿
'Am I in God's stead?'
GENESIS 30:2

All our mercies are to be traced up to our God, and all our miseries to ourselves. We are constantly making ourselves wretched, by departing from our God, or by putting creatures in His place. We often put persons and things in God's stead in reference to our affections, loving them inordinately; in reference to our dependence, trusting them instead of Him; in reference to our worship, idolizing them instead of adoring Him; and in reference to our expectations, expecting them to relieve, comfort, or deliver instead of Him. But insufficiency is written upon every created object. No creature can fill the place of Jehovah, take the richest, the wisest, the kindest, the nearest relative or friend, and you must exclaim, 'Vanity of vanities, all is vanity.' But Jehovah can fill the place of all; He can be instead of father, husband, child, wealth, health, yea, of all things. Creatures may say, Am I in God's stead? If not, why look to me? why depend on me? why expect from me? why grieve so to part with me? Am I in God's stead? If so, He will remove me, or I shall disappoint you. Never, never put any thing in God's place.

> *Heavenly Adam, life divine,*
> *Change my nature into Thine.*
> *Move and spread throughout my soul,*
> *Actuate and fill the whole!*
> *Now my fainting soul revive;*
> *There for ever walk and live.*

🌿 EVENING 🌿
'Who hath abolished death.'
2 TIMOTHY 1:10

Death is our *foe*. It is an implacable enemy. It has slain millions. It has robbed kingdoms of their deliverers, churches of their ornaments, families of their supports, and individuals of their beloved connections. It is powerful, irresistible, cruel, insatiable, the king of terrors. It is a foe that might fill us with fear, and keep us in constant alarm; but we have a *friend*, a friend who is infinitely great, and incomparably good. He knew us thoroughly, loved us infinitely, pitied us tenderly, engaged for us heartily, came to deliver us cheerfully, suffered for us indescribably, and conquered our foe completely. He abolished death. That is, He changed its nature: it is now quiet sleep; He changed its office: it is not an executioner, but a waiting servant; He changed its work: it is now only to take down the prison, and let the prisoner escape; He changed its end: it was truly fearful; it is now divinely glorious. He deprived it of its authority and sting. This He did by fulfilling the law; satisfying the claims of justice; spoiling principalities and powers; wresting the keys from the destroyer's hand; and sending us the good news of complete salvation. Are you *prepared* for this foe? Do you *know* this friend? Do you believe this fact?

> *Did we but trust our heavenly Friend,*
> *And on His faithful Word depend,*
> *Then should we fearless view the grave,*
> *And death itself no sting would have.*

OCTOBER 27

🌿 MORNING 🌿
'The LORD will give grace and glory.'
PSALM 84:11

This is good news, for except the Lord give us grace we shall never be sanctified; and unless He give us glory we shall never be glorified. All must be the free gift of free grace. If anything good was required of us to entitle us, we must sit down in despair; but now all is of divine bounty; we can hope; we need not be afraid. The Lord has given grace to thousands. He has given grace to us; and He will give more grace: grace to fit for duty, grace to support in trial, grace to sanctify the heart; and He will give glory, which is grace in perfection. Brethren, let us endeavour to believe that our God is as kind, bountiful, and beneficent as His Word declares. Let us confess our sins before Him, seek grace from Him, and look to be glorified with Him. Our all is in God; our all must come from God; and all the glory should be daily given to God. Whenever we want grace, let us ask it of God, for He giveth liberally and upbraideth not. Let us approach His throne this morning, and be this our prayer, 'Lord, give us more grace. Give us grace daily, grace to devote us to Thy service, and fill us with holy love.' O for more grace, that we may give God more glory.

Blest is our lot whate'er befall;
Who can affright, or who appal?
Since on Thy strength, our rock, our all,
Jesus we cling to Thee.

🌿 EVENING 🌿
'Who remembered us in our low estate.'
PSALM 136:23

Our state by nature was truly a low estate. We had no liberty, being the slaves of Satan; no ability, being dead in trespasses and sins; no honour, being allied only to traitors and rebels; no real pleasure, being tossed about by desires and disappointments; no prospects, except eternal woe; no profitable employment, for the fruit of our toil was death. Our nature was fearfully depraved; our condition truly deplorable; and our destiny most alarming. But in this state, the Lord remembered us; and it was with reference to it that He made His covenant; sent His Son; promised His Holy Spirit; prepared and gave us His gospel; employed His wise and holy providence; exerted His divine power on our behalf; opened the storehouse of heaven for us; and raised us up to know, love, and realize union to Jesus. And He did this of mere mercy, and because His mercy endureth forever. Mercy fixes on her objects, cleaves to those on whom she fixes, and continues to regard them with peculiar concern. Mercy wrote our names in the book of life; gave us the promises of the everlasting gospel; pleads for us before the throne above; and visits us often to cheer, rescue, and bless.

All-gracious God, Thy pitying eye
View'd the low state in which we lie;
And as an act of sovereign grace,
Sent Thy salvation to our race.

OCTOBER 28

🌿 MORNING 🌿

'Son, go work today in my vineyard.'

MATTHEW 21:28

Some are God's sons only by creation; the Jews were so by national adoption; believers are so by regeneration. They are born of God, and adopted by God. Our God never intended that His children should be idle; He says to every child, *'Son, go work.'* This is the command of a Father: it contains affection; it flows from authority. We are to work for His glory, for the good of others, and to lay up for ourselves treasure in heaven. Working for God is creditable, profitable, pleasant. Our work is in His vineyard; the church finds work for all. Some are employed to plant, some to weed, some to water, and some to watch. The command is 'WORK TODAY.' The present is the period. Today, while you have light, strength, and opportunity. Remember, it is but a day, a short period at longest, but it often proves to be but a short day. Are you standing all the day idle? Go into the vineyard. Are you discouraged? Imitate her who did what she could. Look to the Lord; He will give ability, opportunity, and crown with success.

O give me, Lord, an upright heart,
Well nurtured with a godly fear,
Which from Thy precepts will not start,

When clouds and threatening storms appear,
But onward press with even pace,
Refresh'd and fortified by grace.

🌿 EVENING 🌿

'Sitting at the feet of Jesus.'

LUKE 8:35

This poor man had just been rescued from Satan. He felt under the deepest obligation. He was filled with wonder at his Deliverer's power. He was charmed with His preaching, and he took his seat at His feet. This was the posture of a learner, the place occupied by a disciple. *We* may still enjoy this privilege. Jesus speaks to us now. Let us sit down at His feet, and hear His Word with attention, receive His doctrine with affection, and own Him as our Lord and Master. It is the posture of humility. The feet of Jesus is our proper place. There we are safe. There we shall receive blessings. There we shall learn the most important lessons. It is the evidence of attachment. How much we have to attach us to the Lord Jesus. How much we have already received. How much we want, which He only can supply. How much we shall need, as we prosecute our journey, which it is vain to look for from any other quarter. Let us therefore sit down at His feet, and meekly receive His Word. Let us keep our place, not suffering anything to draw us away. Satan will if he can, but he well knows that he cannot injure us here. Sinners will if they can, but while we are in this posture our conduct will reprove them, and exalt the grace of God.

O that I may attentive sit,
In humble faith at Jesus' feet;
Imbibe His spirit, prove His care,
Preserv'd from guilt and slavish fear.

OCTOBER 29

🌿 MORNING 🌿

'The love that God hath to us.'
1 John 4:16

Who shall describe it? What tongue or pen can set it forth? It is infinite, and what can finite mortals say? It is eternal, and how can we who are but of yesterday declare it? It is the present heaven of the saints, to know and believe the love that God hath to them. None can reveal it to us, or shed it abroad in our hearts, but the Holy Ghost. He can direct our hearts into the love of God, and into the patience of Jesus Christ. He is in office to show the saints the things of God, and enable them to believe and enjoy them. Let us, beloved, daily pray that we may know and enjoy the love that God hath to us; it will be an antidote to all our miseries, a source of joy under all our sorrows. Our friends and frames may change, but the love of God is unchangeable. Our temporal prospects may be all blighted, but if we know and enjoy the love of God, we cannot be unhappy. *Who, or what shall separate us from the love of God?* Jesus has told us that we shall never perish; neither shall any pluck us out of His hand. The love of our God is the source of our happiness, and the cause of our safety. O, to know and believe the love which God hath toward us. *God is love.*

> *What shall I do my God to love,*
> *My loving God to praise?*
> *The length, and breadth, and height to prove,*
> *And depth of sovereign grace?*

🌿 EVENING 🌿

'A bruised reed shall he not break.'
Matthew 12:20

So tender is the heart of Jesus, so gentle His disposition, that the feeblest need not fear, the most timid may take courage. He notices the first risings of desire, the secret inclination, the buddings of faith, and He admires and approves of them. He knows the strength of our corruptions, what terrible conflicts we have, what poor creatures we are, and for our comfort assures us, that though weak and worthless as a bruised reed, He will not reject us, or crush us by His power. He will bind up the bruised reed. He will encourage the desire. He will foster the little faith. He will receive the imperfect prayer. He will accept and bless the discouraged soul. He is represented as a Lamb, to inspire us with confidence; as a Shepherd, to preserve us from alarm; and as a Saviour, to attract us to His throne. He will not break the bruised reed Himself, nor will He allow others to do it. Beloved, are you bruised by Satan, by unbelief, and by an evil world? Do you feel weak and worthless? Are you discouraged and filled with fear? Fear not; Jesus is gentle, kind, and gracious. He despiseth not any. He rejects no applicants. He binds up the broken in heart, and healeth all their wounds. He says, 'I will in no wise cast out.'

> *No, I find He never will,*
> *(Jesus is a Saviour still,)*
> *He who kindled my desire,*
> *Will not let the spark expire.*

OCTOBER 30

🌿 MORNING 🌿

'Take heed, and beware of covetousness.'
Luke 12:15

This is a warning from the lips of our beloved Lord. He knows our weakness and our foes, and He cautions us against them. We want but little here below, for we shall not be here long; and we are going to the land of plenty, rest, and joy. A little with the Lord's blessing is enough. We ought not to be anxious about temporals; only let us be careful that the world is not a loser by us, and we need trouble no further. The Lord will give us enough if we are living by faith upon Him, and walking in communion with Him. We are all prone to be covetous, and it is a fearful sin. Covetousness is idolatry. It steals the heart from God, and sets it upon base and sordid things. It prevents our enjoying either temporal or spiritual blessings. A covetous man must be miserable, must be unholy, must be lost for ever; well may our dear Lord say, *'Take heed, and beware of covetousness.'* It is sly and insinuating, it is deceitful and powerful; and if it once becomes rooted in the heart, nothing but omnipotent grace can root it out. Covet only the best gifts, spiritual blessings.

Great things we are not here to crave,
But if we food and raiment have,
Should learn to be therewith content;
Into the world we nothing brought,
Nor can we carry from it aught;
Then walk the way your Master went.

🌿 EVENING 🌿

'He shall be great.'
Luke 1:32

So spake the angel, announcing the birth of the Lord Jesus, and the prediction is fulfilled. He is great, and His greatness is unsearchable. Great, in the dignity of His nature; in the depth of His humiliation; in the glory of His righteousness; in the merit of His blood; in the provisions of His gospel; in the number of His converts; in the extent of His kingdom; in the tenderness of His sympathy; in the variety of His offices; in the grandeur of His works; in the estimation of His people; in the conquest of His foes; and in the punishment of His determined enemies. His greatness is stamped upon every promise He has made, every pardon He grants, every blessing He gives, and every victory He gains. Believer, thy Saviour is great. Therefore He saves great sinners, confers great grace, bears with great offenders, treats with great kindness, and will confer on us great glory. But His greatness will more clearly appear, when all His people are collected, when the curse is removed from our world, when the glowing predictions of the Old Testament are fulfilled, and He reigns before His ancients gloriously. His greatness shall fill His people with everlasting joy, and His foes with never-ending woe. He shall be great on earth, in heaven, and in hell.

Now, Saviour, in my soul be great,
Thence bid all guilt and fear retreat;
My powers into subjection bring,
And reign supreme as God and King.

OCTOBER 31

🌿 MORNING 🌿

'Call upon me in the day of trouble.'

Psalm 50:15

Keep the straight path of duty, and if troubles come, or difficulties arise, thy God invites thee to call upon Him. He will come to thy help and bring all His boundless resources with Him. He is always within call. His ear is never heavy, that it cannot hear; His arm is not shortened, that it cannot reach or save. He can make thy greatest troubles prove thy choicest blessings; He can give thee cause to bless Him through eternity, for thy sorest trials. O, trust Him, and fear not! Run not to creatures; but, 'Arise and call upon thy God.' Look not to others, until thou hast proved that He cannot, or will not help; and that will never be. His heart is too kind; His Word is too faithful. Art thou in trouble this morning? If so, you have a *special* invitation from thy God to pay Him a visit, and lay thy whole case before Him, expecting His sympathy, interference, and blessing; He says, *'Call upon me in the time of trouble. I will deliver thee, and thou shalt glorify me.'* He is faithful who hath promised. O, trust Him, for so you honour Him; expect from Him, and you cannot be disappointed. Wait for Him, and you shall not be ashamed.

> *Dear refuge of my weary soul*
> *On Thee, when sorrows rise,*
> *On Thee, when waves of trouble roll,*
> *My fainting hope relies.*

🌿 EVENING 🌿

'He healeth the broken in heart.'

Psalm 147:3

Sin has so hardened the heart, that nothing can effectually impress it but grace. No one feels and mourns over the hardness of the heart, but he whose heart has been softened by the Holy Spirit. Nothing will thoroughly break the heart but a sense of God's forgiving love. When the soul is quickened by the Holy Spirit, sin is discovered, guilt is felt, fear is experienced, and the heart begins to relent; a conflict commences, and very often much distress is felt before pardon is enjoyed. Satan is busy, unbelief is strong, our knowledge of the gospel is imperfect, repentance is difficult, the heart is oppressed, and the spirit is wounded. When the man is really broken down before God, is willing to submit to God's righteousness, and to embrace a salvation all of grace, deliverance is near. The Lord sends His Word to heal, applies the balm of a Saviour's blood, speaks peace to the conscience, and lets the oppressed go free. The wounded, broken heart is healed; salvation is come to the soul; and Jesus is most precious. Reader, if thy heart is broken for sin, thy God will heal it. Look to the Lord, and hope in His Word.

> *Nor shall the sinner's hope be vain,* *The mourning sinner's broken heart,*
> *Behold, with all His glorious train,* *Guilt, fear, and bondage all depart,*
> *The King of glory enters.* *When once on Christ he ventures.*

NOVEMBER 1

🌿 MORNING 🌿

'O thou preserver of men.'

JOB 7:20

We have neither wisdom nor strength to preserve ourselves; we are daily liable to fall; and unless God preserve us we certainly shall. Our hearts are so deceitful, our corruptions are so strong, and Satan is so vigilant, that we need look to God as our *Preserver* every hour, and call upon Him to uphold us every moment. He can preserve; He doth preserve; but only in the way of obedience. Except we are watchful, prayerful, and walking humbly with Him, we have no security; we may fall into the grossest sins, and commit the greatest crimes. O believer, never think thyself safe, but as thou art leaning on Jesus, calling upon thy heavenly Father, and cultivating communion with the Holy Ghost! Indeed, thou art in danger; Satan, the world, and thy corruptions, are all leagued against thee; nothing but omnipotent grace can keep thee. Cease from man, trust not thy own heart, but keep close to the good Shepherd. He is able to keep you from falling, and to present you faultless before the presence of His glory with exceeding joy. Thy Preserver is also thy Observer; He notices every thought, word, and deed.

> *Every foe must fly before Him,*
> *Earth and hell shall feel His power;*
> *Heaven and earth with joy adore Him!*
>
> *Hail the long expected hour:*
> *Hallelujah!*
> *Jesus has almighty power.*

🌿 EVENING 🌿

'A Prince and a Saviour.'

ACTS 5:31

The Man of Sorrows is now raised to princely dignity. He is seated at the Father's right hand. He has all power in heaven and in earth. Every knee must bow to Him. He is Lord of all: the Prince of peace, the Prince of life, the Prince of the kings of the earth. He has a princely heart. He possesses all the wealth of the universe. He gives in a princely manner. But He is also a Saviour: a princely Saviour. He saves by His own merit, by His own power. He saves for His own glory. He saves freely. He never barters with sinners, but bestows salvation upon the lost as a princely gift. There is nothing in which He so much delights as in saving sinners. He *can* save to the uttermost. He *will* save every applicant. He came into our world to save sinners. He agonised in Gethsemane and died on Calvary to save sinners. He is now exalted at God's right hand to be a Prince and a Saviour, for to *give* repentance to Israel, and forgiveness of sins. Go to Jesus as to a mild, beneficent, peaceful Prince. Go to Him as a powerful, kind, and willing Saviour, whose work and delight it is to save sinners, even the chief. Honour Him by trusting His Word, relying on His blood, and expect salvation as a free gift at His hands.

> *In Thy state of exaltation,*
> *Answer, Lord, its end in me;*
> *Give me free and full salvation,*
> *Now my Prince and Saviour be.*

NOVEMBER 2

❦ MORNING ❦
'They were tempted.'
Hebrews 11:37

That is, they were tried; and the design of their enemies by these trials was, to draw or drive them from the Lord. Their trials were of the most cruel kind, but they found that as their day, so was their strength. Brethren, we shall be tempted; Satan is not dead, no, nor yet asleep; the world is not reconciled to godliness; nor are we free from indwelling sin. It is not our sin to be tempted – this is our trial; but it is our sin if we yield. God has promised strength, wisdom and grace; and we should seek these, that we may be able to withstand, and so overcome every trial. We may expect to be tempted daily, for Satan goeth about; and if at any moment that we are off our guard, that is the time he is most likely to beset us. Let us keep close to Jesus, the great Shepherd of the sheep; let us keep our eye on our Father's house; and let us aim in all things at God's glory, and temptation shall not harm us. 'Blessed is the man that endureth temptation; for when he is tried, he shall receive the crown of life, which the Lord hath promised to them that love Him.' If the enemy come in like a flood, we may still sing:–

> His oath, His covenant, and blood
> Support me in the sinking flood;
> When all around my soul gives way
> Jesus is all my hope and stay;
> On Christ the solid rock I stand;
> All other ground is sinking sand.

❦ EVENING ❦
'Why is thy heart grieved?'
1 Samuel 1:8

This was the enquiry of a kind husband to an afflicted wife. Let us suppose that the question is proposed to ourselves, and try and turn it to some good account. 'Why is thy heart grieved?' Is it from conviction of sin? If so, the blood of Jesus Christ cleanseth from all sin. If we confess our sins, God is faithful and just to forgive us our sins. Is it from desertion, or the loss of the Lord's presence? He will turn again; He will have compassion upon us. His covenant is sure; His promise is true, though He may hide His face from us. Is it from unfruitfulness? He will be as the dew unto Israel, and they shall revive as the corn, and grow as the vine. He will prune the branch by affliction, and cause it to bring forth more fruit. Is it from poverty? The silver and the gold are the Lord's, entirely at His disposal; and He will supply all our needs in His own time and way. Is it from bereavement? He will not leave us orphans; He will come unto us; the Lord will take us up, and will be better to us than ten such relatives. Is it from hardness of heart? He will melt us and try us. He will turn His hand upon us, and purely purge away our dross and take away all our sin. His love will both soften and sanctify us; therefore grieve not.

> Then let not griefs o'erwhelm thy breast,
> To Jesus fly, He'll give thee rest;
> Hope thou in God, His smiles shall raise,
> And fill thy soul with songs of praise.

NOVEMBER 3

❧ MORNING ❧

'What would ye that I should do for you?'
Mark 10:36

So spake Jesus to the sons of Zebedee, and so He speaks to us. Beloved, have you your petition ready this morning? Jesus is at the pardon office; He is on His throne of grace; He is in a loving temper; He is ready to bless. He says, 'Ask what I shall give thee?' O Jesus! give me sanctifying grace. Subdue my corruptions. Purify my heart. Make me a vessel of honour, meet for Thy use. Why should sin be allowed to work so powerfully? Why should Satan be permitted to have so much power over me? Why should the world attract and lead me astray? Lord, I would that Thou shouldest make me holy, and make me useful; fill me with Thy Holy Spirit; write Thy Word on my heart, and enable me to write out Thy precepts in my life. O Saviour! I would that Thou shouldest make me like Thyself; as meek, as humble, as diligent, as disinterested, as useful to God and man. May I be holy, harmless, undefiled, and separate from sinners. O, make me shine to the honour and glory of Thy free and sovereign grace, and do so at once!

Holy Ghost, no more delay;
Come, and in Thy temple stay;
Now Thine inward witness bear,
Strong, and permanent, and clear;
Source of life, Thyself impart,
Rise eternal in my heart.

❧ EVENING ❧

'Thou hast done right.'
Nehemiah 9:33

The Lord cannot but do right, this is generally acknowledged; but to be persuaded of this, to realize it, and be influenced by it, under severe and heavy trials is exceedingly difficult. But the Lord never acts but according to the plan which He has drawn, which plan is the perfection of wisdom, and proceeds from His infinite love. What He does, He purposed to do; and He purposed to do it, because it was the very best thing that could be done. We are poor, hasty, selfish, dissatisfied creatures, ready to sit in judgment upon what God does, and to complain of His dealings without the least cause. But there are times when looking back upon our losses, crosses, sufferings, and trials, we can say, and say it heartily, 'Thou hast done right.' Doubtless Jacob felt this, when he embraced his son Joseph in Egypt; and Job also, when God had blessed his latter end more than the beginning; and Daniel also, when he was taken up out of the den and no manner of hurt was found on him, because he believed in his God. But it is to feel it *in* the trial, to confess it *under* the affliction, that is most desirable. Let us then, when the Lord tries our graces, or buffets us for our faults, endeavour to say, '*Thou hast done right.*'

With peaceful steps thy race of duty run,
God nothing does, nor suffers to be done,
But thou wouldst do thyself, couldst thou but see
The end of all events as well as He.

NOVEMBER 4

❦ MORNING ❦

'They ... limited the Holy One of Israel.'

Psalm 78:41

This was Israel's sin, and has it not often been ours? Our God is the Holy One, and will do what is most for His glory; He is the Holy One of Israel, and will therefore consult His people's welfare. We must not limit His wisdom, for it is infinite; we must not limit His power, for it is omnipotent; we must not limit His mercy, for it is as high as heaven and deep as hell; we must not limit Him to time, for He will display His sovereignty. He will not be tied to walk by our rules, or be bound to keep our time; but He will perform His Word, honour our faith, and reward them that diligently seek Him. However tried, beware of limiting the Holy One of Israel; say not, 'It is too difficult, or it is too far gone;' this was the fault of Martha and Mary, but Jesus convinced them that they were wrong. Rather say with Jonathan, 'It may be that the LORD will work for us; for there is no restraint to the LORD to save by many or by few;' Jonathan honoured the Lord by trusting Him, and the Lord honoured Jonathan by giving him a victory over the enemies of Israel. Exercise unlimited confidence in God, for He will fulfil every promise He has made.

Wide as the world is His command,
Vast as eternity His love;
Firm as a rock His truth shall stand,
When rolling years shall cease to move.

❦ EVENING ❦

'My God shall be my strength.'

Isaiah 49:5

This was the language of Jesus, our living head, and bright example. He lived by faith on His Father's word. He was deeply tried by his Father's enemies. But He lived by the Father, and we should live by Him. We are loved with the same love, interested in the same covenant, and entitled to the same promises. Let us therefore, in the prospect of great and sore trials, severe conflicts, distressing changes, and the approach of the last enemy, say, 'My God shall be my strength;' for He has said, 'I will strengthen thee;' and when we feel weakest let faith be strongest, for He says, 'My strength is made perfect in weakness.' God has been our strength, and it is having obtained help of Him, that we continue unto this day; let us therefore trust Him for the future, and say in reference to every duty, and when about to engage with any foe, 'I will go in the strength of the Lord GOD: I will make mention of thy righteousness, even of thine only.' If God is my strength, then I shall overcome; I shall persevere; I shall arrive safe at home; I shall praise His sovereign grace for evermore. Let us lie down tonight rejoicing in our privilege, and exercising our thoughts upon this glorious fact, 'My God is my strength.'

What if the springs of life were broke,
And flesh and heart should faint?
God is my soul's eternal rock,
The strength of every saint.

NOVEMBER 5

🌿 MORNING 🌿
'Be ye also enlarged.'
2 CORINTHIANS 6:13

Contraction is a great evil, enlargement is a great blessing. We need to be enlarged in our knowledge, love, hope, liberality, faith, and every grace. Our God disapproves of contraction. The apostles set a different example. Provision is made in the covenant to gratify enlarged desires. The promises warrant enlarged expectations. Jesus bids us ask largely. The gospel calls for enlargement in prayer, benevolence, pity, and compassion, and in our efforts for God's glory. Let us beware of narrow views or feelings, for the heart of God is large; the love of Christ is large; the provision of mercy is large; the gospel commission is large; and the mansions of glory are large. We are not straitened in God, nor in His gospel, but we are straitened in our own bowels. O Jesus, enlarge our narrow hearts; expand our contracted souls! Fill us with all joy and peace in believing, that we may abound in hope, by the power of the Holy Ghost. May we be full of goodness, able also to admonish one another. O, to be filled with the Holy Ghost and with power! O for large hearts, large expectations, and large communications from God!

With holy fear and reverent love,	*And stay myself on Thee alone.*
I long to lie beneath Thy throne;	*Teach me to lean upon Thy breast,*
I long in Thee to live and move,	*To find in Thee the promised rest.*

🌿 EVENING 🌿
'What hath God wrought?'
NUMBERS 23:23

For our *nation*: in delivering it from paganism and popery; and in conferring so many and such great blessings upon it, so that it may well be the wonder and envy of the world. For His *church*: in redeeming it by the sufferings and death of His beloved Son; in quickening, converting, and sanctifying its members; in gathering them together from the ends of the earth; in providing for all their wants, watching over their persons, and keeping them by His power through faith unto salvation. For our *souls*: delivering us from the power of darkness, and translating us into the kingdom of His dear Son; pardoning all our sins through His blood, and justifying our persons in His righteousness; working faith in our hearts; giving us a good hope through grace; making us the temples of His Holy Spirit; conquering for us all our foes and subduing within us our iniquities. What hath God wrought? Wonders. For whom hath God wrought? Sinners. Why hath God wrought? That He might be glorified. Beloved, the past should encourage us in prospect of the future; what He hath done is a pledge that He will do all that He has promised.

What sweeter pledge could God bestow,	*But unbelief, that hateful thing,*
Of help in future scenes of woe,	*Oft makes me sigh when I should sing*
Than grace already given;	*Of confidence in heaven.*

NOVEMBER 6

🌿 MORNING 🌿

'Thou art no more a servant, but a son.'
GALATIANS 4:7

It would have been a great mercy if God had made us His servants, after we had proved His enemies; but He has adopted us as His sons, and taken us to the bosom of His love. He is now our Father, and wishes us to call Him so; we are His children, and He wishes us to walk and act as such. We are not mere servants, therefore we should not be servile; we are sons, therefore we should love, obey, and delight in God as our Father. 'Beloved, now are we the sons of God.' We are delivered from bondage, introduced into favour, have the promise of eternal life, and should rejoice with joy unspeakable, and full of glory. It was free grace which adopted us; the Holy Spirit, by the Word, begat us to a lively hope; and the gospel proclaims our privileges, and invites us to enjoy them. Let us today think, 'I am a son of God. My Father is holy, His children are holy, His Word is holy, He loves holiness, and commands me to be holy; I will therefore lift up my heart to Him; seek grace from Him; and in all things aim to glorify Him.' A filial spirit will lead to filial obedience.

> Pronounce me, gracious God, Thy son,
> Own me an heir divine:
> I'll pity princes on the throne,
> When I can call Thee mine;
> Sceptres and crowns unenvied rise,
> And lose their lustre in mine eyes.

🌿 EVENING 🌿

'Be thou faithful unto death.'
REVELATION 2:10

God is faithful to His people. He always keeps His word. He never disappoints their hope. He exhorts and encourages them to be faithful too. This was spoken to the angel, or pastor of the church; such should be faithful in preaching the Word; in watching for souls; in suffering for Christ; and in seeking by all means to promote the prosperity, peace, and holiness of the flock. It includes the people. Believers should be faithful: to the *truth*, holding it fast, striving for it, spreading it in every direction; to *conscience*, listening to its dictates, observing its warnings, and obeying its demands; to their *profession*, maintaining it, adorning it, and endeavouring to make it answer the end designed in it; to *God*, believing His Word, doing His will, and suffering in His cause; to *sinners*, warning them of danger, telling them the tale of mercy, and leading them to Jesus; to *saints*, reproving their sins, soothing their sorrows, and supplying their needs. 'Be thou faithful unto death.' If it expose you to death, be faithful; the crown of life is the reward. Until removed by death, persevere calmly, patiently, courageously, industriously, until the Master calls, 'Come up higher.'

> Saviour, help me by Thy pow'r,
> In temptations dangerous hour;
> Give me fortitude and faith,
> Make me faithful unto death.

NOVEMBER 7

❦ MORNING ❦
'Go forward.'
EXODUS 14:15

Beloved, there is no standing still in religion; we are either going forward or going back. Our Captain's command is, *'Go forward.'* This is our direction. Go forward in the Lord's way, in the Lord's work, to the Lord's kingdom. The command contains great encouragement. Go forward, remembering the Lord's wisdom, trusting in the Lord's power, and believing in the Lord's love. Go forward in union with the Lord's people, with zeal for His glory, until summoned into your Master's presence. Go forward, notwithstanding difficulties, fears, and discouragements. Go forward, because God has bidden you; He has promised to go with you; He will crown your journey's end. Let us imitate ardent and holy Paul, who said, 'Not as though I had already attained, either were already perfect; but I follow after, if that I may apprehend that for which I am also apprehended of Christ Jesus.' Let us look for, and hasten to the coming of the day of God. There is nothing behind us worth a thought, if compared with what is set before us by the gospel. Be this then our daily motto: *'Forward, forward.'*

Much in sorrow, oft in woe,
Onward, Christian, onward go;
Shrink not, fear not, dare not yield,
Never quit the battle field:
Forward press and win the prize,
Then to endless glory rise.

❦ EVENING ❦
'He thanked God and took courage.'
ACTS 28:15

The kindness of friends cheered the apostle; for this he gave God thanks, and then went forward courageously. Every mercy should be thankfully acknowledged. Whatever does us good comes from God. He is the only source of all good, and to Him our praises should daily ascend. The Lord has brought us through many dangers; He has delivered us out of many difficulties; He has bestowed on us many favours. Let us therefore tonight thank God, and take courage. He has provided for all our future wants; He has given us many, exceeding great, and precious promises; He has assured us that all things shall work together for our good; and we have His Word, that He will never leave us nor forsake us. Let us then thank God, and take courage. Our journey may be rough, our foes may be strong, our troubles may be great; but our strength is equal, our supplies are certain, and the end will crown the whole. Listen not to Satan, yield not to unbelief, fear not the future; He that hath delivered, doth deliver, and in Him let us trust that He will yet deliver us. Look at what He has done, review your mercies, think of His promises, and then thank God, and take courage.

Jesus, on Thee our hope depends,
To lead me on to Thine abode;
Assur'd our home will make amends
For all our toil while on the road.

NOVEMBER 8

❦ MORNING ❧

'As having nothing, and yet possessing all things.'
2 Corinthians 6:10

The Lord's family are generally poor; men may look at them as having nothing valuable, important, or calculated to make them happy; but in reality they possess all things, because God is theirs. Our God has said, 'I am their inheritance,' and we say, 'Thou art my portion, O LORD.' His eternity is the date of our happiness; His unchangeableness, the rock of our rest; His omnipotence, our constant guard; His faithfulness, our daily security; His mercies, our overflowing store; His omniscience, our careful overseer; His wisdom, our judicious counsellor; His justice, our stern avenger; His omnipresence, our sweet company; His holiness, the fountain from which we receive sanctifying grace; His all-sufficiency, the lot of our inheritance; and His infinity, the extent of our glorious portion. This is the blessedness of the people of the Lord: they have God for their God, and all His perfections engaged to make them blessed. O love the Lord! Live upon the Lord! Glorify God in the day of visitation! Make Him your portion and everlasting all! He is enough in the absence of all besides.

> To us the privilege is given
> To be the sons and heirs of heaven;
> Sons of the God who reigns on high,
> And heirs of joys beyond the sky:
> O, may our conduct ever prove
> Our filial piety and love.

❦ EVENING ❧

'Serve the LORD with gladness.'
Psalm 100:2

Our God is infinitely happy, and He loves to see His creatures happy. He provided every thing necessary to make them happy at first, but sin disturbed and destroyed much of God's fair creation. He would have us happy now, happy in His service. Therefore He has provided for our happiness in the everlasting gospel. He says, 'Believe and I will give you a free pardon, I will confer on you a perfect righteousness, I will purify your hearts, I will supply all your wants, I will admit you into My presence for holy fellowship, I will keep you by My power, I will give you grace while you live, and glory when you die.' Is not this enough to make you happy, to induce you to 'Serve the LORD with gladness?' Brethren, in God's service we should be cheerful; but if so, we must realize our adoption, and serve Him as dear children who are fully persuaded of a Father's love. Let us serve Him out of love. Let us serve Him on earth, under the impression that we shall reign with Him in heaven. Let us serve Him in the world, in our families, and in the church; and let it be legibly written out on our conduct, so that all may read it, 'I serve God, I serve Him cheerfully. I would not be otherwise employed.'

> Lord, disperse my sin and sadness,
> Speak salvation to my heart;
> Then I'll serve with joy and gladness,
> And my noblest powers exert.

NOVEMBER 9

🌿 MORNING 🌿

'O God, thou hast taught me from my youth.'

PSALM 71:17

The psalmist was called early, and he ascribes it to divine teaching. None but God can teach us experimentally; and the lessons He teaches are always useful and important. He teaches all His scholars to know themselves: their depravity, poverty, and slavery. He teaches them His law: its purity, claims and penalty. He teaches them His gospel: its fulness, freeness, and suitability. He teaches them to know Himself: as a reconciled God, as their Father and faithful Friend. His teaching is accompanied with power and authority. Are we taught of God? We may know divine teaching by its effects: it always produces humility to sit at His feet, dependence upon Him, abhorrence of sin, love to God as a teacher, obedience to the lessons taught, thirst for further attainments, and brings us daily to Jesus. Let us earnestly seek divine teaching: it preserves from dangers, sorrows, and snares; and if suitably improved, it brings great glory to God, and honour to the cause of religion. Our God says, 'I will teach thee.' Lord, teach me, and make me entirely Thine! He that is taught of God is wise, holy and useful.

> O, let my heart be wholly Thine,
> Thy property alone;
> No longer let me think it mine,
> Or call myself my own.

🌿 EVENING 🌿

'Your redemption draweth nigh.'

LUKE 21:28

That is, your complete deliverance. Your Redeemer hath appeared once, and paid the price necessary for your honourable release. He is now waiting at His Father's right hand, having all power in heaven and on earth, and He will soon come and claim the purchased possession. You may fall asleep in Jesus, you may slumber peacefully in the grave for a little time, but Jesus will soon come, and then He will raise you from the dead as His brethren. You will arise and shake off the dust of death, and put on the beautiful garments of immortality. You will be publicly acknowledged as the sons of God. You will be put in possession of purity, power, and perfection. You will be introduced to your heavenly Father, to the whole of the redeemed family, and to your everlasting home. Then your redemption will be complete. Well, it draweth nigh. Every day, every hour brings it nearer. Are we longing for it? Can we use the language of the apostle, and say, 'Ourselves also which have the first-fruits of the Spirit, even we ourselves groan within ourselves, waiting for the adoption, to wit, the redemption of our body.' If so, rejoice, for your redemption draweth nigh; for now is your salvation nearer than when ye first believed.

> Then shall I see, and hear, and know,
> All I desir'd or wish'd below,
> And every power find sweet employ,
> In that eternal world of joy.

NOVEMBER 10

❦ MORNING ❧

'Behold the Lamb of God.'
JOHN 1:36

Sin requires a sacrifice, and the sacrifice must be in proportion to the offence, and the dignity of the offended; such a sacrifice could not be found, but God condescended to provide one, which was no less a person than His only-begotten Son. This Lamb was provided to expiate and remove sin, to honour the divine government, and reconcile us to God. Let us daily direct our attention to the Lamb of God, who verily was foreordained before the foundation of the world, but was manifested in these last times for us. He is set forth to be the propitiation through faith in His blood, and to be the daily object of our faith, desire, and affection. Provided by God, He presented to God an infinite atonement, and we have redemption through His blood, even the forgiveness of our sins. The Lamb is to be presented daily to God by us, in our prayers and praises; and all our expectations are to be founded upon what He is, what He has done, and what He is doing now before the throne of God. Take off your attention from all other subjects, and *'Behold the Lamb of God.'* Look to Him daily, and look until guilt and fear depart.

> Cast thy guilty soul on Him,
> Find Him mighty to redeem;
> At His feet thy burden lay,
> Look thy doubts and fears away;
> Now by faith the Son embrace,
> Plead His promise, trust His grace.

❦ EVENING ❧

'Take away all iniquity.'
HOSEA 14:2

Nothing troubles a real Christian like sin, and there is nothing for which he prays more frequently, or more heartily, than for complete deliverance from it. He is delivered from its guilt, being justified from all things. But he longs to be delivered from its working. It annoys, irritates, and distresses him. It darkens his evidences; disturbs his peace; and troubles his conscience. Therefore he prays, 'Take away all iniquity.' But the prayer is put into the mouth of a backslider by the Lord Himself, and it is the first thing he should seek. By iniquity he fell, and by sanctification only can he arise. He fell by his own folly, but he can only rise by the Lord's mercy. And will the Lord take away all iniquity? He will. The guilt of it He will remove by applying the atonement, the power of it by bringing home His Word, and the very being of it at death. Let this then be our daily prayer, 'Lord, sanctify me wholly, and preserve my whole spirit, soul and body blameless unto the coming of our Lord Jesus Christ.' And if this flows from our hearts, it proves our regeneration, and will be answered in our complete sanctification, for 'faithful is He that calleth you, who also will do it.' He will take His own time, and work in His own way, but He will do it.

> More than for ease in mortal pain,
> For purity I pray;
> Whatever trial may remain,
> O take my sins away!

NOVEMBER 11

MORNING

'I say unto all, Watch.'
MARK 13:37

The hour of death is uncertain, and the second coming of Jesus is equally so; therefore we are commanded to be always ready, and to be on the WATCH. His coming is the grand object of our hope, and should be our daily desire and prayer. It will be awfully grand. We are deeply interested in it. It is certain, necessary, and will be sudden. We know not the day, month, or year. God has purposely concealed it, in wisdom, in mercy, and for our good. He commands us to AWAKE, and keep awake; to be at our post, and employed in our calling. In order to our watching we must be daily believing Jesus will come, thinking and praying to be found ready. We should watch the signs of the times; the workings of our own hearts; and over our daily conduct. We should walk as we wish death or Jesus to find us; and transact every business as though Jesus was at the door. Would you, beloved, wish to be found idle, contentious, at enmity, or murmuring, or indulging in any sin? If not, watch against these things; put off the old man, and put on the new; behold, the Judge standeth before the door.

> Behold, the awful day comes on,
> When Jesus on His righteous throne
> Shall in the clouds appear:
>
> With solemn pomp shall bow the sky
> And in the twinkling of an eye,
> Arraign us at His bar.

EVENING

'He shall sit as a refiner.'
MALACHI 3:3

His people are His precious metals. Afflictions are His furnace. Purification is His design. He therefore puts them into the furnace, and He keeps them there until His end is accomplished. But He superintends the whole process of refining, Himself. He regulates the heat, watches the operation of it, and sits waiting for the fulfilment of His design. He will not be disappointed, for if one affliction does not produce the desired end, another shall. Beloved, perhaps you have wondered why one trial has succeeded another in your experience; but the reason is this: the dross was not removed. Thy sorest trials are among thy choicest mercies, because they are intended to make you meet to be a partaker of the inheritance of the saints in light. Think not that you are left alone in your sorrows, your Lord sits by; He intently watches the purification, and as soon as thy pride, obstinacy, worldliness, and opposition to His will is gone, the fire is drawn; your troubles will end. There shall not be one furnace more than is necessary, nor shall you continue in suffering one moment more than is needful. Your Saviour, who died for your sins, is your Refiner; and He sits by the furnace during the whole process of refining; He is preparing you for glory.

> With me in the fire remain
> Till like burnished gold I shine;
> Meet through consecrated pain,
> To see the face divine.

NOVEMBER 12

❧ MORNING ❧
'The Lord is my helper.'
Hebrews 13:6

This is a very encouraging view of the Most High God: He is the helper of His people, and therefore it is that they are more than conquerors. Beloved, let us remember this, when called to perform self-denying duties, or to pass through great and sore troubles. We can do nothing aright, apart from God; but we can do all things through Christ who strengtheneth us. He will help us in every distress, bring us out of every trouble, lead us through the world with honour, and land us safe on the shores of the heavenly Canaan; all this is promised to every one that trusts in Him, waits for Him, walks with Him, and aims habitually to glorify Him. What sweet encouragement is this: we have an *omnipotent Helper*; God in the person of His Son is our *Deliverer*. Let us come up out of the wilderness leaning on our Beloved. Let us not grieve His love, or dishonour His grace. Let us keep a clear conscience, maintain a holy walk, exercise simple faith on our covenant God, and then we may boldly say, '*The Lord is my helper*, I will not fear what man can do unto me.' If God helps us, no power can overcome us.

> To look to Jesus as He rose,
> Confirms my faith, disarms my foes;
> Exalted on His glorious throne,
> I see Him make my cause His own;
> Then all my anxious cares subside,
> For Jesus lives and will provide.

❧ EVENING ❧
'What have I done?'
Jeremiah 8:6

A very necessary enquiry with which to close this day. We too seldom examine our hearts, or compare our conduct with God's Word. Let us then tonight seriously ask ourselves a few questions. What have I done *against* the Lord? Have I not broken His law, and disbelieved His gospel? Have I not grieved His Spirit, and slighted His beloved Son? Have I not murmured at His providence, and opposed His will? Have I not neglected His ordinances, and felt my heart rise against His sovereignty? Have I not doubted His love, and questioned His faithfulness? Have I not forsaken Him, the fountain of living waters, and preferred His creatures to Himself? What have I done *for* the Lord? Have I visited His sick, and relieved His poor? Have I instructed His ignorant ones, and encouraged the desponding? Have I assisted His ministers, and filled my place in His church? Have I pleaded with sinners, and endeavoured to restore backsliders to His fold? Have I kept His glory in view, and sought to advance His kingdom in the world? What have I done, compared with my means, my opportunities, my professions, and with what others have done? Alas! alas! wise to do evil; to do good I appear to have no knowledge.

> Lord, with this guilty heart of mine
> To Thy dear cross I flee;
> And to Thy grace my soul resign,
> To be renewed by Thee.

NOVEMBER 13

❦ MORNING ❦

'Speak evil of no man.'

TITUS 3:2

Speak of no man from an unholy motive, or with a design to injure him; this is decidedly wrong. We are commanded by our beloved Saviour, to love our enemies; to do good to them that hate us and despitefully use us; to pray for them and seek their salvation. If we speak evil of them we dishonour God, bring guilt upon our consciences, grieve the Spirit, and spoil our peace of mind. If we can indulge in detraction without feeling guilty and distressed, our consciences must be blinded, and our hearts hardened through the deceitfulness of sin. Our tongues are not our own, they are bought with a price, and should be employed in the service of their proper owner. Never indulge yourselves in thinking evil of another; or in feelings of jealousy, envy, revenge, bitterness, anger, or malice; for these are earthly, sensual, and devilish. How unlovely it is to hear one professor speaking evil of another; the hearer speaking evil of the minister; the rich speaking contemptuously of the poor, the mistress of servants; much more ministers of ministers. Speak not evil one of another, brethren, for this is not becoming the disciples of Christ.

Whene'er the angry passions rise,
And tempt our thoughts and tongues to strife;
To Jesus let us turn our eyes,
Bright pattern of the Christian life!
How mild! How ready to forgive!
Be these the rules by which we live!

❦ EVENING ❦

'The Just One.'

ACTS 7:52

This is one of the titles of Jesus. He was holy in His nature, and perfectly righteous in His conduct. He rendered to all their due. As a Son, He honoured His Father by filial obedience to His will; as a Servant He always did those things which pleased Him; and as the Substitute of His people, He did what was demanded of them, and suffered in their stead what they deserved. He magnified the law and made it honourable. He bore our sins in His own body on the tree. By one offering He perfected for ever them that are sanctified. He is still *the Just One*: just to every character He sustains, to every name He wears, to every office He fills. He will justly punish His foes, and with equal justice save all who believe on His name. His Word He will never falsify. His character shall never be sullied. He will not cast out one coming sinner. He will not neglect one of the lambs of His fold. He will not turn a deaf ear to one who calls upon His name. He will not deny salvation to any self-condemned soul who seeks it at His feet. He will justly reward His servants, not overlooking even a cup of cold water given in His name. He will appear *'the Just One'* in the doom of the wicked, and in the everlasting happiness of His saints.

O Thou Gracious, Wise and Just,
In Thy hands my soul I trust,
Make me holy, be my Guide,
And for all my wants provide.

NOVEMBER 14

🌿 MORNING 🌿

'Consider how great things He hath done for you.'
1 Samuel 12:24

We are very apt to dwell upon our miseries, and forget our mercies. If we are injured by man, how seldom we forget it; but if we are favoured by God, how little attention we pay to it. Let us this morning consider how great things the Lord hath done for us. He gave His Son to be our ransom. He has given His Spirit to be our guide, and His Word to be our directory. He called us by grace, when we were posting to perdition; wrought a change in our hearts, when we were enmity against Him; and pardoned our sins when we expected to suffer His fiercest displeasure. He has given us faith to trust Him, promises to plead with Him, and proofs of His faithful regard, without number. He hath supplied us through all our journey, corrected our mistakes, conquered our foes, and no good thing hath He withheld from us. Let us consider these things, and praise Him for the past, and trust Him for the future. He that is our God, is the God of Salvation; He hath done great things for us, and He will do greater things, that we may glorify Him forever. My soul, consider thy obligations, and give glory to thy God: do so practically; do so daily.

> O, may I ne'er forget
> The mercy of my God.
> Nor ever want a tongue to spread
> His loudest praise abroad.

🌿 EVENING 🌿

'Behold, he prayeth.'
Acts 9:11

Saul, the Pharisee, had long used the form of prayer, but never until now had he really prayed. He was now created anew in Christ Jesus, he had spiritual life, he was under divine teaching, he felt his need of salvation, and therefore he prayed. None really pray but those who are born again; but all quickened souls do pour out their hearts before God. They feel that they must pray or perish. They must pray or sink under the burden they have to carry. The heart is too full to hold, it must have vent; the desires are too strong to be suppressed, they will escape. Words may be wanting, but prayer will ascend; for prayer is rather the language of the heart than of the lip. Reader, there was a time when you did not pray. You were then dead in trespasses and sins. There was a period when you began to pray; that was the time when you were quickened by the Holy Spirit. You cannot live without prayer now, though you feel dull, dead, dark, cold, and stupid; this is the evidence that you are alive unto God. God admires the prayers of His people, and calls *us* to behold the pleasing fact: a persecutor prays. He always attends to praying souls, therefore *continue in prayer*. Pray for grace to pray, when you feel that you cannot pray.

> O Thou, by whom we come to God,
> The life, the truth, the way!
> The path of prayer Thyself hast trod;
> Lord, teach us how to pray.

NOVEMBER 15

❧ MORNING ❧

'He will be very gracious.'

ISAIAH 30:19

We are often very miserable, always very unworthy; but the Lord is very merciful, and He will be very gracious. He will glorify His grace before angels, men, and devils, in His exceeding kindness towards us; therefore if a sense of our deep depravity and entire unworthiness discourage us, let us appeal to the graciousness of our God, and rely on that. 'He will be very gracious unto thee at the voice of thy cry; when he shall hear it, he will answer thee.' He has said that when, forsaking our evil courses, we return unto Him, He will prove Himself gracious. 'Then shalt thou call, and the LORD shall answer; thou shalt cry, and he shall say, "Here I am."' Yea, He will prove Himself very gracious, for He says, 'Before they call I will answer; and while they are yet speaking I will hear.' O the infinite grace of a gracious God! Lord, keep it uppermost in our minds, and before our eyes continually; let it be our encouragement under all the discoveries of depravity we make, and our comfort under all the trials we endure. Let us endeavour to give our God credit for being *'very gracious.'* He is so whether we believe it or not.

> What from Christ my soul shall sever,
> Bound by everlasting bands?
> Once in Him, in Him for ever,
>
> Thus the word of promise stands:
> None shall pluck me
> From the strength of Israel's hands.

❧ EVENING ❧

'God imputeth righteousness without works.'

ROMANS 4:6

This is one of the great and gracious mysteries of revelation. Man has no righteousness of his own. God cannot justify without one. The Lord Jesus comes into our world and produces one. The righteousness of Jesus is infinitely meritorious. He wrought it out in our nature, as our Substitute. It was accepted for us and is placed to our account. Before we have done one good work, altogether irrespective of good works, the moment we believe, God places the righteousness of Jesus to our account. It is ours, ours by free gift; as much ours as if we had wrought it ourselves. It is in this that we are justified. In this we are truly righteous; therefore we are accepted of God, and no charge lies against us in the book of God. All is met. All is answered. The just God acquits us from all charges, pronounces us righteous, declares us to be free from all condemnation. Thus, 'Christ is the end of the law for righteousness to every one that believeth.' Beloved, when Satan tempts you, when fears distress you, when your past conduct generates despondency, when the claims of the law disturb you, endeavour to exercise faith in this glorious fact, that God imputes righteousness without works.

> Jesus, how glorious is Thy grace!
> When in Thy name we trust,
> Our faith receives a righteousness,
> Which makes the sinner just.

NOVEMBER 16

❦ MORNING ❦

'Arise ye, and depart, for this is not your rest.'
MICAH 2:10

There is no permanent rest for the believer on earth; here briars and thorns will be with him; and a voice is daily sounding in his ears, *'Arise ye, and depart.'* Here you are not to loll at ease, or to idle on your journey; here you are not to expect to find satisfaction, for it is an enemy's land, and you are only passing through it to your heavenly home. If your march is quick and your conduct scriptural, be not surprised if the dogs bark at you; they know you not, nor did they know your Master. He was pursued, annoyed, and at last put to death by them; and in agony of soul He cried out, 'Dogs have compassed me; the assembly of the wicked have enclosed me; they have pierced my hands and my feet.' Lay not up for yourselves treasures upon earth, where moth and rust doth corrupt, and where thieves break through and steal; but set your affections on things above, where Christ sitteth at the right hand of God. Use the world, but do not abuse it; pass through it, but never seek a home in it; remember it is peopled by the enemies of your God, and your enemies too.

> When snares and dangers line my way,
> Jesus is all my strength and stay;
> Cheerful I'll walk the desert through,
> Nor fear what earth or hell can do:
> Jesus will ease my troubled breast,
> And shortly bring my soul to rest.

❦ EVENING ❦

'Jesus Christ the same.'
HEBREWS 13:8

Immutability is one of the essential perfections of Jehovah. He claims it as His right. He presents it as a source of comfort to His people, when He says, 'I am the LORD, I change not; therefore ye sons of Jacob are not consumed.' But the Lord Jesus is immutable, because He is divine. He changes not. He is the same in all the glories of His person, in all the purposes of His heart, in all the doctrines of His gospel, in the greatness of His love, in the omnipotence of His power, in the tenderness of His sympathy, in the merit of His blood, and in His hatred to sin. Is Jesus immutable? Then let us adore Him as divine. Let us trust Him with implicit confidence. Let us hold fast the precious truths of His holy gospel. Let us seek comfort in Him, when our earthly gourds wither, and all our cisterns are broken. He is the same in darkness as in the light; when we are cast down, as when we are filled with joy; when providence frowns, as when all things around smile and rejoice. He is always Jesus, the Saviour; the kind, the condescending, the faithful, the tender Saviour. He is the same tonight, as when we first tasted His love; and as when our hearts danced at the sound of His name.

> His purpose and love are the same,
> Whatever the changes I find,
> A trifle may alter my frame,
> But nothing unsettles His mind.

NOVEMBER 17

🌿 MORNING 🌿

'Be ye reconciled to God.'

2 Corinthians 5:20

Is there any thing but love between God and your souls? There ought not to be. God hates nothing but sin. He is offended with nothing but sin. This we profess to hate and forsake. We were once enemies, but Jesus died to reconcile us to God. We are now professedly friends, but do we act towards God, and speak of God, as though we were His friends? Are we offended at any thing in God, or at any thing done by God? Why should we be? His nature is love. His ways are all infinitely wise. His tender mercy is over all His works. He desires that we should be on the best terms with Him. How wonderful! He offers a pardon for all our sins, grace to sanctify our natures, and heaven to receive our souls! *He beseeches us to be reconciled.* As though His tender love could not rest, as though He could not be happy, or content, unless we are friends with Him. Beloved, are you living or walking at a distance from God? Is there any shyness between God and your soul? God beseeches you by me, and I pray you in Christ's stead, 'Be ye reconciled to God.'

Sprinkled now with blood the throne,
Why beneath thy burdens groan?
See the curse on Jesus laid,
Justice owns the ransom paid:
Bow the knee and kiss the Son.
COME AND WELCOME, SINNER, COME!

🌿 EVENING 🌿

'I shall die in my nest.'

Job 29:18

Job's nest was very comfortable, and appeared to be very secure. It was on high, and not to be easily reached. He knew that death could reach it, but he thought that nothing else could disturb it. His conduct was consistent, and his conscience was quiet; God was his Father, and providence his friend. 'Then I said I shall die in my nest.' But, alas! Suddenly a storm arose, the nest was destroyed, and the poor bird lay bleeding and exposed. No earthly nest is out of danger. Temporal comforts are only lent. The higher the tree in which we build, the more exposed to the whirlwind and the storm. The inhabitant of the low place enjoys the shelter. Here we have no continuing city. In one day we may be brought down. Let us therefore endeavour to leave our matters more with the Lord, and learn to be content with His appointments. We must die. But *when*, and *where*, and *how*, should be left with the Lord. Five minutes after death, it will matter very little, whether we died on a bed of our own, in a spacious chamber, surrounded by friends; or at some rich man's gate, neglected and alone. Present comforts may all leave us, our soft nest may be scattered to the winds, but our union to Jesus nothing can disturb.

I would not contend with Thy will
Whatever that will may decree;
But O, may each trial I feel
Unite me more firmly to Thee.

NOVEMBER 18

❧ MORNING ❧

'I will be as the dew unto Israel.'
HOSEA 14:5

Our hearts by nature are like the dry, dead, and barren earth; there would be neither life, beauty, nor fruit, but for the grace of God. And even after regeneration, we are as much dependent upon God, as the earth in the east is dependent upon the dew. If there be no dew, there will be no fruit, and if there be no grace, there will be no real religion. But our God has said, 'I will be as the dew unto Israel.' What the dew is to the earth, God will be unto His people. Does the dew cool and refresh the earth? So will the Lord cool and refresh our souls with the sense of His love, and the tokens of His favour. Does the dew soften and break the clods of the valley? So will our God soften and dissolve our hard and impenitent hearts. Does the dew prepare the ground for the seed, and cause the same to vegetate and grow? So will our God prepare our hearts to receive the Word, and cause it to grow and bring forth fruit. Does the dew fall insensibly, and in the evening, when most needed? So will our God come unto us, when we most need His quickening and fructifying operations.

> Come, Holy Ghost, as heavenly dew,
> My parched soul revive:
> The former mercies now renew,
>
> Quicken and bid me live:
> Thy fertilizing power impart,
> And sanctify my barren heart.

❧ EVENING ❧

'Leaning upon her beloved.'
SONG OF SOLOMON 8:5

Jesus is the object of a believer's love. To him the world is a wilderness. Heaven is his Father's house and his home. He is passing through the wilderness in company with Jesus. He is represented as the bride leaning on her Beloved. This is indicative of weakness in herself, and confidence in her Beloved. He is her strength as well as her guide, her support as well as the object of her affection. She leans on Him as well as converses with Him. He supports as well as comforts her. Believer, keep close to thy Saviour's side. Never leave Him while in this waste howling wilderness. Lean on Him, and when you feel weak *lean hard*. His strong arm is put forth to support thy weak frame. He will bear thee up. He will lead thee on. The more you lean on Him, the more you will love Him; and the more you love Him, the closer you will cleave to Him. Yield to His guidance, trust in His love, lean on His power, walk by His side, and commend Him to others around you. In His company you are safe, in communion with Him you will be happy; like the two disciples of old, your heart will be warmed, and you will be at the end of your journey before you are aware of it. He is always at your side; believe and prove Him near.

> On thy Saviour's love and power,
> On His righteousness and blood,
> Lean in every trying hour,
> Lean till you sit down with God.

NOVEMBER 19

🌿 MORNING 🌿

'It is good for us to be here.'

MATTHEW 17:4

So said Peter when on the mount with Jesus, and so we have said when enjoying His presence and His love. It is good to live and walk in communion with God. It is good to be numbered with God's people, and to occupy a place in His church. It is good to be in the present world, because we have an opportunity of bearing witness for Jesus, and against its course; we have talents to use, and opportunities for usefulness whereby we can glorify God. Is Jesus honoured by our patient suffering? Then, when on the bed of affliction, we should say, 'Lord, it is good to be here.' Is our God glorified by our industry, forbearance, and testimony to the power and grace of Jesus? Then, when in our business, or in company with those whom we are trying to benefit, we may exclaim, 'Lord, it is good to be here!' Yes, Christian, it is good to be any where, and any thing, so that thy Jesus may be glorified, and the end of thy creation, redemption, and sanctification obtained. O, to aim always to honour God, and then we may every where say, 'Lord, *it is good to be here.*' But if it is good to be here, how much better to be alone!

> *Great Comforter, descend*
> *In gentle breathings down;*
> *Preserve me to the end*
> *That no man take my crown;*
> *My guardian still vouchsafe to be,*
> *Nor suffer me to go from Thee.*

🌿 EVENING 🌿

'Ebenezer.'

1 SAMUEL 7:12

We have *required* help, for as creatures we are exposed, weak, and foolish; and as Christians we are surrounded by snares, opposed by enemies, are timid and fearful, and easily turned aside. We have *received* help, and help in every time of need. It was through divine assistance that we were able to overcome unbelief and evil habits; to break away from our old connections; to take up our cross and bear it after Jesus; to stand our ground amidst storms of temptation, and powerful opposition; to persevere in the good old way. Having obtained help of God we continue to this day. Let us then set up our Ebenezer, and acknowledge the help we have received. Its source was divine; it came from above. The supply has been sufficient, well timed, exactly suited to the circumstances in which we are placed. The manner of communication was at times direct: we can say, 'The Lord helped me'; at other times indirect: 'The Lord helped us by others.' What should be the result? Praise: hearty, grateful, constant praise. Prayer: fervent, faithful, frequent prayer for help in future. Patience: giving the Lord time, and waiting in quiet expectation for the fulfilment of His Word. Testimony: God is faithful.

> *Here I raise my Ebenezer,*
> *Hither by Thy help I'm come;*
> *And I hope, by Thy good pleasure,*
> *Safely to arrive at home.*

NOVEMBER 20

🌿 MORNING 🌿

'Brethren, the time is short.'

1 Corinthians 7:29

Then our sufferings must be short, for they are bounded by time, and are confined to the present world. Consoling consideration this. Then our opportunities to glorify our God below must be short; therefore we ought to seize them and improve them with all our might. Then the triumphing of the wicked is short, and the contradiction of sinners against us will soon be ended. Let us therefore be patient, and prayerful, and diligent, for our redemption draweth nigh. The time is short; then we shall soon see our Jesus, enjoy the company of our sanctified brethren, and be for ever with the Lord. The time is short, but eternity is long. Let us therefore be laying up for ourselves treasures in heaven, where neither moth nor rust doth corrupt; and let us be daily preparing for our last remove. The time is short; it flies away: our dying day will soon be here. It remaineth therefore, that both they that have wives be as though they had none; and they that weep, as though they wept not; and they that rejoice, as though they rejoiced not; and they that buy as though they possessed not. Let us use our little time to a good purpose.

> O, may my soul maintain her ground,
> From faith to faith go on!
> At the last day in Christ be found,
> And form the circles that surround
> His everlasting throne.

🌿 EVENING 🌿

'The word of His grace.'

Acts 14:3

This is one of the titles of the blessed gospel. It is God's gracious word – His gracious word to graceless sinners. It originated in grace, and was once a mighty thought hid in the depths of the mind of God. It was introduced into our world by grace, and by grace alone it has been continued until now. It publishes grace, or a free pardon to all sinners who believe in Jesus; a hearty welcome to the Lord's throne; a fulness opened in the Redeemer's person to supply all our wants; and a legal title to heaven by faith in Christ Jesus. It is made effectual by grace, and is the instrument by which the Lord produces the work of grace in our hearts. It is essentially different from law, or legal requirement; for it speaks of favour shown, it presents blessings of inestimable value, and proclaims everlasting liberty as an act of sovereign grace. Beloved, beware lest you legalize the gospel, or turn it into a law requiring, rather than what it is, the joyful sound of the Jubilee, proclaiming pardon, peace, liberty, and restoration to an everlasting inheritance. It is the good news of God's favour, the glad tidings of a full salvation for the poor, lost, and degraded children of men; of every blessing man can need, without money and without price.

> O Lord! the treasures of Thy love
> Are everlasting mines;
> Deep as our helpless miseries are,
> And boundless as our sins!

NOVEMBER 21

🌿 MORNING 🌿

'My peace I give unto you.'

John 14:27

Peace is an invaluable blessing – it is the gift of Jesus. None but believers know the sweetness of the peace He bestows. He made it by shedding His blood. He proclaims it in the everlasting gospel. He bestows it upon us when we believe, and it is enjoyed in the heart under the influence of the Holy Spirit. It is peace with God; a peaceful conscience; the beginning of heaven in the soul. He gives it often when in the midst of trouble; and it makes every burden light, every trouble less, and the sinner happy in every situation. O Jesus! give us Thy peace this morning! Let it reign and rule in our hearts this day. Believer, look only to Jesus for peace, for *'He is our peace.'* Believe His Word, receive His atonement, trust in His perfect work, aim to show forth His praise, and peace which passeth all understanding shall fill your mind. Let it be your daily prayer, that you may enjoy this peace in death; for then you will die happy, honourably, and safely. Seek it as a gift of grace, and you shall enjoy it to the honour of God. You can receive peace from God, though you cannot make your peace with God.

> *Close to my Saviour's bloody tree,*
> *My soul untired shall ever cleave;*
> *Both scourged and crucified for me,*
> *With Christ resolved to die and live:*
> *My prayer, my grand ambition this,*
> *Living and dying to be His.*

🌿 EVENING 🌿

'Is thine heart right?'

2 Kings 10:15

This is an important enquiry. With some the head is right – it has clear views of doctrine, and can make correct statements respecting Christian experience; but the heart is not right. Reader, is thine? Is it broken *for* sin? Is it set *against* sin? Is it *fixed* on the Lord Jesus? Do you embrace the Lord's Word, rest for acceptance on Jesus' finished work, and endeavour so to walk as to please God? Is your heart glowing with love to the saints, pity for the world, and zeal for the glory of God? Can you live comfortably, without living upon Christ? Can you be satisfied without fellowship with God? How is your heart affected towards the Bible, the Lord's day, and the means of grace? Are you humbled under a sense of your sinfulness, and filled with wonder at the exceeding grace of God towards you? If so, your heart is right. But it will not be long right unless it is kept near to Jesus. You must often visit Gethsemane and Calvary, you must have fellowship with Christ in His sufferings, or you cannot keep the heart right. If it is not right, are you mourning on account of it? Do you take it to Jesus? Perhaps you are saying,

> *If mine were right, it could not be,*
> *Good God, so contrary to Thee,*
> *So prone to every sin:*
> *It must remain an evil heart,*
> *Till Thou Thine hallowing grace impart,*
> *And Christ is formed within.*

NOVEMBER 22

🌿 MORNING 🌿

'I will correct thee in measure.'

JEREMIAH 30:11

Sin procures correction, and love sends it. Every child is chastened, because every child sins. But though we are corrected for sin, yet not according to the desert of sin. Our Father chastens us in measure, not in wrath, but in love; not to destroy, but to save us. There is no wrath in His heart, for He has sworn that He will not be wrath with us; yet He will visit our sins with the rod, and our iniquities with stripes. He is reconciled to our persons, but not to our follies. Therefore He says, 'As many as I love, I rebuke and chasten; be zealous therefore and repent.' Let us not despise His chastening, nor faint when we are rebuked of Him; for it is the common lot of all His children, and if it drives us to Him, and humbles us at His feet, it is evidently sent in love. It is a painful blessing; a mercy sent to purify and cleanse us. If we sin and are not chastened, our sonship is questionable; for what son is he whom his father chasteneth not? But if we are chastened, God dealeth with us as with sons; and our sufferings are the fulfilment of His promise. He corrects us for our profit, to make us partakers of His holiness.

> *Though ten thousand ills beset thee,*
> *From without, and from within,*
> *Jesus saith, He'll ne'er forget thee,*
> *But will save from hell and sin:*
> *He is faithful*
> *To perform His gracious Word.*

🌿 EVENING 🌿

'He shall direct thy paths.'

PROVERBS 3:6

Are you in perplexity? At a loss which way to take, or what to do? Does providence baffle all your schemes, and leave you in confusion and trouble? The Lord is teaching you the lesson which He taught His prophet Jeremiah, who said, 'O LORD, I know that the way of man is not in himself: it is not in man that walketh to direct his steps.' You must go to the Lord for wisdom, as well as for grace; and look to Him for direction, as well as salvation. He has marked out your path, but you cannot see the lines; go to Him in child-like simplicity and ask Him to throw light upon it, and then it will be all plain. Seek His direction before every movement. Beseech Him to go with you in every enterprise. 'In every thing by prayer and supplication with thanksgiving, let your requests be made known unto God.' 'In all thy ways acknowledge Him, and He shall direct thy paths.' His eye is upon thee for good. His ear is open to thy prayer. He will be very gracious unto thee at the voice of thy cry; when He shall hear He will answer thee. Consult His Word, seek His blessing, honour His love, keep His company, aim at His glory, and He shall direct thy paths. He only can direct you aright, and He has promised that He will.

> *Commit to Him thy doubtful way,*
> *Rest on His care, and trust His hand;*
> *His goodness shall thy path display,*
> *And soon a prosperous end command.*

NOVEMBER 23

❦ MORNING ❧

'Open thy mouth wide, and I will fill it.'
PSALM 81:10

The Word of God affords all possible encouragement to earnest, fervent prayer; men ought always to pray, and not to faint. Believers should ask all they want of God as their heavenly Father; they should ask of Him because He has bidden them, and expect to receive because He is faithful. Are our wants many this morning? Our God bids us open our mouths wide, and promises to fill them. We should ask largely, for God considers Himself honoured when we ask for much, and expect much. He rejoices over us to do us good. He looks upon us as His dear children, and pledges Himself to give all that we want, or can use to His glory. Let us then ask for a supply of every want; let us continue to plead His largest promises; and let us continue to plead in the name of Jesus until we receive. Our God heareth prayer; and if we, being evil, know how to give good things unto our children, much more will our heavenly Father give good things unto them that ask Him. Let us therefore come boldly unto a throne of grace, that we may obtain mercy and find grace to help us.

> Thou art coming to a King
> Large petitions with thee bring;
> For His grace and power are such,
> None can ever ask too much:
> He Himself has bid thee pray,
> Therefore will not say thee nay.

❦ EVENING ❧

'Mourning every one for his iniquity.'
EZEKIEL 7:16

Such is the effect of real conversion to God. The sinner under alarm may weep, he dreads the punishment of his sin; but the assured believer will mourn, because he has sinned against a God of love, and broken a law that is holy, just, and good. He will mourn over the sin that dwells in him, which no one knows but himself, as well as for the iniquity that is discovered by his fellow men. He daily mourns, because he daily sins. Yet he is not unhappy. He knows that the blood of Jesus Christ cleanseth him from all sin. He knows that to him the Lord will not impute sin. He knows that he is accepted in the Beloved. These things make him mourn. The greater his confidence in God, the sweeter his enjoyment of a Saviour's love; the closer he walks with God, the more he mourns for his iniquity. His is repentance unto life; godly sorrow, which needeth not to be repented of. Beloved, do you mourn for your iniquity? Has there been any sorrow for sin working in your heart today? You daily sin; you must daily repair to the fountain opened for sin; and you should daily mourn for your iniquity. Mourn, but do not despond. Mourn, but hold fast your confidence.

> Dear Lord, may I a mourner be,
> Over my sins and after Thee;
> And when my mourning days are o'er,
> Enjoy Thy comforts evermore.

NOVEMBER 24

🌿 MORNING 🌿
'I will see you again.'
JOHN 16:22

The presence of Jesus is the happiness of His people; when He is present manifesting His love, we are filled with joy and peace; but when He hides His face, we are troubled. Nor is it any wonder, for then generally, Satan comes in with his temptations; our corruptions rise and trouble us; and for a time every thing seems to be against us. But if Jesus hath once visited, He will come again; and He will manifest Himself unto us as He doth not unto the world. In every season of desertion and darkness, let us plead this precious promise given us by our adorable Lord. He sympathises with us, and says, 'Ye now therefore have sorrow; but *I will see you again*, and your heart shall rejoice, and your joy no man taketh from you.' Precious Lord Jesus, let us this day enjoy Thy presence and Thy love; come and visit us, or rather, come and take up Thy abode with us, to leave us no more for ever. Our souls thirst for Thee; we long to enjoy Thy love, as we have done in days that are gone by. O, manifest Thyself unto us this day, and unite us closer than ever unto Thyself! O make us like Thyself and dwell with us for ever!

> *Then let us sit beneath His cross,*
> *And gladly catch the healing stream;*
> *All things for Him account but dross,*
> *And give up all our hearts to Him;*
> *Of nothing think or speak beside;*
> *My Lord, my love, is crucified.*

🌿 EVENING 🌿
'Christ died for the ungodly.'
ROMANS 5:6

Not for the weak merely, but for the wicked; for those who were totally depraved, and entirely unworthy of His notice; who had lost the image of God, were alienated from the life of God, and were enemies to God. What wondrous grace is this! Had He died only for the moral, or the amiable, or those who had something to recommend them to His notice, we might have given way to despair, and have concluded that He could not have died for us; but it was for the ungodly, just such as we are. Actually for us if we believe in Him: in our stead, as our Substitute, that we might never die. He was made sin for us, who knew no sin; that we might be made the righteousness of God in Him. Let us then draw comfort from this fact, that Jesus died, in order that ungodly sinners might live for ever. He bore our sins in His own body on the tree, that we being dead to sins might live unto righteousness. We therefore, as believers in Jesus, shall never die. Our sins are atoned for. For us expiation is made. We are entitled to life. We have it. For Jesus said, 'Verily, verily I say unto you, he that believeth on me hath everlasting life.' O Thou glorious Redeemer, how shall we sufficiently praise Thee for Thy wondrous love!

> *Was it for crimes that I had done*
> *He groan'd upon the tree?*
> *Amazing pity! grace unknown!*
> *And love beyond degree!*

NOVEMBER 25

🌿 MORNING 🌿

'I trust in thy word.'

PSALM 119:42

It is unsafe and improper to trust our feelings or fancies; to listen to suggestions, or judge by appearances; the Christian's guide is God's Word, and this should be the object of his trust. If we cannot take God's Word and depend upon it, what can we trust? It is true; on all necessary points it is plain; it has been tried and always found faithful. We should believe it, rely on it, plead it, expect its fulfilment, and comfort ourselves with it, especially when surrounded with difficulties, when in darkness or filled with forebodings, because God delays and our prayers are not answered. Trusting in God's faithful Word will bring peace to the mind, experience to the soul, and deliverance in every time of trouble. If we trust God's Word we may be confident, for our supply is certain. Trusting a naked promise is difficult, but it is attainable, and truly desirable. The promise is God's bond, and is intended to set our minds at rest. If we trust it calmly and implicitly, we shall enjoy peace, quietness, and confidence. Trusting God's Word, we need fear no foe, or dread any trouble; all is safe, and safe for ever. Lord, work faith in my heart this day.

> In Thee, O Lord, I put my trust:
> Mighty, and merciful, and just,
> Thy faithful Word I prove;
>
> Thou canst, Thou wilt my helper be;
> My confidence is all in Thee,
> The faithful God of love.

🌿 EVENING 🌿

'I would not live alway.'

JOB 7:16

Yet we should be willing to live as long as God pleases. He will keep us in this world no longer than He can in some way get glory by us. Still, pain and suffering make life appear long, and death desirable. It is generally the sufferer who says, 'I loathe it, I would not live alway.' But the language is suited to us, for if we were to live alway, we should sin alway, we should mourn alway, we should be alway passing through tribulation. Who would live alway at a distance from home, in a state of exile? But such is our state now. Well, we shall not live alway, nor shall we live long; our remaining days may be very few. Let us not therefore be much concerned about how long we shall live, but let us aim to live to some good purpose. Let us live while we live. Let us live for God, for the good of souls, for the spread of the gospel, for the improvement of the church, for the honour of Christ, and for the destruction of sin. Let us endeavour so to live, as neither to fear death nor life, being prepared for the one, and useful in the other. Let us live expecting everlasting life, where the satisfaction will be perfect, and the appetite for enjoyment will be always fresh. Let us live *upon* Christ, *for* Christ, and be as much *like* Christ as possible.

> No; I would not always live,
> Always sin, repent, and grieve,
> Always in my dungeon groan,
> Always serve a God unknown.

NOVEMBER 26

🌿 MORNING 🌿

'An heir of God, through Christ.'
GALATIANS 4:7

By nature we are children of wrath; but union to Jesus exalts us to the highest pitch of honour and happiness. All our mercies flow through Jesus; we must ever look to Him as the medium of access to God, and of union with God. If we are one with Jesus, we are heirs of God; to us He has willed all the riches of grace, and all the riches of glory. The testament is made and sealed, and all is secured to us by the oath of God, and the blood of our dear Saviour. O, what an honour! To be the heirs of God! To possess and enjoy throughout eternity all that God can impart! Unutterable grace! We have enough secured to us while on earth; and we shall be put in full possession at the resurrection. Let us then ascertain beyond a doubt, that we are the sons of God; that we have received the spirit of adoption; that we are united to Jesus; and daily walk with God. Let us live expecting the day when we shall be put in possession, and preparing for that glorious event. Let us walk worthy of the vocation wherewith we are called, with all lowliness and meekness, watching unto prayer.

Let earth no more my heart divide;
With Christ may I be crucified:
To Thee with my whole soul aspire;
Dead to the world and all its toys,
To idle pomp, and fading joys,
Be Thou alone my one desire!

🌿 EVENING 🌿

'He hath settled on his lees.'
JEREMIAH 48:11

This was the effect of prosperity. He was now wise in his own wisdom, and strong in his own strength. All was calm and tranquil, and he was settled down in self-satisfaction. This would soon be the case with us, if it were not for trials and temptations. We should, like Israel, forget God our Saviour, and lightly esteem the Rock of our salvation. To a certain extent this is sometimes the case: we settle down, and then prayer becomes formal, spiritual good tasteless, the things of God mere common-place matters. There is no wrestling with God, no direct communion with God, no savoury spiritual conversation; the form is maintained, but the power is gone. When this happens, if we are really Christians, we may look out for troubles, for they will surely come; our God will stir us up, as the eagle stirreth up her nest. He will send one trial upon another, one message after another, until He brings us back to Himself with weeping and supplication. Moab *may* settle on his lees, but Israel *shall not*. Therefore beware of sinking into such an unbecoming state. 'Woe unto them that are at ease in Zion.' Now is the time for diligence, for activity in God's cause, for carrying out the Saviour's precepts. Let us work, not sleep; be active, not settle on our lees.

Be wise to run thy race,
And cast off every load;
Strive to be rich in works of grace,
Be rich towards thy God.

NOVEMBER 27

🌿 MORNING 🌿
'I am the good shepherd.'
JOHN 10:11

Beloved, are you in the fold of Jesus? Are you numbered with His sheep? Are you feeding and resting among them? Jesus presents Himself to us this morning in a very lovely character; He says, *'I am the good shepherd.'* There is no other shepherd so good or so great as He. He has the tenderest affection for His flock. He affords them His powerful protection. He finds them plenty and suitable provision. He gave His life to redeem them. He sends His Spirit to sanctify them. He is preparing a place in heaven to receive them. He will eternally dwell among them and bless them. O, how great is His goodness! He is indeed abundant in goodness and truth. He says, 'My sheep hear my voice, and I know them, and they follow me; and I give unto them eternal life; and they shall never perish, neither shall any pluck them out of my hand. My Father, which gave them me, is greater than all; and no one is able to pluck them out of my Father's hand. I and my Father are one.' What glorious security! What honour is conferred on the flock of Jesus! *Good Shepherd*, keep us near Thyself. Never let us wander, no, not for a moment; but may we be always delighted with Thy love.

The least, the feeblest of the sheep,
To Him the Father gave;
Kind is His heart the charge to keep,
And strong His arm to save.

🌿 EVENING 🌿
'Wash me and I shall be whiter than snow.'
PSALM 51:7

David was no common sinner. His crimes were of a crimson colour. His views of his sin were vivid and powerful. But so exalted were his views of the efficacy of the atonement, that he felt persuaded that if it were applied, it would entirely remove the stain. He believed that if the Lord washed him, He would do it thoroughly; that every spot and trace of sin would be taken away, and that he should be pure as an angel of light. He has realized this. He is enjoying it at this moment. Beloved, however black thy crimes, however deep the stains of sin may be on thy soul, the precious blood of Jesus can remove the whole. If thy God wash thee, He will purge out every stain; He will make thee perfectly clean. It is said of those above, who were once sinners like thee below, *'They are without fault before the throne of God.'* And it is said of Jesus, to His eternal honour, that He is able *'to present you faultless before the presence of his glory with exceeding joy.'* You never can estimate the value of the Saviour's blood. You never can have too exalted views of its efficacy, for it *cleanseth from all sin.* Precious blood! The blood of Incarnate Deity, may it cleanse my soul completely and for ever!

See, see the fountain flows,
To purge thy guilty stains,
Till whiter than the purest snows,
Descending o'er the plains.

NOVEMBER 28

❦ MORNING ❦
'The day shall declare it.'
1 Corinthians 3:13

The day referred to is the day when the Lord Jesus shall be revealed from heaven in flaming fire, when the dead shall be raised, and the judgment commence. O, what a day will that be! Then every covering shall be removed, and every secret exposed. It will be a revealing day, a convincing day, a confirming day, a condemning day, a justifying day. Then our motives will all be discovered, and our intentions laid bare. Hypocrisy will be condemned, and deception punished. O beloved, let us live as having that day before us; let us act as though persuaded that then all will be discovered. Are we sincere? – the day will declare it. Are we aiming at God's glory, or self-exaltation? – the day will declare it. Are we conducting our business on Christian, or worldly principles? – the day will declare it. Are we honest and humble? – the day will declare it. Is our profession from principle, from faith in, and love to Jesus? – the day will declare it. O that that day may declare that we are humble, holy, watchful, diligent disciples of the Lord Jesus! Let us daily live expecting that day; it will come upon many suddenly.

Before me place in dread array
The pomp of that tremendous day,
When Thou with clouds shall come
To judge the nations at Thy bar;
And tell me, Lord, shall I be there,
To meet the joyful doom?

❦ EVENING ❦
'Yet will I trust in Him.'
Job 13:15

Nor can you do better. Nay, you cannot do so well. It is the very best thing you can do. But suppose He strip me of my property, bereave me of my children, deprive me of my health, sever me from my friends, and hide His face from me. Still trust in Him. Not only so, but if He appears to stand over you as an executioner, with the axe uplifted, ready to strike the fatal blow, still trust in Him. You have His Word, and He cannot deny it, He will not falsify it. He *must* be faithful. He *will* be kind. He never can turn away from the imploring eye of His afflicted child. He never will refuse to honour His word of promise, when it is pleaded at His throne. Trust in Him, for He is only trying thy faith, deepening thy experience, and laying a foundation for thy future happiness. Trust in Him, and you will some day bless Him for this very trial. Trust in Him, and when He hath tried you, you shall come forth as gold. Though Satan tempt you, though corruption rage within you, though the world may frown upon you, though Christian friends are unkind to you, though all things appear to be against you, still say, 'Yet will I trust in Him.' Let nothing shake your confidence in God.

Why should I dread Jehovah's hand,
Though it might crush to dust?
'Tis love that gives His arm command,
And in that love I trust.

NOVEMBER 29

❦ MORNING ❦

'I will mention the lovingkindnesses of the LORD.'
ISAIAH 63:7

What subject so suited as this to engage the thoughts, fill the memory, and flow from the lips of the Lord's people? Let us mention the provision made for all His poor, for all their wants; the promises given to all His people, comprehending all their desires; the prayers answered in all times of trial, granting relief and defence. Let us mention the lovingkindness of the Lord to those who are seeking Him, it will encourage them; to those who are complaining, it may silence them; to those who are tempted, it will support them; to those who have backslidden, it will convince, and perhaps restore them. Let us speak of His kindness to ourselves, to check murmuring, produce gratitude, and raise hope. Let us mention the lovingkindness of the Lord, at the Lord's throne, in pleading and intercession; and prayer and expostulation; in praise and thanksgiving. Let us often speak one to another, and let this be our daily subject, *'The Lovingkindness of the Lord.'* This will comfort, strengthen, and sanctify our minds; it will bring us peace.

> *We'll speak of all He did and said,*
> *And suffer'd for us here below;*
> *The path He mark'd for us to tread,*
> *And what He's doing for us now;*
> *Discarding every worldly theme,*
> *Our conversation fill'd with Him.*

❦ EVENING ❦

'The day of small things.'
ZECHARIAH 4:10

The work of grace in some persons is scarcely discernible. Their faith is so weak. Their knowledge is so small. Their love is so feeble. Their reserve is so great. They cannot open their minds to any one. They are held in perpetual bondage. Yet they are the Lord's. They have light enough to see the emptiness of the world, the vileness of sin, and the value of Christ. They long for the enjoyment of His love, and desire above all things an interest in Him. They cannot say they love Him, but they heartily desire to do so. They have many fears and few joys. They say they do not pray, and yet they could not live without going to the throne of grace. In their esteem nothing is to be compared with union to Christ, no people are so happy as the Lord's people, and they feel that they would give a world to be like them. It is with such the day of small things, but there are the things which accompany salvation. There is the acorn from which the oak will grow. There is the dawn which will introduce the perfect day. Beloved, do not despise the day of small things. God does not; Jesus does not; you should not.

> *The first faint spark of good desire*
> *Which feebly would to heaven aspire,*
> *Its kindler God will not despise;*
> *The spark into a flame shall spread;*
> *And bless'd by Him the smallest seed*
> *Of faith into a tree shall rise.*

NOVEMBER 30

❦ MORNING ❦

'Return unto thy rest, O my soul.'
PSALM 1816:7

There is no rest for the Christian but at the feet of Jesus; when we live near to Him, and exercise our faith upon Him, we are at rest. Conscience is silent, or commends us. The law has nothing to say against us. The world has but little influence over us. Satan is weak, and cannot overcome us. But if we wander we become weak, we lose our courage, and darkness, perplexity, and trouble frequently fill our minds. But we *may* return, for Jesus is still inviting us; we *must* return, or we cannot enjoy peace. Let us therefore return unto our rest this morning. O Jesus! we come to Thee! Receive Thy wandering sheep, restore unto us the joy of Thy salvation, and let us find rest at Thy cross. O, to rest on Thy faithful Word, with Thy faithful people; to rest from slavish fear, worldly care, and distressing anxiety; to rest in Thy boundless love, satisfied with the dispensations of Thy special providence. Return, return, my soul, from all thy wanderings, and find thy rest in Jesus, thy faithful Friend and Saviour. Sweet assurance, 'He will receive us graciously.' O Jesus, be my rest, and the solace of my soul this day!

Indulge me, Lord, in that repose,
Which only he who loves Thee knows;
Lodged in Thy arms I fear no more

The tempest's howl, the billow's roar;
Those storms must shake th' Almighty's seat,
Which violate the saint's retreat.

❦ EVENING ❦

'Before honour is humility.'
PROVERBS 18:12

The Lord always humbles, before He exalts. He strips us, before He clothes us with the best robe. He empties us, before He fills us with His grace. We must take our seat on the dunghill, before we are raised to sit with the princes of His people. It is the weak that He strengthens, the poor that He supplies, the condemned that He justifies, the homeless that He receives, the totally unworthy that He crowns with glory. We must lie low, if we would rise high. We must be nothing, if we would inherit all things. We must be quite empty, if we would be filled with all the fulness of God. He giveth grace unto the humble. Joseph must lie in the dungeon, before he is seated in the second chariot of Egypt. David must be hunted like the partridge upon the mountains, before he is raised to fill the throne of Israel. Paul must be a poor blind sinner, before he becomes the great apostle. This is God's plan. The righteous who are now accounted the off-scouring of all things, are destined to shine as the sun in the kingdom of their Father. Beloved, fear not to go down; the lower you descend in humility, the higher you will rise in glory; the deeper your penitence, the sweeter your joys. God resisteth the proud, but He giveth grace to the humble.

He draws from human littleness,
His grandeur and renown;
And humble hearts with joy confess,
The triumph all His own.

DECEMBER 1

🌿 MORNING 🌿

'The Lord God omnipotent reigneth.'

REVELATION 19:6

Our God is the author of all good, the only object of religious worship and fear, the infinite, all-controlling Being. He can do all things, and do all things with ease, swiftness, certainty, and precision. He is on the throne; His reign is merciful, just, glorious. He reigns universally over every empire, kingdom, state, parish, person, thing. Everything that takes place is either appointed or permitted by Him. Everything is overruled, for nothing escapes His notice, frustrates His purpose, or disorganises His plan. All things are tributary, and bring honour to His name. Does the Lord God Omnipotent reign? Then let us fear to offend Him; aim to please Him well in all things; trust in and rely on Him; call upon and prove Him; live in the daily remembrance of His reign. This will conquer fear, prevent sins, strengthen faith, nourish all the graces of the Spirit, and inspire us in our obedience. If the Lord God Omnipotent reigneth, be sure He will take care of His children. He will manage all their affairs. He will secure their best interests.

> Behold the King of Zion rise
> To endless glory in the skies!
> Hail, Fount of blessings! placed in Thee,
>
> Our life, our strength, our all we see;
> While in thy God thy joys endure,
> In Thee our blessings rest secure.

🌿 EVENING 🌿

'Grace to help in time of need.'

HEBREWS 4:16

The term 'grace' includes the wisdom and strength which may be necessary to enable us to act aright, under all circumstances. We daily need grace. But there are seasons in which we need grace especially: as in prosperity, to keep us from getting proud and presumptuous; in adversity, to keep us from complaining or desponding; in temptation, to preserve us from its snares; and in death, that we may die to the Lord's glory. Grace is to be had. There is a throne erected on purpose to dispense it. It is given to the most unworthy. It is to be had in answer to prayer. 'Let us therefore come boldly unto the throne of grace, that we may obtain mercy, and find grace to help in time of need.' Let us not attempt anything in our own strength, or fancy that we can accomplish anything by our own wisdom; but let us live under a deep sense of our need of grace, of God's willingness to bestow it, and of the incalculable benefits to be derived from it. Thus let us approach the throne, pleading the name of Jesus, so we may be supplied. O for grace to keep me in health, to cheer me in sickness, but especially to make me victorious in death!

> The grace I every moment want,
> The fresh supplies of faith and love,
> God of exhaustless mercy, grant,
> In answer to my Friend above.
> Increase my faith, confirm my hope,
> Until I yield my spirit up.

DECEMBER 2

MORNING

'From this day will I bless you.'

HAGGAI 2:19

What day? The day we begin to seek the Lord. The day we decide to be on the Lord's side. The day we publicly and honestly profess Him. The day we heartily engage in His work. The day we return from backsliding, and repent of our sin before Him. The day we identify ourselves with His people in heart and soul. What does the Lord promise? To bless us: He will bless our temporal mercies; He will bless our trials; He will bless our labours; He will bless our families; He will bless our souls; He will bless us with light, liberty, strength, peace, contentment, and success. Beloved, let us be decided for the Lord, and always walk in His ways. Expect His blessing, for He has given you His Word, and confirmed it with a solemn oath. Be diligent in the use of all means. Constantly look to Jesus as the only medium through which all blessings flow. Plead this precious promise before thy God this morning, and many times today; yea, and every day; so shall thy peace be like a river, and thy righteousness as the waves of the sea. He will bless thee, and thou shalt be a blessing.

Then let no care perplex me now;
My only wish and care be Thou,
Be Thou my sole delight;
Bid every sigh of rising thought,
And every pant of breath go out
For Jesus day and night.

EVENING

'I believe God.'

ACTS 27:25

The most reasonable thing in the world, and yet at some times most difficult. He has spoken to us in the plainest terms, He has confirmed His promises with the blood of His dear Son, He has made everyone of His saints a witness to His faithfulness, and yet we do not half believe Him. We do not absolutely doubt the truth of His promises, or His faithfulness to them, but we question their application to us. Yet He has described our characters, presented us with examples as much like ourselves as possible; but unbelief is so strong, Satan is so active, and present things have such influences, that we do not believe God. May He deeply convince us of the sin of unbelief, humble us for it before His throne, and send His Holy Spirit to work faith in our hearts. Beloved, do you, as you read, or hear His precious promises, say, 'That is true. God will perform it. He will make it good in my experience. Therefore, I cannot want. I will not fear. I will only trust in His Word, rely on His power, plead at His throne, and wait for the fulfilment of the promises in His own time and way'. Such should be the language of all our hearts. But, alas! how few of us use it. Our Lord corrects and encourages us tonight, by saying, *'Be not faithless but believing.'*

Now learn in every state,
To make His will your own;
And when the joys of sense depart,
To walk by faith alone.

DECEMBER 3

🌿 MORNING 🌿

'Believe in the LORD your God.'

2 CHRONICLES 20:20

The proper object of faith is God in Christ, not God as the God of nature. In Christ He is gracious unto us, ever with us, ready to help us, and takes pleasure in us. He is our covenant God, all sufficient, and ever propitious. We should believe in His Word, which is true and faithful; in His presence, for He will never turn away from us; in His power, for nothing is too hard for Him; in His character, which He will never allow to be dishonoured; and in His faithfulness, which is like the great mountains, and abideth for ever, We should believe in God, though men rise up against us; though Satan worry and distress us; though doubts and fears arise within us. We should believe in God, for strength to perform duty, deliverance out of every difficulty, and for courage in every conflict. Believing in God will produce contentment, zeal, and humility. Let us have faith from God – it is a gift which He is willing to bestow; and let us have faith in God – it is an exercise which He requires and approves. If the Son of Man were to come, would He find faith in our hearts? O Saviour!

> Let us trust Thee evermore;
> Every moment on Thee call,
> For new life, new will, new power;
>
> Let us trust Thee, Lord, for all!
> May we nothing know beside,
> Jesus, and Him crucified!

🌿 EVENING 🌿

'Thou, O God, hast proved us.'

PSALM 66:10

Every man's profession shall be tried, and everyone's principles shall be proved. It is easy to talk of faith, but it is not so easy to exercise it. It is easy to boast of what we will do under certain circumstances, but it is the circumstances which try us. Boasters always fail. A haughty spirit goes before a fall. We are never safe, but as we renounce our own strength, and rely on God's faithful Word. The dark night, the fierce foe, the fire and water, the much tribulation, will prove us. Many appear to start well, but when they come to be proved, they have not the root of the matter in them; in the time of trial they fall away. Many young Christians, in the warmth of their first love, sadly reflect on more advanced believers; but when they come to be tried they are not more eminent. We do not know what we are, but as God shows us; for the heart is deceitful above all things, and grievously infirm. By the teachings of the Holy Spirit, by the temptations of Satan, and by the mysterious dispensations of His providence, He proves us and shows us what our profession is worth. He says, 'I will melt them and try them. I will bring the third part through the fire'. May we stand the proof, shine brighter, and be more useful for being tried.

> O Lord! how wondrous are Thy ways,
> To try our faith, our souls refine;
> So, passing through the furnace blaze,
> The silver flows more pure to shine.

DECEMBER 4

🌿 MORNING 🌿

'I will go in the strength of the Lord GOD.'

PSALM 71:16

Our own weakness would dismay us, but God's strength is offered to us; in His light we see, and in His strength we work. We have duties to perform, difficulties to encounter, and foes to overcome. Let us therefore go in the strength of the Lord. It is promised to us, and may be received by us; we must ask it of God, we must expect it in faith, and go forth believing that He is faithful who hath promised. Never let us attempt any thing in our own strength; if we do, we shall be sure to fail. Let us first take up God's promise, rely on His veracity, and so go forth to duty, conflict, and danger. Then the battle is not ours, but the Lord's; then we are sure of success, succour, and victory. The Lord will then be our strength and song, our refuge and certain salvation. His strength is made perfect in weakness, and His grace is glorified in the unworthy. Let us not fear, let us not loiter, let us not despond, but let us go in the strength of the Lord, and we shall be more than conquerors. He giveth courage to the faint, and to those who have no might He increaseth strength.

I know the God in whom I trust,
The arm on which I lean;
He will my Saviour ever be,
Who has my Saviour been.
Strong in His strength my foes I face,
Assured of victory through His grace.

🌿 EVENING 🌿

'His fruit was sweet to my taste.'

SONG OF SOLOMON 2:3

The Lord Jesus is incomparably lovely. His personal excellencies baffle the powers of description. Every beautiful figure which nature can furnish is employed to set Him forth. But a spiritual perception is necessary to discern and delight in Him. Everyone who perceives His glory, applies to His fulness; and everyone who applies to His fulness, receives and enjoys His communications. Here He is compared to the apple tree amidst the trees of the wood, as affording refreshing shade and delicious food. 'His fruit was sweet to my taste.' His fruit includes the promises He has made, the pardons He bestows, the reconciliation He has effected, the peace He imparts, the fellowship He has with His people, the assurances of His love, the joys of the Holy Ghost, the hope of eternal life, access into God's presence, and the precious foretastes of glory which He sends. These are sweet, incomparably sweet to every spiritual mind. Sheltered from storms, protected from foes, preserved from the sultry sun, and fed with fruits of salvation, the believer is happy, and his Saviour is precious to his soul. And while the fruits of Jesus are sweet to him, sin is bitter; he has no relish for the follies, vain amusements, and sinful pleasures of the world.

O sweet repast of heavenly love,
How rich these royal dainties prove;
In Thine embrace 'tis life to be,
So sweet Thy fruit and shade to me.

DECEMBER 5

❦ MORNING ❧

'Create in me a clean heart, O God.'
PSALM 51:10

Such a prayer implies a conviction of sin, a sense of pollution, a desire for holiness, a knowledge of weakness, grief for inconstancy, and the possession of true wisdom. It is the prayer of every Christian. Let it be our prayer this day. Let us lift up our hearts and voices to our God, and cry, 'Remove guilt and pollution, produce purity and peace in our hearts. Cleanse us by Thy Word, the blood of Jesus, and the influence of the Holy Spirit.' Purity of heart can only be produced by God; it enters into the very essence of religion; we cannot be godly except we are holy. If we love sin, if we can indulge in sin, or if a sense of having sinned does not pain us, and cause us to adopt this prayer, our religion is spurious; we are destitute of the power of godliness. No real Christian can live in sin. He is called to holiness. He is the temple of the Holy Spirit. Holiness is his element and health. His God says, 'Be holy, for I am holy', and he cries, 'Create in me a clean heart, O God.' Let us be holy in all manner of conversation, looking for and hasting to the coming of the Lord Jesus.

> Supreme High Priest, the pilgrim's light,
> My heart for Thee prepare;
> Thine image stamp, and deeply write
> Thy superscription there;
> Ah, let my forehead bear Thy seal,
> My heart the inward witness feel.

❦ EVENING ❧

'God now accepteth thy works.'
ECCLESIASTES 9:7

When? When He has accepted thy person, and is reconciled to thee. For God never accepts our works while we are His avowed enemies. This would be to accept the works of a rebel, of a traitor, of one who is at enmity against Him. God accepts our persons when we accept His Son. Jesus is presented to us in the gospel as God's free gift, as a Saviour suited to our case, as a blessing which includes all we do, or can need. This gift is rejected by men in general: they put it from them, and treat it with contempt. We did this once. But when the Holy Spirit quickened our souls, enlightened our minds, and wrought faith in our hearts, then we gladly embraced Him. Having received Christ from God, we are received by God from Christ; we are accepted in Him, and entitled to all spiritual blessings through Him. God now accepteth our works, poor, imperfect, and worthless as they are, because they are the works of a beloved child, the efforts of a feeble friend, the productions of a loyal subject. The cup of cold water, the will to do, or give, when we have not the power, is accepted, and placed to our account. Sweet thought, our God has pardoned our sins, accepted our persons, and now He accepteth our works.

> Accepted in Jesus and living on Him,
> His promise I trust and His precepts esteem;
> I strive to be holy, I labour for God,
> And my works are approv'd thro' His merit and blood.

DECEMBER 6

🌿 MORNING 🌿
'And delivered just Lot.'

2 PETER 2:7

Lot was a godly man, justified before God by faith, and justified before man by his good works. But he was a weak man. He chose to dwell in Sodom because it was a wealthy place; he aimed at a fortune, but he was vexed and grieved daily, by seeing and hearing of the unrighteous deeds of his neighbours. His children married into the world, and were ruined; and he himself, though delivered by a gracious and faithful God, suffered severely. His sons and their wives perished in Sodom; his own wife was made an example of on the plain; he was hurried away without a solitary servant, or any property of importance, and had to take up his dwelling in a cave. See the folly of being led by appearances. Let not the heart follow the eye. See also the certainty of being chastened for sin: just Lot could not escape; the faithfulness of divine love towards its wayward children; and the importance of being distinct from the world. The Christian in the world is like Lot in Sodom, and if he chooses his place from the same motives, the Lord may deal with him after the same rule. Gracious Lord, choose our inheritance for us!

> O! to be brought to Jesus' feet,
> Though sorrows fix me there,
> Is still a privilege, and sweet
> The energies of prayer:
> Though sighs and tears its language be,
> If Christ be nigh and smile on me.

🌿 EVENING 🌿
'I am Alpha and Omega.'

REVELATION 1:8

This is the Saviour's testimony to His own dignity and glory. He takes the first and last letters of the Greek alphabet, which enclose and include all the rest, and says, 'I am Alpha and Omega'. These letters form the words which reveal and make known facts: Jesus is the great manifester of God; by Him the divine nature and perfections are brought to light. These letters include all that is necessary for communication, among all who use the tongue. Jesus is the All-sufficient One. He possesses in Himself all that is necessary for our preservation, salvation, consolation, and glorification. He comprehends in Himself all wisdom and knowledge, all worth and wealth, all time and eternity. He is the source and end of salvation. From Him it flows, and He is the centre round which it revolves. To be all this He must be God. He is naturally, essentially, and eternally divine. He includes in Himself all that is great, good, and glorious. Therefore believers are never weary of hearing of Him, or speaking of His praise. In Him sinners will find all they need. Sweet view of Jesus this. Four times in this book does He take this title. Therefore we should often dwell upon it and derive benefit from it. It is full of precious food and sterling worth.

> When o'er the Word my eye is cast,
> There Jesus is the first and last,
> And all the blessings there made known,
> Their Alpha and Omega own.

DECEMBER 7

❦ MORNING ❧

'Cast not away therefore your confidence.'

HEBREWS 10:35

Every believer is confident that Jesus Christ is the Messiah, the sent of God; that He is the only Saviour, and the eternal God. He is confident that heaven is promised to all true believers, and is certain to all holy disciples. He gives credit to God's Word, which reveals the same, is fully satisfied of its truth, and finds courage and boldness to profess the same. His confidence being produced by the Holy Spirit, and grounded on the divine Word, will lead him to commit his all to the divine blessing; to surrender all to the divine will; to part with all in Christ's quarrel; and to rest on the word and veracity of the Lord Jesus. His confidence will often be assailed and sharply tried; but it must be maintained, for we are made partakers of Christ, if we hold fast the beginning of our confidence steadfast unto the end. It has great recompense of reward: in the present life a hundred-fold for all it parts with for Christ; and in the world to come life everlasting. Beloved, let us hold fast our confidence and rejoicing of hope firm unto the end, for if any man draw back God will have no pleasure in him.

Protect me in the dangerous hour,
And from the wily tempter's power,
O, set my spirit free!

And if temptation should assail,
May mighty grace o'er all prevail,
And lead my heart to Thee.

❦ EVENING ❧

'All these things are against me.'

GENESIS 42:36

What things? These losses, crosses, bereavements, persecutions, sorrows, and sicknesses. Against you! Never. They are not against you unless they lead you into sin, bind you faster to this world, alienate your mind from God, and prevent your being useful in your day and generation. They cannot be against you if they wean you from earth, lead you to God, endear the Saviour, render the Bible more valuable, and make you long for home. They are not against you but for you; you forget that they come according to the arrangements of a gracious providence, and that your heavenly Father sends them for your good. Leave off complaining, for it springs from ignorance of God's Word, or forgetfulness of your many mercies and sins; or from unbelief and a bad temper; and it reflects upon the love, care, and kindness of your God. These things are painful, trying, and perplexing; but they are intended to do you good, and while you are complaining, they are working together under divine direction for your present and everlasting welfare. Beloved, how apt we are to mistake the design of our trials, and to lose sight of God's promises.

Let saints their gloomy fears restrain;
No reason have they to complain,
Whatever ills befall;

No troubles from the dust can rise,
For God is holy, good, and wise,
And overrules them all.

DECEMBER 8

❦ MORNING ❦

'I rejoice in thy salvation.'

1 Samuel 2:1

God's salvation is a deliverance from the worst of evils, of freest grace, for the best of purposes. He saves the poor and needy, the guilty and the distressed, who call upon Him, and believe in Him. And we, who have obtained mercy, should with Hannah rejoice in God's salvation, as those who have received an invaluable favour; as those who are laid under, and are ready to acknowledge their infinite obligations. Salvation is the proper source of our joy and rejoicing; and while some rejoice in property, some in power, and some in earthly prospects, let us rejoice in the salvation of our God. It is a cause for rejoicing in sickness and in health, in poverty and in plenty, in life and in death. Although the fig tree should not blossom, neither should fruit be on the vine; though the labour of the olive should fail, and the fields should yield no meat; though the flock should be cut off from the fold, and there be no herd in the stalls: yet we may rejoice in the Lord, and joy in the God of our salvation; for not one thing shall fail of all that He hath spoken. Delightful truth, *'Salvation is of the Lord.'* And the Lord's salvation is for lost and ruined sinners.

Join heaven and earth, to bless	With cheerful heart and voice;
The Lord our righteousness;	In Him complete I shine;
In Him I will rejoice,	His life and death are mine.

❦ EVENING ❦

'My God, we know thee.'

Hosea 8:2

It is a great mercy to know God. No one does except he is taught of God. We did not once, if we do now. We can only rightly know God, by knowing Jesus, for He hath revealed Him. To know Him as revealed in the broken law, only fills us with terror and alarm, for there we only learn His justice, requirements, wrath, terror, power, majesty and jealousy. But to know Him as revealed in the gospel, as made known in Jesus, fills us with joy and peace, for there we see His pity and compassion, His love and grace, His power and mercy, His kindness and attention, His friendship and benevolence, united and agreed to do us good. If we know God, we shall trust in His Word; we shall love His perfections; we shall perform His precepts; we shall cleave to His people; we shall be often at His throne; and we shall delight to do His will. To know God is to be truly wise, and to possess everlasting life; for 'This', said Jesus, 'is life eternal, to know thee the only true God, and Jesus Christ, whom thou hast sent.' The knowledge of God comes from reading His Word, watching His providence, studying His works, and the teaching of His Holy Spirit. Can we say tonight, *'My God, I know Thee? My God, I love Thee?'*

Come, Holy Ghost, unfold Thy Word,
Reveal the Saviour's name;
Fill with the knowledge of the Lord,
The infinite I AM.

DECEMBER 9

🌿 MORNING 🌿

'Walk in love.'

EPHESIANS 5:2

Religion is love: the love of God shed abroad in the heart, transforming our nature into love. The blessing is bestowed to be exhibited; we are to let our light shine, and walk in love, under the influence of love to God, for His mercy towards us, and love to man for God's sake; by the rule of love, doing unto others as we would they should do unto us; seeking their spiritual and eternal welfare, letting it be clearly seen, that we indulge no envy, jealousy, malice, or ill-will in our hearts against any; but that we wish them well, and desire to promote their best interests in any way we can. Love should run through the whole of our actions, and be the ruling motive in our souls. God acts towards us from love. The Holy Spirit is the Spirit of love; and love is the brightest and surest evidence of regeneration. Let us not be satisfied to feel that we love, but let us manifest it; let us *'Walk in love'*; this is the way to be happy, useful and honourable. Bitterness, wrath, censoriousness, and selfishness, prove that we are under sin; but love is of God; and he that loveth is born of God, and knoweth God.

May I from every act abstain,
That hurts or gives my brother pain;
Nay, every secret wish suppress,
That would abridge his happiness.
And thus may I Thy follower prove,
Great Prince of peace, great God of love!

🌿 EVENING 🌿

'The gift of God is eternal life.'

ROMANS 6:23

Our desert is eternal death. With this the law threatens us. But God hath given to us eternal life, and this life is in His Son. Jesus is the true God, and eternal life. We have the promise of eternal existence, of eternal existence free from sin, pain, sorrow, grief, and disappointment; of eternal existence in the enjoyment of ease, holiness, honour, wealth, peace, pleasure, and satisfaction; eternal employment and enjoyment. This is given us, given us freely. It is the expression of Jehovah's love to us; a display of His sovereign and distinguishing grace. Angels sinned, and are thrust down to hell; we sinned, and our God, against whom we have sinned, has given to us eternal life. Every believer has the principle now. He is quickened together with Christ; he is alive unto God. Beloved, let us live in hope of this eternal life. Let us press onward to the enjoyment of it. Jesus has promised it to all His sheep. He says, 'I give unto them eternal life; and they shall never perish, neither shall anyone pluck them out of my hand. My Father, which gave them me is greater than all; and no one is able to pluck them out of my Father's hand.'

Answer then Thy blest design,
Bring to me the life of grace,
Bring me larger life divine,
Fill my soul with holiness,
Fit me for the life above,
All the life of heavenly love.

DECEMBER 10

🌿 MORNING 🌿

*'Neither pray I for these alone, but for them
also which shall believe on me.'*
JOHN 17:20

Beloved, when Jesus was praying for His disciples, He prayed for us; His prayer extended to all who believe, however fearful, weak, and timid. He prayed that we may be one with Himself; one with His church, as members of the same body, children of the same family, heirs of the same inheritance, and parts of the same spiritual temple. He prayed that we may be so one as the Father is one with Him, and as He is one with the Father; that we may have the same love influencing us, the same object always in view, and may exhibit the same virtues. What glorious privileges our Saviour here prays that we may enjoy! What honours He seeks for us! What unspeakable blessedness! Think of being one with God, one with God as Jesus is, one with the Father, Son, and Holy Spirit; to be of one mind, one will, and, as it were, of one soul. Gracious, gracious Lord, hasten on the time when this all-comprehending prayer shall be fully answered in our experience! Let us, beloved, daily pray for this blessing; nothing can be greater, sweeter, or more important.

Thy revealing Spirit give,
Whom the world cannot receive.
Fill me with Thy Father's love;
Never from my soul remove.
Dwell in me, and I shall be
Thine through all eternity.

🌿 EVENING 🌿

'He is Lord of all.'
ACTS 10:36

Jesus has supreme authority. He rules over all. He has all power in heaven and in earth. He doth according to His will. All creatures are under His control, and must subserve His purpose. He claims all as Creator, He reigns over all as Mediator. He uses all to fulfil His pleasure. He is worthy of our highest praise. All men should honour the Son, even as they honour the Father. We can go to no place, and justly say, 'Jesus does not reign here.' We cannot lay our hand on anything, and say, 'Jesus has no claim to this.' We can refer to no event, and say, 'Jesus will not overrule this.' He knows all existencies. He claims all He knows. He presides over all He claims. He uses for His glory all over whom He presides. Everything is at His beck: the fish of the sea, the fowls of the air, the beasts of the field, the angels of God, the devil and his host, the lost souls in hell, the glorified in heaven, sinners and saints on earth. He is Lord of all. He sits at God's right hand in the heavenly places, far above all principality, and power, and might, and dominion, and every name that is named, not only in this world, but also in that which is to come. As the supreme Lord, He is to be loved, feared, and obeyed.

Worthy the Lamb of boundless sway,
In earth and heav'n the Lord of all;
Him all the hosts on high obey;
Let men before His footstool fall.

DECEMBER 11

🌿 MORNING 🌿

'Why dost thou strive against Him.'
Job 33:13

A believer strive against his God! Yes, it is sometimes the case; he may strive against some of the doctrines of His Word; or, against some of the dispensations of His providence; or, against some of the commands He has issued. But why dost thou strive against Him? His wisdom is infinite. His love is unchangeable. His ways are all righteous. His methods may be mysterious, and His dispensations trying; but His designs are all gracious and good. It is your privilege to believe and trust. It is rebellion and treason to strive against Him, for He giveth not account of any of His matters. It is the glory of God to conceal a thing. He is not accountable to any. He will not be questioned by the curious, or called to an account by the proud. He demands our acquiescence on the ground of His perfections, promises, and Word. He will make all plain and clear to us by and by, and then we shall know as we are known, and be perfectly satisfied. He says, 'Be still, and know that I am God.' 'Be silent, O all flesh, before the LORD.' My soul, yield thyself unreservedly to thy God!

> O, let me live of Thee possess'd,
> In weakness, weariness, and pain!
> The anguish of my labouring breast,
>
> The daily cross I still sustain,
> For Him that languish'd on the tree,
> But lived, before He died for me.

🌿 EVENING 🌿

'The true light now shineth.'
1 John 2:8

Our land was once shrouded in the darkness of paganism. This was dispelled by the introduction of the gospel. Then it became enveloped in the darkness of Popery. This was partly dissipated at the Reformation. Clouds of superstition still hang over some parts of it, but the true light nevertheless shines. It shines from the written Word, and it shines from hundreds of pulpits. It has shone upon us. It has shone into our hearts. We have by it discovered our real state by nature; Jehovah's true character; the way of life and salvation; the source of true pleasure; the principle of acceptable obedience. It shines around us now, mildly, clearly, and constantly. It shines to display God's free grace: to enable us to *walk* in comfort, to *work* with pleasure, to *fight* with confidence, to *fly* with certainty, and *to go home* with satisfaction. Does the true light now shine? Then let us be thankful, for multitudes are still sitting in darkness and the shadow of death. Let us improve our opportunity, walking in the light as our God is in the light, and living in fellowship with Him. Let us diffuse the light in every direction to the utmost of our ability. Let us beware of every false light, cleaving to the pure and inspired Word of God.

> O! to rescue men from ruin,
> Let the light within us shine;
> Sinners to the Saviour guiding,
> By an energy divine.

DECEMBER 12

❧ MORNING ❧

'He is the Saviour of the body.'

EPHESIANS 5:23

The church is the body of Christ. Jesus and His people are one. They are His elect whom He hath chosen; His seed which He hath begotten; His portion which He hath received; His delight and glory, in which He constantly rejoices. He saves them by substitution; He took their place, their obligations, and their sins. He saves them by communication; giving them grace and His Holy Spirit, with every spiritual blessing. He saves them by instruction, for they are all taught of God. He saves them by separation, bringing them out of, and delivering them from this present evil world. He saves them by visitations; He grants them life and favour, and His visitations preserve their spirits. He saves them by translation; first out of the kingdom of Satan, into His kingdom of grace; and then out of the present world, into His kingdom of glory. He saves them to display His perfections; confound His foes; exalt His name; satisfy His love; and from sympathy with them. All who are saved form part of His body. Salvation is entirely of God. What happiness to be saved thus! It is honourable, it is holy, and it is free!

Joyful truth, He bore transgression | *All for Him we count but loss:*
In His body on the cross. | *Jesus for the sinner bleeds,*
Through His blood there's full remission, | *Nothing more the sinner needs.*

❧ EVENING ❧

'Have I no power to deliver?'

ISAIAH 50:2

This is a question for unbelief: For *your* unbelief. If God can deliver, if He has promised to deliver, why then these fears, this gloom, and this perplexity? Look your difficulty full in the face, walk round it and examine it on every side, and when you have done so, answer your Lord's question, 'Have I no power to deliver?' You may apply it to sin, its guilt, its power, its consequences. You may apply it to Satan, his malice, his craft, his determined opposition to you. You may apply it to the world, its snares, its persecution, its spirit. You may apply it to any, and all the circumstances in which you can be placed by an adverse providence. Cannot your God deliver you? Is His arm shortened, that it cannot save? Or is His ear heavy, that He cannot hear? If not, why then doubt? Why art thou cast down? Hope thou in God, for thou shalt yet praise Him. He hath delivered, He doth deliver, and He will yet deliver you. Grieve Him not by your unbelief, but trust in His Word, call upon His name, look to His arm, and He will show you that He has power to deliver, and that He will exert it on your behalf. He says, 'Call upon me, and I will deliver thee'.

Jesus, the wonders of Thy name | *No end is of Thy mercies found,*
Today as yesterday the same, | *We cannot stop Thine arm, or bound*
We all are call'd to prove. | *The omnipotence of love.*

DECEMBER 13

🌿 MORNING 🌿

'Ask what I shall give thee.'

1 KINGS 3:5

We are not straitened in our God; He has boundless resources, and is constantly calling upon us to ask and receive. What do we want this morning? Is it not more holiness? We want our understandings enlightened, our wills brought into perfect conformity to the will of God, and our affections fixed on holy and heavenly things. Let us agree to ask these things of our God. He will give freely, cheerfully, and plentifully. Let us ask as Solomon did: *Wisdom*, even that wisdom which cometh from above, which is pure, peaceable, easy to be entreated, full of mercy and good fruits. This wisdom will guide our hearts and direct our ways; it will lead us safely to a city of habitations; it will lead us to do God's will with pleasure, promptness, and delight. It will make us wise to escape from Satan's snares, to avoid temptation, and to do good unto all men. How important is this wisdom! How necessary for us! Well, Jesus stands before us this morning, saying, *'Ask what I shall give thee:'* In Him dwelleth all the treasures *of* wisdom and knowledge, and every *one* that asketh receiveth. O Jesus, give me Thyself!

> O sovereign Love, to Thee I cry;
> Give me Thyself, or else I die:
> Save me from death, from hell set free,
> Death, hell, are but the want of Thee!
> My life, my crown, my heaven Thou art!
> O, may I find Thee in my heart.

🌿 EVENING 🌿

'Mine anger is turned away from him.'

HOSEA 14:4

God has been angry. He is angry with the wicked everyday. His anger against them is *judicial*, roused by their sin. It is fearful. Its consequences are dangerous, dreadful. It was displayed in the flood, more clearly in Gethsemane and Calvary. Hell is the eternal manifestation of God's just anger against sin. He is sometimes angry with His people. His anger against them is *paternal*, roused by the conduct of His child. He is angry because He loves. His love to the person rouses His displeasure against the conduct. He shows His displeasure by afflictions, privations, and distresses. But His paternal anger is momentary. He chastens His child, and is angry because it is obstinate: but as soon as it relents, mourns at His feet, confesses its sin, appeals to His mercy, and pleads the atonement, the frown gives place to a smile, and He kindly says, 'Mine anger is turned away from him. I will receive the prodigal. I will still love the child. I will restore the wanderer to his former place, privileges, and honours. I will love him as though nothing had happened; his sin shall only be remembered by himself.' Sweet thought to lie down with tonight, 'The anger of God is turned away and He loves me.'

> Though His righteous anger rises,
> Anger in a moment dies;
> Mercy still His heart devises,
> Life within His favour lies.

DECEMBER 14

❦ MORNING ❦
'The author and finisher of our faith.'
Hebrews 12:2

All Christians have faith, but some of us have but little faith. He who gave us what we have can increase it; and He will if we apply to Him, plead with Him, and wait upon Him. We need more faith, to enable us to escape the many dangers that are in our path; to do and suffer the Lord's will with patience; to hold fast the faithful Word which we have been taught; to grow in grace and holiness; to exercise forgiving love towards those who have grieved, offended, or injured us; and to honour God, by believing His promises, trusting His providence, expecting His interference, being active in His service, and leaving our concerns in His hands, to be arranged, directed, and brought to pass. We are encouraged to pray for more faith, by the nature of the request, and the design with which we ask it; by the promises which God has given; by the precepts of His holy gospel; by the examples of faith set before us in the Word; by the well-known character of our God; and by the blessed results which must follow from having such a prayer answered. He who first gave unasked, will answer prayer for more.

Author of faith, I seek Thy face,
The work of faith in me fulfil.
Confirm and strengthen me in grace,

To do and suffer all Thy will.
From hell, the world, and sin secure,
And make me in my goings sure.

❦ EVENING ❦
'He doeth according to His will.'
Daniel 4:35

The will of God is infinitely perfect. It rules all events. What God wills He works. What He requires of us, shows what He approves. What He accomplishes by His power and providence, shows what is necessary to be done. His eye is in every place. His hand is in every event. The glorification of Himself is the object He keeps constantly in view. He has so connected His people with Himself, that what glorifies Him, benefits them; and what does them good, brings glory to His holy name. He is carrying out His plan, performing His work, accomplishing His purposes, quietly, constantly, and certainly; amidst all the bustle, confusion, and opposition of men. His will is law. It is the highest rule of right. To attempt to oppose His will is treason. If it could be effectually resisted, disorder, misery, and wretchedness must be the result. But the will of God is united to omnipotence. Whatever He wills His power accomplishes with ease and certainty. By Him all the inhabitants of the earth are reputed as nothing; and He doeth according to His will in the army of heaven, and among the inhabitants of the earth; and none can stay His hand, or say unto Him, 'What doest thou?' Believer, God wills and effectually works thy sanctification.

In heaven, and earth, and air, and seas,
He executes His firm decrees;
And by His saints it stands confessed
That what He does is ever best.

DECEMBER 15

🌿 MORNING 🌿

'Make your calling and election sure.'

2 Peter 1:10

Put your religion beyond a doubt; let there be no reason to question whether you are sincere or not. Calling separates us from sin, Satan, and the world, to holiness, Christ, and the church. Election is the root of calling; it is God's choice of us from others, in Christ, by grace, to holiness, for His glory. We know our election of God, by our being led to choose Christ, holiness, and heaven; to choose them freely, heartily, and habitually. If we thus choose them, we shall use every means to obtain them. We know that we are called of God, by our calling upon God secretly, heartily, constantly, for holiness, salvation, and fellowship with Himself. When we thus call on God we carefully avoid all evil, and follow after everything that is good. Let us give all diligence to know our election, for it is worth all the pains we can take, or the time we spend. Let us follow on to know the Lord, give up ourselves entirely to God, exercise ourselves unto godliness, seek the witness, earnest, and sealing of the Spirit, and cleave unto God with full purpose of heart.

Nothing is worth a thought beneath,
But how I may escape the death
That never, never dies!

How make mine own election sure,
And, when I fail on earth, secure
A mansion in the skies!

🌿 EVENING 🌿

'Thou shalt call me, My father.'

Jeremiah 3:19

Our God loves us to realize His paternal relation to us, and to acknowledge the same in our approaches to Him. A father can do what no one else can. He can forgive the basest conduct. He can love the most deformed child. He can receive the most ungrateful prodigal. He can bestow the most costly favour. He can exercise the greatest patience. So our God because He is a Father, pities us, pardons us, provides for us, loves us, blesses us, acknowledges us, and rejoices over us to do us good. Let us dwell upon this sweet view of the Almighty. Let us pray as to a father. Let us work as for a father. Let us expect as from a father. Let us trust as in a father. Let us love God as a father. Let us speak of Him as of a father. Let us place confidence in Him as in a father. Let us seek the Spirit of adoption, if we have it not, to bear witness with our spirit that we are the children of God; to cry, 'Abba, Father,' in our hearts; and to enable us, without fear or wavering, to call him our Father. O how much gloom and sadness it would prevent, how much comfort and peace would it bring to our souls, if we lived under the impression that our God is our Father! Beloved, endeavour to keep this view of thy God ever before thine eyes.

Abba, Father, Lord we call Thee,
(Hallowed name!) from day to day:
'Tis Thy children's right to know Thee,
None but children Abba say.

DECEMBER 16

MORNING

'The righteous shall hold on His way.'
JOB 17:9

The way to the kingdom is rough and rugged, our strength is often small, and our fears are very many. But if we are justified by grace, sanctified by the Spirit of truth, and pursue a consistent course, there is no doubt of our safe arrival at our Father's house; for 'the righteous shall hold on His way, and he that hath clean hands shall wax stronger and stronger.' The true believer shall hold on, for the promise of God secures him; the fulness of Christ supplies him; the Spirit of grace influences him; the new nature urges him; occasional love-tokens encourage him; and attachment to the Lord and His people prevents him forsaking the right ways of the Most High. Beloved, let us be concerned to have a blameless conversation; let us live near to and walk with Jesus; then our graces will flourish, we shall become rooted in Christ, our daily conquests will give us courage, and our God will give as He hath promised, even grace and glory. It is not for us to be timid; it is not for the righteous to despond, *for he shall hold on his way.* 'They go from strength to strength; every one of them in Zion appeareth before God.'

> They may on the main of temptation be tossed,
> Their troubles may swell like the sea;
> But none of the ransom'd shall ever be lost,
> The righteous shall hold on his way.

EVENING

'Man also knoweth not his time.'
ECCLESIASTES 9:12

All the future is unknown; a dark cloud hangs between us and it. We know not what shall be. We know not the time of trial, when our graces, our strength, and resolution shall be tried. We know not the time of temptation, when Satan will be allowed more particularly to assault us, and try his strength upon us. We know not the time of danger, when there is but a step between us and a grievous fall, when our foes stand ready to triumph over us. We know not the time of our death: it is fixed, it may be very near, but we are ignorant of it. This should teach us humility: let us not presume, but humbly wait upon our God. It should produce caution: let us not be high-minded but fear. It should stimulate to duty: let us work while it is day; the night cometh, and it may very soon be here. It should lead to watchfulness: let us watch and pray, lest we enter into temptation. It should stir us up to prayer: let us pray always with all prayer and supplication in the Spirit. It should prevent carelessness, self-confidence, and lukewarmness; our foes are on the alert, the snares are laid for our feet, the Master is coming, the hour of death may be just at hand. Let us therefore be sober, and watch unto prayer.

> Amidst a thousand snares I stand,
> Upheld and guarded by Thy hand;
> Still let Thy presence be my stay,
> And guard me in this dangerous way.

DECEMBER 17

🌿 MORNING 🌿

'Let the word of Christ dwell in you richly.'
Colossians 3:16

The word which Jesus preached, or the word which His servants wrote, the whole Word of God, is the word of Jesus. Believer, look at your Bible as containing the word of your best Friend, loving Saviour, and final Judge. Let it find a home in your memories, affections, and hearts. Let it keep house, ruling, feeding, and directing your souls. Let it dwell in you plentifully, and know how to apply the different portions to different persons, and different cases. Let it dwell in you richly, that you may have that to plead in prayer which God will notice, approve, and accept; to form, guide, and preserve your judgments; to curb, bound, and regulate your desires; to raise, confirm, and direct your expectations: to silence, enlighten, and purify conscience; to enable you to resist and overcome Satan; that you may be able to reprove sin, and speak a word in season to the weary. Let the word of Christ have the best room in your souls: let it be your daily meditation, food, and directory. *'Let the word of Christ dwell in you richly in all wisdom.'*

> Lord, let Thy wisdom be my guide, That I from Thee may never stray:
> Nor take Thy light from me away; O, let Thy Word within me dwell,
> Still with me let Thy grace abide, Inspiring me to do Thy will.

🌿 EVENING 🌿

'Call His name, Jesus.'
Matthew 1:21

That is, a Saviour. He deserves the name, for He undertook to save, He came into the world to save, He fulfilled the law, was made a curse, and atoned for sin that He might save, He lives and pleads in heaven to save. He *can* save any character. He *will* save all His people. He *does* save all who come to God by Him. He *has* saved myriads already. He saves *freely*, as an act of grace. He saves *fully*, or *from* all evil *to* all good. He saves *eternally*, placing His people beyond the possibility of perishing. He saves consistently with all the perfections of God's nature. He saves without infringing any of the principles of the divine government. He saves millions without injury to one. He saves for His own glory, in obedience to His Father's will, out of pure love to His degraded people. My soul, call Him Jesus, for He has saved thee. Tell all around that He is Jesus, and can save them. His work is to save. His office is to save. His delight is to save. He is the *only*, the *all-sufficient*, the *omnipotent* Saviour. He saves though all hell opposes, He saves though sinners are ungrateful, and He saves though those He saves doubt and distrust Him. He is now exalted at God's right hand, as a Sovereign, to give repentance unto Israel, and the forgiveness of sins..

> Trust in His name, and you shall know,
> Shall feel your sins forgiv'n.
> Anticipate your heav'n below,
> And own His love in heav'n.

DECEMBER 18

🌿 MORNING 🌿

'They are enemies of the cross of Christ.'
PHILIPPIANS 3:18

The cross of Christ is the Christian's glory, and few things would give him more pain, than to be considered its enemy. It embraces the whole doctrine of salvation by grace, and is viewed by the Christian as the foundation of his hope, and the object of his faith; as the end of the law, and the antidote of misery; as the centre of truth, and the subject of the church's song; as mercy's sceptre, and the Saviour's throne; as the mirror, in which Jehovah displays all the perfections of His nature; and the key that opens the gates of the celestial paradise; as the glory of eternal wisdom, and the mystery of incarnate love; as the destruction of death, and the gate to everlasting life; as the object of the angels' wonder, and the cause of the devil's everlasting confusion. Beloved, let us fix our eyes and hearts upon this glorious, this surprising object; and never, never let us, by our conduct or conversation, bring a disgrace upon it; but let us endeavour to advance its triumphs, spread its glories, and bring sinners to admire, love, and trust in it. 'God forbid that I should glory, save in the cross of our Lord Jesus Christ; by whom the world is crucified unto me, and I unto the world.'

> O, may my single aim be now,
> To live on Him that died,
> And nought on earth desire to know
> But Jesus crucified.

🌿 EVENING 🌿

'The holy people.'
ISAIAH 62:12

Such are all the Lord's people. He convinces them of sin, sets their hearts against sin, and they give up the practice of sin. They were chosen to be holy. Jesus gave Himself for them that they might be sanctified. The Holy Spirit takes possession of them, in order to make them meet to be partakers of the inheritance of the saints in light. Holiness becomes their element and delight. They sigh for it, seek it, and endeavour to practise it. They were once very impure, but they are washed, they are sanctified, they are justified in the name of the Lord Jesus, and by the Spirit of their God. Justification lies at the root of sanctification. If the man is justified, he will be sanctified; and it is only by sanctification, that he proves his justification. In vain we talk of sin being pardoned, if it is not subdued. The man who can live in sin is neither just nor holy; he gives no evidence of interest in Jesus, or that he is a partaker of the Holy Ghost. All holy persons discover their unholiness, mourn over it, pray to be delivered from it, strive against it, and long to be perfectly free from all that defiles. Such are the holy people, the redeemed of the Lord. Are you one of them? Is this your present experience?

> Jehovah is a holy God;
> Christ will alone the pure confess;
> Angels are holy, and the road
> To heaven, is that of holiness.

DECEMBER 19

🌿 MORNING 🌿

'If ye love me, keep my commandments.'

John 14:15

Here is the Christian's grand rule of action, the commandments of his dear Saviour. Jesus commands us because He loves us; because He desires our present welfare; because He will prove the sincerity of our profession; and because He approves of the obedience of faith. He commands us to imitate Himself; He is our great pattern and example, and we should endeavour to imitate Him in His Spirit, and design, and actions. He commands us to believe Him, profess Him, obey Him, and continue in His love. Here we have the Christian's grand motive and spring of action: love. Spiritual love is always loyal to the King of Zion; jealous for the glory of the Lord of Hosts; and determined in the cause of the Prince of peace. The obedience of love is easy, hearty, and thorough. Love is the strongest incentive to obedience: it conquers fear, furnishes with zeal, equips with courage, devises the means, surmounts difficulties, and triumphs over opposition. Let us inquire from what does our obedience spring? By what is it regulated? Is our motive and rule, holy love?

*Love is the fountain whence
All true obedience flows;
The Christian serves the God he loves,
And loves the God he knows:
May love o'er every power preside,
And every thought and action guide.*

🌿 EVENING 🌿

'Christ's servant.'

1 Corinthians 7:22

Every Christian is a servant. Jesus is his Master. The precepts of the gospel are his rule. He is bound to obey. He has pledged himself to do the will of God from the heart. He that is not willing to serve Christ, has no evidence whatever that he is interested in Him. The Christian was purchased to be a servant. He is converted that he may devote his powers to the Lord. Let us then enquire tonight, Is Jesus our Master? Do we view Him as such? Do we consult His will in all we do? Do we act as under His eye? Do we often ask ourselves the question, 'Will this please my Master?' Do we look to Him for our supplies, for our orders, and for our reward as servants should? O may the Holy Spirit daily impress these thoughts upon our minds. I am Christ's servant. He is my wise, holy, and generous Master. My business is to please Him. My one object should be to secure His approbation. The world can have no claim upon me. Satan has no right to me. The flesh ought not to rule in me. Beloved, have you been serving Jesus today? Have you consulted His Word? Have you sought His grace? Are you upright before Him?

*While with my lips I call Thee Lord,
O let my heart its Lord confess;
My life be govern'd by Thy Word,
In all the paths of righteousness.
I'll labour to perform Thy will,
And rest upon Thy holy hill.*

DECEMBER 20

❦ MORNING ❦

'I will give you the sure mercies of David.'
ACTS 13:34

The mercies of David are *suited* to a sinner's wants: they comprise all he needs for time, for body and soul; and all he will need through eternity. The mercies of David are *covenant* mercies: the Father has engaged to bestow them through the doing and dying of Jesus; the Son has secured their bestowment by His vicarious sufferings and death; and the Holy Spirit will put the Lord's people in possession of them. They all flow from free grace, are revealed in the promises, and are stored up in the fulness of Christ. The mercies of David are *sure* mercies: they are unconditionally promised to all comers; are received by simple faith; and are bestowed by Jesus as the appointed trustee and administrator of the covenant of grace. They are sure, for God has sworn, and will not change His mind, or remove His covenant of reconciliation. The mercies of David are *given* mercies: no desert is requisite to establish a claim; no hard conditions are laid down to entitle; no price is fixed, or money demanded; but it is, *'Come and receive freely.'*

> Thy favours, Lord, surprise our souls;
> Wilt Thou indulge Thy creatures thus?
> The stream of full salvation rolls,
> To strengthen, cheer, and comfort us;
> How rich the grace! how kind the Word!
> All praise and glory to the Lord!

❦ EVENING ❦

'All things are become new.'
2 CORINTHIANS 5:17

Such is the feeling of the young Christian, and such is the fact in reference to every Christian. He has a new life, which is spiritual. He feeds upon new provision, the bread which came down from heaven. He is engaged in new employments, which are holy. He acts from a new motive – the love of Christ constrains him. He aims at a new end, even at God's glory. He joins a new society, the church of God. All things become new. He has a new federal head, the second Adam. He is introduced into a new paradise – peace and reconciliation to God. He is under a new covenant, the covenant of grace, not of works. He enters into new relations: God is his Father; angels his servants; Christ is his Brother; the Holy Spirit his Comforter. He stands in new relations: to God, he is a child; to angels, a charge; to the world, a witness; to Christ, a servant; to the Holy Spirit, a temple. He experiences new desires, new hopes, new fears, and new joys. He looks for a new heaven and a new earth, wherein dwelleth righteousness. He is not *as* he was, cursed. He is not *what* he was, carnal. He is not *where* he was, in Adam; he is in Christ. 'He is a new creature, old things are passed away, and behold, all things are become new.'

> Now, Lord, I would be Thine alone,
> And wholly live to Thee;
> 'Tis grace indeed that Thou should'st own,
> A worthless worm like me.

DECEMBER 21

🌿 MORNING 🌿

'Oh, keep my soul, and deliver me.'

PSALM 25:20

What a mercy to have a God to go to, a throne of grace set before us, and the precious name of Jesus to plead. How encouraging the examples set before us in God's holy Word. Let us imitate them who spake as they were moved by the Holy Ghost. We are going into the world; the business of the day is before us; our hearts are false and fickle. Let our prayer be, *'Oh, keep my soul'*. Keep me from sin, let me not indulge it in my heart, or commit it in my life; keep me from Satan – suffer him not to lead me astray from Thee; keep me from men – let them not prevail against me. Keep me in Thy way, in Thy truth, in Thy church. Keep me by Thy Word, Thy Spirit, Thy presence, or Thy rod. *'Deliver me'*: from guilt and condemnation, from fear and shame. Keep me at Thy footstool, and deliver me from my own wandering heart. Let me be clothed in the robe of righteousness; cleansed in the fountain of my Saviour's blood; accepted in His glorious person and perfect work; and be crowned with lovingkindness and tender mercy. 'Keep me as the apple of the eye.'

> *Ah, will not He who ransom'd man,*
> *A Saviour's work fulfil?*
> *Almighty is His power – He can;*
> *Boundless His love – He will.*
> *Saviour Divine! deliver me,*
> *O, keep my soul still near to Thee!*

🌿 EVENING 🌿

'Hast thou faith?'

ROMANS 14:22

If you have, God gave it you, for it is the gift of God. If you have now, you had not once, for all are destitute of faith by nature. If you have faith, you feel the power of unbelief, struggle with it, and pray to be delivered from it. Hast thou faith in Christ? Do you believe that His claims are valid? That His Word is true? That His sacrifice is sufficient to atone for thy sin? That He is the proper object of trust, love, and worship? That as a believer, He will save thee with an everlasting salvation? Have you faith to trust His Word? To rely with confidence on His finished work? To profess your dependence on Him alone? To commit your soul into His hands to be saved by His grace? Have you faith to venture in His cause, and boldly to avow yourself to be on the Lord's side? Have you faith in God as your Father? Can you believe that He cares for you, that He will supply your needs, that He will guide you by His counsel and afterwards receive you to glory? Can you trust His faithfulness, rest on His promises, and leave your concerns in His hands? Have you faith to believe that you are delivered from the law, that you are in friendship with God, and may walk at liberty? Daily feed your faith with God's promises, and watch against unbelief.

> *True faith refines the heart,*
> *And purifies with blood;*
> *Takes the whole gospel, not a part,*
> *And holds the fear of God.*

DECEMBER 22

❧ MORNING ❧

'They shall not be ashamed that wait for me.'
Isaiah 49:23

Waiting for the Lord supposes that we want Him to do something for us, bestow something on us, or fill some relation to us. It implies that we have sought Him, that He has promised, but that He delays to answer our request. It proves that no substitute can be found. This promise *suggests* that there may be fears, lest He should not come, lest after all we should be disappointed. This supposes that there may be temptations to distrust the love, faithfulness, and goodness of God, to think they shall be ashamed of having sought, believed, or expected that the Lord would appear. But this precious promise *secures* the waiting soul from shame, disappointment, and confusion; it *assures* us that the Lord will appear, answer, and bless in His own time, and in His own way. Are you tempted? wait for the Lord. Are you afflicted? wait upon God. Are you sorely tried? wait patiently for the Lord. He will not suffer you to be ashamed. Abraham waited, and received the promise. Joseph waited, and was raised to honour. David waited, and had all his desire.

Affliction is a stormy deep,
Where wave resounds to wave;
Though o'er my head the billows roll,

I know the Lord can save.
I'll wait, and bow beneath the rod;
My hope, my confidence is God.

❧ EVENING ❧

"I have given you an example.'
John 13:15

Are you prepared to copy His example? Do you study it? Do you admire it? Do you heartily desire exactly to resemble it? In vain do you hope to be saved by His sacrifice, if you do not imitate His example. He left us an example that we should follow in His steps. Look at His faith in His Father's word, His love to His Father's name, His zeal for His Father's glory, His submission to His Father's will, His diligence in His Father's work. Look at His love to His people: at His patience, His forbearance, His longsuffering, His pity, His tenderness, His self-denial, His faithfulness, His humility, His meekness, His sympathy, His readiness to help them. Look at His pity for sinners. Hear Him pray for them. See Him weep over them. Observe how He seeks to benefit them. How He stoops to them. How patiently He endures their contradiction against Himself. He is your example. You are daily to imitate Him. You should every evening compare your conduct through the day with His. It would do you good often to ask, 'How would Jesus act in this case?' What would He do under these circumstances? O to be like Him! To copy His example daily, exactly! Holy Spirit descend, and give the power!

Be Christ our pattern and our guide!
His image may we bear!
O may we tread His sacred steps,
And His bright glories share.

DECEMBER 23

🌟 MORNING 🌟

'His soul shall dwell at ease.'
PSALM 25:13

The man that fears God must have faith in His Word, love to His character, a desire to please Him in all things, a fear to offend Him in anything, a realization of His omniscience, and be looking forward to His appearing. Beloved, is this our character? It is said of such, *'His soul shall dwell at ease;'* free from slavish fears; from soul-distressing cares and anxieties; in a state of contentment and solid peace. And well he may; for he has God for his portion, the eternal covenant as his stay, the precious promises as his security, the glorious atonement for his plea, complete salvation for his shield, providence as his friend, Christ as his constant Advocate, Captain, and Man-of-War, daily fellowship with God as his relief, and heaven as his final home. His soul shall lodge, or dwell in goodness: so some read it. The goodness of God is the storehouse of every blessing, and will supply his every want, silence all his fears, contradict all his unbelieving doubts, and exalt him to peace and honour. Beloved, let us not be anxious about anything, but casting all our cares upon God, let us dwell at ease.

> *Once the world was all my treasure;*   *Since the Lord has made me blest;*
> *Then the world my heart possess'd,*   *I can witness,*
> *Now I taste sublimer pleasure,*   *Jesus gives His people rest.*

🌟 EVENING 🌟

'The Sun of righteousness.'
MALACHI 4:2

That is Jesus. There is but *one sun*, and our Jesus is the only Saviour. This figure may set forth His greatness, His exalted station, His sufficiency, His beauty and glory, His immutability, His usefulness, and that He is a common benefit. He is the Sun *of righteousness*: This implies the perfection and excellency of His person; the rectitude of His government; the relation in which He stands to His people – He is their righteousness. All light is from the sun; so all our righteousness is from Jesus. He is the source of holiness, and He wrought out that obedience in which we are justified. As there is light enough in the sun for us all, so there is righteousness enough in Jesus for us all. As the light of the sun flows to us freely, so Jesus gives His righteousness freely. As it would be folly to look to any other quarter for light, while the sun is shining, so it is folly to look anywhere for righteousness, but to Jesus only. As the sun decks creation with beauty and glory, so the righteousness of Jesus makes us beautiful and glorious. Sun of righteousness, may we walk in Thy light, receive Thy communications, and point sinners to Thee for life and peace!

> *Christ whose glory fills the skies,*   *Triumph o'er the shades of night:*
> *Christ the true and only light,*   *Day-spring from on high be near;*
> *Sun of righteousness, arise,*   *Day-star in my heart appear.*

DECEMBER 24

🌿 MORNING 🌿

'Whom resist, stedfast in the faith.'

1 Peter 5:9

Satan is the Christian's unwearied foe, he is the enemy of all righteousness, and aims at our destruction. He is especially the enemy of our faith, comfort, prosperity, and usefulness. He is our enemy before God, and he gets access to our hearts; he excites to sin, accuses of sin, and terrifies for sin. We are called upon to resist him, steadfastly believing God's Word, faithfulness, and love, steadfastly believing what Christ is to us, as Satan's grand opponent. Is Satan a deadly serpent? Jesus is the brazen serpent which heals. Is Satan a roaring lion? Jesus is the lion of the tribe of Judah who prevails. Is Satan a destroyer? Jesus is a Saviour. Is Satan an adversary? Jesus is a Friend. Is Satan a wolf? Jesus is the good Shepherd. Is Satan a tempter? Jesus is a Deliverer. Is Satan a deceiver and a liar? Jesus is the truth. Is Satan an accuser? Jesus is an Advocate. Is Satan the prince of darkness? Jesus is the light of life. Is Satan a murderer? Jesus is the resurrection. Is Satan god of this world? Jesus is *God over all*. Resist the devil in the faith of this. Jesus is all you need.

All power is to our Jesus given;
O'er earth's rebellious sons He reigns.
He mildly rules the hosts of heaven,
And holds the powers of hell in chains.
Jesus, the woman's conquering seed,
Shall bruise for us the serpent's head.

🌿 EVENING 🌿

'Buy the truth and sell it not.'

Proverbs 23:23

You need the truth. It is necessary to enlighten the mind, sanctify the heart, cheer the soul, and regulate the life. All goodness flows from truth, and all evil from error. Therefore *buy* the truth. It is to be had, but it must be bought. It will cost you something if you obtain it. But you cannot buy it too dear. It *has* fetched a very high price: some have given their liberty, all their comforts, and their lives for it. It is in God's book, as in a mine. It is in Christ's person, as its centre and home. Labour in the mine. Study Christ. Be diligent, laborious, and determined to have the truth if possible. Pray. Strive. Honour the Holy Spirit, who alone can put you in possession of it. It is His office to *teach* the truth; He *leads* into it, by degrees, by exercise, by a variety of means. Having bought the truth, never *sell* it. No one can bid you a sufficient price for it. You can find no substitute for it. You will be sure to need it, to direct you in perplexity, to comfort you in sickness, to cheer you in sorrow, and to support you in death. Pleasure may bid for it. Honour may bid for it. Wealth may bid for it. But *sell it not*. Study it, profess it, enjoy it, and practise it; make it your companion, your food, and your solace.

O Thou the living way,
The truth, the life, bestow
That holy light whose vital ray
Shall lead, all truth to know.

DECEMBER 25

❦ MORNING ❦
'I will be glorified.'
LEVITICUS 10:3

This is the great end Jehovah has in view in all He performs, and all He permits. He created and He preserves the world, that He might be glorified. He redeemed His people by the blood of His Son, and He will glorify His saints with Himself, to the same end. He will be glorified in His sovereignty, doing as He will; in His supremacy, commanding as He pleases; in His wisdom, disposing of His creatures to secure His design; in His grace, saving an innumerable company of the lost and wretched, to sound His praise forever; in His goodness, supplying the wants of all His creatures, though in rebellion against Him; in His justice, punishing the daring impenitent offender. Beloved, it is our duty to aim at the glory of our God in all things. Does Jehovah command? then we should observe His commands and obey them. Does He graciously promise, and in wisdom and mercy provide? then we should trust, rely, and depend on Him. Does He work in providence and grace? then we should acknowledge His hand, submit to His wisdom, bow at His throne, fear to sin against Him, or grieve His love. Our *business* is to glorify God.

> Lord, turn the stream of nature's tide;
> Let all our actions tend
> To Thee their source; Thy love the guide,
> Thy glory be the end:
> In all we think, or say, or do,
> Thy glory may we still pursue.

❦ EVENING ❦
'Jesus was born in Bethlehem.'
MATTHEW 2:1

When Jesus was born, we do not exactly know, God hath concealed it; but THAT He was born, is most plainly revealed. We know *where* He was born, and *why* He was born. He had eternally existed as God. He was one *with*, and equal *to* the Father. But He became man. He was conceived in Mary's womb. He was born in Bethlehem. He was a weak and helpless infant, and yet at the same time the Mighty God, the Everlasting Father, the Prince of peace. Deity and humanity united in His person. He took our nature to take away our sins. He became a man in order to be a Saviour. He came on purpose to save sinners. This was His object. This was His work. For this He lived, and laboured, and suffered, and died. He came to be our substitute. He was born once, that we might be born again. He died once, that we might not experience the second death, but live forever. His love passeth knowledge. His birth was the greatest display of condescension, which heaven or earth ever witnessed. It was introductory to His obedient life, meritorious death, victorious resurrection, triumphant ascension, and glorious second advent. He *was* born in Bethlehem, in weakness and poverty; He *will* soon come to earth again, with power and great glory.

> God is in our flesh reveal'd,
> Heaven and earth in Jesus join,
> Mortal with immortal fill'd,
> And human with divine.

DECEMBER 26

🌿 MORNING 🌿

'This honour have all His saints.'

Psalm 149:9

What honour? Of being redeemed by the blood of the Lamb, out of every nation, country, people, and tongue; of being born again, not of corruptible seed, but of incorruptible, by the Word of God which liveth and abideth forever; of being acknowledged as the sons of God – 'Beloved, now are we the sons of God, and it doth not yet appear what we shall be; but we know that when He shall appear we shall be like Him, for we shall see Him as He is'; of being closely allied to Jesus – He is not ashamed to call them brethren; of being heirs of God – 'If children then *heirs*, heirs of God and joint-heirs with Jesus Christ'; of being delivered from slavery to serve God in liberty – 'that being delivered out of the hands of our enemies we might serve Him without fear, in holiness and righteousness before Him all the days of our life'; of being appointed to sit in judgment with Christ – Know ye not that we shall judge angels? *'This honour have all His saints.'* Are we saints? Do we walk as becometh saints? Are we living under the influence of these great privileges? Let us admire, adore, and obey.

> Pause, my soul, adore and wonder;
> Ask, 'O, why such love to me?'
> Grace hath put me in the number
> Of the Saviour's family;
> Hallelujah!
> Thanks, eternal thanks to Thee.

🌿 EVENING 🌿

'Should it be according to thy mind?'

Job 34:33

Many appear to think so. If we may judge by their conduct they think that the Most High should have consulted their ease, their fancy, and their aggrandizement. The gospel is not just what they would like it to be. Providence does not work as they desire. Few things are exactly as they should be. Complaining mortal! Should it be according to thy mind? Is not thy mind carnal? Is it not selfish? Is it not prejudiced? If it were according to thy mind would not God's glory be obscured? Would not others suffer? Would not thy lusts be fed? Would not thy temptations be stronger? Would not thy danger be greater? Is not thy God wiser, kinder, and holier than thou art? Does He not love justice? Are not His mercies over all His works? True, you may be afflicted, you may be poor, you may be sickly. What then? You are wishing for health, for a competency, for freedom from trials, but, 'should it be according to thy mind?' Beloved, let us guard against such a spirit: it is common, but it is unreasonable, it is criminal, it is dangerous. The thing is impracticable. Your God must govern; He is wonderful in counsel, and excellent in working. His ways are just, His plans are wise, His designs are merciful, and when the work is complete, every part will reflect His glory.

> Let saints proclaim Jehovah's praise,
> And acquiesce in all His ways,
> He keeps eternity in sight,
> And what His hand performs is right.

DECEMBER 27

❧ MORNING ❧

'I would have you without carefulness.'

1 Corinthians 7:32

Anxiety, or carefulness, is very injurious; it divides the heart, distracts the mind, chokes the Word, leads to distrust, and destroys our peace. It is inconsistent with our profession; we have resigned all into the hands of the Lord, and should leave all to His blessing. We should do everything as for the Lord, and consider our families, our property, and our business, as the Lord's; so should we be holy and enjoy peace. Anxiety, or inordinate care, dishonours God; it reflects upon His sufficiency to supply all; upon His omniscience to discover all; upon His authority and ability to manage all; upon His mercy, bounty, and liberality, as if He would leave us to want; upon His veracity, fidelity, and immutability, as though His Word may be forfeited or His promise broken. Carefulness injures our own souls: it is opposed to contentment and resignation; it nourishes impatience and unbelief; it hinders our usefulness, and hardens our hearts; it cuts off supplies, and procures the rod and the frown. We should therefore aim to be without *carefulness*, for the Lord careth for us.

> How sweet to have our portion there,
> Where sorrow never comes, nor care,
> And nothing will remove.
>
> We then may hear without a sigh,
> The world's destruction to be nigh,
> Our treasure is above.

❧ EVENING ❧

'With thee is the fountain of life.'

Psalm 36:9

All life is from God. All creatures are sustained by God. He giveth life, and breath, and all things. Our existence here is dependent on His will; so also is the comfort of our life. But from Him proceeds spiritual life: the energy that quickens us, the divine principle which exists within us. We are born of God. He holdeth our souls in life. He also revives us and makes us lively. Beloved, do you feel dull, lifeless, and inactive tonight? Are you sighing for a deeper sense of the Lord's love, and for more enjoyment of the Saviour's presence? Fix your mind upon this precious truth: With your God 'is the fountain of life'. He can easily direct one of its streams into your soul. He can revive you in one moment. If He lifts up the light of His countenance; if He whispers pardon and peace; if the Holy Spirit but gently breathes upon you, you will be happy, all will be well. Go then direct to the throne of grace, lay your whole case before your God, tell Him how dull and lifeless you feel, appeal to Him as the fountain of life, plead the powerful name and precious blood of Jesus. Expect God to honour this plea; persevere in your application though you meet with discouragements, and He will revive you again, and your soul shall give thanks to His name.

> Life, like a fountain rich and free,
> Springs from the presence of the Lord,
> And in Thy light our souls shall see,
> The glories promis'd in Thy Word.

DECEMBER 28

❦ MORNING ❧
'Let us not be weary in well-doing.'
GALATIANS 6:9

It is not enough for us to be doing; we should be doing good. We are redeemed and created anew for this purpose. Let us *act* as before God, for the good of man; let us *communicate* advice, encouragement, or relief, in the fear of God and for His glory. What is done well, is done in a good spirit, even the spirit of love, humility, and prayer; is done from a good motive, even the love of Christ; is done by a good rule, the commandment of the everlasting God; is done to a good end, the glory of Him who hath called and commanded us. But we are prone to get weary of doing, especially if we are hasty; or meet with disappointments; or look at creatures; or consult our own ease. But let us not lose heart in the work, neither let us give it over; for in due season we shall reap if we faint not. This is sowing time, but reaping time will come. Let us therefore go on in divine strength, with holy fortitude, with fixed determination, and resigning ourselves daily to God. We shall reap in *due season* if we faint not; for God is orderly, faithful, bounteous, gracious; He will not forget our work and labour of love; but will reward even a cup of cold water, given to a disciple in His name.

> Put thou thy trust in God,
> In duty's path go on;
> Fix on His Word thy steadfast eye,
> So shall thy work be done.

❦ EVENING ❧
'Therefore are they before the throne of God.'
REVELATION 7:15

Why? They were in great tribulation for Jesus' sake. They endured persecution, temptation, the inward conflict, sickness, sorrow, and a variety of afflictions, looking unto Jesus and seeking to please and glorify Him. They were *in* great tribulation, but they were not *overwhelmed* by it. They passed through it with courage, being divinely supported. They frequently contracted defilement in this filthy world, but they hated sin and often loathed themselves on account of it, and they washed their robes and made them white in the blood of the Lamb. They knew, they prized, they used, and they enjoyed the open fountain. *Therefore* are they before the throne. They are now safe, accepted, approved, happy. They serve God day and night in His temple. They serve without weakness, weariness, or drowsiness. They serve Him cheerfully, perfectly, and uninterruptedly. They are freed from all want and pain. They hunger no more. They thirst no more. God *dwells* among them. They know nothing of lassitude, opposition, or sorrow. The Lamb feeds them in person, rules them in love, and leads them to the ever-flowing fountain of life: and God has wiped away every tear from their eyes. They are blessed far beyond their expectations.

> With wondering joy they recollect
> Their fears and danger past,
> And bless the wisdom, power, and love
> Which brought them safe at last.

DECEMBER 29

🌿 MORNING 🌿

'All things work together for good.'
ROMANS 8:28

All the Lord's people love God. They do not love Him as they desire, yet they cleave to Him, and follow on to know Him. He is their God, and has called them according to His own purpose and grace, which was given them in Jesus Christ before the world began, and it becomes the Christian to view everything as having its place in God's economy; and its work to do in accomplishing God's purposes. Angels, men and devils, but perform His pleasure. All things are connected by the infinite wisdom and good pleasure of the Most High. He superintends every movement of every one of His creatures; and directs them to answer His purpose and end. He overrules everything for our good; we never lose anything worth keeping by any of His dispensations. We may gain by all that occurs; we may gain wisdom, holiness, matter for prayer or praise, work for faith, patience, or hope. However, our best interests are secured; everything is working for the good of the church; and though it be rough, it is a right way to our heavenly Father's house.

> *All things on earth, and all in heaven,*
> *On God's eternal will depend;*
> *And all for greater good were given,*
> *And all shall in His glory end.*
> *This be my care! and this alone;*
> *Father, in me Thy will be done.*

🌿 EVENING 🌿

'Their heart is far from me.'
MATTHEW 15:8

And yet they appeared devout. They passed among men for very religious characters. Their devotions were formal. There was no life in their service. They were without sincerity, fervency, or desire. They were satisfied with the form, without the power. They had a name to live, but they were dead. This is the case with too many now. They pass for saints, but are not sanctified. They are considered worshippers, but their hearts are far from God. Now the man is as his heart is. God looketh at the heart. Beloved, is your heart near to God tonight? It is when our desires go out after Him, when our love is fixed upon Him, when the soul bows in reverence before Him, when the expectation is from Him, when our lively and interested thoughts are employed about Him, when all our powers are prostrated before Him, or presented to Him. God is *now* looking at your heart. Do you sigh and desire to get near Him? Do you mourn and grieve over your distance from Him? If so, He looks upon you with pity, and accepts the willing mind. They who live near to God here, will live with God forever. But they who are satisfied with formal worship and distance will be kept at a distance throughout eternity.

> *Why should my foolish passions rove?*
> *Where can such sweetness be*
> *As I have tasted in Thy love,*
> *As I have found in Thee?*

DECEMBER 30

🌿 MORNING 🌿

'I will never leave thee, nor forsake thee.'

HEBREWS 13:5

If the Lord is with us, all will be well; but He has promised to be with us always, even unto the end. Anyone but our God would have left us long ago; but He is longsuffering, full of compassion, and of great mercy. He will go through the whole journey with us, He will be our God to all eternity, and will conduct us through life with safety. He will be with us in every trouble, to support us; in every trial, to comfort us; in every difficulty, to provide for us; in every danger, to deliver us; and under all circumstances, to bless us. He will be with us as our heavenly Father; as our firm and faithful Friend, and as our God; and we shall be with Him by and by, as His children, dependants, and jewels, to be glorified with Him forever. Beloved, let us rejoice in this, that God will never leave us. Death may rob us, friends may leave us, troubles may come upon us, but our God will not forsake His people for His great name's sake, because it hath pleased the Lord to make them His people. Having loved His own, He will love them unto the end.

Since He has said, 'I'll ne'er depart',
I'll bind His promise to my heart,
Rejoicing in His care.

This shall support while here 1 live,
And when in glory 1 arrive,
I'll praise Him for it there.

🌿 EVENING 🌿

'Cleanse thou me from secret faults.'

PSALM 19:12

No one but a Christian will heartily use this prayer. It intimates such an acquaintance with the human heart, and such a desire for true holiness, as none can experience except taught of God. Some never confess known, open, evident faults; nor do they desire to be cleansed from them. And here is one, who supposes that there are faults which he has not detected, follies which have escaped his notice, and he prays to be cleansed from them. He would not only have them pardoned, but the stain of them erased; he desires to be kept from them in future. Our secret faults are numerous; they often spring from inattention, from giving way to our natural inclination, from the unspiritual state of our souls. But the fountain of a Saviour's blood will cleanse from them all; and the power of the Holy Spirit can preserve us from a similar course in future. We need to be filled with the Spirit if we are to keep our hearts with all diligence, if we are to preserve a watch over our souls in private as well as in public. Let us seek this blessing. Christians once enjoyed it, and we are exhorted to possess it; for the apostle says, 'Be not drunk with wine wherein is excess, *but be filled with the Spirit.*' Seek it as a gift, and expect it as a favour.

Lord, who can all his wanderings know?
Or watch where guilt begins?
Then let Thy grace my heart renew,
And cleanse from secret sins.

DECEMBER 31

🌿 MORNING 🌿

'A friend loveth at all times.'

PROVERBS 17:17

Where shall we find such a friend? He that redeems from slavery, and delivers from bondage, is such a friend. But Jesus does this. He that restores to the favour of the judge who condemned, or the Lord who delivered over to bondage, is such a friend. But Jesus does this. He that admits to intimacy with himself, out of pure love, notwithstanding disparity of condition, is such a friend. But Jesus does this. He who counsels in trouble, and gives the best advice in perplexity, is such a friend. But Jesus does this. He who rescues from foes and renders their attempts to injure us abortive, is such a friend. But Jesus does this. He who takes in the rejected and homeless, who clothes the naked and feeds the hungry, is such a friend. But Jesus does this. He who exposes himself to pain, injury, insult, and death, to do us good, is such a friend. But Jesus has done this. He who expends all his property for our welfare, is such a friend. But Jesus did this. He who kindly reproves our faults in prosperity, and visits, comforts, and relieves in adversity, is such a friend. But Jesus does this. He who loves us through life, in death, and forever, is such a friend. But Jesus doth so. *He is the friend who loveth at all times*; changing scenes change not His affection. His friendship flows from purest love, and is founded in a perfect knowledge of our persons, wants, dispositions, and propensities; His friendship is maintained by infinite patience, boundless pity, and the prospect of our being glorified with Him forever. He knows our frame, consults our welfare, and is determined to do us good. He will not allow us to lose by any of His dispensations; but will increase our spiritual wealth by all means. The friendship of Jesus secures all good, and prevents all evil; He will never fail us nor forsake us. He commenced His friendship with a view to extend it through eternity; and it is the same at the close of the year as it was in the beginning. O Jesus! let us love Thee with pure affection, walk with Thee in sweetest friendship, and prove ourselves Thy friends in every place! Be thou our Friend, Counsellor, Brother, Saviour, Lord, and God, in life, death, and forever. Amen.

One there is, above all others,
Well deserves the name of Friend:
His is love beyond a brother's,
Costly, free, and knows no end:
They who once His kindness prove,
Find it everlasting love.

Which, of all friends, to save us,
Could or would have shed his blood?
But our Jesus died to have us
Reconciled in Him to God!
This was boundless love indeed,
Jesus is a friend in need! Amen!

DECEMBER 31

🌿 EVENING 🌿

'God hath dealt graciously with me.'

GENESIS 33:11

Is not this our language tonight? Brought through another year; a year of trials, temptations, and storms, and yet a year crowned with innumerable mercies. Every want supplied, every promise fulfilled, ten thousand evils prevented, unnumbered blessings bestowed. What sins we have committed! What duties we have neglected! What privileges we have slighted! How faithless we have been, and yet how faithful our God. Not one thing has failed of all that He promised; all is come to pass. Our obligations are infinite; our praises should be constant; our lives should be entirely devoted; our persons wholly consecrated to God. Yes, He hath dealt graciously with me, in pardoning my sins, in hearing my prayers, in subduing my foes, in protecting my person, in guiding my feet, and enabling me to hold on in His good ways. O my soul, trust in the Lord; He is thy help and thy shield! Call upon Him in every future trouble. Surrender to Him all that is dear and valuable in thy esteem. Live upon His Word. Look to His fulness. Act for His glory. Cleave to His saints. Rest in the Lord, and wait patiently for Him, and trust Him more heartily than ever.

Then in the history of my age,
When men review my days,
They'll read His love in every page,
In every line His praise.

Also available from Christian Focus Publications ...

978-1-84550-183-9

Morning and Evening

Daily Readings

C. H. Spurgeon

Devotions to bookend and bless your day.

In his devotional writing, Spurgeon's love for God's word intersects with his love for God's people. The result: a wealth of timeless Biblical meditations with applications that are relevant for contemporary Christians.

Dated from 1st January to 31st December, each day's morning and evening devotion is complete with a scripture reference and accompanying exposition.

Spurgeon's characteristically pithy comments hit home with a wit and elegance rarely found in other writing. Christians young and old will find his words challenging and stimulating.

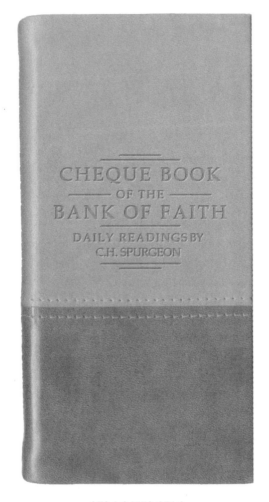

978-1-84550-071-9

Chequebook of the Bank of Faith

Daily Readings

C. H. Spurgeon

A short reading for every day.

Spurgeon wrote this selection of readings to encourage believers to enter into the full provision that their relationship to Jesus entitled them to realise, on a daily basis.

He explains we have to present the promises of Scripture to God in prayer and faith, anticipating that he will honour what he has said.

Each day's devotion therefore begins with a verse of scripture and is followed by a brief exposition to exhort and encourage believers to continue walking with God.

Dated from 1st January to 31st December, and drawing on verses from throughout the Bible, Spurgeon assures readers of the necessity and relevance of God's word for each and every day.

Christian Focus Publications

Our mission statement
Staying Faithful

In dependence upon God we seek to impact the world through literature faithful to His infallible Word, the Bible. Our aim is to ensure that the Lord Jesus Christ is presented as the only hope to obtain forgiveness of sin, live a useful life and look forward to heaven with Him.

Our Books are published in four imprints:

CHRISTIAN FOCUS
Popular works including biographies, commentaries, basic doctrine and Christian living.

MENTOR
Books written at a level suitable for Bible College and seminary students, pastors, and other serious readers. The imprint includes commentaries, doctrinal studies, examination of current issues and church history.

CHRISTIAN HERITAGE
Books representing some of the best material from the rich heritage of the church.

CF4KIDS
Children's books for quality Bible teaching and for all age groups: Sunday school curriculum, puzzle and activity books; personal and family devotional titles, biographies and inspirational stories – because you are never too young to know Jesus!

Christian Focus Publications Ltd,
Geanies House, Fearn, Ross-shire,
IV20 1TW, Scotland, United Kingdom.
www.christianfocus.com